The Wedgwood Family

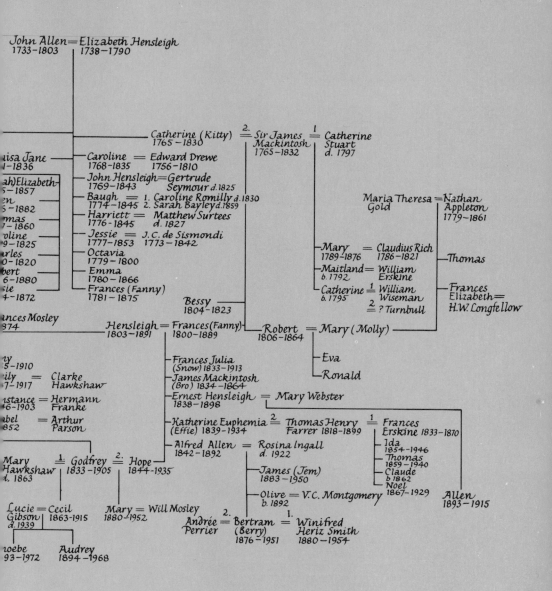

John Allen = Elizabeth Hensleigh
1733–1803   1738–1790

Catherine (Kitty) = 2. Sir James Mackintosh = 1. Catherine Stuart
1765–1830   1765–1832   d. 1797

Caroline = Edward Drewe
1768–1835   1756–1810

John Hensleigh = Gertrude Seymour d.1825
1769–1843

Baugh = 1. Caroline Romilly d.1830
1774–1845   2. Sarah Bayley d.1859

Harriett = Matthew Surtees
1776–1845   d. 1827

Jessie = J. C. de Sismondi
1777–1853   1773–1842

Octavia
1779–1800

Emma
1780–1866

Frances (Fanny)
1781–1875

uisa Jane
1–1836

ah)Elizabeth
5–1857

en
5–1882

mas
7–1860

oline
9–1825

arles
0–1820

bert
6–1880

sie
4–1872

nces Mosley
874

Bessy
1804–1823

Maria Theresa Gold = Nathan Appleton
1779–1861

Mary = Claudius Rich
1789–1876   1786–1821

Maitland = William Erskine
b. 1792

Catherine = 1. William Wiseman
b. 1795   = 2. ? Turnbull

Thomas

Frances Elizabeth = H.W. Longfellow

Hensleigh = Frances (Fanny)
1803–1891   1800–1889

Robert = Mary (Molly)
1806–1864

Eva

Ronald

Frances Julia (Snow) 1833–1913

James Mackintosh (Bro) 1834–1864

Ernest Hensleigh = Mary Webster
1838–1898

Katherine Euphemia (Effie) 1839–1934 = 2. Thomas Henry Farrer 1818–1899 = 1. Frances Erskine 1833–1870

Alfred Allen = Rosina Ingall
1842–1892   d. 1922

Ida 1854–1946
Thomas 1859–1940
Claude b 1862
Noel 1867–1929

Allen 1893–1915

James (Jem)
1883–1950

Olive = V.C. Montgomery
b. 1892

y
5–1910

ily = Clarke Hawkshaw
7–1917

istance = Hermann Franke
46–1903

abel = Arthur Parson
852

Mary Hawkshaw = 1. Godfrey 1833–1905 = 2. Hope 1844–1935
d. 1863

Lucie Gibson = Cecil 1863–1915
d. 1939

Mary = Will Mosley
1880–1952

Andrée Perrier = 2. Bertram (Berry) 1876–1951 = 1. Winifred Heriz Smith 1880–1954

oebe
93–1972

Audrey
1894–1968

The Wedgwood Circle
1730~1897

25 June 1982

For Irma Wolf —
with love
and happy memories
from my childhood
of your many kindnesses
and white Persian kittens!
Barbara Wedgwood

Etruria Hall, home of Josiah Wedgwood I
From an engraving, c. 1770

The Wedgwood Circle 1730~1897

Four Generations of a Family
and Their Friends

Barbara and Hensleigh Wedgwood

STUDIO VISTA
London

A Studio Vista book
published by Cassell Ltd.,
35 Red Lion Square, London WCIR 4SG
and at Sydney, Auckland, Toronto, Johannesburg,
an affiliate of
Macmillan Publishing Co., Inc.,
New York

ISBN 0 289 70892 3

Set in 10 on 11pt Baskerville,
by Colset Private Limited, Singapore.

Printed in the United States of America
by Vail-Ballou Press, Inc., Binghamton, N.Y.

Designed by Rupert Kirby

Contents

List of Illustrations

Picture Credits

Preface

The Wedgwoods of the eighteenth and nineteenth centuries would be famous even if they had never made a piece of pottery, for they possessed a kind of genius for recognizing the genius in others: in some instances, as with the Darwins, they had the good sense to marry it. They themselves took a lively interest in science, art and politics, and their friends included some of the leading figures—scientists, artists, men of letters and public servants—of the day. This book is the story of four generations of Wedgwoods and their friends: what they were like as individuals and what the world was like in which they lived.

To be of interest to readers other than direct descendants, a family history must contain several strong figures round whom the rest cluster. Josiah Wedgwood, Thomas Wedgwood, Charles Darwin, Mary Rich, Hensleigh Wedgwood and Snow Wedgwood were such figures, and if many other members of the family were undistinguished except, in later years, for their wealth and privileged background, there was within each generation of Wedgwoods at least one outstanding individual whose vision extended beyond his own time. But while the more famous few displayed their insights and individuality, the others plodded along, reflecting the attitudes of their class and era, upholding traditions and obligations, living and dying unmemorably. The epitaph of one obscure Wedgwood, however, strikes an unexpected note of farce:

SACRED TO THE MEMORY OF
CAPTAIN ANTHONY WEDGWOOD
ACCIDENTALLY SHOT BY HIS GAMEKEEPER
WHILST OUT SHOOTING
'WELL DONE THOU GOOD AND FAITHFUL SERVANT'

Our notions of biography have changed over the centuries: in the eighteenth century it was looked upon as gossip or a source of anecdote; the nineteenth century expected a biography to glorify its subject. In the twentieth century we generally want to know what the subject was like as a person. But while his contemporaries may have left diaries or letters, or have written lives of him, their standards of importance do not always agree with ours. Sir James Mackintosh, politician, historian, and brother-in-law of Josiah Wedgwood II, solemnly pronounced in 1807: 'The three greatest geniuses of our age are Baillie, Goethe and Madame de Staël.' Quoting Mackintosh's sage opinion, one nineteenth-century letter-writer considered it unnecessary to identify Joanna Baillie but thoughtfully explained that Goethe was a German poet.

If biographical facts do not change (unless they were wrong in the first place), opinions and attitudes about them certainly do, and all biographers, consciously or unconsciously, make judgements based on their own backgrounds and prejudices. It is comparatively simple to describe what a person did, but *why* he or she did it is far more interesting — and more a matter of opinion with the dead than with the living.

Family history is an all-or-nothing proposition. One cannot claim only the good while denying the bad. In each generation there have been geniuses and simpletons, rationalists and mystics, do-gooders and do-nothings. A close examination of one's origins may be a humbling experience as well as a boost to one's ego.

The idea for this saga of four generations of Wedgwoods came from a scrapbook of some hundred letters, photographs and sketches put together in 1897 by Frances Julia ('Snow') Wedgwood (1833–1913) for her niece Mary Euphrasia Wedgwood. The scrapbook begins with a letter from the first Josiah Wedgwood (1730–95) to Thomas Bentley dated 16 March 1768, and includes letters or personal recollections of James Mackintosh, Madame de Staël, Napoleon I, Claudius Rich, Sir Walter Scott, Sir John F. W. Herschel, Sydney Smith, Maria Edgeworth, A. J. Scott, Harriet Martineau, Samuel Rogers, Florence Nightingale, Henry Wadsworth Longfellow and Francis Newman, to name but a few.

For any family, famous or obscure, to pass on its private history for two centuries or more, there must be in each generation not only a strong personality but at least one amateur archivist who hoards letters and diaries and keeps scrapbooks and photograph albums. Such a person was Snow Wedgwood. She was also a moralistic editor who destroyed whatever she considered unfavourable to herself or to anyone she admired. The most interesting letters are, of course, the few that have survived with 'Burn this!' written across them in her distinctive hand in vivid purple ink.

Some of the material for this book was gleaned from the scrapbook, and from other letters, journals and photographs in the Wedgwood family's possession. Most of it was drawn from three major collections of documents deposited in the Wedgwood Archives at the University of Keele. If some individuals and branches of the family appear to receive more attention than others, it is because these people left letters and pictures which their descendants preserved.

Apart from this 'factual' material, though, there are the legends and anecdotes which have come down through the family by word of mouth: how Hope Wedgwood, for instance, either in the distraction of grief or in a fit of plain absent-mindedness, left the ashes of her late husband Godfrey on the luggage rack of a railway carriage on her way back from London after his cremation; or how Cecil Wedgwood, in the next generation, uttering the immortal words 'I will not have a roasted cat on my conscience', ordered the placers to spend two days drawing an ovenful of ware at Etruria because a stray kitten had wandered into the kiln and could not be enticed out before the fires were to be lit.

Now that no member of the Wedgwood family any longer has an active part in the management of the pottery that still bears our name, it seems the more important for the family aspects of the firm's history to be researched and recorded. Historians and collectors of Wedgwood will, we hope, gain a somewhat different perspective on the firm's history than has usually been the case. If the emphasis appears to be more on social concerns than on the pottery itself during the nineteenth century, this is only as it should be, for that is where the family's chief interests lay.

Snow Wedgwood, herself an esteemed author and literary critic, set standards for a biographer which we believe hold true today and which we have tried to follow. In an essay in the *Spectator* in 1882, Snow wrote:

> How far a life is suited for a biography depends on circumstances to some degree independent of the scale of its achievements. It is possible that a great career had better be left unportrayed. Sometimes its own interest is of a kind that should not be revealed, sometimes there is little to say about it but what it has said for itself. And some lives that are anything but great are full of interest in the hands of a worthy biographer.... The only question we would ask a biographer, even of an obscure life, is '*Can* you tell your story?'

HENSLEIGH CECIL WEDGWOOD and BARBARA WEDGWOOD

Doughty House
Richmond, Surrey
July 1979

Acknowledgements

We thank Josiah Wedgwood & Sons Limited, its chairman, Sir Arthur Bryan, and the Trustees of the Wedgwood Museum, Barlaston, for making available for study the Wedgwood archives at the University of Keele. We are especially indebted to the Archivist, Dr Ian Fraser, without whose expert knowledge and generous co-operation this book would not have been possible. Additional help at Keele was given by Dr Hugh Torrens and by Frank Doherty, Senior Lecturer in the Department of English Literature.

We also thank Peter Gautrey of the Cambridge University Library; Dr Sydney Smith of St Catherine's College, Cambridge; Philip Titheridge of Down House; Professor K. J. Fielding of the University of Edinburgh; and Dr Nancy Mautner of the University of Pennsylvania, for assistance with Wedgwood–Darwin documents.

Many members of the Wedgwood family contributed photographs, letters, family legends and personal reminiscences. In particular, we would like to thank Iris, Lady Wedgwood; Margaret Wedgwood Boxall; Sir John Wedgwood; Dame Veronica Wedgwood, O.M.; Nancy Wedgwood; Dr John Wedgwood; Anne Makeig-Jones; Cecilia Makeig-Jones Hampshire; and Martin Wedgwood.

We also wish to thank for help in providing information and photographs Dr Michael Tellwright of Maer Hall, and Wedgwood collectors Byron and Elaine Born, Elizabeth Chellis, Dr Stanley Greenwald, John and Una des Fontaines, David Buten of the Buten Museum of Wedgwood and Gaye Blake Roberts of the Wedgwood Museum, Barlaston.

H.C.W. and B.W.

Prologue

Tuesday, 22 June 1897

A glorious sun warmed the streets of London, where thousands of men, women and children lined the nine-mile route of the Royal Procession, their faces glowing with expectation and good will, mingled with patriotic pride. Many of them had been queuing since the night before to catch a glimpse of the seventy-eight-year-old Queen whose Diamond Jubilee they were celebrating.

For four generations of Victoria's subjects, the popular, high-minded sovereign had come to typify not only a period in time but a unique combination of ideas, attitudes and institutions. Imperialism was at its apogee, and the traditions and pageantry of Empire still roused confidence and self-satisfaction in most British hearts; but now, as the century and the Queen's long reign both neared an end, the old order was beginning to slip away. The minds of some thoughtful persons were already turning in a new direction.

Such a person was Frances Julia Wedgwood, a spinster of sixty-four, who that morning, as the Queen was helped into the royal carriage at Buckingham Palace to begin the five-day festivities, left Notting Hill in a hansom cab for Euston Station. The eldest child of Frances and Hensleigh Wedgwood, Frances Julia—or Snow, as she was called by her family and close friends—had been born in a heavy snowstorm on 6 February 1833. Deaf since childhood, she was in some ways as isolated from ordinary beings as was the Queen. Her world, as she herself often said, was 'the world of the spirit'. A novelist, biographer, historian and literary critic well known in intellectual circles, Snow had, like the Queen, a sincere spiritual yearning for perfection. She, too, regarded being amused—or amusing— as somewhat vulgar and beneath her dignity. The Queen and Snow were both small in stature, less than five feet tall, and Snow weighed only ninety-five pounds; yet each possessed a large sense of purpose and a righteous determination to assert her own individuality.

Also Snow sensed that her life, like that of the Queen, might soon be coming to an end. She had been feeling unwell, had recently consulted a doctor and learned that she had a tumour, possibly malignant. When she was kneeling in church the week before, she had experienced a vision, followed by elation and then a morbid depression which still had not left her.

As almost everyone else in London was watching the Jubilee Procession, at Euston Snow found she had a railway compartment to herself. Her sister Effie, Lady Farrer, and her husband had offered her a place in the peers' stand in front of the National Gallery, from which she could view the Royal Procession with them, as she had done at the Golden Jubilee ten years before. But the glittering spectacle now seemed to her exhausting, and unreal. She had more important things to do. Her valise, bulging with old letters, notes and manuscripts, was safe on the seat beside her as the train moved slowly out of the almost empty station. She intended to spend the next three weeks quietly at her sister's home, Idlerocks, in North Staffordshire, sorting out which of these family papers were important enough to keep and which ought to be burned.

Apart from her own small house in London, at 16 Lansdowne Road, Notting Hill, Idlerocks was the place where Snow felt most at home and where she would spend her final days if God granted her a choice. It was the home of her youngest sister, Hope, who had married their first cousin, Godfrey Wedgwood. Godfrey, though he was the same age as Snow, had retired from the management of the Wedgwood pottery almost a decade earlier because of ill health. He was now a Justice of the Peace and a director of the North Staffordshire Railway. Neither of these offices occupied much of his time, so he sketched, produced surprisingly good watercolours of landscapes, and occasionally debated theological issues with his sister-in-law. Snow was not sure she had convinced him that all questions could not be answered rationally and that trust was God's gift.

In the family, making money out of trade and industry had never been considered quite respectable. One or two male Wedgwoods, in the four generations since the founding of the pottery, had managed it simply out of sense of duty, and this dedication and self-sacrifice had enabled other members of the family to turn their energies towards good works and the socially acceptable accomplishments of ladies and gentlemen of fashion. Of Snow's contemporaries, Cousin Laurence at the age of fifty-three still took an active part in the works management; but most of the burden now fell on the next generation — Godfrey's son Cecil, Clement's son Frank, and Laurence's son Kennard who was at present in South Africa.

Looking out of the window of the railway carriage at the green fields, Snow thought it would hardly be a cheerful summer for Godfrey and Hope's nineteen-year-old daughter Mary Euphrasia. Being confined to the company of ailing old people could depress even the heartiest and most jovial young person, and Mary was anything but jovial. All of the family, including Mary's half-brother, Cecil, who was twice her age, fussed over the child until she was hardly capable of doing anything on her own. Still, she was Snow's favourite among the nieces, nephews and young second cousins. Mary was the one for whom she intended to put together a scrapbook of family letters. Snow's sisters had often told her how very careful, thorough and fastidious she was; her opinions carried weight. It would be hard, however, to decide which letters to keep and which to burn. Most difficult of all would be her own letters to and from her beloved Emily Gurney and her letters to and from the two men who had meant most in her life — Robert Browning and Thomas Erskine of Linlathen. Snow fingered the lock on the valise beside her. So many decisions to make and so little time. Though she longed for death and the blessed union with God, she really had not been expecting it so soon.

When the train steamed into the station at Stoke, Cecil was waiting on the platform. A tall, handsome man with blue eyes and a full blond mustache, he was the person on whose strong character Snow expected both the family and the Wedgwood factory to depend in the future. For that reason she had secretly set up a trust fund for him alone.

Cecil greeted her affectionately. He told her that Hope, having suddenly decided she felt well enough to travel to London and to take Snow's place in the peers' stand with the Farrers, had left late the afternoon before. Lily von Hafen, a former governess, who still lived at Idlerocks and was now in effect a member of the family, and whose brother worked in the accounting department at the factory, had accompanied her.

Snow indicated her trunk, which Richard the coachman and an elderly railway porter hauled to Cecil's carriage. Taking his tiny cousin by the arm, her heavy valise swinging easily in his other hand, Cecil led Snow out of the station past the enormous bronze statue of their illustrious forebear, Josiah Wedgwood, holding his copy of the Portland Vase. Cecil let go of her arm for a moment to tip his top hat to the statue. He winked saucily at Snow.

She thought about the heavy losses the pottery had recently suffered, two years after being incorporated as a private company with the family owning all of the fifty shares. She could not ask Cecil about this now or on the drive to Idlerocks; the coachman would surely overhear and spread tales. Everyone, it seemed, shouted at her. Because her deafness was almost total, she herself never overheard anything. The outer world had been curtained off, as she told herself, in order to make audible the inner voices that were her constant companions.

All the way to Idlerocks, an hour's drive through pleasantly winding lanes in the warm sunshine, Snow watched Cecil's lips, reading the amusing stories he was telling about his pretty Irish wife Lucie and his two charming baby girls. Having been so absorbed in her own misery, she felt a sudden lifting of spirits at being with someone who was young and hopeful and happy.

Her cousin Godfrey, however, was neither happy nor well. He walked with a stick and sat with his leg propped up on a stool in front of him. Young Mary was sulky, disappointed that her mother had not taken her to London to see the Royal Procession and the Illuminations in Hyde Park. Cousin Amy, who had come over from Barlaston for tea, as usual did nothing but complain about the incompetence of her servants and about how the younger members of the family, especially her brother Clement's children, seldom paid her any attention. To Snow she was a tiresome, selfish, narrow-minded spinster of the sort Snow at times feared she herself had become. For that reason, once they were grown, Snow had never really liked Amy.

Cecil, too, stayed for tea. The strain of reading so many lips exhausted Snow. Once Amy had gone back to Barlaston and Cecil to Leadendale, she went upstairs to the small bedroom with the writing desk at the back of the house. On the wash stand, on a starched linen runner, were a blue-printed Wedgwood basin and ewer. On the desk were a vase with roses from the garden, blue writing paper, pen and an ink pot with the purple ink she preferred. This cosy little room had always been hers since Idlerocks was built nine years before.

A maid had unpacked her clothes, hung her dresses in the wardrobe, folded her undergarments and nightdresses and placed them neatly in the drawers of the mahogany chest. Strange how times and customs changed: eighteen years ago, when Godfrey and Hope had married, she wouldn't have travelled anywhere without her own maid Louisa, who had been with her for three decades. Now, towards the end of her life, when she most needed help, she journeyed alone.

Her valise was on the floor beside the desk. She unlocked it and took out several bundles of letters and an untidy manuscript which she doubted would ever be finished now. Two more packets of letters, tied with white tape, she placed in the centre drawer of the desk. Then she lifted out another packet, heavier than the rest, with larger envelopes and tied with brown cord. She stared at this packet for several moments, seemingly weighing it in her hands. Then she firmly put it down, took up the pen, dipped it in the ink pot and wrote across the envelope on the top of the packet, 'Burn this.'

She took off the small wire-rimmed spectacles, which pinched her nose, and rubbed her eyes. Up close everything was blurred. Through the window she could faintly see the Wrekin, twelve miles away in Shropshire. At Idlerocks there was a belief that if one could see the Wrekin, there would be rain; if not, the weather would be fair.

Rain it would be. There was so much to do. She had to determine priorities. Her own literary reputation would, she supposed, rest on her biography of Wesley and on *The Moral Ideal*, a major philosophical work which had taken twenty-two years to complete. She feared that her novels, critical essays and other philosophical works, such as *The Message of Israel,* would have little appeal for future generations. A disappointment. No matter how often she chastised herself, she could not free herself of vanity. 'I could not bear for the most loving eye to see me as I see myself,' she had confided to Emily Gurney years before, 'but I know that all who walk with me must sooner or later see my weakness—the large place that self takes in my thoughts and the way that it colours and distorts my opinions of others.'[1]*

Tomorrow morning she would arise, as usual, at 5 a.m. She would sit at this desk and read through the manuscript notes and letters, sorting them into four categories: (1) 'To Burn'; (2) 'For Mary's Scrapbook'; (3)

---

* Superior figures refer to the Notes on Sources at p.357.

'Confidences To Be Left in Effie's Care'; and (4) 'Letters Written by Josiah Wedgwood I', with notes for a biography of him which she had intended to write and which someone else might have to finish. The biographies of Josiah I by Llewellyn Jewett, Eliza Meteyard and Samuel Smiles were each, from the family's point of view, inadequate and frequently inaccurate. In her own 1882 essay on 'Biography' Snow had written: 'Biography, which is but a part of history, if it is to have any value must contain the materials for moral judgement; and if it is not a transcript from fact, these materials are worthless.'[2] Passing moral judgement on an ancestor was more difficult than sifting truths and untruths concerning those whose lives had no bearing on one's own existence. At the end of a life, as Snow was now at the end of hers, perhaps it was only natural to search out the roots. Perhaps that was why she was here now.

Wedgwoods had been listed in Staffordshire parish registers as far back as 1370. The name itself originated as an obscure hamlet on the verge of a small wedge-shaped wood straddling the boundary between Cheshire and Staffordshire. Not until the latter part of the sixteenth century were the Wedgwoods known as potters. Not until the middle of the eighteenth century did Josiah Wedgwood raise his family from obscurity. 'Genius', as Snow's parents' friend Thomas Carlyle had said, was 'an infinite capacity for taking pains'. It was, she herself believed, far more than that. To search out that something more was part of the reason why she was putting together the scrapbook for Mary, and why she had come back now to this particular place at this particular time.

1

In the Beginning
(1730 – 1762)

Burslem, Josiah Wedgwood's birthplace and 'The Mother Town of the Potteries', was in the early part of the eighteenth century an unlikely place for nurturing genius. Because of the availability of clay and of coal for fuel, it had long been the centre of the pottery industry. Virtually isolated from the rest of England, this Staffordshire backwoods was hardly touched by outside influences and the growing culture in the south.

In 1730 forty-three pot banks were operating in the district, yet there was only one horse and one mule and scarcely any carts. Coal was carried on men's backs. There was no need of carts in any case because there were no roads, only narrow, deeply rutted, muddy tracks impassable to wheeled vehicles in the winter and made worse by the habit of the local potters of digging their clay wherever they found it, thus leaving 'pot-holes' which rapidly filled with water whenever it rained.

The output of the potteries then consisted of redware butter pots, clouded and mottled ware, knife handles, cottage ornaments and white glazed stoneware. A pottery such as the one Josiah Wedgwood's father owned consisted of one oven and several workshops surrounding a courtyard where chickens scratched and pigs rooted. Behind the pottery a small crop of oats or barley was grown. A cow or two grazed the adjacent waste land. Workmen made up to a shilling a day and the value of goods produced in all of the potteries together amounted to less than £7,000 per annum.

By 1760 the population of the whole district was a little over 6,000 people. Burslem was a mere village of thatched cottages with strips of gardens crowded together on the crest of a low hill. There were five shops, two of them belonging to butchers. Letters were brought once a week by a postman on horseback who sounded his horn as he approached; in any case few of the inhabitants could read or write. The major entertainments were drinking, bear-baiting, goose-riding and cock-fighting.

The alehouse was the centre of social life. Here the potters gathered while their wares were being fired. As rough and crude as the ware they produced, they brawled with travellers or hawkers or simply among themselves. The parish constable would often tie the most violent man to a signpost in front of the Red Lion until he sobered up.

On a visit to Burslem, near where he founded Methodism, John Wesley wrote in 1760 of the potters who gathered to hear him preach that 'deep attention sat on every face, though as yet accompanied by deep ignorance...'. As he prayed 'five or six were laughing or talking till I had near done, and one of them threw a clod of earth which struck me on the side of the head, but it disturbed neither me nor the congregation.'[1]

At the time Wesley was receiving this unappreciative reception from the crude potters on Mow Cop, Josiah Wedgwood, thirty years of age and a Master Potter, had only recently begun in business for himself. He was an energetic young man, lame, with a face scarred from smallpox. His eyes were lively and clear blue; he dressed neatly in a frock-coat like a gentleman, and he was affluent enough to have a horse. Even though he himself was a strong Unitarian and wary of what seemed to him Wesley's fanatical evangelism, he rode over to Mow Cop to attend the open-air revival meeting. Any celebrated man who passed through the district interested him, and Wesley's Oxford education and his journey to America, as well as his dedication to educating the minds and converting the souls of 'the forgotten poor', aroused Josiah's curiosity. As he observed the congregation sprawled on the grassy slope, the rowdy behaviour of these vulgar Staffordshire peasants, many of them his workmen and neighbours, reinforced in him the determination to improve himself and his position in the world.

Baptized in the parish church of Burslem on 12 July 1730, Josiah was the youngest of the twelve children of Thomas and Mary Wedgwood of the Churchyard House works. The small pottery had been in the family for several generations, Thomas having inherited it from his father who, in turn, had inherited it from his father; now in 1760 it belonged to Josiah's eldest brother, another Thomas. The Churchyard works was as it had been for the past three generations, and produced, like most other potteries in the district, mottled and cloudy pottery of little refinement.

Josiah's mother was the daughter of a Unitarian minister of Newcastle-under-Lyme, the Revd Samuel Stringer. She had more intelligence and ambition, and was better educated, than the wives of most of the local farmers and potters, and instilled ambition in at least two of her daughters and two of her sons. Of the seven of her children who lived beyond childhood, the others were as unimaginative as their father.

There were other Wedgwood potters, cousins who had been more successful. Another Thomas Wedgwood, an expert thrower, and his brother 'Long John', the best fireman in town, so far succeeded with their salt-glazed ware that by 1743 they had amassed a considerable fortune and built the first house in Burslem to be roofed with slates — an elegant three-storey Georgian brick structure with white facings on a commanding hill-top site, which they immodestly called the Big House. Here they lived and worked in confirmed bachelorhood until 1758 when Long John, at the age of fifty-three, married Mary Allsop by whom he then had six children. Seven years later, at the age of sixty-two, Thomas also took the plunge and married his cousin Mary Wedgwood.

These two brothers were more enterprising than most of their fellow potters. They made considerable improvements in their product and traded directly with London and Liverpool, rather than supplying goods to local hawkers and travelling cratemen. Though extremely cautious with their money, which they invested in land and coal mines, they were nevertheless good hosts and impressed their less sophisticated neighbours with the lavish scale of their entertainment.

After the death of his father in 1739, and having had only two years of schooling, at a day school in Newcastle-under-Lyme, Josiah began work for his brother Thomas. Because their father had died insolvent and the estate was already so heavily mortgaged that nothing could be borrowed on it, the legacies of £20 each he had left to five of his children were not settled until Josiah himself paid them some thirty-five years later.

At the time when Josiah left school and began work, England was at war with both Spain and France. Walpole's power was slipping; opponents of the Government were protesting with a new tune and in the resounding words of Thomson's 'Rule Britannia'. Anson had just returned from a four-year voyage circumnavigating and charting the globe — but, in the isolation of rural Staffordshire, nine-year-old Josiah was hardly aware of such events. In London, where the death rate had outrun the birth rate, Johnson, Hogarth and Fielding were commenting on the human scene and the horrors of 'Gin Lane'; in Burslem hardly anybody commented on anything apart from local gossip.

The boy Josiah spent almost all of his time in the pottery, first carting clay and then, with his brother Richard, learning the art of throwing. Richard was older and stronger than Josiah, but he had neither interest nor aptitude. Josiah had both. He was also a natural acquirer, making a collection of fossils and rocks which the men who led the pack horses from the near-by coal mines gave to him.

When he was eleven, an epidemic of virulent smallpox broke out in Burslem. The disease left Josiah scarred and permanently crippled, with a stiff and painful right knee. No longer able to work as a thrower, he spent long hours modelling in clay, his lame leg propped up on a bench in front of him. For two years he walked with a crutch. Eventually, at the age of fourteen, with the support and encouragement of his mother he was apprenticed to his brother Thomas for five years, to 'learn the art, mistery and occupation of throwing, turning and handleing which the said Thomas Wedgwood now useth'.

In the indentures of apprenticeship witnessed by his mother and two paternal uncles, Abner Wedgwood and Samuel Astbury (who had married Thomas Wedgwood's sister Elizabeth), Josiah promised that

> ... the goods of his said Master he shall not embezil or waste, nor them lend, without his Consent to any; at Cards, Dice or any other unlawful Games he shall not Play. Taverns or Alehouses he shall not haunt or frequent; fornication he shall not Commit — Matrimony he shall not Contract — from the service of his said Master he shall not at any time

depart or absent himself without his Masters leave; but in all things as good and faithfull Apprentice shall and Will Demean and behave him-selfe towards his said Master....[2]

There wasn't much else he could do but dream and scheme to improve the narrow world around him.

At the Big House he met another cousin, Sarah or Sally Wedgwood, who was four years younger than he. Sally was the niece of Thomas and Long John. Her father, Richard, had not followed the family tradition of pot-ting, but had done well for himself in the making and selling of Cheshire cheese, acting as a private banker on the side. Widowed early in life, Richard had only two children, a boy, John, and his daughter Sally. He was accustomed to ride over from his house at Spen Green to visit his brothers at Burslem with Sally riding pillion behind him. Josiah was fasci-nated by this delicate young cousin with the pale skin and reddish-blond hair. She was better educated than he and much richer and somewhat haughty, so he set out to impress her.

The three brothers, the one at Spen Green and the two at the Big House, were not the only comparatively wealthy Wedgwoods. Katherine Wedg-wood Egerton, granddaughter of the first Thomas Wedgwood of the Churchyard works, was an heiress who displayed a generous and kindly interest in her relatives at the Works. A dominant and colourful person-ality, Kate Egerton could neither read nor write, but she was practical and shrewd in her business affairs. Her father, a yeoman who died a quarter of a century before Josiah was born, had left her extensive properties includ-ing several coal mines. After his death she married a cousin, another Richard Wedgwood, son of Aaron Wedgwood, potter of the Overhouse works. He died within a decade, leaving the prosperous pottery to her. Married and widowed twice more, she acquired in the process more properties in and around Burslem.

In January of 1756 she decided that she herself was about to die and set about the practical tasks not only of giving away her possessions, from coal mines and potteries to 'a silver soop-spoon' and 'the featherbed where I now do lye', but also of planning her own funeral. 'I devise there may not be above Sixty persons invited to my funeral, the women to have gloves and the men hatbands and gloves, and it is my desire to be interred either under my father or my mother's Grave Stones....'[3] Having no living children of her own and following the accepted practice of primogeniture, Kate Egerton left the bulk of her considerable estate to Josiah's eldest brother, the dull and plodding Thomas. Legacies of £10 each were also bequeathed to the other children, including Josiah.

At the end of his five-year apprenticeship, Josiah was confident enough of his own abilities and eager to try out new methods, so he proposed a partnership. Brother Thomas declined and thereby made the greatest mistake of his mistaken career. Josiah then entered into partnership with Thomas Alders and John Harrison. All of his other brothers and sisters had either married or left the house beside the Churchyard works. His mother had moved back to her home town of Newcastle-under-Lyme, where two of her daughters were living, so Josiah took board and lodgings in near-by Stoke with the family of Daniel Mayer, a draper.

After less than a year, Josiah discovered that he had made a mistake in his choice of partners. Alders and Harrison cared more for making money than for producing good pots, and were not particularly successful in either endeavour. In 1754 Josiah went into partnership with Thomas Whieldon, a progressive and successful potter at Fenton Low who had the same love of perfection and accuracy in workmanship as his young partner. Eleven years older than Josiah, Whieldon was an astute business-man who had taken on several promising young apprentices, one of whom was William (the block-cutter) Greatbach. Another was Josiah Spode. The snuff boxes and knife handles which Whieldon made were of excellent quality. Together he and Josiah produced white salt-glazed stoneware, imitations of tortoise-shell and agate, redware and Egyptian Black.

At the beginning of the partnership Josiah prepared models and moulds. In the evenings, when he was alone, he began a series of experiments and started to keep the Experiment Books in which he systematically recorded, in a secret code, the thousands of trials he made of clays, mineral earths and metallic oxides in an effort to perfect new bodies, glazes and firing techniques. In the first of these books, the young potter summed up his future goals: 'I saw the field was spacious and the soil so good as to afford an ample recompence to anyone who should labour dilligently in its culti-vation.'[4]

While he was with Whieldon, Josiah again became seriously ill and was forced to spend several months confined to bed in his lodgings over the draper's shop. The Mayer family were kind to him, though they were busy with their own work. He was often visited by his mother and his two married sisters, Margaret Byerley and Catherine Willet. Catherine had married the Revd William Willet, pastor of the Unitarian church in New-castle. Some thirty years older than Josiah, Willet was a kindly and cultured man who loaned his young brother-in-law books and then came to discuss them with him.

Cousin Sally, who by this time had become a tall, delicately pretty young women of twenty-two, also came to visit and brought books. The child-hood friendship now blossomed into a romance, which was thwarted at every turn by Sally's father. Because of his wealth and superior social status, Richard was in no mood to see his only daughter matched with a comparatively poor potter. He told Josiah that he would consider his suit when he could match guinea for guinea the £4,000 which Richard proposed to settle on his daughter as her dowry. On the face of it, this seemed to Josiah an impossible condition. Yet Sally had agreed to marry him and to wait until he could meet her father's stipulation. She had confidence in him even if her father didn't. Nor did Richard Wedgwood appreciate the extent of Josiah's tenacity and his imagination.

During his long illness Josiah was seen by young Dr Erasmus Darwin, who had just settled in Lichfield and whose fame as the most skilled diag-nostician in the Midlands was spreading; he was called in for consultation by the local doctor because Josiah's case — a knee infection which weakened still further his crippled leg — was a difficult one. This illness and lengthy convalescence was crucial in the development of the man Josiah would become. If he had not found time for introspection and self-evaluation before, he found it now. He realized that his frail health would continue to be a handicap in the physical exertion of making pots and that the road to success lay in training others to do the work for him. He was not the first man to turn a seeming disadvantage into an advantage. With the optimism of youth and the single-mindedness of the exceptionally gifted, he set about reading and improving himself in the same way he set about improving his pots.

The partnership with Whieldon ended amicably in 1758, and Josiah's successful experiments with new glazes persuaded him of the feasibility of setting up on his own. He was not of a disposition to remain for long a junior partner in any enterprise in which he felt himself competent. Old Richard's stern conditions for marrying Sally had encouraged him to gamble on making his fortune quickly. So, with his £10 legacy from Cousin Kate Egerton, savings of a similar amount which he had accumulated from the partnership with Whieldon, and help from Thomas and Long John of the Big House, who leased him a small building called the Ivy House for £10 a year, the twenty-eight-year-old Josiah set up on his own as a Master Potter.

It was not the easiest of times to start a business. The Seven Years War with France, 1756–63, had severely curtailed the export trade. The Government had failed to solve the problem of recruiting for His Majesty's Navy, and while patriots were singing that 'Britons never never shall be slaves', press gangs roamed the countryside as well as the city streets. In a single night as many as a thousand men had been known to be kidnapped or, more politely, 'pressed' into service for King and country. Fortunately, however, Josiah's healthy self-interest meant that he paid more attention to commerce than to war.

In the beginning he set himself the task of developing a new kind of workshop and a new kind of product. He employed on a regular basis about fifteen workmen, some of them mere children. He trained them in a way no other English potter before him had done. Discipline was strict, his authority absolute. He personally superintended everything from the clay on the wheel to the final firing and decoration of the ware. Drunkenness, irregular working hours and lack of an orderly routine in the workshops were not tolerated.

In order to gain good will and loyal customers, Josiah accepted small commissions, such as the replacement of a single item — a favourite delft bowl or platter — which other potters refused. He synthesized the ideas and improvements of earlier potters such as Thomas Astbury and Enoch Booth, to perfect a cream-coloured earthenware with a body and glaze which was entirely unlike anything that had gone before. Soon the staple product of the district, salt-glazed stoneware, was seen to be too brittle and pock-marked of appearance to stand up to the competition of this new ware.

Two main methods of decoration were employed. The tableware was either hand-painted with simple flower, fruit or geometric borders, much of the work being done by the widow Warburton of Hot Lane, or else it was printed. Six years earlier, in 1752, John Sadler and Guy Green of Liverpool had perfected a process by which intricately engraved patterns could be transferred, in monochrome, from a copper plate to the surface of pottery. A semi-mechanical process, this was a major step forward technically and one which Josiah exploited to the full. There was, however, one major drawback: the undecorated ware had to be sent to Liverpool for processing and then returned to Burslem for firing. Packed in panniers on the backs of donkeys, the ware was frequently broken or stolen during the rigours of the journey and under the appallingly primitive conditions of transport.

In spite of the difficulties Josiah prospered. By the time Wesley was preaching on Mow Cop in 1760, he was successful enough to hire as a supervisor, at £22 a year, a cousin, still another Thomas Wedgwood. Four years younger than Josiah, this Thomas too had served an apprenticeship to Josiah's brother Thomas before working as a journeyman at Worcester. Josiah had watched this younger cousin's progress for several years and knew him to be competent in his craft, dependable in his habits and capable of pursuing new methods. At the same time Josiah also persuaded his own brother John, who had made a success as a merchant in London and now operated as a trader from the 'Sign of the Artichoke' in Cateaton Street, to represent him in the capital. A complex, restless man of mercurial charm, but given to black depressions, John too had risen above his humble origins and acquired expensive tastes.

Three years after setting up on his own, Josiah needed larger premises. In 1762 he moved from the Ivy House to the Brick House, leased to him by another potter, William Adams, for £35 a year. The first dwelling in Burslem to be made of brick, this was a gracious house, elegant enough for a Master Potter and a soon-to-be-married man: it had a garden in front and a range of two-storey workshops and several bottle-shaped ovens at the back, separate from the house. An unusual feature of the works was a large bell hung in a bell coney by which the workmen were summoned to work instead of by the usual practice of blowing a horn.

Josiah's pottery was now one of the largest in Burslem. He was already more successful than his brother Thomas, in spite of Thomas's having not only the Churchyard works but also the Overhouse works and 150 acres of good farm land which he had inherited from old Kate Egerton. Richard Wedgwood, prodded by his determined daughter, watched the young Josiah's rising fortunes with a grudging admiration. Twice a month now, on Sundays, Josiah rode over to Spen Green to call upon Sally, her pleasant brother and her cantankerous old father.

He also occasionally made trips on horseback to Liverpool, where he bought cobalt and did business with Sadler & Green and with various exporters. On such a trip in the spring of 1762 he had an accident. On one of the narrow, muddy lanes, the wheels of a wagon passing in the opposite direction bumped against Josiah's horse, shoving horse and rider into a fence. Josiah's bad knee was injured again.

In considerable pain, he managed to ride on to the Golden Lion Inn, where he usually stayed in Liverpool. There the innkeeper called in Dr

Matthew Turner, a good surgeon and a practical chemist. One of the founders of the Liverpool Academy of Art, Turner was himself a draughts-man, a classical scholar, a Nonconformist and a ready wit, who had done much to foster literary and artistic taste in Liverpool. He gave Josiah laudanum for the pain and told him that he would have to remain in bed for some weeks.

After a few days, when the pain had eased, Josiah felt restless. He worried about what was going on in Burslem at the new works; even though Cousin Thomas was proving himself a competent manager, Josiah was never one completely to delegate authority. Newspapers and an occasional letter from Sally helped to relieve the boredom, but Turner, as shrewd a psychologist as a physician, saw that his patient was lonely. On one of his visits he therefore brought along a friend, a man called Thomas Bentley. This chance meet-ing completely altered Josiah's life.

2

Expanding Horizons
(1762–1765)

Thomas Bentley was the sort of man Josiah Wedgwood would have elected to be if he could have chosen his own background and personality. The son of a Derbyshire property owner, Bentley was the same age as Josiah and, like him, a strong Dissenter. He had attended a Presbyterian academy, completed an apprenticeship to the cotton and woollen trade, travelled to Europe where he studied French and Italian, returned to Liverpool and set himself up in business as an import and export warehouseman. After the death of his young wife Hannah in childbirth, his sister-in-law Elizabeth Oates moved into Bentley's large and elegant house in Paradise Street, acting as housekeeper and hostess to his many friends. Bentley's business was successful in spite of his outspoken opposition to the slave trade which at the time was an important part of Liverpool's economy. Five years before his meeting with Josiah, he had taken into partnership Samuel Boardman, a man of sound judgement and integrity though lacking in imagination.

Bentley was as prominent in the political and cultural affairs of Liverpool as in its business life. As a member of the Liverpool Corporation, he wrote pamphlets and articles and was an influential go-between with those who represented the city's interests in Parliament. He helped to found and build the Octagon Chapel in Temple Court where the congregation, mainly Presbyterian, had its own liturgy. With Matthew Turner and several other liberal Dissenters, he established the Warrington Academy, which soon became famous not only as an educational institution but as a centre for literary, political and philosophical discussion.

Almost daily Bentley called on Josiah at the Golden Lion. They discussed religion, politics, commerce, canal navigation, art, pottery, logic and poetry. Pottery was the only one of these subjects on which Josiah was better informed than Bentley. Their relationship became in a sense that of pupil and teacher. Bentley's favourite poet was James Thomson; Josiah immediately began reading Thomson's works. That Josiah eagerly sought his opinions and emulated his taste naturally flattered Bentley and encouraged his vanity.

When he was well enough to get around on crutches, Josiah went to stay with Bentley and met some of his friends, including Joseph Priestley who also stayed with Bentley when he came from Warrington to Liverpool. Priestley, at least by name, was no stranger to Josiah. A Unitarian minister, he was acquainted with Josiah's brother-in-law William Willet, who had criticized some of his theological writings and had stimulated his interest in magnetism and optics. Turner, who had made the first commercial preparation of sulphuric acid, had recently given Priestley his first chemistry lessons at Warrington Academy.

Though Priestley had been brought to Warrington Academy by Bentley and Turner as Tutor in Languages and Polite Literature, he thought of himself as first and foremost a theologian. The pupils at Warrington Academy thought of him first and foremost as an eccentric. Walking in a kind of disjointed, birdlike trot, Priestley chattered incessantly, stammering like a woodpecker. Even more disconcerting was the fact that the two sides of his face were so unalike as to cause a marked difference in his left and right profiles.

In spite of his eccentricities, Josiah thought Priestley a genius — as did later the rest of the world. Josiah also thought his new friend Bentley the most cultured, refined and well-informed man he had ever met. He had never in his life known anyone he liked and admired as much. As the three of them sat up late at night in Bentley's book-lined study, smoking their pipes and talking of theology and political affairs, Josiah was awed by the brilliance of the conversation and by the extraordinary chain of events which had landed him in Bentley's grand house. Nothing in Burslem, not even the Big House, could compare with the grandeur of the house in Paradise Street.

Though he was anxious to get back to his business in Burslem, Josiah was reluctant to leave his new friends and the style of life to which he had been introduced. Before he left — taking the post-chaise to Warrington and then going on to Burslem on horseback — he appointed Bentley & Boardman as his sole agents in Liverpool. The firm was to supervise the arrival in Liverpool of clay from Dorset, Cornwall and Devon, to send on these raw materials to Burslem, and finally to export the finished ware to America and other countries abroad. The journey which had begun in misfortune ended three weeks later with one of the most fortunate business decisions Josiah was ever to make.

Back at the Brick House, he was busy from dawn to dusk at the pottery. Still, he 'found time to make an experiment or two upon the aether' which his new friends in Liverpool had discussed. Then, one evening a week or so later, he sat at his desk, sharpened his quill and by the light of a sputtering candle wrote the first letter in an almost daily correspondence that was to span the next eighteen years:

My much esteemed Friend,
    If you will give me leave to call you so, and will not think the address too free, I shall not care how Quakerish or otherwise antique it may

sound, as it perfectly corresponds with the sentiments I have, and wish to continue towards you; nor is there a day passes, but I reflect with a pleasing gratitude upon the many kind offices I received in my confinement in your hospitable Town.

My good Doctor, and you in particular, have my warmest gratitude for the share you *both* had in promoting my recovery, and I know he is too well acquainted with the good flow of spirits (whatever they are) upon the whole animal economy to refuse you your share of the merit in this instance....'[1]

The friendship thus begun became, with the exception of his marriage to Sally, the most intimate relationship of Josiah's life. Undoubtedly Bentley's superior learning, his sophistication and his refined tastes offset to a degree Josiah's lack of education and humble beginnings. Josiah was nothing if not an opportunist, nor was he diffident in the furtherance of his career. As for what attracted Bentley to Josiah, it may have been the admiration of the man of ideas for the man of action. For in spite of his varied interests and activities, Bentley's character had in it more of the sensitive, scholarly teacher than of the shrewd, intuitive leader. Josiah had an exuberant personality, charm, honesty, courage and humour; perhaps Bentley sensed in him, as had William Willet, a mind and spirit capable of greatness.

After his accident on the way to Liverpool, Josiah became increasingly concerned with improvement of the roads. The arrangement with Bentley & Boardman quickly increased his business with America and the West Indies, but he was still hampered by accidents and thefts on the primitive, muddy lanes, which were marked only occasionally by upright stones. At a public meeting in Burslem he proposed that four miles of road be built from the village in the direction of Liverpool. The suggestion was bitterly opposed by the innkeepers at Newcastle, who believed that a new road would take the drinking and other traffic away from them. Josiah persisted, until several years later an Act of Parliament was obtained for the construction of a turnpike and the improvement of paving in the pottery villages.

Now he was confident enough and affluent enough to travel to London. His brother John had been almost as successful in promoting Josiah's ware as Josiah had been in producing it. John not only found new customers but commissioned modellers and engravers, bought gold and enamel colours and borrowed works of art for his brother to copy. With Cousin Thomas competently overseeing the workmen in the pottery, Josiah himself was designing new patterns and advising Sadler & Green on their prints. He also made improvements in the tools of manufacture as well as in the products. And the more successful he became the more he relied on Bentley's taste and judgement — '... as I am about to finish a shelf or two of a book-case, if you would assist me with your advice in the furniture I should esteem it a particular favour.'[2]

The more often he journeyed to London, to Liverpool and to Spen Green, and the more diversified his interests and activities became, the more Josiah needed someone in Burslem who could relieve him of some of the office responsibilities, such as bookkeeping which he particularly disliked. For this purpose he hired his fifteen-year-old nephew Thomas Byerley, a sensitive, high-spirited young man with intellectual aspirations. Josiah's sister Margaret Byerley had been widowed and left with three young children and little else. Her brothers John and Josiah and her brother-in-law William Willet contributed to her support and helped her to establish a small drapery shop in Newcastle. They also provided funds for sending young Tom to school.

Before starting to work for his Uncle Josiah at the Brick House, Tom had gone to London to visit his Uncle John and then on to Liverpool where he stayed with Bentley. Meanwhile, his trunk, which had been sent from school back home to Newcastle, was opened by his mother. In it she found some papers which, Josiah confided to Bentley, 'unravell'd a part of his History which we before were strangers to': young Tom wanted to be an author.

The disgraceful discovery so shocked his family and so embarrassed Tom that he ran away to live in a garret in London where he could put his feelings on paper in privacy. Josiah was astounded by such adolescent longings and wrote despairingly to Bentley: 'What we shall now do with a lad of his turn of mind I cannot tell.'[3] Bentley counselled patience and tolerance, and Tom quickly discovered that loneliness and starvation in a garret were not as romantic as he had imagined. He returned to Burslem and to the less spectacular life of bookkeeping for his Uncle Josiah who now thought him 'a very good boy'.

Josiah possessed a strong sense of family loyalty. Although he had little psychological understanding, he could always be relied upon to help out in practical matters. He frequently visited his mother, who lived with the Willets. He ordered fabrics and household goods from his sister Margaret's shop. He bought vegetables from the farm lands his brother Thomas was trying to cultivate in the time he could spare from his two potteries. He was concerned about his brother Richard who had gone into the Army and who drank too much. He worried about his brother Aaron who was obese, a bit dim-witted, in poor health and without employment. He kept his brother John informed about all of the family news. Just before Christmas of 1763, he reminded John: 'I must hint to you that sister Willet's little lasses will go to bed without their nightcaps soon if they do not receive an old shirt from their Unkle'[4]

By the end of the year 1763, Josiah was able to meet Richard Wedgwood's demand that he match his fiancée's dowry guinea for guinea. He thought it a time for everyone to celebrate, but further objections and delays were contrived by crafty old Richard which disturbed Josiah's Christmas holiday with his mother and the Willets. 'O grief of griefs that pleasure is still denied me,' he wrote to Bentley. 'I own I am somewhat asham'd & greatly mortify'd to be still kept at bay from those exalted pleasures you have often told me attend the marriage state.'[5]

If Josiah was naïve in supposing his future father-in-law would applaud his spectacular success over the past seven years, he was not so naïve in negotiating the marriage contract itself. He talked with Sally and then informed Bentley: '... our Pappa, over careful of his daughter's interest wo'd by some demands which I cannot comply with, go near to separate us, if we were not better determin'd.'[6] Old Richard probably admired him the more for his toughness. Certainly Josiah felt no ill will towards him for his petty objections and wily scheming.

Agreement was reached on 22 January 1764. Josiah was then able to write to Bentley: 'All things being amicably settled betwixt Pappa elect & myself, I yesterday prevail'd upon my dear girl to name the day, the blissful day! when she will reward all my faithful services & take me to her arms! In three words we are to be married on Wednesday next.'[7] The marriage was solemnized on 25 January 1764, in the fine church at Astbury in Cheshire. The couple then returned to the Brick House in Burslem where the small staff of servants had made preparations for the arrival of the new mistress.

Sally was not, even by the fashion of the day, a beautiful woman. What had attracted Josiah most were her intelligence and her determination, the latter of course being a reflection of his own personality. Physically she was tall but slender, her nose and lips thin, her skin milky fair, her hair red and her cheeks rosy. Her grey-green eyes sparkled when she was amused. When she was serious or bent on having her way, those same eyes took on a penetrating stare known, as grandchildren later testified, to wilt frailer and more frivolous natures.

In the early months of the marriage Sally worked closely with her husband, keeping his Experiment Books up to date and entering the accounts when Tom Byerley went to London to help John Wedgwood. Sally was also Josiah's chief critic on matters of design. 'I speak from experience in Female taste,' Josiah boasted to Bentley, 'without which I should have made but a poor figure among my Potts, not one of which, of any consequence, is finished without the approbation of my Sally.'[8]

Their first child Susannah, or Sukey, was born in January 1765. Josiah was delighted, describing the baby to her 'unckle' John as 'a fine, sprightly lass who will bear a good deal of dandleing'.[9] And he ended a letter to his friend Bentley with 'accept the best respects of two married lovers who are as happy as this world can make them'.

In the world larger than that which had brought so much happiness to the young potter in Staffordshire, King George III, who had married Princess Charlotte of Mecklenburg-Strelitz and produced the future George IV, was having more trouble with his Parliament than Josiah was having with his pots. While the King bumbled from one ministerial crisis to the next, orders for Wedgwood in the new improved creamware were coming in at a rapid pace. Among the local aristocracy Wedgwood ware was becoming as fashionable as Dresden and Sèvres porcelain.

Always ambitious to sell more goods, Josiah didn't want his brother John to leave London for a holiday in Paris: 'As to your going to France, I do not believe I can spare you out of London this summer, if business comes in for you at this rate; for instance — An Ord'r from St James's for a service of

Staffordshire ware about which I want to ask a hundred questions, and have never a mouth but yours in Town worth opening on the subject....'

The order came from Miss Deborah Chetwynd, Seamstress and Laundress to the Queen, through a Mr Smallwood of Newcastle whom Josiah thought 'bro't it to me (I believe because nobody else wo'd undertake it) & is as follows. A complete sett of tea things, with a gold ground and raised flowers upon it in green in the same manner of the green flowers that are raised upon the *mehons*, so it is wrote, but I suppose it should be melons.' Having gone into detail about the items in the tea service, Josiah instructed John to get him some gold for 'tryals' and added: 'Pray put on the best suit of Cloaths you ever had in your life and take the first opportunity of going to Court. Miss Chetwynd is Daughter to the Master of the Mint.'[10]

John carried out his brother's request. Josiah was more than ever the perfectionist in his meticulous execution of this first royal order, which so delighted Queen Charlotte that both John and Josiah obtained entrée to Court. Josiah soon went to London to call personally upon his 'good patroness Deborah Chetwynd' at Buckingham House. He wore a new blue surcoat, a scarlet waistcoat resplendent with lace, a 'lite Brown Dress Bobwig' and carried a sword bought at 'Ye Sign of ye Flaming Sword' in Great Newport Street.

This attentiveness to fashion and to Miss Chetwynd paid off. The queen graciously permitted him to style himself 'Potter to Her Majesty' and henceforth to call his creamware 'Queen's Ware'. Elated by this honour, Josiah proudly seized the opportunity of advertising the fact in the *St James's Chronicle* and of describing himself as 'Potter to Her Majesty' on his letterhead and invoices. Both John and Josiah now regularly visited Court, showing samples of new patterns which, as Josiah had foreseen, were eagerly ordered by various friends and relatives of the Royal Family.

One sunny autumn afternoon Josiah arrived at Buckingham House to collect his samples and, he hoped, some orders. Queen Charlotte was near a window examining a vase. To her annoyance the sunlight was directly in her eyes. Protocol would have been for one of the ladies-in-waiting to request a footman to adjust the blind. Apparently no one but Josiah noticed Her Majesty's discomfort. Instead of discreetly getting the attention of one of the ladies, he walked straight to the window and without permission or hesitation pulled down the blind. The Queen smiled and addressed her attendants: 'Ladies, Mr Wedgwood is, as you see, already an accomplished courtier.'

The action was typical of the man. When something needed to be done, Josiah moved immediately in the simplest, most direct manner, accomplishing his purpose without undue embarrassment or fuss. Such candour and social behaviour were unusual in an age of marked social distinctions, when almost all the gentry, great or small, looked down upon anyone in 'trade'.

After the success of the Queen's service, the King gave him a commission for a similar service for himself, but without bands or ribs. This was called 'The Royal Pattern'. Under such powerful patronage Wedgwood ware achieved instant acclaim and was soon seen on the tables of persons of rank and influence throughout England and Europe. No English potter had ever had such a triumph.

Although Wedgwood ledgers began to look like pages from *Burke's Peerage*, not all the customers came from the nobility. Because of its fine potting, excellent design, sanitary features and, above all, because of its relative cheapness, Queen's Ware soon became not only a household word but a household necessity. It was bought by people who before had been satisfied with wooden trenchers and pewter, as well as by those accustomed to Oriental porcelain and silver. During the first half of the year 1765, Josiah reported: 'I have this year sent goods to amount of about £1,000 to London all of which is oweing for and I should not care how soon I was counting some of the money.'[11]

Money was to him not an end in itself but the means of gaining what at the moment he needed or wanted—as it had been in matching Sally's dowry. He was not so foolish as to ignore the importance of making a respectable profit, but as his horizons expanded he became less interested in the day-to-day details which he termed 'piddling' and which he passed on to his young nephew Tom Byerley.

Josiah himself looked at the panorama of the future. The prospect was exhilarating. He experimented incessantly, involving himself in new projects, visiting London to obtain more commissions, attending endless meetings with local landowners to gain their support for the construction of turnpikes, and taking the lead in getting Parliamentary approval for the Trent and Mersey Canal—the single most important factor in opening the way to industrial change in the Potteries.

Canals and Clays
(1765 – 1767)

England was a long way behind France in the building of inland waterways in the 1750s. With the exception of the Sankey Canal, no important canal construction had been undertaken in spite of the small cost and relative safety of transporting bulk cargoes of raw material by water. The Duke of Bridgwater was the first to perceive the advantages of linking his collieries at Worsley by canal with the growing industrial city of Manchester. While the Duke himself was the moving spirit behind the scheme, and his steward John Gilbert was responsible for 'himself overlooking every part, and trusting scarce the smallest thing to be done except under his own eye',[1] the real engineering genius was a friend of Josiah Wedgwood's named James Brindley.

Because of his versatility and inventiveness, Brindley, who carried out many engineering projects without benefit of calculations or drawings, was known as 'the Schemer'. He rented a millwright's shop from those ubiquitous landowners Thomas and Long John Wedgwood, and on a piece of high ground called the 'Jenkins' built a windmill to grind flint in water and thus reduce air pollution in the neighbourhood of the potteries. On the first day the mill was operative, the sails were blown off in a high wind, an event which the philosophical Schemer ascribed to 'bad louck'.

As early as 1759 Brindley had been commissioned by two important Staffordshire landowners, Earl Gower of Trentham and Mr Thomas Anson of Shugborough, to survey the possibilities of building a navigable link between the rivers Trent and Severn. In spite of the obvious advantages of direct communication between the Potteries and Liverpool, there was little public support for such a scheme. The Bridgwater Canal, which was to cut the price of coal in Manchester by half, had to be proved a success before the Staffordshire plan would attract general enthusiasm.

Josiah, however, immediately saw the benefits to be gained from cheaper and surer methods of transport for his bulky raw materials — china clay and china stone from Devon and Cornwall — which had to be shipped by coaster from the south to Liverpool and then brought by pack horse to the Potteries. Just as important was a means of getting finished goods back to Liverpool for shipment to his rapidly expanding overseas markets. Bentley and his influential friend Sir William Meredith, Member of Parliament for Liverpool, also saw the advantages to Liverpool and supported the scheme.

On 11 March 1765, Josiah wrote to his brother John that he had dined with Brindley at the Leopard in Burslem, after which they attended a meeting to rouse support for the navigation scheme. Josiah added that after the meeting he himself 'could scarcely withstand the pressing solicitations I had from all present to undertake a journey or two for that purpose....'[2] So, with characteristic enthusiasm, he began to petition the support of influential people in the area. In Lichfield he sought out Dr Erasmus Darwin.

In the decade that had lapsed since the young doctor first saw the young potter, Darwin himself had become, if not a visitor at Court, at least known to the Royal Family. King George III heard of his skill through Lady Charlotte Finch, governess to Queen Charlotte's children, and asked: 'Why does not Dr Darwin come to London? He shall be my physician if he comes.' But Darwin's practice and his friends were centered in Lichfield.

He had married Mary Howard, a lovely but emotionally unstable young woman, who bore him three sons. He was one of the central figures in a literary and social group which met regularly at the Bishop's Palace in the Cathedral Close. The incumbent of the Palace was Canon Seward, whose beautiful daughter Anna, a minor poet and a prolific writer known as 'the Swan of Lichfield', was the other leader of the group. Romney painted her portrait, and Southey remarked of her, 'more beautiful eyes I never saw.' Anna was in love with Darwin—a love that went unrequited, for although he enjoyed a life-long flirtation with the Swan, as wives and mistresses Darwin invariably chose women who afforded him no intellectual competition.

Darwin's physical appearance made his attraction for the opposite sex unlikely. He was grossly overweight, with coarse features, his skin scarred by smallpox. He dressed carelessly, and his large, full-bottomed wig was often askew. Like Josiah he was lame: having suffered a broken knee-cap in a fall from a carriage which he himself had designed, he now walked with a stiff and clumsy gait. Like Priestley he had a pronounced stammer. Yet numbers of beautiful and intelligent women were enchanted with him.

At the time when Josiah solicited his support for the navigation scheme, Darwin was already a legend in Staffordshire. He spent the greater part of his time tightly wedged into a green chaise with yellow wheels, travelling all over the county calling on his patients. The chaise, which he had designed himself, was called a sulky because it had only room for one person. The inside was fitted with receptacles for books, writing materials and a supply of sweetmeats which the doctor munched constantly while making notes for his books and poems. In winter, when the roads became impassable, he would get out of the sulky and mount his ready-saddled horse, called Doctor, which followed the chaise wherever it went.

Darwin was unwilling to come out publicly in support of the navigation scheme. The issue was highly controversial and might have lost him many

patients. But he lent his anonymous support. In particular, he introduced
Josiah to John Whitehurst of Derby, a clockmaker and watch-repairer who
had achieved local fame by making the clock for the Town Hall. Whitehurst, like Brindley, had no formal education but at an early age displayed
a remarkable understanding of mechanics. Constructing thermometers
and barometers, he also took an interest in contriving waterworks. When
Josiah first discussed the canal project with him, he eagerly became
involved and was able to make a practical contribution out of his knowledge of hydraulics.

Darwin also arranged for Josiah to meet his friends in Birmingham.
Matthew Boulton, the prominent metal-hardware manufacturer, was told:
'I desire you and Dr Small will take this Infection, as you have given me ye
Infection of Steam-enginry.'[3] Josiah enthusiastically reported to Bentley
that in Darwin they had found 'an ingenious and zealous friend to our
cause'.

Towards the end of 1764 Bentley began writing a pamphlet putting forward the advantages of the 'Grand Trunk' scheme, as Brindley called it.
Through his brother John in London, Josiah introduced Bentley to Ralph
Griffiths, publisher of the *Monthly Review* and a former Staffordshire man
who, like Whitehurst, had begun life as a watchmaker. A contemporary of
John Wedgwood's and thus ten years older than Josiah, Griffiths had been
in London more than twenty years; he had established himself as a book-
seller and publisher, producing the first regularly issued literary review in
England, and was notorious for his highly publicized quarrel with his
lodger and assistant editor, Oliver Goldsmith.

Bentley and Griffiths had more than books in common. Both were Presbyterians, and both were widowers who enjoyed living in the grand style.
Griffiths had a house in the fashionable suburb of Turnham Green, and
maintained two carriages. Josiah told Griffiths that he envied his friends
and '... sometimes wish for a pair of wings & a learners seat amongst them,
& had the good Bishop Wilkins' scheme for flying been bro't to any tolerable perfection, you had most certainly seen me fluttering at your Dining
room window at Turnham Green.'[4]

Bentley submitted a draft of his Grand Trunk pamphlet both to the
sophisticated Griffiths and to the provincial Dr Darwin for criticism.
Perhaps because of previous experience with the literary sensibilities of
certain authors, Griffiths had little to say. Darwin was not so forbearing.
Josiah advised Bentley that the good doctor thought the style 'too flat and
tame' — and, he went on, 'be it remembered that he is a poetical genius.'
Darwin, however, passed on some of his criticism to Bentley direct; for, in
another letter, Josiah wrote: 'I doubt not you have rec'd my letter from
Uttoxeter and Derby — & a long, critical and explanatory letter from our
ingenious & poetical friend Doct'r Darwin which I doubt not (if it be such
as he generally favours his friends with) hath afforded you entertainment,
& shook your diaphragm for you whatever it may have done respecting
your Pamphlet on Navigation.'[5]

The criticism shook Bentley's diaphragm, but in a way which Josiah did
not expect. Bentley took such offence at Darwin's criticism that Josiah had

difficulty in soothing his ruffled feelings. 'A pamphlet we must have,' he wrote encouragingly, 'or our design will be defeated, so make the best of the present & correct, refine and sublimate in the next edition. Away with such hypercriticism! & let the press go on.'[6] Actually Josiah himself had a criticism of the pamphlet and was unwilling that the press go on until the changes he wished were made. 'I should like that part about the Pottery pared down a great deal. I am afraid of mentioning too much about our manufacture, lest our Governors should think it worth taxing.'[7]

In November 1765 Bentley's pamphlet was finally made available by several booksellers. Entered at Stationers' Hall in the name of Josiah Wedgwood, it was advertised in all the principal newspapers and quoted at great length by Ralph Griffiths in the December issue of the *Monthly Review*.

Josiah was in London at the time; he and Sally spent October and part of November with Bentley in lodgings belonging to friends of Bentley's in Laurence Lane. While in the city, Josiah transacted business with his good patroness, Deborah Chetwynd; and through introductions provided by her, by his brother John, and by Bentley and Bentley's friend Sir William Meredith, visited the houses of certain of the nobility to inspect and make drawings of their works of art. Wherever he went, he discreetly left copies of Bentley's pamphlet.

The main purpose of the visit to London was, of course, to lobby Parliamentary support for Brindley's Grand Trunk scheme. Josiah himself gave evidence before the House of Commons committee as to how exports and trade generally would benefit. Bentley spoke eloquently about the prosperous future for Liverpool. Brindley pointed to the success he had already achieved with the Duke of Bridgwater's canal, explained technical matters and answered questions. The Schemer was a plain-looking man, a bumpkin in fact; but, as Josiah observed, when he spoke 'all ears listen and every mind is filled with wonder at the things he pronounces to be practicable'.

Opponents of the proposed canal complained, somewhat illogically, that it would dry the springs, drain the rivers and cause such a shortage of water as to stop the mills. Mainly, however, the dispute was not so much over whether it was a good idea to have a canal as in what direction the canal should run.

While the Wedgwoods were in London, Josiah persuaded Brindley to accompany him and Sally and Bentley to a London theatre. Brindley had never seen a play. He found his mind so disturbed by events on the stage that he vowed he would not on any account see another — ever. Josiah and Sally had become more cosmopolitan in their tastes. On the way back to Staffordshire they stopped at the Duke of Marlborough's, spending 'half a day very agreeably at Blenheim House'. But the evening's entertainment was disappointing, as Josiah told Bentley; they 'went with the steward, his daughter & four sons to see a play at Woodstock, but alass, we had seen the London Theatre too lately to have much enjoym't from poverty, rags and blunders on the Woodstock stage.'[8]

The Grand Trunk Bill was finally passed, first through the Commons, then through the Lords. On 14 May 1766, it received the Royal Assent. There was great rejoicing in Burslem, and a general holiday was proclaimed. Before a large assembly Josiah dug the first sod, which was placed in a barrow and wheeled away by Brindley amidst deafening cheers. A barrel of Staffordshire ale was broached; healths were drunk to Lord Gower, Mr Anson and Lord Grey, and Josiah was publicly thanked for his efforts. In the afternoon a sheep was roasted whole. Late at night the festivities ended with a bonfire and fireworks in front of the Brick House.

The following month a Committee was set up to manage the project, the first meeting being held at the Crown Hotel in Stone. Among the Committee members were Josiah, his old partner and friend Thomas Whieldon, Thomas Gilbert, the M.P. for Newcastle-under-Lyme, Darwin's friend Matthew Boulton and Long John Wedgwood of the Big House. James Brindley was appointed Surveyor General, his brother-in-law Hugh Henshall was made Clerk of the Works and Josiah was unanimously elected Treasurer. Flattered by this honour, he was genuinely touched when Mr Sam Robinson 'took me aside very genteelly and offered to join in my security for so much as his Bond would be took for'. The amount of security required was £10,000. Despite the kind offer, Josiah—whose capital assets less than a decade earlier had been only £10—told his brother John: 'I own I should rather have no name but Wedgwood on the security.' He then joked about his new position by listing the Committee officers as follows:

James Brindley, Surveyor General	£200. per annum
Hugh Henshall, Clerk of the Works	£150. for Clerk & Self
J. Sparrow, Clerk to Proprietors	£100. per annum
Jos. Wedgwood, Treasurer	£000. out of which he bears his own expenses.[9]

Josiah was not the sort of person to be satisfied with playing less than a major role in any activity he pursued. Though the post of Treasurer was purely honorary, it was not a sinecure. There were meetings to attend, funds to collect and much negotiating with local landowners and the proprietors of rival schemes. Inevitably to some extent the pottery was neglected. Josiah told Bentley that he wished he could get back to 'the business of making Potts'.

On the other hand the frequent meetings with the local gentry on matters connected with the navigation led to friendships and to patronage by people like the Duke of Bridgwater. Josiah was able to enter the great houses of the region on a basis, if not of equality, at least of mutual respect. He saw at first hand what the gentry admired and placed in their cabinets and on their mantelpieces. He dined at their tables and observed the way in which the various courses were served. All the while he was imagining what he himself could make for these mantelpieces and dining tables.

The Duke of Bridgwater, despite eccentricities, was generous with his hospitality. Apparently be liked Josiah. He took him on a tour of his vast estates and then placed an order for 'the completest Table-service of

Cream Colour I could make'. Josiah also made a dinnerware service with Sir William Meredith's coat of arms on it, presenting it to him as a gift — after which Sir William passed on to him no less than eighteen substantial orders from friends.

So cosy did the two men become that Josiah sought Sir William's assistance in finding some 'genteel employment, not attached with too much fatigue' for his brother Aaron, who is 'deservedly very dear to me'. Sir William obliged by finding a minor official post in Liverpool which demanded little time and even less effort. No doubt Aaron was a bit pompous as well as stupid; Josiah and Bentley referred to him jokingly, but not unkindly, as 'the Alderman'. — 'The Alderman is not quite clever, but sends his best respects to you,' Josiah wrote to Bentley. 'I am going to take him a ride out & shake the dust & rust off his spirits a little....'[10]

Josiah was adept at acquiring patronage. All of the orders for dinnerware and political favours to some degree compensated for his sacrifice of time and energy to the Grand Trunk scheme. None of it would have been possible, of course, had he not had someone at the works skilled in both craftsmanship and management. Such a man Cousin Thomas had proven himself to be. So, in 1766, Josiah took him into partnership for 'Useful Queen's Ware'.

The word 'useful' was aptly chosen. Probably it was an unconscious description of the way Josiah viewed his cousin, as well as a convenient way of defining the limits of the partnership. Josiah needed a craftsman whom he could depend upon to carry out his ideas with the same thoroughness he himself would have displayed. For inspiration and critical judgement, he turned to his brother John, to Ralph Griffiths and, most importantly, to Bentley. Even as he drew up the agreement with 'useful Thomas', Josiah was perhaps envisioning a far more exciting venture with Bentley.

From Cousin Thomas's point of view, the new partnership was a distinct step up in the world. It came at just the right time, for only a few months earlier he had married Elizabeth, daughter of John Taylor, Master Potter of the Hill Top works, Burslem. No doubt Thomas saw Josiah's success as a model for his own life. Indeed there were similarities. Both were the youngest sons of ordinary, unambitious potters; both were open-minded and far more clever and skilled than their older brothers. Thomas, however, lacked the imagination which Josiah naturally possessed and the urbane assurance which he had carefully begun to acquire. If Thomas neglected to perceive these failings in himself, Josiah did not.

About this time Tom Byerley shocked his family afresh, with more adolescent antics of rebellion: he ran off to Dublin to go on the stage. Josiah was not only dismayed but considerably inconvenienced, for he had come to rely upon Tom to handle the loathed paperwork.

Bentley came to the rescue, recommending a young man named Peter Swift whom Josiah engaged for 'the agreed £25. per annum for the first two years & £30. for the third, but if he is dilligent & deserves it, he shall not want encouragement'.[11] Tall, thin, formally dressed in brown suit and bobbed wig, Swift's personality was quite unlike the usual stereotype of an accountant. Given to footnoting invoices with bits of gossip, he was not troubled by correct grammar or spelling; but he was a conscientious young man who eventually became 'Cashier, Paymaster General and Accountant General and without him we should all be in confusion at once'.[12]

Another employee, William Cox, helped in the office and acted more or less as Josiah's personal assistant. Cox, a plodding, middle-aged widower, was quite different in temperament from the cheerful dandy Swift. But from Josiah's point of view they both possessed an important virtue— absolute dependability. It was Cox who visited Matthew Boulton's factory to gather information on engine lathes, of which Josiah had first become aware from reading Plumier's *L'Art de Tourner*, which Bentley translated for him. In 1763, with Cox's assistance, Josiah adapted the metal-turning lathe for fluting and dicing pottery; until that time a primitive pottery lathe had been used simply to pare down inequalities in the surface of the clay.

Shortly after Swift came to work in Burslem, Cox went to London to assist in the first Wedgwood showroom in Charles Street, Grosvenor Square. Even though he was occupied by his own affairs, John Wedgwood continued to exercise general superintendence over his brother's business, and was quite popular with the fashionable ladies who frequented the pattern room in the new showroom. Thus, in spite of Tom Byerley's unexpected departure, Josiah now had all the major divisions of his business under the supervision of dependable and 'useful' men. He was in a position to devote his energies to the larger issues that interested him.

During the 1750s land had more than doubled in value in and around Burslem. Over the past five years Bentley & Boardman had more than tripled the quantity of Queen's Ware being shipped to America and to the West Indies. Now Josiah was anxious to purchase an estate on which he could build a factory commensurate with his increased trade. The Ridge House estate consisted of 350 acres lying between Hanley, Burslem and Newcastle, in an area through which the new canal would inevitably pass. After considerable haggling, Josiah concluded its purchase in July 1766 by agreeing to let the present owner, an elderly woman named Mrs Ashenhurst, have tenancy for life and by 'promising to pay £3,000. at Michaelmas next'.

The mammoth project of building the canal had already encountered difficulties because of the topography of the area to the north of the Potteries. The canal at its highest point was 395 feet above sea level; it was impractical to take it any higher, so it became necessary to build a tunnel, 2,888 yards long, at a place called Harecastle. The long boats were propelled through it by men who lay on their backs on the roof of the deckhouse and 'walked' the barge along by kicking against the roof of the tunnel.

Josiah greatly admired James Brindley, whom he enthusiastically called 'Brindley the Great'. He wrote to Bentley: 'It is an old adage that a man is either a Fool or a Physician at Fifty, & considering the opportunitys I have with the Brindleys and Bentleys of the Age, if I am not a very wise mortal before that age, I must be a blockhead in grain.'[13] It was Brindley who helped Josiah to deal with the landowners who were pressing competing claims, and who, during the excavating operations, which Josiah occasionally watched, found fossils and mineral specimens for Josiah to add to his collection. Brindley's wife, who was some thirty years younger than her husband, often stayed with the Wedgwoods when Brindley was away on business. On one occasion when the two families were together Josiah presented her with a tea set and a handsome mahogany tray. And on Brindley's companionship he was fond of remarking: 'I always edify as much in that man's company as at church.'

When faced with a problem Brindley had the habit of taking to his bed and refusing to get up until a solution occurred to him. One knotty problem laid him low for a week before an ingenious answer presented itself. Designing and constructing a network of canals that totalled over 360 miles, Brindley drove himself at a furious pace both mentally and physically. This troubled Josiah who confided to Bentley: 'I am afraid he will do too much & leave us before his vast designs are executed, he is so incessantly harrassed on every side, that he hath no rest, either for his mind, or Body, & will not be prevailed upon to take proper care of his health.'[14]

A month after he had left for Dublin, nineteen-year-old Tom Byerley informed his Uncle Josiah that he had 'quitted the Stage from a "Conviction of his inability to succeed in any tollerable degree" '. Josiah told Bentley: 'He is gone to London and desires we will get him a writer's place, or some berth in the service of the East India Company. I do not know what we shall do with him to keep him out of mischief and put him into a way of being of some use in the world.'[15]

Forcefully persuaded by his Uncle John, Tom returned to Burslem and being of use, if not to the world, at least to his Uncle Josiah who was quite pleased to have his wayward secretary back again. Josiah told Bentley that Tom had been reduced to 'the humble state of a Potter again; he is to be very good — never to do so again, etc, etc....'[16]

Now that Josiah was about to build a new factory, however, he needed more than his nephew's help. Having experienced the comradeship and intellectual stimulation of Darwin's friends in Lichfield, Bentley's circle in Liverpool and Ralph Griffiths's literary group in London, he felt a need to associate himself with men of culture and learning. More specifically, he wanted his friend Bentley to find him a partner in vase-making, the 'delightfull employm't which I have every day fuller assurance of making as profitable to the purse — as it must be pleasing to the mind — but you know what sort of a Partner it requires; either resolve quickly to join me yourself, or find me out another kindred spirit.'[17]

There were many reasons why a Wedgwood & Bentley partnership would be advantageous for Josiah. From the management of his Liverpool warehouses Bentley had gained marketing experience. He had the education and refined taste which Josiah lacked, and, even more important, he was personally acquainted with some of the most powerful and influential people in the country. He was Josiah's closest friend, and Josiah was invigorated by his company. With Bentley Josiah's creative ideas took concrete form; his confidence in himself was reinforced. Josiah often told him: 'When we have been some time together, I feel but half myself when we are separated.'[18]

There were no such compelling reasons from Bentley's point of view. He had no direct experience of pottery manufacture. His partnership with Boardman was satisfactory, their business in Liverpool successful. With the exception of Josiah, Bentley's closest friends were in Liverpool, and he was involved in community activities there. A project for draining the swamps around Liverpool was at the time receiving even more of his attention than the Octagonians, Warrington Academy and the Grand Trunk Canal. Bentley was a man of urban tastes and urban interests. To move to a dreary backwoods district, where the bleakness of the surroundings was made more depressing by heavy clouds of brown smoke belched out day and night, week after week, by the massive bottle-shaped kilns that dominated the landscape, was more like a retreat than a step forward. Bentley's initial reply to Josiah's proposal was hardly encouraging; but once Josiah had made up his mind to something, that something usually happened. He began to consult Bentley on how to design the new factory, where the new, larger London showrooms should be located and what clays to use in new experiments—the latter a subject about which Bentley surely knew next to nothing.

Many of the Staffordshire potters were interested in finding new raw materials to make a true porcelain that could compete with Meissen and Sèvres. Some pieces of porcelain made from white clay obtained in America had been imported into England and aroused considerable interest. The clay was said to be an earth belonging to the Cherokee Indian nation and to come from a place called Ayoree in Georgia or South Carolina. Josiah was concerned about this new clay on two counts: He did not want the Americans establishing potteries to rival his own, thus curtailing his export trade. Nor did he want any of his Staffordshire competitors to get a monopoly on importing the clay before he could acquire a substantial amount for his own use.

In May of 1767 he set out for London with three objectives: (1) to visit Matthew Boulton in Birmingham on the way, to study the layout of his Soho factory; (2) to find a way of acquiring some of the Cherokee clay without the other potters knowing of it; and (3) to find premises for a larger and more impressive London showroom.

Although Boulton and Josiah were fellow members of the Grand Trunk Navigation Committee, Boulton had been too busy with his various business schemes to attend many meetings. Six years older than Josiah, Boulton was a born promoter; forever developing new ideas and new products, he often took on more than he could reasonably expect to accomplish. The business he had inherited from his father was a small buckle-making factory, hardly more than a country workshop. He quickly expanded the range of items to include what at the time were called 'toys'—that is, buckles, clasps, buttons, hooks, chains, snuffboxes, jewellery and any and every sort of small item that could be produced in metal. With money acquired from marrying, successively, two sisters who were heiresses, and by forming a partnership with John Fothergill, a tradesman who, like Bentley, had connections in foreign markets, Boulton built himself a large and impressive factory which he named Soho. There he began producing candlesticks, pots, bowls, dishes, spoons, tureens, first in the newly invented Sheffield plate and then in sterling silver.

For the past couple of years he had been interested in experiments in steam power, involving his 'philosophical friends' Dr Darwin and Dr William Small of Birmingham. Boulton had sent Benjamin Franklin a model steam engine accompanied by a number of questions about valves— whether it was best to introduce the jet of cold water at the bottom or the top of the receiver, and so on. Then Darwin became enthusiastic enough himself 'to make innumerable Experiments on acqueous, sulphurous, metallic & saline Vapours. Food for fire-engines!'[19]

Josiah was suitably impressed not only by the experiments with steam engines but by what he saw at Soho. First of all Boulton had been shrewd in his choice of property on which to build his factory and his own house, which was some 150 yards distant from the factory. This property, close to the main road between Birmingham and Wolverhampton, already had a stream, canal and mill dam built by its previous owner. The factory which Boulton built was planned in an entirely new way from other factories of the period. The three-floor building was on a grand scale, with an entrance with a clock tower in the middle and on either side wings which formed a large open courtyard at the back. The two upper floors were dwellings for the workmen and their families. Josiah left Soho determined to incorporate some of Boulton's innovations into the factory he intended to build on the Ridge House estate.

Once in London Josiah purchased a map of South Carolina and the Cherokee nation. He consulted various influential people including the Duke of Bridgwater, who advised against applying for a patent or grant but urged him instead to send an agent over to America immediately. Lord Gower's advice was much the same. Furthermore he promised to accredit Josiah's agent to the Governor of South Carolina and to the Attorney General who was under obligation to him since he had secured him his post.

Even more fortuitous, Ralph Griffiths had a brother staying with him who had just returned from South Carolina. Thomas Griffiths retained an interest in a large tract of land in South Carolina although he had failed, through lack of capital, in a scheme for manufacturing maple sugar. For the sum of £50 per annum and his maintenance Griffiths agreed to return to America, to make the dangerous journey into Cherokee territory, to negotiate with the Indians for the purchase of several tons of clay and to bring it back with him to England. The agreement was reached so easily in the pleasant house in Turnham Green that Josiah became suspicious that Griffiths might simply keep the money intended for the clay and never return—'for I have known instances of persons changing their sentiments & principles with the climate & totally forgetting their connections with the friends they have left behind them.'[20] He considered asking Ralph Griffiths to put up a bond for his brother, but then decided that 'I sho'd hardly take the forfeiture if made'.[21]

Josiah was not so lucky in finding a showroom to replace the Charles Street premises. 'And besides room for my *Ware* I must have more room for my Ladys, for they sometimes come in very large shoals together, and one party are often obliged to wait till another have done their business.'[22] But, in spite of the assistance of his brother John and his own stubborn determination to find a '*Large* Room' with six or eight tables to show various table and dessert services 'in order to *do the needful* with the Ladys in the neatest, genteelest and best method ...',[23] suitable rooms were not found on this journey.

Josiah was not really discouraged. On the whole the weeks in London had been profitable and enjoyable. His brother Aaron, 'the Alderman', had accompanied him and was apparently in better health. Or at least his spirits had improved, for 'His Aldermanship' thrived upon good food and drink and pleasant company. The two of them spent an agreeable day at Greenwich. With brother John they visited Ranelagh, a popular pleasure garden in Chelsea where fashionable Londoners dined in theatre-style boxes lining the walls of a huge rotunda and watched other fashionable Londoners walking about a large circular promenade. They dined at other popular inns and clubs and spent a number of evenings in Turnham Green with the Griffiths brothers.

For Josiah it was a happy time. The future was hopeful. He now had two children, his son John having been born a year earlier, and Sally was expecting a third child in the coming month. His business had succeeded even beyond *his* optimistic expectations. By the middle of 1767 it seemed that all things were possible and that nothing could go wrong.

4

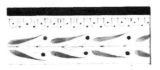

A Time of Crises
(1767 – 1769)

Josiah arrived home safely from London on 12 June 1767, and 'found everything agreeable to my wishes here'. Brindley and Hugh Henshall came to see him the following day to discuss canal business. Then, hurriedly, he dashed off a note to Bentley telling him that instructions were being prepared for Thomas Griffiths's departure for South Carolina within a fortnight. Cheerful and optimistic about his future success and confident that Bentley would eventually be persuaded to join him, Josiah said: 'I am preparing designs, Models, Moulds, Clays, Colours etc. etc. for the Vasework, by which means we shall be able to do business *efectually* 12 months sooner than we could without those preparatory steps, & I have no fear but it will answer our utmost wishes.'[1]

He handed the postman his letter to Bentley, receiving in exchange a letter from William Hodgson, a merchant banker in London. Reading the letter he began to tremble and feel faint: Hodgson informed him of the sudden, tragic death of his brother John.

On Wednesday evening, 10 June, after Josiah and the Alderman had left on their return journey to Burslem, John had gone to see the fireworks at Ranelagh, then on to the Swan where he had dined so recently with his brothers. He stayed until midnight, then asked for a bed. Unfortunately the inn was unable to accommodate him, so he left, and 'in passing the River side, 'tis supposed he slipped in; he was found the next morning about five ...'.[2] Most likely John was robbed and murdered. Josiah would never know. Criminal assaults were so common at that time that men seldom went about the streets of London after midnight except in groups or with an armed escort.

Josiah was unable to return to London immediately, since Sally was about to give birth to their third child. His eldest brother Thomas and his brother-in-law William Willet left immediately to settle John's business affairs and to make arrangements for his burial. Though restive and secretive in his personal life, John had been cautious and responsible enough to leave a will, made less than three months before his death, appointing Hodgson and Josiah as executors. The will listed him as *late* of

Cateaton Street, now of Newcastle-under-Lyme; he had been quite well off financially, and had left gifts and substantial sums of money to relatives and friends.

Two things puzzled Josiah. If John was planning to return to live in Staffordshire, which he disliked, why had he not told Josiah, so that he could make plans to replace John as his London agent? And why had John made a will so recently—as if he anticipated that he might die in some violent fashion? Josiah wrote to Ralph Griffiths about his brother: 'I had long grieved for him as for one who from an unhappy combination of circumstances could enjoy or relish very few of the comforts of life, & but little hopes, alas of ...'[3] The letter was torn, so what hopes alas! died with John.

The inventory Hodgson made of the possessions in John's lodgings showed him to have had what, for the time, was a large wardrobe of elegant and expensive clothes, a gold watch, a gold ring, a seal and a gold chain. Perhaps in deference to John's flamboyant style, Hodgson arranged a grand funeral which included the purchase of a dozen black silk handkerchiefs for the hired mourners and black armbands for the pallbearers. The cost of the funeral was £50. 11s. 7d. —more than twice the amount of the legacy John Wedgwood never received from the estate of his insolvent father. The only members of the family present at the grand funeral were his brother Thomas and his brother-in-law Willet.

For weeks Josiah was depressed, experiencing an uncharacteristic listlessness which lifted only slightly at the birth on 2 July of a second son, Richard. The death of his favourite brother under such strange circumstances was the first major personal loss Josiah had suffered in his thirty-seven years. He was not psychologically equipped to handle disappointments, defeat or disaster; his entire being was oriented towards achievement and a destiny he could control directly. Further upset that Bentley's ill health and problems with his warehousing business had prevented his coming to Burslem to console him, Josiah succumbed to an attack of biliousness. 'The return of my Complaint sunk my spirits,' he reported to Bentley. Then, characteristically, he reasoned that this was something his own common sense could conquer: '... but it is happily gone off without my being very ill, and I have now begun a course of Exercise which I intend to continue, and consists in riding on horseback from 10 to 20 miles a day, and by way of food and Physick, I take Whey, and yolks of Eggs in abundance, with a mixture of Rhubarb and soap just to keep my body open, and I find this regimen to agree with me very well.'[4]

There were other problems which such a regimen was unlikely to cure. Neither Josiah's mother, who was living with the Willets in Newcastle, nor the Alderman, who lived with Josiah and Sally when he was not in Liverpool staying with Bentley, was in good health. Furthermore, Mrs Ashenhurst was creating difficulties over the purchase of the Ridge House estate: she now wanted double the agreed-upon price. 'She scolds and huffs away at a large rate, and seems to be in a good way for making me a hard bargain: I have wrote her by Mr Hodgson, and instructed him to treat with her. If he succeeds, I hope yet to be able to build a Vaseworks the latter end of this summer.'[5]

1-2
Josiah Wedgwood I
and his wife Sarah
*Oils by Sir Joshua
Reynolds, 1782*

3
Overleaf: Wedgwood
wares of the eigh-
teenth century

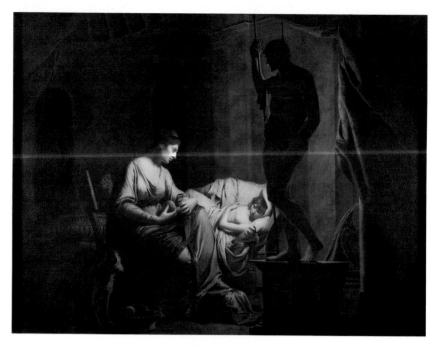

4   *Penelope Unravelling Her Web:* oil by Joseph Wright of Derby, 1783

5   *The Labourers:* enamel on Wedgwood plaque by George Stubbs, 1781

The bickering back and forth through the banker Hodgson continued until December 1767, when, conveniently for Josiah, Mrs Ashenhurst died. The purchase was at once concluded amicably with her son, an Army major quartered in Ireland, and Josiah put into operation his plans for the new vase works.

While he was negotiating with the Ashenhurst family, he was also 'going on with my experiments upon various Earths, Clays, etc, for different bodys, & shall next go upon Glazes'.[6] A year earlier, in 1766, he had first produced the unglazed black stoneware which he named Basalt. Now he had perfected it, made his first medallion and was quite justifiably proud and optimistic about its future. He had also perfected pebbled and marbled wares which were soon to create a 'vase madness', and had begun experiments on bronze and encaustic wares. There was no decrease in the 'demand for cream colour, alias Q'ware, alias ivory. It is really amazing how rapidly its use has spread over the whole globe ... .'[7]

On 8 November 1767, Erasmus Darwin wrote a letter to Josiah introducing his old school friend, Captain James Keir, who wished to look over the Wedgwood factory. When Keir visited at the Brick House he met there John Whitehurst, the instrument-maker whom Darwin had earlier introduced to Josiah and who had helped Brindley and Henshall on the canal project.

Keir and Darwin had been friends in Edinburgh where both completed their medical studies. Though Keir, whose main interest was chemistry, had decided against practising medicine and instead entered the Army, the two had maintained their friendship. Army life, however, began to bore Keir. He decided to sell his commission and put his chemical skills to use in the establishment of a glass factory. On visiting Darwin in Lichfield he hoped not only to make a survey of the various industries in the area and to get Darwin's advice on the site for a factory, but also to find a wife: 'Mrs Darwin can recommend to me some Lichfield *fair* that has more money and love than wit.'[8] Keir and Darwin had much in common: wit, love of women, curiosity about all things chemical and scientific, but also huge appetites and great girths. In their mid-forties, both men weighed more than twenty stone.

Josiah took Keir and Whitehurst through the Brick House works and introduced them to his partner, 'useful Thomas'. Josiah told them of his ideas for the new factory that would be built beside the canal. Keir was impressed by Josiah and by what he saw at the Brick House works, and Josiah in turn was impressed by Keir's knowledge of chemistry and by his ready grasp of the problems then common to all the industries in the area.

As Josiah thought of the difficulties of establishing a new vase-making business and in building a factory some three times the size of the Brick House works, he became obsessed by the necessity of having Bentley as his partner. After the death of John, his need became even more urgent. But in November 1767, when Keir and Whitehurst visited Burslem, Bentley was still not convinced of the desirability of giving up his life in Liverpool to join Josiah in Staffordshire. Josiah applied pressure, appealing to his friend in every way he could, and by the end of the year Bentley had accepted Josiah's proposal of a partnership in the manufacture and sale of *ornamental* ware — with the provision that Bentley would retain his partnership with Boardman. Cousin Thomas was to continue as Josiah's partner for *useful* ware.

Thus the year of 1768 began with renewed hopes. Plans were being drawn up for the factory, which Darwin christened Etruria, the name reflecting the widespread interest at the time in classical pottery. What had been excavated was generally thought to be Etruscan in origin, though in fact it was Attic Greek.

Having already made up his mind that his factory would be modelled on Boulton's Soho, with modifications reflecting the differences in the two industries, Josiah hired a local man, Joseph Pickford, as architect. He also consulted with Darwin, who was designing for him a horizontal windmill 'to grind colours, if it sho'd grind anything'. And he sought advice from the inventive Whitehurst, who had ideas of his own on how a factory ought to be built. None of this made Pickford's job any easier. Josiah knew exactly what he wanted: 'An extensive manufactory, aptly constituted, he viewed in the light of a vast machine, whose different members are mutually sub-servient & perform their several functions under the general guidance & control of the master.'[9]

He concerned himself not only with plans for the factory and with building houses for the workmen, but also with building a house for himself and a house for Bentley. The house for Bentley took precedence over everything. In fact, it was begun even before Bentley had given his final consent to the partnership. Subtlety was not a part of Josiah's character. 'If the Alderman would like to build, I will make him a building lease, if not, I will do it myself for a common rent,' he told Bentley. 'So you may be settling the plan of one house for yourself, and another for my Brother unless you can agree to live together.'[10]

Josiah, having made certain that the new canal would pass not only through his estate but directly in front of his new factory, met with Hugh Henshall to set out the plans. He complained: 'The fields are unfortunately so very level that the Canal will run in a straight line thro' them, at least so it is set out, for I could not prevail upon the inflexible Vandal to give me *one line of Grace* — He must go the nearest & best way, or Mr Brindley wo'd go mad.'[11]

In March of 1768 Josiah and his brother-in-law, Sally's brother John, went to London. They travelled by way of Lichfield, where they stayed with Darwin and viewed the proposed windmill, then went on to Soho, where Josiah and Boulton discussed decorating and mounting Wedgwood vases and other articles with metal. In London they went out to Turnham Green to visit Ralph Griffiths, recently remarried, whose wife was expect-ing their first child. Josiah, who was forever needling Bentley to marry again, wrote: 'I sho'd tell you how happy our host & his Lady are in each other, how happy they made us ....'[12]

On this stay in London Josiah succeeded in finding the showrooms that he had looked for nine months earlier. He leased a new, large house at the corner of Newport Street at the top of St Martin's Lane, and also secured as resident artist David Rhodes, who previously had been an enameller at the Leeds pottery. 'He paints flowers and Landscapes very prettily, prepares a pretty good powder gold, & has a tolerable notion of Colours. He has an Apprentice and another hand ...,' Josiah reported to Bentley. 'The having such a Man as this under the same roof with the warehouse to do Crests, or any other pattern by ord'r, to take sketches, etc. is the most convenient thing imaginable & nobody but ourselves will know what he is doing.'[13]

David Rhodes was not the only artist Josiah hired. A flamboyant modeller named John Voyez, who had first worked with a silversmith and then spent two or three years carving in wood and marble, was also employed. Shrewd, ambitious and unscrupulous, Voyez made a good first impression. Josiah hired him on the spot, an impulsive decision he later regretted.

He acquired on this visit not only new premises and new artists but also one of his most helpful and influential patrons: 'I have spent several hours with Lord Cathcart our ambassador to Russia & we are to do great things for each other.'[14] Actually it was Lady Cathcart, rather than her husband, who was to do the great things. A sister of Sir William Hamilton, British Ambassador to the court of Naples, Lady Cathcart was familiar with the treasures her brother had acquired at Herculaneum, and with Wedgwood's productions; furthermore, she was a woman of superb taste. Josiah agreed to present to Lord and Lady Cathcart a gift of a dinnerware service and a set of vases. It was also agreed that the Ambassador and his wife would exhibit Josiah's wares and accept orders for him, acting in effect as his unpaid agents. Josiah never underestimated the value of employing the right sponsors: 'If a Royal or Noble introduction be as necessary to the sales of an article of *Luxury* as real Elegance & Beauty, then the Manufacturer, if he consults his own interest, will bestow as much pains & expense too if necessary, in gaining the favour of these advantages as he wo'd in bestowing the latter.'[15]

After his return from this successful stay in London, however, things again began to go badly. Some of Josiah's Staffordshire neighbours suggested that he had taken advantage of his position to have the proposed canal run directly in front of the new factory he was building. This was absolutely true, of course, but Josiah was none the less indignant that any ulterior motives should be attributed to him. The dispute was referred to the Committee (of which, of course, Josiah was Treasurer), and the Schemer, Brindley, rather heavy-handedly persuaded the protesters that the best route for the canal was indeed in front of the new Wedgwood factory.

Even though he had won, Josiah was upset by this episode. Anxiety and fatigue were compounded by another attack of pain in his knee. No doubt he had walked too much while he was in London. Still, there was no denying that these attacks — probably osteomyelitis aggravated by the earlier illness and injuries — were becoming more frequent and severe. The medicines which Darwin had prescribed three years earlier were no longer effective. Josiah could not climb the stairs and ladders to the various workshops in the old-fashioned Brick House works. Eventually he could not walk at all.

Darwin consulted with James Bent, a Newcastle surgeon. It was finally decided that the only solution was amputation. Josiah had faced this possibility long before, but to accept the decision demanded courage. There were no anaesthetics; standards of hygiene were low and surgeons often incompetent. Patients as frequently died from the shock of the operation as later from gangrene.

The amputation took place in Josiah's own house on 31 May 1768, a date which he later referred to as 'St Amputation Day'. Bentley came to be with him. Refusing to have the operation hidden from his view, Josiah sat upright in a chair while two surgeons sawed off his leg. He was heavily sedated with laudanum, yet legend claims he watched the ordeal without a shrink or groan.

After the operation was over, the patient remaining alive, Peter Swift appended to an invoice for 'creamware piggins, cream pots, salts, etc.' a laconic postscript to William Cox in London: 'Your favour of the 26th is just come to hand, but can make no reply to the contents. Mr Wedgwood has this day had his leg taken off, & is as well as can be expected after such an execution.'[16]

For several days it was not certain whether the wound would heal or become infected. There was concern in London as well as in Burslem. Lord Cathcart, Lord Bessborough, the Duke of Bedford, the Duke of Marlborough, the Honourable Miss Chetwynd at Buckingham House, Sir William Meredith and many of Josiah's other patrons inquired at the London showrooms for news of his progress. Lord Gower sent a messenger daily to Burslem from his seat at Trentham to get news of the situation.

Five days after the operation the bandages were removed and Bent pronounced the wound to be healing satisfactorily. But the rejoicing was short-lived, for on that same day the baby Richard, then ten months old, died from a severe gastric complaint. Swift again informed Cox: 'I think Mrs W has had severe tryals of late, but the great hopes of Mr W's perfect recovery seems to keep her Spirits up in a tollerable degree.'[17]

Bentley remained with Josiah and Sally for a fortnight, helping with the business and assuring himself that Josiah really was going to be all right. On 14 June Darwin wrote that he regretted he could not come again to visit, but understood that Josiah was better and that their mutual friend Boulton, who had gone to Buxton for his health, was likely to call on Josiah on the way back. Darwin wrote chattily about scientific researches, ending with: 'Mr Edgeworth, a philosophical friend of mine in Oxfordshire, writes me word he has nearly completed a Wagon drawn by Fire, and a walking Table which will carry forty men. This is all the news I can think of to amuse you with in the philosophical Arts.'[18]

Inevitably Josiah took a scientific interest in his own progress: 'My leg is almost healed, the wound is not quite 2 inches by 1½. I measur'd it with the compasses this morning when I dress'd it. Yes! When I dress'd it, for I have turn'd my surgeon adrift, & Sally and I are sole managers now, only we give him leave to peep at it now & then, when he lifts up his hands &

eyes & will scarcely believe it to be the wound he dress'd before.'[19]

Other family crises were taking place as well. Shortly after the death of baby Richard, and while Josiah was still confined to his bed, there were two other deaths in the family: Josiah's mother, who had been in poor health for several years, died in Newcastle, and his brother Aaron, the Alderman, who had been in poor health all of his life, died in Liverpool. Construction on the house for him at Etruria was never begun.

Young Tom Byerley now rebelled for the third time. On this occasion, however, he announced his plans in advance. He was sailing for America in hope of finding a career on the stage in the New World. Josiah naturally disapproved, but realized that there was no way of restraining the impulsive young man. He therefore asked Bentley to arrange a credit of £70 for Tom and to commend him to the good offices of a family in Philadelphia. Never one to miss out on a business opportunity, even from his sickbed, he also suggested: 'If he has a mind to take a few pieces, or 3 or 4 pounds worth of my ware with him, you may let him have so much on his own acc't, & pray advise him to ship himself in the cheapest way for America.'[20] Fortunately for Tom, Bentley was more sympathetic and persuaded Josiah not to send him steerage.

During the time that he was recovering, and confined to his bed, Josiah busied himself by arguing, debating and frequently arbitrarily changing the details of the construction of Etruria. Almost daily he quarreled with Pickford, whom he thought intransigent. With all the changes Josiah had made, Pickford presented a new estimate which was double that of the original one. There were other problems as well. Working capital was in short supply, largely because customers frequently took a year or more to settle their accounts. Josiah asked Cox to collect all of the outstanding debts. The serious-minded but shy Cox disliked talking with customers and most particularly asking them for money. Lacking the supervision of John Wedgwood and through a combination of reticence and ineptitude, Cox had got the accounts in such a muddle that he was uncertain who had paid his bill and who hadn't. There was never any question of Cox's honesty, although Josiah admitted to Sally that to him Cox's character was 'an enigma'. Thus, in spite of selling practically everything he could produce and accumulating orders for delivery months from now, Josiah was very much in need of money to finance the construction at Etruria.

Less successful in selling his wares was his brother Thomas, who found himself unable to manage two potteries, Thomas was producing much more than he could sell, and Josiah agreed to take some of his production off his hands to fill his own orders. He also bought from Thomas the old Churchyard works, which he then leased to another cousin, young Joseph Wedgwood, the son of another Aaron Wedgwood, potter at Longton. Joseph had married the daughter of Josiah's eldest sister Ann. He was a conscientious young man and seemed to Josiah likely to become a good potter — or, in any event, a better potter than brother Thomas.

The first visit Josiah made to London after the amputation of his leg was with both Sally and Bentley, in October of 1768. In London he was fitted with a wooden leg by Mr Addison, a wood carver in Hanover Street. Then he and Bentley began work on the new showroom in Newport Street. There were actually two buildings joined together on the first floor by a large room which extended over both ground-floor shops. The entrance to the showrooms was under an archway in the centre. The first floor was the showroom for the gentry. There dinner and dessert services, teaware and large bas-reliefs, flower pots and bough pots and vases were displayed. The ground-floor shops were for the sale of more ordinary goods including seconds and trial pieces.

The 'vase madness' or craze for ornamental ware really began with the opening of the Newport Street showroom. In the courtyard behind the building an enamelling kiln was built for David Rhodes and his assistant William Croft. The second floor of the building was used as living quarters by Bentley and by Josiah and Sally when they were in town. Otherwise it was partially occupied by Cox and a housekeeper.

They all went back to Burslem, where it was agreed that Bentley would stay at the Brick House looking after his new partner's business while Josiah returned to London, this time taking not only Sally but his sister Catherine Willet and a servant to look after them. The accommodations in Newport Street were pleasant enough for the Wedgwoods to entertain the Hodgsons and the Ralph Griffithses and the Matthew Boultons who were also visiting London.

For several days Josiah and Boulton went 'curiosity hunting together'. They sought items which they could produce jointly. But, with two such dominant and decisive personalities, disagreement was inevitable. Josiah had had some early doubts as to the success of this association and told Bentley that Boulton 'proposed an alliance betwixt the Pottery and Metal branches, viz. that we shall make such things as will be suitable for mounting, & not have that Pott look, and he will finish them with mounts. What do you think of it? Perhaps you wo'd rather he wo'd let them alone.'[21] Probably the difficulty was that Josiah saw the metal as ornamentation for his pots, whereas Boulton viewed the pots as a means of showing to advantage his metal work.

Bentley and Josiah exchanged letters or business notes almost daily while Josiah was in London and Bentley at the Brick House. During this four-month period Bentley's attitude towards the practical arrangements of his new partnership changed. Perhaps he discovered how much he disliked provincial Staffordshire, but knew this would be a sensitive subject with Josiah. Perhaps he realized that he preferred the marketing of pots to their manufacture. In any event, Bentley did not want to move to the Etruria estate.

Fortunately, at the same time, Josiah's extended stay in London convinced him that the sincere but dilatory Cox lacked the intelligence, tact and force of personality to promote the business in the direction Josiah intended. 'I will make all the dispatch I can to ease him of a part of his burden, but I can hardly think of leaving these rooms without leaving a successor in them to do what I fear we shall never get any servant capable of,' Josiah told Bentley; 'and yet this would be laying a plan to keep us ever asunder, the very reverse of what we wish, and what I hope we shall neither of us comply with. Well, we must settle this matter over a pipe when I have next the pleasure of seeing you …'.[22]

Whatever he might say, the success of the business was Josiah's first concern. The partnership books had been opened the previous November. Together Josiah and Bentley had put together the new showroom and hired hands for the partially completed Etruria; but the elegant new house built especially for Bentley would never be occupied by him.

5

The Etruscan Arts Are Reborn
(1769 – 1772)

13 June 1769 dawned bright and clear. Josiah and Sally and their two children Sukey and John, old Richard Wedgwood and his son John, Long John Wedgwood and his family, Thomas Wedgwood of the Big House and his wife, brother Thomas Wedgwood and his family, cousin Thomas Wedgwood and his family, young Joseph and Mary Wedgwood, the Whieldons, the Brindleys and the Henshalls, as well as other friends and relatives, came riding through the pleasant lanes to join the workmen and their families for the opening of the Ornamental Section of the Etruria works.

To celebrate the event Josiah made a brief speech and then donned 'slops', the potter's customary attire. He sat down at the potter's wheel while Bentley turned the crank. With great skill and precision he threw six black Basalt vases of classic Greek shape, which were later decorated with red Etruscan figures and the inscription 'Artes Etruriae Renascuntur — 13 June 1769, Our First Day's Throwing at Etruria'.

The entire company then adjourned to the uplands beyond the factory where a great feast had been laid out on tables beneath the trees. Josiah looked round him and at the hill beyond where the foundations were already laid and construction had begun on Etruria Hall, the small, elegant Georgian manor house he was building for his family. He was now truly a man of property. At the beginning of his fortieth year, for many men a time of internal crisis and change, he had reached a plateau from which he could look back at the distance he had come and see the exhilarating climb still before him. During the past eighteen months he had been through four deaths in his family, faced the possibility of his own death, survived the shock of mutilation and adjusted to the unavoidable physical restrictions resulting from the amputation. Furthermore he had persisted until he gained for a partner the man whose taste and judgement he most admired. By himself he had conceived and built the most powerful and advanced industrial organization in England.

The new Etruria works occupied seven acres and was enclosed by walls on all sides except the one that gave on the canal. In his mind's eye Josiah saw adjoining the factory the village of Etruria now being built for the workmen. Within the next few years it would expand from two dozen to two hundred houses. On this opening day in June Josiah must have felt that he was well in sight of his self-appointed goals. Sally was radiant. Bentley, with his courtly manners, was admired by everyone.

Cousin Thomas, partner in the Useful works still at the Brick House, was very much in the background. He could hardly have been pleased when he learned of the new backstamp 'Wedgwood & Bentley' on each article of ornamental production. That the useful wares might have been stamped 'Wedgwood & Wedgwood' probably never crossed Josiah's mind. Those wares were stamped 'Wedgwood' only, and there was no doubt in anyone's mind who that Wedgwood was.

Bentley, too, was uneasy at the celebrations. If Josiah was insensitive to Cousin Thomas's background role, Bentley was not. Not as in Liverpool or in London, Josiah in Staffordshire was the genial and generous host, in sole possession of the centre of the stage. Bentley could hardly have missed the unconscious symbolism of the opening ceremony. If he remained long at Etruria, he would inevitably be relegated to turning the wheel while Josiah commanded the shape of things to come.

In August of 1769 Bentley and his sister-in-law Elizabeth Oates moved from Liverpool to London, staying first in the apartments over the Newport Street showroom. London at that time was changing rapidly both in appearance and in character: Blackfriars Bridge had been completed, the Gates of the City of London were being removed, and the old symbolic shop signs were fast disappearing. The first Royal Academy Exhibition had just been held. Bentley, partly through his association with Ralph Griffiths, soon found himself part of a group of literary men, artists and scientists, among them Reynolds, Romney, Solander, Banks and Darwin's friend Richard Lovell Edgeworth, who met as a club every Wednesday night at Young Slaughter's Coffee House in St Martin's Lane to discuss art, politics, literature, theology and scientific research. When Josiah was in town he attended the meetings as Bentley's guest. After the third time he presented the club with a service of creamware. Thereafter the group dined only off Wedgwood ware.

Five months after arriving in London, Bentley and his sister-in-law, who was now deaf and in poor health, purchased a large house in Little Cheyne Row, in Chelsea. Bentley chose this particular house not only on its merits and for the beauty of the gardens and surrounding fields, but also because of its proximity to the Chelsea china factory in Cheyne Row which had been making porcelain since 1745. Recently this factory had fallen on hard times and had been put up for sale. Josiah offered to buy the moulds and models, but the proprietors wanted to sell the factory complete, and eventually it was bought by William Duesbury, who owned the Derby china factory. Still, the Chelsea area was the best place in London for Wedgwood & Bentley to recruit china painters and set up a studio.

Josiah made the ware at Etruria, then sent it by wagon to Chelsea, where Bentley directed the work of Rhodes, Croft and other artists who decorated and finished the ware. One disadvantage was the distance between the Chelsea studio and the Newport Street showroom. Bentley could not be in both places at once. The place that suffered most was the showroom. An assistant was hired to live on the Newport Street premises, taking over the duties of head clerk from the enigmatic Cox whose presence was now required at least part of the time in Staffordshire. Cox's previously suspected maladministration became even more apparent just as Bentley was moving to Chelsea, and Josiah quite rightly feared that even more 'confusion and bad consequences' would occur if Bentley were not on hand in Newport Street to examine daily the cash and accounts. Bentley, however, placed his trust in the new assistant, a clever and charming young man named Ben Mather, who proved to be downright dishonest.

In Staffordshire Josiah was having similar difficulties. He could not be both at the Brick House works and at the new Etruria Ornamental works. William Adams, from whom he had leased the Brick House, was anxious for Josiah to vacate the premises. Adams had recently married and wished himself to occupy the house and eventually the pottery as well. Thus, at about the same time that Bentley was moving to Chelsea, Josiah, Sally, Sukey, John and the new baby Jos (Josiah II) moved into Little Etruria, the house originally intended for Bentley. Cousin Thomas carried on at the Brick House works while Josiah, devoting most of his time to the new Ornamental works, laid plans with the long-suffering Pickford for building a new Useful works at Etruria. Anxieties and pressures mounted. Josiah became more irritable and short-tempered.

John Voyez, the artist who had worked at the Brick House during the summer and fall of 1768, was sentenced at the Staffordshire Spring Assizes to be whipped with a cat-o'-nine-tails and imprisoned for three months. Most likely his offense was immoral rather than criminal behaviour. Drinking, wenching and brawling in the local taverns were apparently Voyez's downfall.

Unknown to Josiah or to Cousin Thomas, Voyez had been using one of the sheds behind the Brick House works as a studio where young girls posed for him in the nude. One day Josiah accidentally came on him there, drunk and in the company of the daughter of Josiah's coachman. Josiah was not so much morally indignant as angry that Voyez was neglecting the work he had been hired to do. The other workmen must be made to realize that such behaviour would not be tolerated during working hours. So Voyez was dismissed from his position. Josiah did, however, pay his wages while he was in prison and allowed Voyez's wife to continue living in the Etruria house which had been part of his contract of employment.

Two months before Voyez was to be released from prison, Josiah began worrying that the artist would reveal his secrets to his competitors. 'What then do our competitors stand in most need of to enable them to rival us most effectually?' he asked Bentley. 'Some person to instruct them to compose good forms & to ornam't them with tolerable propriety. V. can do this much more effectually than all the Potters in the Country put together, & without much personal labour, as the ornam't may be bo't or modell'd by others.'[1]

In a futile attempt to prevent Voyez from working elsewhere, Wedgwood & Bentley paid his wages for another six months until his contract with them expired. As soon as he was released from prison, however, Voyez began—first on his own, then in conjunction with Humphrey Palmer, potter of the Church works in Hanley—to copy Josiah's black Basalt. Josiah's ambivalence towards competition expressed itself in a desire to be copied but without the copy being successful. With almost paranoid suspicion he told Bentley: 'I think you sho'd make a point of shewing & selling these [Basalt vases] *yourself only,* lock them up ... *remember Voyez is in Town* & the Warehousemen sho'd not have it in their power to shew a pair of these Vases for sale.'[2] Josiah took out a patent on the encaustic painting applied to the black vases. Yet, only a few weeks earlier, he had declared paradoxically: '... with respect to Rivalship, we will cast all dread of that behind our backs, treat it as a base & vanquish'd enemy & not bestow another serious thought upon it.'[3]

There were similar problems with another bawdy modeller named Boot, whom Josiah threatened to discharge, with Voyez, for being 'loose & wild'; but Boot repented, agreeing to train others at figure-making.

Success and the move from Burslem to Etruria marked the end of the era in which Josiah was the master craftsman personally supervising his workmen in their day-to-day activities. The small family pottery had become big business. There were now two highly specialized factories with 150 employees, 30 of whom were working on vases only. The tight control which Josiah had exercised in the past over all aspects of the business from production to profit was no longer possible, and this made him uneasy. 'I have earnestly requested of him [Cox] in settling the accounts that collecting may go forward without the risque of ruining my Character. I have great need of the former, but am much more solicitous about the latter, as *Cash* may be procured on some terms, but a *good name,* when lost, is scarcely redeemable.'[4]

The winter of 1769—70 was harsh and dreary. Despite his successes—or perhaps because of them—Josiah's mental state was as bleak and dismal as the Staffordshire countryside. His father-in-law Richard Wedgwood fell ill, and Josiah took Sally and the new baby Jos over to Spen Green where they remained for a month. Forever rushing off himself, Josiah disliked being left at home on his own. There were further difficulties with Voyez who was in London circulating a rumour that Josiah was 'broke & run away for no less a sum than Ten Thousand Pounds!'. Upset by such a malicious lie, Josiah declared: 'I have half a mind to frighten the Rascal a little. It wo'd be charity to the Country to drive him out of it, but I am aware that it wo'd be deemed *revenge & pique* rather than *justice* in me to do it.'[5]

He had always been bothered by insomnia. The middle-of-the-night thinking which in the past had proved creative now led to nightmares. A comparatively minor problem with his eyesight upset him far more than the loss of his leg. He consulted an eye specialist who had cured the Duke of Bedford of a similar complaint. The doctor warned Josiah that '... there was always some danger in these cases (Mice Volanti, I think he calls the disorder) but he thinks he shall be able to overcome them.'[6] The main symptoms were headache, a blurring of vision and the perception of little particles floating in the air when he focused on the sky, a landscape, or a piece of paper while reading or writing. The advice of Darwin, who told him that 'everybody at one time of life or other had the same appearances before their eyes, but everybody *did not look at them*',[7] failed to reassure him. John Whitehurst apparently was confident enough of Darwin's medical wisdom, for he sanguinely offered to insure Josiah's eyes for a mere sixpence premium.

The recovery of old Richard and the return of Sally brought a slight improvement, but as long as he had the financial and practical worries of building the new Useful works, Etruria Hall and the housing estate for the workmen, Josiah's eye trouble continued. Indeed, for the rest of his life, whenever under stress, he complained of headache and particles in front of his eyes — probably what in later years would have been diagnosed as migraine. To him at the time and in the throes of his mid-life crisis, the fears were very real. 'I am often practicing to *see* with my fingers, and I think I sho'd make a tolerable proficient in that science for one who begins his studys so late in life, but shall make a wretched walker in the dark with a single leg.'[8]

The death of Darwin's wife added to Josiah's fears and depression. As sometimes happens with well-meaning individuals who busy themselves helping mankind in general, Darwin had failed to perceive the gravity of his wife's condition. He thought her illness to be due to 'the frequency of her maternal situation', she having produced five children, only three of whom survived infancy, within eight years. Only when it was too late did Darwin realize that to relieve her pains his wife had years before taken to 'drinking in great quantity spirits with water'. She died from a disease of the liver at the age of thirty-one.

Despite personal tragedies, both real and imaginary, the Wedgwood business thrived and the 'madness for vases' continued. Six types of ware were being produced at Burslem and Etruria: cream-colour and its variations, black Basalt, Terra Cotta, pebbled and marbled, bronzed, and Etruscan and Grecian.

In St Petersburg Lord and Lady Cathcart's dinner service had attracted the attention and admiration of distinguished Russian guests at the British Embassy. The consequence was an order for four large services, including one for the Empress herself. Josiah and Bentley took as great pains in producing the latter as Josiah had taken with Queen Charlotte's service five years earlier. This first Russian service, a Husk pattern hand-painted in a mulberry pink colour, took a year to complete. In July 1770, Josiah invited his father-in-law, who had recovered sufficiently from his last winter's illness to be spending several months at Etruria, on a trip to London to see the service on exhibition in the London showroom. They stayed with Bentley in Chelsea, where old Richard was suitably impressed by Bentley's hospitality and by the lavishness of his entertainment.

As usual Josiah's energy and inherent optimism rebounded under Bentley's influence. So active was he in walking around the showrooms, the studio and the streets of London that he damaged his wooden leg and sent it off to Addison to be repaired. Fortunately he always travelled with a spare leg. This time, however, he ordered 'a veritable wardrobe of peg legs'. When he got back home he discovered that he had been somewhat absent-minded and wrote to Bentley: 'Send me by the next wagon my spare leg which you will find, I believe, in the closet ... .' Both his good health and his spare leg soon returned. Trouble once again seemed to be in the past.

He was therefore taken aback when, two months after his return, Bentley precipitated the only serious quarrel the partners ever had. Bentley proposed that useful ware should be made at Etruria under the Wedgwood & Bentley partnership. Cousin Thomas was already resentful that Josiah was spending almost all of his time at Etruria and that Bentley received half of the profits from the ornamental business, whereas he, Thomas, received only one-eighth of the profits from the useful business. Naturally Thomas objected strongly to Bentley's newest proposal. Bentley, who may have been irritated that a service as grand as the one made for the Russian Empress and decorated under his own supervision at the Chelsea studio should be classified as useful, reacted by quibbling over the definition of the word 'useful'. Churlishly he enquired if Josiah intended to consider as useful a ewer taken from a drawing in a book on antiquities. Josiah was deeply hurt by the sarcasm, an aspect of Bentley's character which apparently had not been revealed to him before. He was also shocked by Bentley's stated dissatisfaction with the results of their first year of partnership, a sentiment in direct contrast to his own.

'If the first year of a business pays all expenses and furnishes any profit at all, I should not call it a bad one,' he wrote to Bentley,

> but if beyond this it likewise gives a profit of £500, or £1,000 in Cash for goods *really sold* and an increase in stock in manufactured goods *ready for sale* of £1,000 or £2,000 more, surely we ought to be more than barely content. I think we have reason to rejoice, and are robbing ourselves of what is more value than money if we do not take satisfaction of a prosperous and very promising business along with us as a cordial to support us in every hour of toil and fatigue which our avocations necessarily require at our hands.[9]

Bentley was probably as upset as Josiah at the major changes in *his* life—a fact which Josiah, obsessed by his own complaints, failed to notice. The artistic side of Josiah's business was by its very nature speculative, whereas for the useful wares there was always, whatever the economic climate, a market. The economic climate of the early 1770s was certainly not sunny. Trade with America was declining, following the incidents in Boston which led to the Declaration of Independence, and the business done by Bentley & Boardman had already been adversely affected. This, coupled with the uncertainty of the long-range success of the Wedgwood & Bentley partnership and the practically hopeless muddle which Cox had made of the first year's accounts, all contributed to Bentley's insecurity and irritability.

Cousin Thomas naturally felt that Bentley was attempting to undermine him and to usurp his position. Arbitrating between the two and taking infinite pains to be fair to both, Josiah said that he did not feel any inclination to draw an over-nice line between useful and ornamental, and that he had never had any idea that ornamental ware would not be of some use:

> May not usefull ware be comprehended under this simple definition, of such vessels as are *made use of at meals?* This appears to me the most simple & natural line, & though it does not take in Wash-hand basons & bottles or Ewers, & a few such articles, they are of little consequence, & speak plain enough for themselves; nor wo'd this exclude any superb vessels for sideboards, or vases for desert if they could be introduc'd as these articles wo'd be rather for *shew* than *use*.

He then went on to beg for Bentley's continued support and friendship:

> I may not continue long in business, and my life itself is a very precarious one, and whom have I then to leave my business to capable of conducting it in the manner you know I should wish to have it continued but you two; let us therefore, my friend and Brother, live and act like Brothers and friends indeed, and not suffer any small matters to put our peace and harmony in jeapordie. ... Think, my friend, you who can feel for me the situation I must be in. Do you think I could bear it? No, and I am sure you would not wish me to lead a miserable life, continually jarring with those I wish most to be at peace with. Next to *my Wife and Family* my Partners are those with whom I must be at peace.[10]

Bentley regretted his childish quibbling and the anguish he had caused his friend. Soon after receipt of Josiah's letter he left for Staffordshire. There the disagreement was resolved along the lines Josiah had suggested, though Bentley gained an advantage in that the new Etruscan teapots would be made at Etruria.

Other problems were not so easily resolved. On the way back to London, Bentley was attacked by highwaymen, unnerving in itself. Then, in London, he discovered that the patent for encaustic painting had been infringed by Palmer and his London agent Neale. There was much discussion as to whether or not to prosecute. Simply walking into Neale's showroom and buying a vase it could easily be proved that Neale was selling encaustic painted wares. That Palmer was actually making the ware was more difficult to prove. Palmer might have made plain black ware, sold it to someone in London who painted it and who then, in turn, sold it back to Neale. Josiah's lawyer, John Sparrow, contacted Palmer, who freely admitted that he was making the encaustic wares. He said that he would stand trial, as his vases were not an imitation of Wedgwood but were copied from a book on antiquities by Sir William Hamilton which he had bought when abroad. Furthermore, he intended to argue that encaustic colours were an improvement and not an invention, and that Josiah's patent was detrimental to trade. Of course Palmer *had* copied the Wedgwood designs, but it was equally true that the patent was not strictly accurate in describing encaustic painting as a new invention. This dispute and the attendant legal difficulties dragged on for more than a year.

James Bent, the Newcastle surgeon who had amputated Josiah's leg and who was a friend of both Palmer and Josiah, suggested a compromise, which was that Palmer should share in the patent. Because of the decline in trade, which Bentley had foreseen a year earlier, and of the potters joining together to form a protective society, Josiah was willing to accept the compromise. After all, he was constantly meeting Palmer and the situation had become embarrassing. He told Bentley:

> I meet Mr Palmer at our Society and other places frequently and we are, or seem to be, very sociable and friendly; nobody would imagine we were head and ears in Law together, and the People stared abundantly at our walking and talking together so cordially yesterday at the opening of a Bowling Green — a Neighbour joined us and said what a pity it was that two such men (I am only repeating another's words remember) should be at variance and throw our money away amongst people who did not know anything of the cause they were to decide, and that nobody could do it so well as ourselves if we could find in our hearts to talk to one another upon the subject. We looked at each other, I believe very foolishly for some time, and I was obliged to break silence at last by declaring that our Suit at Law had not made any breach in my friend-ship for Mr Palmer and he declared to the same purpose with respect to me. I added that I believed our business could not now be decided any other ways than by Law, otherwise I do not believe we were either of us fond of spending money in Law as to do it for the sake of spending money. Here we were relieved by others coming towards us, so we walked off together talking upon indifferent subjects, and went to dinner, but I rather expect the subject will sometime or other be brought upon the table at our Society.[11]

An agreement was finally reached under which both parties shared in the patent, dividing its cost as well as the legal charges between them.

Competition from another source brought a different response.. The demand for marbled, agate and Basalt vases had so far exceeded production that Josiah tactlessly refused an order from Boulton for vases to be mounted in metal. Boulton took offence. One of his assistants told Cox, who was again visiting Soho to study engine lathes, that Boulton was now determined to make vases himself — black earthenware vases.

The assistant was probably mistaken in his use of the word 'earthenware'. Boulton had been approached by the Comte de Brancas-Lauraguais to join him in partnership for making porcelain in England. Brancas-Lauraguais had discovered kaolin and petuntse at Alençon. In 1766 he had taken out an English patent for vases but hadn't as yet found anyone in England to make them for him. Vases made by a daring and imaginative manufacturer embarking upon a totally new venture in an unfamiliar medium was a different kind of threat from that posed by an experienced and competent copyist-potter like Palmer. Josiah told Bentley: 'It doubles my courage to have the first Manufacturer in England to encounter with—*the match likes me well*. I like the Man, I like his spirit. He will not be a mere snivelling copyist like the antagonists I have hitherto had, but will venture to step out of the lines upon occasion and afford us some diversion in the combat.'[12]

Despite boasts about making his own vases, Boulton soon lost interest in a partnership with Brancas-Lauraguais. He was involved in another partnership, which was for him a far more important venture. On 9 January 1769, James Watt had received a patent for 'a new method of lessening the Consumption of Steam and Fuel in Fire Engines'. Boulton wanted to form a partnership with Watt to build a new factory near Soho where they 'would erect all the conveniences necessary for the completion of the engines and from which manufactory we would serve all the world with engines of all sizes'.[13]

With such a mammoth project in the offing, Boulton changed his mind about making ceramic vases. Josiah tried to smooth over the hard feelings between them. In 1770 the two manufacturers, with their dominant and competitive personalities, were again on friendly terms. Boulton made vases in metal which he and Josiah jovially agreed would appeal to 'those customers who are fond of shew & glitter'. Boulton was also ordering Etruscan painted ware, and Josiah was promising to fill his orders promptly. Still smarting, apparently, from the earlier slight, Boulton commented: 'The mounting of vases is a large field for fancy, in which I shall indulge, as I perceive it possible to convert even an ugly vessel into a beautiful vase.'[14]

Josiah didn't appreciate his vases being called 'ugly', but was able to get his own back in a way that afforded him considerable amusement. In December 1770 he and James 'Athenian' Stuart visited Soho together. Stuart, who had made his reputation with *Antiquities of Athens*, lived in London, designing public and private buildings in the classical style. One of his current projects was remodelling Shugborough, Thomas Anson's home in Staffordshire. Demosthenes' Lanthorn, a garden monument that Stuart had designed for the Shugborough estate, included a huge metal tripod and bowl which Boulton was having difficulty in making.

Josiah described the scene at Soho to Bentley:

The Legs were cast ... but they [the workmen] staggered at the bowl, and did not know which way to set about it. A Council of the workmen was called and every method of performing this wonderful work canvassed over. The concluded by shaking their heads and ended where they had begun. I then could hold no longer but told them very gravely they were all wrong—they had totally mistaken their Talents and their metals. Such great work should not be attempted in Copper or in Brass. They must call in some able Potter to their assistance, and the work might be completed. Would you think it? They took me at my word and I have got a jobb upon my hands in consequence of a little harmless boasting.[15]

The friendly rivalry between Josiah and Boulton, their shared interests in promoting canals and expanding trade, in improving their products for profit and in investigating anything new in the way of mechanics led to their spending time together socially. They both enjoyed the friendships of that 'ingenious philosopher' Darwin who had introduced them, of Darwin's mechanical friend Whitehurst and of Darwin's rival in medicine and in scientific curiosity, Dr William Small. Without any conscious intent of establishing a formal society, these five friends fell into the habit of meeting at more or less regular intervals for dinner and discussion. Thus began the Lunar Circle of Birmingham.

6

The Lunar Circle
(1772 – 1775)

The members of the Lunar Circle began to think of themselves as a club or society in the early 1770s when two other men of science, James Keir and James Watt, moved to the Birmingham area. After his visit to Darwin and to the Wedgwood factory with Whitehurst, Keir had decided to settle in the Midlands, setting up a glass factory at Amblecote. He also found a wife whom William Small described as a 'beauty'.

Watt did not actually move to Birmingham until May 1774, after the death of his wife and the bankruptcy of his partner John Roebuck, who established the Carron iron works and then lost his fortune in coal-mining. As one of Roebuck's creditors, Boulton took over Roebuck's share in the patent on Watt's steam engine. For the past three years, however, Watt had been visiting Birmingham and attending Lunar meetings.

A pattern of holding their monthly meeting at a time when members might return home more conveniently and safely by the light of a full moon gave rise to the name Lunar Society or, as the ebullient Darwin christened them, the Lunatics. Safety was a matter of real concern, for highwaymen roamed the roads and dark lanes, and men who travelled singly seldom travelled unarmed.

Meetings were usually held in the neighbourhood of Birmingham, where Boulton, Watt or Small acted as host. Josiah, Darwin, Keir and Whitehurst attended as often as they could, planning their business trips to coincide with the Monday nearest the full moon. They assembled about midday; dinner was served at two, and the meeting broke up around eight in the evening. The Lunar Circle differed from other provincial societies, and from the London clubs such as the one at Young Slaughter's Coffee House which Josiah occasionally attended with Bentley, in that it had no formal organization. It never elected officers, never kept any records and never published any of its proceedings. Throughout an existence of almost forty years, the society consisted of only fourteen regular members. Friends and distinguished visitors such as Benjamin Franklin, Carolus Linnaeus, and Sir Joseph Banks attended occasionally as guests. There were never at any one time more than nine or ten members, and usually only four or five were at each meeting.

The Lunar Circle served as a clearing house for new ideas and for solving practical problems collectively. Richard Lovell Edgeworth, a young mechanical genius whom Darwin brought into the circle in 1772, observed:

A society of literary men and a literary society may be very different. In the one, men give the results of their serious researches and detail their deliberate thoughts; in the other, the first hints of discoveries, the current observations, and the mutual collision of ideas are of important utility. The knowledge of each member of such a society becomes in time disseminated among the whole body, and a certain *esprit de corps*, uncontaminated with jealousy, in some degree combines the talents of members to forward the views of a single person.[1]

Darwin was undeniably the catalyst of the group and Boulton the organizer, but the member who held them all together in friendship was Darwin's medical rival, William Small. He encouraged and inspired others to do what he himself might have done had he been of a less retiring disposition.

Small first arrived in Birmingham in 1765 with a letter of introduction to Boulton from Benjamin Franklin. Born and educated in Scotland, Small had spent six years in America where he was Professor of Mathematics and Natural Philosophy at the College of William and Mary in the colony of Virginia. His most illustrious pupil there was Thomas Jefferson. Disliking the competiveness in formal organizations, including universities, he returned to England and went into medical partnership with Dr. John Ash, whose principal achievement was the establishment of a general hospital in Birmingham. Small became Boulton's physician as well as his personal friend, while Darwin was physician to Boulton's wife's family. All three men interested themselves in the new 'steam-enginry' which was being developed by Watt. Small put money into the newly formed partnership of Boulton & Watt. Equally importantly, he helped to encourage the dour, pessimistic Watt.

Never were two partners less alike than Boulton and Watt. Though Watt was twelve years the younger, he looked and acted the older of the two. Grey-eyed and at an early age grey-haired, Watt was thin and stoop-shouldered. Simple in tastes, stern in morals and thrifty in finance, he was as cautious as Boulton was bombastic and adventurous. Having none of Boulton's physical stamina, he often conserved his energies by remaining in bed, like Brindley. Though solemn and retiring in his manner, he was by no means shy or diffident. He was so firm in his opinions that some of his Lunar friends considered him stubborn and intolerant. Probably because he was so lacking in humour, he was frequently teased. Josiah often jokingly called him 'my Scottish potter friend', since Watt held a small interest in the Delftfield Pottery.

Being a part of the Lunar Circle was the most stimulating intellectual experience of Josiah's life. To some extent it compensated for the loss of Bentley's company at Etruria. When he visited Bentley in London he travelled via Birmingham so that he could attend Lunar meetings both going and returning, and he timed his journeys accordingly. When not pregnant or ill, Sally usually accompanied him on these trips, and the couple stayed the night in Birmingham, either with the Boultons at their home on Handsworth Heath, or with Watt and his second wife.

Watt was not the only friend to take a second wife. Much to Josiah's delight, Bentley had announced his forthcoming marriage to Mary Stamford, fifteen years younger than he and the daughter of a Derby engineer whom Bentley had known when he was involved with the canal project.

The marriage took place in Derby in the summer of 1772, while Josiah and Sally were in Bath taking the mineral waters for Sally's rheumatism. Since the birth of their fifth child, Thomas, in 1771, Sally had suffered a series of illnesses which confined her to bed much of the time and left her severely depressed.

Josiah also had business interests in Bath, for a few months earlier Bentley had leased showrooms there, in Westgate Buildings, hiring William and Ann Ward (his future wife's sister and brother-in-law) to manage the rooms on a commission basis. Because of delays in decorating and in ordering the ware, the rooms would not open officially until the following autumn. Still, the height of the summer season seemed an appropriate time for Josiah not only to observe his new managers but also to meet on a social basis some of his fashionable patrons as they strolled along the promenade or attended concerts in the Pump Room.

Josiah and Sally were to have returned home from Bath by way of London, so that Josiah could look after the London business while Bentley went to Derby for his wedding. The waters had had little effect on Sally's health, and Josiah, determined that the cure should work, suggested that Bentley postpone his wedding so that they could stay in Bath three weeks longer. Bentley ignored the inconsiderate request and went ahead with his marriage as planned. Sally and Josiah visited the newlyweds in Chelsea on their way back to Etruria.

Sally's rheumatic fever worsened the following month, and her condition was serious enough not only to force Josiah to send for Darwin but for Josiah's sisters Catherine Willet and Margaret Byerley to come to Etruria to stay with their brother during the critical period.

Darwin had another patient in the neighbourhood whose condition had also worsened: James Brindley was dying. Darwin correctly diagnosed Brindley's illness as diabetes, which in those days was usually fatal. Josiah had just as correctly observed that Brindley was suffering from overwork: 'He may get his few thousands, but what does he give in exchange? *His health*, and I fear his life, too, unless he grows wiser and takes the advice of his friends before it is too late.'[2]

As Sally began slowly to recover, Brindley grew steadily worse. Josiah visited him daily at his home at Turnhurst, near Newcastle. He wrote to Bentley that 'Poor Mr Brindley has almost finished his course in this world— He says he must leave us, & indeed I do not expect to find him living in the morning.'[3] Brindley died on 27 September 1772, at the age of fifty-five. His death was in keeping with the way, in life, he had solved his engineering problems. In the middle of the night he awakened from a sound sleep, asked his wife for a glass of water, then said: ' 'Tis enough — I shall need no more.' He went back to sleep and died nine hours later without regaining consciousness.

His brother-in-law Hugh Henshall took over as chief engineer for the canal. Far-sighted enough to form his own carrying company and to build wharves and warehouses along the canal, Henshall and his company soon had a monopoly on the traffic passing from the canal down the Trent. Darwin proposed that 'various Navigations' should place a monument to Brindley in Westminster Abbey, since he was a 'great Genius & whose loss is truly a public one'.

Darwin also suggested that Josiah bring Sally to Lichfield where she could convalesce under his constant care. Perhaps he was aware that even in a household well-staffed with servants Sally was unlikely to have much peace, surrounded as she was by four children all of them under the age of seven.

Darwin's own household at this time was not exactly orthodox. He was living openly with a Mrs Parker, of a lower social class and whom therefore it would be unsuitable for him to marry. The affair had produced two daughters whom Darwin cheerfully acknowledged and raised with his three sons by his first marriage. The youngest of these sons, Robert, was the same age as Josiah's eldest son John. In the Darwin household Mrs Parker had the status of a servant, and on social occasions Darwin was frequently in the company of Anna Seward, the Swan of Lichfield. Josiah had no moral objections to his physician's way of life or to leaving Sally in his household. He himself remained in Lichfield long enough to attend one of the few Lunar meetings held at Darwin's house.

Edgeworth was now living at Lichfield when he was not travelling abroad. Having received an Honorary Gold Medal from the Royal Society of Arts for inventions in mechanics, he had become not only a member of the Lunar Circle but also a regular member of the Lichfield Society. Although he was married and the father of three children, Edgeworth had fallen in love with Anna Seward's best friend, Honora Sneyd, who lived with the Seward family in the Cathedral Close.

Edgeworth's eccentric friend Thomas Day, who wrote a popular anti-slavery epic, *The Dying Negro*, had also moved to Lichfield and had become a member of both the Lunar Circle and the Lichfield Society. Like Edgeworth, Day fell in love with Honora Sneyd, who was herself engaged to marry Captain John André, later executed as a spy during the American Revolution. Having proposed marriage to Honora and been rejected, Day transferred his affections to Honora's sister Elizabeth — and was also rejected by her. Day's difficulties were partly due to his idealistic criteria for the 'perfect wife', but also to his own strange personality. Awkward, absent-minded and ill-assembled, he was obsessed with ridding humanity of its frivolous conceits, and often resorted to insulting speech and crude manners.

When Day moved to Stow Hill, outside Lichfield, he brought with him one of two twelve-year-old orphan girls whom he had legally adopted with the express purpose of training them to be 'ideal women'. One of the two he would then choose as his wife, and on the other he would settle a substantial sum of money. One of the girls failed his training programme during the first six months, and his treatment of the other girl, whom he had christened Sabrina, raised more eyebrows in Lichfield than Darwin's illicit relationship, which was more or less commonplace. To teach her courage in the face of danger, he made her stand still while he fired pistols through her petticoats. Naturally enough she screamed. To fortify her against the dread of pain, he dropped melting sealing wax on her arms. Sabrina could not endure this without flinching. To test her fidelity he whispered pretended secrets, but she told them to the servants. Disappointed that Sabrina showed so little promise of becoming the strong, courageous, loyal and independent character he required, he abandoned his plan, gave Sabrina a generous allowance and placed her in a boarding school in Warwickshire.

The preoccupations of the Lunar Circle at this time (apart from finding Day a wife) were the abolition of slavery, the improvement of telescopes and microscopes, geology, chemistry, Watt's steam engine and Darwin's horizontal windmill. Darwin also invented speaking tubes which he installed in his house so that from various rooms, such as the drawing room or the library, he might communicate with the servants in the kitchen. On one occasion a young delivery boy had come into the Darwin kitchen and was standing in front of the kitchen fire warming himself when, as it seemed, a voice spoke out of the kitchen fire commanding: 'Bring me more coals!' The boy was scared clean out of his wits, refusing ever to enter the Doctor's house again.

Sally seemed to improve during her stay at Lichfield. Josiah returned in November to fetch her, again at a time convenient for another meeting with his Lunar friends. News on the romantic front was that Edgeworth's wife had died giving birth to their fourth child, that Edgeworth had promptly asked Honora to marry him, and that she had broken her engagement to Captain André and accepted him.

Sally's recovery was short-lived, for almost as soon as she was back at Etruria, she began to suffer from nervousness, irritability and fits of depression. Two days before Christmas she had a serious relapse, with fainting fits, chills and a high temperature. 'In this terrible situation she continued for many hours when we thought every moment would be her last ....'[4] The moves from the Brick House to Little Etruria and then to Etruria Hall had been as much of a strain on her as the business moves had been on Josiah. Darwin was again summoned. He bled her and advised that as soon as she could safely travel she should again be taken to Bath and remain there for the rest of the winter.

Throughout January she was unable to leave her bed. In February she was still seriously ill when Josiah's brother Thomas became severely afflicted with dropsy. Two weeks later, however, Josiah felt that both patients were sufficiently recovered for him to make a business trip to London. While he was there, Thomas died, on 23 February 1773, at the age of fifty-six. Josiah was executor of the will. Crêpe and silk hatbands, buckles and sleeve-links were ordered for the funeral attendants from Margaret Byerley's shop.

Thomas died in debt and with his affairs in a confused state. He was survived by five children from his two marriages and a second wife who suffered fits of insanity. One of the boys was mentally retarded and, according to Josiah, '... the foolish talk & behaviour of his mother to him made him for some time quite an Idiot; but he is getting better again, though he will never be qualified to do any business, & what we shall do with him I do not know.'[5] Sorting out his brother's affairs occupied a considerable amount of Josiah's time.

Also in March 1773, when Josiah was having to cope with his deranged sister-in-law, he found himself involved in the mental disturbances of David Rhodes's wife. Arriving one afternoon at Etruria Hall from London, she announced to Josiah that she was losing her mind and that she hated her husband and children. Rhodes arrived a few hours later and, at Josiah's insistence, the couple spent the night with the Wedgwoods. 'Her head was quite gone in the morning,' Josiah said, and then went on to hypothesize: 'I believe the Methodists of whom she has lately been very fond have helped to bring on the disorder, or the beginnings of the disorder sent her amongst the Methodists, I do not know which, but she, her Husband & family are in a most melancholy situation and I am extremely sorry for them.'[6]

As Sally was still confined to the house and as Josiah's sister Catherine Willet, along with several of her children, had whooping cough, Josiah asked his sister Margaret Byerley to close her shop and help Rhodes get his wife to Lichfield to Dr Darwin. By now Darwin was consulted as much in the role of helpful friend as physician. Indeed, apart from Darwin and Small, Josiah had little use for physicians. In July 1773, when Bentley expressed concern about the health of his wife, Josiah had advised: 'Let the Doctors say what they will, don't place too implicit a faith in them. They are often deceiv'd, & look graver than they need to do.'[7]

If health and personal problems were troublesome, at least the Wedgwood business was going exceedingly well. The chief difficulty was in finding competent and reliable workmen. Apart from making the normal range of products, Josiah was experimenting with new and finer clays to develop a purer biscuit body than was generally produced in the Potteries. For the past few years a particular obstacle to his experiments had been a patent taken out in 1768 by William Cookworthy, which gave him a virtual monopoly of all the china clay and china stone of Cornwall. A Quaker apothecary from Plymouth, Cookworthy had been the first to discover true porcelain in England; he founded a factory and later, in partnership with Richard Champion, managed a hard-paste porcelain factory at Bristol. Although his operation was a practical success, Cookworthy was not a good businessman. In 1774 he signed over his unexpired patent to Champion, who then applied to Parliament for its extension for a further fourteen years.

Josiah strongly opposed this extension of the monopoly. He wrote, published and distributed a pamphlet explaining why the clay pits should be open to all, then solicited and gained support from other prominent

Staffordshire potters, particularly John Turner, who joined him in presenting a case to Parliament to defeat Champion's petition.

Behind Josiah's strong feeling and tough action lay a fear that the fickle
public would eventually tire of cream-colour ware and that the addition of
Cornish clay to his earthenware might make the ware whiter. He also
needed the Cornish clays for his experiments in producing a white biscuit
body. While Josiah demanded openness from Champion, he conducted his
own researches in secret, discussing his difficulties and successes only with
Bentley and with the members of the Lunar Society, particularly Small,
Keir and Darwin, who were the most knowledgeable about chemistry.

So secretive and possessive about his own discoveries was Josiah that he
set up his laboratory not in the factory but in Etruria Hall. He stored
barium sulphate and other materials to make his secret mixtures in a range
of cellars partitioned off from other cellar rooms by thick walls and heavy
doors. The means of access was a trap-door and a flight of narrow brick
steps from his study. The steps ended in a wide passage off which there
were two doors, one leading to the room in which the mixtures were made,
the other opening to the outside so that barrels and boxes could be brought
in. The outside door was at the rear of Etruria Hall with steps and a
winding passage protected by a wall so that comings and goings might
easily pass unnoticed. There was also a long secret passage with a stone
floor which connected the cellar of Etruria Hall with the factory. Josiah
along had the keys, though probably he used the passage more frequently
to avoid the inconvenience of travelling in bad weather than for any other
reason.

Apart from issuing the first Wedgwood & Bentley catalogue of cameos,
intaglios and gems, Josiah had another major business project: the execution of a special commission from Catherine the Great of Russia. The
order had been received by Bentley in London from Alexander Baxter, an
Englishman who was Russian Consul in London. The earlier dinner service
in the Husk pattern which had been made for the Peterhof Palace in 1770
had so pleased the Empress that she now wanted a table and dessert service
for fifty people to be used at her Chesmenski Palace. Under the influence
of Lord and Lady Cathcart, the Empress had become interested in English
art, English industries, English social customs and English architecture.
Thus, each of the 952 pieces in the service was to be decorated with a
different English scene, mainly of large country houses. Each piece was
also to bear a crest of a small green frog, to commemorate the site called
La Grenouillière (the Frog Marsh) where the Chesmenski Palace was
located. Since the service was specifically intended for *use* in the Chesmenski Palace, the order should have been filled under Wedgwood's partnership with his cousin Thomas rather than under the Bentley partnership —
or, at least, the honour and the profits should have been shared. Probably
this was never even considered; Cousin Thomas was now thoroughly
eclipsed by Bentley.

Josiah was concerned as to how much the Empress would be willing to
pay for such a varied and magnificent service, how long she would be
willing to wait for artists to complete the time-consuming decoration and,

rather cynically, what would happen if she died before the completion of the order. Baxter, the consul, thought the service should be produced as quickly and cheaply as possible, for about £500. Josiah wanted to do it on a sumptuous scale worthy of his royal patroness. He estimated that it would take two to three years to complete at a cost of around £1,500. The difference was resolved in Josiah's favour when Lord Cathcart spoke to the Empress directly, explaining that in order to do justice to the work the artists could not be hurried and the cost would necessarily be great.

Work commenced in March of 1773, with Edward Stringer, a landscape painter from Knutsford, in charge of sketching most of the views. A portable camera obscura, developed by Johann Kepler a century earlier, was employed extensively by Stringer and other artists as an aid to perspective drawing. It consisted of a pyramidal framework of rods covered with cloth, with a lens at the top surmounted by a plane mirror which reflected the scene on to a sheet of drawing paper on a table inside the tent. The artist would then draw around the objects in the scene and thus determine accurately the relative sizes and shapes. Finding artists competent enough to do the work was a serious problem. David Rhodes supervised the painting in the Chelsea studios. At least two artists, James Bakewell and Ralph Unwin, devoted all of their time for the next year to the painting of the service.

Another problem was the possibility of offending some of Wedgwood & Bentley's noble patrons. Naturally there were more small plates in the service than large dishes. The number of noble lords sensitive about their own importance was considerably greater than the Empress's requirements in soup tureens and 18″ oval dishes. Josiah feared that one gentlemen might be offended to see his elegant house wrapped round a teacup while a neighbouring lord's house, which was no more impressive, was reproduced on—say, a soup tureen. Bentley solved this problem by deciding that the views should be fitted to the items according to their geometric or aesthetic suitability, rather than the importance of the owner. The noble lords would be told this at the time permission was requested to sketch their estates.

The service was finished in half the time estimated and at twice the cost. Surprisingly, neither Josiah nor Bentley had thought to approach the King or Queen for views of the royal estates and palaces. To do so now at this late date when 1,244 scenes of the homes and gardens of the lesser nobility had already been copied would have been tactless and probably harmful to business. Again Bentley solved this embarrassing contretemps by suggesting that the quality of the service would not be fitting for royal estates—in obvious contradiction to what had been told the nobility whose estates were painted.

Before the service was shipped to Russia, Josiah and Bentley put it on exhibition in London. As early as 1772, the partners had realized the need for new and larger showrooms than they had in Newport Street. With Matthew Boulton, Josiah had considered renting one of the new houses being built in the Adelphi by the Adam brothers, but then had decided that the location was not suitable—or, just as likely, that it would be unwise to be next to Boulton. At the end of 1773, and well after work had begun on the Russian service, Wedgwood & Bentley completed negotiations for two adjacent houses at Nos. 12 and 13 Greek Street, Soho. The exhibition of the Russian service in new premises was likely to gain the attention of the fashionable London gentry whom Wedgwood & Bentley wanted as customers.

In May 1774 Sally was well enough to be pregnant again and to accompany Josiah to London while old Richard Wedgwood went to Etruria Hall to stay with his grandchildren. The showrooms had actually opened in April 1774, with the Bentleys moving their residence into No. 13, the smaller of the two buildings. Bentley's ailing sister-in-law retired to Chesterfield where she lived for another twenty-five years on an annuity given her by Wedgwood & Bentley. For several months the Newport Street showrooms were maintained as well. On 8 June 1774, a notice appeared in the *Public Advertiser* announcing the exhibition of the Russian service:

> 'WEDGWOOD & BENTLEY inform the nobility & gentry that those who chuse to see a TABLE & DESSERT SERVICE, now set out at their new Rooms in *Greek Street*, may have free *Tickets* for that Purpose, at the Warehouse in Great Newport Street, & that none can be admitted without Tickets.'[8]

Josiah and Sally returned to Etruria before the exhibition opened, but its success was as great as the partners had hoped. The service remained on exhibition for two months and was seen by Queen Charlotte and her brother Prince Ernest of Mecklenburg, both of whom expressed their pleasure at viewing so magnificent a service. Bentley wrote in great detail to Josiah about the Royal visit.

By this time, however, Josiah's interest and energy were focused elsewhere. He resumed his experiments with the fine biscuit body, announcing to Bentley: 'I believe I shall make an excellent white body, and with *absolute certainty*, without the fusible Sparr.'[9] His interest in politics had increased considerably with the successful lobbying for the Grand Trunk Canal, and this interest had a directly correlation with the influence political affairs had on commerce, and most particularly on the trade in pottery. Throughout 1772 and 1773 he and Bentley, with the assistance of Lord Gower, were in negotiation with the Lords of Trade over the elimination of duty upon ware exported to France.

In November 1774, Sally's only brother John, who had taken over his father's cheese factory, was stricken with a severe illness. Josiah went to Spen Green and, after seeing him, immediately sent for Darwin. Nothing could be done, and he died on 18 November 1774. Old Richard was inconsolable, and let himself be persuaded by Sally and Josiah to return with them to Etruria. There, twelve days after her brother's death, Sally gave birth to their sixth child and second daughter, who was christened Catherine. Josiah told Bentley that Sally was fine and that he hoped to see her downstairs soon, '... for it is becoming fashionable here for the Ladies in the Straw to become well and leave it as soon as they are able; and even a Lady of Fashion may be seen in her Carriage again without shame, in ten days, or a fortnight after delivery.'[10]

These optimistic predictions were hardly justified, for within two weeks Josiah admitted in a postscript to Bentley that 'Mrs W and her little lass are poorly'. Having so recently lost his son, Richard was now even more concerned about the health of his only other child. Unlike Josiah, Richard pampered his daughter, encouraging her to conserve her strength rather than pretend to a robust health she had never had. Richard was prepared to remain with her until she was fully recovered. From that time on Etruria Hall became his real home, and the property at Spen Green was eventually sold. Josiah bore no grudge towards his father-in-law in spite of his earlier opposition, and he gladly welcomed him into the family group. Indeed, because old Richard's business judgement was both shrewd and sound, Josiah frequently sought his advice.

Richard was also popular with his grandchildren. Both Sukey and John, or Jacky, had been sent off to boarding schools in 1772, when she was seven and he six. Sukey went with her two little Willet cousins, Polly and Kitty, to a school at Bolton near Manchester, kept by Mr and Mrs Phillip Holland. John was first sent to school at Hindley, then later, with his cousin John Willet, to the Hollands'.

Josiah took as great an interest in education as did his Lunar friends Edgeworth and Day, who had attempted to put into practice Rousseau's principles of total freedom and 'back to Nature'. Their experiment with Edgeworth's son was a complete failure. Rousseau himself admitted his theories were a mistake when confronted with Edgeworth's wild, uncontrollable boy.

Since at this time neither King nor Parliament saw any necessity for the mass of the population to be literate, there was a good deal of interest among the ambitious middle classes in how to acquire an education; naturally enough, they wanted to improve their own circumstances. Dissenters were barred from the established academies and universities; as Priestley said, 'It is not, I believe, usual for young persons in Dissenting academies to think much of their future situation in life. Indeed, we are happily precluded from that by the impossibility of succeeding in any application for particular places.'[11]

Because of Sally's frail health and the frequent illnesses in the Willet family, Josiah took the responsibility of escorting the children to and from school. Occasionally his sister Catherine Willet accompanied him, but usually he was alone with the children. These journeys he enjoyed, probably because he was able to be with the children for longer intervals than when he was at home and preoccupied with business, experiments, personal correspondence and family problems.

School was not all Josiah had hoped it would be. After Sukey's first year with the Hollands, he decided it was necessary to take her to Liverpool because '... poor Sukey ... after sitting & sewing at school for twelve months is so full of pouks and boils and humours that the salt water is absolutely necessary for her, as Buxton is for Mrs W who is very lame.'[12] Sukey was not completely debilitated, for on the journey with her father and cousins she '... was in high spirits, playing her pranks upon a high Horse Block, miss'd her footing & pitched with her head upon a stone which was sharp enough to make a wound....'[13] Fortunately, as Josiah later noted, her skull proved to be of the 'thick rather than paper thin variety'. The care of three little girls with their schoolgirl pranks was almost as frustrating to him as Sabrina had been to Day. After making the long journey to Liverpool and spending five days there with the girls, he noted wryly: 'I must leave early in the morning, though I have not yet been able to persuade the lasses to Bathe, but they promise & I must leave them to the management of their good Doctor.'[14]

Sukey was then and continued throughout Josiah's life to be the favourite of all his children. She was very like her father both in appearance and in temperament: aggressive, quick-witted and extroverted. In contrast, young John was introverted, serious and lethargic, more anxious to please than to assert himself. Because of their mother's frequent illnesses and their father's various activities which took him away from home, it was probably to the advantage of all of the children when old Richard moved permanently to Etruria Hall.

The end of 1774 and the beginning of 1775 which had seen so many changes and adjustments in the Wedgwood family saw changes in the Lunar Circle as well. Whitehurst had supplied a clock for the country home of the Duke of Newcastle, and the Duke was impressed by his skill and precision. After the passage through Parliament of the Act for a better regulation of gold coinage, Whitehurst was appointed, on the Duke's recommendation, as stamper of the money-weights. This appointment meant that he and his wife would move to London.

An even greater loss within the Lunar Circle was the death of William Small on 25 February 1775. He had long been in poor health and knew that there was no hope for his recovery. In the last few weeks he placed himself not in the care of his partner Ash but instead in that of Darwin. Other members of the Lunar group were kept informed of the 'melancholy scene' by Darwin who remained in Birmingham with his patient and friend, giving 'assiduous and affectionate care' until the end.

Small's death deeply affected all of the Lunar members. Day, who had hurried from Brussels to Birmingham and arrived a few hours after Small's death, seemed never to recover from his grief. Boulton was so distressed that he told Watt: 'If there were not a few other objects yet remaining for me to settle my affections upon, I should wish also to take up my lodgings in the mansions of the dead....'[15] Watt, the dour, unsentimental Scot, replied that Small himself had believed that it was '... our duty as soon as possible to drive from our minds every idea that gives us pain, particularly in cases like this, when our grief can avail us nothing.... It is your duty to cheer up your mind and to pay a proper respect to your friend by obeying his precepts.'[16]

Keir, Darwin and Day all wrote elegies. Of all of them, however, Edgeworth probably came closest to the truth when he said: 'Dr Small formed a link which combined Mr Boulton, Mr Watt, Dr Darwin, Mr Wedgwood, Mr Day and myself together — men of very different characters but all devoted to literature and science.'[17] Without Small those 'very different characters' would begin to assert themselves and the harmony of the past turned into quarrels and misunderstandings.

7

A Seed of Consequence
(1775 – 1780)

The Lunar Society was a curious combination of individualism and co-operation, of the profit motive and altruism, of science and crack-pot fantasy. Here, supposedly, religion and politics were not allowed to intrude: Dissenters, Anglicans and atheists joined together in scientific and literary discussion, Whigs and Tories overlooked their differences—at least until the beginning of the American War of Independence.

Most of the Lunar members believed the cause of the Americans to be just. Darwin, Day, Keir, Whitehurst and Josiah were all enthusiastically pro-American. Boulton, on the other hand, was a loyal Tory and a devoted member of the Church of England. Possibly he was sincere in his beliefs; but there were practical reasons for his supporting the Government against the Opposition: Lord Dartmouth had aided his petition for the establishment of the Birmingham Assay Office; Darmouth's support was needed again for the Bill renewing Watt's patent which was being obstructed by Edmund Burke, leading member of the Opposition. Watt, with his strong conservatism, tended always to take a 'my country right or wrong' attitude. Edgeworth, an Irishman, tactfully preferred not to take sides.

Josiah joked with his 'Scottish potter friend' and with Boulton about their anti-American attitudes. Day, on the other hand, was indignant. He ended a letter to Boulton demanding repayment of a loan with: 'It is unnecessary to add anything from myself, except that America is un-conquer'd, the King is—England will be—& then what will become of button-making?'[1]

Perhaps with the intent of filling the gap left in the Lunar Society by the death of Small, Darwin wrote to Dr William Withering, a physician with a gentle, conciliatory disposition similar to Small's. Ten years younger than Darwin, Withering was the Doctor's protégé, and like his mentor had attended Edinburgh University. For the past seven years he had practised medicine in Stafford where Darwin, who had more patients than he could handle, often referred cases to him. Withering discovered digitalis and its importance in the treatment of heart disease. He was one of the few doctors of his generation who disapproved of bleeding and purging.

Darwin suggested that Withering should meet Boulton, who, after the death of Small, was suffering 'an inconceivable loss'. The result of the meeting was that Withering moved to Birmingham, took over Small's medical practice and became a member of the Lunar Circle. He, too, was a strong advocate of American independence.

Josiah had first met Withering in 1771 when he came to look at the Etruria works and to order some dinnerware. They soon discovered a common interest in chemistry and mineralogy, and Withering was the first to interest Josiah in the relatively new science of botany. He was then in the process of compiling his *Botanical Arrangement of All the Vegetables Naturally Growing in Great Britain, According to the System of the Celebrated Linnaeus*.

Withering also owned property in Staffordshire, including three mills at Moddershall, which he leased to Josiah for grinding some of his raw materials. Withering had recently discovered barium carbonate, a greyish-white mineral occurring in crystals and masses, which was named Witherite in his honour, just at the time Josiah was experimenting with various barium compounds in the development of his white biscuit body. In the early autumn of 1774, he and his father-in-law made a journey to Derbyshire in search of minerals and 'Spath fusible'. But the most reliable substance was barium sulphate or cawk, which Josiah was already using and which eventually became the principal ingredient of the new body, and he and Withering compared their findings on the barium compounds.

'This is the first experiment of its kind,' Josiah told Bentley, 'and I believe a seed of cosequence.' The new body was dense, white, silky to the touch; it was easily stained with colouring. Josiah named it Jasper after the coloured quartz so highly esteemed by the ancient Greeks and Romans. A year after producing his first 'seed of consequence', he wrote to Bentley: 'The blue grounds are out of the last kiln & the Cleopatras, both of which are the finest things imaginable. It really hurts me to think of parting with these Gems, the fruit of twenty years' toil, for the trifle I fear we must do to make a business worth our notice of it.'[2]

For the next five years there were difficulties, however, especially in the firing, and experiments continued using different ingredients and different colours. And however valuable Bentley was as a business partner and artistic adviser, he had no understanding of the problems of ceramic engineering. To talk over these problems, Josiah needed a chemist like Keir or Withering, or a fellow potter.

In May 1775 Champion's Bill asking for an extension of fourteen years, in addition to the seven years remaining of Cookworthy's patent on the Cornish clays, came before Parliament. Champion was one of the chief supporters of Edmund Burke as Member for Bristol; consequently he expected Parliamentary support for his private Bill, and he got it: the Bill passed the House of Commons without amendment. In the House of Lords, however, Josiah's friend Lord Gower gained important concessions. The patent was extended, but to cover the use of china clay and china stone *in porcelain only*, the one product ever made by Cookworthy or Champion. From 1776 onward other potters were allowed to use the same material in earthenware bodies.

After Champion's Act was amended in the House of Lords, Josiah and John Turner, another Staffordshire potter, decided to make a journey through Cornwall. Their purpose was to examine the clay and, if possible, to take a lease on some clay pits. They were accompanied by Thomas Griffiths, who had returned from South Carolina with specimens of the Cherokee clay Josiah desired, but which had turned out to be far too costly to import in large quantities. The fourth member of the party was eighty-seven-year-old Henry Tolcher, a chemist from Plymouth, who enjoyed '… a remarkable share of health & spirit for a man of his great age, & nothing flatters him so much as telling him how young he looks, & how many years he may yet expect to live'.[3] Indeed, Tolcher informed Josiah that he had no notion of dying. He did not think he should die, for he had never felt anything like it yet, never having had a day's sickness in his life.

Josiah seldom travelled anywhere without a business purpose. None the less, at the age of forty-five he was aware that by so doing he had missed something important, for he noted in his journal:

> It is impossible to pass through these finely varied scenes and comfortable haunts of men, without wishing to spend more time amongst them than these hurrying chaises will allow, and I often form hasty resolutions, that the next time I visit such places, I will take more time to stop, & indulge myself with a ramble amongst them; but the next time is like the preceding — every journey has its main object, & all others are sacrificed to that.[4]

When the party reached Land's End, after a particularly hazardous river crossing in carriages at Penzance, Josiah climbed over the stones as far as he could, handicapped by his peg-leg. He wanted to say that he had been to the very farthest point. There he and the others 'gazed for some time with a kind of silent awe, veneration & astonishment, at the immense expanse before us. The day was clear enough for us to have a good view of the Scilly Isles, after some time spent in this situation so singular & new to us, we turned about, and it was with a transport of joy that I cried. Now I set my face toward Etruria again….'[5]

Sentimental as he was over the landscape, he nevertheless drove a hard bargain in his dealings with people. Having found the raw materials he and Turner wanted, he negotiated for a lease to dig for clay and stone on a farm. The farmer's wife wished to sell the clay and stone outright, by the ton, explaining that if her husband had any large sum of money he would waste it all in drink. Josiah refused; he wanted a yearly lease. The farmer suggested 20 guineas. Josiah offered 10, which was grudgingly accepted. Griffiths was then left behind to direct the initial digging.

Both Josiah and Turner considered the trip a success. Towards the end of the journey, however, old Tolcher became somewhat of a trial — '… if he had not his own way in everything, there was no peace with him either in the chaises or in the inns; and above all, his continued quarrels with the chaise boys for driving too fast or too slow, or over the wrong ground & likewise with the waiters at every inn, & for every cause, made us often wish the old gentleman safe at home again.'[6]

After their journey Champion's associate Thomas Pitt wrote to Champion: 'Wedgwood says your specification is a lighthouse, teaching the trade precisely what they are to avoid, which will only bring them safely into Port. The two grand pillars of our Porcelain are the Clay and the Stone, and the rest is near corrective or manufacture, of which, depend upon it, then WEDGWOOD after such an experience knows more than all of us put together....'[7]

When Josiah got back to Etruria, he found that another traveller had returned home also: Tom Byerley was back from America and once again seeking employment. His theatrical and literary ambitions had no more been fulfilled in the New World than in the Old. Unspecified indiscretions had landed him in jail within six months of his arrival in Philadelphia. After his release he quickly spent the enormous sum of £800 ('... and nobody knows what he has done with it')[8] and then moved to New York. There he succeeded in getting a job as a schoolmaster, though his qualifications were certainly minimal and his dedication even less.

The years abroad had, however, matured Tom. Having reached the sensible conclusion that 1775 was not the most propitious year for an Englishman with loyalist sentiments to be in America, he returned to Etruria. Grumbling and criticising (though secretly pleased), his uncle took him back into the firm in his old job of clerk. The reformed Tom was sober and industrious and reliable. Furthermore, he found new ways to be of use, translating and answering letters in French and also acting as Clerk to the Committee of Potters which Josiah was instrumental in forming.

During that same summer of 1775, Bentley and his wife Mary came to Etruria for a visit. It was decided to send Sukey, aged ten, back with them to London, where she could attend school with the Bentleys as surrogate parents. Young John, who was quiet and never complained or stated his wishes one way or another about anything, returned to Bolton to continue his own schooling.

Being in London, Bentley was more closely in touch with the artistic world than Josiah was. In the autumn of 1775 he commissioned John Flaxman, the son of a maker of plaster-of-Paris casts in Covent Garden, to model 'a good Tablet for a Chimney Piece'. Though Flaxman was only twenty, he had already won several prizes from the Society of Arts. He not only modelled the chimney piece but also two vases, four bas-reliefs of the Seasons, several plaques of the ancient gods and goddesses and two cups and saucers, all to Josiah's satisfaction. On one point, however, Josiah was adamant. Major decisions were to be made by the manufacturer; the individuality of the artist had to be subjugated to the over-all character of Wedgwood products. Surprisingly, Flaxman had no objections. If he perhaps preferred carving statues from slabs of marble, he recognized that his daily living came from executing designs for manufacturers.

The commission of Flaxman as an artist and the perfecting of the new Jasper body fortunately coincided with the neo-classic revival in design. Tired of baroque and rococo extravagances, fashionable people acclaimed the discoveries at Herculaneum. Josiah fully appreciated the importance of aristocratic patronage. Alone among the Staffordshire potters he enjoyed the favour of ambassadors and the honour of being represented by them. He wanted his products to fulfil in a contemporary world the place that statues and urns and ceramics in general had played in previous ages. Of the bas-reliefs which Flaxman had sculpted, he shrewdly predicted: 'They want nothing but age & scarcity to make them worth any price you could ask for them.'[9]

After the success of the Russian service exhibition and the issue of the first catalogue, Josiah was even more convinced of the importance of advertising and of display. And he was proved correct. 'Your shew will be vastly superior to anything your good Princes & Customers have hitherto seen,' he told Bentley. 'I am going upon a large scale with our Models which is one reason why you have so few new things just now, but I hope to bring the whole in compass for your next Winter's shew and ASTONISH THE WORLD ALL AT ONCE. For I hate piddleing, you know.'[10]

It was a time for thinking in large terms. The war with America had virtually ruined the export trade, and after the Americans formed a military alliance with France, many Englishmen, including Bentley, feared an invasion of England. Josiah was more sanguine. 'How could you frighten me so in your last?' he wrote to Bentley:

> it was very naughty of you. I thought nothing less than some shelves, or perhaps the whole floor of vases & crocks had given way, & you were sinking down with them, 'till … I found it was only the nation was likely to founder in a french war, & having been fully perswaded of this event for some time past, I recover'd, from my shock & bless'd my stars & Ld North that America was free … from the iron hand of tyranny…. We must have more war, & perhaps continue to be beat — to what degree is in the womb of time. If our drubbing keeps pace with our deserts, the Ld have mercy upon us![11]

Before the French took up the cause of the Americans, Bentley had made a trip to Paris. He surveyed the potential market there and made tentative arrangements for the distribution of Wedgwood products in France, but relations between the two countries were too uncertain for these arrangements to take effect. Upon his return he was struck with a severe attack of gout. Josiah wanted to go to London to be with him, but he had injured his hip and was himself forced to remain in bed:

> The accident I have met with was occasioned by a stupid *Man Animal* throwing a bundle of Weeds over a hedge into the Highway, just before my horse's head, upon which he turned about so hastily as to whirl me out of my Demi Peak, and I tossed upon the hard ground just upon the point of my hip bone. This has given a terrible shake to the joint and made it too sore to be moved without extreme pain, but I have no constant pain, nor any sympton of inflamation in the part, and I am very thankful that the joint is not dislocated, for my surgeon tells me that it could not have been reduced again, for want of a Leg to pull by, and I

should probably never have been able to put on my Artificial one again, which would have been a terrible accident to me....[12]

When he recovered and was able to get about easily, Josiah visited John at school in Bolton and made the decision to send the two younger boys, Jos and Tom, there the summer of the following year, 1777. Tom was then only six years old, but he was a precocious child. His father commented to the Revd Holland that Tom and Jos were practically inseparable and that in spite of Tom's young age he would be 'a pretty little sort of scholar'. Young Catherine, now called Kitty, was an active two-year-old. Her twelve-year-old sister Sukey, who was still at school in London, wrote to her mother: 'I have at last learnt embroidery & I am doing a very pretty picture.... I will buy some silk to work a purse without troubling anybody as I have learnt the stitch by seeing the Ladies work. I have done a small one to try upon which I intend to give to little Sweet Kitty as she has got about the same quantity of money which it will hold so I think it will suit very well.'[13]

In spite of Sally's frail health and bouts of incapacitating depression, she gave birth to another daughter, whom they named Sarah, in September of 1776.

The beginning of the year 1777 had seen a number of changes. The sudden, unexpected death of David Rhodes, the firm's chief artist, left the London decorating department in confusion. Bentley and Mary moved to Turnham Green to be near the Ralph Griffithses, and were thus at a much greater distance from the London showroom which, after Rhodes's death and the dismissal of the dishonest Ben Mather, more than ever needed Bentley's supervision.

Under the direction of Hugh Henshall the Trent and Mersey Canal was finally completed, at a cost of nearly £300,000. It was 140 miles long, with 75 locks, 5 tunnels and 269 aqueducts and bridges. Freight rates were reduced from 10*d* to ½*d* per ton mile, and the risk of breakage of the finished pottery was considerably reduced, thus fulfilling all of Josiah's happier expectations.

Josiah had not been able to attend as many of the Lunar meetings as he would have liked. The meetings, though supposedly rotating among the members' houses, were usually held in Boulton's home. His hospitality was generous, the surroundings both elegant and comfortable. Probably the Lunar members found the atmosphere in the Boulton household more congenial than in that of his partner Watt. The widower Watt had married for the second time a Scotswoman as conservative and thrifty and tidy as he was, and their household included four children and two pug dogs who, like the children, were trained never to cross the clean-polished flagstones of the hall without wiping their feet on the mats placed at every door.

Even when he was unable to attend meetings, Josiah kept up a regular correspondence with Boulton, Darwin and Edgeworth. In 1776 Edgeworth and Honora, who now had two children of their own as well as the four by Edgeworth's first wife, returned to England and bought a house at North Church, just outside London. They then visited at Soho, Birmingham and

Lichfield. In August 1777, they arrived at Etruria. Edgeworth was as ebullient and inventive as ever, immediately interesting himself in the horizontal windmill which Darwin and Watt were building for Etruria. He also had ideas for new products, suggesting to Josiah a design for a chamber-pot with a cover. Josiah improved upon the design, eventually manufacturing 'airtight vessels for various uses'.

The Edgeworths' visit was a success with all of the family. Sukey and Maria Edgeworth, who was a year younger, were compatible as playmates, and when Sukey returned to school in London, she spent the Christmas holidays at North Church with the Edgeworths. 'It is with pleasure I can inform my dear Papa how very happy I am here,' she reported. 'It is impossible to be otherwise in Mrs Edgeworth's company. I think Mr E. is very different to what I always thought him to be. I took him to be a very grave sedate man & now I think him to be just the contrary; he sings all the day from morning till night. Mrs E's sister is here who is my bedfellow....'[14]

More and more the subject of education was occupying the attention of the Lunar members. Edgeworth did an about-face in his theories, becoming a strict disciplinarian. When young Henry Edgeworth began observing and collecting as a hobby, his father noted wryly that at least he would never come under Darwin's definition of a fool: 'A fool, Mr Edgeworth,' said Darwin, 'is a man who never tried an experiment in his life.'[15]

Darwin probably had as much common sense and insight into human nature as any of the Lunar members. On education, he concluded: 'If once you can communicate to children a love of credit and an apprehension of shame, you have instilled into them a principle which will constantly act and incline them to do right, though it is not the true source whence our actions ought to spring, which should be from duty to others and ourselves.'[16]

Unfortunately, as with his first wife, Darwin failed to apply his perceptions to those closest to him. He had great expectations for his eldest son Charles, who was keenly interested in science. At the age of sixteen Charles was sent to Oxford, where he found the emphasis on classical studies both boring and impractical. His attitude probably influenced his father's opinion, for Darwin advised Josiah that it was useless for 'boys intended for trade to learn Greek and Latin'. In 1778, while Charles was at Edinburgh completing his studies in medicine, he was dissecting the brain of a child when he cut his finger. The wound became septic, and he died on 15 May at the age of twenty. Darwin, who had rushed to Edinburgh hoping personally to save him, was inconsolable.

All of his hopes had centred on this favourite son. His second son, Erasmus junr, was of a sensitive, introverted disposition, inclining to mysticism, which his father found effeminate and irritating. The youngest son, Robert, who was the same age as John Wedgwood, now became the focus of Darwin's ambitions. Within a matter of weeks from the death of his brother, twelve-year-old Robert was being referred to as 'the young Doctor'. Like his father, this son was large and clever and articulate; but he had no interest in medicine or mechanics, and shortly thereafter began to suffer frequent headaches and depression.

Three days before the young Charles Darwin died in Edinburgh, Josiah's brother-in-law William Willet died in Newcastle. Josiah told Bentley: 'This truly good man's death was of a piece with his life, calm, serene & sensible to the last moment.'[17] At about the same time Josiah also received news of the death of his only remaining brother, Richard, but he felt less emotion about this than about the death of Willet. Richard's career in the Army had been a failure; he had taken to drink and, according to Josiah, had 'long been lost to the family'.

In early June Josiah went to London to visit the Bentleys at their new house in Turnham Green and to help Bentley plant his garden, as well as to discuss business matters. On the way to London he had stopped in Lichfield to be of what comfort he could to the grieving Darwin, who had decided to publish posthumously an essay that had won his son Charles the first gold medal of the Aesculapian Society of Edinburgh. Josiah naturally encouraged his friend in this, and also encouraged him to come to Etruria and to bring with him his gold-leaf electrometer so that they might try some experiments in fixing 'Lichtenburg configurations' of powdered enamel on porcelain by firing. Darwin agreed to come later in the summer and to bring Robert with him.

Usually the London — Etruria journey took four to five days, with Josiah spending one night in Birmingham and another in Lichfield; but on the return journey this time the charm of his companions caused him to carry on straight through without stopping to call on any of his friends. 'Mr Lloyd, a banker, & one of the people called Quakers, was my *conversing* companion. The Lady had been at Portsmouth & seen all the fine shews there, & was returning to her husband at Birmingham.... She was not overstock'd with ideas, but was lively and sang like an Angel. She was our *singing* companion, & altogether the time ran on very smoothly....'[18]

Back at Etruria, Josiah made another week-end trip to Lichfield, '... to assist at a consultation about a windmill of Dr Darwin's invention, which has likewise been perfecting under the hands of Mr Edgeworth & Mr Watt.'[19] Edgeworth and Honora were also in Lichfield. For many months Honora had been in poor health, and Darwin now accurately diagnosed her trouble as tuberculosis, and advised travel to a milder climate.

About the time Josiah heard the gloomy news about Honora, happier news came from Thomas Day, who at long last had found a wife: Esther Milnes, an heiress who was almost as eccentric as he. Small had introduced them five years before, but Day had refrained from proposing marriage because he feared his friends might think he was marrying the lady for her money. On the contrary, his friends were astonished and delighted that Esther would have him. 'Thank you for the news of Mr Day's marriage,' Josiah wrote to Bentley. 'I hope he will contrive to be happy & to make his lady so. They are good people & I hope will not sacrifice real solid happiness to whim & caprice.'[20]

During the same month Josiah told Bentley that 'Mrs Wedgwood yesterday morning presented me with another fine girl & with as little trouble to herself & family as could be expected. She sent for the midwife whilst we were bowling (after making tea for us as usual in the afternoon) without so much as acquainting me with the matter, slipt upstairs just before supper, & we had not risen from table before the joyfull tiding of a *safe delivery, & all well* was brought to us....'[21]

Now that Sally was in better health, Josiah had reached the conclusion that all the fuss about childbirth was nonsense — 'a sort of decorum establish'd amongst the sex, originally intended, no doubt, to impose upon us poor men, & make us believe what sufferings they underwent for us & our bantlings ...'.[22] Sally felt otherwise; she did not have Josiah's stamina, nor did she share naturally his wide range of interests. But Josiah expected perfection from his wife just as he expected perfection from his workmen.

On the whole, the summer of 1778 was a happy one with all of the family, including Grandfather Richard, in good health. Sukey had become quite accomplished at the spinet and was impatiently awaiting the arrival of a new one which Josiah had bought for her when he was in London. While she performed, the other children sang and played musical games. Kitty had a clear, sweet voice, and young Tom had begun to study the violin. Josiah did chemical experiments in which the boys could participate. Every morning he gathered all of the children together 'for reading stories'. When the weather was warm, they spent many hours outdoors, riding, fishing, bowling, rolling hoops and spinning tops. They made their own small gardens and, in imitation of their father, began gathering rocks and minerals for their own collections. Josiah told Bentley: 'We have filled up some time lately in arranging our shells which has several uses to us. It teaches us something of order & arrangement in general, & induces us to read a good deal of french without the formality of saying lessons.'[23]

This was one of the few quiet periods in Josiah's life, when his attention was focused primarily on family and cultural interests. Bentley had told him that Joseph Wright of Derby was showing six paintings at the Royal Academy Exhibition that year. Five years earlier, with Sir William Meredith, Josiah had been to Wright's studio in Derby, where he contemplated commissioning a painting connected with the pottery industry.

Replying now to Bentley's news of Wright's exhibition, Josiah said:

> I am so glad to hear Mr Wright is in the land of the living, & continues to shine so gloriously in his profession. I should like to have a piece of the Gentleman's Art, but think Debutades's daughter would be a more apropos subject for me than the Alchymist, though one principal reason for my having this subject would be a sin against the Costume. I mean the introduction of our Vases into the piece for how could such fine things be supposed to exist in the earliest infancy of the Potters Art....[24]

Wright had established a reputation for combining the classical style with present-day scientific and industrial imagery, but what Josiah wanted was a painting that would tastefully and appropriately show off his vases. In September he and his lawyer John Sparrow were on a 'navigation embassy' to visit Sir William Bagot. At the same time Josiah managed also to meet with Wright and have 'some little talk upon the subject of a picture for me, but my stay was too short to conclude upon anything, only that we are to meet again, & he has almost promised me a visit in the spring'.[25]

At the same time Josiah was having business dealings with another renowned painter, George Stubbs, who had become interested in enamel painting. Having found it difficult to obtain sheets of copper large enough for full-size pictures, he asked Josiah to produced for him large ceramic tablets; in lieu of payment, he would do some work for him. Josiah readily agreed to this, anticipating that Stubbs would paint portraits of himself and Sally. He hoped to make tablets as large as 36″ × 24″ but found it difficult to succeed with anything larger than 30″. In October he told Bentley: 'When you see Mr Stubbs, pray tell him how hard I have been labouring to furnish him with the means of adding immortality to his very excellent pencil. I mean only to arrogate to myself the honour of being his *canvas maker*. But alass, this honour is at present denied to my endeavours though you may assure him that I will succeed if I live awhile longer undisturbed by the French, as I only want an inclin'd plane that will stand our fire.'[26]

The French fleet was effectively preventing all trade with the European continent, and commerce with the colonies also being at a standstill, a general depression had resulted, with workmen being laid off from the factories. Though many small potteries went out of business, the Potteries as a whole were not as hard hit as the Lancashire cotton mills; but Wedgwood & Bentley found themselves with much heavier inventories than they wished. Josiah, however, took a confident, good-humoured attitude, informing Bentley:

> Not recollecting where I left off, & feeling just now very chagrinish at being stopped in my career, & not permitted to proceed in the invention of new pots & pipkins for my own amusement first, & afterwards for the emolument & entertainment of all the world besides, because, forsooth, nobody will part with their money. — This being the case I begin my letter in abusing the world & everybody in it, for a blind, sneaking, paltry, foolish world & lamenting my own hard fate in coming into it at a time when people know or practice no better.[27]

The almost daily correspondence between Josiah and Bentley had by this time become voluminous. Bentley's treasured letters, which Josiah often re-read, making reference to them months or even years later, were bound into a thick and ever-expanding book. Josiah's sisters Catherine Willet and Margaret Byerley teased him by referring to it as 'Josiah's Bible'.

The Bentleys visited the Wedgwoods, bringing with them Mary's niece Ann Ward, who later became the popular novelist Mrs Radcliffe. Whitehurst also came for a leisurely visit while Watt was at Etruria trying to install Darwin's windmill. Darwin himself came over to try his electrical gilding experiments. Electrifying had become something of an obsession with him: when the Wedgwoods' youngest child Mary Ann suffered convulsions during teething, Darwin lanced her gums, placed her in a cold bath and electrified her.

The health and education of his children was now a major concern of Josiah's, which he approached with the same thoroughness, coupled with the willingness to experiment, that he brought to problems of ceramic engineering. John Warltire, who had been teaching chemistry at Warrington Academy, began a series of chemical lectures in Newcastle to which the subscription was 30 guineas. Josiah sent for his son John to come home from school to attend the lectures. 'Doct'r Darwin has sent his son Rob't to attend the course, & my Jack & this young *doctor is to be* have both taken the infection very kindly. They both attend Mr Warltire every morning for private instruction which is of much greater consequence to them than public lectures. I too am a lecturer in my turn, & have the place of sec. to their private experiments.'[28]

Tom Byerley, who had assumed the duties of travelling salesman as well as Josiah's personal assistant, put to practical use the schoolmastering experience he had acquired in New York. During the school holidays he taught his young cousins French and Latin, and with Josiah's assistance, he began instructing the Wedgwood sons in the family business. 'We have all our little folks about us now, & I am travelling through England with Mr Byer: ley & take the young men along with me. We examine what orders are taken & business done as we go along which makes the route edifying to us all.'[29]

In the autumn of 1779 all three of the Wedgwood sons were at school in Bolton and all of the daughters at home having instruction from their governess Everina Wollstonecraft, sister of the feminist Mary Wollstonecraft. In October the Wedgwoods received a letter from the Revd Holland saying that young Jos was ill. Josiah and Sally both went to Bolton, encountering rioting workmen along the way. Once there they decided to bring both Jos and Tom back with them and to keep them at home until after the Christmas holidays. Byerley was again recruited to teach French, Latin, English, writing and accounts.

The two boys were so improved by their stay at home that Josiah, in consultation with Bentley and Darwin, decided to establish his own home school which he called the Etruscan school. It was attended by his three sons, their sisters Sukey and Kitty, and three sons and one daughter of Josiah's partner-cousin Thomas Wedgwood. At irregular intervals young Robert Darwin attended also. Josiah himself planned the curriculum, recruiting his accountant Peter Swift and a Unitarian minister, the Revd Edward Lomas, to help Byerley with the instruction.

At this point, when the Wedgwood sons were aged fourteen, eleven and nine, Josiah, like Darwin, had more or less made up his mind what he expected their futures to be: '... Jack is to be settled as a gentleman farmer in some desireable situation with as many acres for himself and his tenants to improve, as I can spare him. Jos and Tom to be potters, and partners in trade. Tom to be the traveller and negotiator, and Jos the manufacturer.'[30] It never occurred to either Josiah or Darwin that their sons might have ideas of their own.

Darwin had engaged a French prisoner-of-war to teach Robert French. The two eldest Wedgwood boys were sent to Lichfield to have lessons also. These lessons were so successful that Josiah decided to engage the prisoner,

M. Potet, to teach for a year at the Etruscan school. At the beginning of the next school term, John returned alone to Bolton for a final half-year to complete his studies.

During that spring of 1780 Edgeworth and Honora moved back to Lichfield. Edgeworth believed that if anyone could save his wife Darwin could. But at the time neither Darwin nor anyone else knew how to treat tuberculosis, and Honora grew steadily worse. A few months earlier Kitty Willet, Josiah's niece and Sukey's close friend, had died of tuberculosis at the age of eighteen. Honora knew that she was dying and extracted a death-bed promise from her husband that he should marry her sister Elizabeth, if Elizabeth were willing.

After Honora's death Darwin and young Robert came to Etruria on a visit; no doubt Edgeworth knew that Darwin would tell Josiah the details of his tragic loss, for on 10 May, he wrote simply: 'Let me address this letter to the firm of W & B to ask whether I can have 12 profiles of my dear Mrs Edgeworth done in white on pale blue from a profile by Mrs Harrington & an excellent picture by Smart — I lost her Sunday — & you both know she is a real loss to YOUR FRIEND R.L.E.'[31]

Honora's sister Elizabeth was willing, and Edgeworth stayed a few months longer in Lichfield, consulting by letter with Boulton, an authority on the problems of marrying one's deceased wife's sister, he having done the same thing a few years earlier and successfully avoided excommunication by the Church of England.

From the time Bentley first moved to London eleven years earlier his health had steadily deteriorated. Over the past five years in particular he had suffered various mysterious disorders and a slow, progressive decline. The Greek Street showroom, which previously had been a dissecting room, was never fumigated — a procedure unheard of in those days — and a good many of the employees became ill over a period of time and left their jobs there. During the summer of 1780 Bentley and Mary went to Margate for the sea air, thereby escaping the riots that terrorized most of London during the month of June. In July and August they visited the Wedgwoods.

After the Bentleys returned to Turnham Green, George Stubbs came to Etruria and stayed for several months. Josiah had at first feared that both Stubbs and Wright would be at Etruria at the same time and wondered if they would 'draw kindly together'. Wright, however, was in poor health and postponed his visit. Josiah then changed his mind and decided that Stubbs rather than Wright should do the family portrait which he had already told Wright he wanted him to do.

In exchange for the ceramic tablets, Stubbs modelled a large plaque with a lion attacking a horse. He also gave the Wedgwood children drawing lessons and lectured on perspective. In his own way he was as tough and autocratic as Josiah; for the family portrait he insisted that the children be posed on horse back. Predictably, he and Josiah had a number of disagreements over the portrait. Josiah told Bentley: 'Time and patience are absolutely necessary in these cases, & methinks I would not be a portrait painter upon any condition whatever. We are all heartily tired of the business, & I think the painter has more reason than any of us to be so.'[32]

At the end of October, about the time the portrait was completed, Edge-worth came to stay for a few days with the Wedgwoods before eloping with Elizabeth Sneyd. His tactful comment on the portrait was that 'there is much to praise and little to blame'. Josiah wrote to Bentley asking him to contact a frame-maker and to choose a pattern with which to frame the portrait. He had no reply to his request until, a few weeks later, he received a letter from Ralph Griffiths telling him of Bentley's illness: 'Our poor friend yet breathes; but, alas! it is such breathing as promises but a short continuance. Almost every hope seems to have foresaken us! I dread the thought of what will be the content of my next! adieu! R.G.'[33]

This was a complete shock to Josiah. Bentley's health had always been frail; he had suffered from gout, asthma and a predisposition to colds and infections. Yet he was only forty-nine years old. His health had become suddenly worse after he left Etruria three months before. He complained of headaches, an over-all wasting away and a lack of energy, yet the correspondence between the partners had continued as always.

Josiah started for London immediately after receipt of Griffiths's letter, but when he arrived at Turnham Green, Bentley was dead.

8

Wedgwood after Bentley
(1780 – 1785)

The death of Bentley was a painful shock from which Josiah never fully recovered. He remained in London for his friend's burial on 2 December in a vault within the church at Chiswick. Back at Etruria, he was forced to take to his bed with headache, a loss of vigour and a series of chills and stomach upsets. Mentally and physically he had aged a decade or more in a matter of weeks. The exuberance, humour and optimism of his customary outlook on life were replaced by irritability, intolerance and depression. He developed a trembling in the limbs, reflected in the sudden shakiness of his handwriting.

Christmas of 1780 was a sad one at Etruria Hall. Neither Sally nor the children could distract Josiah from his grief. Samuel Boardman, Bentley's partner in Liverpool warehousing, wrote to him on 31 December 1780: 'Our esteemed friend Bentley, during the short time he was with us, spent a happy and useful life. He has left us with a noble example of virtue and goodness which I hope will never be forgotten in our actions, both in public and in private life.'[1]

Letters of condolence came from Darwin, Priestley and Edgeworth, but Josiah was incapable of responding with his usual openness of feeling. Towards the end of January 1781, he tried to return to something like his old routine and wrote to Edgeworth congratulating him on his third marriage. In London on Christmas Day 1780, with Thomas Day as one of the witnesses, Edgeworth had married his former sister-in-law, Elizabeth Sneyd. Day at this time was writing children's books with the ill-concealed purpose of teaching independence of character and the habits of industry and fortitude. He had just finished the first volume of *The History of Sandford and Merton*, destined to become one of the best-loved books in English literature and to remain in print for more than a century.

Another wedding of an old widower friend took place a few months later, when Darwin married Elizabeth Chandos-Pole, a former patient, recently widowed, and some fifteen years younger than he. Now in his late forties, he had become so corpulent that to accommodate his girth during meals a semi-circular hole was cut in his dining table, and was hardly a sight to inspire romantic passion; and yet he had won an attractive and wealthy young widow who had several other suitors. Mrs Parker, his mistress of more than a decade, must have been disappointed, as was the Swan of Lichfield, Anna Seward. Still, Anna and Darwin maintained their friendship with its flirtatious overtones for another twenty years, sometimes writing love poems to one another in the persons of their respective cats, Mr Snow and Po Felina.

A new wife and the start of a new family helped Darwin overcome his grief at the death of his son Charles. He had now edited and published what he claimed were his son's medical discoveries, found in his student papers. Unfortunately he edited them a bit too much, incorporating into them some ideas of his own which were far beyond a young medical student, however brilliant. If these liberties on the part of a grief-stricken father were understandable, Darwin's crediting Charles with Withering's discovery of digitalis, and the assigning wholly to Charles of a case on which Withering and Darwin had been in joint consultation, was carrying paternal devotion too far — or at least so it must have seemed to Withering. The matter was never openly discussed, but a coldness now developed between the two doctors. They no longer had anything to do with one another professionally or socially, though both continued to attend Lunar meetings, where they preserved at least an appearance of cordiality.

Josiah was attending Lunar meetings more often than in the past three or four years. After the death of Bentley, the Wedgwoods' social life centred almost entirely on the members of the Lunar Circle and their wives. Without Bentley, business matters forced Josiah to spend more time in London, and he planned his visits so as to be in Birmingham on the Sunday nearest the full moon.

On one London visit he commissioned his friend 'Athenian' Stuart to erect a monument to Bentley's memory in the Chiswick church. He also agreed with his partner's widow, Mary Bentley, to manage that part of her income which lay in canal shares and in mortgages. The final dissolution of the Wedgwood & Bentley partnership was signalled by a public auction of the entire Wedgwood & Bentley inventory. This unprecedented sale of china, conducted by Christie and Ansell, began on 12 December 1781, lasted for 11 days and consisted of 2,200 lots.

Mary Bentley sold the house in Turnham Green and moved to Gower Street, then a new and fashionable section of London. She occasionally visited Etruria, and often received parcels from Staffordshire in the boxes of ware sent to Greek Street; but the feelings on both sides appeared to be more duty than genuine affection.

If no one person could replace Bentley as a friend, no single person could take his place in the business either. Josiah sent his nephew Tom Byerley to London to live in Greek Street and to take over the management of the showroom and warehouse. Tom was then thirty-four years old and engaged to marry Frances Bruckfield of Denby. He was also the man within the business upon whom Josiah relied the most. Still, the seventeen years difference in their ages and the memory of Tom's adolescent misdemeanours kept the relationship more on a father – son basis than one of equal friendship.

At about the time Tom went to London, Josiah hired Alexander Chisholm to come to Etruria as his scientific adviser and as tutor to his sons. Chisholm was then more than fifty years of age. For the past thirty years he had been mechanical assistant to Dr William Lewis of Kingston-upon-Thames, a prolific scientific writer who had died about the same time as Bentley. The laboratory at the works became Chisholm's headquarters, and the experiments which Josiah had previously conducted at Etruria Hall, in his study or in the secret laboratory cellars, were transferred there. Chisholm was a scholarly man with a practical, inventive mind and a gentle and kindly disposition. He taught the Wedgwood boys arithmetic, geometry, chemistry and Greek. Happily he developed an affection for all three boys, but most especially for Tom. Though frail and suffering poor health from childhood onwards, Tom with his fair hair and light eyes was the handsomest of all the Wedgwood children. He had a personal charm and, even at the age of ten, showed 'an independent spirit to a degree uncommon in childhood'. Though his brother Jos later insisted that he was never impertinent or obstinate, Tom displayed 'a disregard of authority unless accompanied by argument or a coincidence of sentiment and opinion in his own mind'.[2]

The oldest boy, John, at the age of sixteen was so reserved and lacking in aggression as to cause his parents concern. His seriousness and his overwhelming need to be of use, prompted no doubt by his father's pronouncement of an eleventh commandment, 'Thou shalt not be idle ...', made him much more of a follower than a leader. The middle son, Jos, was equally serious but neither an idle dreamer nor a leader. He was a practical, plodding child who had no difficulty in distinguishing reality from illusion, right from wrong, or the possible from the impossible. The three older girls, Sukey (now called Susan), Kitty and Sarah were all clever, strong-minded and more interested in intellectual pursuits than most girls of their age, though none of them had any personal ambitions — which, of course, their father would have thought unfeminine. The youngest child, Mary Ann, was apparently retarded both mentally and physically.

In early 1780 their grandfather, old Richard Wedgwood, who had suffered a series of illnesses, died. He was much missed by his grandchildren and by his daughter. No one was left now on Sally's side of the family except her uncles Thomas and Long John. Josiah had only his two widowed sisters and his partner and cousin Thomas Wedgwood, who remained in the background even after his rival Bentley's death.

With the help of Chisholm, in the spring of 1782 Josiah completed a series of experiments on heat measurement. He sent to the Royal Society a paper on the pyrometer he had invented, which could measure degrees of heat above the range of existing mercury thermometers. This instrument consisted of two brass gauges so placed that they were wider apart at one end than at the other. Degrees of heat were marked on scales on the gauges. Small cones of clay and alum were placed between the gauges, fired along with the ware in the ovens and withdrawn at intervals. The higher the temperature became the more the cones shrank and moved along the graduated scale. Before this invention the method most frequently used was one discovered by Thomas and Long John Wedgwood, in which changes in colour were observed through progressive degrees of heat. Josiah had used this method to regulate his own firings, but it was too uncertain for the sophisticated works of art he now produced.

Because he was particularly proud of this invention, which gave him a specific claim to membership in the same circle as Darwin, Edgeworth and Watt, Josiah, accompanied by Sally, made a special journey to London to be present at the Royal Society when his paper was presented. 'My Thermometer paper was read in the RS last Thursday, 'he wrote to Watt. 'It underwent the examination of many chemists & philosophers here before that time & they gave it their approbation very fully. I will send you some account of the degrees at which various bodies are changed, when I have a few moments time.'[3]

Watt had recently undertaken a somewhat delicate mission for Josiah. When Josiah and Turner visited Cornwall, they had seen Newcomen's fire engine, used for pumping in the tin mines. Upon their return, Turner installed a similar engine at Lane End to pump water over a water wheel at his pot bank. Later Spode took over Turner's pottery, thus acquiring the engine. Naturally curious, Josiah asked Watt to survey existing water-powered mills at Trentham and Lane End. In particular, he asked him to observe Spode's fire engine and engine mill. When he sent Watt a letter of introduction to Spode, he added a postscript in the accompanying note: 'Get the facts first & deliver the letter afterwords.'[4]

Josiah experimented with two of Watt's rotative steam engines, first 1782 and then again in 1784, but the experiments were not successful. The firm of Boulton & Watt had gone through a difficult period, and the relationship between the two partners was strained.

Although the Soho factory provided skilled labour and made some of the small parts, Boulton & Watt did not manufacture complete steam engines. Other smiths and founders, particularly Priestley's brother-in-law, John Wilkinson, made the larger parts. Not only did Boulton & Watt not manufacture their own products, they did not actually sell them either. Instead they acted as designers and consultants to the companies which used their machines, and which paid, not for the machines themselves, but for the amount of fuel saved by the new machine over the old one which the company had been using. This method of payment led to difficulties, as some company directors and owners of mines devised methods of faking the amounts of fuel consumption; moreover, a depression in the mining industry caused many miners to default on their payments.

The general depression which had affected all the manufacturing industries had been particularly disastrous to the firm of Boulton & Fothergill, which in 1781 was barely able to pay its workmen's wages. Fearing that if Boulton & Fothergill collapsed it might bring down Boulton & Watt as well, and hoping that somehow engines might be used to rescue buttons, Boulton acquired a loan for Boulton & Fothergill with part of the profits on the Boulton & Watt steam engines as security. Watt was furious, and a bitter quarrel developed between the partners. It was further aggravated by

Watt's intention to prosecute defaulters and by Boulton's wish to be accom-modating even to the point of investing his own dwindling capital to rescue some of his customers' failing businesses. At this point, Josiah stepped in and loaned Boulton £5,000. Darwin and Day made loans of £2,000 and £3,000 respectively. By the start of 1784 both of Boulton's companies once more were making a profit, and Boulton and Watt were again the best of friends.

During the early 1780s unemployment and inflation throughout the country spread gloom and despair among the poor. In 1782 almost all of the crops failed. There was a scarcity of provisions through the cold, wet winter. People were without sufficient food and fuel, and riots broke out spontaneously throughout the country. Wedgwood, though faring better than most factories, was not entirely exempt from the troubles caused by the general misery and suffering of the poor.

In March of 1783, when Josiah was in London, a riot broke out in the Potteries. A boat loaded with grain intended for Manchester docked briefly at Etruria. The potters believed that the grain had originally been intended for them but was now being sent on to Manchester because higher prices could be got there. An angry mob followed the boat on to Longport, seized it and brought it back to Etruria where the contents were auctioned off at prices agreeable to the mob. After this success, the rioters, who now numbered several hundred, among them women and children, looted small buildings and attempted to set fire to houses belonging to wealthy land-owners. For a while the Etruria factory seemed destined for destruction, and the crate house actually was burned. Several master potters spoke to the mob but were shouted down. Sally and seventeen-year-old John attempted to reason with four of the men who came to Etruria Hall demanding food and drink, as they intended to stand by all night to guard the corn, flour and barley taken from the boat. Wisely Sally gave the men what they requested.

Order was finally restored two days later by the arrival of the Stafford-shire militia under the command of Major Edward Sneyd. The Riot Act was read by two magistrates, and the crowd dispersed. Two men were arrested and tried two weeks later at Stafford. Young John Wedgwood attended the trial and wrote to his father that the two men were found guilty. One was hanged and the other publicly flogged.

Naturally Josiah was concerned at such violence and lawlessness taking place on his own doorstep. He supported the abolition of slavery and the American Revolution, yet poverty and distress among his own workmen evoked a different response. He wrote and published a pamphlet entitled *An Address to the Young Inhabitants of the Pottery*, in which he expressed his disapproval of 'the late riots' and exhorted the young inhabitants not to be misled by the violent actions of their elders. He said how much better off the workmen were now than in the days of his youth — and then proceeded to take much of the credit for this himself:

Industry has been the parent of happy change — A well directed and long continued series of industrious exertions, both in masters and servants, has so changed for the better the face of our country, its buildings, lands, roads, and notwithstanding the present unfavourable appearance, I must say the manner and deportment of its inhabitants, too, as to attract the notice and admiration of countries which had scarcely heard of us before; and how far these improvements may still be carried by the same laudible means which have brought us thus far, has been one of the most pleasing contemplations of my life.

That a general rise in the standard of living was naturally accompanied by a rise in expectations was something Josiah failed to grasp. The endless patience and perseverance which he displayed in his craft were lacking in his relations with his workmen. People were not as easy to perfect as pots. While he could easily dispense charity to the humble who begged, he could also in good conscience refuse wage increases to the skilled workmen who demanded them.

Although few of the young inhabitants to whom he had addressed his pamphlet were capable of reading the address, let alone comprehending its contents, he issued another for their further edification, this time entitled *An Address to the Workmen in the Pottery on the Subject of Entering into the Service of Foreign Manufacturers*. Having described the misfortunes of misguided men who left their native land to seek employment in potteries abroad, he patriotically concluded:

> Englishmen, in arts and manufactures as well as in arms, can only be conquered by Englishmen: the enemy must first gain over some traders and renegades from among ourselves, before they can obtain any decisive advantage. Is there a man among you then who will stand forth, and acknowledge himself to be that traitor to his country and fellow workmen? Who will openly avow, that for the sake of a paltry addition to his own wages for a few years, he would betray their interests, and wantonly throw away into the hands of foreigners, perhaps of enemies, the superiority we have thus laboured for and obtained!

At the time, of course, England was still far behind both France and Germany in the manufacture of porcelain; but, as sometimes happens, native pride and self-interest overrode truth. Also, now that the war with America had ended, Josiah was afraid that his recently resumed export trade would be curtailed if the Americans established potteries of their own. He was equally fearful that 'unprincipled Frenchmen' would steal his secrets and copy his designs, thus ruining the European export market.

Without Bentley, Josiah had no close friend whose income was from manufacturing yet whose political and moral opinions could extend beyond enlightened self-interest. Both Boulton and Watt were inevitably conservative, if not downright reactionary; Keir was more interested in his chemical researches than in the profitability of his glassworks. Other friends, such as Darwin and Edgeworth and Withering, were not businessmen; their idealism was not likely to conflict with their professional and financial interests.

ARTIST FRIENDS OF JOSIAH WEDGWOOD I

6-9
Self-portraits of Sir Joshua Reynolds *(top right),* 1753; George Stubbs *(centre· right,* on a Wedgwood plaque), 1781; Joseph Wright of Derby *(bottom right),* 1767; *(above)* John Flaxman: oil by Romney, *c.* 1790

Dear Sir

All matters being amicably settled betwixt my Pappa, Clerk, & my self. I yesterday prevail'd upon my dear Girl to name the Day, the blissfull day! when she will reward all my faithfull services, & take me to her Arms! to her Nuptial bed! to — Pleasures which I am yet ignorant of. and you my dear friend can much better conceive, than I shall ever be able to express: in three words, we are to be married on Wednesday next. — On that auspicious day think it no sin to wash your Philosophic evening pipe with a glass or two extraordinary, to hail your friend, & wish him good speed into the realms of Matrimony. Adieu my good friend, I am very busy to day, that no business may intrude on my pleasures for the rest of the week.

My best respects wait on Miss Oats. believe me most sincerely your very affect.te friend

& hble Serv.t

Josiah Wedgwood

Burslem 23 Jan.ry 1764

Can you write two letters of Congratulation on one joyfull occasion

10　Letter from Josiah Wedgwood I to
Thomas Bentley, 23 January 1764

11   Richard Wedgwood   *Oil by George Stubbs, 1780*

12   Thomas Wedgwood of the Big House

13   The Churchyard House works, *c.* 1750

14   The Ivy House works, *c.* 1760

15   The Brick House, *c.* 1762

16   The Brick House works, *c.* 1762

17   Thomas Bentley *Oil, ascribed to Joseph Wright, 1780*

18-19   *Opposite above:* James Brindley
             below: The Roundhouse and Etruria
                     works beside the Grand Trunk
                     Canal, *c.* 1775

ARTES ETRURIAE
1769-1786

20-23
(Top left) 'First Day's Throwing'
vase — Basalt with encaustic
painting, 13 June 1769; *(top right)*
plate from the Imperial Russian
service, 1774; *(above)* the Portland
Vase — black and white Jasper,
1st edition, 1793; *(right)* 'Apothe-
osis of Homer' vase — pale blue
and white Jasper, *c.* 1786

24-25
Dr Erasmus Darwin
and his second wife
Elizabeth, *née* Collier
Oils by Joseph Wright

26   Matthew Boulton

27   Dr William Withering

28   Richard Lovell Edgeworth

29   John Whitehurst

30   Joseph Priestley

31   James Keir

32   James Watt

33   Thomas Day

34 Thomas Byerley
*Wedgwood portrait medallion
by William Theed, 1810*

35 Portland House, the Wedgwood showrooms
in Greek Street, *c.* 1775

36   Tom Wedgwood   *From a chalk drawing, c. 1800*

TOM WEDGWOOD'S
CIRCLE OF FRIENDS

37-40
(Top) Samuel Taylor Coleridge;
(centre left) Dr Thomas Beddoes;
(centre right) Robert Southey; *(left)*
Humphry Davy

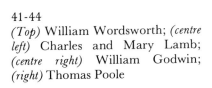

41-44
(Top) William Wordsworth; *(centre left)* Charles and Mary Lamb; *(centre right)* William Godwin; *(right)* Thomas Poole

45-46   The York Street showrooms, *c.* 1810

Edgeworth, however, had to some extent been affected by the general depression. In 1782 he returned to Edgeworthstown in Ireland to take charge of his lands and his investments. A year earlier Darwin's new wife, Elizabeth, had announced her dislike of Lichfield (and probably of Anna Seward as well), so the Darwins, including five children from their previous marriages and a new baby, Violetta, moved to Derby. At about the same time, Day and Esther bought an estate in Surrey, later described as 'one of the most unprofitable farms in England'. There they set about improving their land, educating their tenants and giving away food and money to the poor.

Now that Boulton was making a profit again and proclaiming his success to 'all the world', Day asked him for repayment of the loan which he had made to him and which, along with those from Josiah and Darwin, had been partially responsible for saving Boulton's business. Boulton was a man of ostentation and pride; he disliked being reminded of his debts. Day, on the other hand, lacked both pretence and tact. When Boulton neglected to answer one of his letters, he lost patience, demanded immediate repayment of the loan, and bluntly remarked that he had spent three years in the 'unentertaining ceremonial of soliciting'. Boulton paid, but the personal rift between them continued.

Changes in residence and personal disputes had altered both the composition and the character of the Lunar Society. Distance now made it impossible for Day or Edgeworth to attend meetings, and Darwin was unable to get to Birmingham as frequently as he had in the past. The most influential new member of the group was Josiah Priestley.

Because of his radical political opinions, Priestley had been dismissed from his job as librarian to Lord Shelburne. He then moved his family to Birmingham to be near his brother-in-law, John Wilkinson, and to take up an appointment as minister at the New Meeting House. Until this move in 1780, Priestley's visits to Etruria had been rare, though Josiah frequently saw him in London at Shelburne's town house. Between meetings they corresponded on scientific matters, and Josiah supplied him without charge with every piece of scientific apparatus that could be made in earthenware. In providing Priestley with the requirements for his chemical experiments, Josiah perfected a new composition for mortars and pestles. The invention was tested and approved at the Apothecaries' Hall. Soon it was in demand by chemists all over the world.

Priestley's income was small. To help him pursue his investigations without worry over personal finances, Josiah organized a subscription fund for his benefit. Annual contributions were made by Josiah, Darwin, Withering, Keir, Wilkinson, Boulton and Samuel Galton junr., the Quaker arms manufacturer. Josiah tactfully explained to Priestley that the money was in support of his work, and Priestley gratefully and graciously accepted it.

Josiah and Priestley were elected Fellows of the Royal Society at the same meeting in 1783, Priestley being honoured for his researches in chemistry and electricity, and Josiah for his invention of the pyrometer. At that time the Royal Society had greater prestige than any other club or society. It had not yet barred Dissenters from its membership. Darwin, Edgeworth and Whitehurst were already among the distinguished Fellows.

Chemistry was the subject that now interested Lunar members the most, and the addition of Priestley to the circle increased the number of chemical experiments made. In 1784 Benjamin Franklin sent a description of balloon experiments and an essay on gases to be delivered to Priestley, 'who is apt to give himself airs (i.e., fixed, dephlogisticated, etcetera) and has a kind of right in everything his friends *produce* upon that subject.'[5]

The Lunar Society had already become interested in balloons through Aimé Argand, the Swiss scientist who was also a business associate of Boulton. Argand gave a demonstration of his balloon before the King and his family at Windsor, and then went to Birmingham where a meeting of the Lunar Society was held. Darwin wrote to Boulton that he was unable to attend but had sent to the Society an 'air-balloon, which was calculated to have fallen in your garden at Soho; but the wicked wind carried it to Sir Edward Littleton's'.[6]

Boulton, however, had already launched his own balloon in Cornwall, for the amusement of his children. After Argand's visit, he and Watt, with the assistance of Priestley, designed an experiment with a balloon to determine whether the rumblings of thunder were due to echoes or to successive explosions. They invited their Lunar friends and their families as well as the townspeople to gather in front of the Soho factory to watch the ascent of the 'fire balloon' which was filled with one part common air and two parts 'inflammable air'. The experiment was a failure. When the balloon exploded, shouts of astonishment and fear from the spectators drowned out the effects of the explosion. Watt walked away in disgust muttering his familiar pessimistic philosophy: 'Of all things in life there is nothing more foolish than inventing.'[7]

Darwin wrote to Edgeworth proposing the use of a balloon for transporting manure up the hills on Edgeworth's estate in Ireland. Edgeworth sensibly rejected this scheme, no doubt foreseeing that Irish tempers might explode as well, should the airborne manure be driven by the wind in the wrong direction and accidentally deposited, say, in the village square, or perhaps in the midst of some neighbouring squire's garden party. But the problem naturally intrigued him, and he began a series of experiments on giving direction to balloon flight by the addition of sails and fins.

Another import from France to England which involved Benjamin Franklin again, and which aroused the interest of the Lunar Society at about the same time, was mesmerism. Though Franklin had befriended the Austrian Mesmer and distributed copies of his *Précis historique*, he apparently had no faith himself in animal magnetism. Darwin pooh-poohed the whole idea, and Priestley solemnly concluded that it would not stand the test of repeated experiment. Still, in London in 1785, mesmerism became a popular fad.

Josiah was then often in London, though he had little time for such esoteric pursuits as mesmerism. He was involved in government affairs directly affecting his own business as well as the nation's commerce in general. Richard Arkwright, who had lost the lawsuit challenging the patent on his water frame, had organized a meeting in London of all patent-holders to protest the judgement against him. Though Josiah had taken out only the one patent on encaustic painting, and in principle disapproved of the monopolies which patents encouraged, he supported Arkwright and came to London to attend the meeting. Both Darwin and Watt had previously testified in Arkwright's favour at the trial. Still, the patent was cancelled on the grounds that specifications had been given with deliberate intent to confuse and that there was reason to doubt the originality of the invention. Arkwright was so angry that he threatened to publish descriptions and illustrations of all of his machinery, thereby revealing his manufacturing secrets to the entire world as well as to his English competitors.

While Josiah was not much taken with Arkwright personally, finding him limited in interests and ideas apart from mechanics, he knew that what happened in the cotton mills in Lancashire might also happen in the potteries in Staffordshire. Without the legal protection of patents, workmen might spread about any new formulae or techniques of manufacture. Nothing new and in demand could remain a secret for long.

Josiah had preserved his secret formula for Jasper for several years, but it was at last successfully imitated by Turner and by Adams and then by other Staffordshire potters. In 1785 he had perfected a method of 'Jasper dip' in which objects were coated with Jasper instead of being formed of that body throughout, thus considerably reducing the cost of the finished product. Eventually that too would be copied; but, on the whole, he didn't care as long as he felt himself a step ahead of his competitors. 'A competition for *cheapness* and not for *excellence of workmanship*, is the most frequent and certain cause of the rapid decay and entire destruction of arts and manufactures,' he wrote in the Preface to one of his early catalogues.

To help Arkwright, Josiah arranged a meeting with Sir Joseph Banks, president of the Royal Society and a member of the Board of Trade. He also suggested that Arkwright go to Birmingham and discuss the whole subject of patents with Watt. In a letter to Watt, Josiah said that '... you two great geniuses may probably strike out some new lights together which neither of you might think of separately.'[8] But the cautious Watt, though he sympathized with Arkwright's particular case, thought it unwise to make a public issue over the cause of patents in general, as it might encourage attempts to test the validity of other existing patents, including his own.

A conflict between public interest and self-interest was a new phenomenon for manufacturers. Before the advent of specialization and mechanization, there had been no need for either workmen or industries to look upon themselves as separate entities. In 1785 a Chamber of Commerce calling itself the General Chamber of Manufacturers was formed in London to watch over the interests of English manufacturers; Josiah was elected the first president. The Chamber was essentially a federation of various societies, such as the Potters' Club of Hanley, which had already banded together to protect the overall interests of their particular trades. The impetus to form the Chamber had been given unintentionally by the new Prime Minister, William Pitt, when he proposed the Irish Trade Treaty. Basically this allowed goods to pass between the two countries duty-free; in exchange for free trade concessions, the Irish, should their depressed economy improve, were to be taxed for the defence of Irish shores which the English provided. There was an immediate outcry among English manufacturers who feared that lower taxes and the lower labour costs in Ireland would force English manufacturers out of business.

Josiah himself testified against the Irish Proposals before the House of Commons on 12 May 1785. So successful were he and other officials of the Chamber of Manufacturers in fostering mistrust and resentment between the two governments that the Dublin Parliament ultimately rejected the Proposals, which had been designed to free Ireland from unfair burdens previously imposed. As president of the Chamber, Josiah was no longer simply a successful manufacturer who had improved his craft and gained personal wealth and recognition. He was a power in the country with whom even the Prime Minister had to reckon.

9

The Power and the Glory
(1785 – 1790)

Josiah was not always consistent in his political beliefs. His instinctive liberalism inclined him towards free trade, while his manufacturing interests argued for protection. He was capable of advocating with complete sincerity one point of view on one day and the opposite on the next.

Naturally Edgeworth was disappointed in the attitude of his old friend towards the Irish Proposals. He told Josiah: 'You have no idea of the inaptitude to adventure, which is endemical in Ireland. ... Do you think these people will suddenly become traders? — No, they may be soldiers, Sailors, labourers & may follow the joint occupation of Weaver and farmer, but they will not manufacture for their own consumption during our life time.'[1] The anti-Irish sentiment among his Lunar friends caused Edgeworth pain, but he was not a man to abandon old friends over political differences. He even forgave Darwin, who, perhaps unconsciously, revealed his own prejudices by ending a note to Edgeworth with 'God help you from whiskey — if He can.'[2]

In 1786, Edgeworth wrote to Josiah: 'I think oval baking dishes for meat pies, in the shape of raised paste pies, with bunches of grapes, etc. etc. on their outside made of cane colored ware, not glazed, but nearly as possible the colour of paste would be saleable articles.'[3] Josiah replied: 'I made a clay pye and shewed it to my children as the best judges, but they not knowing that it was intended for, convinced me at once that it was wrong, and I have not yet made another essay.'[4] The children were wrong. Twenty years later game pie dishes were staple items with Wedgwood.

Thomas Day was equally critical of the activities of Josiah and the General Chamber, but for reasons different from Edgeworth's. To Day the freedom of the country depended upon the freedom of the farmer; the manufacturers were seizing power from the landed gentry. Day was achieving national fame with *The History of Sandford and Merton*, the first two volumes of which had now been published. James Keir believed that the volumes would influence the moral conduct of future generations. 'It is of little use to write for grown-up people; their acquired habits will generally prevail; but young unformed minds may be influenced into action and habit.'[5] Edgeworth took a different view, maintaining that Day was wasting his talent: 'The strength of Hercules could not throw a feather farther than it can be thrown by an infant.'[6] Thus, differences among the members of the Lunar Circle grew and became more acrimonious.

During the 1780s the Circle, three of whose members had withdrawn from regular attendance, gained in addition to Priestley three other new members—Samuel Galton junr., Robert Augustus Johnson and Dr Jonathan Stokes.

When Darwin moved to Derby, Withering sponsored Stokes, a young medical colleague and protégé, for membership in the group. Like Withering, Stokes had taken up botany as an avocation. After the death of Boulton's partner, John Fothergill, in 1781, Stokes had been asked by the executors of his will to compile a catalogue of the greenhouse plants in Fothergill's famous botanical collection, which was to be auctioned. Through this work and through his friendship with Sir Joseph Banks, Stokes became acquainted with Boulton, Watt, Whitehurst and Josiah.

Robert Augustus Johnson, a retired army officer with a keen interest in chemistry, in 1788 was elected a Fellow of the Royal Society. His scientific interests and his residence at Coombe Abbey, less than twenty miles from Birmingham, made him a likely candidate for membership in the Circle. In the early 1780s he visited both Soho and Etruria, introducing himself to Boulton and to Josiah and ordering special equipment from both factories for his scientific laboratory.

Samuel Galton junr. came from a wealthy family of merchants, bankers and manufacturers. A collector of scientific instruments, he first became friendly with Boulton and with Josiah when he subscribed to the fund for Priestley. Unlike many of his contemporaries, Galton disapproved of living idly off inherited wealth; he worked first in the family bank and then as the manager of a gun foundry owned by his father and uncle. An individualist, he refused to give up the manufacture of firearms even when told that it was against Quaker principles. When he was disowned at a monthly Meeting, he sent a large donation to the Society of Friends and continued to attend Meeting for the next fifty years, always contributing generously. In 1785 he and his family took up residence in Staffordshire, at Great Barr House, which, after Boulton's house, became the most frequent meeting place for the Lunar Society.

Galton's daughter Mary Anne, who was later denounced by her brothers and sisters for her malicious lies, described in her memoirs one memorable meeting of the Lunar Society at Great Barr House. On that occasion dinner was interrupted when a large black snake wriggled out from under the dining table and began to slither around the room.

'Oh, it's mine,' said Stokes. 'It's quite harmless. Just let it alone.'

Mrs Galton, however, disliked the distraction of the snake sliding around the room and slipping over her guests' feet. 'Go and catch the snake, Mary Anne,' she told her ten-year-old daughter.

While the obedient but frightened Mary Anne stalked the equally frightened snake, Stokes explained: 'I was riding along the road when I observed this animal, as I thought, frozen to death on the side of the bank. I picked it up, intending to dissect it when I got home. I forgot that it was in my coat, but apparently the warmth of the room has thawed it.'.

Mary Anne pounced on the snake, grabbed it and, concealing her distaste, proudly held it up for all to see.

'Well done,' said the Lunar members in a chorus.

'As a reward for your prowess, you may keep it,' the absent-minded doctor told the dismayed child.

During 1785–6 Sally seldom accompanied Josiah on his London trips. Although he disliked travelling alone and preferred her to be with him, he realized that their youngest child Mary Ann required her attention at home. The child had been sickly from birth, and had periodic fits which resulted in partial paralysis and temporary blindness. Her older brothers and sisters frequently mentioned her state of health in letters to their parents when they were away from Etruria. When Sarah was eight, she wrote to her father that the six-year-old Mary Ann bore bathing very well and 'cryed out distinctly mamamama & smiled but she said gna gna when I asked her if she would send her love to you & when I asked her if she wanted to see you'.[7] Mary Ann died in 1786, at the age of eight.

While in London looking after the concerns of the Chamber of Manufacturers, Josiah visited Whitehurst and Ralph Griffiths as well as Tom Byerley. Although Byerley, who now had as many children as his years of marriage, had in no way replaced Bentley in Josiah's affections or confidence, he was doing well in some of the areas of the business in which Bentley had been most successful. Byerley had a gift for conversation and was popular with the customers, particularly the ladies, who visited the showrooms. Now that the war with America had ended, there was no shortage of customers; in fact, demand was outrunning supply, and Byerley was constantly complaining to Josiah that the factory had not produced sufficient quantities of certain articles. He also enjoyed dealing with the modellers and painters, a side of the business which during the 1780s involved many fine artists: George Stubbs, Sir Joshua Reynolds, John Flaxman, Henry Webber, John Devaere, John Coward, William Hackwood, Angelica Kauffmann, Lady Diana Beauclerk, Lady Elizabeth Templeton, James Tassie and Camillo Pacetti were all advising on, creating or copying works of art for Wedgwood in this period.

The success of the Jasper ware was far greater than even Josiah had anticipated. It was made in a variety of colours, including shades of blue, black, green, yellow and lilac, and in items ranging from small cameos to tea services to portrait medallions and large plaques. Josiah began directing his efforts towards ornamental chimneypieces which had become popular in Ireland. Some of his finest ceramic compositions were combined with marble.

He seldom copied exactly, but would obtain an idea from an antique object and then vary the form, adding his own versions of flowers and festoons. Items such as candlesticks, flowerpots, sphinxes, tritons, dolphins and crouching lions first produced in Basalt were later made in Jasper.

The Portland or Barberini vase, as it was originally called, of dark-coloured glass with white cameo figures, had been excavated from a tomb outside Rome in the middle of the seventeenth century. The sarcophagus, dated *c*.A.D. 235, was deposited in a museum in Rome, but the vase, which legend claimed held the ashes of the Roman Emperor Alexander Severus and his mother Mammaea, was sold by Cardinal Francesco Maria Bourbon del Monte to Cardinal Francesco Barberini, nephew of Pope Urban VIII, for 600 *écus*. The vase remained in the Barberini family for more than a century. It was eventually purchased by the archaeologist James Byres, who then sold it to Sir William Hamilton for £1,000. In 1784 Sir William brought the vase to England and sold it to the Duchess of Portland for £1,800. The following year the Duchess died suddenly, and her son the Duke put up her art treasures for auction.

Josiah knew of the vase through Sir William Hamilton, had seen engravings of it published in Montfaucon's *L'Antiquité expliqué*, and had attempted to copy it in Jasper. This proved difficult from the engravings alone. He tried to purchase the vase from the Duke prior to the auction, but the Duke had refused, wanting to keep the vase for himself. The auction took place at the late Duchess's residence in Privy Gardens, Whitehall, from 24 April to 7 June 1786. Being the most esteemed piece in the Duchess's private museum, the vase was the last of the 4,155 lots. Josiah attempted to outbid the Duke, but when the bidding went over £1,000, the Duke sent a note to Josiah that he would be willing to lend him the vase for copying. Josiah agreed, and the vase was bought in at £1,029.

Three days later it was delivered to the Wedgwood showrooms, and Josiah signed a receipt: 'I do hereby acknowledge to have borrowed and received from His Grace the Duke of Portland the Vase described in the 4,155 lot of the catalogue of the Portland Museum ... & I do hereby promise to deliver back the Said Vase ... in safety into the hands of His Grace upon demand....'[8] The same receipt covered the loan of a cameo, a medallion of the head of Augustus Caesar, which was listed in the same catalogue. Josiah's note of possession and promise of return was witnessed by Byerley.

Josiah wrote immediately to Sir William Hamilton telling him of the loan of the vase, now called Portland, and consulting him on the problems of reproduction. He had chosen Henry Webber to model the figures, but the availability of competent craftsmen concerned him:

> ... for how few Artists have we in this branch whose touches would not carry ruin with them to those beautiful & high wrought figures? And suppose one or two could be found equal to the task, would such artists be persuaded to quit a lucrative branch of their profession, & devote half a life to a single work, for which there is little probability of their being paid half so much as they earn by their present employments: for I do not think £5,000 for the execution of such a vase, supposing our best Artists capable of the work, would be at all equal to their gains for the work they are now employed in; and the taste of the present age, you well know, Sir, is not awake notwithstanding all you have done to rouse it, to works of much time and great expense.[9]

The subject of education continued to concern Josiah even though the eldest among his children had now outgrown his Etruria school. In 1786 Susan was twenty-one and interested in music, parties and the comings and goings of fashionable society. She often visited the Darwins at Derby. Her three brothers, now aged twenty, seventeen and fifteen, had all spent some time in the pottery learning the various aspects of the business. Tom and Jos were now at Edinburgh University. John had studied for a year at Edinburgh and then worked in the London showrooms. At his father's suggestion, he accompanied Byerley on a trip to Paris; travelling with them were Watt and Boulton and Boulton's son Matthew Robinson Boulton.

Josiah himself never went abroad; he would always find some pressing reason to remain in England—such as, at this particular time, lobbying Parliament in favour of the Commercial Treaty with France. He had the provincial's mistrust of foreigners and foreign ways; at the same time he wanted his sons to travel, to become fluent in foreign languages and to be at ease in societies different from their own.

Byerley was an ideal guide and companion for a young man making his first trip abroad. Nineteen years older than John, he had experience and maturity; yet he remembered the ambitions and adventures of his own youth. John, however was not one for adventure. After only a few weeks in Paris, during which time he called upon the Duc de la Rochefoucauld and dined with Lavoisier, he asked his father's permission to move out of the city and into the country because '... it would be almost impossible to learn the language in Paris where there are so many things to be seen & to distract the attention from that object'.[10]

John took equally seriously his assignment of learning the intricacies of foreign trade and of gaining a working knowledge of the firm's overseas markets. Writing to his father about the Commercial Treaty with France, he noted: 'It is the report here that it will be vigorously opposed in Parliament and that Mr Pitt has said that if the Manufacturers do not support for, he will not — it will be certainly worth supporting for — great commerce may be carried on in this kingdom though perhaps not so much just in Paris, except in the second order of people for the first order have either plate or fine Porcelaine.'[11]

Having been defeated on the Irish Proposals by the Chamber of Manufacturers, the Prime Minister planned his campaign for the Commercial Treaty with France more carefully. While refusing to deal directly with the Chamber as such, Pitt called in Josiah and Boulton and a few others for private consultation. When both Josiah and Boulton came out in favour of the Treaty, many of the members of the Chamber of Manufacturers felt that Josiah in particular, having so recently opposed the Irish Proposals, had changed opinions — and sides. He was widely accused of double-dealing for his own interests. In a letter in the *Morning Chronicle*, one critic who called himself 'Friar Bacon's Ghost', described Josiah as an 'evil genius and reprobated by the nation at large, as a courtly sycophant, a disinterested deserter of the public cause, and a base betrayer of the interests of his country'.[12]

Josiah was not psychologically equipped to tolerate such criticism; he believed power and glory ought to go hand in hand. 'I am just wearied out with the nonsense of some & the pertness & abuse of others,' he wrote to Boulton, '& if I am not supported from the country soon, either by letters or by some of the members arriving at the Chamber, I must quit my post, for I have been buffeted & teased beyond human patience.'[13]

Human patience was also being tried in his relationship with his eldest son. John had returned from his first trip abroad restless and dissatisfied with being in business and with Staffordshire life in general. Josiah might have been more sympathetic towards him had his son expressed some particular ambition or displayed some definite talent. But John neither knew what he wanted, nor did he excel at anything in particular. His lethargy and his solemn silences irritated his father, who finally resolved to send him abroad again on a more extended continental tour which would include Germany, Switzerland and Italy. This time he was accompanied by the modeller Henry Webber, who was going to work and study in Rome, where it was hoped John might do likewise.

As John was about to embark upon his Grand Tour in the summer of 1787, his two younger brothers returned from their studies at Edinburgh. No doubt to John's relief, they took over duties which had previously been assigned to him. Jos spent most of his time acting as personal assistant to his father, as Byerley had done a decade earlier. Tom, with the assistance of Josiah and Chisholm, set up his own laboratory and began a series of experiments on the relations between light and heat. He corresponded with Keir and Priestley, both of whom were encouraging to him. Yet for much of the time he was unable either to work or to study; he suffered from headaches, lethargy, depression, trouble with his eyesight and an intestinal disorder diagnosed by one doctor as semi-paralysis of the colon, by another as chronic dysentery and by the down-to-earth Darwin as 'worms'.

Josiah himself was not in good health. When he was in London during the spring of 1788, he consulted Dr William Heberden for his headaches. Naturally he discussed his problems with Darwin, telling him: 'I sigh that I am becoming an old man — that age and infirmities overtake me, and more than whisper in my ear that it is time to diminish rather than increase the objects of my attention.'[14] Such melancholy reflection was prompted not only by a gradual decline in his own health, but also by the death of John Whitehurst in February 1788, and then a few weeks later by the sudden, unexpected death of his cousin and partner, Thomas Wedgwood. In one way, however, Thomas's death resolved a problem for Josiah, at the same time causing him seriously to consider the future of the business.

From Josiah's point of view the twenty-two-year partnership between the cousins had worked well, with only the one serious disagreement about items which Thomas considered 'useful' and which Bentley thought 'ornamental'. Thomas had been competent and hard-working, but also realistic, inventive and capable of viewing events in a wide perspective — the same traits which had made Josiah successful. Without such a partner, Josiah would have had less time for his experiments and for his other interests. He would also have made less money. The arrangement was ideal for him. That Thomas viewed it somewhat differently came as a shock.

Josiah and Sally had gone to Blackpool for Josiah's health, in the spring of 1788, when he received a letter from his son Jos telling him that it was rumoured '... that you and T. W. are going to part at Martinmas ... it gives me pain to write anything to you while you are unwell which may be disagreeable ... but I would not hear these things without informing you of them.'[15]

Cousin Thomas had been well aware of the value of his contributions and of his comparative lack of recognition. Josiah was world-famous, associating with men of genius and with the nobility; Thomas, who was now fifty-four, was still little more than a works manager. For a number of years he had hoped to break away from Josiah and set up his own business, but his hopes ended when he left the factory late on a dark evening during a heavy rain storm, slipped into the canal and was drowned. Thomas having conveniently died before publicly announcing the dissolution of the old partnership, a certain amount of embarrassment was avoided for Josiah.

Erasmus Darwin once said that he always felt best just before he was about to be ill. Josiah, on the other hand, usually felt depressed just as he was on the verge of some remarkable achievement. As his numerous trials on the Portland Vase were about to succeed, he became more irritable and more despondent. Both he and Darwin were further depressed by news of the untimely death of Thomas Day on 28 September 1789, at the age of forty-one. The third volume of *Sandford and Merton* had just been printed when Day rode over to visit his mother who lived in a near-by village. One of his cherished theories was that animals should be trained by kindness alone; therefore his horse was undisciplined. Passing a farmyard a short distance from the village, the horse, startled by the sudden appearance of a labourer bearing a corn screen, shied and threw Day on to the stone road. His skull was crushed and he died before his grief-stricken wife could reach him. Esther went into a kind of catatonic stupor, became a recluse and refused ever to go out of her house in daylight. Two years later she announced to the wife of a tenant farmer who looked after her that she no longer wished to live. She got up from her bed, went downstairs, drank a cup of coffee and dropped dead.

Both Keir and Edgeworth wrote biographies of Day, but it was Keir's more sentimental tribute that Esther chose to have privately printed and distributed to their friends. Keir wrote of Day's goodness and of his achievements, passing over his eccentricities and the more controversial aspects of his character; Edgeworth, on the other hand, wrote tolerantly of Day's peculiarities, presenting him in a light which must surely have seemed truer to his Lunar friends, if not to his wife.

In 1789 another Lunar publication appeared: the second part of Darwin's didactic poem *The Botanic Garden* — published before the first part and entitled *The Loves of the Plants*. Darwin had begun the work twelve years earlier but had delayed publication because he feared that appearing before the world as a poet might adversely affect his medical practice. Now, at the age of fifty-eight, he was successful and secure enough not to care about losing or acquiring patients. In any event, his fears were groundless. *The Botanic Garden* was the most highly acclaimed literary work of the period. Darwin was compared with Ovid, Homer, Shakespeare, Milton and Dante; the work was not only thought 'divine and sublime' by the average reader but also by other poets such as William Cowper and William Hayley. Horace Walpole said: 'Dr Darwin has destroyed my admiration for any poetry but his own.'[16]

In March of 1789 Darwin sent an advance copy of the poem to Josiah, asking him to use his influence with Ralph Griffiths to get the book a favourable notice in the *Monthly Review*. Naturally Josiah agreed; he was himself so impressed by the poem that he spoke admiringly and imitatively of his friend as 'the powerful magician who can work wonders, who can liquify the granite and still harder flint into the softest poetic numbers, and with the breath of his mouth waft their very productions to the most distant ages.'[17]

Six months later Josiah sent Darwin the first perfect copy of the Portland Vase, accompanied by a warning not to show it to anyone outside his own family. But Darwin could not resist the temptation: 'I have disobeyed you and shown your vase to two or three; but they were philosophers, not cognoscenti. How can I possess a jewel and not communicate the pleasure to a few Derby philosophers?'[18]

After more than thirty years of friendship Josiah and Darwin had reached the pinnacle of their respective careers at the same time. They shared their triumphs and were generous in their praise of each other. A bond was forged between the two families which was to continue for another three generations.

10

Wedgwood, Sons & Byerley
(1790 – 1795)

On 16 January 1790, Josiah took into partnership his three sons and his nephew Tom Byerley. He realized that his sons were too inexperienced and not sufficiently interested to carry on the business alone after his death. It was ironical that Byerley, who had been so unreliable in his youth, was now the only man in the business upon whom Josiah could rely.

From Rome John had written to his father that he was aware that upon his return he would be expected to 'fix ultimately on some plan of life'. His plan then was that he should become a Member of Parliament 'Unconnected with any Party', and that 'By this means I shall not be prevented from following the business but shall rather add credit to it.' He added that he was reluctant to work full-time in the pottery as he would thereby 'lose a great deal of the liberal eduction I have received'.[1]

Josiah had no more sympathy for John's youthful and impractical dreams than he had had for Byerley's. It seemed to him that his indolent son had been corrupted by 'foreign ways', and he determined not to send either of his other sons abroad except for the purposes of business. Jos, who had looked forward to the sort of Grand Tour John had had, was sadly disappointed.

After John returned home in 1789, he so annoyed his father by his 'foreign manners' that Josiah agreed to his making a leisurely tour round England with the mineralogist John Hawkins, whom John had met in Switzerland. A few weeks later the twenty-one-year-old Jos embarked, not on the dreamed-of Grand Tour, but on a six-month business trip through Holland and Germany with Byerley.

Before the trip, Jos suggested to his father that a friend of his, William Sneyd of Belmont, accompany them; Sneyd had travelled extensively, spoke German fluently and was of a 'mild and gentlemanly manner'. Josiah objected, because he suspected that Jos, like his brother, might be influenced by Sneyd to pay more attention to entering society and enjoying himself than attending to business. Jos stuffily replied that he was well aware of the social distinctions between 'men engaged in business and gentlemen'. He requested that his father should settle the matter with Sneyd, as 'I should think a strong representation of the *dryness* of such a journey to him might perhaps cause him to decline it—if it did not, I should feel myself in an awkward situation & I should hardly know how to refuse his company without giving him offence which I should be extremely sorry to do.'[2]

The purpose of Jos's and Byerley's trip was to display a copy of the Portland Vase, which had been on exhibition in London and received a certificate of merit from Sir Joshua Reynolds; they also took orders. Byerley introduced Jos to various important customers, helping him to gain a knowledge of the firm's overseas markets, just as he had done with John four years earlier.

When they returned, Byerley suffered an attack of gout and was unable to resume work. As the showroom had been neglected during his absence, Jos (who was no more anxious to return to Etruria than John had been) volunteered to take it over until his cousin recovered. Josiah was at first pleased, then vexed, when Jos added that any arrangement for his acting as a salesman would have to be temporary: 'I have been too long in the habit of looking upon myself as the equal of everybody to bear the haughty manner of those who come into the shop.'[3]

Both his older sons had acquired an arrogance which Josiah found distasteful. Jos, however, was dependable and possessed common sense; John's imagination darted from one scheme to another, and he was finding it increasingly difficult to settle on any plan for the future. Though he did not want to be a potter 'full-time', he had abandoned his notion of running for Parliament. For a while he contemplated living the life of a country gentleman and asked his father to investigate the purchase of Maer Hall, an estate near Etruria which belonged to William Bent, a chemist and brother of the surgeon James Bent, who had amputated Josiah's leg. The price of £17,000, however, discouraged him. Then he decided abruptly that he wished to live in London.

Exasperated, Josiah stepped in and made some firm decisions for him. He bought him a house in Devonshire Place and a junior partnership in Alexander Davison & Co., a banking house just then being formed in London. Banking was at the time a fashionable occupation for young gentlemen; without becoming 'tradesmen', the junior partners met several times a year with the City men who were actively in charge of the bank's main business, which was to supply capital to expanding industry.

Tom, whom Josiah described as '... very good; he labours too hard at his studies & the works together ...', had completed two experiments whose results were presented in papers read before the Royal Society by Sir Joseph Banks. In the first he described how a substance could be made luminous by reducing it to powder and sprinkling it on a warm iron plate. The second paper, on making different substances red-hot, established from an experiment gilding a piece of earthenware the physical law that all substances begin to glow at a particular temperature.

With his father's permission, Tom had invited the scientist and mathematician John Leslie, whom he had met when they were both students at Edinburgh, to Etruria to help in the laboratory and to instruct himself and his brother Jos in scientific studies. Tom had hoped that he and Leslie could set up a household together away from Etruria Hall. In a letter to Jos he set out his desire for a quiet, intellectual life, suggesting, in an accompanying note, that Jos show the letter to their father so that it might seem the idea for Tom's moving away had come from the old man himself. the scheme failed. Josiah saw no need for his son to move away from home and told him: 'Even knowledge itself, if receiv'd in exchange for the blessings of society & the family charities, would be dearly bought.'[4] Tom protested, but eventually deferred to his father's wishes.

Leslie had recently returned from America where he had been private tutor to the two sons of the Randolph family of Virginia. Five years older than Tom and having no inheritance or regular income, he immediately accepted the invitation to come to Etruria. 'The idea of residing with a young man whose heart is of the same mould, and whose mind is so benevolent, so generous and so enlarged is beyond measure delightful....'[5] Leslie was effusive, pompous and sycophantic, but apparently fitted well enough into the Wedgwood family, for he remained at Etruria for two years. Josiah was sufficiently impressed by his 'philosophical ingenuity' to give him a letter of introduction to James Watt.

Watt, in the early 1790s, had reached the apex of his career. Under Boulton's guidance, his machines had revolutionized the operations of the mining industry, the textile industry and the iron industry. Even Watt himself was beginning to see new potentialities in his scheme of 'parallel motion in the double acting engine'. Now that the company of Boulton & Watt was secure financially, Watt bought a grand house and forty acres of land at Handsworth Heath, less than a mile from the Soho works. Rooms in his house, his office and the Soho showrooms were steam-heated. Though he was no longer critical of his partner's operational methods, his dour disposition had not improved. Infringements of his patent resulted in his spending a considerable amount of time in litigation, grumbling and cursing those who usurped his ideas: '... since the fear of God has no effect upon them, we must try what the fear of the Devil can do.'[6]

The Lunar member for whom all was not going well now, and who did indeed seem to be pursued by the Devil, was Joseph Priestley. Both his religion and his scientific theories made him appear a threat to ordinary, unthinking men for whom the events in France in 1789 had aroused new hopes and old hostilities. The issue was not so much whether one was French or English as whether one was for or against the Revolution. Dissenters were looked upon as a political faction as much as a religious sect; radical by temperament, they were reformers by design. Priestley was the most famous Dissenting minister of his time; he had also been honoured in France for his scientific discoveries, and was made a member of the Academy of Sciences and an honorary citizen of The First Republic.

The majority of Lunar members, as well as the majority of Dissenters, ardently supported the French Revolution, at least in the beginning. Josiah wrote to Darwin: 'The Politicians tell me that as a manufacturer I shall be ruined if France has her liberty, but I am willing to take my chance in that respect. Nor do I yet see that the happiness of one nation includes in it the misery of its next neighbour.'[7] And Darwin told the skeptical Watt that he felt himself 'becoming all french both in chemistry & politics'.

After July 1789, when the Garde Française had itself sided with the people in the taking of the Bastille, many conservative people in England began to wonder just what changes the radical philosophers who so strongly supported the French revolutionaries might try to bring about in their own country. In Birmingham, which had for years been a stronghold of reactionary conservatism, Priestley was denounced from Anglican pulpits as an enemy of the state and a threat to the Established Church. 'No Presbyterians, Damn Priestley' was scrawled on walls throughout the city.

On 14 July 1791, a dinner to commemorate the second anniversary of the fall of the Bastille was planned to take place at 3 p.m. in the Hotel in Temple Row, Birmingham. Keir, a member of the Church of England as well as a member of the Revolutionary Society which Priestley had helped to organize, was chairman. Priestley himself declined to attend for fear of inciting violence. The meeting was advertised in the *Birmingham Gazette*. Tickets, on sale in advance at five shillings each, included a bottle of wine. Eighty-one ticket-holders turned up at the dinner and were jostled, shoved and hissed as they entered the hotel. Anticipating even more trouble, the diners, having drunk nineteen toasts and sung several songs, adjourned before 6 p.m., leaving quietly in small, inconspicuous groups.

By 8 p.m. a riotous mob had surrounded the hotel. When informed that the dinner was over and that those in attendance had gone home two hours earlier, the rioters broke all the windows in the hotel. They then moved on to the New Meeting House which they burned to the ground, shouting their slogan 'No philosophers—Church and King forever!' In no mood to disperse, the mob proceeded to attack the Old Meeting House, destroying pulpit and pews with axes and crowbars and setting fire to the building itself. Not being restrained by magistrates, clergymen or other officials, all of whom were strangely absent, the rioters chanted 'We want Priestley' and marched towards his house, the Larches. A friend of Priestley's drove in his chaise to warn him.

Unaware of the approaching mob, Priestley was playing a game of backgammon with his wife. They left quickly by a back road and took refuge with a neighbour. Their house was burned, Priestley's library and scientific laboratory destroyed. A barrel of ale had been left on the front lawn in the hope of distracting the mob, but the disappointment of not finding Priestley himself, coupled with the boldness inspired by drunkenness, made the mob seek out other prominent liberal spokesmen. Withering, who had not attended the dinner either, was also warned of the mob's march towards his house. He escaped by disguising himself as a workman driving a wagon loaded with hay, under which were his choicest books and mineral specimens.

Priestley's friends persuaded him that it was too dangerous for him to remain in Birmingham. Josiah, who was in London, immediately sent word that the homeless Priestleys were welcome to stay at Etruria Hall. 'Assure yourself, my good friend, that I most earnestly wish it. Believe this of me — act accordingly, instruct me in the means of doing it & I shall esteem it as one of the strongest instances of your friendship.'[8]

With the assistance of his friends and his brother-in-law, John Wilkinson, Priestley decided instead to go to London. There he took up an offer to teach at Hackney New College and to preach at the Gravel-Pit Meeting House. The week-end following the riots Watt, who travelled armed with two pistols, was at Etruria. He gave young Jos a first-hand account of the riots which Jos then passed on to his father in London:

> Watt says that he firmly believes the inhabitants of Birmingham would easily have quelled the riots in the beginning if they had associated & armed with firearms, or even if they had armed the constables with fire-locks instead of mop staves. But it appears that the magistrates possessed neither activity nor resolution, or that they were not heartily desirous to put a stop to their excesses.... It is certain however that Mr Keir offered to quell the riot if they would give him a written order but the magistrates gave him no answer. An officer in the town offered to head the recruits against the mob but they would not authorize him. Mr Keir armed several of his men & put himself in a posture of defence, & employed scouts, as the mob had sent him word they would visit him to which he replied that he should be very glad to see them.... Dr & Mrs Priestley were within 50 yards of their house all the while it was plundered & did not go to their chaise at a distance until morning. The Dr could hardly be persuaded to go to London & would scarcely believe that he was in personal danger.[9]

Jos ended his letter with the happier news that Sir William Hamilton had visited Etruria and was very pleased with the Portland Vase. Sir William himself wrote to Josiah from Newcastle:

> I am now just returned from your house, and much disappointed at not having had the pleasure of finding either you or my Naples acquaintance [John] at home. However, I have accomplished one of my great objects, which was the seeing your wonderful copy of the Portland Vase. I am so well acquainted with the original, and the difficulties you may have met with, that I really think it is so. The sublime character of the original is wonderfully preserved in your copy, and little more is wanting than the sort of transparency which your materials could not imitate, to induce those not quite so knowing as you and I are, to mistake it for the original. In short, I am wonderfully pleased with it, and give you the greatest credit for having arrived so near the imitation of what I believe to be the first specimen of the excellence of the Arts of the Ancients existing....[10]

Unlike Priestley, Withering was able to return to his house, which had been saved from destruction by the eventual, though late, arrival of the militia. He was, however, shaken by the experience, and he decided to move to Lisbon where he hoped the warm climate would prove salutary to his consumptive condition.

Apart from his illness, two other unpleasant circumstances had dis-illusioned Withering, making him willing to leave Birmingham and his medical colleagues. The rift with Darwin continued, with Darwin still failing to credit Withering with the discovery of digitalis. Darwin also disregarded Withering's statements about the proper dosage, often with serious consequences. Withering was highly offended but remained silent, at least publicly, until Darwin published papers in competition with and in contradiction to Withering's botanical researches. At this additional insult, Withering became furious, taking out his rage on the twenty-two-year-old Robert Darwin, who was just beginning his medical practice. Withering and young Darwin had both seen a certain patient and prescribed different treatments. After the patient's death, each accused the other of incompetence, publishing letters which did credit to neither man nor to the medical profession.

The other unpleasantness occurred with Stokes, whom Withering had employed to help him prepare an updated second edition of his *Botanical Arrangement*. Apparently, the two had not reached a satisfactory financial agreement before beginning the work. Stokes later claimed that the second edition had been done entirely under his guidance and was in effect 'his book'. Withering, who had acknowledged his debt to Stokes in the Preface to the first edition, denied this and accused Stokes of being overambitious. He offered to pay Stokes a fixed sum and then end their arrangement, but Stokes refused, claiming a portion of the profits and the copyright in his part of the work. This Withering refused. Attempts made by Josiah and by other Lunar members to mediate in the dispute failed. On 23 January 1790, Withering sent a formal demand to Stokes that he return herewith all specimens of plants, books and correspondence 'relating to a Botanical Work preparing for the Press.' At first, Stokes claimed that Withering had given him the books, which were extremely valuable, in gratitude for his services. Withering denied this, and Stokes then agreed to return immediately those that were not necessary to the work in progress and to return the remainder within three months. When the books were finally returned, they were damaged beyond use. Withering was appalled. Stokes claimed that part of their verbal agreement had been that he be allowed to 'cut out' any of the illustrations that might be of use to him.

Neither man ever spoke to the other again. In the Withering – Darwin quarrel, the other Lunar members had remained aloof, refusing even to acknowledge the disagreement. After the Withering – Stokes quarrel and the incident of the mutilation of the books, all of the Lunar members (except Darwin) sided with Withering.

About the time Withering's controversial second edition was published, Samuel Galton junr. published anonymously *The Natural History of Birds,* compiled from the work of Linnaeus, Buffon, Latham and others. Far from being intended as a significant ornithological contribution, the book, with its 116 illustrations, was intended for the 'amusement and instruction of children'.

That other instructor of children, Edgeworth, returned to England shortly after the Birmingham riots. He moved his family, which still included nine of his twenty-two children, to Clifton Spa, near Bristol, so that his son Lovell could take the waters and recover from what was feared to be consumption. Josiah wrote to Edgeworth: 'I am truly sorry for the occasion of your visit to Bristol Wells, & shall be happy to learn that they have the desired effect in restoring & establishing your son's health.' Josiah was fond of Lovell, who had written a flattering poetical description of the Portland Vase, which he sent to Josiah. 'It is highly pleasing to see so large a portion of the father's taste & genius descending to the son ...,'[11] he told Edgeworth in the same letter. At the time he made that remark, Josiah was feeling just the opposite about his own three sons, none of whom was turning out as he had planned.

In April 1792, only a few weeks short of his twenty-first birthday, Tom Wedgwood experienced a nervous collapse. Suffering from exhaustion, depression, trouble with his eyesight and headaches so severe that he would sometimes throw himself to the ground screaming, he resolved to give up his scientific experiments, including the photographic experiments which he called his 'silver pictures'. Darwin examined him and prescribed a change of scene, Josiah obligingly sent him to Paris to attend a fête in celebration of the third anniversary of the fall of the Bastille. It can hardly have been a relaxing journey. France was in upheaval, the downfall of the monarchy imminent, and war between England and France only months away. Tom returned even more depressed.

His brother John was depressed as well. He was beginning to have doubts about banking as a suitable occupation. And, Jos, like his sister Susan, was preoccupied with social matters, which interested him far more than the pottery.

In August 1792, Jos and Susan went to the Haverfordwest Assizes where they met Elizabeth (Bessy) Allen, the eldest of nine daughters of John Allen of Cresselly. Never one for doubts or indecision, Jos knew immediately that Bessy was the woman he must marry. A first glimpse of the charming, extro-verted woman who was to be his hostess for a week, and he was deeply affected. He wrote home to his father, 'You are so kind as to say you shall be prepared to see me and my sister, but I hope you will have no objection to me staying a little longer, as much on my sister's account as on my own, for I am afraid she has little chance of bringing Miss Allen back with her.'[12] Being of a gentle nature, Bessy was somewhat awed by the determination of this grave young man who was five years younger than she. But if at first sight she was not as passionately attracted to him as he was to her, she at least found his character impressive and his attentions agreeable. She was also anxious to escape from the tyranny of her widowed father.

John Bartlett Allen, squire of Cresselly, in Pembrokeshire, was domineer-ing and possessed of a vile disposition, quarrelling with his neighbours and making life practically intolerable for his two sons and nine daughters. He expected much of these daughters. If they did not provide charming company and clever conversation, he beat them. Fortunately — or perhaps because of such harsh discipline — the daughters were all highly articulate and entertaining.

Bessy did return with Susan and Jos to Etruria. Four months later, in December 1792, with the approval of both families, Bessy and Jos were married at Cresselly. Before returning to live in Little Etruria, the house that had originally been built for Bentley, and which Josiah was remodelling for them, the newlyweds stayed three months in London with John.

Jos wrote from Devonshire Place thanking his father for a wedding gift of £3,000, which he left with John to invest for him. He also thanked his mother for the gold watch she had given to Bessy. Susan was also in London, staying with John before going on to Bath to take the waters. Like her mother and her brother Tom, she suffered chronic ill health, and was often journeying to consult some new doctor or to try some new treatment. Darwin and Josiah had reached an understanding long before that Susan and Robert Darwin would marry when Robert had established a successful medical practice. The couple themselves took a practical rather than a romantic approach. Before becoming engaged, Robert, who remembered his mother's mental instability and who now observed disturbances in his brother Erasmus junr., asked his father if he thought alcoholism or insanity were hereditary. If so, Robert felt he should not have children and that it would not be fair to marry on the condition that the woman remain childless. His father wrongly assured him that he should have no fears. Susan was now a frequent visitor to Derby, giving her future father-in-law piano lessons as well as attending dances with Robert.

After his return from France, Tom's health grew steadily worse. In April 1793, he decided to resign his partnership in the firm. At the same time John announced his intention of marrying Jane Allen, a sister of Jos's wife Bessy and considered to be the beauty of the family. He also stated that while he wanted no active part in the Etruria management, he was nevertheless prepared to leave the bank rather than give up all of his Etruria shares.

Irritated, Josiah made little effort to conceal his disappointment at having to make provision for a son so little interested in the business 'which has done me no discredit and I hoped it would do none to any of my children'.[13] Josiah told John that it was too soon to know if the banking venture would turn out satisfactorily and that John could retain shares in Etruria so that he might return at a later date if he wished. Thus, a new seven-year partnership agreement was drawn up, with John and Tom taking a progressively larger percentage of the profits. Josiah hoped that Tom's health would improve sufficiently for him to return to the business. He and the rest of the family were, however, aware of changes in Tom's appearance as well as in his personality. Jos later described his brother's physical condition as a 'general wasting away'.

During periods when he was free from depression and incapacitating headaches, Tom read and wrote on a wide variety of subjects, usually concerning himself with the betterment of mankind through science and medicine. One of his projects, reminiscent of an early preoccupation of his father's, was spreading information about inoculation as a preventive against smallpox. Another shared interest of father and son was the investigation of medicated 'airs' as a cure for consumption. Both Tom and his father made sizeable contributions to the establishment of a research laboratory in Bristol called the Pneumatic Institute.

More and more Josiah was withdrawing from the active day-to-day management of the business, letting Jos handle the factory and Byerley the London showrooms and warehouse. His political activity was also diminishing. When Byerley urged him to join one of the numerous patriotic associations being founded to support the Constitution and which were a reaction against the excesses of the French Revolution, he refused. 'I shall let my actions speak for me,' he told Byerley, '& continue to perform what appears to me to be my duty to all around me. I shall certainly love my friends & if I cannot arrive at the perfection of loving my enemies likewise I will not injure them unless in my own defence.'[14]

He made his will on 2 November 1793, appointing as executors his eldest son and his lawyer James Caldwell. He had already made over a large portion of his personal estate to his children, but now that Jos was the only member of the next generation in the business, the factory and the bulk of the property, including Etruria Hall, were left to him. To the other five children he left sums of £25,000 or £30,000 each. He also remembered Alexander Chisholm, Byerley and his children, as well as various other nephews, nieces, servants and long-time employees. The making of a will was simply a practical sorting out of his affairs. He was not preoccupied with death. Despite the frequent headaches and loss of energy, he had no real reason to suppose he would not live for years.

At the onset of Josiah's final illness in 1794, the Lunar Circle had to all practical purposes ceased to exist. Whitehurst, Day and Small were dead; Priestley was in America; Withering had gone to Portugal and Edgeworth had returned to Ireland. Stokes had been eliminated from the Circle, partly by distance, with his move to Kidderminster, and partly by tacit agreement among the other members. During the quarter of a century that had passed since the first informal Lunar meetings, Darwin, like Josiah, had slowed the hectic pace of his travels and numerous activities. Now that they were all in their late fifties and sixties, old friendships and the memory of shared struggles seemed more important than new, co-operative experiments. If they met infrequently as a group, they kept up individual contact and corresponded with one another. Edgeworth, in a sentimental mood, said of the group that it was 'such a society as few men have had the good fortune to live with: such an assemblage of friends as fewer still have had the happiness to possess and keep through life.... This mutual intimacy has never been broken but by death.'[15]

Josiah and Sally spent several months in the autumn of 1794 first at Blackpool and then at Buxton in the hope of restoring Josiah's health. More than anything else he seemed simply tired. When they returned, he felt himself improved, in spite of a sudden, painful swelling in the right side of his jaw, which he thought was only a toothache. He wrote a cheerful and reassuring letter to Darwin in the early part of December 1794. And Darwin replied: 'You know how unwilling we all are to grow old. As you are so well, I advise you to leave off the bark and take no medicine at present.'[16]

A week later the optimism that had so often been justified in the past was no longer possible. Though all of the children, Byerley and his family, and Josiah's sisters Margaret Byerley and Catherine Willet came to Etruria Hall, it was a sad and depressing Christmas. By then all of them, including Josiah himself, realized that the pain was more than a toothache. His decline was swift as the inflammation and swelling passed from his jaw to his throat. Two local physicians were in attendance and Darwin was summoned from Derby. Sally was always resilient and indefatigable in times of crisis. The three daughters helped her to look after him, but the patient grew steadily worse. Susan was so deeply affected by this last illness that she became ill herself. Byerley found he was unable to concentrate upon the business.

It was the sense of vitality and ambition, of life lived to the full, that in retrospect gave pathos to the end. He who had done so much and overcome so many trials in the past was too tired now to battle this new pain that consumed all his strength. He was conscious and as determined to be in control of his own death as he had been of his life. His old friend Darwin, who was never too precise about dosages, gave him a supply of laudanum which he could take as he wished.

Throughout his life Josiah had behaved with consideration, modesty and dignity, always conscious of the fitness of things. His death was the same. On 2 January 1795, he told Sally and Susan not to disturb him, that he would sleep soundly through the night. In the morning it was discovered that his bedroom door was locked from the inside. The carpenter, Greaves, got a ladder, climbed through the window and found him dead in his bed.

11

The Three Brothers
(1795 − 1800)

When Josiah Wedgwood died in 1795, he had more employees at Etruria than all of the Five Towns had had inhabitants in 1730, the year of his birth. Having begun his career with a legacy of only £10, he died worth half a million pounds. 'The death of Mr Wedgwood grieves me very much,' Darwin wrote to Edgeworth. 'He is a public as well as a private loss.'[1] Within a single generation Josiah had lifted the Wedgwood family from provincial obscurity to national importance. He had given his sons all of the advantages that accompany wealth, fame and power, but they were very different from their father. Josiah was a man for all seasons; John, Jos and Tom were very much of their own time, country and class.

No one was more aware of or affected by the differences in the generations than Sally who, at the time of her husband's death, was only sixty years old. She was not a sentimental woman. She did not save letters from her children, as Josiah had done, nor did she keep the many letters of condolence she received after his death. After his casket was lowered into the frozen earth, she left the Stoke churchyard with her son John in a falling snow. All six of the Wedgwood children and Tom Byerley attended the simple service and returned to Etruria Hall with her.

Jos, the second son and namesake, who was twenty-six, inherited Etruria Hall, the Etruria factory and an estate of 380 acres. He was a patient, plodding man, domineering yet averse to taking risks. From the beginning he had possessed no more enthusiasm for being a potter than either of his brothers. Unlike John, however, he was wise enough not to incur his father's displeasure by telling him so.

Less than four months after Josiah's death, Jos withdrew from the day-to-day management of the pottery, though he still retained the over-all control. He and Bessy and their two children, Elizabeth and Josiah III, called Joe, left Staffordshire and moved to Stoke d'Abernon, Surrey, where Jos established himself as a country squire. From Surrey he issued orders like royal commands to the unfortunate Byerley, who, at the age of forty-eight, was now in the impossible position of managing both the factory and the London showrooms and warehouse.

The leases on the Greek Street premises were about to expire. Application for a renewal had been refused even before Josiah's death, and a new location had to be found quickly. Jos chose a site on the York Street corner of fashionable St James's Square, the purchase of which Byerley spent months negotiating. St James's was a residential square, unsuited for commercial purposes; the York Street rooms, however, were elegant and lofty, the staircases wide, and there was ample space for showrooms, offices, storage of ware and living accommodation for staff and for members of the family when visiting London. The site was outrageously expensive.

Jos wanted to dissociate himself from the pottery and from the image of the despised tradesman. Early on he had made the distinction between gentlemen and men engaged in business, a distinction he felt keenly. By marrying into the Allen family, which claimed direct descent from the Cecils, both Jos and John had elevated themselves into the established landed gentry. As a further sign of social advancement, the brothers abandoned the Unitarian Chapel of their childhood and joined the Established Church, an act that would certainly have distressed their father. Jos, however, was as naturally conformist as his father had been nonconformist. His ambitions were to live a quiet, cultured life in the seclusion of his family, to acquire large and profitable estates, to experiment with improving breeds of sheep and to indulge in the gentlemanly pursuits of shooting and riding to hounds. He was single-minded in pursuit of his ambitions and what he saw as his duty. If his actions in pursuing those ambitions seemed devious, opportunistic and inconsiderate of others, it was of little concern to him. He had clearly defined in his own mind where his duty lay and the extent of that duty.

John was incapable of the single-mindedness and ruthlessness that characterized Jos. He was kind, gentle, unobtrusive, weak and easily influenced by others. Unlike Jos, almost all of the major decisions in his life were made impulsively and emotionally rather than carefully and rationally. Silent to the point of appearing almost inarticulate, he was unable to confront any unpleasantness. Thus, consciously or unconsciously, Jos had assumed the role of head of the family while John, happy to be relieved of the responsibility, followed his younger brother's lead.

After Jos's decision to move to Surrey, John thought that he too would like to be a squire. He sold his London house in Devonshire Place and bought Cote House, a country estate at Westbury outside Bristol. Cote House was far larger and grander than Etruria Hall and not as isolated as Jos's estate in Surrey. It soon became a fashionable gathering place for the Wedgwoods and the Allens and for such promising young intellectuals as Southey, Coleridge, Joseph Cottle, Thomas Poole, Thomas Beddoes, Gregory Watt, Basil Montague and James Mackintosh. John's wife Jane, who was as gregarious as her husband was reserved, enjoyed giving parties, and John, too, enjoyed the company of people who had more conversation and were more energetic than he. Not having any active duties related either to his partnership in the bank or to the pottery, he pursued his study of horticulture, in which he had become interested through the Darwins, both Erasmus, senior and Robert, and through his father's friend Withering. At Cote House he built a greenhouse where he cultivated pineapples, peaches and grapes, as well as exotic plants. He experimented successfully with dahlias, chrysanthemums, camellias, roses, carnations and tulips. He planted orchards, acres of vegetables and flower gardens. So well known were the gardens at Cote House that William Forsyth, gardener to King George III, came to visit and not only advised John but sought advice from him.

At Cote House young Sarah Wedgwood, who was tall and stately and fair-complexioned, turned down a proposal of marriage from the widower Basil Montague. Sarah had inherited her mother's reserve and her father's strong will—a combination that fascinated some men and intimidated others. Also at Cote House, about the same time, Kitty Allen, the dark, moody intellectual among the Allen sisters, accepted a marriage proposal from another widower, James Mackintosh, who travelled the Norfolk circuit with his friend and fellow barrister Montague. Mackintosh had no private income. He was a genial, self-educated Scotsman who had first studied medicine, then law and now seemed destined for a dual career as a politician and a man of letters. Though he was balding, small in stature, with a thin, high-pitched voice, he had a quick wit and a pleasing personality that impressed both men and women. In 1796 most of the young intellectuals who frequented the Cote House gatherings expected Mackintosh to be one of the most influential men in the coming century. At this time only four of the nine Allen sisters—Octavia, who was dying of consumption, and the three youngest girls, Jessie, Fanny and Emma—remained at Cresselly with their father and two brothers. Caroline Allen had married the Revd Edward Drewe, a kindly but ineffectual man; Harriett Allen had also married a clergyman, the Revd Matthew Surtees, a selfish, stingy, fanatical man, almost as disagreeable as the father from whom she was trying to escape.

Another frequent visitor to Cote House was the ailing Tom Wedgwood, who did not share the natural reserve that characterized his older brothers. Tom had little difficulty in articulating his feelings either in writing or in conversation. He was the favourite son and the only one who had inherited his father's scientific talents. He immodestly thought of himself as a genius, and possessed the sensitivity, impatience and unpredictability that are often part of the exceptionally gifted temperament. All of this was aggravated by his ill health and reinforced by the obedient attentions of his family and his friends.

After the departure of Jos and Bessy, Tom had felt constrained at Etruria Hall with only his mother, his three sisters and his old tutor Chisholm for company. In the hope of restoring his declining health he went on a five-month walking tour of Germany, with John Leslie as his paid companion. There his health seemed to improve. One feature of his illness, which at intervals seemed to be arrested, was an abrupt swing in mood from almost manic elation to incapacitating depression.

After the German trip Tom bestowed upon the brilliant but impecunious Leslie an annuity for life of £150. With the approval of his brothers and sisters, he then commissioned Leslie to write a biography of Josiah. Like his father, Tom was generous with money in large matters and penurious in small ones. While he would gladly grant a life annuity or donate £1,000 to a cause he believed in, he would at the same time and with equal fervour economize on writing paper. This was a trait he was aware of in himself as well as in others, noting in his journal: 'Great generosity of character is often accompanied by indolence, and sometimes by petty sensualities and selfishness. A man of this temper makes a greater effort in running out of one room into another for a friend, in resigning a bonne-bouche to a longing child, or in parting with a favourite penknife, than in giving away hundreds.'[2] While he failed to note that most people were not in the fortunate position of being able to give away hundreds and thereby compensating for the childishness of their dispositions, he did give an accurate description of himself.

Shortly after his return from Germany in 1796, Tom once again fell into a mood of deep despondency. After staying with Jos in Surrey, he went to visit his sister Susan at The Mount, the house overlooking the river Severn in Shrewsbury which Robert Darwin had built for them when they married, after the year of mourning following Josiah's death. Like his father, Robert was inclined to look upon Tom's illness as one of the mind as much as of the body, a theory which Tom himself refused to accept. Robert had an exceptional ability to read not only character but on occasion even the thoughts of someone he had met only briefly. His memory and his intuitions were almost infallible, so much so that sometimes his powers seemed supernatural — an impression he did not discourage.

A gigantic man, six feet five inches tall and weighing almost 300 pounds, he had enormous reserves of energy, but occasionally suffered lengthy bouts of fatigue. For a man so large, he was surprisingly agile and quick-moving. Equally surprising, and in contrast to his great bulk, was his thin, high-pitched voice, an obvious target for mimicry, though few would have dared to mimic him within his hearing. Like his father, Robert Darwin enjoyed attention and affected eccentricities, dressing only in shades of beige or yellow — jacket, waistcoat, breeches always matching. He rode in a small chaise painted bright yellow which fitted him exactly with no more than an inch to spare on either side. The chaise, with its sleek black horses and handsomely attired coachman, was a familiar and impressive sight, racing along the country lanes. Robert sat as erect and motionless as a statue, his expression thoughtful and unimpassioned. Unlike his father, he did not use his chaise as a study. Travel for him was a time for rest, not work. Because of his great bulk his coachman often preceded him into the houses of the poorer patients to see if the floorboards and the staircases could bear the strain of the Doctor's weight.

Robert's advice to his brother-in-law Tom was that he consult several other doctors. Tom then travelled to Bristol to visit John and to seek medical advice from Thomas Beddoes, a jovial and erratic physician who had married Richard Lovell Edgeworth's daughter Anna. Beddoes was an extraordinary man, some of whose ideas were well in advance of his time. He advocated temperance and cleanliness in an age which cared little for either, and was one of the first doctors to lecture on the prevention of disease. Holding the unpopular opinion that women were *not* mentally inferior to men and should be given equal opportunities in education, he was also the first to deliver medical lectures to women. He had great faith in Withering's digitalis as an anodyne and stimulant. Founder of the Pneumatic Institute, to which Tom and his father had each donated £1,000, Beddoes was a great believer in the efficacy of 'airs'. Tom himself had more hope than faith in Beddoes's scheme, having written to Jos: 'I think I shall contribute as the attempt must be successful in part if it only goes to show that "airs" are *not* efficacious in medicine.'[3]

Because of the difficulty of procuring a suitable house, due to rumours that the gases to be used on the patients were dangerously explosive, the Pneumatic Institute was not yet established when Tom came to Bristol in the autumn of 1796. Beddoes, however, had other experimental remedies to offer, and recommended that Tom inhale the breath of cows. He often suggested that a patient whose disease he was unable to diagnose ought to live over a butcher's shop or, better still, move into a cowshed warmed by a stove. The latter was not an entirely impractical arrangement, since dairies in English houses often had a room for making butter and cheese that was clean and attractive, the floor and walls tiled. Ladies took as much trouble over the pattern of earthenware tiles in the dairy as over the dinnerware for their dining tables, and the Wedgwood company made a line of dairy items, including cream skimmers, large stirring spoons and settling pans. In spite of this, the cow treatment did not appeal to Tom's fastidious disposition — nor, if he tried it at all, did it improve his health.

After spending a few weeks in the Beddoes household, he returned to Cote House where John and Jane had just had their third child, whom they named after his uncle Tom. The whirl of parties at his brother's house lifted Tom's spirits, and he drifted into one of his agitated periods when he could not bear to be alone.

At one of the Cote House parties he met Thomas Poole. Stout and plain-faced, with blunt speech and rough manners, Poole had by his own energy and intelligence raised himself above his class and his surroundings. Successful as a farmer, tanner and land agent in Somerset, he was a great friend and admirer of Coleridge, whom he had met when Coleridge and Southey came to Poole's village of Nether Stowey seeking recruits for their Pantisocracy — Coleridge's grandiloquent name for the commune they hoped to found in America on the banks of the Susquehanna River. It was inspired by the social philosophy of William Godwin who had visited Etruria before Josiah's death and had been in correspondence with Tom about various schemes for reforming society.

Impressed by Tom Wedgwood's intellect and refined manners, the hospitable Poole invited him to Stowey. Tom accepted immediately, attracted by Poole's liberal convictions, but also impelled by his own restlessness to seek out new places and new experiences.

In 1797, when Tom first visited Stowey, Coleridge was living in an adjoining small cottage which belonged to Poole. His household at the time consisted of his wife Sara (whose sister had married Southey), a baby son, and Charles Lloyd, son of the wealthy Quaker banker whom Josiah had met on a coach trip from London to Birmingham nine years earlier. Young Lloyd had literary ambitions and was being tutored by Coleridge. The £80 a year paid by Lloyd and the generosity of Poole, who not only provided housing but supplied the family with milk and fresh vegetables, lessened Coleridge's financial worries, and he had high hopes for his future. Cottle had published his *Poems on Various Subjects*, which went into a second edition, including poems by Charles Lloyd and by Coleridge's old school friend Charles Lamb. Exuberant, vain, impractical and irresponsible, Coleridge was then at the height of his powers. His poetic imagination was stimulated not only by Poole but far more so by William and Dorothy Wordsworth, who had been living at Racedown House in Dorset, and were now at nearby Alfoxden House.

It was inevitable that Tom would be attracted by Coleridge, with his keen sense of humour, irrepressible zest for life and great talent for conversation. It was likewise inevitable that Coleridge, in his straitened financial circumstances, would be impressed by Tom's wealth. Each recognized the exceptional intellectual gifts of the other; they had the same political beliefs, metaphysical interests and need for supportive friendship, just as, to some extent, they had the same weaknesses. Both acted impulsively; both procrastinated and exaggerated their own feelings, at one moment full of enthusiasm and the next plunged into despondency.

Shortly after his first visit to Stowey, where his friendship with Poole and Coleridge was reinforced by leisurely philosophical conversations over mugs of Taunton ale in Poole's garden, Tom went off to spend five days with the Wordsworths. A legacy of £900 left him by a friend had enabled Wordsworth to retire to the country with his brilliant but emotionally unstable sister Dorothy, to establish a routine of plain living and high thinking. Tom and Wordsworth had mutual friends not only in Coleridge and Poole but also in the Bristol manufacturer James Tobin, who accompanied Tom to the Wordsworths', and in Basil Montague, who had unsuccessfully proposed marriage to Tom's sister Sarah and whose small son was living with the Wordsworths. And both Tom and Wordsworth had been influenced by the philosophical writings of William Godwin.

Although Tom was deeply impressed with Wordsworth's intellect, he never felt with him the instant *rapport* and almost schoolboy-like excitement he experienced with Coleridge. Dorothy Wordsworth was a more congenial companion for Tom even though her obsessive devotion to her brother made her reluctant to display her own talents. Unlike the fun-loving Coleridge, Wordsworth had little humour. Not given to joking himself, he seldom appreciated the jokes of others. A solemn, awkward man with strong and acute sensibilities, he viewed his vocation as a poet with immense seriousness. The needs and feelings of others had to be subordinated to the sacredness of his mission.

Tom had a similar Messianic complex about his own writing. He was then in the process of analysing sensation, both physical and mental, tracing its origin in the processes of association which result in either pain or pleasure. His goal was to discover how to manipulate human behaviour deliberately and rationally in order to develop a superior generation imbued with good will towards humanity. He wished to establish a system of education founded on scientific principles. His observations were derived from the subjective study of his own sensations and the objective study of the behaviour of Jos's young children, Elizabeth and Joe. He made extensive notes on the relationship between sensation and perception and how they are affected by emotion, and all of this he had discussed with Coleridge and with Poole. Now he wanted Wordsworth's opinions and advice as to the planning of a curriculum for a new generation of healthy, happy, intelligent and self-sufficient individuals. But Wordsworth was more interested in the philosophy of poetry than in the philosophy of education. He disagreed with Tom's theory that strict control of a small child's sensory impressions would result in emotions and ideas devoid of pain and distraction.

After Tom left the Wordsworths, his health worsened. He suffered a recurrence of his intestinal malady and excruciating headaches. He disliked Etruria Hall even when he was feeling well, so he went to Stoke d'Abernon where he could always count on the sympathy of Jos. Since early childhood Tom and Jos had been practically inseparable, and though Tom was now leading the wandering, adventurous life of a wealthy, invalided young bachelor while Jos was the stable country squire with responsibilities towards his family and his tenants, each needed the other's companionship in the same way that Josiah had needed Bentley's. Fortunately Bessy was tolerant of her brother-in-law's experiments in her nursery, and calmly adjusted the routine of her household to the eccentric and at times irritable demands of an invalid.

Following a more sensible bit of Beddoes's advice, Tom went to Penzance in December 1797 where it was hoped that the milder climate would alleviate his headaches and melancholy. Jos went with him, and in Penzance they renewed their friendship with James Watt's son Gregory, who had also been sent there by Beddoes. Gregory introduced them to Humphry Davy, whose mother ran the boarding house where he was staying. Davy was then only nineteen years old and an apothecary's assistant, but his scientific genius was already apparent. He and Tom quickly formed a close and lasting friendship. They both liked hunting and fishing, and in the evenings had discussions on chemistry and exchanged notes on their researches on light and heat and on the beginnings of Tom's 'silver pictures'.

Through the influence of Tom, Gregory Watt and other mutual friends, Beddoes was persuaded to invite young Davy to Bristol to be an assistant in Chemistry at the Pneumatic Institute, which finally opened in 1798 at Dowry Street, Clifton. Tom, Gregory Watt and Coleridge were among its first patients. Inspired by the gift of £1,000 from a grateful patient named John Lambton, it was a small experimental hospital set up to treat diseases by the inhalation of medicated gases or chemically modified air. Beddoes hoped that by experimenting with airs he might cure cancer, ulcers and paralysis as well as consumption. His early supporters and patrons included not only Tom Wedgwood and his father, but Darwin, Keir,

Edgeworth, Withering, the Duchess of Devonshire, William Reynolds, Dr Ewart of Bath and Dr Thornton of London. The equipment for producing and administering the gases was made and donated by James Watt in the vain hope that Gregory's consumption might be cured.

At the start the Institute attracted the fashionable aristocracy as well as young intellectuals like Tom, Southey, Coleridge and Cottle. Coleridge, like Tom, was beginning to suffer from a variety of ailments, including neuralgia, asthma, rheumatism, toothache and an intestinal malady. Both Tom and Coleridge had enormous medical curiosity, prompted in part by the need for relief from their own ailments, but also by the desire for new sensations and adventures.

The few cures claimed by Beddoes were apparently the result of faith healing rather than the medicated gases. One patient, suffering from paralysis, was so convinced by the charismatic Beddoes that the new treatment would cure him that when Davy placed a thermometer under his tongue to take his temperature he assumed that this instrument was itself the miraculous cure, and in a burst of enthusiasm declared that he was already experiencing the effects of its benign influence throughout his body. Davy wisely said nothing. For a fortnight the man visited the Institute where they did nothing more than take his temperature. He was dismissed, satisfied and cured.

Another result of the experiments at the Pneumatic Institute was Davy's discovery of the effects of the inhalations of 'laughing gas' (nitrous oxide), which he administered to dozens of his friends. Coleridge felt a highly pleasurable warmth and an inclination to laugh, and Southey wrote to Tom: 'Davy has invented a new pleasure, for which language has no name ... it makes one strong and so happy! and without any after disability, but instead of it, increased strength of mind and body. O, excellent air-bag! Tom, I am sure the air in heaven must be this wonder-working gas of delight....'[4]

Tom's report on the experiment was written with greater objectivity:

> I called on Mr Davy at the Medical Institution on 23 July.... I had six quarts of the oxide given me in a bag undiluted, and as soon as I had breathed three or four respirations, I felt myself affected, and my respiration hurried, which effect increased rapidly until I became as it were entranced, when I threw the bag from me and kept breathing furiously with an open mouth and holding my nose with my left hand, having no power to take it away, though aware of the ridiculousness of my situation ... before I breathed the air I felt a good deal fatigued from a very long ride I had had the day before; but, after breathing, I lost all sense of fatigue....[5]

Intrigued with the unexpected results of the 'wonder-working gas of delight', Davy and Beddoes seemed for awhile to have turned their laboratory into an amusement centre. Some of their friends and patients dashed about wildly, others danced and giggled, and a few unfortunates became sick at their stomachs. Occasionally the gas was administered while wine was being drunk; the exhilaration remained the same.

There was, of course, a public outcry against such rowdy and unseemly goings-on, and conservative colleagues in the medical profession accused Beddoes of quackery. Neither the optimistic Beddoes nor the fun-loving Davy was unduly disturbed. Having produced such merriment with nitrous oxide, Davy then proceeded to test nitrous gas on himself, painfully damaging his teeth and tongue. Next he tried inhaling carburetted hydrogen gas and nearly killed himself. Concluding that discretion was the better part of valour, he stopped experimenting on himself and administered new medicated airs to hundreds of hapless frogs, puppies and kittens.

Before the opening of the Pneumatic Institute, Beddoes had recommended opium to both Tom and Coleridge, as well as to Coleridge's pupil Charles Lloyd. The drug was commonly prescribed at the time for a variety of ailments. Mixtures containing opium were sold under a variety of names, such as Godfrey's Cordial, Batley's Sedative Solution, Mother Bailey's Quieting Syrup and Kendal's Black Drop. Pain was soothed, but many patients died from overdoses, while others became addicted.

At about the time that Coleridge and Tom began taking opium, Coleridge's publication *The Watchman* failed, and Lloyd departed, leaving him without any immediate source of income. His debts were mounting. He was offered a place as minister to the Unitarian Church in Shrewsbury at a salary of £150 a year, and through Poole, Cottle, the Wordsworths and other literary friends tried to dissuade him from abandoning poetry and philosophy, he was desperate. On 14 January 1798, he preached his first sermon in Shrewsbury; Robert and Susan Darwin were in the congregation.

Hearing from Poole of the distressing situation, Tom and Jos sent Coleridge a gift of £100, which he refused on the grounds that it would soon be spent and he would still be in the same intolerable circumstances. Tom then persuaded Jos that they should jointly offer Coleridge an annuity of £150 for life, each of them contributing £75. No conditions were attached; Coleridge was to be free to pursue his interests and to write at leisure.

When Coleridge received the letter written by Jos, he was at Wem, near Shrewsbury, staying with the Hazlitts, whose son William was at first an admirer, then later a caustic critic of his work. The Wedgwood annuity, which Wordsworth described as 'one of the noblest acts of mankind', was gratefully accepted by Coleridge. He immediately returned to Stowey by way of Bristol, where he met Tom at Cote House.

During the next few months Tom and Coleridge saw one another frequently. Together they began to experiment with hashish. Tom experienced powerful illuminations which he wished to understand in the pure, cold light of science: 'If Madmen should outnumber us in our senses, we shall change places with them and become the Madmen of the day. For what is Madness, but a difference of opinion from the majority?'[6]

Coleridge's talents were at their zenith. He had already completed the first part of *Christabel* and was within a few months of writing *Kubla Khan* and of finishing *The Rime of the Ancient Mariner*, which he had begun on a walk with the Wordsworths. But, with his financial worries seemingly solved and a growing disenchantment with his pretty but unintellectual wife, he yearned for more excitement than the quiet life at Stowey afforded. Tom had described enthusiastically the trip he had made through Germany; now Coleridge suggested to the Wordsworths that the three of them go there. Their serious purpose was to learn the German language, to make translations and to interpret German philosophy and poetry. Tom thoroughly approved the project. The poets took his advice and planned to visit the same places as he and Leslie had gone to—Göttingen, Goslar and the Harz mountains. The annuity made the trip possible for Coleridge, and Tom loaned the Wordsworths the money for the journey.

After they departed, Tom's health became suddenly worse. He became even more emaciated, and suffered terribly from chills. Depression and restlessness increased.

There was a solidarity among the six Wedgwood children that extended beyond loyalty and affection to a sincere enjoyment of each other's company. Stoke d'Abernon was too great a distance from the rest of the family, and in 1797 Tom and Jos had decided that they would buy estates near one another, either in Somerset or Dorset. They enlisted Poole's assistance and made a number of journeys together looking at various properties.

In August of 1799, Jos acquired Gunville, an estate in Dorset. There were several other large properties in the area for Tom to consider. He had already bought and sold three smaller estates at a considerable profit. Meanwhile he spent some time at The Mount in Shrewsbury with the Darwins and at Etruria Hall with his mother and his sisters Kitty and Sarah. As always Etruria depressed him. He wrote to Jos, 'I wish most sincerely that you should sell Etruria Hall.'[7] The plans were that Sally and her two unmarried daughters, now aged twenty-three and twenty-five, would find a house in the vicinity of Bristol near John and Jane. Sally objected to leaving Etruria Hall, which had been her home for three decades and which both she and Josiah had assumed would be the family residence of one of their sons. None of her children had any desire to live near the pottery, a constant reminder that their origins as well as their continued income were in trade. Sally concealed her resentment at being, from her point of view, needlessly uprooted. Never demonstrative, she withdrew even further any outward display of affection towards her children and grandchildren, and became increasingly demanding of material comforts.

On 12 November 1799, the enthusiastic Beddoes, who once having got hold of an idea was loath to let it go, wrote to Tom that 'for mere temperature, living with cows is the most delicious thing imaginable; perhaps the fumes would give a salutory stimulus to the surface of the lungs, which might communicate itself to the whole system ...'.[8] But Beddoes's advice or the happenings at the Pneumatic Institute no longer raised Tom's hopes or even held his interest. Davy, who had gone to lecture at the newly founded Royal Institution, invited Tom to visit him. He had published an account of his work at the Pneumatic Institute, *Researches, Chemical and Philosophical.* He had also accurately predicted that his discovery of nitrous oxide might be of use as an anaesthetic in surgical operations.

Tom refused Davy's invitation. While Jos and Bessy were in the process of moving to Gunville, he decided instead to visit John and Jane. He found Cote House restful and the company of his beautiful sister-in-law soothing to his raw nerves. With little persuasion he agreed to remain at Cote House with Jane for several weeks while John went to London. John himself was in a highly agitated state. The journey to London was not one of pleasure but an attempt to stave off a disaster which he hoped to conceal from Jane.

12

A Promise Unfulfilled
(1800 – 1805)

John had received word that Alexander Davison & Co., the commercial bank in which he was a partner, was in severe financial difficulties. Not confiding his worries to either his brother or his wife, he hurried off to London. Once there, he discovered that he would be unable to resign his partnership in the bank without forfeiting his investment, which represented most of the inheritance left him by his father. He was further distressed because he had never fully explained his financial situation to his wife Jane. Extravagant and self-indulgent, Jane had no interest in business matters; nor was John the sort of man who could discuss unpleasant realities with anyone. Until he received word of the bank's difficulties, he had been quite unaware of having any problems.

Deciding not to alarm the sensitive Jane or to worry his mother and sisters, John revealed his predicament only to his brothers and to his brother-in-law, when they all assembled for a family gathering at Cote House during the first week in February, 1800.

Robert Darwin, whose profession demanded that he come to terms with the unpleasant realities of life and death and whose disposition inclined him to seek rather than to shrink from confrontations, told John bluntly that he would have to accede to the bank's request for more capital from the partners. He added further that John would not only have to take a more active part in the bank's affairs but that, for the sake of his family, he would have to manage his personal finances in a more responsible manner. Unable to answer directly what he felt as a personal attack, John developed a nervous condition that showed itself in a physical trembling, particularly a shakiness of the right hand and arm.

That Robert could talk in a tough, intimidating manner was witnessed to by a number of his patients. One woman was causing her husband distress by fits of crying and by taking to her bed in despair over comparing herself with her husband's deceased first wife. Robert told her that she was indeed inferior to her predecessor in both appearance and intellect, and that the only way she could retain her husband's affection and the respect of the community was by maintaining an amiable disposition. He then told the husband that if his wife ever had another uncontrollable fit of crying to threaten her with 'sending for the Doctor'.

Robert's toughness towards John was, however, brought on in part by his own irritability and depression. The Mount had recently had its own share of problems. Child bearing was difficult and depressing for Susan; she had been confined to bed during most of her second pregnancy. Remembering the lively parties at Cote House and unaware of her brother's problems, she wrote despondently to John: 'Everyone seems young but me.'

Robert was further troubled by the suicide of his brother Erasmus junr., who walked into the river Derwent during a violent thunderstorm on the night of 29 December 1799. For several years prior to his fortieth birthday Erasmus junr. had shown symptoms of withdrawal, with occasional periods of disorientation, described by his father as 'a defect of voluntary power'. He procrastinated and was unable to make decisions; then he would act impulsively and often irrationally. He neglected his business affairs and refused to pay his bills or to collect his debts. He had never married, nor had he ever really enjoyed being a lawyer. Apart from his thwarted desire to enter the Church, his interests were in statistics, genealogy and collecting coins. Like Robert, he had unusual intellectual powers. He possessed a photographic memory for dates and numbers; ten years after he had completed the first accurate census of Lichfield, he could recall the precise location of each house and the number of its occupants. Only a few months before his death he had bought the small estate of The Priory, near Derby, where Erasmus senior told Robert he would probably 'sleep away the remainder of his days'. A week before his death Robert received from him a little cross made of plaited grass gathered from the tomb of their brother Charles, who had died twenty years earlier. Neither Robert nor his father, both respected physicians who were certainly aware of psychological factors in their patients, anticipated his suicide. As was customary in such cases, his death was attributed by the family to 'a temporary fit of insanity'.

Depression seemed contagious. Unlike Susan or John, Robert expressed his unhappiness in hyperactivity. In company with his father, he was interested in botany and zoology. He raised pigeons and spent much of his spare time in his greenhouse. The gardens at The Mount contained some of the finest and rarest plants and shrubs, which were often compared with and exchanged for specimens from Cote House. An inveterate collector, Robert built up a splendid library. He was also one of the first collectors of Wedgwood ware, having begun his collection in 1793 by ordering a Portland Vase, busts of Washington and Franklin and two Sydney Cove medallions. As shrewd a businessman as he was a doctor, he invested in stocks and in real estate for development as well as in smaller, tangible assets. All of these interests, coupled with a successful and wide-ranging medical practice which frequently kept him making calls for fifteen or sixteen hours a day, left little time for companionship with Susan. He also liked to give dinner parties for some of his prominent patients. In company, both Robert and Susan appeared extroverted and articulate; alone, they were subject to silences and depressions.

Jos and Tom more or less agreed with Robert's assessment of John's circumstances, but they were less outspoken in their criticism. Tom was absorbed in the problem of his own failing health. He had decided to go to the West Indies, where it was hoped that a change of scenery and climate might arrest the mysterious disease that was ravishing his body and imprisoning his mind. Through the ever-helpful Poole, a young man from Bristol named Richard King was found to accompany him. Perhaps with the untimely death of Erasmus junr. in mind, Tom made his will, conferring power of attorney on Jos while he was out of England.

All the Wedgwoods, two of the unmarried Allen sisters, and the Darwins assembled at Cote House for a farewell party before Jos journeyed with Tom to Falmouth where he and King were to set sail. Jos apparently felt that Tom's health had worsened to the point where this might be their final parting. Normally reserved in writing as well as in speech, he bared his feelings in a letter to his brother following his departure:

> The distance that separates us, the affecting circumstances under which we parted, our former inseparable life and perfect friendship, unite to deepen the emotion with which I think of you, and give an importance and solemnity that is new to my communication with you.... It is not so necessary for me to see you, as to know that you are well and happy. Nothing can be more disinterested than the love I bear you. I know that my wife and children could alone render me happy, but I see with the most heartfelt concern that your admirable qualifications are rendered ineffectual for your happiness and your fame by your miserable health.[1]

Sarah and Kitty, who accompanied their mother on her first visit to Jos and Bessy at their new home, Gunville, wrote more cheerful letters to Tom. Kitty reported that the Duchess of Gordon intended to call on Kitty Mackintosh and to attend James Mackintosh's lectures on social and political justice at Lincoln's Inn in London. Sarah wrote that she and her sister had left Cote House without any prospect of finding a house for themselves in the neighbourhood, and that when they arrived at Gunville, 'I was very agreeably surprised in the place. I think it is very snug and almost pretty & I expected to see the ugliest place I ever saw in my life....' She then told Tom that there was a rumour that the neighbouring estate of Eastbury was going to be sold: 'Jos would like very much to buy it himself; perhaps he will take us as his tenants if we should find it as impossible to get a house near Cote as we have done hitherto....' Having reported that their mother was well, that John and Jane had gone to visit the Surteeses, that the Darwins' oldest child Marianne was over the worst of the whooping cough, and that Susan 'goes on much the same, never quite well & never very ill', Sarah described events at the Pneumatic Institute: 'We left Dr Beddoes in very good spirits about his gaseous oxy'd; another paralytic patient has just recovered the use of an arm by taking it six weeks.... One paralytic patient Mr Oliver has just destroyed himself. I hope this will not get the air a bad name.... Ralph Sneyd has been some weeks out of the cow house and continued to get better even after he had left it, but he has had a little relapse and gone to Bath....'[2]

John wrote to Tom that their mother 'still feels the pain of parting with you and though she, as well as your other friends, flatter themselves with your speedy return in good health yet the chance of her witnessing it is not so great as ours who have not so many years over our heads....' He told Tom that although he and Jane were postponing a trip to London, they and Emma Allen had gone to visit Harriett Surtees and her husband, who 'pleasant I am sorry to say I do not believe he can be. He is actively charitable & seems to have the good of the poorer part of his parishioners at heart but where he has been offended unrelenting in his anger & resentment. In his family he has the manners and habits of a recluse & is never visible to his wife but at meals.'[3]

Tom was deeply moved by the affectionate attentions of his brothers and sisters, replying that his emotions as well as his physical frailties left him strength to write only one letter, which was for all of them. During most of the seven-week voyage he remained in his cabin, troubled not only by headaches, lethargy and stomach pains but also by seasickness.

As Tom crossed the ocean to the New World, the seven-year partnership agreement, which had been drawn up under Josiah's supervision, and which had included John as an inactive partner and Jos and Byerley as active partners, expired. As Josiah had foreseen, John did indeed need the pottery to fall back upon, both as an occupation and a source of income. He was drawing more money from the business than was covered by his rightful share of the profits, and unlike Byerley, he was contributing nothing directly or personally to the operation of the pottery.

After the revelation of the bank's difficulties and further conversations with Robert Darwin, who promised Jos that he would never allow John's annual income to fall below £1,000, Jos wrote to John:

> I am most deeply concerned for you, and I have long been so, for it has not been difficult to perceive that your mind has been in a distressed state. I have always thought, & do still, that you might save yourself the greatest part of the pain you suffer by a short easy exertion of resolution. I mean by making a statement of your affairs, which would remove the uncertainty that discourages you. By ascertaining your property & income you would be able to judge what course it is proper for you to pursue, nor do I believe the result of the examination would be so very unfavourable as you expect.... The first step would be to get a statement of your banking concern. I am anxious to make a settlement with Mr Byerley who will come down first week in August. By that time we shall receive a statement of the expenses & produce of our trade for the first 6 months of this year and upon that result come to some resolution. — Your business may easily be done by that time and when once done you will lose a great deal of the bitterness of your feelings....[4]

John took his brother's advice; he then met Jos at Etruria in July 1800. The account of the pottery's trade was far worse than Jos had anticipated, and he felt it his duty to impress upon his brother the seriousness of their position. As Robert had done earlier, he emphasized the necessity of John's living within his income. In spite of the previous warning, John seemed taken aback by the unpleasant news that he was spending more than was rightfully his. He found himself unable to express his feelings or to control the trembling in his right arm, even when Jos offered to cancel all of his debts to the firm.

John was staying with his mother and sisters at Etruria Hall while Jos, Bessy, their three children and servants occupied Little Etruria. The Sunday morning following their talk in their father's old office at the works, John suddenly decided that he would like again to take up an active role in the pottery. He sent a letter by one of the servants to Jos.

'To anyone but yourself I should think it necessary to apologize for the manner in which I yesterday received your communication,' he wrote.

> I was not silent from want of feeling how infinitely I was obliged to you for taking upon yourself a task so irksome as that of communicating unpleasant intelligence & also of your most generous offer which terminated the account. I could not speak not from want of feeling but from excess, & that excess arising from various causes of a very mixed nature. Gratitude to yourself for every act of kindness which I and mine have long experienced from you was at least equal to any other feeling but accompanied by a most poignant sensation of grief for what Jane will suffer when she becomes acquainted with the real state of things.... Having passed nearly a sleepless night I cannot sufficiently collect my thoughts to enter into the subject but I do feel the necessity of finding something which will give me occupation without which I shall be a torment to myself and to all around me. Assist me then, Dear Jos, to form some plan which may be followed up by constant industry & which may have if possible the appearance at least of some use. What has hung heavy on my mind for a considerable time is that I do not appear to be of any use.... I feel that if put in the right way I could be useful but all is lost for want of method & that energy which I never possessed in any great degree but which has been dissipated by a series of unfortunate events. Give me a dispatchment & I do think that I may still be of use to the manufactory....[5]

Partly because he sincerely wanted to help his brother, partly because he recognized that someone would have to take over some responsibilities from the overworked Byerley and partly because he himself wished to spend as little time as possible at the factory, Jos agreed to John's rejoining the company as an active partner. A new partnership agreement was drawn up with Jos holding a half-interest and Byerley and John a one-fourth interest each. John did not pay for his share but was in effect loaned the money by his brother. He paid annual interest of 5 per cent on the loan. This arrangement apparently satisfied everyone—John at last felt that he was being of some use, Byerley was getting the assistance he had long requested, and Jos had satisfied the needs of both of his partners without making any major changes or sacrifices in his own life.

Tom's voyage to the West Indies was a failure. At about the time that his brothers and cousin settled their new partnership, he returned to England and was again writing to Coleridge and to Poole. Coleridge had returned from Germany and moved his family to the Lake District, where the Wordsworths had settled, then came back alone to Stowey for a lengthy stay with Poole.

Tom spent the first few months of his return in a whirlwind of visits to his brothers and sisters. He decided to buy Eastbury Park, the estate adjoining Gunville, and to settle his mother and two unmarried sisters there. But the house needed extensive remodelling, and because Byerley was moving his ever-growing family back to Etruria to live in Etruria Hall, Sarah and Kitty arranged to move temporarily, with their mother into a house found by Poole and purchased by Tom. Like Robert Darwin, Tom had a gift for making money by buying and selling properties.

John planned to move into Little Etruria for three months to supervise factory production. He wrote to Jos: 'My sisters have done very much to prevent my mother seeing Chettle 'til it is ready for her reception as, if she dislikes it, she will have enough time in it to be made comfortable & even if she likes it, I don't suppose she will think it pleasanter than Gunville....'6

Tom didn't want to bother himself with the irksome details of moving house. Finding the round of parties and activities at Cote House exhausting, he had decided to spend the autumn at Gunville following another of Beddoes's suggestions, which was that he live for several months in a completely closed apartment with double windows, double doors and a stove which would keep the temperature at seventy degrees. Jos had consulted with James Watt as to fitting out such an apartment, but all the preparations for an invalid's convenience had not been completed. When Tom heard this, he impulsively decided to go to London. He took temporary quarters in the building in St James's Square where the Wedgwood showrooms were. More and more he was looking for entertainment and companionship. Like Wordsworth's, his criteria for friendship were exalted: 'The refined man does not meet with one in a hundred whose society gives him pleasure, the peasant does not meet with one in a hundred from whom he cannot extract pleasure.'7

Above all Tom was a refined man. During the year 1800 his sense of propriety had received shocks from two of his closest friends, Poole and Leslie. Both men had expressed a desire to marry into the Wedgwood family. Just as Tom was about to depart for the West Indies he received a letter from the pompous Leslie requesting the hand of Tom's youngest sister, Sarah. It began:

On the eve of bidding a tender adieu, may I venture at last to communicate a matter of the most serious and delicate nature? Long has the thought fired and tortured my brain. Often I have been on the point of disclosing it and as often have I been restrained by timidity or a sense of propriety. Still I hesitate. Shall I, by one rash step, provoke your displeasure? That reflection would be the torment of my life. Yet to whom should I unbosom myself but to my early and tried friend, who has felt such a lively interest in all my concerns, and who on this occasion is called by the most sacred ties to interpose his counsel? ... Not to keep you longer in suspence, I have the temerity to think of soliciting an alliance in your family. You startle at this declaration. It may appear presumptuous and romantic. I must intreat you to suppress your emotions until you have finished the perusal of this letter....

The ornate and inflated prose continued for several pages before ending with: 'This is the most momentous crisis of my life. My heart swells with anxiety. I tremble to hear your advice. A few words will suffice, but let it be from your own hand. If it shall be in the least consolatory, it will give buoyancy to hope — it will in part open the prospect of earthly elysium. A contrary presentiment weighs me down. Alas! is all the future to be shrouded in despondency? I fear I have already committed folly. Destroy this letter. Farewell!'[8]

If it wasn't folly, it was certainly an indiscretion which appeared to Tom as audacious opportunism. Leslie, then thirty-five, was still undecided in his career. His main source of income was the £150 annuity bestowed upon him by Tom. He had not then written his textbooks on mathematics, invented the differential thermometer or that most useful household appliance, the ice-making machine. Leslie's biography of Josiah had displeased all of the Wedgwoods. Even in a romantic and sentimental era, his literary style seemed flowery and insincere. Though Leslie was paid for the work, there was no question of publishing his manuscript. Since he was also known as a misogynist, his proposal of marriage seemed hypocritical. Neither Jos nor Tom wanted Leslie for a brother-in-law. Tom told him so in no uncertain terms.

If Leslie's proposal seemed presumptuous and opportunistic, no such ulterior motives could be attributed to Poole's desire to enter into correspondence with Kitty Wedgwood, with 'a possible view to marriage'. Unlike Leslie, Poole was fond of women, had formed a number of affectionate friendships with them and in the past been deeply hurt by his cousin Penelope Poole, who had rejected his proposal and married someone else. Also unlike Leslie, Poole was a man of considerable wealth and influence. He had met Kitty Wedgwood on a recent visit to Gunville, where he had certainly been accepted as a social equal. Unfortunately, those who preach equality do not necessarily practise it; when it came to someone marrying into the family, such was the case with both Jos and Tom. Kitty herself did not care either for Poole's appearance or for his rough, clownish manners, nor did she answer his letter to her. Jos answered with a firm rebuke that expressed the snobbish feelings of all the family.

The kind and humble Poole was hurt by such an immediate and decisive rejection. Ten months later, he declined an invitation from Jos to visit Tom at Gunville: 'Most glad should I be to meet you and Mr T. Wedgwood, but at present I feel I should neither contribute to your pleasure nor my own by paying you a visit.'[9] Still, Poole was not one to bear a grudge: at the same time, he was settling an estate at Combe Florey which he had sold for Tom to a Mr Totterdale. Tom apparently thought it no imposition to ask Poole to sort out his furniture and dispose of his kitchen utensils. In gratitude he sent him two dozen pounds of honey.

While he was living in London, Tom frequently dined with James and Kitty Mackintosh. The Mackintoshes had a wide circle of friends, entertained often and were themselves entertained even more often. At one of the Mackintosh dinner parties a social club was formed and christened 'the King of Clubs'. It lasted for twenty-four years, meeting at the Crown and Anchor tavern in the Strand. In addition to Mackintosh and Tom, the members included Mackintosh's brother-in-law, John Hensleigh Allen; Lord Holland; Lord Lansdowne; Sydney Smith, the witty Canon of St Paul's; his brother Bobus Smith; John Tobin the dramatist and his brother James; John Scarlett, a barrister and Member of Parliament who would later become the first Baron Abinger and Lord Chief Baron of the Exchequer; Richard 'Conversation' Sharpe, a successful hat manufacturer with a keen interest in politics and literature; and Tom Campbell, the young poet, whom Tom Wedgwood helped to clear his debts by a gift of £100. Campbell described the King of Clubs as a gathering place of 'brilliant talkers, dedicated to the meetings of the reigning wits of London'.

Tom was impressed by Mackintosh's literary compositions and lectures as well as by his gift for conversation, and in 1801 gave the barrister a retainer of £100 to sort out his notes on metaphysics and write them up in a form for publication. His own failing eyesight, crippling headaches and lack of energy made it impossible for him to attempt the work himself. Mackintosh had an initial enthusiasm for the task, but, like Coleridge, he was a great procrastinator, forever taking on more than he could reasonably expect to accomplish.

Tom was already well acquainted with Mackintosh's failure to live up to his promises. He and the rest of the Wedgwood family had been waiting six years for Mackintosh to write an epitaph for Josiah, which was to be inscribed on a tablet sculpted by Flaxman and placed in the parish church of Stoke-on-Trent. At Tom's request, Mackintosh helped Coleridge to get a position as a journalist, though from the time the two had first met at Cote House, Mackintosh and Coleridge had never liked one another. They tolerated each other's company only for Tom's sake.

While he was in London, Tom also found time to see his old friends Gregory Watt and Humphry Davy. Watt was now dying of consumption. Davy was busy with new experiments and giving a course of lectures on galvanism at the Royal Institution. Both Tom and Coleridge, who fancied himself an amateur chemist, attended Davy's lectures, and Thomas Poole made a trip to London especially to attend the series.

Tom had at this time a sudden remission of his disease which made it possible for him not only to lead a fairly active social life but also to attempt additional experiments. Davy had access to the laboratories at the Royal Institution, and there the two men returned to the problem of Tom's 'silver pictures'. Davy was also assistant editor of the *Journal* of the Royal Institution, where in 1802 he published an essay entitled 'An Account of a Method of Copying Paintings upon Glass and of making Profiles by the Agency of Light upon Nitrate of Silver, invented by T. Wedgwood, Esq., with observations by H. Davy'. The essay showed how a copy or silhouette of an object could be obtained when its shadow was thrown on a piece of white paper or leather which was impregnated with nitrate of silver. In like manner a silhouette of a picture painted on glass could be obtained by placing the glass on a sensitized surface in the sunlight. Unfortunately Tom failed to discover any method of fixing the pictures, and the copies made had to be kept in the dark. But the essay firmly established Tom as the first photographer, though neither he nor Davy realized that his discovery was the first step towards the creation of a completely new art.

As abruptly as Tom's condition had appeared to improve, it began to worsen. Obsessed now by his own death and by the short time he had left in which to make his contribution to the advancement of human knowledge, he dissipated his energies. He and Davy conducted all sorts of experiments on their own perceptions, examining their hallucinations, dreams and visions, often under drugs. From 1801 onwards Tom suffered paranoid depressions and was at times psychotic. It was his emotions rather than his powers of reason that were affected. At Mackintosh's insistence he consulted the well-known London physician Matthew Baillie, who reported to Jos: 'Your brother's complaint seems to me to be hypochondriasis. It is very apt to last long and is but very little under the influence of medicine. He should endeavour as much as he can to amuse his mind among objects which are new and interesting & by travelling in foreign countries.'[10]

Jos forwarded Baillie's letter to Robert Darwin, who wrote back directly to Tom:

> I have seen Dr Baillie's report of your case to your brother Josiah — I do not doubt its accuracy and truth. In all states of health, like yours, I believe there is a certain degree of organic disease which often, for years, renders the general mass of sensation uncomfortable though unattended with danger to life.... I should rather prefer, in such a situation as yours, a palliative plan and trusting the radical cure to time. If you do not irritate and injure your enemy, your enemy will not hurt you.... In all chronic ill health, there is a great deal of sympathy or action & reaction between different parts of the system. As your disorder affects your mind, let your mind affect your disorder, try travelling, change of climate, & collect circumstances that amuse your mind....'[11]

Before Robert received Tom's reply that he would accept his brother-in-law's advice and indeed that he was already making arrangements for a tour of the Continent, word came of the sudden death of Erasmus Darwin.

Darwin had never fully recovered from the impact of the suicide of Erasmus junr., which he himself described as the worst shock he had received since the death of his son Charles some two decades before. Erasmus junr.'s affairs had been left in a chaotic state. Much of the old Doctor's spare time over the past two years had been spent settling his son's estate. Having finally completed the painful and difficult task, Darwin with his wife Elizabeth and four of their seven children moved into Erasmus junr.'s house, The Priory, during the first week of April 1802. The inevitable upheavals were an emotional and physical strain. The evening before his death, while walking in the garden with a friend of his wife's, Darwin mentioned quite casually that he did not expect to live long. They then went into the house for a pleasant and cheerful dinner.

On the following morning, Sunday, 18 April, Darwin arose before his wife and went downstairs to his study, where he began a long and affectionate letter to Edgeworth, describing his new residence. He was interrupted by a servant. With feeble explanations the servant attempted to justify his failure to obey Darwin's instructions about looking after the horses during the move. Darwin, who abhorred cruelty to animals, got into a violent rage at the man's stupidity. After he dismissed him, he felt a general shakiness and an extreme thirst. He went into the kitchen, drank a glass of buttermilk and warmed himself by the kitchen fire, telling the surprised maid that it was unnecessary for her to work on Sundays merely to supply him with fresh butter. He then suffered a shivering fit, became cold and faint, and told the maid he would return to his study and lie down on the sofa, but not to disturb Mrs Darwin. The alarmed maid summoned Darwin's wife anyway. She and her daughter Violetta went into the study, moved the shivering Darwin from the sofa to an armchair by the fire and covered him with blankets. They sent a servant to fetch a local doctor. Darwin died before the doctor arrived.

Robert was certain that heart disease was the cause of his father's death and that his father had known that he had the disease. Darwin had often said he had no fear of death. Had he a choice he would surely have chosen to die in the way he did, with only brief pain and with very little fuss. Still, after his father's death Robert lapsed into one of his brooding withdrawals. Susan, pregnant again with their third child, was confined to her bed for several months.

Tom left London on 7 May 1802 for an extended tour of the Continent with Giovanni Bianchi, an Italian violinist, as a companion. In less than a week he was disenchanted with Bianchi, who had coarse manners in mixed company and was suffering ill health himself. Bianchi was dismissed and Tom proceeded to Brussels alone. Brussels disappointed him except that the food was good and the accommodations cheap. He arrived there with letters of introduction and was given a month's membership in the Literary Society, which he found dull. He hired a German tutor whose services also included finding a likely companion for Tom. When no companion was found within a week, Tom decided to go on to Paris. Sick of carriages which were slow and tended to break down, he made the journey through Flanders on horseback, casually discarding most of his luggage.

In Paris he met up with some of his King of Clubs friends — Mackintosh, Sharpe and Scarlett. Poole was also in France, making the Grand Tour and improving his French. Tom agreed to join him on a tour of Italy, but depression and a sudden worsening of his physical condition again altered his plans.

Returning to England in September 1802, he immediately went to Bristol and placed himself under the care of the indomitable Beddoes, who at this point was recommending valerian, chloroform and strychnine. Not surprisingly, Tom's internal problems grew worse. Again he sought relief in opium and the companionship of Coleridge. Coleridge's own health and spirits had improved. He wrote to Tom about his future plans for writing a history of English prose, about a visit he had had from Leslie, and ended with an invitation for Tom to visit him at his home, Greta Hall, Keswick. Tom answered with the suggestion that the two of them should go to France again and that Coleridge should meet him in Bristol as soon as possible. Coleridge was full of enthusiasm. Two hours after receiving the letter, he replied: '... barring serious illness, serious fractures, and the et cetera of serious unforeseens, I shall be at Bristol, Tuesday noon, November 9th....'[12] By the time the two met in Bristol, Tom had changed his mind again and made new plans. He had also brought his sister Sarah with him, and the three of them went to visit the Allens at Cresselly.

One evening at Cresselly Coleridge read aloud to the assembled family and guests from a copy of Wordsworth's unpublished poem 'The Leech-Gatherer', which Dorothy Wordsworth had recently sent to him. Unfortunately, twenty-one-year-old Fanny Allen, the youngest of the sisters, got a fit of the giggles while Coleridge was reading a particularly sombre passage about the old man's skin being so withered and dry that the leeches wouldn't stick — a passage which Wordsworth later wisely omitted. Fanny's unsuccessful attempts to suppress her giggles finally brought on shrieks of mirth from the other girls. Highly offended, Coleridge folded the manuscript and remarked: 'Of course the poem seems absurd to a person of no genius.'

Tom eased the awkward situation by saying: 'Well, Coleridge, you must admit it's not a very fitting subject for a poem.'

Never troubled by modesty, Coleridge wrote of his own social success at Cresselly to Lamb, who noted: 'Tom Wedgwood was a dangerous companion, for he was an amateur in narcotics....'[13]

Kitty Wedgwood had received from Emma Allen a different and less flattering version of Coleridge's impressions of the Allen family. She candidly reported to Tom that the Allens, as well as some of the Wedgwoods, thought Coleridge conceited, rude, coarse and irresponsible, with 'too great a parade of superior feeling'. She also believed that Coleridge was taking advantage of Tom's financial generosity — 'I have never recovered his so willingly consenting to be so much obliged towards you.'[14]

After the controversial trip through Wales, Tom and Coleridge left Sarah with the Allens and then decided to go to Coleridge's home, stopping along the way to visit the Wordsworths. At the time Wordsworth, Coleridge, Southey and Charles Luff, a once-fashionable young gentleman who had lost his fortune and escaped to the north to avoid his debts, were all living in the Lake District.

When Tom and Coleridge arrived at the Wordsworths' home, Dove Cottage, Wordsworth informed Coleridge that a daughter, his fourth child, had been born the previous day. The two men hurried on to Greta Hall, arriving there on Christmas Eve, 1802. Coleridge was elated over his new and only daughter, but Tom fell into a painful state of irresolution and despondency.

After the first of the year Tom moved to the Luffs, who, though married five years, were childless. For a few weeks the situation seemed ideal. Tom paid housekeeping expenses and enjoyed the company of Luff for hunting and fishing. For conversation he had the company of Coleridge and the Wordsworths who were only nine miles away. But within a month the old restlessness had overtaken him. Possibly, too, the supply of drugs had run out.

Hearing that Jane was ill and that John was obliged to be at Etruria, he went off to be with her at Cote House. He was also contemplating suicide. In a letter marked 'Private' and headed 'Read this by yourself', he had written to Jos: '... If that fail [a scheme for buying property in Wales] I will neither distress myself nor my friends by continuing a vain struggle with Nature, but in complete resignation yield to her an existence which she will not allow to be anything but a burden to myself, and a perpetual source of anxiety to all around me. I feel a comfort from this resolution which maintains me in my most gloomy moments....'[15]

Meanwhile Coleridge had fallen in love with Sarah Hutchinson, the sister of Wordsworth's wife Mary. Always one to dramatize his own circumstances, he wrote to Tom about his unhappy marriage and his wife's ill temper: 'O dear Sir! no one can tell what I have suffered. I can say with strict truth that the happiest half hours I have had were when all of a sudden, as I have been sitting alone in my study, I have burst into tears.'[16]

His marriage soon deteriorated to the point where he left his wife. Without making adequate provision for either her or the children, he went to live with the ever-hospitable Poole. Weekly letters were now exchanged between Coleridge at Stowey and Tom at Cote House. Both advanced wild new plans for travel. In a return to the Pantisocracy scheme, Coleridge proposed the establishment of an intellectual community in Italy consisting of himself, Tom, the Luffs and the Wordsworths who, hopefully, would bring along Sarah Hutchinson. Poor Southey was expected to stay at home and look after Coleridge's family.

Wordsworth's brother John, a sea captain, was a new source of supply for the drugs upon which the two men were now dependent. Sir Joseph Banks, president of the Royal Society, also sent them a four-ounce parcel of bhang, a drug made from hemp. Coleridge told Tom: 'We will have a fair trial of Bang. Do bring down some of the Hyoscyamine pills, and I will give a fair trial of Opium, Henbane and Nepenthe. By the by, I always considered Homer's account of the Nepenthe as a *Banging* lie.'[17]

The times as well as Tom were becoming slightly paranoid. In the autumn of 1803 all of England was expecting the French invasion which never came. In anticipation of the enemy's arrival, Tom insisted that his mother and Kitty and Sarah move to Cote House. John was spending a great deal of his time now at the pottery. Both he and Jos purchased commissions, commanding regiments which were made up largely of men from the factory who enjoyed having time off from work 'to drum and fife'. Tom wanted to command a regiment, too. Hearing that Luff and a number of men living in the Lake District wanted to form a company but were unable to cover the costs, he financed the arms, uniforms, living expenses and service pay for the men. The company, which was commanded by Luff, became known as 'Wedgwood's Mountaineers' and wore felt hats ornamented with brass strips engraved with the company name. According to Wordsworth, they were a splendid group of men fit for immediate service.

Meanwhile Tom returned to London and set himself up in an apartment with a young man named Frederic, who played the flute. He had fancied he would enjoy cooking and other household chores. Within a few weeks, however, he found such domesticity not at all suited to his tastes or talents. In spite of the threat of war, he and a young artist companion named Underwood went to France. Again Tom changed his plans. Instead of proceeding to Paris, he crossed the Channel back to England on 16 May 1803, the day war was declared.

In despair he returned to the closed apartment at Gunville. Wanting no responsibilities at all, he sold Eastbury Park to Jos at prime cost and wrote to Poole that he had sold property in Launceston for a clear profit of £4,500. 'In the last three or four years I have bought upwards of £100,000 worth of land & find myself a gainer.'[18] At the same time Jos, who felt he needed some property near Etruria even though he refused to live at Etruria Hall, bought Maer Hall from William Bent for £30,000. This was an hour's ride from the Etruria factory.

In January 1804 Mackintosh received a knighthood and a Government appointment as Recorder of Bombay. Kitty was presented at Court, an event which caused great excitement among the Allen sisters. Mackintosh had his portrait painted by Sir Thomas Lawrence, Court painter to the Prince Regent; he had Kitty's portrait painted by John Hoppner, Court painter to George III. He was preparing himself for a future in politics. Meanwhile, he looked upon his stay in India as an opportunity for him to devote himself to his writing, including the sorting of Tom's notes on philosophy.

Tom was one of the few members of the family who did not go to London for the round of farewell parties for the Mackintoshes. Too ill to leave Gunville, he had written to Coleridge that he would isolate himself from the world and resign himself to death. Coleridge, always the optimist no matter how great the distress, naturally opposed the idea. 'What good can possibly come of your plan?' he wrote.

> Will not the very chairs and furniture of your room be shortly more, far more intolerable to you than new and changing objects! more insufferable Reflections of Pain and Wearisomeness of Spirit? O, most certainly they will! You *must* hope, my dearest Wedgwood; you must act as if you hoped! Despair itself has but that advice to give you. Have you ever thought of trying large doses of opium in a hot climate, with a diet of grapes, and the fruits of the climate?[19]

He then suggested that the two of them travel to Malta, Madeira, Jamaica or Egypt. Tom declined. Two months later, with a loan of several hundred pounds from Wordsworth, Coleridge set off alone for Malta and never saw Tom again.

These were the darkest months for Tom. Obsessed by his own death, he lapsed into self-pity and morbid introspection. All of his friends seemed to have fulfilled their early promise. Mackintosh had received his prestigious appointment; Poole was in London working on the Poor Laws: Leslie was soon to be appointed to the chair of Mathematics at Edinburgh and was finishing his book, *An Enquiry into Heat and Electricity*, which he dedicated to Tom. Beddoes was one of the most famous physicians in England. Davy, firmly entrenched in the Royal Institution, was making his most brilliant discoveries and was hailed as a genius both in England and on the Continent. Southey was writing the poems that were soon to make him Poet Laureate; Wordsworth was at the height of his powers, producing his finest poems; Campbell had achieved popularity with his martial lyrics 'Ye Mariners of England' and 'Hohenlinden'. Lamb, secure in his position as a clerk in the East India House, had published *John Woodvil*, a poetic tragedy, and was now collaborating with his sister Mary on what would eventually become *Tales from Shakespeare*. Only Tom and Coleridge seemed still adrift, health and youth fading, promise unfulfilled, haunted by fears of opportunities missed.

The months of isolation in the warm apartment at Gunville improved neither Tom's health nor his spirits. His body weakened. Mentally he turned more and more inward, resigning himself to the pain and loneliness of his destiny. 'Solitude is not in itself above half the evil which we ingeniously make it by increasingly comparing it with the state [of being in] society, instead of cultivating it as an occasional and unsalutory change,'[20] he wrote in his notebook.

Much of his time had been spent in putting down in notebooks his philosophical observations. In the preface to one notebook he wrote: 'How animating is the thought that if by the labour of my life, I should add one idea to the stock of those concerning Education, my life has been well spent!'[21] His eyesight had become so impaired that reading was difficult and his handwriting became almost illegible. Unable to stand the noise and presence of Jos's children in the household at Gunville, he went to Cote House. Jane was ill with her sixth pregnancy, and depressed over John's failure to manage his business affairs properly. The demands Tom made upon even the most sympathetic members of his family became even greater. He could not bear to be alone for even an hour. 'I am very low at present,' he wrote to Jos, 'having had constant fever & headache since I have been here & have lost 4 lbs. of flesh. This is the third attempt I have lately made to reduce my opium. I cannot do it — my spirits become dreadful — the dullness of my life is absolutely unsupportable without it.'[22]

He had at this point lost the vision of one eye and suffered extreme distortion in the little remaining sight in the other. After a visit to Poole at Stowey, accompanied by his friend Tobin, he went to the Luffs for a few weeks. He was not happy anywhere. He became hypercritical of his friends and totally incapable of making a decision and sticking to it. 'I shall stay here as long as I can,' he wrote to Jos, 'but some people and their wives are very intolerable company.'[23]

He now asked Jos to soundproof the temperature-controlled room at

Gunville. Jos suggested that Tom move back to Eastbury Park. At first Tom dismissed this idea, saying that he did not wish his mother and sisters to witness his final agony. Jos had begun soundproofing the room at Gunville, when Tom wrote that he had changed his mind and preferred to be at Eastbury Park with his mother. Jos began making preparations for similar accommodations at Eastbury Park. Tom then wrote he would like Jos to meet him in London, where they would take an apartment together. Next he requested that arrangements be made for him to go to the south of France. Finally he decided to return to Gunville, his irrational suspicions having increased to the point where he believed his own sisters were plotting against him. Travelling back to Gunville, he wrote to Jos: 'If they dine with you from Eastbury on Tuesday, Wednesday or Thursday, I should like to find some mark on your outer gatepost — a scarf or two or dirt on it, or a bit of paper on a stick on the bank within.'[24] In the end, it was at Eastbury Park, not Gunville, where he spent his final days.

He had been there only a few weeks when he began making preparations for another voyage to Jamaica. This not only involved the usual difficulties of finding a sympathetic companion, but was further complicated by a rather paradoxical wish to take with him various species of English songbirds, so that while in Jamaica he might have the atmospheric sounds of the English countryside. Preparations began for procuring various larks, blackbirds, robins, nightingales and thrushes; experiments were made as to whether young birds or old birds travelled best and as to which species suffered the least from a change in climate. Robert Darwin, who had long predicted that Tom would die either in frenzy or paralysis, found a medical student to accompany him on the voyage.

A few days before he was to set sail for Jamaica, he went for a drive in an open chaise with his ten-year-old nephew Joe. They were caught in a sudden summer shower. The sky, the fields, wildflowers all took on painfully brilliant colours. The smells of rain and grass and wet leather nearly overwhelmed Tom. When he got back to Eastbury Park, he had a chill and severe internal pains. He went to his bedroom, requesting not to be disturbed. At midnight he rang his bell and told his servant to look in on him again in two hours' time and to call Jos at 5 a.m.

When Jos came to sit at his bedside, he at first thought that Tom was sleeping but then realized that he was unconscious. He immediately sent for the local physician, who told him that his brother was dying. Twelve hours later, at seven in the evening of 10 July 1805, without regaining consciousness and with Jos still at his bedside, Tom died. He was a few months past his thirty-fourth birthday.

13

His Brother's Keeper
(1805 – 1810)

With Tom's death a part of Jos died too. If his father had felt 'but half myself' when he was apart from Bentley, this was even more true of Jos without his younger brother. Without Tom's imagination and initiative, Jos would never have known such talented and ambitious men as Coleridge or Wordsworth or Davy. Without Tom's wit and love of conversation he would have found himself ill at ease with Mackintosh and Sydney Smith and the other King of Clubs friends. With Tom gone the challenging, adventurous part of life was over.

Jos wrote to Coleridge in Malta, asking him to write a sketch of Tom's life, but received no reply. Coleridge neglected even to acknowledge Tom's death until some two years later. Letters of sympathy came from Wordsworth, Southey, Luff, Campbell and Davy. Poole wrote that he hoped Mackintosh would now be stimulated to complete the sorting of Tom's papers for publication. From far-off India, Mackintosh assured Jos that the work was in progress and asked him to send '... the dates of his Birth, of his various Courses of Study, reading, or meditation, of his travels, of his illness, in short, of the few occurrences of his too short life, with such Anecdotes as have impressed themselves on your mind....'[1] Mackintosh intended to put together a memoir of Tom as a preface to the metaphysical works he was editing.

Jos spent nearly eight months compiling the material. 'I rely fully on your promised discretion,' he told his brother-in-law, 'and I have written almost without reserve (to write altogether without reserve I do not find possible) but I am not ignorant that my honest opinion will to others have the appearance of unmixed eulogy & that my subject being so nearly related to myself is a circumstance that is unfavourable to what I say.'

Jos wanted some permanent record of Tom's life and work, which he believed himself incapable of assessing:

> ... Though we lived together in the closest union, I did not partake in any degree in his speculations, and though he communicated all his discoveries to me as he made them, I was not aware of their importance, nor

did they connect themselves with my own trains of thought so as to be recollected by me; & my incapacity for discussions on these topics must certainly have been a great check on his communications, which would no doubt have been more frequent and more detailed if I had been fitted to receive them.[2]

Jos's own ambitions had been modest. In 1803 he was selected Sheriff of Dorset, a position he enjoyed. He was a man of the country; towns, with their noise and gossip and the bustle of people going about their daily business, disturbed him. Crowds, whether of friends gathered for some social occasion or groups of employees working in the factory, made him uncomfortable.

During the same year, 1803, that he had bought Gunville and Eastbury Park from Tom, Robert Darwin had loaned him the money to purchase Maer, an estate of about 1,000 acres, nine miles from Etruria. The thirty-year leasehold cost £30,000 — £13,000 more than William Bent had asked of John Wedgwood thirteen years earlier. At the same time as he purchased the leasehold on Maer Jos also bought the freehold of a near-by cottage, Parkfields, for his mother and two sisters. He originally considered both Maer Hall and Parkfields as second residences, used by himself and his family only two or three months out of the year, the amount of time he had thought 'required to keep matters at Etruria in a tolerable trim'.

He was, of course, wrong. Matters at Etruria went from bad to worse. Profits continued to decline. The war with France not only curtailed export orders but made foreign debts more difficult to collect. Even more distressing was the fact that all three partners were living beyond their incomes; they did so, at least in part, because until the accounts were audited each year, none of the partners had the slightest idea of what the total income of the pottery was.

In May of 1805, only a few weeks before Tom's death, Jos had gone to Bristol to sort out matters with John. There were more difficulties with the bank, which now had changed its name to Davison, Noel, Templer, Middleton, Johnson & Wedgwood, and moved its offices to 34, Pall Mall, John sold Cote House at a considerable loss, and Jos told Tom:

> ... I left John and Jane well, both still pleased with the proposed plan of living at Etruria. I have had occasion to write very undisguisedly to TB [Byerley] about his expenditures, & at the same time to request him to give up his house to John which he agreed with a good grace. He is also settled that he shall live in town by his own choice, it being what John and I intended to propose to him, if he had not mentioned it first. John will be exceedingly useful at Etruria in the manufacturing branch, but he will not so well manage the general arrangements of business, to these TB will very well attend in London, for they would not go on well together, and I *must* spend a great deal more time at Maer. If I do not live there altogether, I must return then for the hiring when we shall have many new arrangements to make. John wants ballast & you sometimes tell me I carry a good deal. There is every likelihood of the plans

TB & I arranged last year proving very good for making clay and saggars in great part by machinery & John has begun the process of heating with great success. I suppose John will get into the house in the course of the summer. He is to get a vinery built immediately & I shall be glad if he can maintain his taste for the garden, for at present his mind runs riot on the manufactory, to the exclusion of almost every other thought....[3]

Jos missed Tom as a confidant and adviser on both business and family matters. Two years earlier, when neither a buyer nor a tenant could be found for Etruria Hall — and indeed who but a potter would want a pottery on the front lawn, so to speak, of one's country estate? — Jos had leased the Hall to Byerley. Socially the Wedgwoods looked upon themselves as superior to the Byerleys in spite of their being first cousins. On a visit in 1804, Emma Allen observed that Etruria Hall was 'much too good for its present inhabitants'. In many respects, the partnership between Byerley and Jos was similar to the partnership between Josiah and his cousin Thomas Wedgwood a generation earlier. Business and socializing were distinct and separate functions. Living at Etruria Hall, however, had given the younger generation of Byerleys ideas beyond, if not their station, at least their means.

Byerley's eldest sons, another Josiah and another Thomas, had been employed at Etruria, Josiah in the counting house and Thomas in the Ornamental works where he mixed the clays, kept the workbooks and settled the wages. Apparently, he settled a much larger than usual wage upon himself and, following in the footsteps of his father, 'eloped' — only to return penniless a few months later. Meanwhile his brother Josiah had incurred the displeasure of his cousin-employers by his laziness and by his haughty attitude to the job, which he felt to be beneath both his capabilities and his social status — an attitude reminiscent of the Wedgwood brothers fifteen years earlier. Byerley begged Jos for his indulgence: 'I need not tell you that I have constantly many anxious hours about these boys, who are, however, truely good, but the variety of my avocations and cares has not left me the power to lead them on as I ought to have done, and something has perhaps been defective in my plans.'[4]

Despite his cousin's appeal, Jos dismissed the Byerley sons from the works. By increasing his indebtedness to the Wedgwood company, Byerley raised sufficient capital to set up his son Josiah as an independent earthenware manufacturer at near-by Fenton. There he made blue and green-edged ware, some of which was sold to Etruria. Through the offices of Lord Auckland, a post in the East India Company was procured for Tom Byerley junr., who went off to Bombay and became friendly with the Mackintoshes.

Mackintosh was having financial problems of his own and had appealed for a loan from his brother-in-law, Jos, himself already in debt to another brother-in-law, Robert Darwin. Proving perhaps that people are most annoyed by the failings in others which most resemble their own failings, Jos not only refused Mackintosh the loan but lectured him on conquering his shortcomings: 'A coach and four seems to be as expensive, except for the taxes, in Bombay as in England; and a man would not drive four horses in his carriage here if he were determined to save a considerable fortune from a limited income. I cannot help fearing that your expenditure is formed on the habits of men who make fortunes on the savings of moderate incomes. Saving is an art you have to learn....'[5]

Jos himself often dashed across the country from Dorset to Staffordshire, as Poole said, 'like Royalty'. His splendid closed carriage with velvet curtains was drawn by four white horses. Coachman, postillions and footmen were all in handsome red livery.

'A Wedgwood living out of Staffordshire must lose something of his proper importance,'[6] Mackintosh observed. Perhaps this thought was of some comfort to Jos in resigning himself to what in a greater man would have been called his destiny. At the age of thirty-seven, he was returning permanently to Staffordshire and to a way of life he had rejected ten years earlier. He sold the Dorsetshire properties, which included half a dozen estates other than Gunville and Eastbury Park, to John James Farquharson for £52,000 — an increase of £1,270 over the original investment, though considerably less than the value of the improvements made to the various properties.

John Wedgwood lived for a while at Maer, arranging for the alterations Jos wished made to the Hall and to the grounds. He had not lost his enthusiasm for horticulture. Shortly after he moved back to Etruria, he wrote to Forsyth and several other prominent horticulturists suggesting that they get together in London to form a society for the exchange of ideas and information. The suggestion was received with enthusiasm. John drew up a list of regulations for the proposed society and circulated it among potential members. Six months later the first meeting was held in London at Hatchard's, the booksellers in Piccadilly. John presided, though afterwards he chose to become treasurer rather than president. As always, he preferred not to assume a position of leadership but to remain in the background. In spite of his reticence, however, history recorded him as the founder of the Royal Horticultural Society.

When John had first wished to retain his partnership in the pottery, but without taking any active part in the management, Jos had maintained that 'a brother should not be ashamed to take from a brother Now he felt differently. For over a decade he alone had managed his father's estate, which had saddled him with Etruria while giving his brothers and sisters cash legacies. Because of the pottery's debts, these legacies had not yet been settled, and the money remained invested in the pottery. Tom's estate, which was to be divided equally among his five brothers and sisters, would have brought approximately £10,000 to each beneficiary, but partly because Josiah's estate had not been settled, Tom's estate could not be settled either.

As Jos feared, John's mind did run riot on the manufactory. In 1805, John offered the management of a new transfer printing department to their second cousin, Abner Wedgwood, a son of Josiah's old partner Thomas. Abner, who had been working as a potter in Burslem, eagerly accepted the new assignment, thus giving John even more time to devote to developing new bodies and new patterns, an aspect of the business that he enjoyed. Following his own personal tastes and interests, he supervised the execution of a range of expensive botanical printed patterns, some of which required as many as forty-seven separate engravings. He reorganized the firing department and established a rigid quality-control system in the painting and decorating departments. He recognized that tastes were changing and that the classical style which had long been associated with the Wedgwood factory was no longer in general favour. To keep pace with new demand meant a whole new range of shapes and patterns. Decorations had to be more elaborate, colours bolder. When orders declined and profits diminished still further, he began a building programme to enlarge the works. During the year John was at Etruria and Jos was still in Dorset, Tom Byerley optimistically wrote of these changes to Jos: 'Your brother is extremely active and is fast paving the way for a radical reform, and will greatly benefit the concern.' But such major changes and radical reforms were not all to Jos's liking. He began to wonder where John's enthusiasm would lead him next.

If there were problems before Jos moved back permanently to Stafford-shire, there were even more with the two brothers working together. Byerley was a problem as well. He was ageing, ill with a fatal cancer, and no longer capable, if indeed he ever had been, of the over-all management of the sales and warehousing. Despite the introduction of John's patterns, Byerley continued to complain that there were not enough new items to offer and that the designs were not sufficiently ornate or Oriental. Jos began to doubt Byerley's competence. The famous swindler Mrs Roberts came into the London showrooms disguised as an aristocratic lady. Personally assisted by Byerley, she ordered a large dinner service in the new Blue Peony pattern with gilt edges to be delivered immediately to a fashionable address. Within a single day, Mrs Roberts made the rounds of the china showrooms, ordering thirteen of the most expensive dinnerware services available. The following day she and her accomplices, who had posed as servants, disposed of the services for ready cash and departed the fashionable residence without, of course, paying the rent. Byerley later bought back at auction for £7 the service for which he had charged £17. An assistant, John Howarth, took over the York Street salesroom.

Like John, Byerley seemed constitutionally incapable of living within his income. In London, with eight of his thirteen children still living at home, he found that he could not afford to maintain the house he had leased in Sloane Street, Chelsea, then an expensive and partly rural section of town. He sought permission from Jos to move into the building in York Street even though '... the kitchen is a miserable dark one ... and the cooping up of so large a family in the front two rooms would be most objectionable ... but my wife and I do not have anything to sacrifice that we cannot cheer-fully give up to obtain any permanent relief from our present sufferings'.[7] Knowing that this was no satisfactory solution, Jos refused him. Howarth and his family moved into the York Street premises, and Byerley moved his large and troublesome family into a more modest house in Charlotte Street.

As neither John nor Byerley could provide Jos with the business judgement he sought, Jos turned more and more to Robert Darwin for advice. Robert was as clever at business matters as John was inept. His understanding of accounting was superior to Jos's, a fact Jos humbly acknowledged by sending him the annual accounts of the Wedgwood company. Robert would audit the accounts, and offer suggestions on fiscal matters.

Shrewsbury was only twenty-five miles or a long day's ride from Etruria. Now that all the Wedgwoods were back in the area — Jos and Bessy at Maer, John and Jane at Etruria, Kitty and Sarah with their mother at Parkfields — frequent visits were exchanged between the Darwins and the Wedgwoods. The favourite among all the family houses and the most frequent gathering place was Maer. A large Elizabethan house set on a slight hill overlooking a small lake, it was approached by a long, curving drive lined with rhododendrons. Extensive gardens, originally laid out by Capability Brown and recently altered by John Wedgwood, stretched down to the lake and were bordered on either side by acres of woods. Here partridge shooting, fishing, skating, boating, riding, gardening and walking were enjoyed by three generations of Wedgwoods which now included Sally's twenty-one grandchildren.

Robert Darwin, who had 'a dislike to much exercise and rural diversion', did not join in the shooting or other sporting activities at Maer. Never reluctant to express his opinions, Robert had been outraged by the publication in 1804 of Anna Seward's biography of his father, *Life of Doctor Darwin*. Both Robert and his stepmother felt the book inaccurate as to facts and harsh in its judgement of Darwin's character. Anna described the Doctor as 'that large mass of genius and sarcasm'. She was particularly scathing about his reaction to Erasmus junr.'s suicide, stating bluntly that Darwin had disliked his son, whom he considered 'a poor insane coward', and that he received the news of his death with more satisfaction than sorrow. Robert wrote to Anna Seward demanding that she publish a retraction in several prominent journals. He threatened that unless she complied he would publish some of his father's papers 'which would have been as unpleasant for you to read as for me to publish'.[8]

Anna did publish a retraction of her description of Darwin's conduct at the time of his son's suicide, but however much Robert protested that her judgement of his father was merely the vituperative revenge of a scorned and bitter old woman, the damage to the Doctor's reputation had already been done. Jos attempted to persuade Robert that it was best to forget the matter, but Robert could not. The image of his father as gross, coarse and cruel was as painful to him as the actual loss of his father.

Other deaths had taken place within the Wedgwood circle. The old generation was passing. John Bartlett Allen died in 1803, little mourned. His son John Hensleigh Allen became squire of Cresselly, living there with his three unmarried sisters, Jessie, Emma and Fanny. Cresselly seemed a different house. Now all the Allen sisters and their brother Baugh, who was a master at Dulwich College, enjoyed returning for visits. Also in 1803, after an honorary Ll.D. was conferred on him unsolicited by the University of Philadelphia, Josiah's old friend Ralph Griffiths died at Turnham Green at the age of eighty-three.

In 1804, the year of Priestley's death in America, Josiah's only surviving sister, Catherine Willet, died at the age of seventy-eight. Alexander Chisholm, who with his housekeeper had continued to live rent-free in the Gate House at Etruria, died in 1807 at the age of eighty-three. The following year Thomas Beddoes died suddenly of a heart attack at the comparatively early age of forty-nine, causing Southey to lament that he 'had expected more from him than from any other man'.

Matthew Boulton, who for several years had suffered from a painful kidney ailment, died in 1809 at the age of eighty-one. His son Matthew Robinson planned a lavish funeral. The hearse and nine mourning coaches were followed by a procession of six hundred workmen from the Boulton factory. From Soho House to the parish church of St Mary, Handsworth, the route of the procession was lined by thousands of spectators. The only surviving friends from the days of the Lunar Society were asked to the service — Watt, Keir, Galton and Edgeworth. James Watt junr. told Matthew Robinson that it was not necessary to invite the young Wedgwoods, as '... the two families have not been friendly for years'.

'Old friendships should not be abandoned from trifling considerations, such as the common plea of business and want of time, 'Edgeworth wrote to Jos shortly after he returned to Staffordshire. But Jos was not moved by such nostalgic sentiments. In many ways, he was sentimental, but not about his father's old friendships or about his own childhood. Apart from his own family, which included the Darwins and the Allens, he had little need for society, but he did place a value on relative positions within the social structure.

Thomas Poole had recovered from the Wedgwood family's snobbish rejection of him seven years before. He was in correspondence with Jos about the breeding of merino sheep at Maer. In one letter to Jos, he asked: 'With your property, do you never think of putting business out of the question, and allotting it to your second or other sons? In this case I think I would breed Jos [Joe] to the Bar, though he never practices. One may fancy, in a concern like yours, each generation may establish an Elder Son as a Man of Property. This, I grant, is an aristocratic notion, and I don't know if you will like it.'[9]

Jos liked it very much. Aristocratic notions were just what he did have; they were the cause of his being constantly vexed at having to be a manufacturer at all. When Edgeworth sought Jos's advice with respect to establishing his son William as a potter in Ireland, Jos replied:

> I should think it a very hazardous employment of capital to endeavour to establish a manufactory in a new country, and the hazard is much increased if, as in the case of pottery, the success of the process depends much on the skill of the workmen.... In general the master potters have been journeymen, and those who have not been originally of that class are not likely to take a young man and instruct him in their processes, as every manufacturer keeps them as secret as he can.... I see so much difficulty in uniting a good education with the habits that are requisite to form a potter, than I am very doubtful if any one of my own sons will succeed me in my business....[10]

Sons do not always turn out as their fathers intend. Jos's two oldest boys, Joe and Harry, had been pupils of Coleridge's brother George, who was master of Ottery Grammar School in Devon. In 1810, when they were fifteen and eleven, they were sent to Eton. Joe was so solemn and lethargic that when his parents consulted Robert Darwin and other physicians about their eldest daughter Elizabeth's curvature of the spine, they also sought advice regarding Joe's 'disinterested temperament'. Joe was not stupid; he was extremely dull. Harry, on the other hand, was frivolous. His interests were artistic and literary. By joking, day-dreaming and avoiding his lessons whenever possible, he was forever annoying his father. Jos decided that the two younger boys, who were being tutored at home, would be sent to Rugby. Frank, at the age of ten, displayed a strong will and no more interest in his studies than his older brothers. Hensleigh, at the age of seven, was recognized as the scholar in the family. Perhaps because he resembled his uncle Tom in appearance and precocity, Hensleigh was his father's favourite son.

John also had four sons. In a family business the three partners in which were unable to live within their incomes — and Jos was painfully aware that he was guilty of the same failing of which he accused John and Byerley — there would certainly not be places for eight members of the family, to say nothing of the other thirteen sisters and cousins who would inherit a share in the company.

Jos and Robert Darwin met at Maer during the first week in July, 1810, to discuss events which Jos considered had reached crisis proportions. Orders in Council had been passed which stopped both the continental and the American trade. With approximately half its business from the export trade, Wedgwood was bound to be adversely affected, and many smaller potteries, such as Josiah Byerley's works at Fenton, were forced to close. The potteries that were able to continue in business accumulated large inventories originally intended for export, and prices and profits fell. Jos stopped the building programme which John had begun at the works. Major changes had to take place within the Wedgwood company. Thomas Byerley was bedridden and given only a few months to live. As he would die in debt, it would be necessary to make provisions for his widow and younger children, an expense likely to be carried by the firm for many years.

When Robert Darwin came to Maer, Bessy and Jane were leaving Staffordshire to spend the month of July in London, shopping and visiting friends and relatives. It was an established pattern in their lives — part of the summer in town, back to the country to receive visitors in their own homes, then during the month of September a visit to Cresselly. July was also the month for the auditing of accounts at the works and a time when Jos, like it or not, had to devote himself to the business. This summer, however, was different from the previous two.

As the women were about to depart, Jos received some alarming news which he decided to conceal from the women. John was insolvent, unable to meet his debts as they fell due. For the past decade, he had withdrawn yearly from the pottery approximately three times the amount due him on his investment. He was in debt to Jos for more than £5,000 and to Robert Darwin for an even greater sum. Robert was more concerned, however, about John's involvement with the Davison bank in London and the indebtedness of this bank itself. Certain loans which the bank had made carried 'extents', which meant that land and other tangible assets might be seized to recover debts due the Crown. At worst, the pottery itself could be taken over by the Crown, if Jos were held liable for John's debts.

Banking throughout the country was in a precarious state. Since 1797 the Bank of England, with Government permission, had suspended its obligation to honour its notes in gold. Freed from this obligation, both the Bank of England and the country banks increased the amount of their note issues and the volume of their lending. Cash reserves of the private banks were held partly in gold but mainly in Bank of England notes. In the country, bank loans were often made to farmers with livestock as security, and to businessmen such as John, on personal security only. The country banks assisted the double flow of capital from industry into agriculture and from agriculture into industry. Now industry was stifled by no longer being able to export. The Government continued its inflationary methods of financing the war, with the result that prices were rising alarmingly. Individuals as well as manufactories were going bankrupt. Jos told John that he could no longer continue as deputy managing director at the works, that he would have to return to the inactive partnership arrangement and that he and his family would have to vacate Etruria Hall.

John's response was predictable. He was shocked into a nervous collapse and more than willing to turn over all his affairs to Jos to sort out for him. Jos was tired of being his brother's keeper. He despaired of John ever being able to manage his own affairs and contemplated how with impunity he might eliminate him from the business entirely. But this was not a subject he cared to discuss immediately with either Bessy or Jane.

Bessy and Jane arrived at John Allen's house in Albemarle Street in London during the second week in July. Their sister Kitty Mackintosh had just returned from Bombay, leaving her husband behind. It was something of a family reunion, with John, Jessie and Fanny Allen in residence as well. Bessy looked forward to these three weeks in town with her brother and sisters. She and Jane had made the obligatory visit to the Byerleys their second day in town: that sad and unpleasant duties should be got over first was one of Bessy's rules. Then they could enjoy their shopping.

There were evenings at the opera and at the theatre. Dinner parties, concerts, breakfasts and visits to friends at Hampton Court, Richmond and Ealing would occupy almost all of their waking hours. For the Allens the structured seasonal round of social events was the accepted way of life. Bessy liked parties. She could see only two possible reasons for unhappiness in the Allen clan. First, Kitty had returned from India ill both physically and mentally. Her stepdaughters Mary and Maitland had never fully accepted her, and during their adolescence had contrived to make life even more difficult for her. A few months after Kitty's first nervous collapse, Mary, then eighteen, had married the brilliant young Orientalist Claudius James Rich; to Kitty's relief they left shortly for Baghdad. A year later, in

1809, Maitland married William Erskine, the clerk whom Mackintosh had brought with him from England. But even with her stepdaughters no longer under the same roof, Kitty found existence in Bombay unbearable. Mackintosh's erratic behaviour, his sudden enthusiasms, his extravagances, his tendency to take on any and every cause and his inability to manage his finances, left her anxious and uncertain. She suffered from migraine. Finally, in a depressed and indecisive frame of mind, she returned to England with the three younger children. Mackintosh was uncertain about the future, but expected to leave India in approximately nine months. Kitty seemed to Bessy on the verge of another breakdown.

The second potential blight on the Allen happiness was the news that Caroline Drewe's husband was slowly dying of consumption. As with Byerley, the end was expected daily, so that with every post the Allens were expecting to be called to Exeter. But the sad news the post did bring, by a messenger from the York Street showrooms on a sunny Saturday morning, was not the death of Edward Drewe. Bessy received two letters from Etruria, one from Jos and one from John. After a quick glance, she concealed them both from Jane.

Bessy had known for quite some time that the works were in a bad state, as indeed were almost all businesses with a large export market. She had known for an even longer time how extravagant both John and Jane were and how hopelessly muddled their finances. Jos had often been annoyed by what he termed 'John's gadding about'. Still, she was shocked and a little frightened that her husband was making so little effort to save his brother's reputation, which to her was the reputation of the entire family. 'It appears to me a very great importance to both the concerns that there should not be the appearance of a smash,' she wrote back to Jos.

> It would be much better for the family to advance John a few hundred to keep up appearances than that the eldest son of the family should appear in a disgrace situation. If the works are indeed in an improving way, perhaps a year or two may weather the storm. I own I can hardly bring my mind to anticipate all these things done in the most public and obtrusive manner without very painful feeling.... We are all of one family, the disgrace of one is the disgrace of all; let us therefore all join in keeping John's head above water and double our industry to restore matters at the works. It will materially shake the credit of the Bank also that John should be thought to be a very poor man. And the first moment it is suspected that our trade is in a decaying way, everybody will go to other shops. For God's sake, don't be hasty, and don't abate from your attention at the works from considering the matter hopeless.[11]

John's letter to Bessy was pathetic, fearful of the effect that his reduced circumstances would have on Jane. He was concerned that Jane might hear the news before he could collect his thoughts sufficiently to write to her. He was also apologetic over asking Bessy to speak with Jane and over becoming a burden to his brother. Bessy felt the burden, too, but it was a different sort of burden. Jane was her flesh-and-blood sister as well as her sister-in-law.

Her maternal as well as her sisterly instincts were aroused. Jos had thought it prudent for her to talk to Jane as soon as possible, but, having discussed the situation with her brother John, Bessy felt differently. It seemed to her that Jos had exaggerated the dangers of the situation and overreacted. Already he was talking of retrenchments and of the position not being quite as bad at the factory as he had first thought. She knew she would have to be tactful; for once Jos made up his mind to a course of action, he was seldom swayed from that course.

'I think £1,400 is quite a wonderful retrenchment considering how little appears, and what an expensive year the last one was,' she wrote to Jos.

> Therefore it does not strike me to be at all necessary to poison her [Jane's] happiness by speaking to her on the subject now. The bad state of the works might be spoken of a little time hence as affecting us both and when she sees us laying down our horses and turning off our servants she will feel less difficulty in assenting to any further reforms. The works are certainly now in an improving way and even if a few hundreds were necessary to keep up a little for a year or two it would be better to do so than to make an ostensible hastle. This is my real opinion and therefore I shall say nothing to her — as for dissipation, getting rid of a thing of this kind, I know by my own experience that nothing is so unpleasant as going into company with a heartache.[12]

Keeping a secret among five members of a family who were, of course, having hurried, whispered discussions proved impossible. Jane suspected something was amiss. When John Allen accompanied Kitty to the East India Company to protest the heavy duty imposed upon personal possessions she had brought back from India, and Jessie and Fanny went out calling on friends, Jane questioned Bessy. Having no longer any choice in the matter, Bessy told Jane the truth or, at least as much of the truth as Jos revealed to her. She was relieved by Jane's manner and by her acceptance, though, of course, she knew that depression would set in later. 'Jenny's [Jane's] mind is happily of a very elastic nature and her spirits soon rise by excitement, so I hope John will make himself as easy as he can about her.'[13] A decision was taken to carry on with their social activities as if nothing had happened. That evening, Bessy and Jane were taken to the opera by their brother Baugh and his friend Stamford Caldwell.

The following morning four of the sisters — Bessy, Jane, Kitty and Fanny — set out in their carriage to visit friends at Hampton Court. Jane was extremely dejected on the drive. The others offered both comfort and advice, but no one had any truly practical solutions. Jane felt she could not return to Staffordshire with Bessy, nor did she want to go to Cresselly. Bessy strongly believed that both Jane and John should have an extended visit in Pembrokeshire where they would have time to recover and make sensible plans for their future. She told Jane that Jane's older girls could live at Maer and that she and Jos would see that their four boys received a gentleman's education. She did not tell Jane that she had received a stinging letter from Jos who disagreed completely with her concern for appearances. Nor did she say she feared worse news yet to come.

14

This Evil Destiny
(1810 – 1812)

John had not the slightest suspicion that Jos wished to be rid of him completely. He had, in fact, looked upon Byerley's imminent death as possibly advantageous to himself. Someone would have to assume the responsibilities which Byerley had carried. John Howarth, the showroom manager, was a competent man but he had neither the background nor the manner for a more important position. Josiah Byerley, who had failed with his own pottery, now applied to his cousins to take over his father's duties. He assured them that he was a reformed character, but privately both Jos and John thought him incompetent as well as unreliable.

John believed that by making himself of use to his brother he might help to make the pottery profitable again. This was his best, if not his only, chance of regaining at least part of his fortune and of restoring his family to their former standard of living. During the month of August, while he was in London keeping up appearances for Jane's sake, he occupied himself with plans for improving the business and, consequently, his own circumstances.

'With regard to my own matters,' he wrote to Jos,

> as far as I can at present form any opinion I think London will be my future residence & somewhere about Westminster the place. The schooling at Westminster is 12 guineas a year for each boy & boarding at home we might give them a good education very cheap. As for our own comforts we must endeavour to render them as compatible as possible with a rigid economy. If you see no objection to my superintendence of the warehouse in York Street I think I could undertake it to a certain degree by giving a daily portion of my time to it. I should be strange at first but I hope I should soon be able to get the arrangement in my head & be of some use — at least, I would endeavour not to make things worse.[1]

As Jos neither rejected nor discouraged his suggestions, John began to think of his wishes as realities:

I have now been considering very much the nature of the concern in York Street where so large a stock of ware is lying dead. Now I do think by having a sale in the City as well as a sale at this end of Town a great part of the old stock ought to be got rid of & you might again open the rooms with a new assortment of goods. The capital thus called in would be very useful to you & the room gained would be a great advantage & I think that even tho' no change should take place in the firm yet, a sale might be made to make room for a new assortment.... I think the warehouse will not maintain itself without the sale of China & would it not be worthwhile to do as others do — buy the plain ware & paint it ourselves. This might be done & a stock prepared to open the rooms well after a sale had taken place. In the meantime your own express wishes as to making a china body would be going on & you would not then be in any hurry before you were sure of success. These things have been floating in my mind & seeing the brilliancy of all, even the little shops, I feel very convinced that you will never succeed without selling china & that richly ornamented. I throw this off for your consideration as the result of my observation since coming up to Town.[2]

Wedgwood was practically alone among the major English potteries *not* producing a china body. Josiah Spode II first used calcined bones in porcelain around 1800. This new china united the advantages of both hard-paste and soft-paste porcelains and was quickly imitated by Minton, Davenport, Ridgway, Worcester and Mason. Wedgwood alone seemed incapable of keeping pace.

As the weeks passed, John built up in his mind the picture of a new life in London where he would devote half his time to the affairs of the bank and half to the business at the Wedgwood warehouse. He had a conversation with William Leake, the bank's solicitor, who told him in confidence that Templer might retire and John be asked to replace him as resident at the bank. Nothing could be determined until Davison, the senior partner, came to town in January. Nothing would really be changed in the Wedgwood partnership until after Byerley's death.

John and Jane went to Cresselly the first week in September and then on to Tenby. Jane's anxiety and depression seemed to abate in the fresh sea air, though she continued to be plagued with ear trouble: progressive deafness afflicted at least five of the nine Allen sisters, and later a number of their female descendants. John's response to the crisis and uncertainty in his life was physical exhaustion coupled with a mental hyperactivity which he was unable to express except in writing. He was given to staring into space in a cataleptic silence. At the age of forty-five, he was without home or position, his children dependent upon the charity of relatives. Some of the bills his creditors presented to Jos for payment John could not even remember incurring. He had no more idea of what he owed than of what he earned. As neither he nor Jane could bear any confrontations or spoken unpleasantness, neither could really come to grips with the cause of their problems. Like children they were waiting for someone strong and wise to sort things out and then tell them what to do.

When Byerley finally died on 11 September 1810, John's truest feeling was one of relief. Now at last things would begin to happen. He would no longer be idle. 'I suppose it will be quite necessary for the business to go on some time longer at least under the old firm,' he wrote to Jos,

> as the estate could not be accurately settled for a good while to come & the Irish business must of course be our concern if you mean to close it finally. I should think that Fayle [an import-export broker] would be a useful assistant in winding up that concern if he could spare time this autumn to go over to Dublin & see how matters are going on & in that case I might meet him there. Of course you will see him & will settle with him what will be best to be done. Will it be worthwhile to enquire about Mr Green's clay in Wicklow? As my name has never appeared in the late partnership will it be necessary that any notice of it should be taken by adding it to Josiah Wedgwood? If I am ever wanted to sign bills & receipts, etc., I can do so by procuration & as for drafts I had rather have nothing to do with them more than is absolutely necessary. This you may enquire about also & if it is thought advisable that any addition to J.W. should be made I shall be perfectly satisfied with a simple co. being added.[3]

Jos made no reply about changes in the partnership. Instead he offered two other suggestions. As John was already in Wales and had nothing in particular to do, he might make a journey to Cornwall to look over the clay mines. Secondly, he suggested that John should put up for auction all of his furniture, plants and household goods at Etruria Hall, as Jos wished to lease the Hall in order to gain additional income. John acquiesced, saying he had only delayed leaving because his mother and Kitty were there at present while Parkfields was being remodelled. He then asked Jos to find an auctioneer and to make the necessary arrangements.

Jane took a less sanguine approach, noting that John was suffering such nervous feelings as to be unable to write about the arrangements. 'When our things are sold,' she enquired of Jos,

> don't you think it worthwhile to keep those Beds as we must want? Such as ours, one of the Pink Garret Beds for the two Girls & the common Tent Bed for the Boys & Children? I should have thought it might have been as well to rescue some tables & 1 or 2 common wardrobes, not my handsome one; but I am quite incompetent to judge on these points, not knowing what prices old furniture will be likely to fetch in Staffordshire or what we must give for what we cannot do without in London. I am only anxious to do with as little of the luxuries of life as possible. Would to God I had done so sooner! If we have in store our bare essentials I still however hope to do well. I say *if* because I have some suspicion from your letter that there is still more evil in store for us & a further reduction may be necessary....[4]

She added a postscript: 'If you like our piano, I think it would be a good plan for you to take it but don't just do it on our account unless you do like it.'

John took off for Cornwall, assuring Jos that he would not leave there '...
until I have settled everything that will lie in my power to do. At present I
am totally ignorant of the whole act of clay getting as well as that of getting
stone but with Samuel Mellows' assistance I may possibly gain sufficient
knowledge to form a tolerable judgment of what will be best to do & also as
to erecting any machinery for returning the water. I will also go to the works
at Hendra.'[5] But his spirits were flagging. The decision about his taking up
residence at the bank in London having been postponed until March, the
prospect now seemed less likely than it had a month earlier: 'Having given
up hope, it does not much signify whether the struggle is carried on & I
think there will be less actual discomfort in the deprivations one must
submit to residing in Scotland than if we reside in London where everything
is so dear & where the temptations will be so much greater,' he told Jos.
'Having made up my mind to the material present & having no pleasure in
store or in retrospect I endeavour to make the most of the passing hour & to
enjoy the good company I am at present with.'[6]

Actually, of course, John had not given up hope. More than ever he was
hoping to prove himself useful by assisting the firm's agent, Joseph Edwards
of Truro, to resolve disputes about pumping water on to various lands and
about the quantity of clay to be taken from specific places. Returning to
Cresselly a month later, he and Jane and their seven children spent Christmas with the Allens. In January John went to London, leaving Jane and the
three youngest children, Charles, Jessie and Robert, who were ten, six and
four, at Cresselly. He had sent the two older girls, Eliza and Caroline, to live
with Jos and Bessy. The older boys, Allen, aged fourteen, and Tom, aged
thirteen, were sent to board at Westminster School. John himself took
cheap lodgings without meals at the White Horse Cellar and set about
trying to salvage something for himself from his two partnerships.

On 1 January 1811, the York Street showroom sent out several hundred
copies of the following letter, over the signature of Josiah Wedgwood II:
'The dissolution of the partnership of Josiah Wedgwood and Byerley, by the
death of Mr Byerley, having made it necessary to collect without delay the
debts due to the late firm, I take the liberty of sending your account, and of
requesting you would be pleased to pay the same to me. The business will be
continued under the firm of Josiah Wedgwood, here, and at Etruria in Staffordshire, where your commands will be thankfully received and punctually
executed.'

John chose to ignore the fact that not only was his name not added to the
firm but that neither was the simple '& Co.' which he had suggested. As a
result of the demanding notice some accounts were paid, though by no
means all, and the firm was better able to assess the real difficulties of its
financial position.

Many customers among the aristocracy and gentry simply, as John himself had done, neglected to pay their bills. The account sent to the Marquis
of Donegal, for example, revealed that he had not paid his bill since March
of 1795, an oversight of almost fifteen years which had failed to deter him
from ordering or the firm from continuing to supply him with goods. An

estimate of the accounts outstanding at the time of Byerley's death was £41,477 — a sum greater than the total assets of the factory.

With considerable justification, John believed that if the firm collected the accounts due, cleared its old inventory, introduced new, more saleable products, improved methods of production, particularly in the firing, and opened shops which catered to the general public, substantial profits would again be made. If substantial profits were made, he would be able to settle his own debts. Both Jos and Davison had promised to come to London in March. Davison did come, and quarrelled with Templer over the proposed conditions for Templer's resignation from the bank. The solicitor Leake told John that no changes would be made in the near future. Because of an unexpectedly high number of large withdrawals, the bank was again in severe difficulties and borrowing heavily from the Bank of England. John's services were really unnecessary.

What was even more depressing, Jos saw no need for John to take an active part in the management of the firm. So there was nothing for him to do in either of his partnerships. Even more painful was Jos's hiring of twenty-three-year-old Josiah Byerley again, on a temporary basis, to assist in the York Street showrooms, the position which John had suggested for himself.

Jos had four reasons for succumbing to Josiah Byerley's plea to be given a job. Firstly, Jos had an immediate need for someone experienced to take stock at the York Street showrooms and at the Dublin warehouse; secondly, he hoped that by employing Josiah he would reduce his own financial burden in supporting the Byerley family; thirdly, Josiah was an executor of his father's will, and Jos would thus be forced to deal with him over the settlement of Byerley's share in the firm and of his personal indebtedness to it. Last of all, employing Josiah meant that there would be no position left open for Jos to offer to John. Jos had no illusions about young Byerley's character or about his abilities. In fact, he found him an extravagant and arrogant young man whose ambitions exceeded his talents. Still, he could command and control Josiah in a way in which he could not command or control his own brother.

Like John, Josiah Byerley had the annoying habit of spending beyond his means and of offering his opinion on aspects of the business where that opinion had not been sought. When Jos was not in London Josiah occupied Jos's own bedroom in York Street. He requested permission to have an extra room as his private sitting room and to employ a manservant to look after him. 'Mr Mason of Lane Delph is in town and he called upon me,' Josiah informed Jos with unconcealed self-importance,

> and in the course of conversation said that we should sell immense quantities of china here if we had it — and that he should be very happy to make it for you. His china is, I believe, very good, & he has great orders for it. I only submit it for your consideration, whether you think it would answer, if Mr Mason were to manufacture the china & you were to have it enamelled at Etruria? ... The stock of old enamelled patterns is very large — I am convinced that nearly all of it might be disposed of to

respected dealers in town on condition of taking some of the more modern goods.... A blue printed Chinese Landscape pattern, light blue, seems to be very much wanted & would probably sell very well....[7]

Jos told his young cousin that he was prepared to pay him a salary of 150 guineas a year and no more. He had paid for Thomas Byerley's funeral; extended the legacies from his own father's will to include the younger Byerley children who were born after the death of Josiah I; and, in the year following Byerley's death, made several gifts of such sums as £30 and £50 and £100 to Byerley's widow. From Jos's point of view he was behaving honourably and generously towards the Byerleys by providing them with funds which he considered appropriate to their needs. But the Byerleys did not like seeing themselves as 'poor relations', and were desirous of living in a manner similar to that of the Wedgwoods.

John's grand manner of living continued to confound Jos as well as to concern him. From Wales, John had written to Jos requesting him to visit John's tailor in London. As the brothers were the same size, Jos could be measured for a new cape, coat, waistcoat, breeches, etc. which John would be needing. Then, ten days after John left London in May of 1811, having decided against taking a house in the city because of the high cost, he told Jos that he had decided instead to take a year's lease on a house in Southend, a popular seaside resort.

Jos suspected that John and Jane would see much of the fashionable gentry who frequented Southend during the summer season and consequently would continue to live beyond their income. Despairing of John's being able to comprehend the need for economy, Jos explained to Jane his reasons for opposing the move. Jane showed the letter to John, who responded with uncharacteristic anger, insisting that neither he nor Jane were 'desirous of entering into the amusements of a watering place'. Jos withdrew his disapproval when John explained:

In the first place we were driven by necessity to make an immediate choice of some place where to retire to & it was necessary that we should retire to some ready furnished house & that that house should contain as much room as would be sufficient to lodge my family. We did not look for elegance nor for anything more than the common conveniences of life without any wish to enter into society or any of the expenses attendant upon such scenes.... At present I see no reason to think that I shall soon be called on to reside in London & therefore I have totally banished this idea from my mind & I have felt the extreme disagreeableness of being entirely without a resting place so very strongly that I could not bear the idea of continuing in that state any longer. There is but one thing that could render that state supportable & that is the knowledge that those who interest themselves in our welfare disapprove the choice we have made of a dwelling.[8]

Jos knew that although Bessy had accepted his decision *not* to pay off John's debts with more of the firm's money, she had disagreed with his reasoning. This made him uneasy. He had perhaps built up false hopes by encouraging her to believe that the situation at the factory was improving. Actually, the reverse was true. Practically all the economies that could be made had been made. Expenses still exceeded income. Some way had to be found to increase sales within the home market. Josiah Byerley, along with Howarth and the travelling salesman Josiah Bateman, backed up John's criticisms and suggestions: 'I send you a black milk-jug lately sent up,' wrote Byerley, 'to shew you the faults in the blackware, which I imagine to be owing to the glaze which in pouring in the inside has slopped over & has not been properly wiped off before firing in the gloss oven—& I believe the Teapots etc. are all injured in the same way in the gloss oven & not in the Black biscuit oven....'9 At the same time Byerley sent him a china teacup from the Derby manufactory and promised to follow it with a piece of Worcester china which was generally considered to be the best.

Jos was now on the verge of perfecting a Wedgwood china body. He had forwarded a trial sample to John, who he reluctantly admitted had been more directly involved in the development of the china body than he had been himself. John replied:

> I have received yours and the china saucer. This latter may be improved & I have no doubt that in a few more trials your glaze will be made to run more fully over the body which is rendered very adverse to a smooth surface by the introduction of so much calcarious earth in the bone. I should wish that constant trials might be made of the Coalport body which contains no bones & takes a very superior glaze. The few trials A.W. [Abner Wedgwood] made were spoiled by accident but you may see some trials of it in Mr Brown's room. The colour was ruined by having rust mixed in the pan in which it was ground. You will see that the glaze has run most beautifully over it & if you can succeed in it, it will be a much superior body to what any bone body can be made....10

In the autumn of 1811, when farmers had had as bad a year as manufacturers, Jos felt that he might be obliged to sell Maer and move back to Etruria Hall in order to carry on the business. Robert Darwin continued to express his concern over the extents, or liens, for which Jos had allowed himself to become liable through his brother's losses, and Jos himself felt somewhat stupid and embarrassed over this. To hand over to the Crown either the York Street building in London or the Etruria pottery itself because of an unwise investment of John's which Jos had endorsed would be a disaster for all members of the family. But there were few personal economies left to be made. Jos dismissed three more servants, so that the staff at Maer consisted of only five menservants, three boys and seven women. The family kept only one large carriage and one chaise.

As the battle to save the business was more immediate than a French invasion, Jos, as his brother Tom's executor, cut off Luff's captain's pay and all the other expenses connected with the Wedgwood Mountaineers. He also withdrew his half of the Coleridge annuity, although he continued to pay Tom's part. Finally he decided to act on a decision he had taken months before: he would ask John to resign his partnership in the pottery.

It was a difficult letter to write. Jos made several first drafts, keeping them in his desk drawer for a few days before composing another draft which he then discussed with Bessy. She held to her view that it would be an embarrassment to the family if it were known that the eldest son had been asked to resign from the family business. She also believed that an outright dismissal would inevitably cause hurt feelings and that most of the family, at least on the Allen side, would think John had been shabbily treated by his brother. Jos insisted that the possibility of the loss of the entire business was of far greater importance than personal feelings within the family. Still, he revised the letter so that John had a choice and so that resignation seemed more a persuasive suggestion than an outright demand:

> I have thought a good deal both of your affairs and of my own. The result is that I think it desirable for both of us to dissolve the partnership.... Your income is so small that any further diminution of it would be exceedingly inconvenient to you; so much so that you cannot with prudence risk any part of it for the chance of a profit. The business last year has not afforded you a profit equal to the interest due by you for the sum overdrawn and has therefore diminished your income in that year. The same reasoning may be applied to your property. It would be very distressing to your family to have the amount of it diminished, but it appears that your share in the Trade has diminished in value, being worth less than half what you paid for it, though that purchase did not include the outstanding debts due to the concerns & they are now included in the valuation of your share. The burdens upon the Trade are so great, owing to the Partners having drawn too much, that a very serious responsibility attaches to your property from your having a share in the Trade. You must take into consideration too what would be your situation in the case of my death.... The business is now not worth carrying on, and if I could withdraw my capital from it, I would tomorrow, but that is impossible; & I must continue it, if it be only to pay the interest of the money borrowed and to get a rent for my building.... On my side it is desirable to dissolve the partnership, to simplify the concern, to eliminate the difficulties of the settlement of my affairs in the case of my death, that would arise from a partnership, and to relieve me from the risk, whatever it may be, arising from my partner having a share in a bank, subject to an Extent in certain cases....[11]

Although there had been numerous indications from Jos that such a move was likely, John refused to face reality. Money matters perplexed and bewildered him. More and more he depended upon Jane's judgement. While Jane was extravagant, she was more cautious than John in her dealings with people. He didn't want to upset her with more evidence of his inability to manage his own affairs. Furthermore, he suspected she would see Jos's action as a betrayal, so he said nothing to her. He retired to his study and impulsively replied to Jos's letter by return post:

Long as I have been aware that I have been a burden & canker I was not till now aware how much & consequently did not know how far my obligation extended to you. During the last 8 years of my life I can truly assert that little has occurred but what has fully convinced me that my name in any concern was enough to overwhelm it & that all my endeavours to render myself useful to society are vain. Under these impressions, even were those others produced by your letter omitted, I should not have hesitated a moment to comply with your request of dissolving our partnership so ruinous to you & which I have rendered so unavailing to myself. My mind is so broken down that I cannot find terms to express my feelings & they often seem to put an entire stop to all perception & I find myself at a void unconscious of anything passing within me until recalled by some external sensation. I am not however less sensible of the many & continued instances of your active kindness for which I am indebted to you tho' without the slightest prospect of ever repaying them in any way.... If not absolutely necessary, I should wish that the dissolution of the partnership should not be put in the Gazette.[12]

That John replied immediately and capitulated without any protest at all brought great relief to Jos, although he suspected that John hadn't the faintest idea of the consequences of what was being asked of him. Also, he suspected that John had not discussed the matter with Jane. Bessy reported having received a letter from Jane which made no mention of the matter. Jos concluded that all that was necessary now was to dissolve the partnership through legal means, to prevent, if possible, the dissolution from bringing public disgrace on John by being 'gazetted' and to advise and reassure John about his future. 'I do think, if you take a calm survey of your situation, that it is not such as should make you unhappy,' he told his brother.

Your property and income are certainly not such as you anticipated in the outset of life, but they are sufficient for your wants.... It is fortunate for your family that they are young enough to accommodate themselves to the situation in which you may place them & as to enjoy in time as much happiness as they could have done in any, and this I say with a perfect conviction of its truth. For yourself & Jane, I think much will be done if you have exerted, or can call up resolution enough, to be perfectly explicit to her with respect to your affairs. The advantages of complete confidence are so obvious and you love and rely upon her so entirely that I am persuaded that it can only be the apprehension of giving her pain, as the difficulty of the effort to communicate one thing unpleasant, that would prevent you from living at all times quite open with her. I wish very much to know what you have acquainted her with of the present state of things and if she is not completely acquainted with them that you will give me leave to write to her.[13]

Jos then pointed out that the Davison bank was quite likely to make a provision for at least one of John's sons, that their mother had property of which John would inherit a part and that all of the children had prospects

for a sizeable inheritance from Kitty and Sarah if they remained unmarried — as became more likely with each year that passed.

Letters from Southend and Etruria crossed in the post. John's second
letter dismayed, then angered Jos. John's self-reproach and his professed
gratitude to a brother who wished to be rid of him put Jos on the defensive.
He who was trying to do the right thing for all members of the family was
suddenly cast in the role of the family villain. Bessy's argument that it would
appear to others that Jos had treated his own brother shabbily seemed to
have more validity now. But the one thing Jos had always prided himself on
was his fairness. Uncertain of his own ability to lead the company successfully through this difficult period, which his father would have considered a
challenge, he was sure that John was more of a liability than an asset. But he
wanted to be certain that John understood the fairness of the proposal and
was not, childlike, simply doing as he was told in order to please those
responsible for his affairs.

'I have always found that actual feeling is too strong for abstract reasoning,' John had begun his second letter. — Abstract or practical reasoning
was precisely what Jos considered most essential. Feelings, he feared, would
confuse the real issues and cause the ruin of the family's fortunes. 'My own
peculiar despondent feelings have arisen from a long & anxious examination of the past events of my life,' John explained, 'Many things have pressed
on me to make this examination & sorry am I to add that the result has been
a confirmation of my worse fears. In every commercial speculation in which
I have engaged to be useful to my family, I have utterly failed ... the pottery
partly through my own fault & partly this evil destiny. I am afraid I cannot
be convinced that my name is not a name of evil destiny.'[14]

The phrase 'evil destiny' alarmed Bessy and exasperated Jos. The more
Jos thought about John's second letter and the more he observed Bessy's
response to it the angrier he became. All the old resentment at having to
assume the responsibilities of an older brother because of John's instability
and incompetence came to the surface. He had sent his brother a gift of two
brace of partridges and three hares but now he delayed for two weeks in
answering this last letter. Even after two weeks his fury had not abated. He
began his next letter with the observation that he would like to have known
what had prompted John to reach so quickly the decision to resign his
partnership. He was inclined to think that John had not fully acquainted
himself with all of the ramifications of such a course of action. While his
own consideration had since 'rather confirmed than weakened the opinion I
expressed to you', the dissolution of the partnership was too important a
matter 'for us to trifle with or to take any hasty resolutions upon'. Conceiv-
ing that his brother might 'have thought my proposal deriving from other
motives', Jos begged him to consider again the whole matter and to write to
him 'freely and openly for I do sincerely assure you that I shall not object to
continuing as we are if you determine on mature reflection that it is for your
interest, taking the burdens into account as making up your mind to incur a
proportionate share of the risks.'[15]

John again answered by return of post. This time the tone of his letter was
different. John, too, was angry. 'In reply to your observation that I did

not enter into the particulars of the statement you first sent me I did not think the circumstances of the case called for it,' he wrote.

If you turn to your letter accompanying the accounts I think you will see that there could be no necessity on my part to enter into any details. Where so much was owing on my part & where it was stated that my continuance in the concern would be injurious to my family, where there was a possibility that my connection with the business might be the means of involving the whole concern in ruin by bringing on it an Extent from the Crown, I think you will allow that I had no option & that I must have been made of very strange materials to have hesitated one moment in my reply.... I felt the extreme injustice of continuing in a concern having abandoned all share in the active management of it, and feeling that even though I gave my time & attention to it, yet they were worth nothing.... Could I again take an active share in the business & could I live in the country I would accept your offer contained in your last letter with the highest satisfaction, but I do not think since you wrote your first letter that either your own opinion or any circumstances have changed so as to render that eligible now which was then ineligible & I have only to lament that I must still remain in my present unsettled plan of life which is rendered so much more irksome by want of employment.... I shall conclude this ungrateful subject by saying that I shall never cease to regret that circumstances have rendered this separation necessary ... & I do most sincerely hope you may never feel in the slightest degree what I have felt in forming this resolution.[16]

This letter was received only ten days before Christmas. Jos had planned to spend a week in London shortly after the first of the year. After discussion with Bessy he decided to leave Etruria the day after Christmas and go immediately to Southend where he and John could talk over matters face to face. He took with him a plum cake and presents for all of John's children. Jos could not remember when he had felt such misgivings about his own motives. He was certain that the dissolution of the partnership would benefit himself, his children, his two unmarried sisters and his sister Susan and her six children. He was also certain that John's eldest son Allen would be even more of a liability to the business than his father. As the head of the Wedgwood family as well as the head of the business, he was obsessed not only with appearing to be fair to everyone but in genuinely being so. He was not a superstitious man. He did not believe in evil destiny, but if his brother were to be afflicted by such a destiny, he did not want to be the cause of it.

15

The Game of Life
(1812 – 1814)

If Jos considered himself the head of the Wedgwood family, Bessy considered herself the heart of the Allen family. Jos grappled with practical problems; Bessy made sure the ties of affection among the Allens and the Wedgwoods and the Darwins were not neglected. Aware of her husband's faults as well as appreciative of his strengths, she was a shrewd enough psychologist to know when to intervene in the family business affairs and when to keep silent. Jos's conscience was somewhat clearer after he relented and offered to take John back into partnership. But, secretly, Bessy as well as Jos breathed a sigh of relief when John refused. The dissolution of the partnership provoked neither the scandal nor the overt hard feelings within the family that she had anticipated. Yet, the relations between the brothers and between the sisters would never be quite the same again.

Jane, like her sister Kitty Mackintosh, had come to terms with the unfortunate fact that she had married a kind but weak man. 'I can no more play the game of life than I can play the game of Whist,' Mackintosh observed of himself. The observation was equally true of John. Bessy noted that both her sisters now suffered severe depressions, fatigue, migraine headaches and a seemingly endless series of physical ailments. The hereditary deafness from which they both suffered was also a tidy means of protecting themselves against more bad news.

Jos had been right about Southend being an impractical place to live. Bessy hoped now that John and Jane would move to Shropshire where they would not only be close to them at Maer and to the Darwins at Shrewsbury, but also to old Sally Wedgwood who was now aged seventy-eight and in poor health. Instead, John and Jane preferred Exeter, where they would be near the widowed Caroline Drewe. However polite and friendly Jane might appear on the surface, she would never be as close to Bessy as in the past. This saddened Bessy. After Jessie, Jane was the sister who meant most to her. She could not help but feel some resentment towards Jos, yet, now that the deed was done, she tactfully refrained from further comment.

John had permitted his second son Tom, aged fifteen, to join the Scots Fusilier Guards. His eldest son Allen went on at Westminster School, but it now seemed less and less likely that a place would be found for him in the Davison bank. Bessy concurred with Jos in feeling that the frail, introverted Allen would be a liability in the pottery. So both were relieved when John himself, some time later, remarked of the boy: 'I am so entirely at a loss about him that it is a very sore point with me. He has less of vigour than any young man I ever saw. I see nothing in him which leads me to think that he will ever make a man of business....'¹ That Allen was an exaggerated version of John, but without his attractiveness, escaped no one, except possibly John himself.

Meanwhile Bessy was feeling some concern over her own eldest son Joe, who now preferred to be called Jos — which some of the family did, despite frequent confusion with his father, while others continued to call him Joe. Bessy had as usual gone to Cresselly in August, taking her two oldest daughters, Elizabeth and Charlotte, as well as Joe. The party stopped for several days at Shrewsbury to visit the Darwins and again to consult Robert Darwin about Joe's lethargy and chest pains. Like his cousin Allen, Joe had always been sickly, introverted and unathletic, but the pains naturally gave rise to fears of tuberculosis. Robert advised rest and sea bathing. Bessy wrote to Jos from Wales that Joe seemed 'very weak, not without some return of the pain in his chest, a few more bathings will I think determine whether it agrees with him or not.... As to his going to Edinburgh, I don't think either you or I should feel very easy to have him at such a distance while this pain continues. It is not fixed to any particular spot but wanders about from one place to another.'²

Joe had completed one year at Edinburgh University, where Professor Playfair had been his tutor. One of the older lecturers, who remembered Jos, confused Joe with his Uncle Tom — having, as Joe expressed it, 'so little chronology in his head'. Joe's father, like his father before him, took a great interest in his son's study curriculum, and had noted: 'I am somewhat disposed to envy your present situation, or more truly, I am deeply impressed with the value of the objects that you have the means of attaining and rather regret that I did not, at your time of life, more fully understand them and systematically appraise them.' He then went on to observe that if he himself had persevered in his studies 'during the golden period of youth, I should now have reaped the harvest of former exertions.... But, fathers live again in their sons, and it would indeed be happy if they could impart their experience to their children, but tho' this cannot be done to the extent of their wishes, yet the voice of disinterested affection will be listened to with kindness, and if the judgment of the monitor be entitled to respect, his opinions will have some weight.'³

Joe had been unwell during part of his first term, and was concerned not only over attending the lectures his father wished him to but also over making the acquaintance of the proper families. 'I can't say that I have made many yet, having been only twice up [i.e. out] since I came to Edinburgh,' he told his father; 'but I suppose I shall get on in time, however I should be glad of one or two letters of introduction if you can get them.' He then described a riot which took place on New Year's night in the streets round the university. A mob of young men 'formed a conspiracy, took an oath and had a watchword upon which they sallied forth, knocking down with bludgeons everybody they met and robbing them of their money and watches. One or two persons have since died in consequence. They have however taken up as many as forty or fifty of whom a good many will pay pretty dear for their evening's amusement.'[4]

Jos had decided opinions on all that his son reported, telling Joe that 'A man's character is very much determined by the company he keeps & no man can be sure that he can keep himself untainted if his companion are loose.' He then went on to commend Joe upon 'the habit you have formed of drinking water' and confiding his over personal observations of the disastrous effects on mind and body of 'immoderate use of fermented liquor'. His final word was about money: 'You are in a house with tried young men whose fathers are much richer than I am. Do not attempt to vie with these in expense.'[5]

Joe's chest complaints of the following summer were as much psychological as physical. He was at a critical period in life when decisions about his future were expected of him. But he was not a decisive personality, nor was he a scholar. Going to the University of Edinburgh was a duty, not a preference. He had no more desire to enter the family business than his father and uncle before him had had. But, unfortunately, during the first seventeen years of his life he had displayed no particular talents in any other direction, nor had he developed any strong interests. Joe was a person who observed rather than acted.

His sisters Elizabeth and Charlotte, aged eighteen and fifteen respectively, entered into all activities with the energy and enthusiasm that their brother lacked. They enjoyed the parties and excursions that Joe detested. Charlotte was delighted when her mother permitted her to attend a ball in Tenby, even though she had not yet had her formal coming-out. Balls were less exciting for the hunch-backed Elizabeth, only a little over four feet tall, who knew it was unlikely that she would seriously attract someone of the opposite sex. From early adolescence she had seemed to accept with equanimity the fate of spinsterhood, developing close and affectionate relationships with her five spinster aunts—the two Wedgwood aunts, Kitty and Sarah, and the three Allen aunts, Jessie, Emma and Fanny.

The three Allen aunts, in this summer of 1812, were going through their own personal and emotional upheavals and were agitated by uncertainties. Their brother John, now aged forty-three, had announced his impending marriage to Gertrude Seymour, daughter of Lord Robert Seymour. John's sisters both married and unmarried were unhappy at his choice, fearing their future sister-in-law possessed both a gloomy character and an inadequate dowry. Their only other brother, Baugh, still a bachelor and a master at Dulwich College in London, was coming to Cresselly later that summer. No one had actually expressed to John disapproval of his forthcoming marriage, mainly because he seemed so happy. The sisters' emotional turmoil was heightened by the fact that Jessie, Emma and Fanny would have to move from the house where they had lived all of their lives and where, after the death of their father, they had had such a happy and secure life. John wished his sisters to find a house in the neighbourhood, but they had misgivings as to whether this wish was shared by his future wife. It was finally decided that the three sisters would make no permanent commitment but would make extended visits to their other sisters, beginning with the Wedgwoods at Maer and then going to the Mackintoshes when they were settled in London.

Three months earlier James Mackintosh had returned from India, leaving there his daughter Maitland and his son-in-law and former secretary, William Erskine, who had recently been appointed clerk to the Court in Bombay. With Kitty he had gone to the Lake District, where they visited Wordsworth. He reported that Wordsworth, his wife and family were in good health, though less than a year later Jos Wedgwood had a sad letter from Dorothy Wordsworth enclosed with an order for some pottery: 'I cannot close my letter without saying a word or two on the state of our Family,' she wrote. 'We have within the last nine months suffered great affliction in the sudden death of two of my brother's children: He has only three remaining. My brother is in good health and begs to be respectfully remembered to you.'[6]

Relations between Jos and Mackintosh were somewhat strained. Not only was Mackintosh still in debt to Jos, but he claimed that the book he had completed of Tom Wedgwood's philosophical observations, as well as all of Tom's notes, had been lost at sea on the return voyage from India. Jos doubted Mackintosh's story.

Mackintosh's own interests were now focused on politics. Through the influence of his old friend John Scarlett, now Lord Abinger, he had been offered a seat in Parliament, and agreed to stand in the next election for the county of Nairn. This decision was a considerable relief to Kitty, who had been harassed by the uncertainties of her husband's career and income.

Jos, too, was being harassed from a number of different directions. The news that the Mackintoshes as well as the three unmarried Allen sisters intended to make extended stays at Maer caused him to defer for a year moving his family back to Etruria Hall, which was now vacant. Though the move would have meant considerable savings, at a time when retrenchment was essential, he was glad of an excuse to postpone it.

Along with his brother John, Jos was one of three executors of the estate of their cousin Thomas Wedgwood of the Overhouse works, who had died in 1809. This Thomas Wedgwood had left six young children and a wife, Benedicta, the third executor of the will. An even worse businessman than his grandfather Thomas, Josiah I's eldest brother, he had left legacies totalling £15,000, but his estate was proved in Chancery to be worth less than £1,000. The entailment was cut and the Overhouse property sold. Unfortunately, Benedicta was still unable to make ends meet. As John had left Staffordshire and was in any case too much absorbed in his own financial problems to be of practical assistance, she turned to Jos with requests for loans, complaining that the will of her husband's grandfather had never been satisfactorily settled.

Other cousins were asking for money as well. Josiah Byerley could not curtail his expenses and was constantly in debt. His superior attitude towards those who came into the showroom and towards the other employees annoyed Jos, even though he himself had behaved in a similar manner at the same age. Howarth and young Byerley disliked each other and quarrelled frequently. Finally, Jos told Byerley that he would have to find another job. Byerley begged his cousin not to dismiss him, promising to do better and reminding him of his poor widowed mother and sisters. Jos relented but not with good grace.

At about the same time, Jos's practical-minded sister Kitty proposed to him that £50 be deducted annually from the incomes of the family — herself, Sarah, Jos, John, their mother and the Darwins — to assist the Byerleys. It was a solution which satisfied everyone and which Jos probably should have thought of himself. After several more unsuccessful attempts at borrowing money from Jos, Byerley married and emigrated to Sierra Leone where he was no more successful in business than he had been in England. A few years later he was borrowing money from his cousin Sarah Wedgwood, who was more soft-hearted than her brother Jos.

In 1812 Sarah was thirty-four years old and her sister Kitty thirty-eight. They lived a quiet life with their mother at Parkfields, an existence which, with its proximity to the Jos Wedgwoods and the Darwins and with society provided by other prominent families in the neighbourhood, was agreeable to all three women. Neither Sarah nor Kitty was any more inclined towards adventure than towards marriage. Both were devoutly religious and cared little for material possessions. Since the incident with Basil Montague at Cote House, Sarah had received numerous proposals of marriage, but, like her brother Tom, she was too idealistic and too fastidious to come to terms with the prospect of marriage. Apart from Tom, whom she had idealized, Sarah's deepest feelings were reserved for those of her own sex. Jessie Allen and Jos's daughters Elizabeth and Emma touched her the most. Still, she kept up a coquettish manner with eligible men. Over the past decade she had maintained a lively flirtation with Baugh Allen — a relationship which members of both families, as well as Baugh himself, at first anticipated might develop into something more than friendship.

Kitty's disposition was more serious than Sarah's. The least attractive among the six brothers and sisters, Kitty took a rational, unsentimental view of life. She had a quick mind for figures and a lively interest in politics, economics and religion. Robert Darwin remarked of her that 'she thought more clearly than almost anyone he knew, man or woman'. Sarah, on the other hand, in her tender, impulsive disposition was most like her brother John. Taking money for granted, she contributed generously to a never-ending series of worthy causes. Widows, orphans, the sick and the old found in her a sympathetic supporter. All of Jos's children were devoted to her, but most particularly the youngest girls, Fanny and Emma, the pets of the family, who were affectionately called 'the Dovelies'.

During the summer of 1812 the Dovelies, aged four and six, stayed with their aunts and their grandmother at Parkfields while their mother, sisters and oldest brother were in Wales. The three other brothers, Harry, Frank and Hensleigh, were away at school. Jos, who was obliged to spend more time at the factory, dined with his mother and sisters twice a week and reported to Bessy that the behaviour of the Dovelies was 'good and agreeable'.

At the end of Bessy's visit to Wales, and a month before John Allen married, Jessie, Emma and Fanny Allen left Cresselly, returning with Bessy to Maer for an unspecified length of time. Shortly after they all got back to Maer, the Mackintoshes and their three children came for a week's visit on their way back from Scotland.

Mackintosh was again in poor health. The family noted how the eight years in India had aged him. He had lost weight, his skin had become sallow, what was left of his thinning hair had turned white. Though his physical energy had never equalled his mental energy, any more than his accomplishments matched his ambitions, he seemed much older than his forty-seven years. Aware of dissipating his energy in too many directions, he remarked about himself that 'medical men agree, notwithstanding the obstinacy of my symptoms, that they do not arise from organic disease, so that nothing but time seems to be thought uncertain'.[7]

After the visit at Maer the Mackintoshes planned to spend a couple of months in Bath before going to London. Then Sir James, whom the family called Mack, would begin the masterful project he had outlined for himself of writing a History of England. The session of Parliament in which he was to represent Nairn would not commence until the following June.

Jane came up from Exeter with her seventeen-year-old daughter Eliza. Six of the eight Allen sisters had a merry reunion, saddened only by Jane's report that the daughter of their sister Caroline Drewe was ill with the dreaded consumption. While the sisters shared their reminiscences and confidences, which comforted the three homeless spinsters and lifted the forebodings about uncertain finances from Jane and Kitty, Jos and Mack discussed Napoleon, politics and trade. The three young Mackintoshes became acquainted with their Wedgwood cousins. Fanny Mackintosh was a high-spirited twelve-year-old who could ride and climb and play games as well as her cousins Harry and Frank; the nine-year-old Hensleigh viewed her with considerable awe. In October the Wedgwood boys went back to school and the Mackintoshes departed, having extracted a promise that all the sisters would come for another reunion in London as soon as the Mackintoshes were settled there.

Eight months later when the three unmarried Allen sisters, accompanied by Bessy, left for the Mackintoshes' house in Great George Street, Westminster, Jos determined that the time had come to move his family back to Etruria Hall. 'I am glad the rides about Etruria are so much prettier than you expected,' Jessie Allen wrote the next summer to her niece Elizabeth. 'And tho' it is not so delightful a place as that dear Maer, I have no doubt that you will be as happy there, for happiness is like heaven, more a state than a place.'[8]

After the quiet of Staffordshire and the gentle family life of the Jos Wedgwoods, life with the Mackintoshes in London was something of a culture shock for the spinster Allen sisters, who were now all in their middle thirties. 'I have found out that taking one's pleasure, usually called idleness, is the busiest thing in the world,'[9] Jessie Allen observed to her niece.

Exciting events were taking place in London, at which, because of Mackintosh's influence and popularity, the Allen sisters and the Wedgwoods found themselves front-row spectators. The scandal of the year was the trial before the House of Commons of Princess Caroline, wife of the Prince Regent, for adultery. 'The extreme unpopularity of the Prince Regent and the natural interest inspired by a wife abandoned by her husband, had a great effect. The result of these causes, combined with the most stupid blunders on the part of the other side, had given her the most complete victory. All the world is with her, except the people of fashion at the West End of town,'[10] Mackintosh wrote in his journal.

Though Mackintosh supported the Princess, he was enough of a political animal not to offend the Prince Regent, who had given him permission to study the Stuart manuscripts in Carlton House. A great amount of Mackintosh's time was also spent at Holland House where he formed a particularly close relationship with Lady Holland as well as Lord Holland. He took up residence there for a month or so at a time while Kitty and the children remained at Great George Street. Kitty's nerves became more and more strained or — as Jessie said — 'Kitty's head was in a gale of wind', so the three unmarried sisters, though often visiting at Great George Street, took lodgings for themselves in Dulwich near their brother Baugh.

Their social life, however, continued to centre upon the Mackintoshes. They sometimes went to the House of Commons to hear the debates, especially when Mackintosh was speaking. He spoke passionately and eloquently in support of a bill introduced by his friend Samuel Romilly to abolish the death penalty for stealing from shops, but the bill was voted down in the House of Lords by 26 to 15; among the majority were 5 bishops and 2 princes.

The most talked-about exhibition of the season was of Sir Joshua Reynolds's portraits, which had been sent from all over the realm by their owners. It was a gallery of almost all the beauties, wits and heroes of the past sixty years. The fashionable gentry came to see themselves, their ancestors and friends, but most of all to be reminded of a leisurely era in the not-too-distant past, before the French Revolution and its aftermath had torn asunder what had seemed to them a just and rational world.

The sisters attended plays and operas and concerts, some of them featuring the celebrated soprano Angelica Catalani, then at the height of her popularity. They also heard much of the fashionable literary salons in which Mackintosh was a central figure. He had remained friendly with his old King of Clubs friend Thomas Campbell, who that season was giving a series of lectures at the Royal Institution as well as editing an anthology of English poetry.

During the early part of May, before Bessy returned to Staffordshire, Richard Lovell Edgeworth, his fourth wife and his daughter Maria came over to London from Ireland. With the publication of *Tales of Fashionable Life* — issued in six volumes, the last three of which contained *The Absentee* — Maria had established herself as one of the most popular contemporary novelists. 'Miss Edgeworth is a most agreeable person, very natural, clever and well-informed,' Mackintosh wrote in his journal. 'Mr Edgeworth is like his daughter, with considerable talents and knowledge....'[11] The twenty-five-year old Lord Byron, whose *Bride of Abydos* had sold over 6,000 copies in a single month, was averse to sharing the limelight with anyone. He dismissed Maria's works as of no consequence and described the seventy-year-old Edgeworth as 'a tiresome and conceited old bore'.

During the summer and autumn of 1813, the most celebrated literary figure in London was Madame de Staël. Her prestige was further enhanced when Napoleon exiled her from France. If princes and leaders of nations cowered before the First Consul, Madame de Staël as an individual did not. She openly complained that 'in meeting Buonaparte oftener, he intimidated me daily more and more. I confusedly felt that no emotion of the heart could possibly take effect upon him. He looks upon a human being as a fact or a thing but not as a fellow creature. He does not hate any more than he loves; there is nothing for him but himself; all other beings are so many ciphers. The force of his will lies in the imperturbable calculation of his selfishness.'[12] Mackintosh was intrigued by Madame de Staël. Her grasp of the wider political and social issues of Europe and her vision of the direction in which this new century ought to be headed, fascinated many insular English intellectuals who elevated her beyond the status of a successful novelist.

In July of 1813 the Mackintoshes held an evening party with a dozen or more celebrated literary figures, including Madame de Staël and Lord Byron, as guests. The party was a disaster. Byron, the 'gloomy egotist', as his critics described him, took an immediate dislike to Madame de Staël, though later a strong friendship developed between them. At the time of the Mackintosh party, however, Byron was still recovering from his much publicized affair with Lady Caroline Lamb. He was contemptuous of Wordsworth, Coleridge, Southey and almost all of the older, acclaimed authors.

The dozen or more less celebrated guests, including the three Allen sisters, had been looking forward to hearing one of Madame de Staël's famous harangues against Napoleon. Unfortunately, she arrived in low spirits. The jealous Lord Byron, whom Jessie Allen described as 'pale' with a 'severe expression' and 'looking ill-natured when in speech', behaved rudely to her. Ignoring her and directing the conversation towards his own affairs, he announced that he was travelling from Greece to Persia and India. In front of everyone, he asked Mackintosh for a letter of introduction to his son-in-law Claudius Rich, the East India Company Resident in Baghdad. Madame de Staël affected disbelief that such a man as Byron could leave England, suggesting 'the misery of finding himself alone, abandoned and dying in a distant land'.

'One is sufficiently fatigued with one's friends during life,' replied Byron. 'I should find it hard to be bored with them in death also.'

'Ah! my Lord, you are happy,' exclaimed Madame de Staël. 'You have felt the happiness *d'être entouré, moi je crains d'être abandonné.*'[13]

A less subtle incident took place between the poet Samuel Rogers (who had once claimed that his voice was so weak no one would listen to him if he did not say unkind things) and William Ward, the third Viscount Dudley. Upon coming face to face with Dudley, Rogers pointedly turned his back on him and left the party. Dudley then proceeded to insult literary figures in general and some of the other guests in particular. He maliciously mocked Campbell's recent poem 'Pleasures of Hope'.

After the party ended, at half past twelve, Kitty retired with a sick headache. Jessie was appalled to discover from Mackintosh that he had invited Madame de Staël, her son and daughter, Campbell and his wife and a few other friends to a breakfast which he wanted the Allen sisters to give on the following Tuesday. Without consulting any of the sisters, Mackintosh had invited and received acceptances from fourteen people. The dining room in their rented lodgings could seat no more than eight, so Jessie was obliged to borrow Baugh's room at the College. Though the party went off smoothly, it caused considerable inconvenience, and Jessie told Bessy later that she found little pleasure in the company of literary people who, after all, put forth their best efforts in their writing. 'I would much rather read their works,' she said. 'That is surer than their society, which fails in giving one pleasure at least six times for once that it succeeds, and then it is seldom equal to one's expectation.'[14]

All of the fashionable salons in London, at least among the Whigs, sought the presence of Madame de Staël. Her lover, Albert-Jean-Michel Rocca, a Swiss army officer twenty-two years younger than she, was pointedly snubbed by British society. Consequently Madame de Staël selected Mackintosh as her favourite escort. 'She treats me as the person she most delights to honour,' Mackintosh wrote in his journal. 'I am generally ordered with her to dinner, as one orders beans and bacon; I have, in consequence, dined with her at the houses of almost all of the Cabinet Ministers. She is one of the few persons who surpass expectation....'[15]

Though Madame de Staël was forty-seven, dissipated and grossly overweight, she continued to attract men sexually as well as intellectually. Her taste in clothes was flamboyant, at times even vulgar. Invariably her gowns were cut too low and revealed too much, the sleeves also too skimpy to serve any useful purpose. She favoured turbans and scarves in exotic hues of red, pink and purple. With such a brilliant, sensuous and unconventional woman, neither Kitty Mackintosh nor any other gentle-bred English woman could hope to compete. But if Kitty withdrew from the scene, one formidable woman remained to challenge Madame de Staël, both for political influence and for Mackintosh's attentions. Lady Holland, who had made Holland House the most celebrated of the Whig salons, was ten years younger than her rival. She had a history of amorous adventure which, though equally titillating, was more in line with the English view of socially acceptable scandal. Her first husband, Sir Godfrey Webster, had divorced her in 1797 after she had given birth to a son by her lover Lord Holland. Though Lord Holland married her and they then produced four more children, her reputation as a *femme fatale* continued, intriguing ambitious men and annoying respectable women.

During the previous year, Lord Holland had been urged in vain by Lord Grey to take over the leadership of the Whig Opposition. As he had been

Lord Privy Seal in the Grenville ministry and had held a seat in the Cabinet after the death of his uncle, Charles James Fox, he seemed an appropriate choice. Also the Prince Regent had no particular dislike of him, as he had of other prominent Whig Members. But, unlike his wife, who relished being at the centre of the stage, Lord Holland preferred a supporting and consequently less demanding role in life. Still, whoever wished to rise to a position of power in the Whig Party needed the backing of those in the Holland House set, which included Lord Grey and Henry Brougham, Princess Caroline's legal adviser and recent advocate.

Mackintosh's aims were ambivalent. He wanted an active, influential position in the political world, but also to be a historian and scholar removed from conflict and competition. His gifts lay not only in his charm and wit but also in his ability to persuade others that they, too, were charming and witty. He spoke eloquently about trivial as well as great matters. He was, however, highly sensitive and often indecisive. Jessie Allen commented on his sensitivity: 'How unfit for public life M. is. His unresenting nature lays him open to every coward. I wish he had the baton of Diogenes to lay about him a little.'[16] Lord Holland remarked of him that he was the only Scotsman he had ever known who felt 'the delight of lounging'.

Mackintosh's attractiveness to women was legendary and, in part, the cause of some of the tensions within his marriage. His sister-in-law Fanny Allen was more than a little in love with him. To women like Madame de Staël and Lady Holland he was the perfect confidant and escort, being intelligent and imaginative enough to amuse them, yet compromising and mild enough not to pose any competition. Madame de Staël referred to him as her 'English cicerone'. He took her where she chose to go, advising her on which invitations to accept and which to refuse. Not to be outdone, Lady Holland insisted that Mackintosh spend much of the summer of 1813 in residence at Holland House, sleeping, as he noted in his journal, in Charles James Fox's bed. Jessie Allen wrote to Bessy that she was afraid that Mackintosh would not be well enough to cut much of a figure in Parliament, as 'Lady Holland and Madame de Staël ... divide the prize, and terribly does he lose his precious time between them'.[17]

Emma Allen was apparently less concerned with Mackintosh's health than with the effect his conduct with women was having upon Kitty's health. When she approached him on the subject, he bristled with indignation. Emma found she had opened an uncomfortable breach between them: 'Since I have lost half my pleasure in Mackintosh's company, I feel very little disposed to go to George Street without Jessie's or Fanny's support, for he is always so glad to see them that going with them secures me a kind welcome also....'[18]

In the autumn of 1813 Sarah Wedgwood went to London, spending part of her time with the Allen sisters and part of it with the Mackintoshes. The literary scene was enlivened by the success of the first play by Anne Caldwell, the Wedgwood's friend and neighbour at Linley Wood in Staffordshire. Gossips were also delighted by old Edgeworth's irritable comment that the glorious reception given to the immoral Madame de Staël rendered valueless the public favour the 'pure' Maria Edgeworth had received. And

Madame de Staël cancelled the visit she had planned to Edgeworthstown.

After the first of the year Mackintosh himself cancelled all evening engagements except those in his own home. Both he and Kitty were in poor health. During the eighteen months since he had returned from India, he had made no progress on his history nor had he achieved any particular distinction in the Commons. As always there were financial problems. Tensions and misunderstandings between him and Kitty increased to the point where they had only superficial communication, though Mackintosh himself professed to see nothing wrong in the marriage. Kitty grew more depressed and unable to cope with the demands imposed upon her. As hostess at a dinner party for the de Staëls, she failed to instruct the servants properly. The food was inadequate and poorly cooked. A series of blunders on the part of the servants occupied more of her time than she devoted to her guests.

Beyond 'having her head in a whirl-wind' Kitty had come to recognize the painful truth that the hopes and ambitions she had for her husband were never going to be fulfilled. Furthermore, she realized that she was no longer in love with him. In the fall of 1814, Madame de Staël left England for Paris. When Mackintosh followed shortly thereafter, ostensibly to do research for his history in the archives of the French Foreign Office, Kitty experienced most of all an overwhelming sense of relief.

16

Return to Etruria
(1814 — 1815)

The move back to Etruria Hall had not been as disagreeable to his family as Jos had supposed it might be. Nor, unfortunately, had it proved as great a saving as he had hoped. The place needed repairs which he had no intention of undertaking. Most of all he disliked returning to the home of his childhood because it reminded him that the source of his wealth and, consequently, his position now in society, came from the despised pottery belching forth clouds of black smoke which were clearly visible from the windows of the drawing room of Etruria Hall. He could not escape his industrial inheritance. There was no way in which he could dispose of the business and by so doing acquire sufficient capital to provide for all of the family dependent upon him. In the past, money matters had been handled in an extremely casual manner, all members of the family drawing from the same trust account, borrowing from each other, then attempting to settle at the end of the year. Without his bailiff, John Wilmot, Jos would have been at a complete loss; yet inevitably, it seemed, Robert Darwin found some errors in the accounts which Jos felt foolish at not having spotted himself.

The Darwins were one branch of the family without financial worries. Robert's medical practice brought in a substantial income, and he was shrewd in his investments. 'I have often thought of buying an estate, principally as the most secure position for our daughters,' he wrote to Jos, 'merely intending to buy land for the sake of property & income, not for situation or other consideration, therefore where I could get most for my money would suit me best.'[1]

At the same time Jos was fearing that his own indebtedness might force him to dispose of Maer. 'I have for some time thought that I shall find it necessary to sell Maer,' he told Robert, 'but I am unwilling to do it till I am obliged because I can see the estate is in a very improving state and will pay very well for keeping a while. I have thought it might be practicable to devise a plan for offering the estate at a valuation to the parties to whom I shall be indebted on the division of the Executors' estate but I have not completed any such scheme.'[2] Robert replied: 'I hope you will not think of selling Maer but to your family.'[3]

During that summer of 1813, Susan and her younger children, Kitty and Charles, aged three and four, joined Bessy and the Dovelies for a seaside holiday. The four older Darwin children, Marianne, Caroline, Susan and Erasmus, went to visit their Wedgwood cousins at Etruria Hall.

Jos had handed over responsibliity for his older children to the governess, Miss Dennis, and to his sisters at Parkfields. Escorting Susan and Bessy and the four little ones to Wales, he returned by way of Exeter, where he visited with his widowed sister-in-law Caroline Drewe and with John and Jane, who were to take possession of a new house the week after Jos left. Jos reported to Robert Darwin that John's new house was 'very pleasant and affords no obstacle to economy, but I am afraid they will find they have not yet made all the sacrifices necessary to bring their expenses within their income'.[4]

Whenever Jos was most frustrated by failures at the pottery and by his own inability to extricate himself from debt, he became more critical of John. Whatever John proposed to do in his private affairs, Jos found objections. In all conscience, however, he knew that John was a casualty of the currency crisis and could hardly be held responsible for depreciation in the value of bank notes, unfavourable foreign exchange or the precarious state of the Bank of England after an unprecedented increase in the number of bills discounted. That a private bank such as Davison & Co. found itself entangled in forgeries and unwise speculation was a circumstance over which Jos felt John and his partners ought to have exercised better judgement. As John continued to borrow money for himself personally and also to request that loans be made to Davison & Co., Jos considered a division in his father's trust. Such an arrangement at this time would be inconvenient, when the income from the pottery was declining. Jos told Robert: 'I cannot be easy if you suffer your loans to me in any degree to interfere with your plans. I have a very large surplus of property beyond my debts but not convertible at once into money.'[5]

His mother was now too feeble to be bothered with money matters. His sisters, anxious to be helpful, were agreeable to any plan suggested. 'Kitty has been observing that you ought not to give us five per cent,' Sarah wrote to him. 'I never thought of that before but we have certainly been cheating you for some years of one per cent at least; it will be easy I think to alter this in the past accounts as well as to make it only four per cent (if it ought to be so much) in future.'[6]

But the division of the trust proved more complicated than Jos had imagined and beyond the capabilities of Wilmot, whom Robert Darwin jokingly referred to as 'our Chancellor of the Exchequer'. Thus, matters continued in the same haphazard manner as they had for the past twenty years.

Affairs at the factory were 'muddled through' in much the same way. The bone china which had been introduced in 1812 was not a commercial success. The demand for Jasper and for Basalt had declined sharply. Some of the bold florals with wide-bordered coloured groundlays and the Japan patterns which John initiated had proved popular, but the quality of the decorating varied considerably. There were no modellers or artists at the factory of the calibre of Flaxman, Webber or Croft. No one in particular was responsible for developing new products and new designs. The workmen themselves more or less made what they felt like making.

The John Wedgwoods settled into Baring Place, their new home in Exeter, with a much-needed feeling of again putting down roots. John took up his horticultural hobby again and built a greenhouse where he grew rare tropical plants. He cultivated a rose garden and a vegetable garden. Jane and her widowed sister Caroline found themselves particularly congenial. The three unmarried Allen sisters and Kitty Mackintosh and her three children came for a lengthy visit. Emma Allen wrote to Bessy: 'the furniture in this house is so good; it abounds so with flowers and there is such an air of elegance about it, that you cannot feel its lovely mistress is misplaced in it.'[7] There was a party-like atmosphere reminiscent of earlier, happier days at Cote House.

Beyond the pleasant façade at Baring Place, however, John and Jane had anxieties, not only about their finances but about their sons as well. Charles suffered chronic ill health and was feared to be consumptive. The eldest son, Allen, had completed his studies at Westminster School but was so withdrawn that his parents were concerned over his mental stability. Their second son, Tom, who had an adventurous but volatile disposition, was with his regiment abroad, so there was an ever-present concern about his safety.

Jos's sons were faring considerably better. In 1814 Joe, who had returned to his studies at Edinburgh, went to Paris for eight weeks to improve his fluency in French. First he spent a week in London, making arrangements and collecting introductions for his stay in Paris. His brother Harry, now fifteen, was still at Eton, and the younger boys Frank and Hensleigh were at Rugby. Though neither Joe nor Harry had shown any exceptional ability or ambition, they were both amiable. Frank and Hensleigh had more of their grandfather Josiah in their make-up. Highly articulate, Hensleigh distinguished himself at school in science and in mathematics. He had his grandfather's imagination, patience and perseverance. Frank, though not a scholar, had a dominant personality and a dogged determination to succeed.

When Bessy was getting the two younger boys ready to return to Rugby, she found a guinea in one of Hensleigh's handkerchiefs. Upon questioning him, she learned that he and Frank had saved it from their allowances. She asked for what purpose.

'I don't like to tell,' the eleven-year-old Hensleigh replied.

'Why?'

'I am afraid of being laughed at.'

'I think you can trust me,' his mother said. 'I am not used to laugh at you, but how can I know whether it is a proper use?'

'It is not an improper use,' Hensleigh seriously assured her. 'And we wish to consult you because we did not know what to buy. The writing master has been very kind to us and we wish to give him something, but it must not be before we go away, or he will think, and the boys will think, that we wish to coax him.'

'I don't think any way of spending your money can be more proper than showing your gratitude,' his mother told him. 'Therefore if you will trust me with the guinea, I will execute the commission for you.'[8]

After much consultation about the tastes of the writing master, they agreed upon a volume of Lord Byron's poems. Young Hensleigh was suitably impressed that Lord Byron was a friend of his Uncle James Mackintosh.

Uncle James was at the time visiting Madame de Staël at Coppet, her home in Switzerland. Accompanied by his friends Rogers and Sharpe, he had been part of the entourage surrounding Madame de Staël in Paris. They all attended theatres, operas, concerts, exhibitions and countless parties where literary and political topics were discussed. At Coppet Mackintosh became friends with three of Madame de Staël most brilliant advisors and admirers — August Wilhelm Schlegel, the German philosopher and literary critic; Benjamin Constant, the Franco-Swiss novelist and political writer; and Jean-Charles Léonard Simonde de Sismondi, the Italian economist and historian. In the past both Schlegel and Constant had been lovers of Madame de Staël; their old rivalry had evolved into intellectual competition, and the two bickered jealously and incessantly. Sismondi, on the other hand, was a pompous and clumsy man with a large head and a dwarfish body. But as if to compensate for what he lacked physically, he was gifted with a gentle and kind nature. Clever and cheerful, he had a direct, candid manner, behind his aristocratic pretensions, that drew to him many devoted friends. Mackintosh became one of these.

After several weeks at Coppet, Mackintosh went on alone to Basle where he met his daughter Mary and her husband Claudius Rich, returned from Baghdad. After a separation of six years it was a happy reunion. The three spent two weeks together in Basle. Then Mary and her father decided to make a brief tour of Switzerland, visiting Lucerne and returning by way of Geneva. Claudius went on to Paris to sort out personal problems with the East India Company and to obtain suitable lodgings for himself, his wife and his father-in-law.

When Mackintosh and Mary arrived at Brig, where the new road to Italy through the Simplon Pass had recently been opened, they discovered that the best inn in this popular little border town had been taken over by the Princess of Wales and her party. As they walked away to find accommodation elsewhere, the royal carriage clattered by on the cobblestones. Princess Caroline recognized Mackintosh, put her head out of the window and shouted in her thick German accent: 'Ach, ach! How delightful! Come up come to dinner.'

Mackintosh and Mary found rooms at another inn and visited the seventeenth-century castle nearby. The following day they dined with the Princess, whom Mackintosh described as 'very communicative, very foolish, very good-natured and very undignified — but I rather like her. The dinner was the best I had seen for some time.'[9]

While Mackintosh and Mary dined with royalty and savoured the delights of the Rhône Valley, Claudius, who was on leave of absence for his health, received an unpleasant shock in Paris. His salary as Resident in Baghdad had been cut from £4,000 a year to £900 a year. When

Mackintosh and Mary finally arrived at the Hôtel de Bourbon in the rue de la Paix, where Claudius had found rooms, they all conferred at great length about Claudius's difficulties. Finally they agreed that Mary should go to London and plead Claudius's case in personal interviews with the directors of the East India Company. Some of the directors were personal friends of Mackintosh. Introductions could also be arranged to one or two members of the Cabinet who might bring political pressure to bear on the directors of the East India Company.

As Madame de Staël was coming to Paris with her entourage, which included Rocca and the Duc de Broglie as well as Constant, Schlegel and Sismondi, Mackintosh decided to remain in Paris with Claudius for a few more weeks. Madame de Staël and the gaiety of Paris were preferable to a dreary winter in London with a difficult and uninterested Kitty.

Mary Rich left for England in the early part of December 1814, escorted by Joe Wedgwood, who, conveniently, was concluding his visit in Paris and returning to Edinburgh by way of London. Joe found Mary's company more exhausting than exhilarating, rather an anticlimax after the excitement of Paris. Nor, in Paris, had he found the society of Mackintosh and his exotic friends any more to his liking. Upon his return, Joe told his father: 'I have not written to Sir J. Mackintosh for I do not think he would at all expect it and I find I have nothing on earth to say to him.'[10]

After a four-day visit in London, during which he stayed at George Street with his Aunt Kitty, who seemed more nervous than ever, Joe fulfilled his duties by calling upon his Uncle Baugh, his three spinster Allen aunts and his cousin Dr Henry Holland. He spent considerable time in the Wedgwood showrooms because this, too, was expected of him. Like his father, Joe did what was expected of him.

Back in Edinburgh, he reported to his father: 'I do not find that I have lost more of the lectures than my stay at Paris in my opinion makes up for.'[11] He was now attending lectures in chemistry and natural history and had found a tutor for private lessons in German. The following year he planned to make his Grand Tour abroad.

As the year 1814 drew to a close and the new year began, life seemed much as usual within the Wedgwood circle. No one was prepared for the enormous changes that were to come, both on the international scene and within the immediate family. Though they did not recognize it at the time, the old ways were passing. A new world was beginning.

17

New Ways for Old
(1815 – 1817)

The England of 1815 was a strange mixture of antiquated traditions and new inventions, of great wealth and dire poverty, of elegance and vulgarity, of democracy and unfair privilege. Old King George III, blind and deaf, was confined to padded chambers at Windsor. In intervals of madness he crooned hymns and addressed imaginary Parliaments. At Brighton the corpulent Prince Regent danced, gambled, ate seventeen-course dinners, drank port, made love to Mrs Fitzherbert and acquired ever more fanciful follies to adorn his famous Pavilion. The Prince Regent's patronage had made Brighton the nation's favourite seaside resort, in spite of Dr Johnson's description of the surrounding country as 'so desolated that if one had a mind to hang oneself for desperation at being obliged to live there, it would be difficult to find a tree on which to fasten a rope'.[1]

The rapid increase in population—from about 7,000,000 in the middle of the eighteenth century to more than 13,000,000 in 1815—led to even greater inequalities between rich and poor. For the common people, politics was largely a diversion, symbolized by free beer at pre-determined elections. Power was in the hands of the aristocracy and the landed gentry. A man of property automatically achieved independence and respect. Within the limits of the law, his income and his conscience, a man of property could do as he pleased. Such security fostered self-confidence which was often expressed in arrogance and a taste for eccentric behaviour.

Most of London's main streets were now lit with gas. A few enterprising individuals replaced the oil lamps in their houses with gas despite complaints that the smell made sensitive ladies and gentlemen sick while the fumes 'well nigh asphyxiated them'. Changes had taken place in dress as well. Children were no longer dressed in imitation of adults. Copying Napoleon's Empress, Englishwomen wore the Empire gown, long and straight, low-necked, short-sleeved and high-waisted. Discarding uncomfortable tight breeches, men now wore trousers, though these were not yet quite proper for evening wear. Replacing the minuet were two new dances, the waltz and the quadrille. Pipes were no longer smoked, though snuff was taken by men and women alike. Apart from Maria Edgeworth and Lord

Byron, the most celebrated authors of popular literature were Sir Walter Scott and Jane Austen.

The old order was beginning to slip away. Though thousands still flocked to public executions to watch the spectacle , men were no longer hanged for trivial offences. Instead they were shipped to Australia. Economic conditions and unemployment caused many others to emigrate. While Government and Church alike still took the view that the condition of the poor was one to which God had called them, some men, like the high-minded Evangelical Prime Minister, Lord Liverpool, had developed a social conscience. Unlike Pitt and Percival, Lord Liverpool refused to buy votes in Parliament with the promise of peerages. Furthermore, he proposed that ecclesiastical appointments be subject to merit irrespective of influence, a policy that was not put into practice for another quarter of a century. With remarkable tact and prudence, Lord Liverpool struggled successfully to hold together a divided Tory Party, torn apart by the ambitions and ostentatious rivalries of Canning and Castlereagh.

Whatever unseemly disagreements arose within Cabinet meetings, Parliament itself was chiefly concerned with foreign policy, uncertain whether the old enemy France would be governed by King Louis XVIII or by the presently exiled Emperor. Throughout England and on the Continent there were agitating rumours that Napoleon was intriguing to escape from Elba. On 1 March 1815, rumour became reality. The Emperor landed near Fréjus with several hundred men. From the Hôtel de Bourbon in Paris Claudius Rich wrote to his wife:

> Bonaparte at Lyons! the troops, as may have been expected, go over to him as fast as they appear ... all the English quitting Paris in a great & useless fright. The Town quiet — the King tranquil — everyone cries Vive le Roi but not a single proper measure is adopted, & if they knew what they were about the case would not yet be desperate — as it is, I feel the game is up.... Madame de Staël, Rocca, Schlegel and Albertine decamped today for Coppet without beat of drum. I forgot to tell you that on Wednesday Madame de Staël gave a grand concert at which Catalani sang. She has walked off with Walter Scott. I have consulted with Sismondi about what is best for me to do; and he is clearly of the opinion that I should be wrong to start before the Embassy — that I cannot possibly be exposed to the least difficulty as long as any of the Mission is here, and that in short, I ought to remain for the present. Keep your mind tranquil, old Missee, stay where you are, and rely upon it that I know what I am about & shall not be imprudent.[2]

During the past three months in London Mary Rich had met various directors of the East India Company and successfully pleaded her husband's cause. A paragraph countenancing Rich's stay in Europe having been inserted in the Court's Orders to Bombay, Sir Evan Nepian, the Governor of Bombay, was obliged to reinstate Rich. His salary and allowances remained reduced, but not so drastically as had first been suggested. Now that her mission was accomplished, Mary was anxious to rejoin her husband, but he was insistent that she remain in England until relations between the two countries were settled.

Mackintosh returned to London shortly before Madame de Staël left for Coppet. Madame de Staël, who was frequently as active in patching up marriages as she was in tearing them apart, had written to Kitty that in her opinion Mackintosh should retire from politics and devote his energies to writing his History. Kitty no longer cared. Her mind was occupied with her husband's mounting debts and his inability to see any profitable project through to a successful conclusion. Because she had come to believe that Mackintosh was all show and no substance, she suspected others knew it as well. Still, she received kindly into the house in George Street the step-daughter who had been so difficult and disagreeable to her. Six years of marriage had matured Mary, so that she was at least no longer openly hostile. Indeed, she seemed to take a genuine interest in her stepbrother and stepsisters. She was particularly fond of Fanny, who was displaying the same sort of precocious intellect as Mary had done at a similar age. And Fanny, without doubt, as Kitty's favourite child.

Six weeks after Mackintosh's return from Paris, Mary sat up with her stepmother and Fanny Allen until 4 a.m. when her father came back from the House of Commons with the news that war had been declared. In spite of Mackintosh's appeal to her to wait at least another day, until she could have first-hand news from Byron and Scott, Mary stubbornly refused to defer rejoining her husband. She left for Paris the following day, crossing the Channel in an open boat.

Mary's loyalties were strangely divided. Almost fanatically pro-Bonaparte, she and Claudius watched from the balcony of the house of Queen Hortense of Holland the review of the French troops before they marched to Waterloo. Handfuls of violets were scattered from balconies and windows all along the way. When the Queen naïvely asked Mary if England had such fine men, Mary reported 'then my John-Bullism got up'. Still, she noted the Emperor's smile as he looked up at the balcony where Queen Hortense was sitting. Mary was touched with a lively sympathy for him.

Soon after Napoleon and his troops marched northward, Mary and Claudius left for Baghdad by way of Geneva, retracing the tour through the Rhône Valley that Mary and her father had taken six months earlier.

A few days before the start of the battle of Waterloo, in which her seventeen-year-old grandson Tom Wedgwood took part as a foot soldier, old Sally Wedgwood died peacefully at Parkfields. At eighty-one she was the last member of her generation in the family.

Her will was proved at Shrewsbury on 12 June 1815. Kitty and Sarah were the executors. With the exception of small annuities for life to a few spinster nieces, friends and servants, and minor bequests, such as £40 and all her clothes to her housekeeper Elizabeth Moore, the estate was divided equally among her five children. The shares amounted to £1,400 each. John's share, however, was placed in trust, to be administered by his younger sisters. In the event of his death the trust would be transferred to his wife and then to his children. The arrangement had been made at Jos's suggestion when John resigned his partnership in the pottery.

There was still concern within the family circle about John's inability to manage his affairs. In spite of his misfortune four years earlier, he had continued in each subsequent year to spend anywhere between a third and a half again more than his annual income. Nor would he give Jane any idea of how to budget their household expenses. The strain of their indebtedness and the uncertainty of their future brought on more of her migraines and fits of exhaustion.

After an especially bad year at the pottery, Jos determined to work out for John a budget for his living expenses, giving him what, in effect, amounted to a quarterly allowance. John had no objection to this arrangement. 'I do now most sincerely hope that from this time forward I shall give you much less trouble than I have hitherto done,' he replied agreeably. 'I have been studying the different accounts which you have sent me & think I have made myself acquainted with them & I hope also that I may say that our different arrangements will enable us to live within the income we at present possess.'[3]

A month after their mother's death, Jos wrote to John:

Some time ago I requested my mother to give you such part of her property as she might mean to leave to me. Her will was then made and she did not make any alteration in it, relying no doubt upon my carrying the proposal I had made to her into effect. I have accordingly added a codicil to my will, bequeathing the legacy I derived from my mother of £1,400 to you exactly in the terms in which she made the bequest of £1,400 to you. The bequest I thought it best to make in that way to secure this income & principal of it to your family in all events. The interest I will pay to you from the time that I derive interest from it which will no doubt be very soon. Having neglected to pay you for some articles such as wine, piano forte etc., I thought an addition to the sum of £1,400 would be a good way of settling the account & I have accordingly added $600 to the £1,400 making a sum of £2,000 bequeathed to you in the terms of my mother's bequest, and I shall have to pay you an annuity of £100 which I engage to do.[4]

John was indeed desperate for money. His natural reticence and unwillingness to confront anything unpleasant, coupled with an inability to understand the business situations in which he was himself involved, caused him to seek help from members of the family individually and without anyone actually understanding what was happening. The result, naturally, was that they all discussed his affairs behind his back. 'The Dr [Robert Darwin] is so constantly engaged that he desires me to thank you for your letter & offer of receiving the dividends which he told John you would do,' Susan wrote to Jos. 'John seemed to be in haste for the money as he wrote to ask for it one night & the following post brought a letter of attorney for the Dr to sign. Afterwards he sent the security which I will transcribe on the other page & that is all we know of the transaction — I hope he has not been making any hazardous speculation but can't help having some fears from his not having mentioned anything about it to you—but perhaps his great aversion to saying anything about money matters may have occasioned his silence.'[5] The 'security' dated 2 September 1815 which John gave to Robert Darwin was 'the sum of six thousand five hundred pounds 4 per cent stock & to be accountable for the dividends until the said stock is replaced & for which I pledge the property coming to me under the will of my late Brother Thomas Wedgwood....'[6]

At the same time John had asked Jos to give to George Templer, the active partner in Davison & Co., permission to borrow £6,000 of the £9,000 in Exchequer bills which Jos had bought through Davison & Co. John assured Jos of his absolute confidence in Templer and then wrote to Templer that he might 'appropriate to £4,000 of Exchequer Bills belonging to my brother Josiah'.[7] This was, in effect, a final desperate gamble to recoup old losses and make a quick fortune on the crest of a new financial boom. It was a gamble that failed.

Mackintosh also continued to be troubled over finances. Attendance at the House of Commons, the rigours of an exhausting social life and the pressure of mounting debts caused him to put the house in George Street up for sale. During the summer of 1815 he and Kitty and their three children, Bessy, Fanny and Robert, aged sixteen, fifteen and nine, moved from London to Weedon Lodge near Aylesbury. A pleasant, retired spot that offered few neighbours and even fewer distractions, it seemed an ideal place for Mackintosh to resume work on his History.

After the Mackintoshes left London, the unmarried Allen sisters decided to make a tour of the Continent, a rather daring and independent plan for three single women to undertake. Their brother John had wanted them to return to Cresselly and live there with him, his wife and their two babies. The sisters still had reservations about their sister-in-law's hospitality, but they felt it would be a pointed insult for them to refuse their brother's sincere invitation in favour of returning to the Jos Wedgwoods, or to the John Wedgwoods with whom they had already spent many months. Thus, an extended tour of the Continent seemed the happiest solution. At the beginning of September, soon after the Continent was again opened to English travellers, they set out, with John Wedgwood escorting them as far as Paris. John had already spent several weeks in London, consulting with Templer and the other partners in Davison & Co. about new investments. Jane chose to remain at home in Exeter, saying that she did not feel strong enough to enjoy travelling.

In 1816 the Jos Wedgwoods felt sufficiently confident of the increase in sales and profits from the pottery to move back to Maer Hall. Joe Wedgwood had completed his studies at Edinburgh and gone to London to consult with his uncle Baugh Allen and his cousin Dr Henry Holland about making the Grand Tour. His Uncle John Wedgwood had advised him against going to Italy, as there were so many bandits there and English gentlemen were a likely target. Other members of the family disagreed. Finally it was settled that Joe could begin his tour by taking his brother

Harry to Geneva, where he was to attend school. It was also thought fortuitous that the three Allen aunts would be in Geneva for a few months at the same time.

Harry was the son his parents worried over the most. His easygoing disposition and gentle manner were in sharp contrast to the seriousness of the others. His dislike of Eton and his failure to apply himself to his studies brought concern as to his intellectual capacities. While he was worrying about his inability to grow thick whiskers, his mother confided to her sisters: 'I had rather hear that his head was upright on his shoulders than that his whiskers were a yard long.'[8]

In Geneva Harry and Joe and their Allen aunts found that they were fortunate in having Sir James Mackintosh as a relative. Through him they had introductions to the noble, the rich and the talented. Chief among them was, of course, Madame de Staël. She and her daughter Albertine, who had recently married Victor de Broglie, included the Allen sisters in the circle who attended parties at Coppet. There they met Sismondi who, unlike his friend Mackintosh, had actually completed his sixteen-volume *Histoire des républiques italiennes du Moyen Âge*. His fame had spread to England. Almost overnight he had become internationally celebrated.

Sismondi fell head over heels in love with Jessie Allen. She was both astonished and flattered. Her sisters Fanny and Emma disapproved of a romance with such a misshapen little man with un-English manners. Still, all three sisters found him a knowledgeable guide and a considerate companion.

Madame de Staël herself was now ill and incurably addicted to opium. Since the days of her triumph in London, four years ealier, she had become skeletally thin, her skin greyish, forgetful and inattentive to what was said to her. Still she maintained her old way of life, taking her entourage with her, first to Florence, then, in the winter of 1816, to Paris, to set up her salon in the rue Royale. Sismondi remained in Geneva, hoping to persuade the Allen sisters to allow him to accompany them to Italy. Young Joe Wedgwood had already left for Naples, assuring his aunts that he 'saw nothing at all improper in Sismondi's travelling with them as their protector'. Others, including Sismondi's friend Constant, *did* think it improper.

Sismondi finally departed for Pisa alone, and the Allen sisters followed a couple of months later with a *voiturier* and an English gentleman so much younger than they that there could be no possible hint of scandal. Seventeen-year-old Harry, now left alone in Geneva with only his teachers and fellow students who spoke mainly French and German, would no longer be invited to accompany his aunts to grand occasions such as the ball given by the Prince of Mecklenburg. He walked two miles in the rain to wave goodbye to the Allen ladies who drove away in a splendid six-horse carriage.

Back in England there was a great family gathering for a fortnight at Bath. The party consisted of Bessy and her daughter Charlotte, the widowed Caroline Drewe and her daughter Harriet, the John Wedgwoods, the Robert Darwins and Kitty and Sarah Wedgwood. They had all leased a house together for a fortnight. Kitty Wedgwood was appointed 'housekeeper-hostess'. They all took the mineral baths, and in the evening attended parties, learning to waltz as Jessie, Emma and Fanny had done in Geneva. The main topic of romance was not among the young girls but once again with the thirty-nine-year-old Sarah Wedgwood. According to Bessy, she was 'a great deal unhinged by Henry Swinney's appearance among us'.

The older generation of women would gather late in the evenings in the bedroom which Caroline and Bessy shared, 'curling our hair together over the fire and discussing Mr Swinney.' All approved of him except Sarah, who kept him and everyone else in suspense until the last possible moment, when she refused his proposal with the same excuse she had given her other suitors — that 'they were in every way unsuitable'.

While the women were upstairs discussing matters of the heart, John Wedgwood and Robert Darwin sat in front of the fire in the downstairs sitting room discussing business and politics. With the opening of the new session of Parliament in January of 1816, Mackintosh would be returning to London. From accounts given them by their wives, Robert and John knew that the isolation at Weedon Lodge had had a good effect on Mackintosh's physical health but had depressed his spirits. He had accomplished little in his writing. The difficulty of organizing the manuscript material which the Prince Regent had placed at his disposal confused and frustrated him. His tendency to digress on inconsequential matters obscured the over-all structure of the work and impeded its progress. Having decided to return to London and concentrate on affairs in Parliament, he assigned Kitty and the sixteen-year-old Fanny to copying for him some of the letters from the Marlborough papers.

John told Robert that Mackintosh's house in George Street had not yet been sold, the highest offer being only £1,600, though all of the furniture and household goods had been sold at auction. Mackintosh's plan was that he himself would stay with Lord Holland in Bobus Smith's house in Savile Row. Weedon Lodge would be shut up, and Kitty and their two daughters would move to Maer Hall with the Jos Wedgwoods, while young Robert Mackintosh returned to school at Winchester.

Maer was the place where family, friends and neighbours could always be sure of a genuine welcome in times of ill fortune as well as good. There was hardly a time when Jos and Bessy and their children were there alone. Frequent visitors were their neighbours, the Tolletts of Betley, the Sneyds of Keele and the Caldwells of Linley Wood. On their frequent journeys between London and Yorkshire the Sydney Smiths usually stayed at Maer for a week or so. The clergyman Smith, one of the founders of the *Edinburgh Review*, a Whig supporter and member of the Holland House set, had a wit that enlivened any gathering. His jovial personality was in sharp contrast to that of the solemn Jos. 'Wedgwood is a good man,' Smith remarked. 'It is a pity he hates his friends.' And to Jos himself Smith said: 'You and I are exceptions to the laws of nature; you have risen by your gravity, and I have sunk by my levity.'

Smith always cheerfully agreed to preach a sermon in the small church at Maer. This event inevitably lifted the spirits of the congregation, though Smith earlier had observed of his own preaching: 'When I am in the pulpit, I have the pleasure of seeing my audience nod approbation while they sleep.'

The Smiths were, of course, friends of the Mackintoshes and Darwins as well as the Wedgwoods. Young Erasmus Darwin had been staying at Maer with his Uncle Jos and his cousins Frank and Hensleigh while his parents were in Bath with Aunt Bessy and other members of the family. Before the three little boys went back to school, their Aunt Kitty Mackintosh with her daughters Bessy and Fanny arrived for their four-month visit. Bessy described the Mackintosh nieces to their Allen aunts abroad: 'I never saw such two grave girls as the two Mackintoshes, but I think them both clever. Fanny seems to have a very clear head and a great deal of information very clearly arranged. She is a furious politician, as is likely, but I am not clear whether she is aware of the distinction that everybody ought to feel between patriotism and party spirit. Kitty is very kind and indulgent to them, but she has not accustomed them to prompt obedience.'9

Kitty's depressions did indeed seem to lift when she was apart from her husband. And, during this visit, Bessy felt that she and Kitty became closer and more sympathetic towards each other than at any time since their marriages. Both the sisters noted with pleasure and amusement the fascination that sixteen-year-old Fanny held for thirteen-year-old Hensleigh, who offered to help her transcribe some of the manuscripts Mackintosh was using in writing his History.

As for the other young Wedgwoods, Joe returned to Geneva, after a three-month stay in Italy, and wrote to his father that Harry was applying himself to moral philosophy, physics, mathematics, German and drawing lessons. From Geneva Joe then went to Basle and embarked upon a Rhine cruise which ended in Amsterdam, where he met his cousin Allen, who had been sent abroad because his parents were at their wits' end what to do with him. 'Allen does not much approve of the Dutchmen & says the English are as unpopular here as in the rest of Europe,' Joe reported. 'I cannot understand the reason of all this dislike against us. I was talking with a Saxon about it the other day & he seriously attributed it to our wearing long coats which the French look upon as a kind of insult of assumed superiority.'10

After the Napoleonic Wars an era of artificial prosperity set in. Paper money was issued in excess of gold reserves, interest rates were low, speculation increased, the values of stocks fluctuated from day to day, and prices rocketed to dizzying heights. Then followed the inevitable reaction; the markets were overstocked, liabilities could not be met, banks suspended payments and businesses failed.

In the spring of 1816, Davison & Co. entered into its worst and final financial crisis. The bank was unable to meet demands made against it, and the partners were quarrelling among themselves. Some threatened to resign, some demanded resignation from the others. Accusations of forgeries and misappropriation of funds were flung by partner against partner. John Wedgwood was first appalled, then frightened. A considerable share of his property had been invested in the company, and the whole of his property pledged for its debts. He confided the distressing circumstances to Jos who, being in London on business of his own, investigated the rumours and told his brother: 'I cannot conceive that the present partners can hold together for any time or for any useful purpose ... at the very time that you were using every exertion to save the house, D[avison] & N[oel] drew out each of them about £15,000, as if scrambling to get as much as they could from the wreck and that T[empler] sat quietly by & suffered this to be done. Such conduct makes one tremble for the stability of the house.'[11]

As usual John had told neither Jane nor Allen nor any other member of his immediate family about the bank's difficulties. In a panic he pretended that the awful predicament simply didn't exist. Though he had come to London and was going in to the Pall Mall offices daily, he began imagining another new kind of life for himself. When he read in the newspaper of a vacancy in a clerkship in the Canal office in Stone, he thought of applying for the position, and wrote his brother three letters on three successive days. In the third letter he asked Jos if he would 'perhaps speak or write in my favour to some leading man who might not be averse to my appointment. I have no doubt that the candidate recommended by the committee will be the successful one. The idea of eventually doing something to benefit my family by my own personal exertions is I confess consoling.' He then went on to say he had not mentioned this plan to Jane but that he was certain she would be as happy as he to move back to Staffordshire. He concluded: 'I am entirely convinced that a residence as clerk at Stone will lend much more to my happiness than as a partner in Pall Mall.'[12]

Jos replied that not only was such a position beneath his brother's social station but that John knew absolutely nothing about accounting procedures. John countered with a plan of hiring a bookkeeper to do the job for him while at the same time instructing him. Jos said quite firmly that such a plan was nonsense. 'You will be looked upon as a gentleman applying for a situation of business without being able to give the usual evidences in such cases of being competent to the employment.... My own opinion is that it is rather too late in life for you to make so very general & so great changes in your life.'[13]

Jos began to be concerned about John's mental state. As the situation at the bank worsened, he wrote directly to the partner George Templer to see if anything might be done to rescue the company from bankruptcy by advancing additional funds or by arranging for John and Templer to separate themselves from Alexander Davison and Sir Gerard Noel Noel. At this point Noel was in charge of the company and attempting to merge it with a larger bank and recoup his own investment if not those of his partners. After consultation with Bessy Jos decided that not only should Jane be informed of the imminent disaster at the bank but that the rest of the family should know as well.

Kitty and Sarah were at the time visiting the Darwins. All were distressed, though not actually surprised by the news. They stayed up late at night discussing possible courses of action for John to take. The following morning Sarah wrote to Jos:

If there is a probable chance of £5,000 being of any use in this emergency Kitty and I should be very glad to advance it without security, but we must leave to you to determine whether in that case it would be better to risk it or to keep it to assist John with. Sometimes I believe even a few thousands may keep on a house till other things come in. — We have no money I suppose but we could raise it could not we somehow? ... The doctor [Robert Darwin] bids me say that he has £2,500 in 4 per cent all of which you may have....[14]

As Jos had already loaned £9,547 in Exchequer bills to the company and there was considerable scepticism as to Sir Gerard Noel Noel's true intentions, the family decided against putting up more money to rescue Davison & Co. By August the bank was remaining open on a day-to-day basis. John finally told his wife — who of course, as in the previous crisis, had suspected the situation, 'tho' I believe it was proved by the immediate shock it gave me that I feared more that expected it.'

Jane was supportive and sympathetic, writing to Bessy and Jos:

How poor John has been able to endure as well as he has, what has been his lot for the last few months, I cannot tell, but I have the comfort of thinking that his health is not hurt by it, and for the future, whatever may betide us, I am sure his load will be the lighter for our participation. If reserve were not incurable, I should hope he would lose the habit of being so from his late sufferings, and the relief I am sure he has had from opening his mind; at the same time I must bear testimony to the beauty of his temper, which with such a load on his heart has never for an instant been betrayed into the slightest irritation, nor indeed has it made him withdraw from general sympathy in what was happening round him.[15]

Once the situation was known to everyone, Jos and Bessy went to London to be with John and Jane during this anxious time. Kitty Mackintosh and her two daughters stayed on at Maer Hall with the four Wedgwood daughters, who ranged in age from eight-year-old Emma to twenty-three-year old Elizabeth. Bessy Mackintosh, now aged twelve, had become an invalid. To the family's distress, Robert Darwin pronounced her incurable with only ten years at most to live.

On 22 August 1816, Coutts took over Davison & Co., thus rescuing it from the disgrace of bankruptcy. 'It is wonderful to see the composure with which they all bear the wreck of their fortunes, now they are secure of not being in the Gazette,' Bessy wrote from London to her sisters abroad. 'That evil appeared so enormous that everything else is thought light in the comparison. They [i.e. John and Jane] will now stay with us till some arrangement can be made as to their future plans....'[16]

Thus, as the impecunious Mackintoshes left Maer with fading hopes as to Mack's political future, the John Wedgwoods returned destitute and dependent upon the good will of the rest of the family.

18

A Wise and Masterly Inactivity
(1817 – 1823)

After the takeover of the bank, Jos, Kitty, Sarah and the Darwins together gave £6,000 to be placed in trust for John. They all took it for granted that some of the capital invested would be recouped when the Davison affairs were finally settled, though exactly how much this would be was uncertain. Jos's friend and neighbour, James Tollett of Betley Hall, offered John and Jane a house in Betley at a very small rent. He said that he and his family would enjoy the pleasure of their company. After several months at Maer, John and Jane accepted his offer.

Baring Place and its furnishings were sold at auction. The move from Exeter and the close companionship with Caroline Drewe was not such a wrench as it might have been had Caroline herself not been leaving. Her eldest daughter Harriet was marrying Robert, Lord Gifford. It was now all too clear that her two youngest children, like their father before them, were dying of consumption. Caroline had decided to take them and her two older girls, Marianne and Georgina, to Italy. Thus, it was arranged that she would join her three unmarried sisters who were in Pisa.

Sismondi also had met the party in Pisa and declared his love for Jessie. She promptly refused his proposal of marriage, declaring that she could never settle permanently away from England or from her family. Sismondi refused to take no for an answer. They would continue as friends and companions while the Allen sisters were in Italy but with no discussion of marriage. He was convinced that by becoming accustomed to his daily presence Jessie would eventually change her mind.

Back in England, Jos and Robert Darwin tried to sort out the financial tangle which John's misfortune coupled with the economic instability of the country as a whole, had precipitated. Robert wanted to invest in more property, but much of his capital was tied up in loans to his brothers-in-law. 'I have to pay off the remainder of the mortgage on Maer at Lady Day which is £4,000,' Jos told him.

I could not immediately pay more than £3,000 in addition to that but I fully rely on receiving sums on the settlement of Davison's affairs which would enable me to pay £7,000 more and which I hope will be in a very few months. You might rely upon £10,000 from me in a few months. If business should revive, I should not doubt of being able to increase that sum in the course of the present year, but at present, I see no sign of encouragement.... I should conceive the present is a favourable moment for making purchases of land, but much wiser heads than mine are unable to see into the future. The circumstances that have occured since the peace have been so different from expectations that I do not know how to guess at what is to happen.[1]

Jos's expectations from the settlement of the Davison affairs were uncertain also. Various loans which he fully expected to be repaid in full were, according to Davison & Co., subject to Extent. There were discrepancies between Jos's records and those of the bank: certain letters or papers were inexplicably missing and, according to Sir Gerard Noel Noel, nonexistent. When John went to see Sir Gerard, he refused to admit him. Nor would he answer John's letters.

In Parliament, though the Whigs were destined to remain in Opposition for many years to come, Mackintosh was beginning to exercise some influence. In May of 1817 he took up the cause of Mary Ryan, an illiterate woman sentenced to a month's imprisonment after she had made a vain attempt to help her husband escape from prison. Ryan had been convicted of highway robbery and sentenced to public execution. When, on the very day of the execution, the widow with her orphaned infant was forced to begin her own prison sentence, there was a public outcry. Mackintosh spoke eloquently in the Commons for about half an hour before moving a free pardon for Mary Ryan. The speech was well received on both sides of the House. The motion was carried, and Mackintosh himself gained considerable praise. In Ireland Edgeworth and Maria read of the case and wrote to Mackintosh enclosing a donation which they wished him to give to Mary Ryan.

A few weeks later Mackintosh wrote to the Edgeworths telling them he had personally given their contribution to the 'deeply affected woman'. 'Nothing could have gratified me more truly than your approbation of my efforts to obtain retribution for a shocking outrage on the decorum of public justice,' Mackintosh said. He then went on to talk of literary matters, of Maria's work, of Scott and of Southey. 'Madame de Staël', he told them, 'is on her death-bed, full of vivacity and courage.'[2]

Sadly, by the time this letter was received Edgeworth himself was dead. Within the next three years, two other close friends of Josiah I and members of the original Lunar group, Keir and Watt, were to die also.

Madame de Staël's death was as dramatic as her life. In Paris in February 1817, as she was making her entrance in full evening dress, turban and feathers at a grand reception given by a minister of Louis XVIII, she collapsed in front of the gasping assemblage, felled by a stroke. Paralysed and unable to speak, she lived on until the middle of July, when she died of an overdose of opium administered by her close friend and servant, Fanny Randall.

Her death went unmourned and practically unnoticed by the Wedgwoods. During the same week they were caught up in their own family drama. Susan Darwin was suddenly taken ill with severe stomach pains. After forty-eight hours, during which her condition rapidly worsened, Robert sent for her sisters Kitty and Sarah. 'It is impossible to have a worse account than I have to give,' Kitty wrote to Jos.

> The Doctor has not the slightest hope & her suffering is terrible. The pain indeed is gone that was her first illness, but she has such severe vomitings and sickness that he says he does not think her suffering much lessened ... this evening she is worse, & he is very wretched.... He was afraid our seeing her would agitate her & she does not know we are here. Marianne & Caroline are always with her & keep up pretty well.... The Doctor has just been to tell us he does not think she will pass the night & unless I add a postscript in the morning you may conclude all is over.[3]

There was no postscript. Susan died of peritonitis a few hours after Kitty sealed her letter. Sarah wrote to Jos on the following day, Thursday, telling him that the funeral would be on Monday 'but the Doctor would be glad to see you and John sooner if it is convenient to you. He is obliged to go tomorrow to Denbigh to see a patient who is very dangerously ill; he will return on Saturday evening. He thinks the journey and being obliged to think of other things will do him good.'[4]

The Jos Wedgwoods and John Wedgwoods left together in a carriage for Shrewsbury within hours after receiving Sarah's letter. The Darwin boys, Erasmus and Charles, stayed at home from Shrewsbury School. Years later Charles, who was eight years old at the time, recollected little of his mother except her death-bed and the black velvet gown in which she was buried. The women busied themselves comforting the older girls and looking after the little children. No one knew how to comfort Robert. The unexpected death of Susan at the comparatively early age of fifty-two was a blow from which he never fully recovered. 'To know that we have fulfilled our duty towards the objects of affection whose loss we deplore is one of the most sure sources of consolation,' Jos wrote to him, 'and I trust that you will receive that reward for your uniform kind and tender care of my sister. I trust too that our long friendship and brotherly love will suffer no abatement from the removal of her who loved us both so well....'[5]

The feeling of brotherhood between the two men was, if anything, strengthened. From that time on, however, the Wedgwood children protested against being sent on lengthy visits to The Mount, where they were never certain of the Doctor's moods. The depression which occasionally had struck him in the past seemed never to lift now, and the atmosphere at The Mount was one of never-ending gloom. Robert's wit turned to sarcasm and bullying, and he alternated between periods of frantic activity and periods of exhaustion. All six Darwin children were in a state of perpetual tension, and they spent ever more time at Maer.

Following Susan's death, Robert apparently decided not to draw on his share of the pottery's profits for the preceding year. A few weeks earlier, he had given an additional £2,000 to John, instructing Jos to add it to John's trust fund. Jos was concerned as to exactly how this should be entered into the firm's books, 'though John is clear of all claims and encumbrances yet as one can never be sure of what may arise in the Court of Chancery or elsewhere from such great and complicated concerns, I would advise that it should be secured against any possible claims of his present or future creditors.'[6]

In London James Mackintosh, now aged fifty-three and four times a grandfather by his daughter Maitland Erskine, was beginning to feel the pressures of time passing and opportunities missed. 'How few now remain of those who were kind to my childhood, or whom my boyish promise filled with hope and pride!'[7] he wrote in his journal. Still, even at this late stage in his life, Mackintosh seemed more fascinated by the style of his own performance than by either its content or its purpose. 'Dined at Holland House,' he noted. 'Kept up an almost constant laugh, though by means of puns and small jokes. It was only small beer; but it sparkled and produced the effect of noble liquor.'[8] He continued to support the abolitionist cause, associating with Wilberforce, Romilly, Brougham and Stephens. He felt keenly Romilly's suicide in 1818 following the death of his wife. Romilly's niece Caroline Romilly had become engaged to Baugh Allen, though permission had not yet been granted for Baugh, in his position as a don at Dulwich College, to marry.

Mackintosh's most worthwhile project during this period was lobbying in Parliament for a committee to enquire into the means of preventing the forgery of bank notes. The problems within the banking industry as it was then structured had been forcefully brought to his attention by the difficulties of his brother-in-law John Wedgwood.

Mackintosh was, of course, still having his own financial problems. Because he was unable to discipline himself to writing and therefore could not rely on a steady income from this source, he accepted a position as Professor of Law and General Politics at the East India College at Haileybury and moved his family to near-by Mardocks in Hertfordshire. The position required little exertion on his part, as he could use lectures he had given in the past; and he was able to be in London when Parliament was in session. On the whole, he himself was practising what a quarter of a century earlier he had described in *Vindicae Gallicae* as 'a wise and masterly inactivity'.

Equally desirous of a life of 'wise and masterly inactivity' was Jos. After the unpleasantness of John's muddled affairs at the bank, the shock of the death of Susan and the sad news from Italy that Caroline Drewe's two younger children had died of consumption, Jos began to think of some cheerful family project. The travels of Joe and Harry and the social life of the Allen sisters on the Continent stirred his imagination. 'Going abroad is still one of papa's castles in the air,' Elizabeth Wedgwood wrote to her Aunt Fanny Allen, 'but I do not feel as if it would be accomplished.'[9]

She was wrong. In March of 1818 Jos and Bessy and their four daughters, then ranging in age from nine to twenty-four, and John's twenty-two-year-old daughter Eliza, went to Paris for a six-month stay. They took a house in the rue Caumartin in 'the genteelest part of Town'. Through Mackintosh and Maria Edgeworth they had introductions to the fashionable literary salons. At Madame Récamier's salon they met the Queen of Sweden. They attended a soirée at Madame Catalani's, and they were part of the grand procession at Longchamp. Their Staffordshire neighbours the Caldwells had also taken a house in Paris, and Kitty Wedgwood later joined her brother and the Paris group.

Sarah moved into Maer while alterations were being made to Parkfields. In the evenings she had the companionship of her nephew Joe, who was the only member of the family left at Maer. In the absence of his father, Joe was in charge of the pottery, a rather anomalous situation since, at the same time, he was supposedly learning the business. Harry had been sent to Cambridge to study law. Frank and Hensleigh were still at Rugby.

Jos and Kitty returned to England in late May, leaving Bessy and the girls in Paris. Constant and Sismondi, whom Charlotte Wedgwood described as 'not as ugly as he had been represented', were in attendance to escort the six ladies to a seemingly endless round of parties.

The three unmarried Allen sisters and Caroline Drewe were still in Italy. After three years abroad, they were at last making plans to return to England. Jessie had relented sufficiently to tell Sismondi, before he left Italy for Paris, that she would reconsider his proposal on the condition that they not see one another for a year, so as to determine if they could live happily apart. Only as a last resort should they 'take the remedy of marriage'.

Jos had three purposes in returning to England. He wished to check on the situation at the pottery, to collect Frank and Hensleigh from school and to consult with his London solicitor, Robert Dennett, about an unexpected situation which had arisen over the still unsettled affairs of Davison & Co. Jos had recovered neither the sums of money nor the stock owed to him by the late firm of Davison & Co and by Sir Gerard Noel Noel personally. In view of his promise to repay his own debts to Robert Darwin, the situation was highly embarrassing. Worse still, Jos had made serious errors in judgement in allowing some loans which he had not realized were subject to Extents, and by making personal loans to Noel. All of this had been done at John's request and with the advice of William Leake, Davison & Co's solicitor.

After the break-up of the partnership, Leake sided with Noel against John, apparently in the last few months of the bank's existence advising both John and Jos against their own best interests and secretly aiding Noel and Davison to recover their investments at the expense of the other partners. Jos threatened to take legal action against the late firm of Davison & Co. and against Sir Gerard Noel Noel, whereupon Noel obtained an injunction from the Solicitor-General to prevent proceedings against him, at the same time filing a writ against Jos over certain stocks and bills which he claimed had become the property of Davison & Co. The situation had become so tangled and unpleasant that it was now entirely in the hands of the lawyers.

Relations between Jos and John were further strained. John did not want the public humiliation of a law suit with all the attendant publicity and the revelation of the deceptions and blunders within the firm. Jos didn't give a damn about publicity or unseemly revelations; he felt he had been cheated and, one way or another, he wanted his money back. Both brothers sought advice from Robert Darwin. For once Robert agreed with John. There was no chance of recovering all of the money. There would be less to lose with Noel suing John than with Jos suing Noel.

Jos returned to Paris in June with Frank and Hensleigh. He placed the two little girls, Fanny and Emma, in boarding school. Then he, Bessy and the older girls, Elizabeth and Charlotte, and John's daughter Eliza went to Switzerland to put Frank and Hensleigh in M. Chenevière's boarding school where Harry had been.

In September of 1818 the Allen sisters returned with the Jos Wedgwoods to England. Fanny Allen went to stay with the Mackintoshes in Hertford-shire. Emma and Jessie returned to Cresselly to stay with their brother John, his fractious wife Gertrude and their three incorrigible young sons.

Jessie was in a quandary about her feelings for Sismondi. 'I love him more than I would allow even to myself,' she confessed to Bessy, 'and I begin to think I cannot be happy separate for ever from him.'[10] She also confided in her brother John her contradictory desires both to be with Sismondi and at the same time not to be separated from her family and in a foreign land. John's feelings were equally ambivalent. He said that her marriage would be to him the same as if she 'took the veil in a distant country', but that he would rather not see her at all than see her unhappy. This was the attitude of Baugh and of the other sisters, except Fanny who persisted in her dislike of Sismondi, citing what she called his 'physical repulsiveness'. Bessy, how-ever, most strongly urged Jessie not to think of her family at all but to think of herself. 'We have all made our election without reference to you, and you have a full right to do the same.... *We* risk the loss of a very great pleasure, but *you* risk the happiness of your life.... I think you cannot be happy in giving up the man you love, and I see no reason to doubt your being happy with him.'[11]

With this encouragement Jessie wrote to Sismondi accepting his proposal. Two months later he came to England, where he received considerable attention from the London literary world. The marriage of Jessie and Sismondi took place on the morning of 19 April 1819 at Jeffreyston Church, Pembrokeshire. After the ceremony they drove straight off to London. There they spent a few days with the Mackintoshes before leaving England. Bessy was at Cresselly and attended the wedding with the other Allen brothers and sisters, all except Fanny who refused to go to the service. Later on the same day Fanny wrote her first letter to Madame Sismondi:

> You have been fully aware I think that I have noticed you little and avoided being alone with you to spare our feelings. For this reason I went into the garden this morning to avoid seeing you go. But ten thousand wishes for your happiness accompanied you and I do not doubt you will find it as soon as the bitterness of parting is over. Bessy and the girls returned from the church so quickly, that I could scarcely credit they had been there — they all looked so well it was quite a pretty sight. Bessy

then cut the cake and then made up the parcels and we all walked in the garden till 2 talking of you. A couple of years will soon pass away and then we shall see each other again.[12]

Two months after Jessie's marriage, Baugh Allen resigned his mastership at Dulwich College and married Caroline Romilly. The Mackintoshes leased their house in London, and Mackintosh stayed at Holland House while Kitty and the two girls visited Edinburgh for several weeks, returning by way of Staffordshire where they spent another month with the Jos Wedgwoods. Kitty's depressions and irritability, a reflection of her feelings of homelessness and financial insecurity, increased rather than lessened over the years. In the company of her sister Bessy, however, she was more relaxed and seemed better able to accept her lot in life.

'Kitty M. and her daughters went on Wednesday, and her visit here was entirely agreeable from beginning to end,' Bessy wrote to Jessie Sismondi in Switzerland.

She was kind and affectionate to me and good-humoured and agreeable to everybody. I think I may say with truth that no cloud ever interrupted the pleasure I had in her company. Her girls seem very happy with her, and though she gives them multitudes of directions, as she neither insists upon obedience, nor gets out of humour when she is not obeyed, it does not interrupt the general harmony. It had only this bad effect that *Fanny* [Mackintosh] constantly mounts the opposition coach and drives it with the most uninterrupted composure.[13]

At the time Fanny was twenty years old, tall and dark like her mother, scholarly and political like her father, strong-willed and adventurous like her half-sister Mary Rich.

For the past two years Mackintosh had been trying to get a better post for his son-in-law Claudius Rich. He made unsuccessful approaches both to the East India Company and the Crown Office for what he thought were better appointments, such as the Residency at Surat or Customs Master in Bombay. But, at the beginning of 1820, when George III finally died, Rich was still the East India Company Resident at Baghdad.

In the autumn of 1820, after a number of illnesses and arguments with the dishonest despot Daoud Pasha, Rich and Mary, with the Persian secretary Seid Aga, various officers of the Residency and a large retinue of servants, left Baghdad for a six-month visit to Kurdistan, then a country unknown to Europeans and unsurveyed. Mary Rich travelled through the towns like a Turkish lady, in a covered mule litter, so she would not be seen by the male population and thereby undermine the dignity of the party. It was a happy journey, despite heavy rains, the discomfort of their accommodations and Rich's perpetual ill health. He and Mahmud Pasha of Sulimania became close friends, bridging the formidable cultural gap between them. Unfortunately Rich's relations with Daoud Pasha of Baghdad, which had always been poor, worsened during his absence, so that upon their return he and Mary were refused entry back into the city. When they entered anyway, they were held captive in the Residency. The Governor of Bombay demanded their immediate release and public reparation for the insult which the Pasha had dealt the British nation. While the Pasha was certainly treacherous, cruel and greedy, Rich's arrogance and British chauvinism also amounted to insult.

'It is a proud distinction for the British Government', Rich commented, 'that even in these barbarous climes such is the general opinion of its justice and confidence in its honour, that a dispute with it is sure to render the native Prince unpopular, even with the savage clans who can form no opinion on the merits of the case....'[14] Rich and Mary finally escaped by fostering the false rumour that Rich had been offered and accepted the Residency at Surat, as it was well known in Baghdad that Mackintosh had been trying to get the post for him. Daoud Pasha was so anxious to be rid of this annoying Englishman and to return in peace to his corrupt dealings with the East India Company that he believed the rumour and permitted Rich and Mary to leave Baghdad.

Back in Staffordshire Maria Edgeworth visited the Darwins and the Wedgwoods. Like her father, she was sentimental about old friendships. After her father's death, she completed his *Memoirs* and took over the management of the Edgeworth estate. She and Scott became close friends and literary confidants. Though she wrote several distinguished books after her father's death, she was denigrating of her own work. On the Continent her reputation was at its highest; in England it was beginning to suffer from the inevitable comparison with Jane Austen. At Maer, Maria's modesty and humour made her an easy member of the household.

Parkfields, as well as Maer, was coming in for its share of literary activity. Ten years after Mackintosh had reneged on his commission to edit Tom's papers on metaphysics, saying that the manuscripts had been in a trunk lost at sea on his return voyage from India, Sarah Wedgwood decided that she, if no one else, would attempt to put Tom's ideas on paper. John gave her some of Tom's papers which he had found in the cellars at Etruria Hall, and she began work. Unfortunately Sarah was not a Maria Edgeworth. Her comprehension of her brother's intentions was, however, far greater than either John's or Jos's. Still she deferred to their opinions. 'These are part of the papers that you were so kind as to express a wish of seeing,' she told Jos. 'I shall be very much obliged to you if you will read them with a very critical disposition.... I mean that I shall be very glad if you will tell me whatever you think is false, but I still more desire to know what you think too evidently true to be worth mentioning or too trifling, & what parts you think tedious or in any way disagreeable....'[15]

Jos apparently took her at her word, for she wrote again how obliged she was to him for his useful remarks, as 'I am convinced that a great many of the things mentioned as wrong are so, & many other things I shall be able to make much clearer in consequence of your pointing out where they are obscure.'[16] Sarah revised the essay. It was printed privately and circulated among the family and their close friends.

While Sarah was at work on Tom's papers at Parkfields, Kitty Wedgwood went to London with Fanny and Emma Allen. Jessie Sismondi had returned to England for a visit, and the three unmarried women planned to accompany her back to Chêne, her home in Switzerland. There was some concern as to whether Kitty ought to make the journey. She had not been feeling well for several months. Robert Darwin had diagnosed a tumour of the stomach. 'I do not think there is now any degree of soreness in the tumour,' Sarah told Jos. 'She thinks that the soreness the other day was merely owing to indigestion. I believe these accidental things, such as a hard coughing fit, for instance, will occasionally cause that soreness when the tumour itself is not in a worse state than usual.'[17]

Not having seen his sister for several months, John Wedgwood wrote to Jos how shocked he was at 'how huge Kitty has become'. She had gained nearly three stone. John was further shocked by yet another setback in his own affairs. Earlier Jos had suggested to him that he take his family abroad, possibly to Paris, in order to escape all the debts and lawsuits against him. A few months later, at the lawyer Dennett's suggestion, John wrote a letter to Jos in which he assumed all responsibility for the debts which Jos had incurred:

> Considering that you have long had large sums of stocks & money owing to you by the late firm of Alexander Davison & Co & by Sir Gerard Noel Noel, all of which you advanced at my request & refrained from taking proceedings for removing the injunction obtained by Mr Davison against your proceeding to judgement in your suit against them ... I think it proper to assure you that as you have in all these transactions been guided by my desire & acted entirely with a view to my interest — without the possibility of making any profits or deriving any advantage whatsoever from the risks you have incurred or from the length of time you have been without the use of your capital, I owe myself responsible to you to make up in the fullest manner any losses that you may thereby eventually sustain. And whereas I have requested the Attorney General to compromise the questions in dispute between me & Sir Gerard Noel Noel ... I hereby engage & undertake to indemnify you for such sacrifice by paying and satisfying all your said claims....

He then went on to list all the amounts owed to Jos. 'This I believe to be a true account & which I hereby engage to take on myself & shall esteem myself highly obliged to you for your long forbearance & for the assistance you so readily furnished at the time of our greatest need.'[18]

The obvious result of this agreement was that John would sustain all of the losses and forever be in debt to his brother. Even if Jos were forced to contribute more to the upkeep of John and his family, from his point of view this was preferable to the loss of his own investments and source of future income. That Dennett agreed to John's reaching a compromise over the matters in dispute with Davison and Noel was to assume that John had made blunders which did indeed contribute to the decline of the company. Someone had to bear responsibility for the losses and suffer the consequences. As one of a group of naïve bumblers and unethical manipulators,

John was the perfect candidate for scapegoat. If Jos chose to protect his own interests first, he might perhaps be excused in view of his brother's past record of unwise business judgements. At the age of fifty-five John was not likely to develop either the shrewdness or the competitiveness which the world of commerce required. 'Dr Darwin & Catherine & Sarah', wrote Jos, 'have placed £1,500 in my hands as Trustee for you and your family to which I have added the like amount of £1,500 in order to secure an adequate income for your support & a future provision for your family on the occasion of your great loss of the final arrangement with Sir Gerard Noel Noel....'[19]

This was the third trust fund set up by the family for John. The £1,500 which Jos contributed was approximately one-eighth of the loss he would have sustained had John not assumed full responsibility for his brother's losses as well as for his own. That Jos was also guilty of poor business judgement was no secret. John wrote to Jos from Shrewsbury that their brother-in-law Robert, whom he called 'our fat friend', said he hopes 'you have learned your lesson and will sign no more agreements with Extents'.

After a lengthy stay at The Mount, the homeless John and Jane did decide to go abroad for a few months, not to escape the lawsuits which were now over, but to recover from the strain. They were also concerned about the health of their son Allen and their second daughter Caroline, both of whom Robert Darwin had diagnosed as consumptive.

Bessy had gone to London in April of 1821 to stay with Kitty Mackintosh. The sisters wanted a last visit with Jessie Sismondi before she returned to Switzerland with Emma and Fanny Allen and Kitty Wedgwood.

While they were in London, John Allen's father-in-law, Lord Robert Seymour, took Bessy, Jessie Sismondi and Kitty Wedgwood on a tour of the newly built Bethlem Royal Hospital, popularly known as Bedlam. Kitty Wedgwood strongly supported prison reform for women. She had taken considerable interest in improvements made in the conditions at the Liverpool and Stafford gaols. Bessy, who was 'very much interested and not much shocked', described their visit to Bedlam to Jos:

> The first thing that struck me was the magnificence of the building, which is one absurd expenditure of the funds. Lord Robert went over the whole. Every cell was unlocked before us and these cleaner than most gentlemen's houses. The galleries were warmed with stoves but not sufficiently, but there were fires in many of the sitting-rooms and there was no female under constant confinement.... Lord Robert's behaviour to all was strikingly kind, he took many of the poor women by the hand while he comforted them with the hope that if they behaved quite quiet he would represent the case to the Governors which was all he could do; he cautioned us against speaking too much to the prisoners for fear of exciting them. They all knew him perfectly well. The nurses seemed respectable and humane in their conduct, while we were going through one of the Galleries one of the maniacs rushed out of her cell and stood in an attitude that might have been a study for a painting. Her draperies hung about her in a very picturesque manner, her arms were extended

and her ravings were in a voice that seemed more than human, but the nurse put her back into her cell before we had more than a glance of her figure, and she continued her ravings. Kitty stood listening a short time after the door was closed, but the ravings were incoherent about Jupiter and Juno. We went into an enclosed yard turfed with gravel walks and there we found a great many women walking about.... One woman began to rave at us but she was immediately taken off. But what interested me was a very pretty girl among the incurables. She had the prettiest manner I ever saw, she was exceedingly lively, said she was as happy as the day was long, that Miss Forbes the Matron allowed her to call her Mamma, and always told her when she was wrong. She did not seem above twenty.... I felt quite sorry to leave her in this dismal yard surrounded by all the maniacs, some walking about in a melancholy way & some in straight waistcoats and some inclined to raving. This poor girl had been a governess in Lord Bute's family and her sister is confined in a private mad house. The Physician said she was sometimes very outrageous, tearing off her clothes, but nobody could have guessed her to be insane by her appearance or manner. — After this we went among the criminals, they were all dismal and walking backwards and forwards in their cells and some at liberty. After spending two or three hours there Lord Robert put us down at Mr Hope's where we met Mrs Holland and Kitty [Mackintosh] and looked at a fine collection of pictures and all that magnificence could do in furniture.[20]

The Hope family were great patrons of the arts and collectors of Wedgwood. They were among the subscribers to the first edition of the Portland Vase in 1789.

As the Allen sisters parted after their reunion in London, Claudius and Mary Rich arrived in Bushire where the East India Company owned a factory presided over by an agent. There Rich received praise from London, Constantinople and Bombay for his decisive action in Baghdad, but as yet there was no new posting. Both he and Mary were in poor health, suffering from the chills and fever endemic to that part of the world. On 26 June 1821, Mary sailed from Bushire for Bombay, where she would stay with the Erskines while Rich went to the milder climate of Shiraz to wait for orders for his next posting.

In Bombay Mary and the Erskines and their five small children had a happy reunion. Mary soon regained her strength. At the time all was going well for the Erskines. William had been made Master in Equity in the Recorder's Court in Bombay. He was a member of the committee which drew up the celebrated Bombay Code of Regulations. He retained his interest in Persian studies and, following a success with *Babar's Memoirs*, continued to make other translations.

From Persia Rich wrote to Mary of the beginnings of the magnificent week-long wedding festivities of the Prince of Shiraz, the second son of the Shahzada who was the heir apparent to the Persian throne. He wrote to his wife almost daily, giving a journal-like account of his activities. Then the letters suddenly stopped. Each day thereafter when a ship was expected from the Persian Gulf, Mary went down to the docks to ask the captain what was the news from Persia. The news was that an epidemic of cholera was raging across the country. The town of Shiraz was decimated and those surviving panic-stricken. The young prince's wife died during her wedding festivities, and the Shahzada himself fled in terror leaving his own mother to die alone by the roadside. Government ceased to exist. Within two weeks the death toll was over 5,000. A small number of British subjects were confined to their quarters at the Jehan Numa, where they felt comparatively safe in their isolated garden. No place, however, was proof against the disease. On 4 October 1821, Rich, already weakened from his earlier bouts of fever, was seized with sudden violent spasms. Within twenty-four hours he, too, was dead from cholera. He was aged thirty-five.

Three weeks later William Erskine learned of his death in a letter from the East India Company while Mary was at the docks enquiring the latest word from Persia. When Erskine came home from his office and gave her the unhappy news, she fell to the floor unconscious. Overnight her hair turned snowy white. For weeks she appeared dazed. Her sister and brother-in-law feared that her reason might never return. One day as she held her baby nephew Claudius, named after his uncle, she burst into tears and uncontrollable sobbing. From then on she was in perfect control of her senses and reason, but she was a changed personality. She requested that no one ever utter aloud in her presence the name of Claudius Rich.

Back in England, Mackintosh wrote to Mary, urging her to return and live with him and Kitty. Mary, at first, was somewhat reluctant — as, indeed, was Kitty to have her. Mackintosh was instrumental in securing for Mary a pension of £200 a year from the East India Company and in initiating negotiations with the British Museum for the purchase of Rich's vast collection of Oriental manuscripts, coins and sculpture. The collection was eventually purchased for £7,000 — and Mary decided to return to England.

In January of 1822, the Dovelies went to London to Mrs Mayer's finishing school at Greville House on Paddington Green. Frank and Hensleigh were at Christ's College, Cambridge; Harry had finished his studies at Cambridge and was studying mathematics and physical science with the famed Mrs Somerville, for whom Somerville College, Oxford, was named. Joe was at home at Maer. Every day he rode on horseback to work at the pottery with his father.

In the spring Bessy had a bad fall from a horse and broke her arm. She was then fifty-eight years old. 'I think I shall not ride much any more,' she wrote to Jessie. 'I am grown timid, and my arm continues weak. I don't think, however, it would hinder me if my spirit was better. However, when I have got my Shandredan [a small one-horse phaeton] I shall not want to ride.'[21] She never did recover sufficient courage to ride again. Nor did she any longer enjoy the long walks through the fields and over the wild heath of Maer. Not to lose the companionship of Elizabeth and Charlotte, she rode a little donkey named Peggy while the girls walked beside her.

While Bessy was slowly mending, Kitty Wedgwood grew steadily worse. In the spring of 1823 her condition had worsened to the extent that she and Sarah moved to Shrewsbury where she could be under the constant care of

Robert Darwin. It was a long-drawn-out and painful death which exhausted the emotions of everyone in the household. In August of 1823, Sarah wrote to Jos that Kitty 'expired about 7 o'clock this evening. She lived much longer than the Doctor expected, she retained perfect use of her faculties and quickness till within an hour or two of her death when she appeared a little confused. We will write again in a few days to say how everybody is; I hope Marianne & Caroline will bear it pretty well. They have nursed her with heroical fortitude ... the Doctor has had great fatigue, he expects a long sound sleep tonight, which I hope he will have. He is much obliged to you but does not wish to see you just at present.'[22]

Jos was somewhat concerned at Robert's not wanting to see him at that time. He had sent his brother-in-law the accounts, which were audited in July, and which were worse than expected. For the past eleven years, from 1812 to 1823, Jos had been in sole charge of the pottery. He had now reached two major decisions with regard to both the family and the pottery. In spite of Joe's indifference, which his father fully appreciated, he would be taken into the business as a partner. The other decision was that Harry would have to practise law. In Jos's opinion Harry had no more aptitude for business and no more common sense than his uncle John. Under no circumstances was Harry to be brought into the family business.

19

Advanced Christians
(1823 – 1830)

When James Mackintosh first returned from India, he noted that during his absence a new phrase had crept into everyday language. That phrase was 'an advanced Christian'. It had originated in the Evangelical movement and meant good, virtuous and tranquil.

Evangelicalism was a state of mind, a spirit of resolution constantly invigorated by prayer, meditation and self-searching. It was the new 'vital religion' within the Established Church, and it did for the well-to-do, educated classes what Methodism had done for the poor and illiterate in the eighteenth century. Wesley, who died in 1791, had not actually separated the Methodist societies from the Church of England; but, in fact, he had created a new sect with its own organization. It preached the evangelical doctrine of personal salvation through a state of grace. Signs of the state of grace were observance of the Sabbath day, regular prayer, daily Bible reading, abstention from alcohol and gambling, and a stern objection to all frivolous pursuits.

The phrase 'an advanced Christian' was used most frequently in describing the acceptance of personal tragedy. Caroline Drewe became an advanced Christian when she accepted as God's divine will the painful deaths of her husband and three of her children. Caroline influenced the John Wedgwoods, and Kitty Mackintosh who had already been exposed to Evangelicalism through a number of her husband's political colleagues. Apart from Cambridge, the most important concentration of Evangelicals was in South London, the so-called 'Clapham Sect'. It centred on Thomas Macaulay's father Zaccariah Macaulay, a merchant who for fifteen years was manager of the Evangelical journal, the *Christian Observer*. The real leader of the Clapham Sect, however, was William Wilberforce, who had been converted to Evangelical Christianity after a visit to the Continent in 1785. Other members of the Clapham Sect included the wealthy banker and M.P. for Surrey, Henry Thornton, the lawyer James Stephens and the former Governor-General of India, John Shore, later first Baron Teignmouth.

Another person ripe for conversion to Evangelical beliefs was Mary

Rich. Before she returned to England in 1823, her brother-in-law William Erskine had been accused of defalcation and removed from his offices at Court in Bombay. He had to post a heavy security before he and Maitland and their children could leave India. They decided to go back to Erskine's home in Edinburgh, but Erskine's health was so broken by the publicity of his disgrace that the family decided to take the long way round and return to Scotland by way of China. Mary Rich had sailed straight for England.

In England the Mackintoshes were as usual leading an unsettled life. After Mackintosh had completed his final term as Professor at the East India College at Haileybury, they moved from Mardocks back to London, to a house in Cadogan Place. Their daughter Elizabeth had died of cancer, as Robert Darwin had predicted, at the age of nineteen, and was buried in the Hampstead parish churchyard; a tablet inscribed to her memory was placed inside the church. The Hampstead parish church was a stronghold of the Evangelicals. It had a large proportion of Scots in the congregation and also many prominent literary figures, including Joanna Baillie, whom Mackintosh greatly admired. While Jos's daughter Elizabeth Wedgwood was in London visiting the Swinton Hollands in Russell Square, her mother wrote to her: 'I beg you will as much as you can attend to your aunt Mackintosh, whose feelings at this time are, I fear, a little sore, and whose share of happiness is, alas, too slender....'[1]

Within a few months, however, the Mackintoshes were again back in the country, this time as permanent guests at Ampthill Park in Bedfordshire, the country seat of Lord Holland. Ampthill Park was cold and gloomy and in a run-down condition. Lord Holland seldom went there himself. Mary Rich had once again become a part of the Mackintosh household, and the old tensions between her and Kitty were aggravated. Possibly they were too much alike. Both were strong-willed women with jealous and possessive dispositions, both were intelligent and highly articulate, and both were dedicated to humanitarian causes — though they seldom chose the same cause at the same time. Mackintosh himself pompously described Kitty as 'an upright and pious woman, formed for devoted affection who employed a strong understanding & a resolute spirit in unwearied attempts to relieve every suffering under her view'.[2]

Jessie Sismondi wrote to Bessy that she had heard that 'Mackintosh's history was in great forwardness, that he had this winter read parts of the first volume to Lord Holland, who liked it very much, and it would be published in the spring. How I wish the news were true.'[3] At this point everyone acknowledged Mackintosh's brilliance, only no one expected anything to come of it.

For all members of the Mackintosh family the one good thing about the move to Ampthill was their neighbour, Sir Robert Inglis. He and his wife had adopted the two orphaned daughters of Henry Thornton, although the girls were but a few years younger than their foster parents. Lady Inglis and Mary Rich began a friendship that was to last throughout their lives, and Fanny and the Thornton girls, Marianne and Henrietta, became close friends. All were fervent Evangelicals and their proximity reinforced their convictions.

The John Wedgwoods, who were already inclined towards Evangelicalism, were further influenced by the evangelist-physician Dr Henry Baron. After their return from abroad in the autumn of 1824, they went to Gloucester to seek Dr Baron's care for their three ailing children, Eliza, Allen and Caroline. Dr Baron had had some 'miracle successes' in curing consumptives and was recommended by Robert Darwin. The Wedgwoods were soon joined in Gloucester by John Allen, with his wife Gertrude who also had consumption. Eliza and Allen recovered to live lives of perpetual invalidism, but both Caroline Wedgwood and Gertrude Allen died in January of 1825.

These deaths altered the lives of both families. Emma and Fanny Allen moved back to Cresselly to look after their widowed brother and his four children. The John Wedgwoods now became fanatically Evangelical, desiring to convert everyone. One person who might have been thought a likely candidate for conversion was Sarah Wedgwood. Though a religious person, she was not inclined towards Evangelicalism. Like her father, she was an ardent humanitarian, much too concerned with the practical needs of the present to worry about the world hereafter.

After Kitty's death Sarah lived alone, except for two servants and her housekeeper Betty Moore, who had been with the family since the days at Eastbury Park. Jos and Bessy suggested that she come and live with them, but she was too independent for that. Unlike her brothers and sisters, she hadn't the slightest interest in material possessions, preferring a life of spartan simplicity to the extravagant indulgences at Maer. Spinsters of the middle and upper classes — and in mid-nineteenth century England 42 per cent of all women between the ages of twenty and forty were unmarried — were often better off financially than their sisters whose husbands managed, or mismanaged, their financial affairs.

A compromise was reached. Plans were made for building a small house for Sarah on Maer Heath, near Maer Hall. Her house, called Camphill, took three years to complete, and she did not move there until the early part of 1827. At the time she was forty-eight years of age. Although she pursued good works, these occupied little of her time. Like her sister Kitty, she was a far cleverer manager of money than her brothers. She simply decided whether or not a cause was worthy. If so, she generously donated her money, but not her time. The older she got the more critical and aloof she became. Bessy wrote to her sister Emma that Sarah had 'given away more than £1,000 in different acts of benevolence. Who can say that a woman is not as capable of managing a large fortune as a man, or that a single woman has not as many opportunities of doing good as a married one? I wish I could preach singularity among my poor neighbours I know; for I do believe that if nobody would marry who could not maintain a family till they were thirty years old, there would be no poor in England.'4

The Jos Wedgwoods were not enthusiastic converts to Evangelicalism either. Their views on religion were much more casual. On her daughter Emma's confirmation, Bessy remarked: 'I think it would be right in Emma to be confirmed and therefore I hope she will feel no objection.' This confirmation was strongly encouraged by John and Jane, whose own daughter

Jessie was confirmed in the Maer church on the same day, 17 September 1824. Bessy had simply asked Elizabeth to get Emma to read a little on the subject, but if she were averse to it, 'perhaps we ought not to press it, any more than it is better done than omitted, as it is better to conform to the ceremonies of our Church than to omit them, and one does not know that in omitting them, we are not liable to sin.'[5]

For the past five years Elizabeth had been conducting a Sunday school at Maer. The Government had no mandatory educational policy and more than half the population was unable to read or write. Sunday schools, set up by private individuals, were concerned with practical matters as well as with the Scriptures. The alphabet, reading, writing and spelling, along with habits of cleanliness and discipline, were just as important as the catechism. School was held on Sundays only because the children worked on other days. At Maer the pupils met in the laundry or occasionally in the servants' hall. Attendance was secured by bribes of sweets and gingerbread augmented once a year by prizes of Bibles.

> God bless the squire
> and his relations,
> And teach us to keep
> our proper stations.

This prayer echoed at Maer and across the nation. No one questioned it any more than they questioned the unChristian practice of having one church service for the gentry and another for the common folk.

Fortunately, there was as much interest in pleasure as in piety among the third generation of Wedgwoods. The favourite social occasion was the house-party, which usually included a hunt, the new fashionable archery meet and a ball. House-parties were the traditional means for eligible young ladies and gentlemen to meet one another and find suitable marriage partners — just as Jos had attended the Haverford Assizes over thirty years before and found Bessy.

Jos and Bessy's four daughters were not much inclined towards the natural frivolities of life. Pale and solemn, and all wearing spectacles, they were extremely indifferent to clothes and personal appearance — much to the distress of their Allen aunts, who wished them to flirt and charm. Flirting and charming were more the pastimes of the Wedgwood sons, excepting Joe, who was even more silent and serious than his sisters. When Harry pointed out an attractive girl to him at a ball, he replied: 'I suppose she is no worse than other young ladies.'

Of all the nieces and nephews who flocked to house-parties at Maer, Caroline and Charles Darwin were Jos's favourites. Caroline's dominant personality and sense of humour reminded him of her mother in her younger days. Just as Josiah and Erasmus had done a generation earlier with Susan and Robert, Jos and Robert now were rather forcefully letting it be known how happy both families would be if Caroline and Joe were to marry. Joe was, however, slow to take action. At twenty-nine he was still unwilling to commit himself.

Sixteen-year-old Charles Darwin in many ways resembled his uncle Tom

Wedgwood, whom Jos continued to miss although two decades had passed since his death. Like his uncle Tom, Charles was tall and slender, athletic, and passionately interested in hunting and fishing. Also reminiscent of Tom was Charles's passion for collecting, observing and analysing. With his brother Ras, who was five years older, Charles had set up a chemistry laboratory. Because he spent so much time in this laboratory, he was nick-named 'Gas' by his fellow pupils at Shrewsbury School. He collected stamps, coins, plants, birds' eggs and dead insects. His sisters had convinced him it was not a good idea to store bottles of live insects. Also like his uncle Tom, he took to watching birds and making notes of their habits. None of these interests or hobbies impressed the masters at Shrewsbury School, or Robert Darwin who feared that his youngest son would become nothing but a 'dilettante collector and idle shooting man'.

Robert decided to send Charles to Edinburgh University with Ras. At six-teen he was too young to enter medical school, though Robert had already determined that both of his sons would follow him and their grandfather in the practice of medicine. During the summer before the Darwin brothers left for Edinburgh, Charles helped his father attend some charity patients, writing out their case histories. After this initiation, he was permitted a few days holiday at Maer with his Wedgwood cousins.

Bessy wrote to Fanny Allen about all of the young people visiting at Maer following the marriage of Marianne Darwin to Dr Henry Parker, a promis-ing young physician whom Robert Darwin had taken into partnership. Susan and Catherine Darwin and John's daughter Jessie Wedgwood got the most attention at Maer. Like her mother, Jessie was the beauty in the family. Bessy told her sister Fanny that she thought Harry was very much in love with Jessie, though

> whether it will last long after she is gone is another thing, but I believe it very well she is going. They had been dancing every night and last night acting besides. She is looking very pretty, very merry, sitting always by him, and very much taken up with him. Whether she sees her power and her vanity is pleased by exerting it, or whether she is unconscious, I don't know, but as I said before I am glad she is going. At the same time I like her very much, and if he and she could afford to marry, I should desire no better. After all he may forget when she is gone, but I am sure there is danger in their being together, and I don't much like mounting guard every evening till it pleases them to go to bed, or watching them talking nonsense and playing 'beggar my neighbour' or other such lover-like pastimes. Susan [Darwin] comes in second best, and I was in hopes would have caused a diversion, but she has no chance. In short we are just now very flirtish, very noisy, very merry, and very foolish.[6]

The young cousins had performed *The Merry Wives of Windsor*, without Falstaff, for the select audience of Jos and Bessy. Charlotte was the prompter, as no one knew the lines very well. Harry, Hensleigh, Jessie and Susan Darwin all performed very well. Joe's performance was described as very indifferent.

Joe's performance at the pottery was also indifferent. Fortunately, twenty-four-year-old Frank had now left Cambridge and joined the firm, and he showed both more interest and more ability. His mother, with considerable pride, described him as 'right-minded, steady and just what an English merchant ought to be, exact to punctilio in all his dealing, active and industrious'.[7] From the beginning of his apprenticeship, Frank, like his grandfather Josiah, kept a 'Recipe Book' which included various experiments and improvements.

With both Joe and Frank now working regularly at the factory, Jos decided to take Bessy and the four girls to Switzerland and Italy. He confessed to them that ever since his youth he had wanted to see Switzerland. Perhaps after thirty-five years he still felt resentment that John had been given a Grand Tour and he had not. Or, perhaps, he was simply remembering Tom's enthusiastic accounts of his travels through Switzerland.

On 15 February 1825, they left for Geneva by way of Paris, where they had made an arrangement to buy two carriages. They then hired drivers and a guide and set off for Switzerland in grand style. The Sismondis welcomed them warmly and introduced them to Genevois society which was noticeably more sophisticated than the girls had experienced in rural England. Jessie Sismondi taught the girls to curtsy and to dress their hair in the latest fashion. They were sent to a well-known seamstress to have new gowns and bonnets made. Balls, afternoon teas and soirées occupied their days and evenings.

Jos was impressed by the Sismondis' friends and regretted that he did not understand the German language. After five weeks in Geneva, Bessy decided that she did not feel strong enough to make the trip to Italy. She preferred to remain in Switzerland with the Sismondis.

Jos did not want to go to Rome without Bessy, but she persuaded him to carry through the original plan for the sake of the four girls. Jos did so, but he did not enjoy himself in Italy. Nor did he conceal his displeasure. He found travel disagreeable. The carefree attitude of the Italians annoyed him. Punctuality was a Wedgwood obsession, and Jos was especially irritable when planned timetables could not be met.

The girls wrote to their mother that his temper had greatly improved in Rome which 'suited him very much', but Jos himself reported:

All these boasted places only confirm my preference of England and of Maer. I am quite surprised at the attachment of your sisters [the Allen ladies] to Rome, especially as I suppose they had not a carriage constantly, for the filthy habits of the people and the total neglect of the police as to cleanliness, make the town very disagreeable even for a man to walk about in, and intolerable I should have supposed for English women.... I believe I shall quit this country without any desire ever to return to it, but if possible with a deeper detestation of the principles which cause its degradation, and a more heartfelt approbation of the contrary ones which are in operation in our own happy country ... in short I remain at least as good a John Bull as I came out.[8]

Throughout Italy the four Wedgwood girls — all blond and fair-complexioned with rosy cheeks, dressed in similar travel costumes and new Swiss bonnets, and all wearing the same grave expressions and the same kind of wire spectacles — attracted attention. At Sorrento their courier Henri locked them in their rooms to protect them from unwelcome attentions.

From Chêne, the Sismondis' country home, Bessy wrote to Jos that she felt a little uneasy about playing cards on Sunday and hoped that neither Jane Wedgwood nor Caroline Drewe would learn that the Sismondis did so regularly and that out of civility she, too, had obliged. Jos replied: 'One word about your playing cards on Sunday, as you do not think it wrong to do so, why should you object to Caroline or Jane knowing that you did? I am rather afraid of Evangelicism spreading amongst us, though I have some confidence in the genuine good sense of the Maerites for keeping it out, or if it must come, for having the disease in a very mild form.'⁹

Evangelicism was due to arrive at Maer five months later in the very mild form of Allen Wedgwood. while Jos and Bessy were abroad, the living of the little church at Maer became vacant. With his father's approval, Joe offered it to his cousin Allen, who was now thought by the rest of the family to be a permanent invalid and consequently unfit for any other work.

Vicars at Maer, or indeed elsewhere in the country, were seldom chosen on the basis of vocation or even of religious zeal. Most frequently they obtained their posts through being related to the squire, or to someone for whom the squire wished to do a favour. Apart from educational background, very little was required of a vicar. He was expected merely to uphold the doctrines of the Church of England and, from the point of view of the gentry, to instruct the lower classes in proper behaviour.

As Jos wished to be back in England for a Canal meeting in October, he and the family returned to Maer the same week that Allen arrived from Gloucestershire, where the John Wedgwoods had settled at Kingscote. Allen was on crutches. More preoccupied with his health than with church rituals, he lived entirely by the clock, becoming agitated if anything interfered with his accustomed daily routines. He refused, for example, to vary his time of dining by so much as a quarter of an hour. Obsessed by his bodily functions and his 'delicate stomach', he was fanatical about his diet. Certain foods he believed poisoned his system. His eccentric behaviour was often a trial to his aunt and uncle, and his cousins frequently poked fun at him. He was amiable, however, and seemed not to mind being the subject of jokes. He was Evangelical but not energetic. As the one cancelled out the other, religious life at Maer was carried out with minimal observance and not much fuss for anyone. Allen, like his father, had a love of gardening, and under his tender care, the flowers of Maer, if not the parishioners, bloomed.

In the spring of 1826 the Sismondis came to England, visiting the Mackintoshes, the John Wedgwoods and the Jos Wedgwoods, before going to Cresselly for the summer. Harry Wedgwood described Sismondi's bows and continental manners: 'He and I salute one another in the style of the frontispiece to *Les Précieuses ridicules.*'¹⁰

Both Harry and Hensleigh were at the time living in London. Hensleigh, the only real scholar in the family, had left Cambridge with first class honours in mathematics and was made a Fellow of Christ's College with a stipend of £70 a year. He was now studying law and had chambers at Gray's Inn. Harry had already been called to the Bar, was living at the Temple and travelling the Carmarthen circuit. Both young men visited Maer often but enjoyed London, neither working as hard as he might have. Harry enthusiastically described life in the city as 'the freshest news and the freshest fish and to see everybody and everything'. With tongue in cheek, he told his mother: 'The country is a very good place to see good company in, but is very blank by itself, and so I dare say Joe and Allen have found it by this time. What brilliant evenings they must be spending together, what a flow of soul! I pity even Squib [the fox-terrier] when I think of it.'[11]

The Sismondis returned to Switzerland in November of 1826 taking with them their nephew Edward Drewe, who was now twenty-one, and their nieces Fanny and Emma Wedgwood. No longer called the Dovelies, Fanny and Emma were still inseparable at the ages of twenty and eighteen. Their visit to Switzerland was to be for six months, after which it was planned that Frank Wedgwood would go to Geneva and escort his sisters home.

In Geneva, Edward Drewe, who expected to come into a sizeable fortune from a bachelor uncle on his father's side of the family, fell in love with a Swiss girl named Adèle Prévost, proposed and was accepted, much to his mother's distress. Caroline Drewe had sent him to Geneva because of 'the strict morality of the place'. All of the Allen sisters were consulted as to whether Caroline should approve of the engagement or should suggest that Edward delay marriage until he actually had his fortune. Caroline's son-in-law, Edward Alderson, jokingly remarked: 'I declare if I broke both my legs all of Mrs Drewe's sisters would shake their heads and say "Poor Caroline".' The love affair and all its complications also inspired Harry to write a poem:

> Write, write, write a letter!
> Good advice will make us better.
> Sisters, Brothers, Father, Mother,
> Let us all advise each other!

A few months later Edward did marry Adèle and she was happily accepted into the family. Frank, however, did not go to Geneva to collect his sisters, as his father had decided that he would prefer to go himself and let Frank continue with his work at the pottery. Jos also decided to take with him Charles and Caroline Darwin, neither of whom had been abroad, though Charles only went as far as Paris.

Frank, with his sister Charlotte, was allowed to accompany his father and Darwin cousins as far as London. There he stayed with Harry, while Charlotte stayed in Great Russell Street with her cousin Georgiana Alderson. Aunt Caroline Drewe was also there. Aunt Kitty Mackintosh, accompanied by her daughter Fanny, came up to London from Ampthill and invited them to hear the Evangelical Thomas Chalmers preach. Chalmers was well known as a philanthropist and theologian as well as a preacher. All of the family, including Charlotte, went to hear him and also to hear Edward Irving, the founder of the Holy Catholic Apostolic Church. There they saw and heard people 'speak in unknown tongues'.

Kitty was particularly impressed by the sermons and also seemed to be in a highly agitated state. As usual, the Mackintoshes were undecided as to where they wanted to be or where they could afford to live. In July of 1827, Mackintosh, Kitty and Fanny came to Maer for a six-month visit. Young Robert Mackintosh was at the University of Edinburgh, and Mary Rich had gone abroad with their Bedfordshire neighbours, the Inglises. Mackintosh was in a depressed frame of mind. He had been bitterly disappointed earlier that year when he failed to be appointed to Canning's Coalition Cabinet, composed of both Whigs and Tories. Mackintosh felt betrayed by some of his Whig colleagues. The only position offered to him was that of Privy Councillor — which, out of necessity, he accepted. In this frame of mind he decided to devote the whole of the next six months to work on his History.

The routine of the Maer household changed considerably with Mackintosh in the role of resident genius. A room with bookshelves and writing tables had been specially prepared for his convenience. All of the younger Wedgwoods and their Darwin cousins who were visiting were impressed by their uncle's erudition. The captive and willing audience was essential to the nourishment of Mackintosh's ego. Unfortunately, he found the younger generation not very inspiring intellectually, 'more good than agreeable, excepting Hensleigh' whom he thought gifted, though probably destined to a lifetime of ill health. Hensleigh, now aged twenty-four, was suddenly taking a more serious interest in his cousin Fanny, who was three years older than he.

Mackintosh continued in a depressed state over his failure to make his mark in the political sphere. He complained of fits of giddiness which prevented his working on his History, so he delegated more research and copying to his wife and daughter. Kitty often stayed in another room apart from the general activities of the Maer household. Her special project at the time was the reforming of the Smithfield cattle market.

On the whole, however, Mackintosh behaved with his usual charm, which seemed to captivate everyone except his wife. 'He is in a very amiable humour, and so friendly to me that I have begun to love him,' Bessy told Emma Allen. 'We play a rubber every night, which he enjoys very much, and considering he is a genius, he plays very decently. The Darwins go on Monday. I like them very much, but I shall not be sorry to have our party lessened. There is very little pleasure in what the young ones call a row. Hensleigh is gone and him we all regret. He and Fanny Mack are great friends and cronies.'[12]

While Mackintosh was at Maer, he received a summons from Lord Lansdowne announcing the Court at which Mackintosh would be sworn in as a Privy Councillor. Canning's ministry had lasted only four months; under the hatred and malignity with which he was assailed by the Tory aristocracy, Canning's health had broken, and he died — like Charles James Fox twenty-one years earlier — in the house of the Duke of Devonshire. Whig influence had declined still further. In the following months there was a considerable jockeying for position within both parties.

Mackintosh thought he ought to leave for London immediately, even though he was feeling unwell. Lord Stowell had delayed his resignation, to which Mackintosh's appointment was tied, because he had not received a pension, and there might be further complications, since Lord Stowell was not only stubborn but so nearly senile that he could not even remember the name of the Duke of Wellington. 'I thought it unsafe to delay though I feared the Journey & took Fanny with me to read, write, talk & if need were to nurse,' Mackintosh told John Allen. 'I got better however on the road and came to Lansdowne House (my home) pretty well on Thursday, 15th November. I waited three hours on Friday at St James's before we were let in to take the Oath and our Seats. The Duke of Devonshire had 6 hours to wait & stood while *we* were sitting. The King didn't look ill or weak but the contrast of his deeply ploughed & harrowed Face with a youthful Wig gave him a likeness to Blake the hairdresser.'[13]

Mackintosh and Fanny met Mary Rich in London. They decided that the whole family should move to Clapham, to a house next door to one owned by Sir Robert and Lady Inglis. Mackintosh and Fanny then returned to Staffordshire to collect Kitty and to pack up Mackintosh's books and papers.

In Staffordshire, Jos was worried, even more than he had been in the past, about the future of the pottery and the wisdom of carrying on the business at all if the capital could be got out and safer investments made elsewhere. Joe had proven himself dependable, though more punctual than responsible. Frank was tougher and more vigorous, the sort of authoritarian manager who set goals both for himself and his workmen.

In November of 1827, as the Mackintoshes were leaving Maer, Jos took Frank into the business as a partner. He retained one-half of the shares himself; Joe and Frank had a quarter each. The name of the business was changed to Josiah Wedgwood & Sons. At this time Jos also decided to sell the family's interest in the Cornish clay mines. After consultation with Robert Darwin, he purchased more Canal shares with the residue of the trust fund.

Six months later Jos and Bessy went to London to see about selling the York Street building. 'He has long been thinking of doing so,' Bessy wrote to Jessie Sismondi, 'as it has not answered for some years, but the procrastination natural to an uncertain step has hitherto stopped him. I don't know whether it is a prudent thing or not, for I really am in entire ignorance of Jos's finances, nor do I believe he knows his own income, but he says the produce of the works was deficient in a very large sum last year.'[14]

Jos had frequently criticized John for failing to confide his financial situation to Jane, though Jos himself was doing — or, more precisely, failing to do — the same thing. Whereas John agonized over his shortcomings and berated himself for his weaknesses, Jos's pride would not allow him to admit that he was in any way incapable of managing either his own affairs or the over-all affairs of the family.

On 6 October 1828, Bessy wrote to Jessie: 'Jos is just returned from London having sold the house in York Street for £16,000, with which price he is satisfied, yet being more than he gave for it, but whether it will increase or lessen our income remains to be seen. I am the less anxious about that question from never having known what our income was....'[15]

Towards the end of 1828 it was announced publicly that Wedgwood & Sons would close its London business and sell off its stock of goods there on the premises. The sale lasted for ten months, until all of the goods was disposed of, some items for as little as a tenth of their original cost. Moulds, samples and trial pieces were also sold. The goods were ticketed in lots, and medallions, cameos and seals of various periods and in various compositions were grouped incongruously together. Imperfect pieces were lumped with perfect pieces—seemingly without reason and more or less as they were pulled out of the stock room. None of the family showed any interest in purchasing anything.

Jos now wished to sort out the complications of the joint trust fund for the family and to invest the capital elsewhere than in the pottery. Robert Darwin, fearing the expense of a lawyer looking into their affairs, sent Jos a 'deed of gift' which made him trustee for the share of the estate of Thomas Wedgwood that was to come to the Darwin children.

Robert told Jos:

At our marriage I settled £6,000 and your Sister £10,000. The former of these sums I think was exchanged into a cheque to that amount in one of your mortgages, that I suppose on Maer, and perhaps the £10,000 was also so amassed at the same time as I then understood everything except these sums became in my own power. The property from your brother Thomas also became mine. By my will everything I desire in any way from the Wedgwood family is in six shares, one to each of the children; the above £10,000 by a part therefore of, or being nugatory from the property left being more than that amount. All property not part of this & which I call my own, including the £6,000, is by my will divided in 8 shares, two to each son and one to each daughter. By deed of gift I make over the share of T.W. to you for the children and another deed to your two eldest sons as trustees for Mrs Parker [Marianne Darwin].... I apprehend by both these deeds you and your sons have power to lend and therefore if it is expeditious to apply the residues for four canal shares you may lend the balances to me, and I purchase them; and in case of any dispute at a future period, in place of the canal shares, my executor may pay back the balances borrowed. In fact it will be paying from one hand to the other, the only difference being that one hand has eight fingers, and the other six fingers.[16]

The John Wedgwoods and their eldest daughter Eliza had spent all of the year 1828 abroad, most of it in Geneva with the Sismondis. John was now aged sixty-two, still receiving a monthly allowance from his brother and still more or less wondering what he was going to do when he grew up. If he had any sad feelings about the sale of the Cornish clay mines or the closure of the London showrooms, he kept them to himself.

When they returned to England in the spring of 1829, they were still unable to fix upon a settled plan of life or a fixed abode. They again disappointed Bessy by refusing to settle in Staffordshire. Instead they went to Wales and rented a house near Abergavenny called The Hill. In March of 1829, while the sale of the goods in the showrooms was still going on, Bessy accompanied Jos to London. She first visited the Mackintoshes at Clapham, where she became increasingly uneasy about Kitty's mental state — 'I have now and then a nameless fear about Kitty which makes me wish she should be soothed by her family as much as possible, and when I think how short a time we may some of us have together, I am desirous above all things that our last years may pass in harmony and affection.'[17]

Mackintosh was busy with affairs in Parliament. By the repeal of the Test Act which barred Dissenters from occupying official posts in the State, Dissenters, Liberals and the new Evangelicals were now able to take an active part in the decisions which affected the country as a whole. There was even a rumour that the Catholic Emancipation Act would be passed during this Parliament. Mackintosh was far too preoccupied with changes in the nation to notice any change in his wife's behaviour. If he observed anything at all, he attributed it to the tension and rivalry which had always existed between her and Mary Rich. This was just the sort of unpleasantness which Mackintosh chose to ignore: Kitty and Mary ought to love one another, and he refused to acknowledge that in reality they didn't. Bessy failed to make him see what was apparent to everyone else.

Ironically, it was Bessy, not Kitty, who was then on the verge of a serious illness. After her visit to the Mackintoshes she went to stay with her widowed niece Harriet Gifford in Roehampton. There she had a serious seizure, first described as an epileptic fit. Jos came immediately and it was feared that she might not recover. For several months they remained in Roehampton. By the time she had recovered sufficiently to be taken home to Maer, the sale at York Street House was completed and the Wedgwood showrooms closed in London.

Again ironically, the Wedgwood company founded by a Dissenter and expanded during a period of discrimination against Dissenters began its retrenchment at a time when the Government was extending new rights to Christians of all denominations.

20

Cousins and Lovers
(1830 – 1832)

George IV, dispirited, ailing and ridiculed, died unmourned on 26 June 1830. He was succeeded by his bluff, honest, good-hearted and not very clever brother, William IV, who was then almost sixty-five years of age. Short of stature, as well as of tact and temper, William IV, with his pin-shaped head and very red complexion, began his reign the morning after his brother's death by driving up to London with a streamer of black crêpe, known as a 'weeper', flying from his white hat. Instead of weeping, however, the King smiled, bowed and waved to his startled subjects. If there were no expectations of brilliance from the continuation of this unpopular Hanoverian dynasty, at least it seemed unlikely to be dull.

Mary Rich and Fanny Mackintosh accompanied their father to Westminster Abbey for the coronation of William IV, which Fanny described to her cousin Hensleigh as 'a very grand occasion'. Two days later Hensleigh told her about the coronation celebrations in Staffordshire where it rained heavily, '... rather to the Governor's [his father's] relief as it entirely absolved him from walking in procession with the gentlemen of Hanley previous to a grand dinner there at which he presided. He came home around nine o'clock swearing at the horrible dullness of a public dinner with its concomitants of loyal & sentimental toasts. Nature never intended him for a public man. They dined 1,500 poor people in the market hall....'[1]

Jos was now sixty-one years old and much concerned with the future of his sons. Joe at age thirty-five showed not the slightest interest in leaving home or in doing anything else adventurous. He turned over almost all of the business at the factory to his brother Frank. Unlike Joe, the brusque, determined Frank was quite 'set on marrying'. He was simply uncertain whom to choose — or, who would choose him. 'I don't think Frank has given up all hopes of Susan [Darwin],' Hensleigh told Fanny Mackintosh. 'I wish he would propose.'[2]

Both Hensleigh and Harry fancied themselves in love and wanted to marry. Their father feared that neither of the marriages was suitable. Neither Harry nor Hensleigh had a prospect of earnings adequate to support a family in the manner to which they were accustomed. Jos was concerned that he would be obliged to provide permanent incomes for them as well as for his four daughters if they remained unmarried. If the girls did marry, he would of course be expected to provide substantial dowries.

The son who irritated him the most was Harry. For years Jos had despaired of Harry's ever amounting to anything and therefore avoided his company as much as possible. Thus it came as a complete surprise to him — though not to Bessy — that Jessie Wedgwood, the most beautiful of all the girls of the third generation, should accept Harry, particularly when there were so many other eligible young men with substantial fortunes around. Neither Jos nor any of his contemporaries objected on the grounds of genetics to the marriage of first cousins. Indeed, Jos liked to keep his family closely knit. He simply would have preferred Harry to make an alliance with one of the Darwin girls rather than with a daughter of his brother John, whose strained financial position was all too familiar to him.

In his blunt way Jos saw no reason not to make his feelings quite clear to John:

> I heard on Tuesday that Harry had prevailed upon Jessie to enter into an engagement to marry him. On our side there can be but one objection, the small allowance that I can give him & the uncertainty to say the least of his getting much by his profession. He has I believe told Jessie that the utmost that I can give him is £400 a year & that I cannot settle more than £200 of the £400 because 5/10ths of my clear income comes from the Pottery either as profit or rent, both of which would fail together and if any considerable diminution of the present profits should happen I should probably be obliged to lessen Harry's allowance. I trust this may not happen but it is possible and I think you should know it. I am sure Harry has not meant to conceal anything from Jessie but he may perhaps not have sufficiently fixed his own mind & consequently may have failed to direct hers upon the contingency which the continuation of his allowance at the rate of £400 a year must depend.
>
> After what I have said you will know that I do not think the match a very prudent one but they may have many years of happiness ... after all the young & sanguine may for what I know take a wider view of such questions than we codgers & I am sure that when they are old enough to judge for themselves I do not feel confidence enough in my calling to give them the shape of advice. I would venture no further than to put them in possession of information.[3]

Hensleigh's romance with his cousin Fanny Mackintosh came as no surprise to his father or to any other members of the family. Bessy had long before observed that Fanny and Hensleigh 'will never help falling in love with each other so much as they are together'.[4] Like Harry, Hensleigh's prospects in the overcrowded legal profession were not good. Jos told Joe that

> Hensleigh's thinking of leaving the bar and receiving a clerkship in order to practice as an attorney has made me know that his prospects are not considered by him as very promising & has led me to cast about for any

means of improving them. I can do nothing for him but offer him a share in the Manufacturing & I wish to consult you upon that suggestion. To be sure the manufactory does not offer any great advantages & all speculation as to its future state must be mere conjectures—still, I think that capital, skill & industry will probably hereafter command a higher rate of profit than they do now. With reference to yourself and Frank, it might be convenient at my death or in the event of my relinquishing all interest in the manufactory that Hensleigh should be a partner with you & invest his property in the purchase of the effects in trade.... I have not given the slightest hint upon the subject to Hensleigh.... I don't know how Hensleigh would suit the situation but he has talent & industry & good sense. And employment would probably be very beneficial to his health. You will probably think it strange as Harry's prospects at the Bar are probably no better than Hensleigh's, that I have not thought of making the same offer to him. It is because I don't think him qualified to enter into such business. I should like to know whether you are of the same opinion.[5]

Joe rather casually told his father that 'if Harry & Hensleigh wish to join in the pottery, I have no objection whatever, and as to qualifications I do not know that any particular qualifications are necessary—beyond what any man of common understanding possesses'.[6]

Harry was not asked into the firm and Hensleigh declined the offer. He felt that his own talents and interests lay elsewhere and also that it would be unfair to his brothers, as the pottery did not provide a sufficient income for so many partners. From Jos's point of view, this was a disappointment. Hensleigh was the one son whom he believed had exceptional ability. He had come to rely upon his opinion in legal matters in the same way that he relied upon Robert Darwin's opinion in financial matters. Moreover, he had a nagging fear that his one gifted son would follow in the footsteps of his cousin and close friend Ras Darwin, becoming nothing but an idle dilettante. Only a few weeks after Hensleigh declined to join the pottery, Jos informed him:

I have a few words to say to you which are so extremely obvious that you will think I might have kept them to myself. Yet I think I should not do my duty if I did not speak out.... I think your attitude to Fanny Mackintosh induces you to seek her company so often as to interfere very much with the attentiveness that is required by your profession. The habit will grow upon you by indulgence & the motive which if it were properly directed would open you to increased progress in your profession seems to me likely to diminish your industry & your prospect of success....[7]

Jos was not the only person critical of Hensleigh's behaviour towards Fanny. Mackintosh was possessive towards his daughter and jealous of the time she spent with Hensleigh. For two years now Hensleigh and Fanny had been scheming to meet one another without Mackintosh's knowing. They pretended to meet by accident or prevailed on other members of the family who were sympathetic to them, such as Harry or Ras Darwin, to set up social gatherings. Both of them enjoyed the intrigue. Hensleigh told Fanny after they had attended the same party. 'I flatter myself that I behaved beautifully & I do not think that anybody could have guessed that I cared tuppence for you.'[8]

Mackintosh guessed that Hensleigh cared considerably more than tuppence and decided to take Fanny abroad. He was in a highly agitated state, not only because of his daughter's unwelcome romance but because of the break-up of his own marriage. Bessy Wedgwood had been accurate in her apprehensions about Kitty Mackintosh's distraught frame of mind. In the autumn of 1829, Kitty left London, travelling with a companion as far as Paris. From there she went on to Geneva to stay with the Sismondis. She did not tell Mackintosh that she was leaving him, nor did she let him know where she was. He learned that she was in Switzerland from Bessy Wedgwood who was, of course, in correspondence with her sister Jessie. Probably with the thought of going to Geneva himself, Mackintosh, taking Fanny with him, went to Italy to visit Madame de Staël's daughter Albertine, the Duchesse de Broglie.

Meanwhile, at Chêne, the sixty-five-year-old Kitty became more and more withdrawn. She had sudden inexplicable fits of temper and complained of pain in her limbs. On 6 May 1830, she suffered a stroke which left her speechless and paralysed. A week later she died. Jessie wrote to Bessy:

> I cannot but think her death, thus sudden and without suffering, is a most merciful dispensation. She could neither make herself nor others happy and I dreaded the future (which must necessarily have darkened more and more on her as she advanced) so much, that it seems to me as if a great evil was withdrawn from me in its being denied to her. If she could have got Fanny out to her I think she had some vague notion of never returning.... The disorder had been stealing on all the winter and was clearly no one stroke.... Her husband and children will be easily enough reconciled to her loss, alas! she has been long lost to them.[9]

The tug-of-war between her parents for Fanny's affections was ended. When she and her father returned to England, Mary Rich became mistress of the household at Clapham which included herself, Mackintosh, Fanny and young Robert, who had come down from Edinburgh. Eleven years older than Fanny, Mary Rich was as fanatical about morals and manners and conventional proprieties as about religion. She seemed to have forgotten her own romantic life with Claudius Rich in Persia.

Fanny was considerably influenced by her stepsister, whose commanding personality and romantic past held a kind of fascination for her. Fanny and Mary shared the same lady's maid as well as the same political and historical and religious interests. It was at Mary's prompting—though he needed little urging—that Mackintosh had written to Hensleigh early in 1830 that he and Fanny were seeing too much of one another and that Hensleigh's behaviour towards Fanny might be seen by others to exceed the usual bonds of 'cousinly affection'. When Hensleigh came to call, Mary received him with 'glum looks'.

Hensleigh told Fanny: 'I was very sorry to receive Sir James's note as I at first thought that you were to cut me or nearly so, and if it had been less kindly worded I could not have borne it … my answer to Sir James was that I have myself been somewhat afraid that I was being unfair to you in pursuing my line of conduct since it would keep other people off when I have so little prospect of being able to marry you … but that I love you.'[10] He then promised Fanny that he would be more prudent in his manner towards her and said that he was sorry if she thought he 'was angry at Sir James or Mrs Rich, though she is rather tiresome sometimes'.[11]

Actually he *was* angry and most particularly with Mary Rich. Only one day after saying that he wasn't angry, he exploded: 'I can't bear to be met with such looks as Mrs Rich gave me today when I called — she is not your Mother and why should she interfere between you & me? You are quite of an age & judgment to decide for yourself on matters of this kind.' Then he drafted a letter to Mackintosh in which he made his feelings quite clear:

> Fanny is gentleness itself & yields to everybody. Mrs Rich allows herself to direct her as if she were a girl of eighteen … there is something degrading at our age to feel oneself constantly watched & to have nothing trusted to one's discretion as if we had been detected in all the underhand proceedings in the world…. All I wish for is to be admitted on such terms as are natural for so near a relation considering the intimacy that has always existed between our families, when I hope my conduct will be such as to satisfy you. Even if ever I am able to marry Fanny, I should not wish to take her away from you if things could be managed otherwise.[12]

Hensleigh's perception of the situation was accurate: while Mackintosh desired his daughter's happiness, he did not want to lose her companionship. When the two men met again, they did not mention their correspondence. Fanny and Hensleigh continued to see each other as often as before, developing even more elaborate subterfuges. When Hensleigh visited Maer the following summer, he suggested that if Fanny wished to write to him privately, she could write through Frank at the factory. Frank would pass on the letter 'without anyone's being the wiser'.

Fanny had already written to him at Maer before she received his letter. He replied: 'It was so good of you writing again so soon when I had hardly ventured to allow to myself that I had any hopes of any dispatches. It was so satisfactory hearing the Governor when he returned from his ride to the post "Hensleigh, here is one for you" while I was sitting in the library pretending to myself that I could not even hope for one.'[13]

After his father gave him Fanny's letter, Hensleigh took it outside with his ink pot and writing paper, crossed the terrace and climbed up into an old yew tree where he and his brothers used to hide when they were children. There, straddling a large limb and leaning back against the trunk of the tree, he read Fanny's letter and composed one in return:

I must confess it is not easy to write so good a hand with one's paper on a book & one's legs dangling from the branch of a tree as it is sitting at one's ease at a desk. But then you know we are writing to a poor dear little cockneyfied cousin of ours whose ideas are confined to the sunny-side of Bryanston Square so we must try to explain to her what the country means; & this is such a nice study to retire to. A semicircle of thick old yews pushing their branches out into the middle & half filling it up, with oak trees in front & a patch of sky about the size of a dining table over-head. Then there is a bird making such a comical noise I cannot conceive what it is. I am so quiet here on my bough they take no heed of me & I dare say they take me for a great black rook.... This weather and employment makes me very sentimental. I am sure it was walking out in just such a day that Milton wrote his *Penseroso*.... I wish the midges would not bite so, they will fairly drive me away soon. How would writing in gloves be I wonder? It is odd how such little beasts can be so venomous. I must give in.... Indoors again. One of the first things I hear on coming in was Aunt Drewe declaring she had a mind to explore all the old walks. What a pretty to-do it would have been if she had done so & found me on my perch writing away. Do you think she would have guessed who I was scribbling to in that retired spot? ... So give me a kiss & goodbye for the present....[14]

Like Kitty Mackintosh, Hensleigh's 'Aunt Drewe' suffered increasingly severe depressions as she grew older. Caroline was now almost totally deaf, which further emphasized her withdrawal and sense of isolation. She had no permanent home, and paid a constant round of lengthy visits to her three children and to her sisters and brothers. Wherever she went, she was something of a trial.

If Hensleigh's romance appeared beset by complications, there was more serious trouble between Harry and Jessie. In April of 1830, six months after the announcement of their engagement, Jessie declared that she would not marry Harry if he lost a bankruptcy case he had taken on in the law practice he had set up in North Staffordshire. Far from successful, he had already lost several important suits. Still, Jessie's unexpected ultimatum caused considerable turmoil at Maer. Harry went to Tenby to persuade her to change her mind. The Allen aunts and Aunt Sarah Wedgwood were indignant over Jessie's behaviour. Hensleigh, who had been employed to draw up the marriage contract, concluded that Harry must have had a horrid visit at The Hill and that Jessie didn't really much care for her future husband. Still, Harry succeeded in persuading her to change her mind. Hensleigh was summoned to The Hill to finalize the marriage settlement. 'It is very dull of uncle John to keep me here when he has nothing in the world to say which couldn't have been said by letter,' Hensleigh told Fanny. 'The only suggestion he had to make about the settlement was one that I could not allow. I am impatient to get away but can't leave before Tuesday.'[15]

Marriage was in the air. While he was still at The Hill, Hensleigh listened to the ambitions of his cousin Tom Wedgwood who was thirty-three, a colonel in the Army and, like his cousin Frank, 'a good deal set on marrying', though not quite sure to which woman. Ever conscious of his own problems, Hensleigh recommended to Tom a young woman whose name he had forgotten but who was a great friend of the Thorntons and who had an income of £500 a year.

In September of 1830, Harry and Jessie were married at Tenby. Immediately thereafter they set out for Etruria. Jos had agreed that the young couple could live rent-free in the vacant Etruria Hall, shutting off the many rooms and wings of the house they would not need. 'On Friday we all drove over to Etruria to receive Harry & Jessie,' Hensleigh reported to Fanny 'You have no idea what a pretty house they have got. The drawing room is beautiful with four such pretty drawings of Charlotte's in it. Jessie trembled violently on her arrival, it quite shook her arms backward and forward, she is the most nervous person I ever saw.'[16]

Two weeks later Hensleigh noted: 'Harry does not flirt a great deal with Jessie. The principal sign of their marriage is her taking his arm out a-walking. She also jokes him too a little & only fancy poor Allen's clumsiness in joining in with her bantering, as if it were the same thing being rallied by a woman you are in love with & a great awkward brother-in-law. We are all in admiration of their virtue in having him over the very first week of their settlement at Etruria.'[17]

Fanny's father's fortunes just then suddenly took a turn for the better. With the resignation of the Duke of Wellington's Tory ministry on 16 November 1830, a new Whig Government was formed under Mackintosh's old friend Lord Grey. Mackintosh, who had been so often passed over by his colleagues in the past, was finally offered a place on the Board of Control. This was not a particularly important position, as the Board rarely met and was but one of three divisions of the Home Government of the East India Company. But it carried a salary of £1,500 a year, which considerably eased Mackintosh's strained circumstances. On the strength of this, and Mary Rich's pension from the East India Company, Mackintosh decided to move from Clapham to a house closer to the centre of the city, at 14 Great Cumberland Street. At the same time, the first two volumes of his long-awaited *History* were published. The work received much publicity — and mixed reviews.

Fanny Allen, the youngest of the Allen sisters, who was now aged forty-nine, also moved to the centre of London, to a house in Wimpole Street, during the early part of 1830. Although she had received several offers of marriage, she had remained a spinster. Only two men had she ever truly loved. When she and her sisters Jessie and Emma were abroad, she had often been escorted to parties by William Clifford, a wealthy, charming and idle English gentleman whom, she later confessed to her sister Bessy, she would have married if he had been able to return her love. Clifford was not, however, the marrying kind. The other man, whom Fanny had loved since she was eighteen, was her brother-in-law James Mackintosh.

Perhaps at this late stage in her life — and it was even later for Mackintosh, who was now sixty-six — she had hoped that something might develop beyond the close relationship that had always existed between

47 John Bartlett Allen, *c.* 1765

48 Cresselly, the Allen family home in Pembrokeshire

49   Eastbury Park, home of Tom Wedgwood

50   Cote House, home of John Wedgwood

51   Maer Hall, home of Josiah Wedgwood II

52   The Mount, home of Dr Robert Darwin

55-56
Claudius Rich and *(below)* his
wife Mary, *née* Mackintosh

53-54
J.C.S. de Sismondi and *(below)* his
wife Jessie, *née* Allen

57   Madame de Staël

58-59   Josiah Wedgwood III and
his   wife   Caroline,   *née*
Darwin

60-61 Henry Allen (Harry) Wedgwood and
his wife Jessie, *née* Wedgwood
Portraits by George Richmond

62-63   Frank Wedgwood and his wife
Fanny, *née* Mosley

64-65
Hensleigh Wedgwood and his wife
Fanny, *née* Mackintosh
Watercolour of Fanny Wedgwood by
George Richmond, 1832

66-67
Charles Darwin and his wife
Emma, *née* Wedgwood
*Watercolours by George Richmond,
1838-9*

68   Frances Julia (Snow) Wedgwood and
her brother James (Bro), 1838

69   Ernest Hensleigh Wedgwood as a child
Watercolour by George Richmond, 1841

70 Erasmus Alvey Darwin
Crayon by George Richmond, 1841

71 A fantastic zoo, drawn by E.A.
Darwin for his nephew Alfred Allen
(Tim) Wedgwood, 1847

72   Hope Wedgwood

73   Katherine Euphemia (Effie) Wedgwood

74   Robert Browning in 1870
Photograph by Julia Margaret Cameron

75   Thomas Erskine as a young man
Sketch after George Richmond

76   Snow Wedgwood in 1888
Pencil drawing by Edward Clifford

77   Watercolour sketch by Snow Wedgwood of her
drawing room at 1 Cumberland Place, 1872

them. Marrying one's deceased wife's sister was no longer as much disapproved of as it had been a generation earlier. Fanny and Mackintosh saw each other several times a week. She often accompanied him to fashionable political and literary gatherings. Mackintosh appeared to have regained some of his youthful energy and enthusiasm. Still, he was as self-centred as always, no more conscious of Fanny's needs and feelings than he had been of Kitty's. Fanny heard much of the romance of her niece and namesake and how distressing it all was for Mackintosh.

'I found Sir James had been speaking to Aunt Fanny about me,' Hensleigh wrote to his cousin Fanny, 'so I explained to her how things were between us & told her that I believed you were attached to me. I think she is much interested for both of us & I hope may be instrumental in putting things on a more pleasant footing.... I do think I love you more every day.'[18]

Fanny Allen, perhaps sentimental over lost opportunities in her own life, was indeed sympathetic towards the young lovers. She persuaded Mary Rich not to chaperone the couple so closely and suggested to Mackintosh that for his own happiness as well as Fanny's he would be well advised to approve the engagement and to use his influence in getting a Civil Service appointment for Hensleigh which would provide sufficient income for them to marry.

'I called at Wimpole Street this morning and walked Aunt Fanny out shopping,' Hensleigh wrote to Fanny. 'I had a good deal of conversation with her and asked her with some alarm about the subject which interests me most just now, that is how often she thought it would be considered reasonable that I should see you, when, only think, my dear love, how pleased I was when she told me she had suggested to Sir James that perhaps once or twice a week would be about the thing....'[19]

With the Whigs now in power Mackintosh contacted Lord Lansdowne, the Chancellor of the Exchequer, Lord Brougham, Lord Grey and other prominent Whigs about a Commissionership of Bankruptcy for his son Robert. He also endorsed and forwarded Hensleigh's application for the post of Assistant Registrar of Cabs. Hensleigh told his father that he hoped

> to hinder the ladies from stepping too hastily to the conclusion that because Sir James has asked for it he is sure to have his request granted ... as if he fails he will not like to have his failure bruited about so I hope they will not even tell The Hill of it.... There's the chance of the Bills not passing at all & then there must be a great number of competitors for so good a place, for there will always be a great chance of succeeding ultimately to the Head Registrarship, a place probably of £2,500 a year.[20]

In spite of protestations to the contrary, Hensleigh was disappointed when the post was given to a nephew of Thomas Campbell's who was the godson of the King. Robert Mackintosh received his post. After many delays and disruptions Lord Lansdowne spoke to Lord Melbourne who agreed to give Hensleigh preference over any other person equally recommended for the next suitable post. After more delays and uncertainties, Hensleigh was eventually appointed to a Police Magistracy, a stipendiary post which provided sufficient income for him to marry. Then he proposed formally to Fanny.

Now that the Whigs were in power for the first time in years, Mackintosh involved all of his friends and family in politics. Mary Rich disliked social occasions, so Fanny acted as hostess for her father. Once more the social and political and literary worlds overlapped. In March of 1831 they gave a grand dinner at the new house in Great Cumberland Street. The guests included Bishop Copleston of Llandaff; Sir Thomas Denman, then Attorney-General and later Lord Chief Justice; Francis Jeffrey, founder of the *Edinburgh Review* and Lord Advocate; Lord Nugent, M.P. for Aylesbury and the younger son of the Marquis of Buckingham; Richard Shiel, dramatist and Irish politician; Lady Gifford, Fanny's cousin, and Marianne Thornton, Fanny's close friend. Wordsworth, now aged sixty-one and even more temperamental than in his early years, arrived late and peevishly refused to meet Jeffrey who had written critically of his poems in the *Edinburgh Review*. He stated that he was fire and Jeffrey water; if Mackintosh put them together, 'they would inevitably hiss.' Mackintosh, however, succeeded in reconciling them. On the same occasion he also attempted to persuade two of his brothers-in-law, John Allen and Jos Wedgwood, to run for Parliament as Whig candidates.

Politics was an area of conflict for Jos. His way of life was that of a Tory gentleman, yet his inheritance allied him with the Whig manufacturers. He did not agree immediately to Mackintosh's proposal. He was mainly concerned about the effect that life in London might have on Bessy's frail health. She had never completely recovered from the seizure she had had at Roehampton. Naturally enough, Jos sought Robert Darwin's advice.

'Taking everything in circumstance into consideration, I feel inclined to wish you should be M.P.,' Robert said.

> I think Bessy would feel uneasy if you were not to stand & might suspect your motive — and, indeed, if after one session you find any real inconvenience, either on her account, or on any other, you may withdraw from Parliament. If you are elected there must be a serious conversation with your wife that she must lead a quiet regular life in London because when she has been there hitherto, she has I suppose been too much excited, to use the fashionable expression.[21]

Jos stood for the 'rotten' borough of Newcastle which, by leave of the freeholders, belonged to the Duke of Sutherland. The rhetoric of his campaign was straightforward and uninspiring. 'My principles are those of the Reform Bill,' he told the voters. 'If they are yours, you will send me to represent you. Otherwise not.' He lost by a heavy margin to Edmund Peel, the Duke of Sutherland's Tory candidate; but he aroused good will and support among his workmen who contributed to the expense of his campaign fund.

Robert Darwin was having as much difficulty as Jos in getting his son settled. Ras had completed his medical studies at Edinburgh but decided against actually practising medicine, since he 'had become convinced from various small circumstances that my father would leave me property enough to subsist on with some comfort ... and my belief was sufficient to check any strenuous effort to learn medicine'. Thus, Ras had moved to London with nothing more strenuous to do than live the life of a cultured gentleman. He established himself in artistic and literary circles. He read extensively and collected a fine library. He and Hensleigh became even closer friends than they had been as boys, breakfasting together every Sunday; on other days 'their hours didn't much agree'.

In May of 1831, while Fanny was visiting friends in Harrogate, Hensleigh and Ras went off to the Isle of Wight on a botanical expedition. 'It is a great thing,' Hensleigh wrote to Fanny, 'having so patient a friend as he is; there are very few men who would endure to walk with a friend who was constantly stopping and running backwards and forwards.'[22]

Charles Darwin also disappointed his father by deciding against a career in medicine, claiming he could never hope to be as good as physician as his father. Robert made no effort to disguise his displeasure at having two idle sons who continuously overspent their allowances, but he continued to indulge them. Perhaps recalling his own father's bullying behaviour towards Erasmus junr., he decided to send Charles to Cambridge to study for the Church. Charles found this plan more to his liking than the alternative of studying law.

During his three years at Cambridge, Charles paid little attention to formal studies or to the Church. He fell in with a 'sporting crowd' and thoroughly enjoyed hunting, drinking and playing cards. He did, however, find one serious friend in the Professor of Botany, the Revd John Stevens Henslow, with whom he took long walks. Henslow introduced him to the works of John Herschel and Alexander von Humboldt. He also persuaded him to begin the study of geology. In 1831 Charles took his degree at Christ's College, standing tenth on the list among those who did not go for honours.

After coming down from Cambridge, Charles went on a geological tour of Wales with Adam Sedgwick, Professor of Geology at Cambridge. When he returned home, he found a letter from Henslow recommending that he apply for the post of naturalist aboard H.M.S. *Beagle*, which was to make a surveying voyage round the world under the command of Captain Robert Fitzroy.

Though he didn't actually forbid it, Robert Darwin objected to Charles's taking the position. He thought it a wild scheme, unsuitable for a clergyman, another change in profession for Charles and probably a useless undertaking. He also suggested that the offer must have been made to others who turned it down — otherwise Charles would not have received it. Charles modestly agreed that this was probably true and wrote to Henslow refusing the position. 'Even if I was to go, my father disliking would take away all energy and I should want a good stock of that.'[23]

Observing the depth of his son's disappointment, Robert told him: 'If you can find any man of common sense who advises you to go, I will give my consent.' As Charles was on his way to Maer for the opening of the partridge shooting season, he decided to talk over the plan and his father's objections with his Uncle Jos and with his Wedgwood cousins. They were unanimously in favour of his going. Jos immediately wrote to his brother-in-law answering his principal objections. Charles also wrote to his father:

> I am afraid I am going to make you again very uncomfortable. But, upon consideration, I think you will excuse me once again, stating my opinions on the offer of the voyage. My excuse and reason is the different way all the Wedgwoods view the subject from what you and my sisters do ... the danger appears to me and all the Wedgwoods not great. The expense cannot be serious, and the time I do not think, anyhow, would be more thrown away than if I stayed at home. But pray do not consider that I am so bent on going that I would for *one single moment* hesitate, if you thought that after a short period you should continue uncomfortable....[24]

Jos read this letter, which was dispatched with his own. Then he decided that he should escort the timid, obliging Charles back to Shrewsbury and present Charles's case more forcefully himself. Robert listened to the arguments, changed his mind and agreed to finance Charles's making the voyage by continuing his allowance.

Charles assured his father that he would have to be 'deuced clever' to spend more than his allowance on board the *Beagle*.

'They tell me you *are* deuced clever,' Robert replied.

Two weeks later Hensleigh visited Charles's oldest sister Marianne Parker, who brought him up to date on the preparations for Charles's voyage. 'Things are not quite so magnificent as they were reported to be at first,' he wrote to Fanny,

> as it is not certain that they are to go around the world & Charles is to pay for his own outfit (about £500) & £30 a year for board & he is to remain out for three years, unless he chooses to leave the ship, but in spite of all, he is enthusiastic about it & only wishes the voyage was longer before he touches land. He is as busy as a bee in his preparations. Captain F. promises to put him ashore in some healthy port for the winter months of stormy weather. Marianne's account is that they treat Charles like a child & promise to put him ashore whenever there is a storm.[25]

Hensleigh also told Fanny that Marianne was quite pregnant and that her oldest child was 'the most absurd likeness of Dr Darwin that I ever saw.'

When Hensleigh arrived at Maer, he had more news to report to Fanny. Uncle John, Aunt Jane, their daughter Eliza, a maid and a manservant had left The Hill at Abergavenny and moved back to Etruria Hall with Harry and Jessie, a convenient economy for both families. Sixteen years after the dissolution of the Davison bank, John was still being questioned about some South Seas stocks which he had purchased and neglected to put in the bank's records. At Maer there was also more excitement and concern over Charles's forthcoming voyage when Charles himself came for a farewell visit. 'Frank & my father were busy at a reform meeting in the Potteries, poor souls & could not come home for dinner,' Hensleigh wrote to Fanny.

Harry came in just as we had begun. I wonder Charles is not damped in his ardour for the expedition. He says that Patagonia where they are going first to is the most detestable climate in the world, raining incessantly, & it is one vast peat bog without a tree to be seen. The natives will infallibly eat you if they can get an opportunity. They have got some tame Patagonians that they are going to take back & who promise to give up cannibalising but they do not believe a word of their promises. Then their mode of proceeding will be to anchor close to shore & remain there two or three weeks till they have surveyed all the country about & then go on to another place. It is very enterprising to go in spite of such discouraging accounts.[26]

After numerous delays the *Beagle* finally set sail on 27 December 1831. Its twenty-two-year-old naturalist was seasick. Less than two weeks later Hensleigh was also feeling queasy. The occasion that prompted this was his long-awaited marriage to Fanny, which brought most of the Allens, Wedgwoods, Mackintoshes and Darwins to London to celebrate.

21

Beginnings and Endings
(1832 – 1833)

Hensleigh's and Fanny's wedding suffered almost as many mishaps as their four-year romance. The day before the wedding Hensleigh was lying in bed in his chambers at Gray's Inn and thinking himself most unwell. He had just resolved to put off the wedding and had begun a note to Fanny when, according to his sister Fanny, 'his Doctor came and told him he was quite well and must eat a chop and drink a glass of wine. So he wrote to Fanny that he was coming to dinner and begged her to buy a ring, which was certainly not very decorous. However, she told Sophy Thornton to get it, which she did. When he did come, he looked very thin and unbridal; however, he said he was well.'[1]

Apart from his having a position that would bring him sufficient income and prestige, another condition had been imposed on Hensleigh before Mackintosh would give his approval to the marriage. This was that Hensleigh and Fanny would live with him — and also, of course, with his son Robert and with Hensleigh's old enemy Mary Rich. Fanny had no desire to be separated from her father whom she adored, though Hensleigh confided that when it came to the point. 'living with Sir James would be quite a sacrifice'. He was not particularly fond of Fanny's brother either. Robert Mackintosh seemed to him awkward, conceited and much too willing to take advantage of the privileges which his father's friends gave him without, in return, fulfilling the obligations of his privileged position.

After much searching, a suitable house was finally found at Langham Place. The four Mackintoshes moved there five days before the wedding. Then, much to Fanny's dismay, they discovered that they could not be married in All Souls' Church, Langham Place, as they had not lived in the parish for fifteen days. Even though the clerk at the church suggested that they simply swear that they had lived there for fifteen days, Hensleigh 'chose to have a conscience' and refused to do so. Two years earlier he had also displayed a conscience, when he resigned his fellowship at Christ's College Cambridge, because he 'had not done right' when subscribing to the Thirty-nine Articles set out by the Church of England in order to receive his M.A. degree.He had not sincerely believed in the Articles at the time and later found that he had acquired even more doubts.

Then Fanny protested at being married at St Andrew's Holborn, which was Hensleigh's parish. Her objections were that the church was not fashionable and wouldn't look well in the newspapers. After persuasive arguments by her cousins and future sisters-in-law, she finally relented and 'bore her fate pretty well'.

On the morning of the wedding there was even more confusion. Fanny's wedding gown, which was being presented to her by Lady Holland, had not arrived by the time the party was to set off for the church. Fanny Wedgwood who was one of the bridesmaids, had to take off her dress and give it to her future sister-in-law. Then the party set out for the church in a procession of carriages — the bride, Sir James and Mrs Rich in the first carriage. Robert Mackintosh and his cousin Tom Wedgwood set off in another carriage to pick up Hensleigh.

When the bridal party and guests had been assembled in the church for some ten minutes and still the bridegroom had not appeared, they began to fear Hensleigh had been taken ill again or had misplaced the marriage licence. At last, however, he arrived. The service began with both Hensleigh and Fanny behaving with great decorum and neither of them wearing their spectacles. The clerk got confused as to who were bridesmaids; the vicar 'made the service very long by reading the tiresome exhortation at the end', and there were many dirty, poor people in the church who kept pressing in close. Then, as they were leaving the church in their carriage festooned with ribbons, an old woman in the crowd of poor people said: 'Well if I was going to be married, I would not have all those ribbons to tell people what I was about.'

The newlyweds rode back to Langham Place in the carriage with Sir James and Mrs Rich. When they got there, they found the intended gown had arrived. Fanny, however, changed into her travelling dress. There was an elegant breakfast for forty-two people. Ras Darwin, Tom Wedgwood, Robert Mackintosh and Edward, now Baron, Alderson, proposed toasts and were all very merry. The festivities continued long after the bride and groom had departed for a brief honeymoon at Sevenoaks, Tunbridge Wells and St Leonards.

At the wedding breakfast Charlotte Wedgwood met her future husband, the Revd Charles Langton, a clever, jovial man with a disposition more like that of a politician than a clergyman. Two weeks later they were engaged. And two months later, on 22 March 1832, they were married by Allen Wedgwood in the little church at Maer.

Frank Wedgwood married equally suddenly. During the excitement and festivities of Charlotte's engagement, he met Frances Mosley, the daughter of the Revd John Peploe Mosley, rector of Rolleston, at a ball. Like his father before him, Frank fell in love at first sight and instantly made up his mind that this was the woman he intended to marry. Fanny Mosley was blonde and beautiful and frivolous. Like Bessy forty years earlier, she was at first intimidated then overwhelmed by a determined and aggressive young man who managed his family's pottery.

After Frank's decision to marry, Jos asked Harry and Jessie, and conse-

quently John and Jane as well, to vacate Etruria Hall so that Frank and his
new wife (now called Fanny Frank to distinguish her from her sisters-in-law
the unmarried Fanny Wedgwood and the newly married Fanny Hensleigh
Wedgwood) might move there. Bessy feared that John and Jane might feel
further abused and alienated by being asked to vacate the Hall a second
time and only a few months after they had moved back there. Jos, however,
was adamant in his decision. It would be convenient for Frank to be so close
to the factory. Frank, after all, was the son upon whom the future of the
pottery — and, consequently, the Wedgwood fortunes — would depend.
Harry and Jessie moved to a house called Keel while John and Jane and
Eliza, who had become as strange a religious recluse as her brother Allen,
move to Seabridge, which was only a few miles from Maer.

Jos was again asked to run for Parliament in the next election. His misgivings on this occasion centered on the expense of maintaining a residence in
London as well as keeping up Maer. On this matter he sought Hensleigh's
opinion.
    'With respect to your living in Town as Member for Stoke,' Hensleigh
wrote to him,

> I will now mention a plan that I have been thinking of for some time but
> I had some awkwardness about mentioning anything that was so inhospi-
> table to you. I am sure if I had a house of my own I need not say how glad
> I should be for you to come & live with me when you were in Town, but I
> could not ask you, & I know you would not do it, to come & live regularly
> at Sir James's expense so what I propose would be that you should come &
> live with us and pay a moderate board, say two guineas a week towards
> the expense of the household.'[2]

Hensleigh was uncomfortable in his father-in-law's house and embarrassed that Mackintosh would allow Jos to come into his house as a paying
guest. Hensleigh was well aware that Mackintosh and his family had lived
off the Wedgwoods for periods of as long as six months and that Mackintosh
had never paid back money borrowed from his father over two decades
before. The immature, unintellectual Robert persistently voicing his
opinion on matters about which he had little knowledge further aggravated
Hensleigh. Tensions in the household increased. Hensleigh and Robert
argued openly with ill-concealed hostility over the most trivial affairs. Surprisingly, Mary Rich unfailingly sided with Hensleigh. Before any disagreement between Mackintosh and Hensleigh came into the open, Mackintosh
suffered a freak accident.
    At a dinner party on Friday, 2 May 1832, a chicken bone lodged in his
throat. For several minutes he choked and coughed. The incident was
uncomfortable and disconcerting but not thought serious, and the bone was
not removed until the following Monday. The surgeon as well as Mackintosh then thought that he would suffer no more than a sore throat. Unfortunately an infection developed, followed by additional complications, and
Mackintosh died at Langham Place on 30 May 1832, less than a month
after the accident. Fanny Hensleigh, Mary Rich and Fanny Allen, who was

at the time in Switzerland visiting the Sismondis, were all shocked and grieved deeply.

Robert Mackintosh determined to find an historian of stature to finish off the third volume of his father's *History* and to publish his letters and diaries as a kind of memorial. He also decided to move from Langham Place. Hensleigh was secretly relieved.

At about the time of Mackintosh's death a serious outbreak of cholera struck England. In the Midlands the epidemic centered mainly on New-castle-under-Lyme. The disease caused such panic that people landing in France from England were placed in a three-day quarantine. In August, twenty-six year-old Fanny Wedgwood was suddenly taken ill with what the family described as an 'inflammatory attack'. Three days later she was dead. No one was quite certain whether her death was the result of cholera or some other violent intestinal disorder.

Baugh Allen took Bessy and Elizabeth to Wales to help Bessy recover from the shock of the death. Bessy's own health had already been visibly declining. Twenty-four-year-old Emma, who had never been separated from her sister Fanny, remained at home with her father and brother Joe. Her grief was private and poignant.

After the Reform Bill became law in 1832, Jos again stood for Parliament in the new reformed borough of Stoke-on-Trent. This time he won by a hand-some majority even though his campaign speech had been listened to 'with-out applause'. His nearest rival, Henry Davenport, was, however, met with hisses and hootings.

Emma described to her Aunt Jessie Sismondi how she and her sister-in-law Jessie Wedgwood went to Hanley to see the candidates going to Stoke to be nominated:

> Papa went first with his sons and some more gentlemen, his proposer and seconder, in the carriage open with four horses; a few carriages followed and then the tag-rag and bobtail in gigs, carts and phaetons. Then came Davenport, who looked much more numerous, which made us rather low ... the next two days the voting took place, and what a pleasant short affair it is now to what it used to be. There was some rioting and some who voted for Davenport had all their windows broke.... Papa and all of us were very much pleased at his coming in so grandly, especially as he is become too Tory for these Radical Times.[3]

All four of Jos's sons worked to get him elected. Frank not only worked during the campaign for his father's election, he also served on the commit-tee for Sir Oswald Mosley, his wife's cousin. Mosley was elected as well.

In February of 1833, Jos and Bessy's first grandchild, Hensleigh's daugh-ter Frances Julia, was born in a heavy snowstorm from which she acquired the lasting nickname of Snow. In March, Frank's son Godfrey was born, followed a few weeks later by Harry's daughter Louisa Frances.

Later in the spring Bessy and her daughters Elizabeth and Emma went to London to see Hensleigh and Fanny and the new baby. Jos was already in

London for the first session of Parliament. He had rented lodgings near the Commons and spent the week-ends with Hensleigh and Fanny who, with Mary Rich, had moved back to Clapham to the old house next door to the Thorntons. Mary Rich had missed the Evangelical church in Clapham. After the sudden death of her father, she had become, if possible, even more Evangelical. Robert Mackintosh, who had resigned his position as Commissioner of Bankruptcies and was seeking a more prestigious Civil Service appointment, kept lodgings on his own.

Before returning to Staffordshire Bessy and Elizabeth and Emma once again went to visit Harriet Gifford in Roehampton. There Bessy had another serious seizure, during which she fell and permanently damaged her spine. Dr Peter Holland was summoned, and again it was feared that she would not live. Jos, Hensleigh and Fanny drove out in a carriage from London. Joe and Frank came down from Etruria, and Charlotte Langton came from Onibury, near Shrewsbury, where her husband was the vicar. Though Bessy survived what was either a stroke or a serious epileptic fit, she was never able to walk again without assistance. After several months she was moved back to Maer. While she had periods of lucidity, her mind was damaged, and she suffered progressive deterioration both physical and mental.

Jos stayed in Parliament throughout the term 1832–5. Conscientious about attending sessions and voting, he remained quietly on the back benches. He did not stand a second time. He was sixty-four years old and had no more personal ambitions. Nor had he any illusions about the ambitions or abilities of his four sons. His thoughts now centered almost obsessively on settling financial affairs and establishing a secure income for his children and grandchildren.

22

The Quiet Path
(1833 – 1837)

'Our whole family are now assembled, except Hensleigh,' Jos wrote to the Sismondis. 'All well; and I often think that if they have all taken the quiet path of life they have none of them made us ashamed or sorry.'[1]

Three of his children still lived at home at Maer. Joe was now aged thirty-eight. Daily he rode on horseback with his father to the factory, arriving by ten and returning by four. The two unmarried daughters Elizabeth, aged forty, and Emma, aged twenty-five, helped to care for their bed-ridden mother and pursued their different interests. Elizabeth continued her Sunday School, her free medical clinic and her charities of making clothes and household goods for the poor. She distributed vegetables and eggs from the farms at Maer. Emma played the piano, worked in the garden, read the latest novels and wrote in her diary. Both sisters loved animals. Maer was a house that always seemed to have as many cats and dogs as humans. And both sisters visited frequently with their Aunt Sarah Wedgwood, who now lived a spartan existence at Camphill since her old housekeeper Betty Moore had retired.

Problems with servants were constant at Maer as well as in other country houses. Even before Bessy's last illness there had been a 'grand blow up' which Hensleigh described to Fanny—'women brought in & stay all night in the men's rooms (& two men & a woman staying one night in Samuel's pantry). What a pleasant thing it would have been for my mother if she had stumbled across them on one of her nightly rambles after Giss [her pet terrier].'[2] Samuel was dismissed. Another feud developed between the cook and the housekeeper, each threatening to leave if the other remained. After her mother's second illness at Roehampton, Elizabeth took more firm control of the household.

Both Hensleigh and Fanny were by temperament and inclination natural members of the Clapham Sect. Members of the Sect attended the Evangelical Church in Clapham, and many of them actually did live in or near Clapham. They were, for the most part, rich—second- or third-generation wealth. Their money came from business, finance, trade and industry. Their interests were intellectual and humanitarian. They invested their money, as well as their energies, in the encouragement of the arts and in social betterment. Evangelicals, both inside and outside the Established Church, believed that material success was the criterion of achievement and that they could set about making money to the glory of God provided only that they were scrupulous in the spending of it.

After the Hensleigh's move back to Clapham, Mary Rich's religious beliefs took on a slightly more mystical character. Obsessed by death and by the certainty of a life hereafter in which she would once again be joined with her beloved Claudius, she attended weekly prayer meetings and was influenced by 'those who spoke in tongues'. Fanny Hensleigh often accompanied her.

Fanny Allen visited the Hensleigh Wedgwoods in Clapham and accompanied Mrs Rich to meetings on two occasions. She reported that the man speaking in tongues 'raved like a maniac ... with as small a portion of the Spirit, I should have thought, if they had not said otherwise, as any teacher ever had'. On the way home she told Mrs Rich that she would have thought the man 'insane if left to my own judgment; she told me that she thought every repetition that he had used was commanded by the Spirit and quoted the verse 'line upon line' etc. as the authority.'[3]

Hensleigh and Fanny were both believers but in a less strident manner. Hensleigh was conscientious about his magistracy work. He was also absorbed in the study of etymology, which had interested him since his days at Cambridge when he excelled in Latin, Greek and Hebrew as well as in modern languages. The dissection of words was to him what the dissection of insects was to his cousin Charles Darwin. Fanny Hensleigh jokingly complained to her sister-in-law Elizabeth: 'Hensleigh is so busy now with language and metaphysics that it is rather hard to make him spend his holidays. Tomorrow I'm taking him on a round of visits. He is very dissipated dining out.'[4]

Hensleigh and Fanny led an active social life. Like her father before her, Fanny enjoyed parties and the intellectual stimulation of conversation with interesting and influential people, particularly those with literary connections. She was a great advocate of women's rights and tended to choose women friends who were intellectual and active in various social or political reforms. Three of her closest friends were Marianne Thornton, Harriet Martineau and Elizabeth Gaskell — the latter distantly related to the Wedgwoods through her mother Elizabeth Holland. As a girl, Mrs Gaskell had attended a school at Avonbank run by three of Thomas Byerley's daughters. Fanny herself had no pretensions to literary talent, though she considered herself an astute judge of the work of others.

Part of James Mackintosh's work, *A History of the Revolution in 1688*, had been revised by Thomas Wallace, an M.P. friend of Mackintosh's and formerly one of the Commissioners for Indian Affairs. Published with a memoir of Mackintosh as a Preface, it was poorly received and ferociously attacked in the *Edinburgh Review* by Thomas Babington Macaulay, who had been asked by Robert Mackintosh to edit the text himself but had refused. Robert then decided himself to undertake the additional work of editing his father's journals and letters, a project that was encouraged by the rest of the family and by Mackintosh's old patroness Lady Holland. Through the kindness and influence of Lady Holland, Robert was given a series of Government appointments, the first of which was a consulship. 'Erasmus [Darwin] is gone as his clerk,' Emma Wedgwood reported, 'which surprised us all that so idle a man should like to undertake it (viz. the Clerk) as it is supposed he will have a good deal to do. The girls at Shrewsbury tell him they are afraid the King will have a very bad bargain.'[5]

Bad bargain it likely was. Ras was soon back in London, resuming his old leisurely life-style. Apart from the Hensleigh Wedgwoods, his closest friends were Thomas and Jane Carlyle, who had recently moved from Scotland to London. Carlyle had just achieved a popular success with his *Sartor Resartus*, which set out guide-lines for a rather elusive new religious system, and had begun an ambitious historical work, *The French Revolution*. Ras and Harriet Martineau, who was gaining a large following with her stories and dialogues illustrating classical economics, frequently found themselves paired at dinner parties. 'It is curious to see what good order she is in,' Fanny Hensleigh told Elizabeth Wedgwood, 'and how she jumps up when he makes her a sign that the cab is waiting & declines taking her home by Tulse Hill as she proposes ... it is amusing to me to see how entirely married they seem & he minds it as little as she does....'[6]

Robert Mackintosh's publication of his father's memoirs brought almost unanimous approval. Another old literary friend of Fanny Hensleigh's, Maria Edgeworth, wrote to her:

> So many sweet and bitter recollections have come over my mind when-ever I have thought of writing to you that I have still delayed and delayed — still thinking a time would come when I should write with less emotion and perhaps give you less pain.... The *Memoirs* are most interesting at this moment & they must continue to interest as long as the History of our times and the faithful and lively portrait of one of the most distinguished men of his age shall be valued in England, or in any part of the *reading* world that is the civilized world. The character is so fully laid open and is so true to nature that it must keep its hold of the mind. Who ever begins will go on with this memoir. Your brother has, with great skill and judgment, made use in the first place of that which every reader must feel gives the stronger evidence of truth, that is your father's own account of his early life, all his journals and his letters....

Maria concluded by saying how grateful she was for the praise given to her in Mackintosh's journal: The manner in which my father and Mrs Edge-worth are mentioned was delightful to me — and what he says of myself gave me infinitely more pleasure than ever could have been said of my books.'[7]

Fanny was pleased by Maria's comments as she was fond of her person-ally, as well as appreciative of her writing. More and more Fanny sparkled in the company of literary discussion and debate, while Hensleigh with-drew, preferring more the company of his own word studies.

Jos was having literary discussions of another sort. He had been provoked and upset by an article by Thomas De Quincey in *Tait's Magazine.* Published after the death of Coleridge in 1834, the article was titled 'S. T. Coleridge by the English Opium Eater'. It contained three errors with reference to Tom Wedgwood which Jos found unforgivable. First De Quincey stated that Tom owned a butcher shop and, following his doctor's advice, lived above the shop. Secondly, he said that after Coleridge's return from Göttingen in 1799, he attended Tom as a devoted Friend and companion throughout the long illness which brought Tom his untimely death in 1805. Thirdly, De Quincey stated that because of Coleridge's tireless devotion Tom left him the annuity in his will.

Jos felt that, quite apart from being untrue, the article made Tom's motives in giving the annuity seem less worthy than in reality they were. He exchanged several letters with his old friend Thomas Poole, who wanted an authorized version of Coleridge's letters and papers published. Jos didn't want any letters that either he or Tom had written to Coleridge to be published. This disagreement widened the distance between two old friends who had already become more distant than either wished at this late stage in their lives. Both were stubborn men. Their correspondence ceased, and Poole died two years later.

When Hensleigh asked his father why he had discontinued his half of the Coleridge annuity, Jos replied: 'I had my reasons.' There the matter rested. The 'Governor' was not a man who felt obliged to explain his reasons.

Over the years John Wedgwood's character had changed little either. In a letter to their youngest son Robert, who had become a vicar in Wales and had recently married, Jane reported that his father was still 'gadding about'. John had never lost his enthusiasm for canals. During the period when Jos was in Parliament, John got himself appointed to a special committee in Newport to oppose the construction of a railroad in Monmouthshire. As canals had done eighty years earlier, this new method of rail transportation posed a threat to the old order. The Wedgwood family had considerable investments in canal shares. 'If carried into effect the loss to this canal will be £10,000 per annum,' John told Jos, 'for the whole of the Iron will leave us and go by the new road.... It is very important to throw as many obstacles as possible in the way of the railroad.'[8]

Because the Wedgwood family had considerable investments in the canals, or Turnpike Trusts, but also because the Wedgwood company moved its clay and its finished pottery on its own barges, neither John nor Jos wanted to believe that the canals could not withstand the competition of the new railways. But the canals had not been built with an eye to the future. The sizes of the locks varied considerably, and long-distance cargo had frequently to be loaded and unloaded as goods passed from one canal to another. Worst of all, the canals were neither wide enough nor deep enough to switch from horse-drawn barges to steamboats. Railways were the obvious transport wave of the future — the rising tide of a new era. 'I do really begin to believe in the railroad since Frank has been on it,'[9] Fanny Hensleigh announced seriously.

As a family the John Wedgwoods were in their usual undecided, transitory state. They visited their son Robert at Tenby and then went to

Cresselly, where they spent the winter of 1836, with John Allen, his four adolescent children and the two unmarried Allen sisters Emma and Fanny, now aged fifty-six and fifty-five. Their third son Charles, an undisciplined and adventurous young man, had died of a fever in India. Caroline Drewe, the sister to whom Jane was closest, had also died the year before. Her death left a void in Jane's life similar to the deep grief she had felt with the death of her daughter Caroline a decade earlier.

On their way back to Seabridge in Staffordshire, John and Jane and Eliza, who was her parents' constant companion, decided to travel by way of Shrewsbury where they would visit Robert Darwin and his three daughters, Caroline, Susan and Catherine, now aged thirty-six, thirty-three and twenty-six. First, however, they visited the Langtons at Onibury, where Jane confided to her niece Charlotte that she 'had a bad opinion of herself, but that she was not the least depressed by it, and talked about it with the utmost composure'.[10]

Jane felt death approaching, though no one in her family thought her dangerously ill. For years she had suffered headaches, exhaustion, nervousness and a variety of other psychosomatic complaints. But, in appearance, attitude and movement, she seemed much younger than her sixty-six years. Less than a decade before she had been mistaken at a party, not for her daughter but for her grand-daughter. By contrast, John's physical appearance had altered considerably. With his thin white hair, stooped shoulders, hesitant walk, nodding head and increasing shakiness in the hands and arms, he seemed much older than his seventy years. It was therefore a shock to everyone, including Robert Darwin, when the family arrived at The Mount with Jane ill. She immediately took to her bed complaining of chest pains and exhaustion. At first Robert thought she was having a gall bladder attack and would soon recover. A week later she was weaker and had no desire to move from her bed.

The news sent to Maer from The Mount was:

On Tuesday evening the Doctor saw her before he went to bed & found her pulse & every symptom quite good — but about twelve she awoke in dreadful pain. The Doctor was called up & sat some hours by her bedside. He was then much alarmed, and thought her in the greatest danger. This terrible pain lasted all the next day, but abated at night, and she thought she should sleep well — but a restlessness came on which seems to be quite a fatal symptom, and an extreme cold — she was sinking all Thursday — towards evening her mind began to wander & she suffered extremely from restlessness.[11]

Knowing that she was dying, Robert Darwin sent word to her children. Jessie and Robert came immediately. Tom, who was at Cresselly with his fiancée Anne Tyler, could not be reached in time. Allen, like his father, could not bear the emotional strain of a deathbed scene, so he remained at Maer.

They supported her up on the side of the bed. She scarcely knew them, but when Eliza said, 'Mother, you are going to Caroline,' it was the first thing that lay hold on her mind. Eliza then uttered some prayers aloud, and a few sentences of scripture; it instantly had the effect of calming & comforting her. Robert was supporting her head & then continued a few more sentences of prayer which she evidently followed with her mind & very soon all was over in perfect quietness and to see her quiet after such suffering was a relief to them all.[12]

All of the Wedgwood – Darwin – Allen family were concerned as to how John, who had been so dependent upon his wife, would adjust to living without her. He looked 'an altered man' but after a few days recovered his ability to sleep through the night and seemed quite composed. Plans were made for John and Eliza to combine households again with Harry and Jessie. Seabridge was larger than Keel, and now that Jessie was pregnant with her second child, living at Seabridge seemed more sensible. Noting that 'besides losing the object of so much affection, they lose one whose society was the life of them all', Elizabeth Wedgwood thought that 'their settling at Seabridge gives Uncle John constant employment and almost a daily ride there, and we are very glad to see that he is able to take an interest in his new garden, and all the preparations.'[13]

Another family crisis occurred in London at the time of Jane's death. Fanny Hensleigh's three children all came down with whooping cough, and the baby, only seven months old, died. 'What an anxious, distressing time of it you and Fanny have had till your poor little thing went home,' Frank wrote to Hensleigh. 'I am afraid Fanny will feel it very much as the more trouble she had with the poor little helpless thing, the more she would love it....'

As to the other death in the family, he observed: 'I cannot think how Uncle John will ever get over his loss — so wrapped up in her as he has always been — or Eliza — indeed they will all of them feel the gap very much. The funeral is to be on Thursday. Harry & Allen have gone over there [Shrewsbury] where it is suspected they may chance not to meet with a very cordial welcome. The house being full & Tom expected & the doctor unwell and no great reason for their going....'[14]

As he grew older, Robert Darwin's depressions, fits of anger and spells of rapid talking became more pronounced and more intimidating to those around him. He worked hard, daily witnessing suffering and death. He felt deeply the loss of patients and friends, and he brooded upon the frequent helplessness of medical men to effect cures. He was a disappointed, lonely, complicated man whom many feared and few understood. 'The doctor, good as he is, is so tiresome that he takes away every feeling of liberty,' Fanny Allen noted after visiting there. 'I found it was a gain when I got behind even the pillar of the sitting room so that I was out of his observation.'[15] The one event which seemed likely to lift Robert's spirits was the return of his son Charles, who had been away almost five years now.

Charles came back to Shrewsbury on the morning of 5 October 1836, walking into the house just before breakfast. 'We have had the very happiest morning,' Caroline Darwin reported. 'Charles so full of affection and

78-79　　John Wedgwood and his wife Jane, *née* Allen
　　　　Oil of Jane Wedgwood by Sir Thomas Lawrence,
　　　　c. *1800*

80-81　　Josiah Wedgwood II and his wife Bessy, *née* Allen
　　　　Oil of Bessy Wedgwood by George Romney, 1793

82　　*Overleaf:* Wedgwood wares of the nineteenth century

83-84   Sir James Mackintosh and Lady Mackintosh, *née*
Kitty Allen, *c.* 1803
Oil of Sir James by Lawrence; Lady Mackintosh by
John Hoppner

85-86   Dr Robert Darwin and his wife Susannah, *née* Wedgwood

delight at seeing my father looking so well and being with us again.'[16] Charles himself wrote to his Uncle Jos: 'My head is quite confused with so much delight, but I cannot allow my sisters to tell you first how happy I am to see all my dear friends again. I am obliged to return in three or four days to London when the *Beagle* will be paid off, and then I shall pay Shrewsbury a longer visit. I am most anxious once again to see Maer and all its inhabitants, so that in the course of two or three weeks, I hope in person to thank you, as being my First Lord of the Admiralty.'[17]

Charles went to London to wind up his affairs with the *Beagle*, to make arrangements for presenting his collections to the Zoological Museum and to the British Museum and to confer with Hooker, Lyell, Lonsdale, Bell and other scientists about his work and about his future. He visited his brother Ras and with Fanny and Hensleigh. As Hensleigh had been unmarried the last time Charles saw him, Charles was 'much struck with the sight of Hensleigh walking up the street with a bandbox in one hand and a child in the other'.[18]

These were exciting times for Charles and consequently for the rest of the Wedgwood-Darwin circle. For the next few months he went back and forth several times between Shrewsbury, Maer, Cambridge and London. He began preparing his 'Journal of Travels'. The beginning of the year 1837 was for him, his family, his country and indeed for the whole civilized world the beginning of a new era in history.

23

The New Victorians
(1837 – 1843)

In 1837 William IV died of a circulatory disease, and his eighteen-year-old niece Victoria ascended the throne. The new young Queen commanded attention, affection and, most of all, a new hope. Among her subjects one Englishman out of three could neither read nor write his name; two out of three women were illiterate. And yet, this was an era of progress. Railway lines were hurriedly being laid all across the country. People reckoned distance now in terms of hours and talked of 'getting up steam' to do things. Steamships were even crossing the Atlantic Ocean to America.

Under the ageing, aristocratic Lord Melbourne, the Whigs remained in power for another four years. Melbourne had been vindicated the year before in the divorce trial of Caroline Norton who was accused of having an intrigue with him. Caroline Norton, a friend of Fanny Hensleigh and Elizabeth Gaskell, was an exceptionally beautiful and gifted woman with a talent for musical composition. The result of the trial, which was caricatured by Dickens in *The Pickwick Papers*, was not disgrace but greater popularity for her among the fashionable political and literary circles in London.

Within the Wedgwood circle forty-two-year-old Joe at long last fulfilled his parents' expectations by marrying Caroline Darwin. From her sofa Bessy commented that she was as 'pleased as if Joe had won Victoria herself'. Charles Darwin, who was staying in London with his brother Ras, wrote to their cousin William Darwin Fox:

> Caroline is going to be married to Jos [Joe] Wedgwood. I do not know whether you recollect him, he is the eldest son — He is a very quiet grave man, with very much to like and respect in him, but I wish he would put himself forward more. He has a most wonderful deal of information and is a very superior person, but he has not made the most of himself — I am very glad of the marriage for Caroline's sake as I think she will be a very happy person, especially if she has children, for I never saw a human being so fond of little crying wretches, as she is.[1]

Charles finished writing his 'Zoology of the Voyage of the *Beagle*'. Then he took his holiday at Shrewsbury and at Maer, where Hensleigh was the centre of considerable controversy and turmoil. Hensleigh has resigned his Police Magistracy because his conscience would no longer allow him to administer oaths. Charles also wrote to Fox about this Wedgwood family crisis:

> I am sure you will be sorry to hear a piece of bad news with respect to the Wedgwoods. Hensleigh W. who married Fanny Mackintosh (and who is the pleasantest of the whole family) has long had great scruples about the profanation of taking oaths on trifling occasions. A week since, it happened for him to swear *42* oaths!! under the new reign to qualify as magistrate. This he could not bring himself to do and consequently resigned his place of 800£ per annum and is now utterly thrown out of all employment. — He has three children and may probably have more and has scarcely anything to live on. — It is a most distressing case; many thousand people might be searched and not so excellent, clever & admirable a pair could be found as H. and his wife — and now they are actually thinking of going to *America*! — though I cannot but hope that something may turn up.[2]

It was not a new or sudden decision. For the past four years Hensleigh had struggled with his conscience. He had accepted his father's advice, that he should refrain from a hasty decision. He had been particularly influenced by Jos's suggestion that the evil might best be remedied from within the establishment. 'I am in hopes that the arguments for retaining his office will have their view weighed with him,' Jos had written to the Sismondis,

> and especially as his mind is now turned to exertion for the removal of unnecessary oaths, in which he must see that his situation as an acting magistrate will give him a weight which would be lost by giving up his office. If after taking sufficient time to restore the equilibrium of his mind ... he should form a solid conviction that administration of oaths by a Magistrate is forbidden by the gospel, there can be no doubt that it will be his duty to resign; and however great may be one's concern one cannot blame him, though even then he cannot expect to be supported by much of the sympathy, respect, and admiration, which are given to great sacrifices for objects which all men feel to interest human nature.[3]

The same scruples and stubbornness which had caused Hensleigh to resign his fellowship at Christ's College and to refuse to lie about Fanny's residence at the time of his marriage were now focused on the morality of administering oaths. Though Jos did not share Hensleigh's convictions, he must have recognized his own unyielding personality in his son's actions. Not only his father, but his brothers, sisters and cousins, and even more importantly his wife, disagreed with Hensleigh. 'The burden of the sacrifice, if you resolve to make it, will fall with greatest weight on your wife & children,' his father argued, '& it is your duty to take care that you do not injure them without a conviction that a higher duty requires the sacrifice.'[4]

A higher duty called. Shortly after his return to London from Maer, Hensleigh wrote to his father:

> I have been a good deal distracted ever since my return from Maer with doubts as to the lawfulness of oaths of any kind & they have increased so much that I can no longer reconcile it with my conscience to keep my present situation, so large a part of the duties of which consist in the administering of oaths. I am satisfied that nothing but long periods & of being brought up in the middle of the system could allow us to put such a construction upon our Saviour's precept as is usually done. But however this may be, it is impossible for me to go on with a dissatisfied conscience & the arguments in favour of the lawfulness of oaths are far from satisfying me; they appear to me to be mere defences. I think it very possible that it may be lawful for a man to take a judicial oath, but I feel that it is not lawful for me & there is no use in letting £800 a year persuade one's conscience.[5]

Hensleigh then went on to say that he would have difficulty in finding a tenant for the house in Clapham and asked his father if he might send Fanny with her nurse and the new baby Ernie to Maer until he could get his plans settled.

Jos replied: 'Your letter received yesterday is final & it now remains for you to settle your plans for the future in which you will have the most affectionate sympathy & serious respect of myself & our whole family. Will it not suit you best to bring your family here as soon as you can where you may calmly consider of your future course?'[6]

The house in Clapman was leased more quickly than Hensleigh had anticipated, so that the entire family came to Maer, with the exception of Mary Rich, who, having given some thought to settling with the Inglises, finally took lodgings in London near the A. J. Scotts. A former assistant to the popular Scottish evangelist Edward Irving, Scott was an impressive minister who had gathered around him a devoted group of followers, mainly wealthy middle-aged women like Mary Rich.

Hensleigh was undecided where to go or what to do. As Robert Mackintosh was at the time in America, Aunt Fanny Allen told Fanny Hensleigh that she hoped 'that America will not be brought into question' as to where they should settle. 'Hensleigh is led by a clearer light than that which most of us go by,' she said, 'and it was impossible for him not to do as he has done.'[7] Aunt Sarah Wedgwood took the same attitude — that her nephew Hensleigh was superior to ordinary men.

Fortunately, however, for his ordinary wife and children, the Whigs were still in power and distributing political appointments. Through the influence of Lord Russell, Hensleigh could anticipate being offered another Government appointment. His father had other ideas. Again Jos wished to make his youngest son a partner in the firm, and again Hensleigh refused. He said that Fanny preferred living in London to living in the Potteries, that he believed he could find another Government post which would not compromise his principles and that in any event he did not wish to do anything that would deprive either his father or his brothers of income.

Jos replied:

> I wish you to put any such considerations for me out of the question. I have only one object, to act justly toward all my family in the suggestion I made to you of becoming a partner. I wish to add to your income without making an unfair distribution of my property — my sincere & only wish is that you may decide on the course most conducive to your & your family's happiness and I am persuaded your brothers have no other wish & will have no personal feeling respecting your conduct whatever course you may take.[8]

He then went on to suggest that on a probable annual gross profit of £5,000, which was what the pottery had been averaging, Hensleigh could deduct from his income 4 per cent interest on the capital put up for him by his father and deduct a further sum of £100 to his partners until he was competent to manage the pottery himself. Under this arrangement Hensleigh would still have an income of £580.

While waiting for some word from Lord Russell about a Government appointment, Hensleigh devoted more time to his study of etymology. Six hours a day he spent locked in his study absorbed in his books. When no political appointment was forthcoming after six months, Jos once again renewed his offer of a partnership in the pottery.

Hensleigh was spared further argument with his father by the offer of the post of Registrar of Cabs, to which he had originally aspired five years earlier, but which carried a salary of only £400 a year. He accepted despite this: a reduced income was preferable to no income at all. He and Fanny, their three children and their servants moved back to London to a house in Notting Hill on which they took a twelve-month lease.

While Hensleigh was going through his crises of conscience, Charles Darwin was having crises of his own. During the visit at Maer when Hensleigh debated moral attitudes with which Charles differed but still respected, Charles took several long strolls around the walks at Maer with his 'First Lord of the Admiralty'. They went to examines a field which had been spread with quicklime ten years earlier. Jos pointed out to his nephew the large quantity of fine earth continually brought up to the surface by earthworms. Charles concluded that all the vegetable mould over the earth's surface had passed many times through the intestinal canals of worms and would again and again pass through them in the process of ploughing the soil. Spread over the fields not only by ploughing but also by rain, the mould would gradually cover anything left on top of the ground. Charles decided to put forward this unorthodox theory in a paper which he read before the Geological Society of London. It attracted little interest at the time.

Charles had things other than geology and earthworms on his mind, however. Since his return home he had begun to think seriously about his own future and to examine critically the lives of his friends and relatives. For a while he lounged around the Athenaeum Club with Ras, enjoying the leisurely life of a gentleman who had no need to exert himself in making a living. At the same time he observed Hensleigh and his enjoyment of married life in spite of his financial troubles. To his surprise Charles found himself taking an interest in the activities of Hensleigh's children, particularly of the precocious five-year-old Julia, who was called Snow. Charles was even caught up in the excitement of Caroline and Joe's marriage and in the setting up of their first house, Clayton, which was three and a half miles from Etruria.

In June of 1838 there was a party at the Hensleigh Wedgwoods' new house in London, which was next door to Ras's house in Great Marlborough Street. Robert Mackintosh had returned from America. Emma Wedgwood and Catherine Darwin came back from Paris where they had met the Sismondis. All of the travellers, Charles and Ras and Thomas and Jane Carlyle, came to dinner. After this party Charles began to think seriously of marrying his cousin Emma. With characteristic objectivity he had already drawn up a balance sheet, on Maer notepaper, of the advantages and disadvantages of marrying. The paper was headed *this is the question* and divided into columns: *Marry* and *Not Marry*. In the latter column were such notes as 'not forced to visit relatives and to bend in every trifle ...' and '*loss of time* — cannot read in the evenings — fatness and idleness — anxiety and responsibility — less money for books, etc....'

These disadvantages were far outweighed by the comments in the other column: 'My God, it is intolerable to think of spending one's whole life, like a neuter bee, working, working and nothing after all — Only picture to yourself a nice soft wife on a sofa with good fire, and books and music perhaps — Compare this vision with the dingy reality of Great Marlborough Street. Marry — Marry — Marry Q.E. D.'[9]

On the back of the page he had summarized his situation and all of the reasons in favour of his marrying. Then, in August of 1838, he visited Maer again and spent many hours alone in the company of his cousin Emma. The more he saw of her the more he was convinced that she was the woman he wanted to marry, but he was uncertain of her feelings for him. In confusion he left without asking the all-important question. In November, after another bout of the mysterious illness which had afflicted him since his voyage, he returned to Maer. He was determined to ask Emma to marry him, although he was afraid he would be rejected because his face was too plain. On Saturday, 11 November, which he described as 'the day of days', Emma accepted his proposal in the library at Maer.

All of the family were delighted. Robert wrote to Jos: 'Emma having accepted Charles gives me as great happiness as Joe having married Caroline, and I cannot say more. On that marriage Bessy said she should not have had more pleasure if it had been Victoria, and you may assure her I feel as grateful to her for Emma, as if it had been Martineau herself that Charles had obtained.'[10]

The reference to Harriet Martineau was in sarcasm. After a triumphant tour of America, she was at the height of her fame. Robert, however, had taken a decided dislike to her. Her political opinions and her style of writing infuriated him, and he had a horror of Ras's suddenly deciding to marry her. There was gossip about them in London which had spread to the country. So great was Robert's animosity towards the lady that on one occasion, to the younger generation's amusement, 'the Dr read the first article in the *Westminster Review* before he knew it was not hers, and wasted a great deal of good indignation, and even now he can hardly believe it is not hers.'[11]

But, if Robert was outraged at the thought of Harriet Martineau marrying into the family, there were those within the family who considered Ras less than an ideal husband. On learning of Emma's engagement to Charles, her Aunt Jessie Sismondi wrote to her: 'I am grateful to him [Charles] for saving you from Erasmus. I was always afraid of that. I knew you would be a Mrs Darwin from your hands [which apparently were like her Aunt Susan's]; and seeing Charles did not come on, which Fan [Allen] and I used to speculate on and expect in every letter from Maer, I began to fear it was Erasmus.'[12]

That Ras had incurred Jessie's disapproval was not because of anything in particular he had done but because he had never done anything in particular. Nor did he show any signs of ever doing so. In contrast to his energetic and domineering father, Ras was lethargic and gentle and retiring. At times, it seemed almost as if he were destined to live out his father's early, cruel prediction that he was too idle ever to amount to anything — an echo of his grandfather's judgement of his namesake Erasmus, junr., whom he had predicted would 'sleep his life away'. Neither Ras nor Charles ever felt he could live up to his father's expectations. Perhaps as a consequence, both brothers suffered periods of inexplicable exhaustion and spent a great deal of their adult lives reclining on sofas. Ras's virtues were kindness, generosity and a brilliantly analytical mind, which Sismondi thought equal to Carlyle's; his flaws were a lack of confidence and a self-deprecation which harmed no one but himself. He liked women and frequently sought their companionship, but he was not a man to take on responsibilities which might be avoided. Perhaps, too, he was already aware that the woman he really loved was married to his cousin Hensleigh.

Jessie also gave her niece Emma advice on another subject that concerned her — Emma's lack of interest in clothes:

> Now that your person will belong to another as well as yourself, I beg you not to go to Cranbourne Alley to cloathe it, nor even to the Palais Royale.... But be that as it will, if you do pay a little more, be always dressed in good taste; do not despise those little cares which give everyone more pleasing looks because you know you have married a man who is above caring for such little things. No man is above caring for them, for they feel the effect imperceptibly to themselves. I have seen it even in my half-blind husband.[13]

Emma never really outgrew her childhood nickname of Little Miss Slip-Slop. She was as indifferent to houses and fashionable furniture as she was to clothes. After considerable house-hunting, to which Ras as well as Charles devoted his time they selected a furnished house at 12 Upper Gower

Street. It was spacious, inexpensive, located in a convenient neighbourhood and very ugly. Neither Charles nor Emma minded as long as they were comfortable and Charles had room for his specimens. The front attic at Upper Gower Street was to be named The Museum. The front room downstairs, both a laboratory and a study, held more specimens — 'so will allow things to grow, and things will always grow.'

With the prospect of his new life before him, Charles took more interest in social activities than at any time since his early years at Cambridge. He could hardly wait for Emma to join him:

> Erasmus's dinner yesterday was a very pleasant one: Carlyle was in high force and talked away most steadily; to my mind Carlyle is the best mind worth listening to of any man I know. The Hensleighs were there and were very pleasant also. Such society, I think, is worth all other and more brilliant kinds many times over. I find I cannot by any exertion get up the due amount of admiration for Mrs Carlyle: I do not know whether you find it so, but I am not able to understand half the words she speaks, from her Scotch pronunciation. She certainly is very far from natural; or to use the expression Hensleigh so often quotes, she is not an unconscious person....[14]

Anxious as Emma was to join Charles in London, she had mixed feelings about leaving her sister Elizabeth with the entire burden of nursing their mother. But Charles was impatient for the wedding to take place as soon as possible, and as there was little likelihood that Bessy would ever be any better, there was no real reason to delay.

Charles and Emma were married on Tuesday, 29 March 1839, in the little church at Maer. Allen Wedgwood performed the service which was attended by only the immediate family from Shrewsbury and those already in Staffordshire. Bessy's condition had deteriorated to the point where it was impossible for her to leave her bed, let alone attend her daugher's wedding. When Emma went into her room to say goodbye, she found her mother asleep and so they were both spared the pain of a parting scene.

Emma and Charles left Maer in a phaeton packed with sandwiches and bottles of water for the train journey from Newcastle to London. As they waved goodbye, Emma was moved to tears by the poignant realization that from the once large and happy household at Maer there remained only the ageing, patriarchal Jos, the invalid Bessy, and their middle-aged spinster daughter Elizabeth.

Two months after Charles and Emma's wedding they returned for a visit at Maer and then at Shrewsbury. Eliza Wedgwood, John's eldest daughter, came with her father to Maer to nurse her Aunt Bessy so that her cousin Elizabeth could go with Charles and Emma to Shrewsbury and have a little holiday.

The two old brothers, John and Jos, now seventy-two and sixty-nine, were both as reserved as ever. They had a quiet, leisurely visit which brought them closer than they had been in years — though, one evening at dusk, as the shadows darkened the house, Emma entered the drawing room and found them sitting in silence in the dark. John's eyesight had begun to fail. For several years now Jos had been afflicted with palsy. It was the same kind of tremor that had bothered John to a lesser degree all of his life. Jos's deteriorating condition depressed him. He had a fear of being invalided and paralysed like Bessy. Even the slightest change in his physical or mental state he discussed with Robert Darwin.

'Your kind of tremor goes on slowly increasing sometimes to a certain point and then stays and does not seem to get worse,' Robert told him.

I have often known this to be the case, and as far as it may be considered of any analogy to a paralytic nature, it certainly is a kind of safety valve from a real paralysis. I cannot help suspecting and hoping that you have not any greater failure of memory than takes place with anybody at your age and not such as would induce you to take any decisive step of declining any occupation simply on that account. From the same feelings of failure of memory, I have taken several little precautions for the last few years, such as reading all letters twice over before I answer them, and being very particular in not putting off doing anything that can be done at once for fear it should quite escape my attention. With this case I have often a little accident, dropping what I ought to have retained.[15]

One member of the older generation still in excellent health was sixty-year-old Sarah Wedgwood. During Elizabeth's visit to Shrewsbury she came over daily from Camphill to dine with her two older brothers. Conscious of her diet, she was a staunch believer in abstinence from alcohol. She took regular exercise and read omnivorously. In spite of her robust health and charitable disposition, she was not inclined to gentleness or to patience or to the actual doing of practical things herself. She was totally incapable of nursing Bessy as Elizabeth, or in her absence Eliza, did.

Both Jos and John were fortunate in having elder daughters who were devoted, competent in domestic affairs and apparently content to dedicate their lives to their parents — a not uncommon fate for elder daughters in the nineteenth century. Jessie Sismondi, who twenty years earlier had experienced difficulty in separating herself from her family, worried that her two nieces were selflessly sacrificing their own happiness and would then find themselves lonely in their declining years. 'There cannot be a happier or easier task than making the lives comfortable of my father and mother,' Elizabeth assured her. 'There were never people who gave so much and required so little. Indeed it often makes me ashamed and touches me very tenderly to see my father get up to pay me some little kind attention that would come so much more appropriately from me to him.'[16]

Elizabeth had given up teaching her Sunday School. At the time she began her school, there had been no other education offered to the village children. Now the Methodists had a regular five-day school, so the need was no longer as great. Nursing her mother without the help of Emma was exhausting. Although there were nine servants in the house, the job of nursing was considered a family obligation, the duty of a daughter. Now totally helpless, Bessy's last years were spent on what Hensleigh described as a 'water bed' designed by Robert Darwin.

Charles and Emma's first visit back to Maer was spoiled somewhat by Charles's feeling unwell most of the time. 'Charles got some of his father's good doctoring and is much better again,' Elizabeth reported from Shrewsbury, 'but I suppose he is feeling the effect of too much exertion in every way during his voyage and must be careful not to work his head too hard now. His journal is out at last along with two other volumes of Captain Fitzroy and Captain King of the same voyage, but I have not had time to read it yet.'[17]

Hensleigh was also 'working his head hard' with his *Dictionary of English Etymology*, which had developed into a life-time undertaking. He and Fanny, their three children and Mary Rich had just taken a house in Gower Street only four doors away from Charles and Emma. 'We find it a constant pleasure having them [the Hensleighs] so near,' Emma reported. 'They often walk in to drink tea with us, and vice versa.'[18] The Hensleigh's house was larger and more convenient than the ones they had had in Notting Hill and Great Marlborough Street. Mary Rich had her own drawing room in the front of the house. There was another large drawing room at the back of the house which looked out over the garden where the children played.

Snow was now six and a half years old and a remarkably precocious child. Even though she was handicapped by poor hearing, her literary talents and astonishing memory were apparent. The book of 'Snowiana' which her Aunt Elizabeth had begun to collect grew thicker and thicker with anecdotes and childish verses. Before she was seven years old she was asking her mother to write down poems as she dictated them. One evening as she undressed for bed she composed the following:

> In the month of May
> When the fields look gay,
> Nothing seemed to have sorrow;
> Oh, wait till tomorrow
> When there will come a wintry day
> That will drive away this joyful May.
> We, like the flowers, fade away
> For we are made of dust and clay,
> And then comes a wintry blast
> Which drives them away with the wind and the past.
> But for the saints there's another May
> Which is a longer happier day,
> Where they never say good-night,
> Always peace and never fight,
> With crowns of glory on their heads,
> There they never rest on their beds.[19]

If hardly a literary masterpiece, it was a considerable achievement for a six-year-old. It also reflected an early preoccupation with good and evil that was to characterize Snow's mature writing. So gifted a child was naturally aware of the approval and special attention of numerous doting relatives.

Most important to the little girl, and far more influential in the development of her personality than either Hensleigh or Fanny realized, was Aunt Rich who spoke of God and the Heaven into which only the good and the righteous were permitted. The bright little girl who failed to hear when people spoke softly often feared to go to sleep at night because God might call her to Judgement and find her wanting.

At the age of eight she wrote to her mother: 'My dear Mamma, You cannot think how sorry I was this morning to make you so unhappy. I do not think anything made me naughty but pride. I have prayed to God to forgive me & I think you will. I am really sorry. Oh! Mamma, you do not know how unhappy I was to see you so unhappy all today. I know I have been cross for two or three days. I cannot help disliking my lessons but I will try to do them well. Goodbye.'[20]

A few months later Snow asked her mother if she might write to her mother's good friend Harriet Martineau to tell her how much she liked her stories and to inform her what was happening in the Wedgwood family, since her mother was ill and neglecting her correspondence. Fanny agreed and Snow wrote several letters to which Harriet Martineau replied:

I really am much obliged to you for sending me letters — particularly as you do not expect me to answer every one. If you or Bro (whom I find, I must now call Macky) will write to me some times when your Mamma is ill or busy, I shall be very much pleased. It is rather sad, however, that somebody is always ill when you write. If your Mamma had not been able to put in that she was better, your last would have made me very sad. I am glad you like my stories — particularly the last, as there are not to be any more. I find I like reading stories far better than writing them.[21]

She then went on to tell the child a story and ended by describing the flowers in her garden, signing the letter 'Your affectionate friend'.

An opposing force to the pure spirituality of Aunt Rich was the frivolity of Uncle Ras. He brought the Hensleigh children presents, took them on special outings and allowed them more or less to say and do whatever they chose, however blasphemous or irreverent. While Fanny was occupied with the new baby Effie, Ras often amused the three older children by drawing pictures and telling stories.

In December of 1839 the ailing Jos and the selfless Elizabeth visited the Hensleighs and the Darwins in their Gower Street houses. Emma had just given birth to her first child, William Erasmus. Charles was in poor health and consulting Dr Peter Holland. 'It is a great happiness to me when Charles is most unwell that he continues just as sociable as ever, and is not like the rest of the Darwins who will not say how they really are,' Emma wrote to her Aunt Jessie Sismondi, 'but he always tells me just how he feels and never wants to be alone, but continues just as warmly affectionate as ever, so that I feel I am a comfort to him.'[22]

Hensleigh and Charles were finding their different and separate interests remarkably complementary. They were able to debate ideas and each could at the same time be assured of an intelligent and sympathetic response from the other. Hensleigh dissected words and their various combinations while Charles was then most keenly interested in geology and zoology. He sought both ideas and specimens wherever he could find them. For example, he sent word to his cousin Fox: 'Don't forget, if your half-bred African cat should die that I should be very much obliged for its carcase sent up in a little hamper for the skeleton....'[23]

Hensleigh and Fanny and Charles and Emma shared the same social life, had the same friends and read the same books. 'I have been reading Carlyle, like all the rest of the world,' Emma told Jessie Sismondi. 'He fascinates one and puts one out of patience. He has been writing a sort of pamphlet on the state of England called "Chartism". It is full of compassion and good feeling but utterly unreasonable. Charles keeps on reading and abusing him. He is very pleasant to talk to anyhow, he is so very natural, and I don't think his writings at all so.'[24]

The year 1840 brought the new institution of the Penny Post. Now the writer rather than the recipient paid for the letter. Twice as many letters were being sent as had been in the past. Jos wrote to Emma that he would like George Richmond to do a portrait of her for him. He also requested that portraits be done by Richmond of his other two daughters, Charlotte and Elizabeth, and of his daughters-in-law, Jessie, Fanny Frank and Fanny Hensleigh.

The Sismondis visited England in the summer of 1840. They and Fanny Allen travelled from London to Reading by train, then from Reading to Bristol before proceeding by coach to Tenby. At the station both Jessie and Sismondi had their pockets picked. Then there was great confusion with a hundred people running from one railway track to another. 'At Reading we very nearly lost Fanny, and Sismondi by a trick detained the coach, pretending he could not get down after many vain efforts, and the coachman swearing he must drive off, and I with my head out the window screaming "Fanny!" We persuaded the coachman to go himself, which he did, saying to S., "Sir, you are a queer sort of traveller, you first lose your cushion, then your purse, and now your wife." '[25]

While on this trip, Sismondi's fatal illness — a protracted attack of hiccups — began. Jos's palsy, or what is now called Parkinson's disease, which Robert Darwin has suggested might increase to a certain level and then stabilize, continued to increase so that writing and other ordinary manual activity, such as using a knife and fork, became increasingly difficult for him. He spent less and less time now at the factory. He was as self-conscious and uncomfortable in handling the ceramics as in handling the accounts.

In 1841 Jos resigned his partnership in the firm and gave his approval to Joe's resignation the following year. Having sold his share of the business to his brother Frank, Joe bought Leith Hill Place, an estate of some four hundred acres in Surrey. With Caroline and their baby daughter Sophy he retired to live the life of a country gentleman. Frank was left alone to manage the pottery.

In London, the Hensleighs and the Darwins continued to share the same friends and the same interests, if not always the same opinions. Emma and Fanny Hensleigh took the children to Hyde Park to see the illuminations for the Queen's marriage on 10 February 1840. Towards the end of the same year Maria Edgeworth, now aged seventy-three and as energetic as ever, visited London, going to parties, concerts and exhibitions with Emma and Fanny Hensleigh as if she were their contemporary. Apart from Jos and Robert, Maria was one of the few people who could describe from personal experience to the youngest generation of Wedgwoods and Darwins what their great-grandfathers were really like as men. Little Snow and Macky looked upon her with awe.

One conflict between the Wedgwoods and the Darwins which had carried on for three generations was between the sincere Christianity of the Wedgwoods and the agnosticism of the Darwins. It was a conflict particularly painful to Emma who, more than the others, was caught between. Through Mary Rich the Hensleighs had become friendly with the A. J. Scotts. Fanny Hensleigh attended Scott's course of lectures on 'The Connexion of Science and Religion'. With Emma's approval she persuaded Charles to accompany them to one of the lectures, 'but he got so bodily tired before it was over that it had not a fair chance.'[26]

Mary Rich's piety hung as a distinct presence over all of them — somewhat oppressively over Charles, Ras and Hensleigh. Having discarded the authority of the Church and of the Thirty-nine Articles and established his own conscience as an alternative, Hensleigh anticipated the ethical interpretations of James Martineau, Benjamin Jowett and Henry Sidgwick by several years. By contrast Emma and Fanny Hensleigh viewed Mary's fervent spirituality with reverence.

After Sismondi's death in June of 1842, the bereaved Jessie wrote to Emma: 'If I could but have Mrs Rich's firm faith that he was only passed from the visible to the invisible world, and already lives and is waiting for me, oh what happiness it would be.... Alas, my faith seems all hope only and no firmness, and in such discouragement as mine, even hope itself cannot wear her cheerful face....'[27] Selling Chêne and her house in Geneva, Jessie left Switzerland and returned to Wales to live with her sister Harriett Surtees who, after a lifetime of unhappiness, was also widowed. On her way to Tenby, she stopped in London for several weeks to visit the Hensleighs and the Darwins. Like five of her sisters, Jessie too was now almost totally deaf.

While Sismondi was suffering his final illness, Harriet Martineau, already deaf from an early age, fell ill with a serious heart disease. Fanny Hensleigh and Ras thought she was fatally ill or at least likely to be permanently invalided and isolated in the country without close friends or family. Ras was extremely distressed. There was discussion among the Hensleighs and the Darwins and other friends as to how they might help her. Emma described Ras's dilemma of

thinking that owing to her long illness she might be in want of money, to ask if he could help her. He carried about his letter in his pocket for some days without having courage to send it; but he did at last and poor

Miss M. was very much gratified by it, though she would not let him help her. She refused very nicely by openly entering on her affairs with him and telling him exactly what she had, to show him that she was not in want. She has nothing but what she has earned. I am afraid she has little chance of recovery, which I am sorry for. Life was of great value to her, though she seems resigned to quit it.[28]

In spite of Harriet's protests her friends did get together and raise an annuity which enabled her to buy a small farm at Ambleside. There she lived quietly, seeing only a few close friends and relatives and confined mainly to her bed. Her heart condition was neither better nor worse. Then, she experienced a divine revelation which culminated in a miracle cure. After five years of what several doctors had diagnosed as a fatal illness, her health was perfectly restored. It was the sort of supernatural experience which awed doubters like the Darwins and led believers like Mary Rich to praise the Lord and damn sinners into eternal hell. Mary never tired of quoting this glorious instance of the power of faith which had actually happened to an intimate friend of her sister Fanny, a friend who had often visited in the same house where Mary herself lived.

Harriet's brother, James Martineau, a Unitarian minister, was at the time Professor of Mental and Moral Philosophy at Manchester College. His sister's miraculous recovery confirmed him in his belief that the last appeal in all researches into Biblical truth must be the judgement of the human mind. It was indeed rational to believe that miracles occurred in the present decade as well as in Biblical times. — It was also the same decade in which Charles confirmed his own belief in the origin of species which would soon shake the very foundations on which religious faith was based.

After his retirement from the pottery, Jos declined quickly. His posture became stooped. His walk, a short-gaited shuffle with the arms dangling in front of the body, became so difficult that he frequently lost his balance and fell. The tremor in his hands and arms contrasted with a rigidity of facial expression.

In September of 1842, only a few months after Joe had left Staffordshire, Jos fell and suffered the loss of all voluntary movement, though occasionally he had periods of great agitation and uncontrollable shaking. What he had feared most, being helpless and bedridden like Bessy, actually happened. Fortunately, Bessy's mind was now so far gone that she never knew of his illness, which quickly progressed to the point where it was thought he could live no longer than a few days.

Seventy-six-year-old Robert Darwin, who at this time was himself ill and confined to a wheelchair, came to be of what assistance he could to his brother-in-law and closest friend. Joe and Hensleigh were summoned, and Jos rallied without really recovering. Only his senses and his mind remained undamaged.

Charlotte and Charles Langton and their only child Edmund moved back to Maer to help Elizabeth with her two helpless patients. This was convenient for everyone. Langton, like Hensleigh, had suffered a crisis of doubt and reached the conclusion that he could no longer in good conscience continue as a minister in the Established Church. Therefore, they were forced to move from the vicarage at Onibury.

Ten months after the Langtons returned to Maer, on 12 July 1843, Josiah Wedgwood II died peacefully in his sleep. His career had not been brilliant, but he had fulfilled his obligations and done his duty. He alone had preserved the heritage given to him. Now it was passed down intact and unwanted to another lonely man in the third generation.

24

Unconscious Persons
(1843 – 1851)

If sons of famous fathers are handicapped by generational comparisons, grandsons often discover that what was a disadvantage to their fathers is an advantage to them. At the age of forty-three, Frank Wedgwood was quite willing to take advantage of his inheritance. Straightforward, brusque and unaffected in his speech and in his personality, Frank was what his brother Hensleigh approvingly referred to as 'an unconscious person'.

Frank had no illusions about his own talents — or about the talents of his brothers. He knew that his brother Harry was of a frivolous, artistic disposition, lacking in self-confidence yet highly imaginative. By contrast, his brother Joe — the last man in the world to be called frivolous — had the unshakeable confidence of a man totally without imagination, or self-assertion. Hensleigh, on the other hand, had imagination, ambition and an intellect superior to those of his three older brothers. From early childhood Frank had recognized that he would never be the scholar Hensleigh was. He neither resented this nor attempted to compete with Hensleigh. He was realistic and self-confident enough to acknowledge his own virtues of fair-mindedness, industriousness, thrift and common sense. In spite of having married the daughter of an Anglican rector, he turned his back on the Church of England and reverted to the Unitarianism of his grandfather. He attended the church in Newcastle to which Josiah and Sally had belonged and where the Revd William Willet had once preached. Also like his grandfather, he was a great supporter of the anti-slavery movement. In politics, at this point in time, he was a Liberal. All matters requiring judgement were for him either black or white, right or wrong. He accepted that managing the pottery was his duty and his lot in life — at least until his father died.

Having finally settled the estates of his grandfather, great-uncle and father and then finding himself considerably in debt, Frank formed a partnership with John Boyle, who had previously been associated with Herbert Minton. Eventually Boyle was to own a half-interest in the pottery by paying £5,000 initially and a total of £20,000 over a twenty-year period. Boyle was not only a competent potter himself, having first managed his own earthenware factory at Keelings Lane, Hanley, but he had achieved quite a reputation for his fair dealing with workmen. In 1839 he had contributed 'An Account of Strikes in the Potteries in 1834-1836' to the *Journal of the Statistical Society.*

Frank himself had no wish to continue in the pottery business or to continue living in Etruria Hall if either or both could be disposed of at a profit. Thus in 1844 the whole of Etruria village, Etruria Hall, the pottery itself, various works of art and all of the pastures were catalogued and put up for auction. A large portion of the pasture lands and Etruria Hall were sold. The pottery itself failed to meet the reserve price and remained unsold.

Frank decided that if the pottery was not worth its reserve price, a drastic reorganization was necessary. With Boyle's help he began by throwing out all the old records — the correspondence, invoices, ledgers, oven books and pattern books — of his grandfather and father. What would be important historical documents to later generations seemed to him at the time rubbish — and he found a rubbish collector to haul them away. He and Boyle were new captains of industry. They had no patience with old-fashioned eighteenth-century attitudes. This was the mid-nineteenth century and they intended to modernize. Then, unexpectedly, only eighteen months after the partnership agreement was made and less than six months after the Wedgwood factory failed to sell, Boyle died. Frank was again faced with finding a partner, if for no other reason than to put capital into the ailing pottery, which at the time was employing fewer workers and yielding less profit than in his grandfather's day.

In March of 1845 he borrowed £15,000 from Robert Brown, a banker. This debt was paid off in three instalments — in July 1845, in January 1846, and in July 1846. In March of 1846, Frank and Brown drew up a partnership agreement which was to last for twenty-two years. All of the old firm's debts were to be paid by the new firm, or, in effect, by Brown. Two-fifths of the valuation of the firm was to be put up in capital by Brown, who was then to receive two-fifths of the profits for the first four years while Frank would receive three-fifths. After four years profits were to be shared equally. The partnership could be dissolved by either partner at the end of the seventh, twelfth or seventeenth year.

During the 1820s and 1830s the emphasis within Wedgwood, as within other potteries, had been on the virtues of thrift. Josiah II had struggled to secure capital to enable the company to produce the necessary goods for an expanding population at home as well as for an expanding economy abroad. After his death, there were suspicions that parsimony was not necessarily economy. Some pottery owners were, of course, brutal and predatory. On the whole, however, the owners were struggling to convert ignorant, provincial people, accustomed to working in traditional ways at their own pace, into an efficient, machine-handling labour force. The old craftsmen who had seen the first Josiah come into the factory and work the clay as well as any man among them were long since gone. Their descendants, who often held the same job generation after generation, did not have the same sort of personal relationship with their masters as Josiah's workmen had had with him. Ownership and craftsmanship became more and more separate. The idea that the manager of a factory needed any professional training was considered eccentric and rather ungentlemanly. Frank Wedgwood commanded the respect of his workmen not through shared knowledge but through a combination of historical tradition and through being scrupulously fair and dependable. He was so unvarying in his habits that residents of Etruria village could set their watches by the time he passed going to and from the factory.

In spite of the continued shortage of capital and a general lack of interest among members of the Wedgwood family, the 1840s and 1850s were periods of expansion, as they were in the pottery business as a whole. New machines such as pug mills, blungers, clay filter presses, jolleys for shaping the ware and steam slip pumps were invented. Workers who had thought themselves more or less secure because of their skills now felt their livelihood threatened. The Potters' Union, which had been formed in 1836 but had never been particularly successful, encouraged its members dismissed by the larger, more progressive factories to emigrate to America. Using up almost all of its capital, the union purchased land in Wisconsin and established a community which it called Pottersville. Hundreds of potters emigrated from Staffordshire. Largely through poor leadership and lack of organization, this supposed Utopia in the New World failed. More anger and frustration were aroused in the workmen. Mason and Spode bore the brunt of the hostility, largely because these factories were more progressive and because W.T. Copeland, owner of Spode, was also the Conservative Member of Parliament for Stoke-on-Trent. Because of its backwardness, there was comparatively little disturbance at Wedgwood.

For the world at large the decade of the 1840s was one of revolution on the Continent, famine and rebellion in Ireland and the rush for gold in America. In England there was the abolition of the Corn Laws, mass emigration and the 'railway mania' — far greater than the canal mania of the previous century. People not only now travelled at fifty miles an hour, as opposed to twelve, but more people travelled greater distances than they had ever done before. Even seventy-seven-year-old John Wedgwood, who had so strongly protested against the railroad a few years earlier, changed his mind and gave the new transport his approval. In fact, he took to riding the train simply for amusement or, as he put it, 'for a lark'. The nearest railway station to the Potteries was at Whitmore, a distance of five miles. On one occasion John rode the train from Whitmore to Birmingham and back with the excuse of purchasing a pound of brown sugar. This day's adventure caused his son-in-law Harry to spend more than three hours in getting him to the station and then fetching him home again.

The innocent, irrepressible John and the self-righteous, God-fearing Eliza continued to live at Seabridge with Harry and Jessie and their four children. John's eyesight had failed to the extent that he was no longer able to read, and his palsied condition made writing and other manual activities difficult. His greatest pleasure in life was still in his gardening, but the cold Staffordshire winters bothered him more now than in the past, and he was unable to spend much time out of doors.

After the death of Jos, which distressed John more than the family had expected, he and Eliza spent the winter at Tenby with John's youngest son Robert. Even in Wales the winter of 1843 was severe, and John's health became more feeble. Almost overnight he seemed to lose interest in what was going on about him. On 24 January 1844, he died of an attack of bronchitis and was buried in the parish churchyard in Tenby. After the funeral his sister Sarah wrote to the old housekeeper Betty Moore: 'My brother John remained in a state of great weakness for several days and died in the easiest manner possible on Friday afternoon: he had no pain or suffering for the three or four last days, & was not seriously ill quite a week altogether.'[1]

Sarah, the only surviving child of Josiah and Sally, was now aged sixty-eight and in excellent health. By preference she continued to live alone, with only three servants, at Camphill. Although her numerous nieces and nephews and their children called upon her frequently, her immediate affections were lavished more spontaneously on puppies and kittens. She had never cared for children. As she grew older, her character hardened; she became a rather formidable and opinionated old lady. Tall, thin, very upright and solemn, she was like her own mother had been in her last years. Her fastidiousness became something of a fetish. She kept several pairs of gloves beside her so as not to soil her hands while performing various tasks: a pair of loose black cotton gloves was designated for shaking hands with children, while gloves of lighter colours were for cleaner occupations such as reading books.

Charitable almost to a fault, Sarah's sentiments had always been roused most fiercely by those whose distress was at a distance. A quarter of a century earlier she had described herself to Jessie Sismondi:

It is my misfortune to be not of an affectionate disposition, though affection is almost the only thing in the world that I value; I don't know why I should be ashamed to own what I cannot possibly help, an extreme fastidiousness about charm and agreeable qualities; there are very few persons in the world who are agreeable and charming enough in appearance, manner and conversation to give me a lively pleasure, and I seem as if I could not feel affection enough to satisfy me without that. It is partly owing I suppose to my so seldom feeling a lively affection that I feel its sweetness so very sensibly when I catch it, and that I seem almost as if I could not bear to be without it.[2]

The Frank Wedgwoods and the Harry Wedgwoods, who by 1845 had some ten children between them, were within a few miles of the Maer estates. The Langtons and their one child Edmund continued to live at Maer and to help Elizabeth to care for the invalid Bessy. Both Baugh Allen and Harriett Surtees died in 1845, but Bessy, at this stage little more than a vegetable, was oblivious to such losses.

The three other surviving Allen sisters, the widowed Jessie and the two spinsters, Emma and Fanny, continued to live part of the time in Wales and part in London. They made frequent trips to the Continent, though now they all three suffered from the seemingly inevitable Allen maladies of deafness and depression. Occasionally, as in the old days, they visited Maer. Shortly before her seventieth birthday, Jessie sadly remarked to her niece Elizabeth: 'I understand myself no better now than if I was born yesterday.'[3]

Finally released from the dreamy, dozing state which had been her existence for nearly a decade, Bessy died peacefully in her sleep on 31 March 1846. Maer Hall was, and had been for several years, too large and costly in upkeep for the Langtons and Elizabeth to continue living there. Joe had no desire to leave Leith Hill Place, where he had so recently established himself. Frank with his spartan habits felt the cost and the responsibility too great for him. He had recently purchased a hundred acres near Barlaston and was drawing up plans to build Upper House, an unpretentious family house with space enough for half a dozen exuberant, noisy children. Harry had no money either to purchase or to keep up the Maer estate. Hensleigh, who had improved his own income by investments and by joining the boards of several companies, was adamant that both he and Fanny felt their roots to be in the city rather than the country. Thus, Maer — which had been the happiest of all the Wedgwood houses — was sold to the Davenport family, descendants of Jos's old political opponent.

Not only were the Langtons and Elizabeth confronted with finding a new home, but Sarah Wedgwood also had to leave Camphill, which was sold as part of the Maer estate. The Harry Wedgwoods at near-by Seabridge were also adrift. By the end of 1847, all of the family but the Frank Wedgwoods had left Staffordshire. The Harry Wedgwoods settled near Woking, and the Langtons and Elizabeth moved to Hartfield Grove in Sussex, where Elizabeth set up another school. Sarah Wedgwood leased from Sir John Lubbock a house called Petleys, near Downe, in Kent, where she moved with her three faithful servants.

Sarah's main interest in moving to Kent was, of course, to be near the Charles Darwins. Emma and Charles had left Gower Street in September of 1842, moving to Downe, to a house called Down which Robert Darwin purchased for them for £2,200. Charles enthusiastically told his sister Catherine that although the house was ugly and 'looks neither old nor new; walls two feet thick; windows rather small; lower story rather low; capital study 18 × 18. Dining room can easily be added to is 21 × 15. Three stories, plenty of bedrooms. We could hold the Hensleighs and you and Susan and Erasmus altogether.'[4]

The main reason for the move from London was Charles's frail health. It was felt that a quiet life in the country would be more soothing, to the mysterious nervous ailment which periodically attacked him, than the excitement and stress of city life. During the autumn of the Darwins' move, it was Hensleigh, however, who suffered a serious bronchial illness. At the suggestion of Emma and with the approval of Hensleigh's doctor and cousin Peter Holland, the Darwins took the Hensleighs' four older children, Snow, Bro, Ernie and Effie, to live with them at Down. Fanny herself was ill and exhausted from the double strain of nursing Hensleigh and of caring for their new baby, Alfred, who was sickly and cried constantly. After two months in bed Hensleigh recovered and with Ras, Fanny, the new baby and his nurse went to Down for more convalescence.

While at Down Hensleigh and Charles had time for lengthy discussions reminiscent of their grandfather Josiah's treasured talks with Bentley. The late-afternoon conversations which had taken place almost daily when they were neighbours in Gower Street were missed by both of them. The existence of God and the meaning of Christ in everyday life were subjects which had assumed considerable importance in their discussions. Having no doubt about the existence of God, Hensleigh dismissed the absolute authority of the Bible and had developed an interest in spiritualism. Like his father and grandfather before him, Charles had many more religious doubts. With regard to the existence of God, he was wise enough to maintain a complete neutrality, neither affirming nor denying any belief. He was shrewd enough to recognize also that his credibility as a scientist was reinforced by the openness of his attitude.

On 5 July 1844, Charles completed a manuscript sketch outlining his *On the Origin of Species*. He felt that if he died before a major work was completed, he had at least stated the case for natural selection as the means by which the species had descended. He wrote a formal note to Emma which he asked her to keep with his will: 'I have just finished my sketch of my species theory. If, as I believe, my theory in time be accepted even by one competent judge, it will be a considerable step in science. I therefore write this in the case of my sudden death, as my most solemn and last request, which I am sure you will consider the same as if legally entered in my will, that you will devote £400 to its publication, and further will yourself or through Hensleigh take trouble in promoting it.'[5]

Charles had faith that even if his cousin and brother-in-law differed with him in belief — and Hensleigh disagreed with him only with regard to man, not concerning the origin of other species — Hensleigh would at least honour his request to see that his theory of the origin of the species be made known to a world-wide audience and not just to a handful of English scientists who might or might not concur and who might have their own theories and reputations to uphold. Hensleigh was an honourable man. As he had proven by his resignation over the lawfulness of taking oaths, he would perform his duty even if it demanded personal sacrifices.

Charles had reason to think he might not live much longer. His main symptoms were headaches, stomach complaints and an extreme debility which limited the amount of time he was able to devote to mental labours as well as preventing much physical exertion. He was also susceptible to colds and infections. Possibly he suffered from the Victorian malady — chronic arsenic poisoning. At the time, arsenic was regarded by doctors as a panacea — his father had prescribed it for eczema on his hands when he was at Cambridge — and frequently given as a tonic; Charles took some with him on the *Beagle*. During the voyage he was ill several times with tropical fevers, and on one occasion was forced to spend a month in bed on shore in Valparaiso after being attacked by the benchuga, a large blood-sucking bug on the pampas which is a carrier of the micro-organism trypanosoma.

He may indeed in South America have contracted some incurable tropical disease, such as Chagas's disease, which left him debilitated for the rest of his life, but he began the journey with a predisposition towards headaches and intestinal disorders. Certainly also part of his condition was psychological. He had an extreme devotion to and dependence upon his father, who bullied and denigrated him in his youth. Except with his family and a few close friends, he was abnormally shy, and his fear of social occasions inevitably produced stomach complaints. The older he got the more incapable he became of facing any unpleasantness and the more dependent he became upon Emma, who, of necessity, had to develop a toughness to protect them both.

Hensleigh, too, shared the tendency to become ill whenever anything of an emotionally demanding or distressing nature occurred, but his illnesses were less frequent now that he was more secure financially. Along with Erasmus Darwin and Thomas Farrer, he was appointed one of the first trustees of Bedford College. Farrer, a barrister and member of the Board of Trade, had known Sir James Mackintosh and worked with him when he was associated with the East India Company. He had also known Hensleigh when Hensleigh was a barrister at Gray's Inn. They moved in the same social circles and shared an interest in politics and literature as well as education.

The English literary world in the mid-nineteenth century was in a state of transition. In 1843 Wordsworth, at the age of seventy-three, had succeeded Southey as Poet Laureate. Coleridge had been dead a decade, Keats and Shelley much longer. Some of the writers creating the most excitement in London now were Elizabeth Gaskell, Harriet Martineau, Leigh Hunt, Thomas Carlyle, Charles Dickens, Elizabeth Barrett and a young poet named Robert Browning. With the exception of Dickens and the invalided recluse Elizabeth Barrett, all of these writers were friends of the Hensleighs and of Ras Darwin. Also in the same circle were Samuel Rogers, John Ruskin and Monckton Milnes. Ruskin and Fanny Hensleigh shared a concern for social reform and advocated a system of national education for adults as well as children. Both were dedicated to individual fulfillment through the development of creative abilities. Ruskin was particularly kind and helpful to young artists and took an interest in Sophia Sennett, a young friend of Fanny's whose work Fanny greatly admired.

Over the years Fanny Hensleigh's interest in politics and her passion for avant-garde or what, at the time, seemed radical causes, increased. She was a great organizer and fund-raiser. In the early 1850s she and the Carlyles were involved with Giuseppe Mazzini, the idealistic though somewhat impractical Italian patriot who agitated for Italian unity under a republican form of government. Though befriended by Fanny and the Carlyles, Mazzini was not popular with other members of the Wedgwood–Darwin family, including Hensleigh, Ras and Jessie Sismondi who had met him when she visited her husband's mother and sister in Italy.

Robert Mackintosh returned from America with a young American wife, the rich and socially prominent former Molly Appleton from Boston. Her father, Nathan Appleton, a textile manufacturer and merchant banker of national importance, would have found more in common with Josiah Wedgwood I than with his lethargic and somewhat effete son-in-law. At first the energetic Appletons, who believed in nothing if not the individual, entrepreneurial spirit, disapproved of Robert. Fanny Appleton, Molly's sister who three years later married Henry Wadsworth Longfellow, described Robert as having 'quite a good face, an awkward figure, however, laughs spasmodically, is constantly absent when present, & jerks out his words like a badly working pump'.[6]

From Robert's point of view, it was a highly satisfactory union. The Appletons were extremely wealthy and generous with their money. If Robert and Molly remained an ocean away, Robert need never exert himself by working. He could continue to solicit from his father's old friends civil service appointments with titles more impressive than the responsibilities they carried. There was no need for him to concern himself with a salary. Molly's allowance more than provided for a comfortable living, and her inheritance promised to be substantial. They quickly produced two children, Ronald and Eva, and established themselves as part of the London literary and social world frequented by the Hensleighs and Ras Darwin.

The youngest generation of Wedgwoods, Darwins and Mackintoshes often made visits of their own, accompanied by their nannies, to Kent, Staffordshire, Wales and to 'the Shrewsbury conclave', where the two spinster Darwin aunts, Susan and Catherine, and old Robert Darwin, who in 1846 at the age of eighty was confined to a wheelchair, still lived at The Mount. Like his father, his brother-in-law John and his son Charles, Robert spent much of his time in later years in his greenhouse. His chief interest was botany. Both Susan and Catherine had inherited their father's pessimism, so that over the years The Mount became even gloomier. The presence of little nieces and nephews brought only a temporary respite. The passing of the years had not softened the abrasiveness of Robert's disposition. To the end of his life he continued to voice his opinions with regard only for the truth. Nor did he lose his uncanny ability to read other people's characters and often, frighteningly, their thoughts. Hypocrisy practised for the sake of coddling people's feelings disgusted him — as he was fond of announcing before delivering some devastating pronouncement.

Robert Darwin died on 13 November 1848, in his eighty-third year. Upon hearing the news of their father's death, both Ras and Charles became physically ill. Ras sent for Fanny Hensleigh who later went with him to the station to board a train for Shrewsbury. Shortly after he arrived, he wrote to her, telling her Susan was bearing up well but that Caroline was crying and being very wretched because she and Joe had delayed leaving Leith Hill Place until it was too late, and her father was dead when they arrived.

All of the Darwin sisters had taken it for granted that Charles would not attend the funeral because of his illness. He had been to Shrewsbury for a fortnight the month before. His sister Susan wrote to him: 'God comfort you, my dearest Charles, you were so beloved by him.' But even though he was ill and Emma, pregnant again, was unable to accompany him, he arrived in Shrewsbury shortly after the funeral service had begun. He stayed at The Mount with his sister Marianne Parker who was so distraught that she, too, had become physically ill and was unable to attend the service.

Ras had feared that he would not be equal to the occasion either, but at the last moment he managed to join the procession which walked behind the coffin to the church. The four Parker boys were honorary pall-bearers. Following them came Caroline and Joe Wedgwood, Dr Parker with Catherine Darwin and Ras with Susan Darwin. Ras wrote to Fanny Hensleigh that after the service everyone at The Mount was sick but, as Dr Parker observed, from nervous feelings rather than from any known disease.

Robert Darwin had amassed a considerable fortune and left all of his children far better off than any of them had anticipated. He had converted most of the old canal stocks into railway stocks. From his investments, each child was left with an annual income of over £8,000. As Robert had also advised Jos and managed most of his affairs in later years, the Wedgwoods as well as the Darwins benefited from his business acumen.

Shortly after his father's death, Charles went to Malvern for hydropathic treatments. He believed these helped him. The following year he spent sixteen weeks at Malvern. In March of 1851 he was there for a week and returned by way of London, staying with Ras and visiting with the Hensleighs. Ras was at the time seeing a great deal of the Carlyles, and they all went to see the Elgin marbles which had recently been acquired by the British Museum. It amused Ras that what impressed Carlyle most was seeing a resemblance in one of the figures to Sir Robert Inglis.

Charles had left his two sickly daughters Annie and Henrietta to take the waters at Malvern. They were in the care of their governess and an old nurse who would soon be coming back to Down to look after the new baby Emma was expecting in May. Hensleigh remarked to Ras that Charles seemed healthier and happier than he had been in years.

Three weeks later he was back at Malvern. Annie had a fever and had become dangerously ill. As Emma was unable to travel and Ras was unequal to the emotional strain, Fanny Hensleigh went up to Malvern to be with him during the crisis. Charles had never experienced such anxiety and grief. He had mourned his father, but that death was expected; the death of his favourite child was almost more than he could endure. Years later he said he did not believe he could have borne it without Fanny Hensleigh to comfort him and to look after the practical details. Annie died on 23 April 1851, at the age of ten. Three weeks later Horace Darwin was born at Down.

In July of 1851, Charles and Emma had recovered enough from their grief to come to London and spend twelve days with Ras at his new house in Park Street. Apart from being with Ras and the Hensleighs, another reason for coming to London at this time was to see the Great Exhibition at the Crystal Palace which had opened on 1 May 1851.

The Frank Wedgwoods and the Hensleigh Wedgwoods had received invitations to attend the opening celebration of this first grand world trade fair. Artists, industrialists and the nobility were all to share in the festivities. The two Wedgwood couples rode together in a carriage to the Crystal Palace in Hyde Park. A crowd of over ten thousand people had gathered in the park to watch the celebrities arrive. The Duke of Wellington came early amidst loud cheers from the people, some of whom had climbed trees for a better view. It was the Duke's eighty-second birthday.

Preceded by a troop of Life Guards, the Queen and Prince Albert arrived at noon. There was a loud flourish of trumpets from the north gallery as the royal party entered the building, which was divided into two wings. In the western wing were displayed the industrial products of the British Empire, and in the eastern, displays mounted by other countries in all parts of the world. As the Queen proceeded past the line of admiring subjects to a raised platform in the north centre of the building, a choir sang *God Save the Queen*. His Royal Highness Prince Albert read a report of the proceedings of the Royal Commission which had organized the event, then presented Her Majesty with a copy of the report. The Archbishop of Canterbury said a prayer invoking God's blessing upon the undertaking, and the choir then sang the *Hallelujah Chorus.*

The Wedgwoods were all moved by the grandeur of the occasion— Fanny Frank perhaps most of all. She was a sociable woman who enjoyed people and parties and occasions both grand and frivolous. Frank on the other hand had little tolerance for any occasion that lacked a practical purpose, and did not enjoy visits to dissipation-tempting London where perhaps he felt ill at ease with Hensleigh and his intellectual friends. Fanny Frank, who was pregnant with their seventh child, was far from being an intellectual; but she was bored and lonely in Staffordshire with only Frank, their children and a handful of provincial neighbours at a distance. Frank allowed her one trip to London a year.

All four of the Wedgwoods felt a thrill of excitement as the royal procession formed, led by heralds and the architect Joseph Paxton, so that the Queen might view some of the exhibits. In spite of the prominence of the name Josiah Wedgwood and the elevated social position of his descendants, Wedgwood & Brown's was not one of the exhibits selected for the Queen's viewing. Hensleigh and the two Fannys were disappointed; Frank affected not to care.

Actually there was no reason why Wedgwood should have been selected. For the past half-century the company had been declining in prestige, profit, quality and industrial leadership. According to the illustrated catalogue of the Exhibition: 'ETRURIA—the celebrated establishment founded by Josiah Wedgwood ... has sent its *quota* of beautiful works through its present occupants, Messrs Wedgwood & Brown who reproduced some of the best articles originally designed or executed by its famous founder.'[7] Had the Exhibition taken place seventy-five years earlier, the Wedgwood display might have been exactly as it was in 1851. On the other hand, Minton, Spode, Worcester and Doulton had all produced new items and patterns in keeping with mid-Victorian tastes. Frank Wedgwood had little interest in design or in changing fashions. He chose to capitalize on his grandfather's success, reproducing urns, vases, ewers, inkwells and figures that had sold well in the past and eliminating those items that had not found a substantial market. In writing of the Exhibition in a supplement to the *The Times* of 1 May 1851, one reporter noted: 'In pottery the reputation of this country may be safely left in the hands of Minton and Doulton....'

25

A Glorious Pretence
(1851 — 1859)

The Great Exhibition captured the popular imagination of the nation, which was changing rapidly. The 1851 census showed, for the first time, more people living in the towns of England and Wales than in the country. There were fewer small farms, many more large ones: this was the end of the yeoman class. Moreover the census showed that in 1851 42 per cent of English women between the ages of twenty and forty were unmarried. By law a married woman lost all rights to her own property. Activist women like Florence Nightingale announced that marriage not only would rob a woman of her individuality, it was also a kind of moral suicide.

On the whole, however, the decade of the 1850s was a period of quiet prosperity during which the rich got richer and the poor became less poor. The prosperity was based on rising money incomes rather than on rising real incomes; poverty and squalor became more widespread, particularly in urban areas.

When Charles and Emma came up to London in July of 1851, the Hensleighs sent for their two older sons, Bro — called Mack—and Ernie, to come down from Rugby to attend the Exhibition with them. Since the opening, which they had attended with the Frank Wedgwoods, Fanny and Hensleigh had been back to the Exhibition on three separate occasions. Their eldest daughter, Snow, now eighteen, was the only member of the family who chose *not* to visit the Exhibition. Like Florence Nightingale, Snow was determined to assert her own identity and freedom of choice. She had recently returned from a stay at Ambleside with her mother's friend Harriet Martineau, whom she greatly admired. Apart from literature, social reform and a passion for theological debate, the young girl and the older woman had their deafness in common. Harriet had an ear trumpet, which intimidated some speakers, but Snow wanted no object to call attention to her disability. When she and Harriet were alone, they sat face to face and were able to read each other's lips.

During this visit to Ambleside, Harriet took Snow to call on the ageing Poet Laureate Wordsworth at Rydal Mount. For someone of Snow's generation and temperament, Wordsworth was old-fashioned. Personally she found him conceited and disagreeable. As they were about to leave and were waiting for their carriage, a chair drew up at the front door, bearing the shrunken figure of the invalid Dorothy Wordsworth, returned from her daily excursion. Upon hearing Snow's name, the old woman seized her by the arm and inquired eagerly: 'From whom are you spawn?'

Startled and repelled by the old woman's touch, Snow replied haughtily: 'My father is Hensleigh Wedgwood'.

Dorothy Wordsworth's eyes were wild, full of fire and light, but her mind was vague and wandering. 'Hensleigh Wedgwood?' she murmured, 'I know of no Hensleigh Wedgwood. Do you know Thomas Wedgwood?' She then lapsed into a eulogy of Tom Wedgwood as if his death had occurred yesterday instead of nearly half a century before. Snow had barely heard of her great-uncle, but she made a mental note to ask her father more about him. The impression left on her mind by this ailing, half-mad old woman was far more powerful and illuminating than the pompous image of the old Poet Laureate, who died a few weeks later.

Snow developed close friendships with two young women of her own age, her cousin Fanny Erskine, who lived in Edinburgh, and Meta Gaskell, the eldest daughter of her mother's friend Elizabeth Gaskell, whose writing she admired even more than Harriet Martineau's. She had been particularly influenced by Mrs Gaskell's novel *Mary Barton,* which dealt not only with the deplorable conditions of the working classes in Manchester but also with a woman who acquires from misfortune and death an understanding of herself and society. Mary Barton was not a passive, angelic feather-brain, like most of Dickens's heroines, but an active, intelligent character with whom bright young women like Snow could identify.

During the autumn of 1851 Snow accompanied her Aunt Rich to Edinburgh to visit the Erskines. William Erskine, who had never really lived down his disgrace in India, was in poor health. Over the years Mary Rich had loyally stood by her sister Maitland and Maitland's children. For the past decade she had each year visited Scotland, where she became more and more devoted to William's half-brother, Thomas Erskine, a religious teacher. Erskine had inherited the family estate of Linlathen, and with his sister, Christian Stirling, had turned it into a place of religious retreat or a school for religious study and meditation. Nominally Erskine was a member of the Church of Scotland, though he rarely availed himself of its ministrations. He was certainly no Anglican, nor was he a Calvinist. Instead, he formed his own cult. More through the magnetism of his personality than through any profundity in his thought, he acquired wealthy disciples, such as Madame de Staël's daughter, the Duchesse de Broglie, Lady Inglis and Mary Rich. People thought him either a saint or a madman. Meeting Erskine on this first visit to Scotland was one of the most crucial factors in the development of the woman Snow was to become.

With Aunt Rich and her cousin Fanny Erskine, Snow made a pilgrimage to the birthplace of her grandfather, James Mackintosh. She wrote to her mother that the house was now inhabited by an old farmer and his wife: 'It seemed so odd going to see Miss Helen Mackintosh at Inverness and hearing her speak of my grandfather and tell long stories about him, whilst she is still quite a young looking woman. She thought Fanny [Erskine] very like him....'

In the same letter Snow reported on attending her first ball and that Fanny Erskine was quite a social success whereas she herself felt awkward. 'I take sudden fits of dislike to being constantly in company, as I am now — I don't think it is at all my element. I am sure I am always doing awkward things. I shall never go out as soon as I get home — not that I don't enjoy seeing new people, if I did not feel myself obliged to behave like a Christian now. I often deplore my extreme age and wish I could sit down quietly and say nothing to anybody'.[1] Her deafness made being in large crowds of people an intimidating experience. To conceal her fear of misunderstanding what was being said to her, and consequently of making some embarrassingly inappropriate response, she pretended to despise balls as superficial and silly. Her defence was in laughing at the foolishness of others before they could laugh at her.

Upon her return to London, she did not, however, stick to her plan of never going out. In May of 1852, she wrote to her brother Mack, who was still at Rugby: 'I went to a ball at Mrs Taggerts. It was very pleasant and we danced a great deal. In the intervals of dancing I amused myself with admiring Millais [the Pre-Raphaelite painter] who was there. He is the most lovely man I ever saw but he looked rather a fine gentleman. — I had such a succession of idiots for partners that I had quite enough amusement laughing at them....'[2]

In August of 1852 William Erskine died. Mary Rich had gone to Edinburgh to be with her sister. Snow wrote to her that she hoped 'soon to hear that she [Aunt Maitland] takes her place in the family again. It is not often, I should think, that anyone can look back on so many years of married life with so little bitterness mixed with the sorrow as in her case.'[3]

Shortly thereafter Fanny Erskine came back to London with her Aunt Rich to visit Snow. London was an exhilarating experience for a naïve young girl from Scotland. Her Aunt Fanny Hensleigh had inherited the Mackintosh gift for conversation and enjoyment of social gatherings. She was a superb hostess, and the Hensleighs entertained frequently. They gave a series of parties that autumn, not only for their friends but also for the benefit of the younger generation. At one of these Fanny Erskine met her future husband, Thomas Farrer.

Godfrey Wedgwood, Frank's oldest son, also attended a number of the parties given that autumn by the Hensleighs. He was a close friend of Snow's and one of the few young men of her own age whom she did not think an idiot. Though neither deaf nor handicapped in any other physical way, Godfrey had inherited the Wedgwood reserve and lack of humour. He could no more lose his solemnity and enter into a convivial, high-spirited party than could his grandfather Jos or his Uncle Joe. Unfortunately, however, he did not share their toughness. Nor did he possess the assertiveness of his father. Highly sensitive and self-deprecating, Godfrey shared with Snow a feeling of awkwardness on social occasions and confided to her: 'I have my doubts as to the policy of counting on dancing as amusement where one is an utter stranger. I never can manufacture conversation with the least ease.... I mean that on asking a girl to dance where one is an utter stranger, one cannot help feeling that she w'd be much rather dancing with her friend Smith, who carries on an eye conversation with her across your back and so on.'[4]

Godfrey's mother wanted him to be a cultured gentleman. His father wanted him to be a tough sportsman and an even tougher businessman. As the eldest son, Godfrey, at the age of eighteen, naturally had gone into the family pottery. He served as an apprentice or personal assistant to his father. Snow felt indignation that Godfrey would not be going on to Cambridge, as was planned for her own brother Mack the following year. With the sort of directness her Uncle Frank understood and respected, she told him she thought he kept Godfrey too closely confined to 'that nasty old pot shop'.

Soon thereafter Godfrey escorted his sisters Cecily and Rose to Paris for a week. On the journey he read Carlyle's *French Revolution*, which he told Snow enchanted him more than any book he had read for ages. He said he was very much looking forward to another stay in London with the Hensleighs where he hoped he might meet their friend Carlyle. He also reported that his father had bought Thackeray's *Esmond* which the entire family thought frightfully dull, particularly by comparison with Jane Austen's *Pride and Prejudice*.

In November Snow went to Manchester to visit the Gaskells. There she became seriously ill with rheumatic fever. The Gaskells were alarmed and sent for Fanny and Hensleigh to come immediately. They arrived with Aunt Fanny Allen, who had been visiting them in London. When it became apparent that Snow would recover, but that she would have to remain at Plymouth Grove for several weeks, her parents returned to London. Great-aunt Fanny stayed on at the Gaskells' to help nurse her. While she was convalescing, Snow received affectionate letters from both Godfrey and Mack. Godfrey's parents had finally agreed that he could spend more time in London, partly on business and partly attending social and cultural functions. He told Snow that she had missed the Duke of Wellington's funeral but that she probably would not have enjoyed it much since she was not much of a sightseer.

Seventy-one-year-old Fanny Allen felt that she was once again being of some practical use in nursing her great-niece, who was the granddaughter of the only man she had ever really loved. She travelled less frequently now than in the past. She was content to live quietly at Tenby with her two surviving sisters. Robert Wedgwood, his wife and children and his sister Eliza, who had come to live with him after their father's death, lived near by and were kind and attentive to their aunts. It was hard on Fanny being the youngest in a family of eleven children.

Jessie Sismondi's health was rapidly failing. She had developed heart disease, along with the deafness and depression that afflicted so many of the Allen women. Shortly before she died, on 3 March 1853, she experienced a fit of despair over various notes in her husband's journals which she felt had been proved inaccurate by later events. One afternoon while her sisters were out of the house she impulsively burned all of the journals.

Sismondi had intended these for publication, and had left them in her care with instructions that a period of fifteen years from the date of his death was to elapse before publication. She also destroyed the journals that she herself had kept during the time she had spent in Geneva and in Italy. This act was deeply regretted by her sisters, for sentimental reasons, and by her great-niece Snow, who had expressed an interest in editing the journals. As a family, the Allens, like the Wedgwoods, did not see the shape of the future in contemporary events or records. They destroyed more than they preserved.

In the summer of 1854 the Hensleigh Wedgwoods, all six of their children, Aunt Rich, three servants and the A. J. Scotts went to Paris. The Hensleighs always took a lively interest in new places, new ideas and new inventions. In the 1850s Paris set the styles and standards of taste for all of Europe.

From Paris had come the new fashion of the crinoline, with its scalloped flounces, bones, frills, fringes and double skirts. To create a similar, less costly effect, young English ladies like twenty-one-year-old Snow and sixteen-year-old Effie sometimes wore a dozen or more starched petticoats and were driven to balls standing up in their carriages. Every fashionable young lady now owned at least one silk dress in which she attended church, paid afternoon calls or sat at home to receive visitors. Caps were no longer worn beneath one's bonnet, though bright-coloured flowers were frequently tucked under the brim. Women wore their hair smoothly brushed back from a centre parting and gathered at the nape of the neck in a chenille net.

Fanny Hensleigh and her three daughters, including twelve-year-old Hope, all wore new French dresses of silk, with lace collars, at the wedding of their cousin Fanny Erskine and Thomas Farrer at James Martineau's Unitarian chapel in London. Even Aunt Rich, who always wore black, sported a new Paris bonnet for the occasion.

In the year 1854 also occurred Godfrey Wedgwood's twenty-first birthday. He was presented with an address from the workmen of the Wedgwood factory and signed by fifteen of their number whose average period of service at Etruria was fifty years. Two among them, William Heath and William Stanway, had both worked under Godfrey's great-grandfather Josiah I. Heath had joined the Etruria factory in 1784 as a thrower's apprentice and had worked there for seventy years. Stanway began in 1794, only shortly before the death of Josiah I. There was a factory holiday with a picnic for all the workmen and their families. The following evening the Frank Wedgwoods gave a ball in Godfrey's honour, to which all the gentry from miles around came. After this occasion Godfrey confided to Snow that it was not so difficult to make conversation, as all the young ladies were obliged to be polite to him and wish him a ' happy coming of age and a prosperous future'.

Many public events of 1854 were neither happy nor prosperous. While the Hensleigh Wedgwoods were in Paris, their friend John Ruskin was publicly humiliated when his wife was granted a decree of nullity on the grounds of the non-consummation of their marriage. She resumed her maiden name and a year later married the young painter John Everett Millais whom Ruskin had championed, and whom Snow had found so attractive at a ball three years earlier. There were even greater disasters to the nation. The Crimean War began in the spring of 1854, and that autumn on 25 October at Balaclava, occurred the famous charge of the Light Brigade, an appalling catastrophe and possibly the most badly bungled manoeuvre in military history. The episode resulted in furious anti-Russian sentiments among the British public at large and a reshuffling of the Cabinet with Palmerston once again emerging as Prime Minister.

Unencumbered by excessive patriotism, Elizabeth Barrett Browning wrote from Italy that the purchase of a commission did not change a gentlemanly civilian into a trained officer. 'Soldiers should have military education as well as red coats.' She went even further, to say that the faults of the nation as a whole, whether in the Crimea or in the ugliness of London, were due to the English habit of 'incessant self-glorification'. It was the cause of English illiteracy and English corruption. Like Josiah Wedgwood three-quarters of a century earlier, she announced that 'nothing will do for England but a good revolution and a "besom of destruction" used dauntlessly'.[5] It was a rational, if harsh, criticism, and not one likely to make her popular in her native country. A far more reassuring approach, even if it bore out Elizabeth's condemnation, was that of Tennyson, who, having succeeded Wordsworth as Poet Laureate, composed a poem that romanticized the absurdities of the battle into brave and noble sacrifices made for Queen and country. Florence Nightingale was the national heroine. The Victorian upper classes had a glorious time in a glorious world—as long as they pretended. Their entire social structure was based on pretence.

One person who, like Florenee Nightingale, refused to pretend was Snow. Though she was thirteen years younger than Florence Nightingale, the two women became friends through Florence's cousin Hilary Bonham Carter, who had studied art in Paris with the celebrated Madame Mohl, and who was described by Snow as 'one of the most loveable women I ever knew'. Florence Nightingale had repeatedly declined a proposal of marriage from a close friend of the Hensleighs, Richard Monckton Milnes, later Lord Houghton. Snow disliked him, although Florence continued to call him 'the man I adore'. They all attended parties in London and went for a week's stay at Florence's uncle's home, Embley Park, at Romsey, Hampshire.

Snow shared Florence Nightingale's mistrust of marriage and like the older woman had a mystical belief in her own destiny, though her aspirations were in a different direction from Florence's. In the autumn of 1855 she returned to Manchester and took on the task of copying Brontë letters for Elizabeth Gaskell, who was planning a biography of Charlotte Brontë. In other ways, too, she acted as Mrs Gaskell's secretary and research assistant. For recreation she spent time with her friend Meta Gaskell and with her Aunt Rich's friends, the A. J. Scotts, who had moved to

Manchester when Scott became Principal of Owens College, where he also held the Chair of Moral Philosophy.

During this period Snow decided that, like Elizabeth Gaskell and the Brontë sisters, whose letters she was reading, she would become a novelist. Secretly she began her first book, which she entitled *Framleigh Hall*. It was, like many first novels of young authors, a projection of her own emotional conflicts on to imaginary and not very convincing characters. Snow herself was a young woman of extreme passions and fastidious principles. At a crucial point in the story, she described her heroine's feelings:

> The thought that the most intense, spontaneous feeling of her soul was one with which she must struggle as a deadly sin, overwhelmed her with a sense of injustice. At what point was it in her power — when could she have stopped and said, 'Here esteem ends, here passion begins — I will go no farther.' She could remember no such point. She knew her love was hopeless...and yet so much dearer was it to her than any other joy that she wished to sink into nothing rather than survive it.[6]

Fearing ridicule and harsh criticism from her parents and from her intellectually arrogant brother Mack, Snow confided her literary ambitions only to her sister Effie and to Meta Gaskell. She did not expect the family to disapprove of her becoming a novelist, but saw that if she were going to write a novel it would have to be an excellent one, of which the family could be proud.

She finished *Framleigh Hall* in less than a year, sending off sections for Effie to read and criticize. Effie's candour about her sister's writing, which she found 'a bit long and tiresome', was unsettling. Snow began a second novel and somewhat hesitantly showed the first two chapters to Meta Gaskell, whose immediate response was enthusiastic approval. When the firm of Hurst & Blackett offered to publish *Framleigh Hall* if she would make certain changes, she decided to do so and to publish anonymously. Because she was frightened that her parents might see some of the letters from Hurst & Blackett, she rushed down each morning to receive the post and then place it on the hall table as the butler usually did.

The major change the publishers wanted in *Framleigh Hall* was that the villain Mortimer, rather than the hero Maurice, should die at the end. Such a change proved more difficult for Snow than it would have been for most moralistic writers content with the simple but ever-popular theme of the triumph of good over evil. 'I think the deathbed of a very bad man is too awful an idea to be brought into a novel,' Snow confessed to Effie, 'so I am working very hard at trying to reform him, but it will turn out something quite disgustingly mawkish and commonplace.'[7]

Effie was rather more interested in the good and evil that were done in the present world than in promises of a glorious existence in the life hereafter. Naturally she said so, making Snow all the more nervous. 'I do wish you were here, for my dreadful anxiety is that now I shall not be able to keep it a secret from the elders,' she wrote to Effie. 'I sh'd be miserable ever after if any of our people don't like it. I was rather depressed by the way you spoke about it, though you are such a rabid novel reader, & if you did not like it, how much more Mack and all our people who are so dreadfully critical — Oh dear! I have given myself up to be made a pincushion!'[8]

To make the difficult changes in the novel, she decided to take the manuscript to Down, where she felt she could work without being disturbed and with less anxiety about being teased or criticized. If necessary, she could confide in her Uncle Charles and her Aunt Emma. They were, she felt, less critical than her own parents and could be relied upon to keep a secret.

When she arrived at Down on 6 November 1856, she was met with the news that her Great-aunt Sarah, the last surviving child of Josiah Wedgwood I, had died at her neighbouring house of Petleys only a few hours earlier. She was aged eighty. Most of the family were coming to Down for the funeral. Within the next forty-eight hours Snow's parents, her Aunt Elizabeth, her Uncles Joe, Harry, Frank and Allen all arrived, so that instead of the quiet she had anticipated, all the rooms at Down were crowded with relatives.

Sarah's six nephews were honorary pall-bearers. Charles Darwin described the funeral in a letter to his sons William and George, who were away at school:

> The funeral was at 3 o'clock, and Mr Lewis managed it all. We walked down to Petleys and there put on black cloaks and crape to our hats, and followed the coffin which was carried by six men; another six men changing half way. At the Church door Mr Innes came out to meet the coffin. Then it was carried into the Church and a short service was read. Then we all went out and stood uncovered round the grave whilst the coffin was lowered, and then Mr Innes finished the service, but he did not read this impressive service well.... Then we all marched back to the house, Mr Lewis and his two sons carrying a sort of black standards before us; and we then went into the house and read Aunt Sarah's will aloud.... She had left a great deal of money to very many charities....[9]

Snow finished the revisions to her book at Down, confiding her ambitions and her fears to Emma and Charles. They encouraged her to share her success with all of the family and not hide behind anonymity. Snow's intuition that her work would not be popular within her immediate family had, however, been all too accurate. In spite of the book's modestly favourable public reception — and lavish praise from Harriet Martineau, Elizabeth Gaskell and her Uncle Ras — Snow's parents were united in the opinion that the novel was 'foolishly sentimental' and, most hurtful of all, 'boring'.

Upon hearing that the publishers had commissioned a second novel, Hensleigh, possibly hoping that his and Snow's relationship might be similar to that of old Edgeworth and Maria, asked Snow to show him the manuscript before she submitted it so that he might offer his suggestions. In the course of the following spring, she gave her father sections of the book as it progressed. Hensleigh not only made suggestions, but corrections, deletions and additions of his own — changing, in fact, both the story and the moral.

When Snow was back at Linlathen during the summer, she rewrote the entire novel and sent it back to her father. He replied:

My dear Snow, I am sorry you take such an uncomfortable scheme of novel, it quite gives one a pain in the stomach. It is a radically false position in which you place Edward and one in which it is very difficult to sympathise with him. It is a man in a woman's place & the feelings you describe are more those of a woman than a man. You must be content to leave my softening down the scene where Lord Conylsford catches them. It would not have done as it stood & I should like to have altered her exclamation 'do not leave me desolate.' Pray write something more chearful the next time. Your affectionate father,   H. WEDGWOOD.[10]

Such a devastating blow to her pride was mitigated somewhat when Hurst & Blackett accepted the manuscript and published it as she had written it, but the damage to her confidence was irreparable. She did choose, however, to have the novel, entitled *An Old Debt*, published under the pseudonym Florence Dawson. She put aside a third novel halfway through. Thereafter, in spite of protests from her Darwin uncles and the Gaskells, she insisted that she had no imaginative powers and that if anything at all her mind was 'merely analytical'.

Hensleigh had always undervalued his children's abilities, setting standards which none of them felt they could achieve. From early childhood, Snow had been considered exceptional by the rest of the family. Mack and Effie, too, had inherited their parents's intellectual gifts, though they received little encouragement except from their Uncle Ras.

Ras Darwin was, in part, responsible for Hensleigh's harsh patriarchal dominance, which seemed in contrast with his earlier pleasant, tolerant manner. While Hensleigh shut himself up in his study, poring over books in ancient Greek, Latin, Hebrew, Sanskrit, medieval German and the modern European languages, Ras—who had no work at all to do—spent much of his leisure in the company of Fanny Hensleigh and her children. Apart from his brother Charles and his cousin Hensleigh whom he considered his closest friend, Ras had always preferred the company of attractive intellectual women to that of men. Though he was a close friend of both the Carlyles, he was more intimate with Jenny (Jane) than with Thomas. He frequently took her for rides alone in his carriage.

Ras also enjoyed the company of children. Like his cousin Harry Wedgwood, who wrote children's stories as a hobby, he was at ease talking with children and entertaining them by playing games, drawing pictures and making up stories. He had a special love for little girls and most particularly for Effie and Hope. Snow received the affection and encouragement from Ras that were lacking from her father—though, clearly, Effie and Hope were Ras's special favourites. None of Charles and Emma's children, or the Parker children, or Joe and Caroline's three little girls, had lavished on them such love and gifts as Effie and Hope were.

By the early 1850s Ras had discarded most of his former women friends whom he had escorted to dinner parties and taken for afternoon rides in his carriage. He saw Fanny Hensleigh and the Hensleigh children several times a week at least, and when they were not seeing one another, each wrote notes telling the other what he or she was or would be doing. Ras began to address Fanny as 'Missis' and 'the wife'—he spoke of 'our daughters' and referred to Hope as his 'little wifey'. He took a summer place large enough to house the entire Hensleigh family. Hensleigh himself was too absorbed in his work to leave London, but Fanny Hensleigh, Snow and the three youngest children, Effie, Alfred and Hope, all joined him. When Hensleigh and Fanny went on holiday to Germany, Ras had Effie and Hope come and stay with him. And when the Hensleighs and the older children returned from Germany, Ras sent Fanny Hensleigh a note: 'It would be delightful if the wife would pack up her carpetbag and come here and go to the Palatine [a hotel in Manchester]....[11]

On several occasions he and Fanny did actually travel together without Hensleigh and without any of the children. 'You must send me some sailing instructions how to get to Elm Grove and when,' Ras wrote to her in the 1850s; 'perhaps we may meet at the Three Bridges at 10:52 train and that would give time to get on Monday or perhaps I may come a day or two after—it is very horrid to think of and it is necessary to divert the mind from such horrors by thinking of the little wife and co.'[12]

A few years later, when Fanny Hensleigh was planning a visit to Harriet Martineau, she suggested that Ras meet her there and they return together. He replied: 'Your idea of my joining you at Ambleside is so startling that it will require some days to compose my imagination, but I should like well enough to be there.'[13]

When Ras suffered an illness that seemed more serious than the usual Wedgwood – Darwin cult of unhealth, Fanny Hensleigh stayed at his new house in Queen Anne Street to nurse him. Everyone in the family, apart from Hensleigh, it seems, was aware of their devotion to each other. There was no actual rift between Fanny Hensleigh and Hensleigh, who appeared as compatible as ever, or between Ras and Hensleigh. The two men seldom saw each other alone as they had in their younger days. Ras was, however, present at practically all of the Hensleighs' dinner parties—but then, so were the Carlyles. Ras almost never entertained without including the Hensleighs.

In February of 1858, when Charles was visiting London, the Hensleighs had a dinner party so Charles might meet Henry Thomas Buckle, the author of *An Introduction to the History of Civilization.* Later Snow recalled: 'I never remember any other book occasioning quite the same stir of interest & discussion at all events in my circle. The *Origin of Species* did not open so many subjects on which *everyone* had an opinion. Certainly Charles Darwin was more interested in it [Buckle's book] than in any other I ever discussed with him. I remember reading it at Down with absorbing interest.'[14]

As Hensleigh neared the end of his own manuscript and the work that had occupied him for two decades, he seemed suddenly to emerge from his cloister and discover how much *his* family had indeed become his cousin's family as well. Snow was writing books which, though silly, were published; Mack had come down from Cambridge and taken a position in the Colonial Office. Time had passed. Hensleigh must have felt that while he had been secluded, Ras somehow had usurped what should have belonged to him. In typical Victorian fashion, he became all the more demanding and dictatorial. If anyone else in the immediate family sensed that all was not well, it was the oversensitive Snow, who commented to Effie: 'I sh'd not care for any trouble from without if we were not all so cold & sharp to each other....'[15]

Apart from that of Emma and Charles, there were no completely happy marriages among the third generation, though they all maintained the pretence of happiness. Joe was even more of a stern, authoritarian parent than Hensleigh, making his three young daughters stand in line each afternoon to receive their 'treat', which was a spoonful of cream—if, of course, they had been good girls. Joe's wife Caroline was beginning to display signs of mental disturbance similar to those of her grandmother and Erasmus junr. Careless in her appearance and forgetful of the most obvious practical details of managing a house and family, she refused to leave Leith Hill Place, and became an almost complete recluse. But after some twelve years, during which she became more and more withdrawn, she made a spontaneous and lasting recovery.

Harry and Jessie had never had a happy marriage, and Jessie, who had a complaining disposition, must often have wished she had permanently broken off their engagement. She was no doubt further disillusioned by the similarities—their mild manner and complete lack of common sense—between her father and her husband. Because of Harry's inability to make a success of the law, or any sort of business, he was often shunned by the rest of the family.

Frank was even more dogmatic, tyrannical and frugal than his brother Joe. Fanny Frank had neither intellectual resources nor insanity, as had her sister-in-law Caroline, to fall back upon. Over the years she became lonely, fat, embittered and bored. She drank wine to calm her nerves, while Frank spent more and more time at the pottery which, for him, was the lesser of two evils.

In spite of Frank's frequent presence, the pottery was going from bad to worse. Since the death of the first Josiah, the factory's policy had been more or less to let the workmen do as they pleased. Journeymen potters, even though they worked for Wedgwood, were themselves employers in that they contracted to do a job and then took on help on their own responsibility. The result was that there was no discontent among the workmen, but also no distinctive new character in the company's products. The Jasper ware shown at the Great Exhibition at the Crystal Palace had been discontinued forty years earlier by Josiah II. The old eighteenth-century moulds were used, which cut down production costs, and Jasper once again became a staple, though small, part of the company's over-all production. Basalt, pearlware, creamware, stoneware, caneware, drabware and Rockingham glazed ware were all being produced. The bulk of the production was in dinnerware rather than in decorative items, and most of the dinnerware was in transfer-printed pearlware. No one in particular was in charge of design. Patterns were produced if they happened to please Mr Wedgwood or Mr Brown.

All went on in a very routine yet casual and parsimonious fashion, until 1859 when Robert Brown died suddenly of a heart attack. For the third time the Wedgwood factory belonged solely to Frank Wedgwood, who had never really wanted it in the first place.

26

True Dilettantes
(1859 – 1864)

The year 1859 was a turning point in the history of the pottery and in the history of the family as well. After Brown's death, Frank took twenty-six-year-old Godfrey, who had been in the factory for the past eight years, into partnership. Nineteen-year-old Clement returned from abroad to begin his apprenticeship at the factory, and fifteen-year-old Laurence, who had completed his schooling at Overslade, near Rugby, followed in his brother's footsteps by going abroad first to Mannheim and then to Paris. Sending the boys abroad was more to give them a practical education than to expose them to culture. Wedgwood now had offices both in Germany and in France, to which Clement and Laurence were sent to learn the overseas side of the business as well as the languages.

In 1859 the celebrated French artist Emile Lessore came to work at Wedgwood. For several months prior to this he had worked at Minton, but had been unhappy there because of the strict discipline and lack of freedom. He now sought out Wedgwood, where there were no foremen and where artists were left free to paint as they pleased — though this was not so much part of a policy of encouraging creativity as a matter of indifference which accidentally proved beneficial.

When Godfrey became a partner in the firm, he took more interest in the design aspect. Having himself a minor talent for drawing and painting, he appreciated art and artists in a way his father did not. Lessore was hired as a piece-painter of landscapes and figures. He was paid by the square inch. Soon, however, his work proved so popular that he was given a contract at the high salary of £500 a year. Furthermore, he was allowed to live in Paris in the winter and London in the summer, being required to spend only ten days of each summer month at the Etruria factory. Lessore believed that the Potteries — with their smoke-filled air, cold, damp winters and lack of cultural stimulation — was an unhealthy place for himself and his two young children.

Lessore's paintings on Wedgwood plaques, bowls, vases, teaware and dessert services were an instant success — partly because the painting was so unlike anything Wedgwood had produced before. Lessore was also a shrewd psychologist. Instead of protesting against the conservatism and general lack of interest of his employers, which had allowed competitors like Minton and Doulton to take the lead in both design and sales, Lessore praised Frank Wedgwood for refusing to change the old ways of his grandfather simply to meet modern taste. At the same time Lessore himself was painting very much to the so-called modern taste and encouraging other Wedgwood artists to do the same. In a flattering tribute to his employer, Lessore wrote: '...the old manufactory of Josiah Wedgwood, founded in the last century, must remain the same, and continue to give imperishable productions, full of the flavour of antiquity, which delights the true dilettante.'[1]

In the context of the times, dilettantism was admirable. The true dilettante was a gentleman who pursued an art or a science, not because it was necessary for him to earn a living by it, but because it was worthwhile and enjoyable. Two true dilettantes who now found themselves the focus of public attention were Hensleigh and Charles. Within a few months of each other they both completed the books which had occupied them for over two decades. After finishing his manuscript each became ill. Then, again, after the books were published and reviewed, the two cousins and brothers-in-law whose dispositions were so similar once more succumbed to headaches, upset stomachs and a general debility which left them both incapable of any exertion. Charles reclined on a sofa in his study at Down while Hensleigh reclined on a sofa in his study in Gower Street.

On the Origin of Species, of course, attracted more attention than *A Dictionary of English Etymology.* For many of his contemporaries, Darwin's work destroyed the very foundations on which western civilization was based. In his Introduction to the book, Charles wrote: 'I am fully convinced that species are not immutable; but that those belonging to what are called the same genera are lineal descendants of some other and generally extinct species, in the same manner as the acknowledged varieties of any one species are the descendants of that species.'[2]

On the Origin of Language, Hensleigh's Introduction to *A Dictionary of English Etymology,* was equally revolutionary in its premises which supported and reinforced Charles's line of reasoning. Hensleigh came to the conclusion that 'language, like writing, is an art handed down from one generation to another, and when we would trace upwards to its origin the pedigree of this grand distinction between man and the brute creation, we must either suppose that the line of tradition has been absolutely endless, that there never was a period at which the family of man was not to be found on earth, speaking a language bequeathed to him by this ancestors, or we must at last arrive at a generation which was not taught their language by their parents.'[3]

When not just criticism but abuse began to pour in on Charles from all directions, he went to another hydropathic institute, at Ilkley in Yorkshire. While he was away, Fanny Hensleigh brought her ailing husband to Down to calm his nerves. Charles returned from Ilkley without feeling much better but having corrected the proofs of the second edition of *On Origin of Species.* At Down Hensleigh and Charles were able to console one another as well as rejoice in the satisfaction of works completed, whatever their reception.

Snow spent the late summer and early autumn at Linlathen where she came under the charismatic influence of another powerful divine, Frederic Denison Maurice, one of the leaders of the Christian Socialist movement. Maurice, along with Charles Kingsley, preached that the Kingdom of God was of this world as well as the next; he denounced the exploitation of child labour in the factories as intolerable in the eyes of God.

On this occasion, the first visit Snow had made to Thomas Erskine's house without her Aunt Rich, she had a mystical revelation which affected her more profoundly than the Christian teachings she had absorbed there seven years earlier. As a consequence of this revelation, she determined to hold herself in readiness, like Florence Nightingale, awaiting some further sign of what to do with her life. Surprisingly, in spite of her belief in divine guidance, she supported her Uncle Charles's theory of evolution and set about writing an essay which would rebut the theological arguments against it. Charles, who had never publicly denied the existence of God, read her essay, 'The Boundaries of Science', published in *Macmillan's Magazine* (July 1861), and wrote to her: 'I think that you understand my book perfectly, and that I find a very rare event with my critics.'[4] Encouraged both by her Uncle Charles and her Uncle Ras, and by Maurice, Snow undertook a comprehensive study of religious beliefs and conflicts to be developed within a biography of John Wesley. By immersing herself in the analysis of theological doctrines, she hoped to reinforce her own belief, which was always shadowed by a kind of rational scepticism, and to find some spiritual mission or purpose for her life.

While Snow was in Scotland sifting through her emotional and spiritual conflicts, her Aunt Fanny Frank had somehow summoned the courage to try to sort out her own more earthy emotions by taking a two-month holiday in America. She had been to several doctors with complaints of nerves, difficulty in breathing, a tendency to weep for no apparent reason, and a general feeling of anxiety and agitation. In order to sleep at night, she had to drink several tumblers of wine. Like Lessore, she was oppressed by the isolation and dreariness of the Potteries. Two doctors recommended a long holiday with an ocean voyage.

Frank, who was never ill himself and had little patience with those who were, had no intention of taking an ocean voyage. He felt that his wife should simply use a little will power and pull herself together. She had duties towards her home and her family — just as he had duties toward the pottery. All of their seven children were still living at home, from Godfrey, the eldest, to Mabel, the youngest, who was eight.

That Fanny Frank was in the throes of a nervous breakdown was apparent to everyone but her husband. He was tired of her complaints, her indecision and her 'constantly wanting to be on the go'. Actually he was happy to be rid of her for a while, even if she were seeing Tom Appleton with whom she had kept up a mild flirtation when he visited Barlaston. Appleton had extended a general invitation to all of the Wedgwoods to come to Boston to visit him and his other in-laws, the Longfellows, and the Robert Mackintoshes would be in Boston, as well. Frank had no patience with gossip either; but the Hensleighs and the Darwins viewed the matter differently. 'I am very sorry Frank does not grow wiser as he gets older,' Emma told Hensleigh, 'for I really believe this scheme is certainly his.'[5] Frank paid no attention to the objections of his brother and his sister—telling them quite bluntly that he had not sought their counsel on a matter which concerned only him and his wife.

Fanny Frank was as easily influenced as Frank was obstinate. She confided in everyone and sought advice everywhere—making a somewhat frantic round of family visits before her scheduled departure. Twice she cancelled her plans and then just as abruptly reinstated them. The Hensleighs were concerned that the journey alone, or with only a maid, would be seen to be improper even if it wasn't: 'Your letter of Saturday has done no harm,' Emma wrote to Hensleigh.

> ...Charles talked to her [Fanny] about the chances of being ill and Frank having to go and fetch her—and the next day she told my Aunts [Emma and Fanny Allen] he had made her quite low about going but that she was better the next day, and her spirits had got up again—I don't myself believe the world will think it very improper—considering her size and how much older she looks than she is—and if they do think it odd it does not much signify. Time goes so fast she will be back again before half the world know she is gone. I am in greater hopes it will not strike all the world as it does us that neither my Aunts nor Sarah [Baugh Allen's second wife] have taken it the least in that light even after we have put it into their heads.[6]

Despite all misgivings Fanny Frank finally departed. She wrote to her family that the ocean voyage had calmed her nerves and lifted her spirits. Boston and the social life led by the Appletons and the Longfellows delighted her. The Americans admired and respected Longfellow and Emerson in much the same manner as Londoners lionized Carlyle and Tennyson. Fanny Frank went to dinner parties and literary gatherings and thoroughly enjoyed herself. Longfellow wrote out in his own hand and signed for her the lines:

> Let the dead Past bury its dead
> Act, act in the living Present
> Heart within and God o'erhead.[7]

It was a sentiment which corresponded with Fanny Frank's new view of herself. At the age of forty-eight she had indeed acted in the living present. Furthermore, she felt far better for having done so. If Appleton had seemed fascinating when she met him in England, Longfellow was positively heroic in New England. His home, his wife, his children, his style of living, his work and his manner of working—all were quite different from life in North Staffordshire. Molly Mackintosh and her children came to Boston from Antigua for a visit. Molly was ill and homesick for her family and friends. When all of these hospitable Americans urged Fanny Frank to extend her visit, she did so.

Back in Staffordshire Frank discovered that his wife's departure had damaged his own self-esteem. He had a strong sense of his own authority and of other people's duties. Though he himself had goaded her into leaving, he hadn't really expected her to sail across the ocean by herself. When she decided to extend her stay, he was astounded—then angry. Short of going there himself and bringing her back, which his pride would not allow, there was simply nothing he could do but wait. Another six months passed before she finally returned.

While his mother was in America Godfrey took his sisters Cecily and Amy and his cousin Louisa Wedgwood to Switzerland on a holiday. He had invited his cousin Effie to come along also, but she refused with the excuse that she had promised to accompany her mother and Snow and Uncle Ras to Manchester to visit the Gaskells.

'Godfrey is always taken for our father,' Louisa wrote to Effie from Switzerland. 'He overheard a waiter at the Schweigerhof speaking of him as "that gentleman with the three daughters".[8] In many ways Godfrey seemed older than he actually was. Sensitive, solemn and shy, he was anxious, as an eldest son, to live up to his father's expectations, even though he knew that his brother Clement had many more of the qualities his father admired than Godfrey himself had. The incompatibility of his parents and what he perceived as their small, unnecessary unkindnesses distressed him. He wanted to please—and he doubted that he had the ability to please everyone, or indeed, anyone. He wanted a polite, orderly uncomplicated existence. Life should proceed according to a plan. Now that he had become a partner in the firm and thus secured a respectable income, he wanted to marry.

All three of his Wedgwood uncles had married their first cousins. His Uncle Charles Darwin was the son of first cousins as well as having married his first cousin—thus giving rise to the joke that the Darwins were more Wedgwood than the Wedgwoods. Times change, however. There was now talk that possibly all of this intermarrying was not good for the health of future generations. Godfrey's father Frank was fond of pointing to the chronic illnesses of Ras and Charles and Hensleigh—in contrast, of course, to his own robust health. Another family joke was that Godfrey's cousin Henrietta Darwin had 'made invalidism her vocation'. Frank never tired of pointing out to Godfrey that Hensleigh's sons were nothing but 'listless lay-abouts'. This, indeed, was true.

Such criticism could not, however, be levelled at Hensleigh's daughters. Snow, Effie and Hope were formidable intellectual matches for any man. Furthermore, they rivalled their Uncle Frank with their dedication to exercise and to early rising. Godfrey knew that all three young women certainly had more energy and self-determination than he had. For the past five years he had admired Effie, who was vivacious, flirtatious and strong-willed. What made him refrain from proposing marriage to her was not fear of the consequences of another first-cousin marriage but fear that she would refuse him. From conversations with Snow and with his own sister Cecily, he got the feeling that Effie looked upon him in much the same way as she looked upon her own three brothers. Still, he was sure — or thought he was sure — that she was fond of him. He had even been so bold as to ask Snow if she knew what Effie's feelings for him were.

Effie was at the time twenty-one years of age, conceited about her own attractiveness and as immature emotionally as she was precocious intellectually. She was flattered by Godfrey's attentions and had confessed to Snow that she found their soft-spoken, serious-minded cousin interesting. Snow replied: 'I am glad you do appreciate him. Strange to say, I think he is very little appreciated as everybody thinks he is commonplace which, when you get below the surface, he is not. If he had a backbone, I sh'd think him perfect, but that is a fatal want.'[9]

Godfrey's 'fatal want' was the same one that had affected eldest sons of the previous two generations of Wedgwoods. Like his Great-uncle John and his Uncle Joe, he had served his apprenticeship at Etruria, done his duty and attempted to combine the two occupations of managing a factory and being a country gentleman. He was a kind, modest man who would have much preferred someone else to wield power. Effie was very much a woman attracted to power.

In the spring of 1862, when Godfrey visited the Hensleighs in London in their new house at 1 Cumberland Place, Regent's Park, he was both fascinated and bewildered by Effie's unpredictable behaviour. When he asked her if she wanted him to accompany her to an exhibition at the Royal Academy, she replied that she didn't. He couldn't imagine what he had done — or hadn't done — to offend her. On the following evening he and Mack and Ernie took Snow and Effie to a ball. Godfrey asked Effie for a waltz, and she replied that she had already promised it to Clarke Hawkshaw, son of Sir John Hawkshaw of Hollycombe. Godfrey soon found himself dancing with Clarke's sister Mary, who seemed as placid and agreeable as Effie was volatile and difficult.

Four months later, in June of 1862, Godfrey and Mary were married. They spent most of their three-month honeymoon in the Hawkshaws' London house on Eaton Square where they received visitors frequently. Effie's flip comment was that they behaved 'as if they had been married for years'.

People were crowding into London from all over the country for the International Exhibition of 1862. Lessore, spending the summer in London, had painted a number of plaques and large majolica vases to be displayed. He had also persuaded Frank and Godfrey to produce the majolica ware which had proven so successful for Minton and Doulton and other factories. Most of the majolica items which Wedgwood made were, however, from eighteenth-century and early nineteenth-century moulds — thus, game pie dishes, wine and water ewers, Tritons and dolphins, which had previously been made in Cane, Jasper or Basalt, now made their appearance in brilliant colours with a shiny opaque glaze. Wedgwood's display at the International Exhibition was larger and more impressive than it had been at the Great Exhibition eleven years earlier.

The new Exhibition Hall—replacing the Crystal Palace which had been destroyed by fire—was composed of two vast domes of glass, each larger than that of St Peter's in Rome, connected by a nave 800 feet long, 100 feet high and 85 feet wide. Thousands of people thronged to South Kensington to marvel at this new building decked with brightly coloured streamers and flags of practically every nation. But following the state carriages conveying the Royal Commissioners deputed by the queen to open the Exhibition came a cortège with coachmen in black livery, and the black armbands of the Crown Prince of Prussia and Prince Oscar of Sweden, in the royal carriage, were mournful reminders of the untimely death, less than six months before, of Prince Albert, the initiator and co-ordinator of this new International Exhibition.

The nation, which had never really accepted this un-English Prince with his un-English tastes and habits, now recognized its own loss as well as the Queen's. For weeks Victoria had been sunk in grief and despair; then with dignity she put on the dark veil of widowhood she was to wear for the next half-century. Her fortitude, obstinacy and belief in the importance of her own historical role had prevented a permanent collapse. As she left Windsor while the funeral she could not bear to attend was taking place, she was heard repeating to herself: 'I will, I *will* do my duty.' It was the same philosophy that the Wedgwoods had practiced for three generations.

Snow went to this International Exhibition because the Scotts were in London and wanted to go. 'We had a most disastrous attempt at getting away,' she told her Aunt Rich. 'First he [Scott] and I were separated from my mother & were ever so long before we could find her. Next she could not find her parasol & went from one stall to another in despair. After that we found we were at the wrong door and had to walk along that endless row of carriages to look for our own—& to finish up with, the coachman came the wrong way....'[10]

During the same week the Scotts attended a dinner party given by the Hensleighs. A main topic of conversation was Ruskin's leaving England in a great depression because Carlyle and Charles Darwin had shaken his belief in Christianity and it had left a great blank in his mind. Scott later told Snow that he thought Carlyle 'had become entirely fatalistic & that he was too consistent not to follow it [his scepticism] out to all its conclusions.[11]

At Hensleigh's request Joe had sent Carlyle John Leslie's manuscript biography of Josiah I with the notes and corrections that Coleridge had made. This had been kept first at Maer Hall and then later at Leith Hill Place and consequently was not among the old documents discarded by Frank. Carlyle read it and also made a few notes in the margins but agreed with Coleridge that the manuscript could never be made publishable. He himself was not interested in writing a biography of Wedgwood.

Meanwhile, however, Godfrey had received a request from Eliza Meteyard, a London journalist and an acquaintance of Snow's, for permission to look at the Leslie manuscript, which she thought was still at the factory. She had been commissioned by Joseph Mayer of Liverpool to write a biography of Wedgwood.

The Mayers were an old Newcastle family with pottery connections.

Joseph Mayer was himself a distant relative and descendant of Daniel Mayer, the draper with whom Josiah had lived when he was a partner with Whieldon. Mayer's late brother Josiah Mayer had owned a pottery in Burslem, which Eliza Meteyard visited in the course of writing the Wedgwood biography. The real source material for the book, however, came from Joseph Mayer himself. Some seventeen years earlier, while he was in Birmingham and passing through the Snow Hill section where Matthew Boulton had begun his early career, a sudden thunderstorm forced him to take refuge in a near-by waste and scrap shop. Piles of scrap iron, copper, brass and junk of every kind littered the floor. While pacing up and down, waiting for the rain to stop, he noticed on the battered oak counter a pile of old ledger books. Upon closer examination he discovered that the ledgers were from the Etruria factory and related to the wages of the workmen.

The scrap dealer informed Mayer that he sold these books to butchers and shopkeepers to wrap up their bacon, butter and green groceries, the big sheets being a convenient size. The scrap dealer who had purchased these from the Wedgwood factory after the death of Josiah II, when Frank launched his clean-up campaign, took Mayer up into the loft above his shop where he had many more documents. Mayer purchased all of the material from him and devoted his leisure time to arranging the documents. Unable to give time to the writing of a book himself, he made the material available to Eliza Meteyard.

Having learned of Carlyle's negative comments on the Leslie manuscript, Godfrey wrote to Eliza Meteyard that the family did not want the Leslie manuscript to be used as the basis for a book about Josiah Wedgwood I, but that he would ask his father to compose a memorandum of stories told by workmen whose fathers and grandfathers had worked at Etruria. Not knowing of the material his father had given to the rubbish collector years earlier, Godfrey concluded: 'I am sorry such a man should have left so little to chronicle behind him — he appears to have been a man of deeds having little time to leave any memorandum of them behind him. The most that can be known of him will have to be from the works he has left in clay.'[12]

Frank, perhaps embarrassed now that he had taken so little interest in preserving factory material that was of interest to historians and collectors, then changed his mind and asked Godfrey to send Eliza Meteyard the old Leslie manuscript.

In late 1862 and early 1863 there was nearly as much criticism and gossipy correspondence in the Wedgwood—Darwin circle as when Fanny Frank had gone to America four years earlier. Charlotte Langton had died in January of 1862, and within the year Charles Langton had asked Catherine Darwin, who was then aged fifty-three and in poor health, to become his second wife. To the younger generation of Darwins and Wedgwoods, among whom only Godfrey was married, this seemed positively indecent. Both Catherine and Langton had strong wills, quick tempers and depressive dispositions. Snow and Effie in particular disliked the annual visits which they were obliged to make to Shrewsbury. 'What is trying in Catherine', Snow once told Effie, 'is not so much any actual fault of temper as unreasonable lamentations over what cannot be helped — exaggerated fits of dislike to trifling things to which a careful easy companion who takes things lightly would not much mind.'[13]

Despite opposition Langton and Catherine became officially engaged in June of 1863, and were married five months later. To show publicly that there was no breach in the family, Ras Darwin, the Hensleighs and the Joe Wedgwoods all attended the ceremony.

On 26 October 1863, the foundation stone for the Wedgwood Institute at Burslem was laid by the then Chancellor of the Exchequer, William Gladstone. With the backing of the Chamber of Commerce, the Potters' Union, various manufacturers and several wealthy collectors such as Joseph Mayer, the Institute was designed to contain a school of art, a museum and a free library for the inhabitants of the Potteries. Banners were strung across the streets, some reading 'Welcome to the Rt Hon. W. E. Gladstone, M.P., D.C.L.', 'Peace and Prosperity', and 'May Honest Industry Ever Prosper'. The past few years had not been prosperous ones in the Potteries. A terrible winter in 1861-2, combined with the effects of the American Civil War, had led to much poverty and distress in the region.

The Institute was named for the first Josiah, not because the present members of the Wedgwood family had taken any special interest in bringing it into being, nor made any generous contributions to help establish it, but simply because no English potter before him or since was more acclaimed throughout the world. The name itself brought instant recognition, even though none of Josiah Wedgwood's descendants were on the large committee for the establishment of the Institute. Mr and Mrs Frank Wedgwood and Mr Clement Wedgwood did, however, attend the luncheon at the Town Hall after laying of the stone by Gladstone.

The event was given wide coverage by the Press. The Assembly Rooms were repainted, and there was a grand display of pottery from more than thirty manufacturers in the district. Behind the chairman's seat, occupied by the Rt Hon. Earl Granville, were life-sized busts in Parian ware of Victoria and Albert. Behind these were the royal standard and the Union Jack. Every table was ornameted with little vases, busts and statuettes from Etruria and from other potteries in the area. In front of the orchestra was a fine marble bust of Josiah Wedgwood made by Fontana and presented by Joseph Mayer. On either side of the bust was a magnificent vase in Jasper, reproductions of vases in the palace of Fontainebleau.

Gladstone's speech delivered at the luncheon in the Town Hall was reproduced in full in The *Evening Star*. 'England has long taken a lead among the nations of Europe for the cheapness of her manufactures: not so for their beauty,' Gladstone concluded. 'And if the day shall ever come when she shall be emiment in taste as she is now in economy of production, my belief is that that result will probably be due to no other single man in so great a degree as to Wedgwood.'[14]

Frank probably regretted then that he had not insisted that Joe and Harry and Hensleigh come back to Staffordshire for the occasion.

Actually, there were fifteen grandchildren and twenty-eight great-grand-children who might have attended, if anyone had cared.

Hensleigh, as a scholar and historian, was one of the few who did care, but he was preoccupied with immediate family problems. His son Ernie, a polite, jovial young man, had taken a minor post in the Colonial Office which Hensleigh felt was beneath his abilities. The youngest son, Alfred, who had left Rugby without completing his studies, showed no sign of either ability or ambition. In a conversation reminiscent of John's talk with Jos about his son Allen a generation earlier, Hensleigh confided to Frank that he had never encountered any young man so indolent as Alfred. After four years of Alfred's doing nothing but lounging about and annoying his parents and his brothers and sisters by his dullness, occasionally punc-tuated by fits of temper, Hensleigh got him a midshipman's berth and, against Alfred's wishes, sent him off to sea.

Even more distressing to Hensleigh and to the rest of the family was Mack's condition. Like Fanny's sister Bessy, who had died at the age of nineteen Mack—now twenty-seven—had an incurable cancer and was given only a year to live. In a desperate but futile attempt to find some miracle cure, Fanny Hensleigh took him to the warmer climate of Italy. In a state of morbid depression Hensleigh stayed at 1, Cumberland Place with his three daughters and Ernie during the cold, dreary February of 1864.

27

A Romantic Interlude
(1864 – 1866)

Mack's condition, rapidly deteriorating even in the warmth and dry air of Florence, caused Fanny Hensleigh to bring him back to London in early April, three months sooner than had been planned. Because of anxiety, exhaustion and the brevity of their stay, she had not used the introductions Robert Browning had kindly given her to his friends in Italy, the novelist Isa Blagden and the American sculptors Hiram Powers and Harriet Hosmer. She was none the less grateful for his thoughtfulness, particularly since they had known one another only slightly through the Carlyles, Ruskin and Monckton Milnes, though they had other mutual friends in the G. H. Leweses, the Maurices, the Spottiswoodes, the Leigh Hunts, the Edmund Lushingtons, Harriet Martineau and the reticent, unsocial Poet Laureate Tennyson.

On a chilly, grey London evening in late April of 1864, the Hensleighs gave a dinner party which included Browning as well as the Carlyles, the Scotts, Harriet Martineau, Ras Darwin and Snow. Victorian dinner parties of the sort the Hensleighs gave were awesome affairs which began at around eight and often lasted for three or four hours. There were many courses — soup, fish, entrée, pudding, savoury, cheese and fruit, with all the appropriate wines, coffee, liqueurs and port. Ladies retired to the parlour for coffee and personal gossip. Men remained in the dining room where cigars were passed along with the port. Throughout dinner, the well-dressed guests, both women and men, were expected to be clever, agreeable, and *au courant* with art, literature, politics, science and theology. In metropolitan intellectual circles those who did not measure up conversationally failed to survive socially and even occasionally fell back into that uncultured group who, like servants and children, called their evening meal 'tea'. For the intelligentsia and the upper classes, tea remained precisely that — a cup of tea and nothing more.

Elizabeth Barrett Browning had died two years before, and Browning was trying to assuage in a busy social life both his loneliness and his sense of failure as 'the author of unreadable books'. Encouraged by a new literary popularity which he had not achieved during his wife's lifetime, he now eagerly embraced the London intellectual—social scene. An extrovert with charming manners, a loud, resonant voice and a fund of amusing stories, he was a much-sought-after dinner guest.

Snow had met Browning early in the spring of 1863 when, with Aunt Rich and two of her Erskine cousins, she attended a dinner party given by Madame Schwabes at which he was also present. Accustomed to the company of the learned and famous, Snow thrived on literary arguments and found herself fascinated by this poet whom most people considered *the* 'literary lion'. Still, she was confident enough of her own views not to be uncritical of his. It was the sort of confidence Browning admired, especially in a woman.

Snow described the party at Madame Schwabes's to Effie, who was visiting Leith Hill Place:

> ...I had Browning to myself for the chief part of the evening. He was perhaps a little too loud and rollicking. I got into a very comfortable corner between him, Mr Milnes and Madame Mohl who was, as Louisa [Erskine] would say, 'in shouts' all the time—it was all very loud and jovial, & I did wish once or twice that some music would strike up. The great subject was Mr Swinburne's poems. Milnes was attacking Browning for attacking them, & B. defended himself very indignantly from the charge of having dissuaded the publisher from accepting them, in which story he said there was not a word of truth. It was very wrong to fabricate such a legend, but I thought it would have been better taste for Mr B. not to have said so much against these unhappy poems—he said they were a third-rate imitation of Byron which if a man believed, he would jump over Waterloo Bridge, & then went on with very fierce contempt against them,—which he said the author would attribute to the jealousy of a 'brother bard'.

Telling Effie that she had worn to the party Effie's green silk dress and Hope's great hoop, which was painful to sit upon, and made her tremble for the tables when she ventured to move across the room, she then mentioned Browning's personal attentions to her: He was so particularly civil, wanting to know what time he should find Mama at home. When I said she was out of town, hoping we should see something of each other in October, when he comes back to town — I never saw such an un-lionish lion.'[1]

Now, ten months later, Snow looked at Browning across her parents' dinner table, reading his lips with almost as much pleasure as she read his poetry. She was thirty-one; he was fifty-one, famous and handsome in a rugged, masculine way not often associated with poets. Unexpectedly she was attracted to him with the same suddenness of passion that had overwhelmed her spiritually with Thomas Erskine at Linlathen. Like her heroine in *Framleigh Hall*, she was overcome by 'the most intense, spontaneous feeling of her soul...with which she must struggle as a deadly sin'.

Browning was adored by scores of fashionable women, many younger, wealthier and prettier than Snow, who already had the outward appearance of a prim, pious and critical woman. Yet when he looked across the table, he, too, was attracted by something both physical and spiritual in her. In many ways she must have reminded him of his wife in the early days of their courtship. Both women were small and frail and dark in colouring. Both were highly intelligent, with a literary gift and sensibility. They had both received praise for their published writings. Both were outwardly modest and submissive, yet a perceptive man would have sensed that within each was a passionate, rebellious spirit. Browning, whose actions were guided by intuition and whose closest friendships were with women, was excited by Snow as he had not been by any woman apart from Elizabeth. With extraordinary prescience, he guessed that she was capable of understanding him and of stimulating him intellectually in a way that no merely fashionable woman could do.

There were similarities in the two women's circumstances as well. Elizabeth had been a semi-invalid who needed care and protection; Snow's deafness made her appear equally vulnerable. Both were sheltered, unhappy, eldest daughters with brothers called Bro. Elizabeth's Bro had drowned accidentally, bringing about, or at least contributing to, her invalidism and reclusiveness. Snow's Bro was also dying; she was clearly distressed and seeking the same sort of spiritual consolation that Elizabeth had sought. Snow's subservient devotion to the strange, half-mad Erskine had its counterpart in Elizabeth's deep involvement with an Evangelical clergyman, the Revd George Barrett Hunter.

At the dinner table, while Carlyle thundered and raved like Lear about the need for a single heroic figure to rise from the revolutions on the Continent, Browning was suddenly taken ill with a severe migraine, which interrupted the party and greatly embarrassed him. Fanny Hensleigh took him into the study next to the parlour where he could rest on a couch. Snow brought ice packs and placed them on his head while he tried to be resolute against what he later described as 'not pain but the stupidity that accompanies it'. It was an intimate moment recognized as such by them both.

Several days later Browning, who ordinarily would have sent a servant, came personally to call on Fanny Hensleigh with a bouquet of flowers and a note of apology. She was out shopping. Snow was alone in the parlour copying one of Blake's engravings. She had been thinking of Browning — with what Effie described as 'her tendency towards idolatry' — almost constantly since the evening of the dinner party. The unexpectedness of meeting him alone emboldened her to invite him into the parlour and to make a proposal unusual for a young woman of her background and upbringing. As she herself later put it, 'A woman who has taken the initiative in a friendship with a man, as I have with you, has either lost all right feeling or else come to a very definite decision on the issue of all such friendships.'[2]

She asked Browning to call on her once a week to discuss literary matters and moral issues. Their intercourse would be of a spiritual nature, with the clear understanding that the 'man – woman' feelings which so often complicate friendships between persons of the opposite sex would not enter into it. She thought that this stipulation would not bother him since he had already experienced the great love of his life and, in any event, was getting on in years. As far as her own feelings were concerned, there would be no difficulty as she was 'shielded by the deliberate decision of her mature life' never to marry.

In an age in which well-bred young women were taught never openly to mention such matters, Browning was naturally intrigued. That Snow was forthright enough to tell him that she had irrevocably renounced any sexual feelings towards men was novelty enough to be a challenge rather than a deterrent to him. It must also have reminded him of his own idealistic and impossible suggestion to Elizabeth two decades earlier — that if she could care for him only as a friend he would promise faithfully to live with her forever 'as chaste as brother and sister'.

Snow, who not only had a predilection towards older men but also towards martyrdom and tragic endings, probably naïvely believed that to be a spiritual and intellectual companion to a man like Browning would satisfy all of her emotional longings. Perhaps, like Florence Nightingale waiting for her destiny to make itself known, she saw helping him as a possible divinely ordained mission for her future. She wanted very much to help, to serve and to be needed. And, at that moment, she also needed his help in understanding why a just and righteous God should permit her young brother to suffer such a cruel death. That she so clearly needed Browning was an important element in the beginning of their friendship. Browning, too, needed to be needed. And, she made him feel young again. The past was over — he might risk a future.

Charmed and flattered, he accepted her invitation to friendship. On Sunday afternoons, shortly after one o'clock, he took the new Underground train from his house in Warwick Crescent to the Wedgwood home in Regent's Park. 'I dare say that I have managed to give you a notion that the distance between your house and mine is formidable,' he told her. 'The time of the journey from door to door cannot exceed twenty minutes, by railway.'[3]

Throughout the late spring and early summer of 1864 they saw one another once a week, sometimes more often, meeting not always by chance at art exhibitions, musical gatherings and dinner parties. On Sunday afternoons behind the closed doors of the drawing room at 1, Cumberland Place, they spoke of their own writing and what was happening in the literary world in general. Both thrived on gossip and literary analysis; they moved in the same social circles and knew the same people. They discussed God, the teachings of Erskine, Scott and Maurice, the promise of a life in the hereafter and the spiritual role of the artist. Snow confided to him her personal distress and her fears for her dying brother. From the depth of his own sorrow, he comforted her, but the emotions emerging were something more than a mutual experience of grief, and this was observed by others.

Snow's parents felt some apprehension. Hensleigh undervalued his daughter's abilities and frankly wondered why a man of Browning's reputation would pay her so much attention. Fanny Hensleigh liked Browning and found him personally attractive. She also knew that at the time he was calling on Snow every Sunday, his name was also being linked with that of the poetess Jean Ingelow and with Snow's friend Hilary Bonham Carter, as possible second Mrs Brownings. With the instincts and knowledge of a woman of the world whose relations with her own husband as well as her friendship with Ras Darwin were more passionate than was proper in mid-Victorian England, Fanny Hensleigh suspected that consciously or unconsciously Browning's appeal to her daughter was as much of the flesh as the spirit. At the moment, however, the entire family was caught up in the agonizing, protracted death of the eldest and brightest son, and had neither time nor strength to consider Snow's emotional conflicts.

After three years of suffering, Mack — or Bro — died peacefully on 24 June 1864, at the age of thirty. Snow immediately wrote to Browning telling him that at last her brother was at rest. She ended her note, 'I shall very soon wish to see you again, and perhaps you will let me summon you. You will not wonder to hear that my mother is physically worn out, but I think it is the best thing for her mind. When I can see anyone, it will be you.'[4]

Browning responded the same day by himself taking a letter round to Cumberland Place, no doubt in hope of seeing her, but no one in the family was receiving. In his letter he told her:

> ... the circumstances under which I have come to know you may certainly have so operated that, in the meeting of our hands mine has seemed somewhat to lift rather than be lifted by yours. But that has been only a chance — and any day you would help me as much. Simply, I value your friendship for me, as you shall know if you will but wait: and it already seems useless to tell you that wherever I may be of the slightest good to you, it will be my pride and privilege when you count on me. And now — no more assurances of this kind from me, nor surely any need for them will you ever feel.[5]

In this he was quite wrong. Snow needed constant reassurance and seemed totally incapable of believing she could ever be at all important to him. — 'I dread myself, for I know there is in me an exacting spirit that dries up all the love and kindness which it needs so terribly.'[6] She had no more confidence in her worth as a woman than as a novelist. Once she had been wounded, as she was when her father told her that her book made him 'quite sick at my stomach' — the wound was permanent and fatal. There was a neurotic element in her character that was self-destructive and seemed to demand needless suffering and self-sacrifice. 'I find myself imploring bearable pain,' she later wrote, 'not pleasure.'[7]

Since Fanny Hensleigh knew of Snow's note to Browning about Mack's death, and of Browning's immediate personal response, Snow decided to show his letter to her mother. Wishing to allay any suspicions of Browning having matrimonial intentions towards her and to justify her own wish to keep their intimate friendship on the high spiritual plane that she had first dictated, Snow told her mother of the 'man — woman' restrictions she had placed on their friendship. Then, naïvely, she wrote to Browning telling him what she had done and noting that her mother 'was startled at the unusual course I had taken, hers is a mind to perceive very clearly the objections to it, but as she saw I had lost nothing in your eyes by it, she was satisfied'.[8] She also felt impelled to reiterate her conditions to Browning, as if already he had ventured too far: '... if I felt that the mere accident (as I feel it for all its influence on my feelings for you) of your being a man and my being a woman is inimical to its long existence in this personal form, you must remember that what I had before I knew you, perhaps the larger part of your mind, I should still have after our intercourse had ceased.'[9]

Browning failed to heed the warning. He replied: 'I am glad that you showed my letter to Mrs Wedgwood. You know well what is the way of the world with any exceptional mode of proceeding: if one wears a white tie instead of a black one, or calls at 10 rather than 5 p.m. — it has something to say and smile about. It is for you to determine when it is right that I should see you.'[10]

She determined in a matter of days, and his visits increased in frequency from once to twice a week. Rumours circulated in that gossipy little world of fashionable intellectuals whose ambiguities and self-centredness Jane Carlyle perceived so keenly and with such bitterness. Browning heard the rumours, too; but, with more egotism than common sense, he perceived them then as flattering rather than harmful. Snow herself bravely and innocently commented: 'A life of silence as mine is (though it is possible to forget it with you) breeds a peculiar indifference towards the opinion of the world. I know not whether it is for good or for evil, but one who never *over* hears, cares little for and knows little of the surface current of opinion which expresses itself in slight remark.'[11]

On 22 July Snow left London for the obligatory round of visits to her relatives. First she went to the Joe Wedgwoods at Leith Hill Place. This was a sombre house with her silent, autocratic Uncle Joe, her eccentric, secretive Aunt Caroline and their three serious daughters, Sophy, now aged twenty-two, Margaret, aged twenty-one, and Lucy, aged eighteen.

The precious afternoons with Browning were supplanted by an easy and increasingly intimate correspondence. Distance probably made her feel safe from any weakness towards the flesh — and, perhaps, at the same time more daring. Having nothing or little to do at Leith Hill Place, she walked in the dense yet familiar woods and felt 'the regrets, wishes and weariness of life' disappear. She looked around her at the shrubs and distant hills as if they had changed, and 'that is purely because a fellow creature — not spotlessly perfect by any means — tells me that my absence makes a hole in his life, that I am willing, oh! more than willing, to keep my foothold here, while he cares to have me'.[12]

She was hopelessly in love not only with the man Browning but with the myth that surrounded him. That myth, of course, included his dead wife whom she believed, rightly perhaps, to be the true inspiration for his genius. Elizabeth had been all of the things Snow felt were lacking in herself. 'Your wife always seems to me so eminently a woman, the maternal, the conjugal relations seem necessary parts of her character, one feels they were the expressions of herself. With me, all the relations of life are unfortunate, and I do not feel that it just so happens because the beloved and honoured ones with whom I share them are what they are — but because of something in me which grates against all the material bonds of life.'[13]

Had Browning been a less simple man — or perhaps had he not been falling in love again himself — he would have considered her personality more thoughtfully. He would have analysed the reasons behind the limitations she placed on their friendship; he would have questioned her constant reference to their intimacy as 'one perpetual farewell'. Instead, he asked her for her photograph and assured her that he would always tell her the truth and entertained 'no doubt or fear of the future with us two'.

Though she, of course, had no way of knowing it, the romantic imagery and symbolism in his letters to her were similar to — in some instances, identical with — what he had written to Elizabeth two decades earlier. He spoke to both of the palm tree and palm wine as a metaphor for love between man and woman. Light was used to represent both women — to Elizabeth: 'I shall grow old and die with you — as far as I can look into the night I see the light with me.' And, when he was abroad, he wrote to Snow: 'Write and hold out a light, if I am ever to swim across the dark strait from Boulogne to the Abydos of Warwick Crescent.'[14]

After her stay at Leith Hill Place, Snow went to Falmouth to visit Thomas Erskine's niece and her close friend Julia Stirling. She confided her feelings for Browning to her friend and, at this point, may even have thought of revoking the restriction she had placed on their friendship. Her letters took on a coquettish tone. His letters became more bold. They dissected their emotions, used pet names and fretted about whether the post would bring a letter. She teased him about the difference in their ages — 'your grey hairs wd protect you.' They continued to refer to 'palm wine' as love or affection. He spoke of needing from her 'a pin-head-sized drop of palm wine just now, being out of sorts on various accounts and perhaps no-accounts so I hold up the tip of my finger to catch it as having a right, please observe!'[15] And she replied: 'I am not altogether displeased with those no-accounts which sent me an order for a pin-head-drop of palm wine today, which I hasten to supply....'[16]

For the first ten days in October she went to stay with her Aunt Rich and the widowed Lady Inglis at their country home in Milton Bryan. Aunt Rich had already heard gossip about Snow and Browning and was quite as sharp and critical about Browning as she had been about Hensleigh and his attentions to Fanny Hensleigh thirty-five years earlier. She told Snow that she had seen 'your Mr B' at an art exhibition in London and didn't think he looked at all poetical. Snow wrote to Browning: 'I thought it hard to be called upon to account for your looks.'

The visit was hard in other ways, too, disturbing further her already turbulent emotions. The house itself, in which no one so much as dared to open a newspaper on Sunday, gave a sobering view of the narrow existence of two elderly women with only each other and their cats for company. Snow felt 'muzzled' — yet, at the same time, she admired the martyrdom of her Aunt Rich, 'speaking of her past happiness — passionate love whose embers give all the warmth she needs.' Mary Rich believed fervently in only one marriage on earth and then a spiritual reunion of husband and wife in the next world. Claudius Rich had been dead for forty-two years, yet Snow noted: 'So poignant and enduring was her grief that during all my recollections she could never bring herself to use his name.'[17]

Browning, too, worried about her and what Aunt Rich and others were saying about them now. He cautioned her: 'You know the difficulties will begin soon enough: my visits will seem importunate, be remarked on, the usual course of things must be looked for.'[18] Instead of suggesting that he limit his visits or discontinue them entirely, when they were both again in London, he expressed fears about the difference in their ages and that he was preventing her from being interested in others. Clearly he did not believe her vow to remain chaste: 'A better than I, God knows, should have the whole palm tree in its season. There, that's said. Meantime, grow and be happy, and let me sit under the branches to my day's end, come what will.... Forgive all that is stupid in all this, which I dare not re-read: and only mind the main truth that I am ever yours, R. B.'[19] Romantic words which clearly indicated to her, as he intended, that he found her desirable as a woman as well as an intellectual companion.

Two months before she was to return to London, Browning took his son Pen for a holiday in France. Before leaving he wrote to her:

GOODBYE DEAREST FRIEND, I go tomorrow, stay, as I very likely have told you, some two months, and see you prominently on the white cliffs, as a landmark for return. We won't teaze each other with any more 'last words', but take the good of understanding each other without further labour and pains: I will not be older than you like, nor you younger than I want. I daresay nothing but good will come out of it all to you and me. Remember where I will be till I settle — 151 rue de Grenelle, Faubg. St. Germ. and always inform me exactly where you are. I have been reading your admirable article in the 'Reader' — admirable, I mean every letter of the word. So, I stretch out my hand for 'bread' — had you any fancy of the possible attitude in the future of, Yours ever affectionately, R. B.?[20]

Her confidence in the masculine ability to maintain friendship on a purely platonic basis was further shaken that autumn. A few months earlier Godfrey's wife Mary had died from complications after the birth of their son Cecil, and Godfrey had fallen into despair and become ill both physically and mentally, and unfit to work. Various members of the family, including Ras, the Charles Darwins and Snow's own parents, expressed the hope that he would remarry soon. Within the family circle only Mary Rich felt that he should never re-marry but wait patiently until he was reunited with his wife in the next world.

Snow saw the parallel situation of two widowers with only sons, and remarked upon this to Browning. She noted that she could not help shrinking in imagination from the time when 'the absorbing grief shall yield to the mere material want of a new companion. It is so disappointing to see it, it seems to me like a sort of abdication of the rights of immortality....'[21] She made constant references to the perfection of Browning's dead wife and the impossibility of his ever finding another such 'window' to 'look direct into the face of Heaven' — as if she were not only reminding him of the restriction she had placed on their friendship but also telling him how he *ought* to feel about the past.

Mary Rich's influence on Snow was far greater than anyone imagined. Snow postponed her return to London, going instead to Manchester to the Scotts, where she noticed 'coincidence' in Scott's illness with that of her dead brother. She became depressed, extended her stay in Manchester and then instead of returning to London went back again to her Aunt Rich at Milton Bryan.

Browning was impatient for her return, and despite her hints of 'perpetual farewell', he seemed quite confident of their future together. Snow suggested he call upon her mother, which he did. Fanny Hensleigh and Browning liked one another. He would certainly have been acceptable as a son-in-law. The difference in age would not have mattered.

Although Browning possessed a genius which Snow certainly did not have, she was a far more complex personality than he. He did not understand her at all. He ignored such warnings as: 'I am not feminine, they say'[22] — because this was an almost exact repetition of early discussions with Elizabeth during their courtship. She, too, had been bothered as to which of the two of them was feminine and which masculine.

Sensing an old, familiar argument, he happily replied: 'I am 'feminine', if you are not, and bent consequently on having the last word about that palm wine.'[23] He wanted to place her upon a pedestal, a position which made her uneasy and which she refused. Instead, she wished to place him there, but he would have none of it. The endless debate as to who was superior and who was inferior was remarkably parallel to the initial dialogues Browning had had with Elizabeth — a fact which Snow could not have known and which Browning failed to understand, or perhaps he was lulled into a false security by the very familiarity of it all.

Browning's need for self-abnegation was almost as great as Snow's. In Evangelical zeal and romantic aspirations, they were kindred spirits — two strong natures at loggerheads, each reluctant to command, each eager to obey. Snow rightly perceived, as Elizabeth had done before her, that Browning did not see her as she truly was but as the personification of the anima within him. He addressed himself through her to an ideal woman of his own creation. This made her uneasy — as Elizabeth, too, had been during his courtship, when she wrote: 'May God grant that you never see me as I am.'

The crucial difference between Elizabeth and Snow was that Elizabeth saw quite clearly the man Browning was, with all of his flaws as well as his virtues. By some unkind quirk of fate, Snow and Browning shared the same blind inclination to idolatry. Conflict was inevitable. He was a cheerful, hearty optimist; she, a solemn and brooding pessimist. He always expected to be happy — she had never expected it nor believed she was deserving of it. Still, as long as they were apart, they might admire each other from afar until malicious rumors damaged the reality.

When she finally returned to London at the end of November, the Sunday visits were resumed. And so, apparently, was the gossip, which she pretended did not matter. Browning was too absorbed in beginning *The Ring and the Book* to notice any change in her. She cancelled several of his visits because the younger Darwin children were staying at 1, Cumberland Place and had an illness which might have been infectious. Though he himself had cancelled an earlier visit because of his own illness, he replied by telling her that he had walked to the gates of Regent's Park and looked at her house.

On 1 March 1865, a little over three months after her return to London, Snow sent Browning a long letter which abruptly terminated his visits. She took great pains to do it properly, for she made several drafts of the letter which she failed to destroy. Torn between the spiritual and the physical, she was much concerned that he should not think that she wanted to marry him:

> ... I have reason to know that my pleasure in your company has had an interpretation put upon it that I ought not to allow. I have no doubt the fault has been mine, in incautiously allowing it to be known that I made an object of your visits. You will feel at once that it is a mistake which must be set right by deeds, not words. I am reflecting on myself, not upon you. You have only accepted a position into which I invited you — remember, I invited you. Your attitude has been response from the beginning. In anything now that I may wish otherwise you have no responsibility. I have drawn it upon myself. It is no use asking myself how far such an opinion would affect me if I had no one to consider but myself. Tell me, am I not doing what you would wish, if you were in their place? They know that I am the author of all that is peculiar in our intercourse, but I cannot explain this to those others who impute to me anticipations irreconcilable with that fact. I have no reason to think your attitude is misinterpreted but perhaps all the more for this I ought to be careful to correct the view they have of mine. Am I not right, dear friend?[24]

He was stunned. He had not the faintest intention of making a break with her. He had been stimulated by her ideas and unperturbed by the contradictions in her character — all very similar to the ups and downs in his lengthy courtship of Elizabeth. He believed that their relationship was proceeding well until some malicious person began a vicious rumour with the intent of doing *him* harm. Having been hurt when his work was rejected by critics and publishers alike, he was now at the pinnacle of success, in his prime and finding himself adored by half the fashionable women in London. When she asked him to come no more, he was wounded by what he could only consider as her rejection of him as a man, which he could not believe she truly wanted to do. He had pride, and he replied to her generously:

> I thought from the beginning it was too good to last, and felt as one does in a garden one had entered by an open door, — people fancy you mean

to steal flowers. I consider you are altogether right in deciding so—and certainly you are right in being sure that I understand you. I shall talk not another word about it: I 'withdraw'—beyond my visits—exactly as much of my appreciation of you—as, having to go to the house no more, I withdraw my knowledge of in what part of London it is situated and whether it look out on trees or a brick wall.... I left you always to decide (as only yourself could) on what length into the garden I might go: and I still leave it to you. But I would remark—as common sense must, I think—that to snap our outward friendship off short and sharp will hardly cure the evil, whatever it be: two persons who suddenly unclasp arms and start off in opposite directions look terribly intimate. But you know all the circumstances....[25]

Whatever the circumstances were, Snow shared them with Julia Stirling, forwarding to her both a copy of her own letter and of Browning's reply. That other young spinster disciple of Erskine wrote back, '... what a real effort you must have made in your appeal to him to conceal the fact that your heart had betrayed you. If he guesses the truth, he certainly most honourably ignores it—and makes the path easy to you which you have chosen.'[26]

Browning did not guess anything. Aware of Snow's depressions, her constant harping on the perfection of his dead wife and her abrupt changes of mood, quite likely he felt that the cessation of his visits would be only temporary. Later, after the unpleasant rumours had faded, she would change her mind and let him resume the mutually pleasurable visits. Certainly he felt she would want to see his work and that it would be enough to bring them together again.

He could not have been more wrong. They were both victims of their own proud, sensitive natures and of the hypocrisies of the age.

28

Some Refracted Words
(1866 – 1870)

The Hensleigh Wedgwoods rented a large house in Wales, near the Allen relatives, for the summer of 1866. Effie and Hope were with them. Alfred, who had returned after an unsuccessful career at sea, came along, and there were brief visits from Ernest, Snow and Godfrey. Invitations were extended to the Darwins, the Joe Wedgwoods, the Harry Wedgwoods and the Frank Wedgwoods. The annual round of holidays and social visits seemed endless. With the expansion of the railways across the country and on the Continent, Victorian families of the leisure class were constantly on the move.

After the Hensleighs returned to London in September, Snow spent only a few days at Cumberland Place before going to Scotland. A few weeks after terminating Browning's visits and after receiving from him the gift of his *Collected Poems,* she wrote to Thomas Erskine, confiding in him her feelings of misery and seeking his counsel. Erskine responded: 'I know you are in the hands of One who can help you, and who not only sees these dark gropings in you, but who in a certain sense put them there.'[1]

Erskine, whose disciples called him the Beloved One, was now aged seventy-eight, almost totally blind, and partially deaf. His sister Christian Stirling, who had been his constant companion for thirty years, was herself in ill health. Bishop Ewing, Dean Stanley, A. J. Scott, F. D. Maurice and other members of the Linlathen circle had for years been pressing Erskine to gather his writings and teachings into some sort of organized form for publication, but he had made little progress with this. At Scott's urging, when Snow went to Linlathen in the autumn of 1866, she proposed to Erskine that she act as his secretary and editor, and he eagerly agreed.

At first their work took the form of discussions about the meaning of the scriptures. Snow found these not only intellectually exhilarating but helpful in solving some of her own inner turmoil. She decided to keep a journal account of the daily discussions and send it to her Aunt Rich, who was now in her eighties, crippled with arthritis and unlikely to return to Linlathen.

Erskine's absolute certainty—'I am much more sure of the being of a Righteous One than I am of the existence of those chairs'—was reassuring to troubled minds. Snow believed in God and in a life hereafter, but, as she explained to the Beloved One, she had difficulty in reconciling the New Testament with the fact of modern civilization. Erskine replied that the Bible did not condemn civilization, only that part of it which is idolatry.

During the first month of their collaboration there was more discussion than actual writing. Snow reported to Aunt Rich that Erskine had observed with amusement that when she wished to do the talking, she placed him on her deaf side, but when she wished to consult his opinion, she placed him beside her good ear.

As important to Snow as the daily walks and talks with Erskine was the beginning of a new and powerful friendship with Emily Batten Gurney, whose husband Russell Gurney was Recorder of London and Member of Parliament for Southampton. Her mother, a friend of Mary Rich, was descended from the Venns, an old and distinguished Evangelical family.

Emily and Snow were the same age and had met years before when they were first brought to Linlathen as impressionable young women. If there was a question as to whether Browning or Erskine held the most important place in Snow's passions of the soul, there was no doubt that the closest woman friend of her life was Emily Gurney. No man or woman had ever before entered so completely into Snow's feelings as Emily. 'You fit into all the angles of my nature,'[2] she told her friend. At Linlathen they knelt in prayer together with Erskine, and Snow felt 'lifted up from the earth'.

She returned to Cumberland Place in October, but only for a few weeks. More and more she was feeling estranged from her family. Effie was still the one to whom she felt closest, yet Effie's common-sense, rather than spiritual, approach to life somewhat separated them. When in London, Snow found herself spending more and more time with her Aunt Rich, who was living with Lady Inglis on Bedford Square, and with her Aunt Elizabeth who, after Charlotte Langton's death, had taken a small house at 4, Chester Place, opposite the Hensleighs at 1, Cumberland Place.

Apart from her Aunt Rich, the one relative with whom Snow was able to discuss religious matters and with whom she felt a certain sympathy was Godfrey. After the death of his wife, he, too, sought faith but was unconvinced. He told Snow that 'if Darwinian theory could be proved, our longing after perfection would be satisfactorily accounted for'.[3]

Snow told Emily about Godfrey's troubles after his wife's death, and remarked: 'There never was a mental history so mysterious to me as Godfrey's.'[4] Probably because of the similarity of his situation to that of Browning, she seemed determined to convince Godfrey of the existence of God and the possibility of perfecting the spirit through self-denial or martyrdom. Godfrey's chronic depression was hardly alleviated by such conversations with his cousin, and he finally told her that 'seeking God was too arduous a search for one who has the business of everyday work of life to do'.[5]

Unhappy with life in London, Snow went to Down for a week before going to Wales to visit her Aunt Fanny Allen. Emma Allen had died, and the eighty-four-year-old Fanny still lived alone in the house she had shared with her sisters during the last years of their lives. Near her were the children of her brother John Allen and the family of Robert Wedgwood, John Wedgwood's only surviving son.

Fanny Allen had been a girl of fourteen at the time of the death of the first Josiah in 1795, a fact which prompted Snow to call her 'my little eighteenth-century Aunt'. More impressive than her age, however, were her mental alertness and her endurance. It was her daily habit to stand in front of the open fire in her sitting room and read *The Times* from cover to cover, a procedure lasting an hour or more.

The year 1866 ended with more than the usual share of griefs and deaths, and few joys. Catherine Darwin Langton and her husband returned to Shrewsbury where she died on 2 February 1866. Her sister Susan, who had been ill for several years, died a few months later. Ras was particularly depressed by the death of Susan, who had been his favourite sister. Charles, of course, had a recurrence of his illness; and The Mount, which Emma noted had seemed so sunny and yet was so sad, was put up for auction after the three surviving Darwin children — Ras, Charles and Caroline Wedgwood — had taken what possessions they wished. Robert Darwin's collection of Wedgwood, which held little interest for either his Darwin or Wedgwood relatives, was rather casually distributed throughout the family. What remained was included in the auction of household goods, the total of which fetched less than £1,500.

Two other close friends of the Hensleighs, Elizabeth Gaskell and A. J. Scott, died during the winter of 1866. Snow had been with Scott at Linlathen in October. Scott had felt his health might improve there, in the presence of the Beloved One; but, at this point, Erskine was in too poor health himself to be of assistance to anyone.

Snow made several trips back and forth to Scotland, spending almost as much time there as in London, though little was being accomplished on Erskine's book. She complained to her Aunt Rich of Erskine's lack of organization and of his inability to accomplish anything concrete, observing that 'a life of leisure is not conducive to literary work'.[6] Erskine's sister Christian Stirling was now dying, and his other sister, Davie Paterson, who lived in Edinburgh, came to Linlathen with her son and his family to help nurse her sister and ailing brother. It was, to say the least, a gloomy household, brightened for Snow by a brief visit from Emily and by the presence of another young woman, Jane Gourlay, who taught at a school in Edinburgh and who had been brought to Linlathen as tutor to the young Paterson children.

Ernest had lost his position in the Colonial Office. While waiting for another appointment to be procured for him, he accompanied Snow on one of her trips to Linlathen. His boredom and depression and inability to amuse himself there simply increased the gloom. Snow had felt a similar frustration when earlier the idle Alfred. who was given to childish outbursts of temper, had come along in anticipation of being amused.

'I want so much to get on with his [Erskine's] writing,' Snow wrote to her Aunt Rich in June 1866. 'I feel that I really can help him if he will obey me...the misfortune is his immense wish to retouch — he takes all the sap out of what he writes by going over all the fragments.'[7]

Snow's speaking of the Beloved One 'obeying' her was an indication of how senile and dependent he had become. He himself referred to her as 'my governess'. He was incapable not only of completing a chapter of the book or a unified section of a chapter, but of completing a paragraph. He would go over a single sentence compulsively for several hours at a time. Finally Snow decided to take the manuscript as he had originally dictated it and hide the pages from him. She told him she would later edit the manuscript herself and return it to him for final corrections.

One day when Snow was feeling ill with a severe headache and had gone to a doctor to have herself 'galvanized', Erskine searched her room, found the manuscript, got someone to read it to him and then was so dissatisfied that he began to rewrite it all over again. Snow protested, taking the manuscript back from him and hiding it in a different place. Again when she was out of the house, he searched for it, found it and destroyed it.

She was, needless to say, exasperated; but the Beloved One explained that his irrational behaviour was the result of his grief for his sister Christian who died in December. If one believed, as Snow did, that a divine such as Erskine was possessed by the Holy Ghost and destined to guide less worthy mortals such as herself, it was of course a weakness on her part to allow any critical or hostile feelings towards him. With true Christian forbearance she assured Erskine that she would gladly and humbly begin a new manuscript with him the following summer.

Snow came back to London in a depressed frame of mind. During the spring of 1867 she became even more depressed, avoiding social occasions or seeing people at home. Her friend Emily Gurney was the only person whose company she desired. Eventually her parents became alarmed about her withdrawal, which was not unlike that of her grandmother Kitty Mackintosh and several others of the Allen family. Fanny Hensleigh wondered if a resumption of her friendship with Browning might not improve her daughter's spirits.

The Hensleighs took a broader view of sexual morality than most of their contemporaries. Indeed, many of their friends led unorthodox private lives. George Eliot and G. H. Lewes lived together as man and wife, though Lewes was still married to Agnes Jervis, who had given birth to two children by Lewes's friend and literary colleague Thornton Hunt. Harriet Taylor had been the mistress of John Stuart Mill, openly living with him for several years until they married after her husband's death. Ruskin, Caroline Norton and Monckton Milnes had all been involved in scandals of one kind or another — yet all of these people were friends and welcomed into the Hensleighs' home. (Quite likely, however, none of them would have been invited to dinner at Bedford Square by Lady Inglis or Mary Rich.)

Certainly the Hensleighs had no moral objection to Snow's friendship with Browning, though Browning's name was linked with a succession of women not only over his possible remarriage but also over rather silly behaviour. As more than one fashionable Victorian lady testified, Browning in mid-life and later years was given to indiscriminate kissing, patting and fondling of attractive women. Some were flattered; others were repelled and angered. Most, of course, simply tolerated the unwanted petting as a minor flaw in an otherwise admirable man. This was, however, precisely the sort of flaw Snow could not have borne in any man whatever other virtues he might possess.

Without telling her daughter, Fanny Hensleigh invited Browning to dinner again at 1, Cumberland Place. He replied to the invitation by writing to Snow and asking her to refuse it for him: 'The truth is best said. I underwent great pain from the sudden interruption of our intercourse three years ago: not having the least notion why that interruption must needs be, then or now, I shrink — altogether for my own sake — from beginning again, without apparent reason, what may be stopped once more as abruptly and as painfully without reason one whit more apparent.'[8]

Snow wrote back that she had not known her mother had invited him and therefore the disappointment was less. That she still cared for him was obvious because she added a postscript that since they had parted she had seen him twice in the street.

In the summer of 1867, following a riot in Hyde Park, the second Reform Bill was passed. For the first time, the English working man had a vote in managing the affairs of the nation. Now that the American Civil War was over export trade improved, and there was a general sense of prosperity such as had not been seen in the Potteries for nearly a decade.

Though not himself a chemist, Godfrey began experimenting in an amateurish way with bodies and glazes for different products to add to the range of items made by the Wedgwood Company. Lessore was painting on Wedgwood plaques, and, at Godfrey's request, painted a portrait of three-year-old Cecil from a photograph. Lessore also gave Godfrey the benefit of his judgement on various trials being made. 'I like the eggshell look of the enamel marked behind W., the other F.G. looks better as yellowish colour more approaching the cream colour.'[9]

Godfrey was determined to improve upon the quality of the Jasper being produced. Apparently, among other things that Frank had thrown away in his clean-up campaign after the death of the second Josiah, were the old recipe books for Jasper. The formula that had been used in the 1780s simply was not known to the 1860s. Godfrey went to the Museum of Practical Geology in London and asked if they could help him to determine the proportion of cobalt in the old grey-blue Jasper mixture and if they could recommend a young chemist who might be interested in employment at Wedgwood.

Thinking of expanding the colour range of Jasper, Godfrey broached the subject with his father. Frank replied:

As to Jasper — it is so exclusively almost blue & black that I do not think the public would buy anything else — if they wanted variety they would not reject lilac and green and yellow so completely as they do — nevertheless a new colour or two would no doubt be an advantage if we knew how to lay hold of it — but the objection to a chemist is that he would be absolutely ignorant and we should have to pay him whilst he was learning.[10]

Though he was pleased over Godfrey's taking an interest in the firm, Frank was as worried about Godfrey's depressive moods as the Hensleighs were about Snow. Frank's own marriage had disintegrated to the point where he and Fanny Frank led virtually separate lives. She spent as little time in Staffordshire as she could. 'Your mother has come back persuaded by her new doctor (or perhaps more likely having persuaded him) that she is too weak to take her walking exercise,' Frank told Godfrey, 'so she is to take carriage (exercise!) and drink plenty of wine—he wanted her to go to America again but as she cannot do that he advises her to go to the seaside in April or as soon as the weather gets warm. I am very much vexed because I do believe she is just as well & as strong as when she came back from America and it looks to me as if she would never be easy to be six months together at home.'[11]

At age sixty-six Frank was astonishingly robust himself and unable to understand other people's ill health. In Fanny's absence he lived with four of his children at the Upper House. Clement, his favourite son, married Emily Rendel, the daughter of James Meadows Rendel, in November of 1866, and they lived near by in a house called Barlaston Lea.

After Clement's marriage, Frank suggested to Godfrey that he give up his house, Everleigh, and with little Cecil move back to the Upper House with the rest of the family. 'Whatever has a bad tendency to make you live in the past,' he wrote to Godfrey, 'has I am afraid a bad effect on your health—a matter which I need not remind you does not only concern yourself—I do not know whether I might almost say does not even principally concern yourself.'[12]

Godfrey decided to spend the summer abroad and forget the various problems at the factory. In general, and as usual, they all forgot the factory. Frank went to London to visit the Hensleighs and Elizabeth Wedgwood. Then they all went to Down to stay with the Darwins. Frank also stopped by Leith Hill Place and then invited the Hensleighs to Barlaston. They came with all of their children except Effie, who preferred to visit the Bonham Carters, and Snow, who again was headed for Scotland.

The situation at Linlathen was even more difficult than it had been the previous summer. Erskine's other sister, Davie Paterson, was slowly dying. Erskine, now totally blind, suffered paranoid delusions. The saintly disposition of the Beloved One now revealed its dark side. He began threatening violent action, using obscenities and attributing Machiavelli—like plots to his nephew who had taken over the unenviable task of looking after him and the large household at Linlathen.

While Snow was there, she received a letter from Browning, forwarded to her by her mother. Browning said that he was sending her the publisher's proofs of the first two volumes of *The Ring and the Book,* which were about to be published in America. If she were still interested in his work, he would appreciate her giving him the benefit of her critical appraisal. 'It is more than a year since I heard from you—remember, I have no means of knowing that this application comes inopportunely, should it do so. You may be absent, too: but this direct way of writing is better than enquiring through friends.'[13] She replied immediately that she was eagerly looking forward to receiving the proofs. 'The reading will form a very helpful distraction to my occupation here—watching a painful deathbed.'[14]

He, too, answered immediately, dating his letter on Guy Fawkes Day and ending with: 'My sister keeps house here and people come to see her sometimes, —women-people; is the notion that I might see *you,* so—a birth of this memorable Gun-powder-treason-and-plot-day—fraught with fire and brimstone? here or there or wherever I possess my soul I am dear friend, yours ever, R.B.'[15]

Clearly he thought that her interest in his work also indicated an interest in him personally, but she completely ignored his frank, gentle and fanciful plea for the resumption of their friendship. Over the next five months, however, she sent him nine letters criticizing his work. He accepted many of the minor corrections and indeed made changes. Her over-all criticism (which revealed the irony of their works being the exact opposite of their personalities) was that he took a gloomy view of life, pointing out the dark aspects of man's nature rather than the light, spiritual side. He found this view hypocritical, overly sentimental and unrealistic. He felt that she was now rejecting his work, as well as him, and at just the moment when he was receiving the most acclaim. It seemed to him that she equated popular acclaim with lack of worth, and this angered him. 'Yes, the British Public like and more than like me, this week, they let their admiration ray out on me, and at sundry congregations of men wherein I have figured these three or four days, I have seen, felt and, thru' white gloves, handled a true affectionateness not unmingled with awe—which all comes of the Queen having desired to see me, and three other extraordinary persons, last Thursday.'[16] The other three worthies were Thomas Carlyle, George Grote, the banker and historian of Greece, and Sir Charles Lyell, the geologist and close friend of Charles Darwin. They met the Queen at the residence of Sir Arthur Stanley, the Dean of Westminster. Apparently the Queen too felt the occasion somewhat of a strain, for she asked Carlyle if he had been writing anything lately.

In spite of his success, Browning had his problems. Not having found the female intellectual companion he needed, he had swallowed his pride and once again turned to Snow, who not only denigrated his work but reiterated *ad nauseam* that only the dead Elizabeth could be his inspiration. Furthermore, he was having problems with his son Pen, who was not—and would never be—living up to his father's expectations. Browning was at this point in need of a feminine guide; in short, he was ready to remarry.

Snow was also in need of masculine guidance, but more in terms of a spiritual leader than a flesh-and-blood husband. After the death of Scott and the disturbing madness of Erskine, she had turned to F. D. Maurice as her spiritual mentor. Maurice was a friend of the Hensleighs, the Carlyles, the Mills, the Leslie Stephens and other descendants or survivors of the Clapham sect. He had gone from Unitarianism to Anglicanism, a move which Carlyle could not understand. Maurice became Professor of Moral Philosophy at Cambridge in 1866, and from 1870 to 1872 was incumbent of St Edward's, Cambridge. He died there on 1 April 1872.

On one occasion Snow accompanied him to Bath and then on to Bristol, serving as a companion-nurse to Mrs Maurice, who was in poor health. She wrote to her Aunt Rich that Maurice, unlike Erskine, had no respect for patient investigation. 'What I feel the want of in him is of sympathy with the *spirit of search*—it is not like a limitation of his mind but a sort of unfaithfulness in him to a possibility of a higher life.'[17] Whenever Snow was troubled about herself, her friendships with men or her religious beliefs, she turned to her Aunt Rich just as she had done as a child. Mary Rich unfailingly advised humility and self-sacrifice.

One member of the family who had no trouble with religious beliefs and who certainly lacked the 'spirit of search' was Frank Wedgwood. One morning when he and Godfrey were riding to work at Etruria, Godfrey mentioned his conversations with Snow and his own difficulties in accepting the miracles of the New Testament as actual happenings. Frank later told his son that he had never looked into the matter 'because the miracles do not stick in my gizzard as they do in yours, and I find no difficulty in believing they may have been performed in spite of want of satisfactory proof that they were performed'.[18]

In the summer, when Godfrey was on holiday with his mother, Frank wrote to him: 'Do not let your mother go on sponging on Mrs Travers for a bottle of wine—it may be got quite good enough at the Inn on paying a proper price.' He then elaborated upon the religious discussion he had recently had with his son:

> I do not mean that miracles are to be believed without good proof, but you go farther, you not only refuse to believe the miracles without good proof (& quite right too) but you consider the want of proof (a mere accident) as proof of falsehood and the claimer to work miracles, which is illogical unless you know (which you do not & cannot) that they were not worked, or unless you maintain that a miracle is impossible, which is equivalent to saying you know the limit of God's power, or you know how he would choose to act not only in ordinary cases but in a case which need occur once in the history of mankind.[19]

Frank was not the sort of person with whom one could argue and expect to win. As his sister Emma had observed earlier: 'He does not grow wiser as he grows earlier.'

The Hensleighs and the Charles Darwins rented summer cottages from Julia Cameron at Freshwater on the Isle of Wight. Ras Darwin came for a lengthy stay, as did Tom Appleton and his widowed brother-in-law Longfellow. Mrs Cameron took Charles's photograph, which pleased him immensely, and arranged for all of them to call upon Tennyson whom she considered as her 'celebrity in residence'. Neither the Wedgwoods nor the Darwins found Tennyson as interesting as Longfellow.

No poet held any interest for Snow but Browning. Once their correspondence about *The Ring and the Book* had ended, she felt the loss and confided her unhappiness to Emily Gurney, who apparently viewed the situation quite differently from Julia Stirling and Mary Rich. Perhaps now Snow sensed that her pride and her persistent striving for perfection through sacrifice were out of proportion.

As abruptly as she had broken off her friendship with the poet, she attempted to renew it. Five months after he had proposed that she call upon his sister, she ended a letter in which she told him: 'My friendship with you was — and is — the great blessing of my life....' 'I wish I knew your sister.'[20] Now he was no longer interested. He had already told her:

> I lost something peculiar in you, which I shall not see replaced, — is that stated soberly enough? I neither can — ever could, nor would, were I able, — to replace anything I have once had: I think I *have* had things thoroughly and effectually and in a sense sufficingly. You now talk about 'done' something 'wisely or unwisely' for yourself; I shall not believe you ever 'did' anything in the matter, but let *be,* let *do*—wisely, I have no doubt: I think you will not accuse me after my four years' silence, with saying to the contrary, — for I am not given to 'striving and crying'.[21]

She wrote to him that it was 'some refracted words that made it possible for me to do what I did'. Those refracted words, were repeated to her not by her mother or by her father but by someone else who had her interest as much at heart as they, but who was not identified by name. The someone else was, of course, Mary Rich, and the words were nothing more than a quotation from the poem 'A Light Woman' — 'And she, she lies in my hand, as tame as a pear basking over a wall....'[22] Mary Rich implied to Snow that Browning himself had heard this remark and jokingly commented that he looked upon Snow as a '*gêne*'.

Browning vigorously denied that he ever made such a comment. Indeed, he said that if anything he could be accused of over — praising her. The repetition of words that had been painful to him in the past and the constant harping on points which need have been made only once, now made him angry. 'It is useless to speculate upon uselessness. I enjoyed seeing you much — there is a fact — and acquiesced in giving up that enjoyment for any cause that seemed sufficient to you — there is another: and if, of your very own self, you could however fantastically, assure me, "Oh, but it was all done to relieve you from a *gêne!*"—well, I shall say—"you know better!" '[23] He then added in a postscript that he was going, in ten days or a fortnight, to Paris for a month and letters would not be forwarded.

Five months later Browning found himself the centre of even more titillating scandal when he impulsively proposed marriage to Carlyle's friend Lady Ashburton, tactlessly suggesting that his fame would be useful to her whereas her money and social connections could help his son. Lady Ashburton was a great deal harsher in turning him away than Snow had been.

Thomas Erskine died in March of 1870. Snow regretted not only his death but that she had been unable to help him leave a written monument of his work. The death of Erskine, who was rivalled in her affections only by Browning, perhaps prompted her to write once again to Browning. She told him that a close friend of hers (Emily Gurney) had been deeply impressed by the purity of the heroine in Browning's poem which she had herself so disliked. It was, in effect, her way of apologizing for the sharp criticism she had dealt him. It was also, probably, a last desperate hope that their friendship might not only be resumed but develop into something more.

In spite of the uproar over Lady Ashburton, Browning had grown mellower. Still, for him, the romance was over. 'Come, let us go back to the quiet place, where "we do not forget each other". Goodbye, dear friend; it was very pleasant to hear your voice in the dark — though I see no face since years now.'[24]

Whether it was the way she finally wished it to be or not, the importance given to 'some refracted words' had determined the course of Snow's life for the next half-century. Erskine, even in death, had won the battle, if not for her soul, at least for her life on earth. The deaf little girl who had feared to go to sleep at night because Judgement Day might come and she be found wanting, remained for the rest of her life eminently respectable, invincibly intellectual and obstinately asexual.

29

Lead Kindly Light
(1870 – 1875)

"An Empire without religion is like a house built upon the sand," said Queen Victoria, thereby dismissing Darwinism and offering a memorable phrase for future poets. 'Lead Kindly Light' was her favourite hymn. It was also Frank Wedgwood's favourite hym, and he shared the Queen's confidence in divine guidance and in himself pointing the way for others.

After the second Reform Act of 1867, Gladstone's Liberal Government was returned to power until 1874. During that Parliament the sale and purchase of officers' commissions was abolished, the secret ballot was introduced in elections, competitive examinations for the Civil Service were instituted, and Dissenters were allowed entrance into Oxford and Cambridge. With his emphasis on free trade and economies in Government spending, Gladstone was Frank's political hero. Indeed, at times Frank himself seemed to be the embodiment of the ultimate Gladstonian virtue – thrift.

In the ideological sphere, Frank was greatly influenced by that hearty optimist Samuel Smiles, who was then at the height of his popularity. In *Self-Help*, first published in 1859, Smiles brought the self-made man to the public's consciousness just at the time when the phenomenon (such as Josiah I and his contemporaries) was ceasing to exist.

Frank could hardly picture himself as a self-made man, but he did hold that any moral person could rise to eminence by thrift and hard work – a belief which offered hope to all and posed no threat to the class structure. His own children had followed his advice and turned out more or less as he had planned they would and as the children of strong-willed Victorian patriarchs usually did. Clement was the favourite son because he was most like his father in disposition. He and Emily had produced a son who was named after his paternal grandfather. Young Franky was, naturally enough, the favourite grandchild. Old Frank's few dissatisfactions centred on his wife, her ill health, her restlessness and her insatiable desire for travel when everything she could possibly want was in Staffordshire. After her return from America, Frank was, however, more disposed to compromise. In the spring of 1870, when he was aged seventy, he was able to convince himself of the virtue of combining business with pleasure in a trip to France. He and Fanny Frank took their youngest child, Mabel, then aged eighteen, to Paris and left her at a French 'finishing school'. They visited Lessore who promised 'to bring his daughter to see Mabel &/or ask her to Marlotte [his home] to sleep,' Frank wrote to Godfrey. He was later concerned to learn that 'Artistes' were not considered of first-rate respectability and 'Artistes in fayence did not mend the matter'.[1]

Frank had brought along several new dinnerware patterns to show to the import houses. Crossing the Channel on the same boat with the Wedgwoods was Herbert Minton's nephew, Colin Campbell, who was also travelling to Paris to show new patterns.

In Paris, to his annoyance, Frank found his wife always in the carriage wanting to go to see or to buy something. 'I escaped from Paris with a cap, a bustle & 10 pair of gloves — saw the Louvre in 2 hours and thought it full half an hour too much,' he complained. 'I escaped Fontainebleau scot-free, being Monday we could not see the château except outside, which I was glad to see & thought it the most respectable palace I have seen.'

He was not a happy tourist. Like his father Jos half a century earlier vowing never to return to Italy, Frank concluded: 'In spite of good bread, good butter, good beds (no bugs or fleas), good cookery & two good passages, I come back like a true John Bull, more determined than before never to set my foot out of Great Britian again unless I must.'[2]

He also determined that before the year was out he would retire from active partnership in the firm. The business was doing well now. A new tile department, in competition with Minton and Doulton, had been opened while he was away. His three sons seemed able to divide the responsibilities in a fair and congenial manner, despite Godfrey's depressions and frequent ill health. Frank himself would, of course, continue to advise, but by late autumn — November, in fact — he would leave his three sons equal partners in a business now valued at £56,098.

While he and Fanny were in Paris, two tragedies occurred in the family. His brother Harry's eldest son John was drowned in a boating accident. Snow, who was visiting the Maurices, described it in a letter to Emily Gurney:

> An Uncle for whom I have an especial love, and still more pity, thinking him so little appreciated by his wife or any of the family but his eldest son, was out in a boat with this beloved son — the boat overset, my Uncle looked back and saw John, as he thought in his depth. He saved himself by clutching an oar — but the young man was carried away by the flood! He was not a character the least interesting to me (except that he was very sweet-tempered) an empty-headed officer; but he was the one centre of love in his family. With no other strong bond they were all devoted to him. My poor Uncle had to tell the wife who was just recovering from her confinement....[3]

The other tragedy was the death of Fanny Erskine Farrer. Shortly thereafter Thomas Henry (or Theta, as he was familiarly called) Farrer came to visit the Hensleighs at their summer home in Kent. The Charles Darwins and Ras Darwin were there as well. All of the Hensleigh children were spending the summer there except Alfred, who had gone off on a holiday to America. Effie, who was being courted by a don from Merton College, Oxford, had resumed her singing with great seriousness.

'Effie has been singing some of her old songs & has taken my mind so vividly back to the past,' Snow wrote to Aunt Rich. 'I was astonished at his [Farrer's] being able to ask Effie to sing — he sat with his face hid in his hand & there were tears in his eyes when she finished.'[4]

After the death of Thomas Erskine and the termination of the Browning friendship, Snow was without a father figure and spiritual teacher to place upon a pedestal. Erskine had left her in his will the sum of £100. Knowing that Maurice's income was small and his wife in ill health, Snow offered him the money so that he could take his wife abroad for a rest cure. She also offered herself as their courier. 'I was thinking when I was with you last, how much solace there would be to me if I could be anything to Mrs Maurice of what I was to Mr Erskine,' she wrote to Maurice.[5] Although he refused the offer of a holiday abroad, Maurice did recognize her kindness and her need to be of use. He invited her to accompany Mrs Maurice on another trip, to Clifton, where she contributed generously to the expenses of the holiday.

With Maurice's encouragement, Snow took up many of the social causes which Maurice advocated. Upon her return to London in the autumn of 1870, she went each week to pray with the workhouse women. This was not, however, to her fastidious tastes. In spite of good intentions, she was far more at ease in religious discussions held in the parlours of upper-middle-class intellectuals.

At about this time she also become friendly with George Eliot and her husband George Henry Lewes. Snow and George Eliot shared an interest in theology. Snow's biography of Wesley had received favourable reviews in almost all the important publications, including Lewes's *Leader*. George Eliot had just translated Friedrich Strauss's *Life of Jesus* and been converted, though reluctantly, to the view that the historical Jesus was elevated into the Christ. For her Christianity was built on the Christ myth. This was similar to the belief of another of the Hensleigh Wedgwoods' friends, Francis Newman, with whose religious 'modernism', stopping just short of agnosticism, Snow disagreed.

George Eliot invited Snow to tea. Though they disagreed on the question of moral influence in literature, Snow later spoke warmly of both George Eliot and Lewes to Emily Gurney. 'I felt there something that was an element in the holiest conjugal union ... I am sure they are united by love, though perhaps it was a flaw in her that bound them in one.'[6]

Another literary figure of note agreed with Snow about the importance of morality in literature. 'I wish you would write biography for the rest of your days,' Harriet Martineau wrote to her. 'Large & noble subjects, I mean, of course. Sagacity, dispassionateness, power of justice, power of analysis, power of appreciation, and remarkable power of expression in a capital style — these are your characteristics, it seems to me, and these are what I take to be the chief requisites of a biographer.'[7] Harriet Martineau was now nearing seventy and seldom came up to London from Ambleside.

In the autumn of 1871 Emily and Russell Gurney went on a tour of America, giving Snow their cottage at Woolhampton, near Reading. She went there with the intention of doing some writing. Her father, who was making additions to his etymological dictionary and writing a paper on linguistics, accompanied her. Later they were joined by Alfred who had returned from his American journey, which he seemed to enjoy although 'he did not arrange it very well, going over the same ground two or three times, and not seeing a great variety of American scenery—but it satisfied him.'[8] Alfred had spent all of his time in New England, but he had a pleasant visit with the Appletons and with Longfellow. He had little interest in writing or reading, and his father and sister were hard pressed to find something for him to do. At the age of twenty-nine, he was still unable to settle upon a suitable career.

From America Emily Gurney wrote of their travels. She suggested that since Snow's letters were often of general interest, and were important as a record of her development as a writer, they keep their correspondence with a view towards possible publication.

From London Ras Darwin reported that 'Effie is singing her head off, and I am going today to hear her in Brook Street before she had quite worn herself out. Hope on the contrary is magnifying her head, and has just called *en route* to Logic with her 'srip' [script] her last new invention of which she is very proud.'[9] Hope developed her own kind of shorthand with certain symbols for frequently used words and with phonetic spelling. She and Etty (Henrietta) Darwin took geometry lessons together from a private tutor on a rather erratic basis, as one or the other was usually suffering from some illness real or imaginary.

In London Etty went with Fanny Hensleigh and Hope to a party given by the Vernon Lushingtons, where she met R. B. Litchfield, a friend of Maurice and one of the founders of the Working Men's College, where he had taught for seventeen years. A month later Litchfield and Etty were engaged, and two months later they were married in the little church at Down. When Litchfield fumbled around and seemed to have forgotten the ring, Frank Wedgwood became highly agitated, leaned forward and, according to Snow, attempted to direct the whole affair, 'sawing the air as Hamlet instructed his players not to do.'[10]

It was a marriage that pleased friends as well as family. Snow wrote to her Aunt Rich, who was staying at Milton Bryan with Lady Inglis: 'There was a very nice letter from Florence Nightingale about the marriage in which she says the bridegroom is the one man she would like to know!'[11] Litchfield had at one time been considered a possible suitor both of Snow and of her old rival for Browning's affections, Hilary Bonham Carter.

Several month before the Darwin–Litchfield wedding, the Charles Darwins and Godfrey Wedgwood received proofs of a second book by Eliza Meteyard. After the success of her biography of Josiah Wedgwood I, she had taken the material Joseph Mayer had catalogued about the second generation of Wedgwoods, and written a book titled *A Group of Englishmen*.

Both Charles and Emma were critical of the book. They objected to the publication of the names of famous men who had borrowed money from Josiah II and, in some instance, failed to pay it back. 'The recording of the fact that these persons received help from the Wds [Wedgwoods] would be no doubt painful to their families,' Emma Darwin wrote to Eliza Meteyard, 'but the imputation of being unreasonable in their demands is almost disgraceful to them, & whether just or not, every member of our family would think it a breach of confidence to consent to the publication of such a statement.'

The Darwins also objected to statements about Tom Wedgwood 'which almost give the impression that he was insane'. Emma then added that her sister Elizabeth, who was aged twelve at the time of Tom Wedgwood's death, 'is confident that there was no ground for thinking such was the case; but that he was very much depressed and restless.'[12]

Eliza Meteyard was clearly surprised and grieved by the criticism, since no objections had been levelled against her first book, about the elder Wedgwood. 'The majority of the papers used in the biography — as also in this more miscellaneous account of his descendants and friends — were thrust ignominiously forth from Etruria as rubbish and waste,' she replied. 'After multitides of them had been dispensed for use in a low neighbourhood, Mr Mayer, a most worthy gentleman and who honoured Wedgwood in a day when no one cared for his name and few for his works, came upon them by mere chance — and from that day they thus became his property through purchase.' She went on to say that in deference to their feelings she would make a few alterations but that she would not change the whole book in order to fit one point of view. 'I have a duty to perform to Mr Mayer, to my publishers, to myself and what is of still more account — my duty to posterity — who will receive these truths of good — many of them great — men — however chequered by the good and ill of human character — with an interest which *we* cannot conceive.'[13]

Slight changes were made in the proofs, and the book was published two months later. At the same time Eliza Meteyard was in the newspapers, not for the book, but because she had been assaulted on Hampstead Heath by an off-duty officer of the Metropolitan Board of Works. She had been walking on the public highway carrying in her hand some sprigs of fern. Gathering fern on the Heath was a criminal offence bringing a penalty. When an off-duty officer saw her, he yelled at her to stop. Not seeing him and being totally deaf, she continued walking. Furious at what he thought was her disobedience to his authority as an officer, and also probably further angered by drink, the officer siezed her from behind by the shoulder, grabbed the fern out of her hand and threatened her with a stick. The case attracted considerable attention in the news, the issue being whether the officer had used unnecessary violence and brutality. A small, frail woman of fifty-seven, Miss Meteyard suffered considerably from the shock of the attack and later from the attendant publicity. To recover, she went to Liverpool to visit her patron Joseph Mayer.

Eliza Meteyard's acquaintance with Snow, which had never been particularly intimate, virtually ended after the publication of *A Group of English-*

men. The Hensleighs, and most particularly Fanny Hensleigh, did not, however, take offence at the revelation in print of James Mackintosh's borrowing from the Wedgwoods and neglecting to pay back his debts. It was, after all, as Eliza Meteyard herself had pointed out, the truth. The family rift which the Darwins had feared never materialized.

In the summer of 1872 all of the Hensleighs visited Down. Hensleigh and Fanny Hensleigh, who were now in their early seventies, made the decision to live all year round at Ravensbourne near the Darwins. Like Elizabeth Wedgwood they had begun to find life in London a bit wearying. When Elizabeth had come to visit them in London, Hensleigh took her on the new Underground to Hyde Park. On returning they waited more than an hour on the wrong side of the platform. When they finally did get home and told their story, Effie glibly commented: 'That comes of gentlemen taking care of ladies; if the ladies took care of the gentlemen, it would be otherwise.'[14]

Elizabeth was having increasing trouble with her eyesight. During the summer of 1872 both she and her brother Frank were in London consulting doctors— Elizabeth for cataracts and Frank for intestinal problems. After the visit to Down and a longer stay at Ravensbourne, the Hensleighs (who were the perpetual travellers that Frank was not) decided to take Effie and Hope on a holiday to Germany. Snow was going back to Linlathen with Emily Gurney for the annual reunion of Erskine disciples which had spontaneously become a custom in the two years since his death. Ernest was remaining in London at Cumberland Place, and Alfred, according to his brother, went off by himself to the Continent, 'well supplied with the necessary cash which however I have no doubt he will invest in a gross of green spectacles at Paris and we shall have to send and get him out of pawn.'[15]

At Linlathen Snow began the actual writing of her ethical history of the world's civilizations which she had first discussed with Browning eight years earlier. Erskine had inspired her; Maurice encouraged her. The systematic account of the development of civilizations and their aspirations —which she had first called *A History of Human Aspiration* and then later changed to *The Moral Ideal*—occupied much of her time and mental energy over the next twenty-two years. Like her father and her Uncle Charles, she was capable of a sustained intellectual effort which demanded seemingly endless research, patience and imagination. It was the sort of effort that awed her less gifted relatives. While she was in Scotland during that summer of 1872, her brother Ernest told her that she had been sent 'a note from the London Library with a very heavy and learned list books which I observe the Secretary says he is happy to say are at your service. I suppose his happiness consists in getting rid of such works.'[16]

Snow was well aware of her bookishness and that it sometimes placed a barrier between her and others. 'I feel I have all the faults of the intellectual nature, though with so few of its advantages,' she told Emily Gurney, 'and these faults are specially unlovely. I am sure the energy that goes to make study possible is subtracted from a part of the nature by means of which we adapt ourselves to others, and I always long very much to know how much of this one may sanction.'[17]

In the autumn of 1871, Snow and Effie had gone to Staffordshire to visit their cousins — 'chiefly to please my Father,' Effie wrote in her private journal, 'but also in the hope of thawing the ice which had been frozen nine years between Godfrey and me.'[18] The two sisters stayed with Clement and Emily at Barlaston Lea but visited the family at the Upper House. Godfrey called frequently at Barlaston Lea to take them for walks or rides.

Emily told Effie that Godfrey had confided to Clement that he was in love with Effie and wanted to marry her, but felt that she despised him and had never forgiven him for marrying Mary Hawkshaw. Effie told Emily that her pride had been hurt and that she felt a 'coldness and stiffness' towards him. Emily suggested that she give him a chance to explain his feelings, and Effie — like Snow — had a revelation in church that she ought to be more charitable. When Godfrey asked her if she would go riding with him on Tuesday afternoon, she accepted.

On that ride Godfrey made an astonishing confession. After they had agreed how difficult it was to get matters right between persons once they had gone wrong, Godfrey said: 'I've been a brute. I've felt it for years & have been miserable. I wish I could stand and do penance in the market place.' He then went on to say that he could not tell her his old grievance with her because (like Snow and Browning) it involved what someone else had repeated in gossip. So, when he discovered that Mary could care for him, he married her. The marriage was not unhappy until Effie and her sisters came to visit in Staffordshire, and Godfrey, inexplicably, told his pregnant wife that he had always cared for Effie 'and she [Mary] was hurt at what she thought my attentions to you & reproached me going home — it was our one sore thing together. I never felt so wretched in my life as when you called next day.... Mary's death sealed my lips & I was tongue-tied & could not offer any explanation & my loyalty to her made me resolve to see as little of you as possible. I felt it would be treason to her memory to think of you....'[19]

The confession thoroughly rattled Effie, who wasn't at all sure what her feelings for him truly were. Until then she had thought him rather weak in character and bumbling — a not inaccurate judgement in view of his indiscreet confession to his wife. None the less, Effie agreed to think over all that he had said and give him an answer in a month when he came to London.

Clement and Emily were both in favour of the match and did all they could to promote it. Snow, however, was totally unaware of any romance, and Effie chose not to confide in her. Snow was so absorbed in spiritual matters that while they were at the station waiting for their train to take them to Manchester to visit Meta Gaskell, she commented: 'It half vexes & half amuses me that Godfrey should have entirely ceased caring for me. I think he is afraid of any deep intercourse — that part of his nature has shut up & will never open again to anyone I believe. I think he cares more for you now than he does for me!'

Effie noted in her journal that Snow's conversation 'sounded so odd to my ears & made me feel her so utterly ignorant'.[20]

A month later Godfrey came for a week-end visit at Cumberland Place. Effie refused his offer of marriage but said that now the misunderstandings had been aired, she hoped they would be friends.

Six months later she received another proposal of marriage from another widower, Thomas Henry (Theta) Farrer. Again she refused. But, Farrer didn't behave like Godfrey or any of Effie's other rejected suitors. He didn't silently fade away. Instead, he called more frequently at Cumberland Place, telling the Hensleighs and Ernest and Hope and Snow that Effie had made him very unhappy. He then went to Down and told the Darwins that he had proposed and been rejected without any satisfactory explanations. He received sympathy everywhere.

Snow observed that Effie's vanity would be upset by being a *second* wife, though this was more likely a projection of her own attitude in her romance with Browning than of Effie's actual feelings. Furthermore, like her grandmother before her, Effie would be stepmother to three children of the previous marriage. Unlike her grandmother's stepdaughters, and the stepdaughters in most fairy tales, Ida Farrer adored her cousin Effie and took up pleading her father's suit.

Effie abruptly changed her mind. She told Farrer that she would marry him because she couldn't bear his looking so miserable and going around telling everyone that *she* was the cause. They became engaged in November of 1872 and were married on 30 May 1873, at James Martineau's Unitarian chapel in London.

After the marriage Snow was doubly depressed. She feared that Effie had married to please her parents and to please Farrer and Ida, but not to please herself. The other cause of her depression was that this was the last winter that she and her family would spend at Cumberland Place. 'I am mourning over the approaching move, and making a sketch of the Park as seen from our windows that I may look at it in the days to come,' she wrote to Emily Gurney. 'The keenest joy and the keenest pain of my life have looked through those windows with me, and neither can return — no, there is no shadow of change in that quarter, but I think he has given up all hope perhaps too quickly.'[21] Snow apparently had not given up all hope herself that Browning would come back into her life in the chaste marriage of minds she desired. The gossip about his tactless proposal of marriage to Lady Ashburton and her angry rejection of him probably encouraged Snow more than it distressed her. Hers was the same sort of avoidable martyrdom Godfrey had experienced by leaving the relationship with Effie unresolved for nearly a decade.

As long as Effie remained unmarried, Godfrey could continue to hope for a change of heart. Once she was married to Farrer, Godfrey experienced a sadness laced with regret that was similar to his bereavement after the death of Mary. Effie's marriage also coincided with the announcement of his brother Laurence's engagement to Emma Houseman, the daughter of a London solicitor. Godfrey's sorrow deepened into a morbid depression. His nerves and his health suffered. When he was asked to serve on the Town Council, he declined the nomination. 'I have repeatedly felt the length of my tether,' he said in his letter of refusal, 'and I know that by undertaking more work I shall break down again. I am not able to take my full share of work at my business and until I am able to do so, I owe it to my partners not to undertake any fresh occupation.'[22]

Once retired, Frank interfered far less in the affairs of the pottery than his sons had imagined he would. Instead, he transferred his energies to politics. Having supported Gladstone for two decades, Frank now found himself strongly opposed to what he considered Gladstone's weakness in the handling of foreign affairs. Worse still, in his opinion, was Gladstone's 'objectionable and ineffective handling of the Irish problem'. To his family's dismay, he took to public campaigning for Disraeli and to buying up various properties throughout England in order to acquire more votes. His political speeches were more distinguished for the acerbity of their rhetoric than for their relevance to political realities.

Godfrey and his brothers were appalled. Their father's denunciation of Home Rule for Ireland and his railing against foreigners in general were hardly good for business. The more they attempted to silence him, the more he proclaimed his right to speak his mind. Outside the family the situation no doubt seemed more amusing than permanently harmful. 'I feel for you very much in the trouble you must be in now that your father has taken to such bad ways as to electioneering,' Vernon Derbyshire wrote to Godfrey. 'It is one of the severest trials sons have to go through to find their fathers not turning out well. Could you send him to sea? Or would he go to Australia? I have a brother-in-law there who is a shepherd and is doing well. If he won't leave the country, could you not put him in "chancery". I have heard that people are well taken care of there and *never* come out!'[23]

While their father persisted in his electioneering, the three brothers and partners attempted to sort out the complications of their future inheritance resulting from Frank's failure to sell the pottery in 1844. In 1873 they purchased for £17,000 the land, buildings and fixtures which previously had been rented from the estate of Josiah Wedgwood II. They also drew up a new partnership agreement which included the provision that each partner would be allowed to introduce 'as clerk and pupil' one son whom might succeed his father as partner after he had been a pupil for three years and had reached the age of twenty-one.

Gladstone was finally swept out of office in the election of February 1874, despite his promise of the total abolition of income tax. Naturally and paradoxically, Frank was in favour of abolishing income tax; he simply wanted someone other than Gladstone to do it. With Disraeli now in office and Frank, so to speak, having helped to win the battle, Godfrey and his brothers persuaded him to take their mother on a holiday to Guernsey.

They had been in Guernsey only a few days when a tragedy occurred. Carrying a lighted candle through a dark corridor leading to their bedroom upstairs in the inn where they were staying, Fanny Frank stumbled, fell and set her dress on fire. Suffering severe burns on her shoulders, back and legs, she died at the inn eight days after the accident. Throughout the week of her suffering and despite warning from the local doctor, Frank refused to believe that her condition was critical. He wrote to both Godfrey and to Clement that she would be better 'as soon as the wounds begin heal'. He was thus as unprepared for her death when it actually came as were other members of the family who had understood the situation was not serious enough for them to come to Guernsey.

Fanny Frank's adoration of Longfellow and the weird coincidence of her suffering the same agonizing and bizarre death as that of Longfellow's wife thirteen years earlier, impressed itself on the minds of several members of the family. Even Frank, the careless destroyer of family letters and business documents, preserved the scrap of paper on which Longfellow had written the verse for Fanny Frank which he found among her possessions. Perhaps the words had some comfort for him, too. Hardly less opinionated or cantankerous, he was subdued for several months after his wife's death.

During the 1860s and 1870s spiritualism created a stir in fashionable London society, just as mesmerism had a century earlier. Predictably, Frank Wedgwood dismissed it as 'absolute rubbish'. Equally predictably, the Darwins and the Hensleigh Wedgwoods decided to investigate the subject.

One evening during the winter of 1874 Ras arranged a seance at his house conducted by a paid medium named Williams. Present at the seance were the Charles Darwins, the Litchfields, the Hensleigh Wedgwoods, Snow and George Eliot and her husband G. H. Lewes. The group gathered round the dining table in the dark and witnessed the usual manifestations of sparks, wind-blowing, some table rappings and moving of furniture. Lewes was inclined to joke and not play the game fairly. Hensleigh tended to believe there was more to it than trickery; Charles was sceptical, though not disdainful, while Ras was delighted with having provided such an entertaining evening. He continued to hold seances throughout the spring.

The older Ras became, the more affectations he acquired. One of his habits, which delighted small children, was carrying a young kitten in his waistcoat. He liked to feel its warmth and softness. Ras's nephew Frank Darwin also liked cats and often sent up to London by train two or three-week-old kittens for his uncle. Like both his uncle and his father, Frank had studied to be a doctor and then chosen not to practice. His chief interest was botany. In the summer of 1874 he married Amy Ruck, and they settled in a small house near Down so that Frank could work as his father's secretary.

During the same summer Snow visited Down and helped her Uncle Charles finish his translations of Linneaus. One afternoon Snow and Emma discussed spiritualism and how those present at Ras's first seance had reacted to the phenomenon. When describing Charles's view, Emma told Snow: 'I think he has quite made up his mind he *won't* believe it, he dislikes the thought of it so very much. Otherwise I am sure Mr. Williams would be just the sort of man he would have believed.'

Snow replied rather spitefully: 'I thought he used to look upon it as a great weakness if one allowed wish to influence belief.'

'Yes,' Emma replied, 'but he does not act up to his principles.'

'Well, that seems to me what one means by bigotry.'

'Oh, yes,' Emma agreed. 'He is a regular bigot.'[24]

Another sceptical or bigoted member of the family was ninety-four-year-old Fanny Allen. Upon hearing that Elizabeth was going up to London in her own carriage to take part in a seance with the Hensleighs and Ras, Fanny Allen declared: 'The Spirits will not do her any harm ... spirits do not meddle with matter, and when furniture or heavy bodies are moved, it is matter that moves them.'[25]

Fanny Allen's sharp wit and common sense never failed her. Once she was in her nineties, however, her eyesight began to fail. Like her sisters before her, she was totally deaf and too frail to leave her home near Tenby where Allen Wedgwood had also retired to live near his brother Robert.

Fanny Allen died on 6 May 1875, and her great-nephew George Allen wrote to his cousin Emma Darwin: '... she would not let me know that she was so near her end, or any of us. and it seems strange that the only person with her besides her own maids was almost her newest acquaintance Mrs Power, but that seems to have been just what she wished, and also a short illness, as she had a special aversion to keeping her bed.'[26]

She had left written instructions with her maids on a sheet of paper headed *Miss Allen's Message*: 'My love to all who loved me, and I beg them not to be sorry for me. There is nothing in my death that ought to grieve them, for death at my great age is rest. I have earnestly prayed for it. I particularly wish that none of my relations should be summoned to my bedside.'[27]

Only a few months short of her ninety-fifth birthday, Fanny Allen, whom Snow had described as 'my little eighteenth-century aunt', was the last of the generation of Allens who had married into the second generation of Wedgwoods. She also the last member of the family who had personally known Josiah Wedgwood I. On a visit to Down when she was eighty-nine years old, she told Emma that both of her husband's (and her own) grandfathers would have been proud of Charles for what he had accomplished and for being a gentleman about it all.

30

Gentlemen Amateurs
(1875 – 1882)

'I sometimes feel it very odd that anyone belonging to me should be making such a noise in the world,'[1] Emma Darwin observed. Indeed it was an odd situation. Charles was neither a professionally trained naturalist nor a geologist. Apart from conversations with and personal encouragement from men like Lyell and Hooker, he was largely self-taught. In short, he was a gentleman amateur who was far more gifted and dedicated than many of those who claimed to be professional scientists. On occasion, he himself was as surprised as Emma at the honours and attentions thrust upon him.

During the late spring of 1875, Snow went to Kent for a week, staying first with her Aunt Elizabeth and then visiting with the Darwins. As she got off the train at Beckenham, she met Thomas Huxley on the station. He, too, was coming to visit the Darwins and was to be of the party when Sir John Lubbock brought Gladstone to Down to meet Charles. Snow noted Huxley's energy and 'ready pleasantness'.

The following day Charles struck by the 'liveliness of interest' in Gladstone's conversation and by 'the gentleness of his manner'. He was also surprised that a statesman of Gladstone's stature should call upon him and be interested in his opinions on philosophical and political issues. Charles professed a complete absence of the right to an opinion on such matters, not having sufficient background knowledge. None the less, conscious of the tide of history and of his own advancing years, Gladstone asked him: 'Mr Darwin, do you think that in the development of the world's history, the future belongs to America and that the Eastern civilisation is to decay?'[2] Charles considered the matter and said that he was inclined to the affirmative. Later he told Emma and Huxley that he found Gladstone's mind quite remarkably alien to the scientific temperament.

During the same week Snow dined with the Bonham Carters and with the Lubbocks, where the conversation was mainly about politics. She then went on to visit the Farrers at Abinger. Effie had proven herself as competent as a wife and stepmother as in everything else she had undertaken. Farrer's sons Claude and Noel were polite and attentive, and twenty-year-old Ida was devoted to Effie. Snow thought her the most interesting of the three children, there was a spiritual side to her character which appeared lacking in the young men. Ida listened with interest when Snow spoke of Maurice's work and of the old days at Linlathen. Snow told of a religious debate which she had had with George Eliot, who seemed to have come out best. 'There is nothing in Christianity in regard to which I have the slightest difficulty,' the novelist told Snow, 'except that I see no evidence for it whatever.'[3]

Ras Darwin and the Hensleighs, with Alfred and Hope, also visited Abinger that summer. The Hensleighs had discovered that they missed city life and were not of the temperament to remain contentedly in the country. They wanted a residence in London as well as a house in the country, as the Farrers had, for holidays and entertaining. Eventually they sold Ravensbourne, built a house in Surrey near Abinger, which they christened Hopedene, and leased a London town house at 34 Queen Anne Street, only a few doors away from Ras at 6 Queen Anne Street.

On 28 September 1875, the Hensleighs, the Farrers and the Darwins were all invited by Godfrey to the opening of Wedgwood's new London show-rooms in Hatton Gardens. All but the Charles Darwins accepted. Clement and Laurence remained in Staffordshire, but old Frank accompanied Godfrey to London for the occasion, and they stayed with the Hensleighs in Queen Anne Street.

The new showrooms were for the wholesale trade only. Shop owners and buyers from Thomas Goode & Sons, Selfridges, Aspreys and other London stores were invited to view a new range of shapes, patterns and items. Émile Lessore was too ill to come from Paris for the opening, though many of the pieces were his creations or else were inspired by him. It was the final triumph of a successful career; six months later Lessore was dead. His suc-cessor was Thomas Allen who had worked for Minton for over twenty years.

Allen was a different type of artist from Lessore. Educated at Stoke and at the School of Design in London, he was trained in the Sèvres or Minton style of elaborately detailed painting and not in the impressionist technique of Lessore. The understatement long established at Wedgwood was, how-ever, in keeping with Allen's talents. He began at Wedgwood by decorating a costly dessert service with subjects taken from the works of Angelica Kauffmann. In this and in the assignments that followed he achieved a kind of decorum in the handling of nude or semi-draped figures that enchanted rather than offended Victorian sensibilities. Classical taste was being revived in a very nineteenth-century manner.

On 4 December 1875, Carlyle—the grand old man of British letters—received on his eightieth birthday a gold medal and an address of admira-tion signed by his friends, an illustrious circle of scientists, writers and public figures. Among those who signed the address and who later came to call upon the Sage of Chelsea in honour of this special day were Browning, Tennyson, George Eliot, Harriet Martineau, T. H. Huxley, Charles and Erasmus Darwin, Hensleigh and Ernest Hensleigh Wedgwood. Two years later Millais, whom Snow had found so attractive two decades earlier and who had later married Ruskin's divorced wife, began a portrait of Carlyle which he could never complete because he could never satisfy himself that he had truly captured the extraordinary power that emanated from Carlyle's personality.

The year 1876—ten years after her final break with Browning—was a fateful year for Snow. Her essays and literary criticism in the *Spectator*, *Macmillan's* and *Blackwoods* had attracted considerable attention and praise. At the age of forty-three she had become a literary personality of some distinction. Fame did not, however, bring happiness. Like those of her grandmother Kitty, her depressions deepened and became more frequent as she grew older.

She returned for a winter visit to Scotland, staying first in Edinburgh with Julia Stirling and then with Jane Gourlay before going on to Linlathen. She wrote to Emily Gurney from Linlathen: 'we are deep in snow, the ivy outside is turned into a Camellia bush and is laden with heavy blossom, the streets have an hour of transitory deceptive beauty but all will soon be mud.... I think snow is the only aspect of nature I dislike, it seems to me like a prudish hypocrite, piqueing itself on its own immaculate purity and pointing out every speck of dirt in its neighbourhood.' Perhaps she thought it too obvious to point out that what she disliked most had the same name as that which her family had bestowed upon her, she was remarkably naïve about herself and her own feelings of inferiority and self-disgust. 'One morning after fresh snow in the night, I thought the wood looked pretty all veined with silver, but the rocking wind soon sent all that on avalanches,' she told Emily, 'and drifted snow has no beauty—"white as the driven snow"—seems to me flattery, the wind always bring dust. I like to think that you are far away from all these howling winds and bitter cold, but come back!'[4]

At the time, Emily and Russell Gurney were in Egypt. A boat in which they were sailing on the Nile was upset in a squall, and Russell Gurney's three nieces were trapped in a cabin below deck and drowned. The Gurneys themselves were on shore at the time and were unharmed, though Emily collapsed from the shock of the tragedy. Fearing that Snow might read of the accident in the newspaper and be uncertain about her friend's safety, Hensleigh wrote to his daughter assuring her that he had already made enquiries and that both Emily and Russell were unharmed.

When they returned, Emily and Snow became, if possible, even closer. Both were witnessing lingering deaths. Emily's mother, who had been a close friend of Mary Rich's, and Mary Rich were dying. 'Beloved Snow,' wrote Emily, 'I am wondering whether that death bed & that departure will reveal to you any missed light in her who has been so close to you.'[5]

Like many religious people of their generation, Snow and Emily shared an extraordinary curiosity about death and a somewhat fanatical anticipation of death-bed revelations. Usually they were disappointed. Replying to Emily, years later, Snow observed bluntly: 'I cannot say that it did so, but the noble nature was never really eclipsed to me.'[6] Shortly before Mary Rich died in October of 1876, Snow told her: 'All my life would have been different but for that journey you took me to Scotland, dear Aunt Rich—for my Linlathen life would never have come if it had not been for that prelude in those far-off years.'[7]

Within weeks of the death of Mary Rich, Frank Darwin's wife died after childbirth. Frank and the new baby, christened Bernard, came back to live with Charles and Emma, as Frank was already working as his father's secretary. The tragedy of the death of a much-loved young wife shocked and grieved the Darwins and the Hensleighs, although the Hensleighs were at the time concerned with Hope's forthcoming marriage.

No marriage within the family ever created such mixed feelings and controversy. Hope was marrying Godfrey. From a broad-minded, long-term point of view, it was a practical arrangement, a marriage of convenience kept within the family circle. If Godfrey continued to love Effie, well — Hope herself was so deeply attached to her sister that she could not imagine anyone, man or woman, not loving Effie.

After Effie's marriage, the two sisters remained as close as they had been before. Farrer was fond of Hope and happy to have her with them both in London and at Abinger. He also found Godfrey agreeable if somewhat ineffectual.

With justification, Effie felt some lingering twinges of guilt about her harsh treatment of Godfrey. She still cared for him, not as a lover but as a brother. If Godfrey lacked, as Snow put it, 'a backbone', he certainly had more character than either Ernie or Alfred. Effie had the somewhat disturbing habit of taking charge of other people's lives as well as her own. She felt sure that thirty-two-year-old Hope, with her modest but pragmatic temperament, was not going to fall in love in the romantic sense. Unlike Snow, who went to extremes in all of her emotion, Hope was not inclined to grand passions. Twelve years younger than Godfrey, Hope had the same sort of sensitive, retiring nature, the same hypochondria and, apart from travelling, the same interests as he. More than any other member of the family, Hope had been in favour of Effie's marrying Godfrey. Hope — unlike Snow or Meta Gaskell — considered that Godfrey had all of the virtues of a good husband.

With both Effie's and Farrer's encouragement, Hope and Godfrey became engaged during a week-end party at Abinger in the summer of 1876. To most of the family the engagement was a shock. Reactions were mixed. Snow, naturally, thought that Hope was compromising herself by settling for less than a perfect spiritual and material union. Ras Darwin gave his favourite child 'his blessings' and commanded Godfrey to cherish his good fortune. From the beginning Hensleigh had wanted Godfrey for a son-in-law, although he was not sure that Godfrey could make Hope happy if he still loved Effie. Fanny Hensleigh feared that the marriage might eventually cause unpleasantness and jealousy between Hope and Effie, a fear shared by Charles and Emma and by Clement and Emily. Frank thought the union 'a good match' and was relieved that Godfrey had at last found himself another wife. Godfrey's four sisters all disapproved.

His sister Amy was even more strongly opposed when Godfrey told his father and sisters that it was to be a civil rather than a church ceremony and that none of them were to feel obliged to come to London for it. 'At first I thought of taking advantage of your dispensation and not going,' his father told him, 'but before I had got to the turning back place in my ride, I had considered that if nobody of our faction (as Amy would say) was there it might look as if we did not like the match and besides I was not sorry to show that I liked the civil marriage.'[8]

Hope and Godfrey were both surprised and touched that Frank showed up by himself and that eighty-three-year-old Aunt Elizabeth came up from Kent just for the day. After the marriage Frank wrote to Godfrey:

> I am *very* much pleased that my attendance pleased you & Hope ... I felt triumphant over you & Elizabeth when I got to Euston twenty minutes too soon and pounced upon her ten minutes after just going to take her ticket. We had a pleasant journey down and I got here not a pin the worse. Rose and Mabel asked me about the ceremony but Amy begged to hear nothing about it. She wants to be able to say she does not know where it took place. My going off was a surprise to them for I thought your letter to Rose (which she read out at breakfast) had mentioned that the wedding was the next day so I told nobody only sending a message to Emma [Laurence's wife] by Stevens [the coachman] so that they first heard it from her. And it so happened there was nobody in the house at my setting out to say 'where are you going?'[9]

In his old age Frank enjoyed outwitting his children.

Hope and Godfrey leased a house near Barlaston which immediately proved unsatisfactory. As old Frank tactlessly pointed out, the bedrooms were 'small and damp' and there was a 'foul-smelling stench in the parlour' that couldn't be removed. Godfrey had fears that Hope would be bored and rest-less in Staffordshire, as Snow and Effie and most of the Hensleighs always were. Perhaps the memory of his mother's unhappiness and boredom was still haunting him. His sisters-in-law Emily and Emma were absorbed in children and babies. Amy was involved with the Wesleyan schools and with the establishment of a night school to help illiterate workmen learn to read, write and do basic arithmetic. Apart from his commitment to local politics, old Frank was concerned with the establishment of a local branch of the Manchester School for the Deaf and Dumb, on whose board he served. Rightly Godfrey felt that the adjustment from town to country would be difficult for Hope.

There was another adjustment that was difficult for both of them: Godfrey was parsimonious; Hope was extravagant. Having reach the deci-sion that they would have to move to a better house, they dithered between taking Caverswall Castle, a grand establishment which pleased Hope but which was £270 a year more than another house which Godfrey thought suitable. Surprisingly, Frank, who had been far from generous in his own marriage, sided with Hope. 'There are two kind of fools in the world,' he told Godfrey; 'one who runs over his income or who even is so near it as to be constantly in fear of it — the other who pinches & screws all his life all the while laying by money that if properly spent would make all the difference between ease & discomfort. There's a moral sentiment for you — you did not think I was such a Dr Johnson!'[10]

Godfrey leased Caverswall Castle in the autumn of 1878. While decorations were being done, he and Hope went to the International Exhibition in Paris. The Wedgwood Company had a display there featuring the work of Thomas Allen and the new bone china which they had begun manufacturing again after a lapse of more than fifty years. The new china was of a much finer quality than the old. After Paris, which tired Hope, they went on to Italy where the warm climate improved Godfrey's circulatory problems and eased Hope's arthritis.

While they were in Italy, Frank, who seldom visited the pottery once he had retired, wrote to them: 'I do not know whether the change is in me or the Works, but I thought it looked blacker and grimmer than ever it did while I was there. I had no time to see all Clement's improvements — I must go again some time for that.'[11]

More decisive than either Godfrey or Laurence, Clement had an aptitude for the business. Whereas Godfrey was inclined to preserve the heritage, Clement was willing to take risks. He introduced new machinery, reorganized the production assembly and built new workshops. In 1880, at Clement's suggestion, Thomas Allen officially became Wedgwood's first art director. He designed a dinnerware service engraved and printed with scenes from Scott's *Ivanhoe*, and developed a series of tiles showing characters from Shakespeare's *Midsummer Night's Dream*. Cups with moustache guards were introduced. Except on the new bone china, more of the decoration was printed, less hand-painted.

Godfrey was conscious of his own shortcomings as a businessman. He realized that as the eldest son he was merely fulfilling his duty. Commanding or managing people was extremely difficult for him. He had no desire to be the 'Governor'. Dismissing people, for whatever reason, pained him. Confrontations, disagreements or unpleasant situations troubled him far more than they did Clement. Godfrey avoided them whenever he could, and yet he was the senior partner, the one upon whom the final responsibility should rest. 'I do not think your conscience need trouble you,' his father told him after he had procrastinated for months before finally dismissing an incompetent accountant, 'if a Bank was bound to keep all the old incapables it would before long want somebody to keep it.'[12]

If he had had a choice or if he had summoned the courage to take responsibility for the direction of his own life, Godfrey would not have gone into the business world. Now he began to wonder if his own fifteen-year-old son would really choose to enter the pottery if other opportunities were available. He consulted with Cecil's Hawkshaw grandfather as to whether engineering, the traditional Hawkshaw family profession, would be likely to suit Cecil. Since Cecil, who was then a schoolboy at Clifton College, had shown no taste for mechanical things, as Clarke, Cecil's uncle, had done at a similar age. Sir John Hawkshaw thought it unwise to have Cecil become an engineer. After considerable discussion, Sir John and Godfrey came to the conclusion that in a few years Cecil would be mature enough to decide his own future. In the meanwhile, they thought it could do him no harm to go to Cambridge, though neither considered it likely to be of any practical benefit to him.

Cecil was of a different temperament from his father. He actually *wanted* to go into the pottery. After leaving Clifton, he made the obligatory continental tour and then settled in Paris for six months, where he improved his French and was tutored in Latin and Greek for the Cambridge entrance exams. He was not by nature a scholar. Upon learning of his father's persistent ill health and frequent absence from the pottery, he wrote to his stepmother Hope that '... it would be better for me to give up Cambridge & come to work as soon as I leave here.... He has done everything to please me & much as I would like to go to Cambridge I would far rather be at work, as he is so weak, & helping him what I could.' Then, as if echoing his grandfather and his great-grandfather, he remarked: 'I am getting more & more convinced that I am a John Bull: Abroad is not bad for a time, but I should never wish to leave England to travel. It's very odd how few good horses one sees, even all the private ones are more or less groggy about the legs....'[13] He returned to Caverswall Castle and joined the pottery, riding to work each day on a good mare named Polly.

Once Frank had retired from the pottery, he seemed to gain more pleasure from life — as if to make up for all those years he had dedicated to the business. The candour of his speech, which had often been abrasive in earlier years, now seemed more like honest common sense. He had preserved his energy, his zest for living and his sense of humour — so uncharacteristic of his brothers and sisters. Retaining a lively interest in what was going on in the world, he could even summon up a genuine rage when the Liberals unexpectedly won the election of 1880 by a substantial majority and Gladstone was returned as Prime Minister but in a dual capacity, as Chancellor of the Exchequer as well. 'That blundering old fool,' Frank called him — though Gladstone was some nine years younger than Frank.

An unsuspected and no doubt suppressed sentimentality in Frank's nature suddenly emerged in his latter years. He had taken to making annual visits to his brothers and sisters and to Cecily Hawkshaw, the only one of his seven children who had moved away from Staffordshire. 'I had a very pleasant visit to Cecily,' he told Godfrey, 'and found all the children glad to see me which flatters my vanity much because I know it is honest & we grown ups are such confounded hypocrites that nobody knows when we are pleased or when we are only grinning a company smile.'[14]

Frank was no confounded hypocrite. Nor had he overcome the impulse to pronounce judgement, though generally accurate, on other people's behaviour. The family at Leith Hill Place led, in his view, a very dull life. 'I never met anyone silenter than Sophy,' he reported. 'Joe was quite talkative comparatively.'[15]

The Darwins struck him as livelier. He and his brother Harry — who, according to Frank, 'would be as dull as a duck by himself' — went to stay with their sister Elizabeth, and visited the Darwins daily. Frank found Elizabeth better than he had expected 'except that her face looked small'. Now that she was almost totally blind, the sunny, gentle disposition she had possessed all her life reversed itself. She experienced morbid depressions and unrestrained hostilities which distressed Emma and her brothers. 'Troubled with the vivid remembrance of old painful things, she said she should like to have everything past wiped out.'[16] A small, bent figure feeling her way with a stick and followed by her terrier Tony, she spent most of her time with the Darwins. Whenever she came into the drawing room at Down, she would ask anxiously: 'Where is Emma? Where is Emma?'[17]

At Down there was always an open invitation to any relative or close friend to come and stay for a few days. Specific invitations were extended each year to various branches of the family. If there were always more visits exchanged between the Hensleighs and the Darwins, it was because their interests were more compatible and they had been closer in their younger and middle years. Now, in old age, all the brothers and sisters began to draw closer. In June of 1878, six months after Charles had been awarded an honorary Ll.D. at Cambridge, Emma wrote to her daughter Etty: 'We have settled to go to Leith Hill Place on the 5th, Abinger on the 10th and Barlaston on the 15th....'[18]

The year 1880 saw three marriages, two deaths and one birth within the family circle. On 3 January 1880, Horace Darwin married Ida Farrer — another marriage which threatened to cause a rift within the family. Horace, the youngest of the Darwin sons, was sickly, overprotected and undecided upon a career. His brother Leonard said: 'Of all my brothers, Horace was the one whom I should have thought the least likely to make a success in life.'[19] Theta Farrer not only thought so, too, but loudly proclaimed it — much to the annoyance of the Darwins and the embarrass-ment of the Hensleighs. The more various aunts, uncles and cousins protested, the more Farrer insisted that none of the delicate, uncultured Darwin sons was good enough for Ida. Fortunately, Ida disagreed. The marriage took place with a determined bride, an ill bridegroom and a glowering father of the bride. At the reception after the ceremony various factions in the family were not speaking to one another.

Seven months later, in far less dramatic circumstances, Frank's two youngest daughters Rose and Mabel married, leaving Frank alone at Bar-laston with forty-five-year-old Amy, the only one of his seven children to remain unmarried.

Josiah Wedgwood III died on 11 March 1880, at the age of eighty-five. Charles and Emma and Elizabeth were in too poor health to attend the funeral, but the three surviving brothers — Harry, aged eighty-one, Frank, aged eighty, and Hensleigh, aged seventy-seven — all went to Leith Hill Place for the funeral.

Eight months later, on 7 November 1880, Elizabeth died. The Hensleighs, Snow, Ernest, the Farrers and Ras all made the trip to Down. Emma wrote to Frank: 'We shall be most glad to see any of those who loved her for the funeral (on Thursday, probably about 2 o'clock) but I very much hope you will not take a long winter journey.'[20]

Godfrey knew that he was to be one of the executors of his aunt's estate and offered to go in place of his father. 'I mean to go,' Frank told him, 'I could not let her be buried & me not there. Many thanks for offering to save me the journey — but I am quite well & quite up for the journey. Indeed I never find a railway journey tires me.'[21] He went to London accompanied by his butler, Henry Coldrick, and stayed the night with his daughter Cecily. On the morning of Elizabeth's funeral, he went to Down but returned to London immediately after the service with Hensleigh and Snow. The following day he took the train back to Staffordshire.

Almost all of the older generation, now ranging in age from their early seventies to mid-eighties, were ailing in one way or another. Caroline Wedgwood, though recovered from her mental disturbance, had a serious heart condition and seldom left Leith Hill Place. Fanny Hensleigh also had heart trouble and found walking extremely tiring. She had taken to a bath chair and called upon Ras almost every afternoon. Occasionally Hensleigh joined them for tea. Once again he was engaged on a major intellectual endeavour that occupied most of his time. With Frederick James Furnival, a philologist and associate of Maurice's in the Christian Socialist movement and at the Working Men's College, he was planning the *Oxford English Dictionary*, to be edited by Herbert Coleridge,

In the summers Ras visited Charles and Emma at Down but spent most of his time with the Hensleighs at Hopedene. By the winter of 1880, Ras's chronic invalidism had become a real and serious stomach disorder which caused him constant pain and left him in a weakened condition. Now he seldom left his house in Queen Street, though he was constantly cheered by visits from his nephews and nieces, particularly Hope and Effie. When they were away from London, he wrote to them frequently, telling them bits of London gossip and what books he was reading.

They also wrote to him and, at Hope's suggestion, developed the habit of sending on to him letters they had written to each other. This gave him great pleasure. After reading the published correspondence of Mendelssohn's sisters, he wrote to Hope, 'I am more than ever convinced that yours & Effie's letterss must someday be published.' He then went on to tell her about the letters from the Mendelssohn sisters 'which might have been written by you two. They are on just the same terms together as you, and I declare the characters run parallel — also the outward circumstance, so far as they have got two husbands just as good as yours though they differ in respect of being as strong as horses.'[22]

Letter-writing was, of course, a great Victorian pastime, and the published letters of the near-famous as well as the famous satisfied a curiosity about private lives which Victorian reserve excluded from direct discussion. Charmed by the correspondence between Bismarck and his wife, Harry Wedgwood wrote to his sister Emma: 'What a mercy it is good husbands and wives are sometimes parted so as to have to take the world into their confidence. When you and Charles die the world will ask — Had these good people *nothing* to say to each other? What a dull couple!'[23]

Though Charles and Emma were hardly a dull couple, it was true that they were seldom apart and therefore had no need to write to each other. Charles also lacked a literary sensibility. Emma, on the other hand, had a talent for making a letter seem like a personal conversation. Domestic matters received the same serious consideration as world events. Babies were a subject she believed interested everyone.

Mary Euphrasia Wedgwood was born on 15 February 1880. Godfrey was aged forty-seven and Hope aged thirty-six. They had been married four years and had not planned to have children. But, once Mary arrived — 'a fat, bald, red-faced creature who', according to her Aunt Snow, 'howls every time I come near her' — she was greatly loved.

Mary was Frank's twentieth grandchild and Hensleigh's first — and therefore specially loved by Fanny Hensleigh. She was also like a grandchild to Ras Darwin. Hope generously wanted to share her with Effie, so that Mary would always feel that she had two mothers instead of one. Effie adored her, speaking of her as 'our child' — as Ras had spoken of Hope to Fanny Hensleigh three decades earlier. Godfrey made sketches of her and hired an American genealogist to produce a book tracing the Wedgwood family history.

A few years earlier Charles had had the Darwins traced back over the past two hundred years and was pleased with the thoroughness of the research into county and parish records. Ras, the Litchfields and the five Darwin sons had all found the Darwin history extremely dull. Still, Ras told Godfrey: 'Please to put my name down for £20, and I hope your book will be more successful than our attempt to glorify the Darwins, but then we hadn't so many pictures as you will have. — Let me suggest to finish up the volume with a photo of the last and most precious of the generations.'[24]

Ras kept up a cheerful facade even though he was in considerable pain. Charles was the Darwin now chronically depressed. Seeing others of his generation grow old and ill and die weighed heavily on him. He was no longer able to do much work with a microscope, as this tired him. Frank did much of the tedious research for him, while he discussed philosophical ideas and theories with old friends like Hooker and Huxley and Lubbock and, of course, with Hensleigh. Etty Litchfield spoke of her father and her Uncle Hensleigh as 'two old men disagreeing merely for the amusement of starting an argument'. In a depressed mood, Charles wrote to Alfred Russel Wallace: 'What I shall do with my few remaining years of life I can hardly tell. I have everything to make me happy and contented, but life has become very wearisome to me.'[25]

Theta Farrer, now knighted for his work on the Board of Trade, wanted to smooth over the harsh things he had said against the Darwin sons which he knew had hurt Charles. In the autumn of 1880 he invited Charles to come to Abinger to see some Roman remains he had unearthed close to his house. Charles observed how worms had been able to burrow through floors and walls. This revived this interest in worms, which had first been stimulated by his Uncle Jos at Maer.

In December of 1880 Charles and Emma went to Leith Hill Place to visit Caroline, who was now eighty and crippled with arthritis. She was cared for by her unmarried daughter Sophy and by her widowed daughter Margaret, who had returned to Leith Hill Place with her three small children, Hervey, Meggie and Ralph, after the death of her husband, Arthur Vaughan Williams, in 1875. The youngest daughter, Lucy, had married James Harrison, a naval lieutenant, and also was frequently at Leith Hill Place when her husband was at sea.

Emma and Charle found Caroline determined to come to London for what she described as 'a last visit with Ras' whom she had not seen for almost two years. They persuaded her to delay her journey until the summer when the weather would be warmer and when she could visit Down as well.

On Saturday, 20 August, 1881, Caroline and Margaret came to London. They stayed in the Farrers' house which had a bedroom on the ground floor so that the crippled Caroline did not have to climb the many stairs she would have had to do in Ras's house. The Farrers and the Hensleighs and Snow were all at Abinger, but the Litchfields were in London. On Sunday they drove Caroline and Margaret in their carriage to Ras's house where they all five had Sunday dinner. Ras was genuinely touched to see his sister. They reminisced about the old days at The Mount. Ras spoke of a letter he had received from Fanny Hensleigh, saying that she and Hensleigh and the Farrers had left Caverswall Castle, collected the two Farrer boys and gone to Abinger, where they were expecting Horace and Ida. They all laughed when Caroline reported that Theta might be vindicated in his judgement of Horace's 'damned hypochrondiacism'. She and Margaret had just seen Horace and Ida at Down, and Horace, in typical Darwin fashion, was feeling too unwell to travel.

Ras talked of his sadness at the recent deaths of George Eliot and Carlyle; They had offered to bury Carlyle in Westminster Abbey, but according to his own wish, he was buried in Scotland beside his parents at Ecclefechan. Ras grieved for the loss of his old friend, the Sage of Chelsea, and was angered by the mysterious threats of James Anthony Froude, Carlyle's designated biographer, against Mrs Alexander Carlyle, the heir to Carlyle's estate, whose right to some of the Carlyle manuscripts and papers Froude disputed. Neither Hensleigh nor Ras liked Froude and had ignored him socially. Ras, the Hensleighs and other friends of Carlyle's felt that Froude's biography—published almost before the Sage had been lowered into his grave—treated him unfairly and with the malicious purpose of effectually lowering him in the world's opinion. Snow took up the cause and wrote a critical, almost contemptuous, review of Froude's book for The *Edinburgh Review*. 'I am delighted with Snow's article and the way she has administered divine vengeance,' Ras said; 'how he [Froude] must long to put her in the docket.'[26]

The morning following the family gathering Ras arose as usual, but before noon he had a severe attack of stomach pains and nausea. Caroline and Margaret arrived in the middle of the day and sat with him during the afternoon while he lay on the sofa, speaking only occasionally. On Monday night he became worse. The doctor came on Tuesday saying it was only another bilious attack. He was too weak to get out of bed and was unable to eat or drink. Margaret and Etty helped the servants care for him.

Caroline was distressed that she could not see him because of the three flights of steep stairs, but Ras was most insistent that she not make the attempt. The following day, however, she succeeded, Margaret reported, in 'getting up & by caution & waiting before going in, he did not seem annoyed or distressed'. She stayed in the bedroom next to him all the rest of the day 'to be able to go in for a little bit now and then'.

During the afternoon Effie, who had come up to London for a friend's wedding, arrived. 'She just gave him a look but did not like to disturb him just then.'[27] The next day Ras seemed somewhat better and was able to take liquids. Effie, however, had already returned to Abinger to bring her mother back to London. Caroline and Margaret left on Thursday, 25 August, feeling that he was improving and in no immediate danger. Indeed, they left him sitting up in bed reading the newspapers.

On Friday afternoon he had another severe attack, and his butler summoned both the doctor and the Litchfields. Shortly after the Litchfields arrived, Effie came with her mother. Fanny Hensleigh, the true love of his life, stayed at his bedside until the end, which was painless and calm. On Saturday morning Etty sent telegrams to her mother at Down, to her brother George at Cambridge and to her Aunt Caroline at Leith Hill Place: 'He died quite peacefully at 11 o'clock.'

Caroline was grateful that she had been able to make the journey and see her brother one last time. When she thought back over his life and over the conversations that she had had with him at the last, she felt a tenderness towards Fanny Hensleigh and a compulsion to write to her immediately. Since she and Margaret had left London before Effie returned with her mother, Caroline did not know that Fanny Hensleigh had been with Ras when he died. 'Dearest Fanny,' she wrote, 'You will not mind my writing a word to say how I grieve you had not even the consolation of being with him at the last & it is hard on you who have made the happiness of his life ... dear Fanny, I hope the shock has not made you ill.'[28]

George Darwin was an executor of his uncle's estate. He came to London to make arrangements for the burial which was to be at Down and to settle the estate. When he opened his uncle's desk and found a will, he also found a paper attached which he told his cousin Hope, 'I am sure will touch you': 'To Executors: I wish the portraits of Effie & Hope to go to F.E.W. [Fanny Hensleigh] & the Wells & Mason to Effie & Hope. My love to them needs no expression. E.A.D.'[29] Erasmus Alvey Darwin was buried at Down with a phrase from Carlyle's portrait of him as his epitaph — 'One of the sincerest, truest, and most modest of men'.

A week after the funeral, George told Effie: 'The house has just been sold & the place will be dismantled in ten days.' There were letters and photographs and sketches — many by Effie and Hope which George and his Aunt Fanny Hensleigh agreed should be shipped to Down and then sorted through later. Snow wrote a memorial to her uncle which was published in the *Spectator*. She described his playfulness, tenderness, humour, lightness of touch and 'the peculiar mixture of something pathetic with a sort of gay scorn, entirely remote from contempt.... Erasmus Darwin has passed away in old age, yet his memory retains something of a youthful fragrance; his influence gave much happiness of a kind usually associated with youth to many lives....'[30]

Charles Darwin felt his brother's death deeply. He had sensed a sadness in Ras's solitary life. In another phrase of Snow's, it seemed to him that his brother's life was 'something less than it ought to have been'.

During the autumn of 1881 Charles withdrew more and more within himself, though he hardly ever wanted Emma out of his sight. The regimented life he had designed for himself became even more regimented. He breakfasted early, went into his study to read his letters between nine and ten o'clock. At ten, Emma or occasionally Frank, read aloud to him for half an hour. Back to his study until twelve o'clock. Then, if the weather permitted, he would take a walk round the 'sand-walk'. Luncheon was at one o'clock. After dinner there would be a game of backgammon, sometimes music or more reading aloud, often from German scientific periodicals. He retired at half-past ten and expected Emma to accompany him.

In December of 1881 he went to London where he suffered his first heart seizure. He returned to Down as quickly as possible and took to his bed. In January he was back to his established routine, but the strolls along the sand-walk were discontinued. Ocassionally he would walk part of the way to the potting shed and then turn back. Walking brought on chest pains. During February and March his heart condition worsened. Andrew Clark came down from London to see him, and he was visited at regular intervals by Dr Norman Moore, the local doctor.

Some days were better than others, but he sensed that little time remained to him and observed as dispassionately as if he were noting a scientific fact: 'my course is nearly run.'

On the mild spring day of 19 April 1882, he died quietly with Emma holding his hand. A week later he was buried in Westminster Abbey. Emma allowed the nation to honour him, as Sir John Lubbock convinced her was 'clearly right', but she remained at Down. She had said goodbye privately in her own way a week before. In London it was a cold, windy day for the nation to say farewell to one of its most illustrious countrymen. Inside the Abbey was a great black-clad congregation of the famous and the near-famous. All five Darwin sons were present — and Hensleigh, the only Wedgwood, or Darwin, of his generation well enough to attend. Pall-bearers were Hooker, Huxley, Wallace, Lubbock, William Spottiswoode, Canon Farrer, the Earl of Derby, the Duke of Argyll and the Duke of Devonshire. Darwin was laid to rest in a grave beside Sir Isaac Newton as the choir sang: 'Let his body be buried in peace, his name liveth evermore.'

31

Depressions and Recessions
(1882 – 1892)

At the time of Charles Darwin's burial in Westminster Abbey, the country as a whole was in the throes of what even then was called the Great Depression. The first of several Royal Commissions was appointed to report on agricultural problems. Less than 15 per cent of the working population was engaged in farming; the majority of the people now lived in towns where there was a better chance of improving one's lot in life. Yet, even in the cities, there was a loss of confidence by businessmen and by manufacturers.

Potters, like workmen in other trades, had submitted to a 10 per cent reduction in wages, in a settlement between seventy-eight pottery employers and the five pottery unions. When several years passed without any reinstatement of the lost 10 per cent, the pottery unions and the Chamber of Commerce went to arbitration, and again the unions lost. This time, however, they formed a Council of Federated Potters and voted to strike. Some 30,000 out of 50,000 potters stopped work at the beginning of 1882, but the strike, so bravely begun, collapsed within six weeks for lack of funds. In November 1882 a new union, accepting members from all branches of the potters' trade, was agreed, and the National Order of Potters was formally established in 1883. Conciliation and arbitration were its immediate objectives. Most of the pottery owners were anxious to settle. Like other manufacturers, they were suffering from depressed trade, increased foreign competition and the generally reduced prices at which their goods were selling.

Wedgwood suffered less from labour troubles than most other potteries, because of its history of paying high wages to master craftsmen and of allowing these men to hire their own workmen: if the apprentices and the less highly skilled workers were poorly paid, they could blame the skilled workers rather than the factory. Paradoxically, though new machines and new labour-saving methods were being introduced, Wedgwood was hiring more workmen, and expanding at a time when other potteries were retrenching. They were also employing more artists and giving them the freedom to experiment. Thomas Allen proved as competent a director of designers as creator of new designs.

Thus, more or less by fortuitous circumstance and somewhat to their own astonishment, Wedgwood proved an exception to the national trend of recession and depression. The cold, gloomy year of 1882, when people were starving and rioting in the streets of London, was the most profitable year the Wedgwood company had in thirty-five years.

The marriage between Hope and Godfrey developed into a much happier and more affectionate relationship than anyone, other than Hope, had dared to imagine — especially after the birth of little Mary. Still, in a pattern similar to that of his own parents, Godfrey went abroad every year on holiday, whereas Hope, who disliked travelling and had no interest in 'visiting foreign places', remained in England.

During March and April of 1883, Godfrey took a six-week holiday in Greece, where he wrote to Hope: 'I feel I am wasting time here that I might be having with you, precious holiday time, without a conscience about the Works — and I chafe at spending it alone.' Hope had taken three-year-old Mary and gone to London to visit her parents, Snow and the Farrers.

'One thing I am glad of,' Godfrey confided, ' — that I am not ill again for the nth time under Theta's hospitable roof. Not that they don't make it as pleasant a place to be laid up in as to be had away from home.' [1] In spite of his love for his 'own dear wife' to whom he wrote almost daily about how he longed to hold her in his arms again and that when he returned 'teams & cart ropes won't drag me away from you again', Godfrey still had not overcome his attraction to Effie and his uneasiness in the presence of Theta.

While Godfrey was in Greece, the Farrers made a trip to Oxford at the invitation of Benjamin Jowett who also had the Spottiswoodes staying with him. Effie described the visit to Oxford in a letter to Hope which Hope then forwarded on to Godfrey. Thanking her for Effie's letter, he wrote: 'What a power she has of putting the most interesting parts of her visit before you. If I had been at Oxford, I should not have heard or seen so much as she has made me see.... I will keep the letter for I want to read it again.' [2]

In 1883 Emma Darwin moved to Cambridge with her daughter Bessie, her son Frank and her grandson Bernard. They took a house there called The Grove. Shortly after the move, Emma went back to Staffordshire to visit her old childhood friend Ellen Tollett, who was now an invalid. They reminisced with unabashed sentiment about the days of sixty years ago at Maer and at Betley Hall.

When Emma returned to Cambridge, she found that Frank was planning to marry Ellen Wordsworth Crofts, a lecturer in history at Newnham College, and to build a house on part of The Grove fields so that Bernard would not be separated from his grandmother. Emma wrote to Frank that she thought it rash to build a house so soon, and that he and Ellen would be welcome to stay at The Grove until Frank's career at the University was more settled and until he was able to see what the relationship between Ellen and Bernard would be.

'I don't in the least mind talking about it,' she wrote to him, 'but I can write more clearly than speak.' [3] Frank, who was at the time engaged in the time-consuming project of editing his father's autobiography and letters, agreed. Froude's edition of the letters of Jane Carlyle was creating quite a stir at the time. Emma was particularly shocked at how any woman could write such disloyal letters about her own husband. 'But one gets fond of her through everything. She has Carlyle's taste for very disagreeable personal observations,'[4] she wrote to Etty.

Emma and Bessie still returned to Down every summer. The five Darwin brothers and their families came for brief holidays at spaced intervals. But, because three of her five sons were now living in Cambridge, Emma was happy to be there during the winters. She also visited London and frequently saw the Litchfields and the Hensleighs and the Farrers.

In May of 1884, her brothers Frank and Harry, whom Emma called 'my two old gents', came to visit her in Cambridge. Frank continued his pattern of yearly visits to his daughter, to both of his brothers, to his sister-in-law Caroline Darwin Wedgwood and to his sister Emma Darwin. He also called upon several of his Darwin nephews, as well as all of Hensleigh's children — even including the unfortunate Alfred, who had married, without the approval of his parents, Rosina Ingall, the daughter of Richard Ingall, a civil engineer of Valparaiso, Chile. Alfred now had two sons, Bertram Hensleigh (Berry), born in 1876, and James (Jem), born in 1883; he was living near Horsley, Surrey, attempting unsuccessfully to be a country squire.

At the age of eighty-three Frank was as active as he had been at sixty-three. After the incorporation of the new borough of Hanley, he was on the Town Council and took a lively interest in all of its affairs. 'We thought we could not do without a coat of arms,' he told Godfrey, 'so we asked as to the charge & were told it would cost £70 — which on learning from the Town Clerk that no very dreadful consequences were likely to follow if we refused to pay the money, we did so — or rather we dropped the correspondence with the Garter King and made our own coat of arms under which we have flourished ever since in Peace & War just as much as if it had been properly emblazoned at the heralds office.'[5]

Frank's dislike of Gladstone, whom he had met only once in his life, continued, but it was more in the nature of a personal vendetta than an ideological disagreement. Godfrey pleased his father by relating to him some malicious gossip about Gladstone's wife. 'If you can pick up anything more against Mrs Gladstone, pray do,' he replied; 'something in the poisoning line would be very gratifying.'[6]

More directly involved with Gladstonian policies and with the increasing problems of international trade was, of course, Theta, now Sir Thomas, Farrer. As a member of the Board of Trade, which in the mid-1880s was headed by the Radical leader Joseph Chamberlain, Theta, like Frank Wedgwood, began to have severe political and philosophical doubts. Now in his sixties, the hitherto confident Theta experienced a loss of faith in himself and in the Radical intellectual circle of which he was a part. In the past he had been a Liberal, a reformer, a supporter of humanitarian causes. Now, his attitudes had became not just conservative but reactionary. No longer a promoter of free trade, he became a fanatical protectionist. What was good for humanity was now less important than what was good for Britain. The best of all possible worlds naturally would be a British world with British values. Yet, from his privileged vantage-point, he could see that the sun was already slowly setting on the Empire—a sunset that to him was both unavoidable and intolerable. He was one of those Kipling-esque men who in the early part of the nineteenth century had made Britain great, but who in the last quarter of that century had begun to seem slightly ridiculous—and Theta knew it. He became so insular in his views, and so depressed, that Chamberlain wrote to Effie that he 'was uneasy at what I hear from Sir Thomas.... He is always so cheerful about himself that his present state of depression makes me anxious that he should take every care & not worry himself about any office or public business.'[7]

Theta's relatives were less charitable in their feelings towards him. Hope agreed with Snow that he 'did indeed scream and fly into rages when not in his depressed state'. Both sisters were distressed that the independent-minded Effie refused to contradict him or even to express to her sisters privately any disagreement with his opinions.

Snow was working long hours on her book, *The Moral Ideal*, and spending a good deal of time with a new religious teacher, Howard Hinton. In the spring of 1885, she accompanied her parents, both of whom were in poor health, on a visit to Hope and Godfrey. They all made a sentimental trip back to Maer. Though Fanny Hensleigh's heart trouble kept her from taking the old familiar walks through the Maer woods, as she and Hensleigh had done in the days of their courtship, they had a picnic on the lawn.

Godfrey, too, was beginning to have pains in his leg and had difficulty in walking. He and Hope decided to move from Caverswall Castle, which required too large a staff of servants to maintain and which, in the way of old castles, was cold, damp, draughty and in need of constant repairs. Steep stairs and long rides either on horseback or in a carriage tired Godfrey and aggravated his lameness. After much searching, not having found a house to their liking that was close enough to the factory, Godfrey decided to build a house. This was to take some years. Meanwhile, Frank told Hensleigh that he was not going to offer his opinion any more 'because Godfrey is always asking for my advice but never following it'.

Frank's house at Barlaston was still the centre of the four Staffordshire Wedgwood houses, even though, apart from servants and frequent visitors, Frank and his unmarried daughter Amy were the sole occupants. 'Uncle Frank came into the room like a sunbeam,' Snow wrote to Effie.

Frank took much more interest in his grandchildren than he had in his own children when they were the same age. He was particularly concerned with their education. Without being asked, he busied himself in the hiring and firing of governesses and then pronouncing upon their competence or incompetence. Lily von Hafen, Cecil's former governess and Hope's friend, had been with the Laurence Wedgwoods for several years; the Clement Wedgwoods had a number of governesses in quick succession and had finally settled upon a Miss Hill whom Frank considered 'a good hit'. He reported to Godfrey: 'She gives me the impression of sense & brains (if they are not the same thing) and moreover I am much mistaken if she does not know what she is about at the Whist table ... she & I as partners knocked the others into a cocked hat & I cannot take credit for any good play on my part....'[8] At Caverswall Castle, where Cecil lived with his father, stepmother and five-year-old half-sister Mary, an attractive young Irish woman from Cork named Lucie Gibson was hired as a governess in the spring of 1885.

When the Hensleighs returned to London in early June, they and Snow and Ernest and the Farrers attended the unveiling of the memorial statue to Charles Darwin at the Natural History Museum. The Litchfields and four of the five Darwin brothers also attended the ceremony. Emma declined because she preferred 'avoiding all greetings and acquaintances'. Three weeks later, however, she did come to London and stayed at Queen Anne Street with the Hensleighs. One morning Hensleigh took her to view the statue. Unrecognized, she would be able to study it in a leisurely fashion. Her son George had told her that the hands were wrong: considerably larger and more powerful than Charles's hands had actually been. George had already been to have a cast taken of his own hands to be used as a guide in altering the statue. There was also a defect in the eyes which displeased the Darwin sons. Emma was fearful at being disappointed as well. She told Hensleigh that she did not expect to be satisfied with the likeness. But, after the two of them had stared at it in silence for a long while, she remarked: 'I like the attitude. The general look of dignity and repose is of more consequence than a strong likeness.'

In the evening Emma went with Hensleigh and Ernest to a meeting of the Society for Psychical Research. Three years earlier, in 1882, Hensleigh had been one of the founding members of the Society and had been elected a vice-president. Since the time, more than ten years before, when the Hensleighs and the Darwins and the Litchfields first attended seances at Ras's house, Hensleigh's interest in spiritualism had increased. His main preoccupation was with psychic phenomena. He wrote articles for the *Journal of the Society for Psychical Research* and tried to devise a scientific method of studying the evidence of direct communication with the spirit world. He was interested in hypnosis, telepathy and automatic writing. Since Fanny Hensleigh's ill health and her age—she was now eighty-five—prevented her attending meetings of the society, Ernest often accompanied his father, but he was prompted more by filial duty than by genuine interest.

Snow, Effie and Hope all shared their father's preoccupation with the spiritual quest and with life after death. Snow's book *The Moral Ideal* was an attempt to recast religion—to reconcile the old beliefs with historical truth and with the scientific facts Darwinism had forced upon the world. In short, she wanted a rational humanism within the framework of the Established Church. Describing Snow to an acquaintance, her old Linlathen friend Emily Gurney said: 'I consider her essentially Christian— but her mind is much too alive to intellectual difficulties to admit of the Hope and Joy of Faith. She has no special attachments but she values the Holy Communion. She has a very critical and subtle intellect—happily also a deep, tender, humble heart.'[9]

Effie and Hope carried their father's spiritualism one step further and joined the Theosophical movement. The Theosophical Society had been founded in America in 1875 by Madame Blavatsky, whose book *The Secret Doctrine* quickly spread the movement round the globe. The Theosophists claimed to derive their truths by way of intuition or through the revelations of masters or seers; their emphasis was on the individual struggle for wisdom, wholeness and union with God. Closely related to Yoga and to the philosophy of the Upanishads, Theosophy was also allied with reincarnation and occultism—that is to say, with astral bodies, guardian angels and the like.

Inevitably, with those who wish to improve mankind, politics and religion go hand in hand. Several of the founders and leading members of the Fabian Society were also spiritualists. At a spiritualist soireé held at Hensleigh's house in Queen Anne Street, two of the founders of the Fabian Society, Edward Pease and Frank Podmore, first met each other. G.B. Shaw, Graham Wallas, Sidney and Beatrice Webb were all interested in spiritualism and attended meetings. Annie Besant, a union organizer, social reformer and advocate of birth control whose trial, conviction and subsequent mistrial for alleged indecency was a *cause célébre*, was converted to Theosophy as suddenly as she was to Fabianism. In 1891, after the death of Madame Blavatsky, she became the Theosophical Society's most prominent member and was eventually elected international president.

Effie and Hope were both thrilled by Annie Besant's charismatic personality, and her preaching, not revolution but evolutionary socialism, which would achieve the utilitarian aim of bringing the greatest happiness to the greatest number. The sisters were committed to both the new politics and the new religion as revealed by Annie Besant. Like Charles's old advocate T. H. Huxley, Hensleigh, Godfrey and Snow went along with the new politics, but continued their attempts to fit both spiritualism and the new science into the Established Church.

Only a few months after Emma attended the Psychical Research meeting with Hensleigh, Snow's last 'beloved saint', Hinton, fell from his pedestal and away from the Church with a resounding thud when he was found to be a bigamist. He had been living a hidden life with an abandoned woman whose soul he claimed to have saved by going through a marriage ceremony and by continuing to pretend to be her husband. The great Victorian sin was not infidelity, but getting caught at it.

Emma kept to her own faith without contradicting or alienating any of the Hensleighs, just as she had done with Charles and his agnosticism. There were so few of their generation left now that in her view such differences were best overlooked. Frank naturally disagreed. There was nothing he enjoyed more than 'a good debate over an honest difference of opinion'—in other words, an argument. Emma had invited her three brothers, 'the old gents', to Down for a week in September. Harry, too ill to come, died the following month. Hensleigh and Frank came and 'squabbled like children'. Hensleigh had lost most of the hearing in his 'good ear'. Frank's usual voice level was, according to Emma, 'a gentle roar'. Now, he bellowed his support for good old-fashioned Unitarianism at Hensleigh, who fell back on deafness as his defence. Ernest had accompanied his father and uncle to Down and then escorted his Aunt Emma to Leith Hill Place. Ernest was agreeable and amusing but lacking in vigour. He endured his work at the Colonial Office but, like his Uncle Robert Mackintosh, was more interested in prestige than in power. His chief claim to fame was that he was the best whist player among all the Wedgwoods and Darwins.

In 1886 politics took precedence over religion. Lord Salisbury, whose wife, Georgina Alderson (Caroline Drewe's granddaughter), was a cousin of the Wedgwoods, came into power. It was a period of imperialist expansion, of wars in Bulgaria, Egypt and Afghanistan, of tentative alliances with Germany, Russia, Austro-Hungary and with France. In 1887, the year of the Queen's Golden Jubilee, there was a fever of 'new imperialism' which infected almost every British politician except, perhaps, Salisbury himself.

But not all the nation's obsessions were political. The craze for lawn tennis, invented in 1874, had spread among both men and women. Lawn tennis was a feature of week-end parties at the suburban homes of the wealthy and at the country seats of the aristocracy. The first Lawn Tennis Championship for women was held at Wimbledon in 1884, seven years after the first men's competition. A year later, in 1885, women were allowed to play in golf tournaments. Even more important and more liberating was the craze for cycling which swept the country with the patenting of the safety bicycle in 1886. These athletic enthusiasms naturally brought about a change in clothes. Independent, daring women, like Effie, might even wear a neat knickerbocker suit while cycling from Bryanston Square to Regent Street to do a bit of shopping.

Emma Darwin was reading Emerson and telling the less daring, unathletic Etty that she 'really wanted to know what transcendentalism means, and I think it is that intuition is before reason (or facts). It certainly does not suit Wedgwoods, who never have any intuitions.'[10]

Hope and Effie thought of themselves as both practical and intuitive. In further pursuit of self-awareness, Hope became a vegetarian. After Chamberlain's resignation, Theta left the Board of Trade and, according to Hope, 'turned over a new mellow leaf ... he seemed free from something & I suppose it must be the duty of fighting.'[11] Both Theta and Effie then became vegetarians. Theta's health improved, and he was appointed to a post on the newly formed London County Council.

Frank Darwin completed *The Life and Letters of Charles Darwin*, which was published in the autumn of 1887. His mother was pleased with it, and his Uncle Frank Wedgwood wrote to him: 'It is like hearing Charles's voice and seeing the expression of his face again.'[12] His Aunt Caroline Darwin Wedgwood, however, had reservations, which she wrote to Emma: 'I wish some years ago I had known that Charles thought my Father [Robert Darwin] did not understand or know what ability and power of mind he had really. He was so proud as well as fond of him — but I often felt afraid that Erasmus might feel mortified and feel undervalued. I long to strike a pen through that mistaken sentence of my Father's estimation of Charles.'[13]

The estimation of one generation by another may also change again with a third generation. Joseph Mayer died in Liverpool in the autumn of 1886, and on 21 July 1887, the Mayer collection of Wedgwood manuscripts was auctioned in London at Sotheby, Wilkinson & Hodge. Somewhat embarrassed by the criticisms which Mayer, Eliza Meteyard and others had directed at his father, and at the Wedgwood family as a whole, for not appreciating the historical value of Josiah I's papers, Godfrey went to London and bought the lot. He himself was not particularly interested in old manuscripts, and saw no way in which they would benefit the business at present. Thus, in the anticipation that Snow might write a biography, he loaned them to her. She was too absorbed in her own work, so she gave them to her father, who read them and then sent them on to Emma Darwin.

The Hensleighs' household was, at the time, disturbed by a series of unexpected events. Fifty-year-old Ernest suddenly married Mary Webster, an orphaned young woman who had no dowry and who was estranged from her adopted parents. While she and Snow were friendly, though their interests were not compatible, Snow thought it best to abdicate the role of mistress of the house now that her mother was bedridden. Alfred, who had long been out of favour with the family, separated from his wife Rosina, left his house at Horsley, Surrey, and went abroad, placing his two young sons in the care of his sister Snow. That the house in Queen Anne Street with its two frail octogenarians was not the most congenial environment for two active boys also probably influenced Snow's decision, at this time, to take a house of her own.

If Ernest's sudden marriage surprised and disappointed his family, it was mild by comparison with the dismay felt in Staffordshire when twenty-four-year old Cecil announced his engagement to Lucie Gibson, his little sister's governess. The romance had sprung up secretly while Godfrey was on holiday with the Farrers in America and while Hope was in London visiting her parents and selecting furnishings for the new house that was being built. Seven-year-old Mary—who had written to her Aunt Snow about the progress on the building of the house and that she 'enjoyed going out with Father because there is almost always an accident'—accompanied her mother to London, leaving Cecil and Lucie alone, apart from the servants, at Caverswall Castle.

On 9 September 1887, the day before Godfrey's departure for America, Lucie wrote about the excitement—'the talking, the making of plans & altering them again, the solemn consultations over every article of clothing, the grand review of all the boxes, portmanteaux and bags that the house contains (and their name is legion), the packing, and scurrying, and rushing to and fro.'[14] Then, at half-past two, they 'were all electrified by seeing an ambulance van drive up to the door, accompanied by Mr Laurence W and a doctor'—and Cecil on a stretcher with his leg strapped to a splint. He had been escorting a party round the works when he slipped and fell with his leg under him. Though it felt as if something had snapped, he got up and went on until suddenly he fainted.

Lucie Gibson wrote in her diary:

It was nearly two hours before the household calmed after his arrival, and then Mr and Mrs W had to go for a stroll in the garden to compose themselves...then there was a great alarm that we had neglected the packing, and must make up for lost time; so we all rushed up to the Oak Room where all his things were collected, and packed like blacks. They were handing me the things & I was putting them in, and *three times* I had to take them all out and begin again because of some new thing that was or was not to go and that altered the whole configuration of the trunk. Then there was a solemn procession, armed with candles, to the dark passage off the back hall (near C's door) where coats and caps are hung to consult & decide upon his supply of overcoats; C's voice coming through his open door in a cloud of tobacco smoke, delivering his sage opinion on the weighty subject.

All this time the wind was rising steadily — it's blowing a gale now: and by the time dinner was over Mrs Hope was reduced to prowling about the room and looking out of every window in turn out of sheer fidgets. Then we adjourned to C's room and had tea there — his majesty with a 'cage' over his leg, looking dignified & imposing even in his nightgown. But Mr and Mrs couldn't sit still for long; so they went to bed at half-past nine to shorten the day — not reflecting that it would lengthen the night; I am sure they won't sleep a wink...the wind is getting worse & worse! I don't believe he'll go at all!'[15]

The following day Lucie wrote: 'Well, he *did* go; at least they've left the house. I've just been interviewing the doctor who says it is only a sprain after all and will be well quite soon....Aunt Amy (bother her) came pegging over hotfoot to see him and to kick up a fuss. If I hadn't happened to be busy just when I saw the carriage coming, I would have gone and sat on the side of his bed and been there when she came in just to vex her!'[16]

Two days after Godfrey's departure for America, Hope and Mary went to London. Except for the servants and occasional visits from nosy Aunt Amy and the Laurence Wedgwoods, Lucie and Cecil were alone for three weeks. Cecil stayed home from the works even though his leg injury was not nearly as serious as had at first seemed.

Like most nineteenth-century fathers, Godfrey had hoped that Cecil would marry an heiress, certainly not a penniless governess, however attractive and clever she might be. Lucie tactfully went home to Ireland a week before Godfrey returned from America, leaving Cecil and Godfrey to settle the matter. Cecil was a far stronger and more determined character than his father — and Lucie was more determined than both of them together.

In Staffordshire the year 1888 began with heavy snow. Laurence's eldest son Kennard, who was fourteen, had a severe case of measles and was forced to miss half a year of school. Clement had been unwell for several months. He finally went to London to consult a specialist who told him that he had cancer. In a frantic attempt to find some cure, he and Emily left for a spa in Germany where they would remain through the rest of the winter. Franky, now aged twenty-one, left Cambridge and began his apprenticeship in the firm. Their other three boys were off at school at Clifton. Twelve-year-old Cecily moved from Barlaston Lea to Barlaston to stay with her grandfather

Frank and her Aunt Amy. Lily von Hafen, who had been Cecily's governess, now moved back with the Godfrey Wedgwoods to replace Lucie Gibson as Mary's governess.

The cold winter took its toll with old Frank, who suffered several chills. Godfrey did not tell him of Caroline Wedgwood's death until after her funeral. His fears that his father would insist upon travelling in the freezing weather to Leith Hill Place were unnecessary. 'I should have liked to be at the funeral as I was at Elizabeth's and Joe's and Harry's,' Frank told him, 'but it was out of the question even if I had notice of the day with certainty.'[17]

Frank himself had a bout of the flu in February. But, like his grandfather Josiah, he had little patience with doctors—'No doubt the final cause of patients *is* doctors.'[18]

Charles Langton, who was the same age as Frank, died during the cold winter of 1888. Frank had been one of the few Wedgwoods or Darwins who had approved of Langton's third marriage, four years earlier when he was aged eighty-four. 'I see no reason why he should deny himself the comfort of a companion merely because he is old and wants one all the more,' Frank explained to the others. He then went on to point out that Langton's grand-children, whom he had provided for financially, afforded him little com-panionship and that a new wife might 'make him come out of his shell a little'.[19] This proved to be the case. The last years of Langton's life were happier than the previous two decades had been for him.

Also, in February of 1888, when the accounts for the previous year were audited at the factory, Godfrey and Laurence discovered that the factory had made a substantial loss in 1887. The depression that had affected not only the pottery industry but business throughout Britain had finally moved into Wedgwood. Since neither Godfrey, Clement nor Laurence had their father's aptitude for or interest in finance, this loss—the most serious in seventeen years—came as a shock to everyone. Cecil was in Ireland meeting Lucie's family when the news came. Upon his return to Staffordshire, he told his father that he and Lucie were willing to postpone their marriage until the business improved and that the suggestion of the postponement had been Lucie's. Godfrey assured Cecil that such a sacrifice was unneces-sary, as the pottery was not their only source of income. Then he wrote to his future daughter-in-law: 'That you should be willing to defer your marriage for our convenience shews, that whatever it is which renders intercourse between the two generations more difficult than we had hoped, it is only something on the surface, that down below, you do sympathise with us and are ready to make sacrifices for us.'[20]

Whatever disapproval or disappointment had been felt by Godfrey at the forthcoming union was eased by Lucie's generosity and strength of character. Still, her behaviour was not without self-interest. She wanted to be certain that she really was going to be accepted as a social equal and a rightful member of the family. Her flame-red hair was a true indication of a fierce Irish temper. She was an independent and shrewd young woman who correctly understood the temper of her democratic, liberal-minded employers—who were just as bigoted as anyone when it came to marrying into the family. Thus, knowing full well that Cecil would marry her even if it meant his leaving his family and the pottery, Lucie accused Hope, rightly, of trying to dislodge her from Cecil's affections. Furthermore, Lucie suggested that she herself might break off the engagement if she could not be assured of being all that Hope wanted in a daughter.

'I am quite sure — this an answer to a question of yours — that you could be everything in the world to me that you choose, 'Hope replied. 'All but, that is, a daughter & perhaps you will decide aginst that — but do not ever doubt that you have in your hand (beside what you may have for Cecil) help and happiness to an indefinite degree from me.'[21]

The marriage took place in Cork on 18 July 1888. The couple spent a brief honeymoon in Ireland and the Lake District before returning to a small rented house at Chapel Chorlton near Maer. Pleading Godfrey's ill health, Hope and Godfrey did not attend the wedding, but sent a telegram of best wishes.

Snow also telegraphed her best wishes for happiness to the young couple. As a wedding present, she painted two watercolours of Caverswall Castle for them. Snow was happier now than she had been at any period in her life. The passions and inner conflicts which had so tormented her early years had abated. For the first time in her life she had a house of her own and a life more or less independent of her parents. She was now aged fifty-five. *The Moral Ideal* was published during the summer of 1888. The reviews were unanimously favourable; somewhat to her own surprise, Snow discovered that she was a celebrity. Her novels were brought out in new editions under her own name and there was a third edition of her biography of Wesley. Her Aunt Emma Darwin a few years earlier had remarked of F.D. Maurice's major work: '...if I could keep to my resolution of never even trying to understand him I should quite enjoy the book.'[22] Emma and others not only enjoyed Snow's book but understood it and were impressed by the originality of the thought as well as its complexity and clarity. Effie and Hope, who in the past had complained of their sister's 'endless dark sentences of doom and gloom', were extravagant in their praise. Even Hensleigh, who had been so critical of his daughter's imaginative powers, at long last gave the approval that had been withheld for so many years.

In mid-life, Snow no longer needed the idealized masculine figure she had so constantly sought in the past. Erskine, Scott and Maurice were all dead, Hinton disgraced. The only man whose memory or whose real existence still haunted her was Browning. The dedication of her book 'To an old Friend' was, as she confided to her companion Marian Hughes, to Browning. She sent a copy of the book to him at Warwick Crescent. Unknown to her, he was then in Venice, where he died a few months later. His sister Sarianna, whom Snow had never met, returned her letters which Browning had kept for nearly a quarter of a century. If she had known that Browning, who was so fearful of what would be written about him after his death, had destroyed almost all the other letters in his possession, she would have realized how important to him she really was.

Another person who died shortly before he finished reading Snow's book was her Uncle Frank. On 1 October 1888, at the age of eighty-eight, Frank

Wedgwood died peacefully in his sleep. The news was telegraphed to his son Clement in Germany, to Hensleigh in London and to Emma in Cambridge. 'I think his was the happiest old age I ever knew,' Emma told her daughter Etty. 'He was entirely without the faults of old age and wiser and gentler than when he was young.'[23]

Etty and her brother George both offered to take their mother to Staffordshire for the funeral. In the end, they all joined Hensleigh and Snow and the Farrers for the sad train journey up north. Fanny Hensleigh, unequal to the strain of either the journey or the occasion, remained at home in Queen Anne Street with Ernest and Mary. The Darwin faction stayed at the Upper House in Barlaston with Amy, whereas the Farrers and Hensleigh and Snow stayed with Godfrey and Hope at their new house, Idlerocks.

Clement and Emily were unable to return in time for the funeral. When they arrived back in Staffordshire a month later, Godfrey felt relieved that his father had not seen Clement in his present condition. The miracle cures or experimental treatments had not worked, and it was apparent that Clement had only a few weeks or months to live. He and Emily did not return to their home at Barlaston Lea but instead moved into the Upper House, where Amy could help Emily nurse him.

Frank had been the first really sound Wedgwood businessman since his grandfather Josiah I. He died a wealthy man. He also had planned his estate sensibly, avoiding the entailments and confusions that had so bedevilled previous generations. He had made a number of shrewd business investments, apart from the various properties he had bought for political purposes, so that his share of the assets of the Wedgwood factory was less than one-third of the total worth of his estate. His executors were his three sons. His shares in the Wedgwood factory were divided among his seven children in the proportion of four for each son and three for each daughter. Godfrey inherited the family portrait painted by Stubbs for Josiah I, as well as one of the First Day's vases. Clement and Laurence inherited First Day's vases and Clement received a first edition of the Portland Vase.

Clement's sons returned from Clifton College to the Upper House for Christmas. The Laurence Wedgwoods had all of the family, including the newly-weds Cecil and Lucie, for Christmas dinner. But it was a sad Christmas and the last time Clement left the Upper House at Barlaston. He died there on 24 January 1889, at the age of forty-nine.

A few months after the death of his father, Godfrey, following in the family tradition, decided that he would resign from active partnership in the pottery. He was having difficulty with his leg and was further handicapped by his old depressions, which seemed to strike at regular intervals. Now he had not only his father's estate to settle but also Clement's. He had a strong family sense of responsibility, not only in the pottery but in civic and philanthropic activities as well. After handing over the chairmanship of the pottery to his brother Laurence, he became a director of the North Staffordshire Railway, replaced his father on the Committee of the Chamber of Commerce and took a more active part in the local branch association of the Manchester School for the Deaf and Dumb. Now that he was settled in his new house he took more interest in the near-by village church of St John the Evangelist at Moddershall, which had been consecrated eleven years earlier in 1878. There he bought a family pew, made a substantial donation to the church and took nine-year-old Mary with him almost every Sunday. All of this was more conformity than conviction. On the whole, he was more influenced ideologically by Snow's *The Moral Ideal* than by traditional Anglicanism or by his father's 'common-sense Unitarianism' or his wife's Theosophy.

Also following in his father's footsteps, Godfrey became the one member of the family who kept in touch with all of the others. He visited his Darwin cousins regularly and invited Margaret Vaughan Williams to bring her three children, Hervey, Meggie and Ralph, to Staffordshire during the school summer holidays.

In February of 1889 Godfrey was in London on business to do with Clement's estate. The great national event of the day was the vindication of Parnell and the collapse of the case brought against him by *The Times*. That and the policy of imperial unity were much talked about in London intellectual circles. Godfrey stayed at Bryanston Square with the Farrers and visited the Litchfields, with Snow and with the two generations of Hensleighs who, sadly, were not living in such peaceful harmony in Queen Anne Street as Snow and Effie and Hope had anticipated.

Mary Ernest, as she was called, had a quick temper, a sharp tongue and little patience with the problems of the aged. She was also petty and spiteful, frequently refusing small requests for no reason other than to cause discomfort. Then she was given to crying spells, followed by fits of remorse which upset Fanny Hensleigh and provoked Hensleigh to sarcasm and to sharp criticism of her. Ernest refused to take sides, avoiding any conflicts or confrontations and consequently losing the respect of everyone.

Before returning to Staffordshire, Godfrey went to Cambridge to visit his Aunt Emma and his cousins the George Darwins, the Horace Darwins and the Frank Darwins. Godfrey had not seen his Aunt Emma since his father's funeral. Now aged eighty-one, Emma informed them all that she was 'so well and strong, I can't think what is the matter'. Around her were seven young grandchildren, her pleasant though slightly retarded daughter Bessie, her old staff of servants from Down, her little dog Dickie and the inevitable litter of kittens for companionship and amusement. Emma, like Frank, had kept up her interest in the world at large and particularly in politics. She was strongly opposed to Home Rule for Ireland and therefore was irate over Parnell's success. This amused Godfrey and reminded him of his father, for Emma was as blatantly and personally hostile to Parnell as his father Frank had been to Gladstone.

Emma ordered books from the London Library a dozen at a time, reporting that on most days she was able to get through one volume and part of another. Although she enjoyed novels, she was a stern and perceptive critic, becoming as much involved with fictional characters as if they were personal acquaintances. She could be quite abusive towards authors whose characters were unnatural or whose plots were illogical. She always read two books at a time—a 'stiff' book and a 'light' one. Henry James's stories were considered 'stiff'. Mrs Henry Sandford's book *Thomas Poole and His Friends* was 'light' in a derogatory way. Coleridge's letters quoted in the book annoyed Emma. She described them to Etty as 'a mixture of gush and mawkish egotism and what seems like humbug...I can't imagine how my Father ever liked and admired Coleridge. I believe Dr Darwin would have been more acute.'[24]

As her three sons living in Cambridge were more inclined towards scientific than literary interests, Emma discussed books by letter with Etty and with Snow. Though she tried to keep her thoughts in the present, Emma could not help sometimes comparing the world around her now with the world of her youth. 'How like Erasmus Horace is in some things,' she remarked to Etty, 'his being so happy and easy with the pretty girls.'[25]

When her own contemporaries—and there were few of them left now—fell ill or when her grandchildren were going through the usual childhood ailments, Emma frequently criticized the doctors, most of whom she considered inept. She referred back to her own father-in-law with such glowing remarks as: 'I am sure Dr Darwin would never have made so stupid a blunder' or 'I am sure Dr Darwin would have allowed ripe peaches....'

In June of 1889 Fanny Hensleigh, who had been bedridden for two years, died and was buried in the tomb with her father and sister at St John's in Hampstead. After such a long illness her death could only be thought a release. Even Hensleigh, who shortly afterward suffered a serious illness himself, murmured 'Thank God' when Godfrey told him the news of his wife's death. All three of the daughters had returned to Queen Anne Street and had taken turns at her bedside during the last forty-eight hours.

After the funeral service Ernest, Mary Ernest and Hensleigh returned to Queen Anne Street while the three sisters and Godfrey and Theta held a family conference in Bryanston Square. They were all in agreement that it would be intolerable for Hensleigh to continue to live in the same house with Ernest and Mary Ernest. With his deafness and stubborn conviction of the rightness of his own opinions, Hensleigh did not have an easy disposition in his old age. Nor was he one to suffer fools. He was annoyed by the weakness of Ernest's character and by the meanness and ignorance of Mary Ernest. In comparison with his three intellectual daughters, Mary Ernest was stupid, dull and small-minded. The three sisters were afraid that Mary's small-mindedness would result in, if not abuse, at least unkindness towards their father.

Thus, the consensus was to recommend to Hensleigh that he sell the house in Queen Anne Street and move into a house with Snow and her companion Marian Hughes; but, as Effie shrewdly pointed out, it should be made to seem like his idea rather than something being forced upon him. In August of 1889 Effie went with her father to visit Emma at Down where, with Emma's help, the idea of changing houses seemed naturally to emerge. Four months later, Hensleigh, Snow and Marian moved to 94, Gower Street, a spacious house with light, well-proportioned rooms overlooking the gable of the Irving Church which the family had attended half a century earlier.

'When first the idea of keeping house with Snow dawned before me,' Hensleigh wrote to Emma,

> I regarded Marian as a necessary drawback that had to be swallowed, but I have quite changed my views. I now regard her as a great advantage, adding much to the cheerfulness of the house and making everything go smooth. She is extremely handy in making all arrangements, so that neither Snow nor I have the least trouble in housekeeping. And she is a very pleasant companion. She gets on very well with Mary Ernest, only makes her rather jealous when they compare the amount of their weekly bills.

He then went on to tell his sister that he was settled very comfortably and decidedly better off than he had been at Queen Anne Street. 'I go out very little. I do not feel any the better for it when I do, not even more virtuous...so I sit by the fire and muse.'[26]

Hensleigh and Snow were compatible in a way they had never been before. Encouraged by the success of *The Moral Ideal*, Snow began work on a second historical-religious volume which she titled *The Message of Israel*. Hensleigh took an interest in her philosophical pursuits, whereas she accepted his enthusiasm for spiritualism and encouraged his research and writing on telepathy, extra-sensory perception and what Jung would later call synchronicity.

In the new house in Gower Street, Hensleigh had his own sitting room, which was twenty-four feet by eighteen feet, on the first floor, and a bedroom above. There were three servants in the house, a cook, a maid and a gardener. Snow kept up a friendly relationship with Ernest and Mary Ernest. They visited frequently at Gower Street even though Hensleigh never got back his liking of his daughter-in-law. Effie was less charitable — and probably more honest. She had no respect for her brother and sister-in-law, told them so and refused to have anything more to do with them. Not living in London, Hope was able to avoid an open breach. She simply ignored them.

Snow's guardianship of her two young nephews Berry and Jem was less demanding now that the boys were at school at Rugby where both their father and grandfather had gone. Hensleigh took little interest in his grandsons. Though Snow's house was considered the boys' home, they spent part of their holidays with their Aunt Effie and Uncle Theta at Abinger and with their Aunt Hope and Uncle Godfrey at Idlerocks. Snow invited some of the young Darwin cousins to visit in London but was disappointed in the children's personalities, which, she told Hope, were 'exceedingly polite and dull'. Hope replied that she was sorry that the little Darwins were dull. 'We have enough dullness in the family & plenty of virtue — a little vice would make a pleasant variety.'[27] In London and at Abinger there were no cousins of their own age for companions, but in Staffordshire Berry and Jem found playmates in their Uncle Laurence's four children and, of course, their cousin Mary.

Ten-year-old Mary now often came to London with her mother to visit her grandfather and her Aunt Snow. Mary was more at ease with adults than with her own contemporaries. With her mother, her governess Lily von Hafen, Aunt Effie, Aunt Snow and her adopted Aunt Marian, Mary visited churches, museums, galleries and theatres in London. She was a lonely, sensitive child who quickly replaced the two boys as her Aunt Snow's favourite child. Perhaps Snow sensed something in Mary that was akin to the isolation and unhappiness she herself had felt in her girlhood.

Snow took Mary's hurts and disappointments much to heart. It distressed her that her father paid so little attention to his granddaughter and seemed to care so little for her while she tried so very hard to please him. Snow wrote to her Aunt Emma how heartbroken Mary was when her little cousin Mildred Hawkshaw invited her to go with her to a party and then forgot her. Wearing her new dress and standing by the window in the first-floor drawing room in Gower Street, she waited with her grandfather, her Aunt Effie and her Aunt Snow for the Hawkshaw carriage to come. After an hour or so, her aunts gently began to explain how people often unintentionally forgot even very important things. Mary listened attentively and then replied: 'But people don't forget what they like.'

If Hensleigh had little interest in the child Mary, he did enjoy visiting her parents at Idlerocks in the summers. Perhaps, too, these summers in Staffordshire (which had changed so little) made him nostalgic for his youth, even though he had always preferred city life to country life. Godfrey admired his uncle and father-in-law, and he welcomed his visits.

'I am afraid poor Godfrey has bad turns [depressions] from what Hope said to me,' Etty Litchfield wrote to her mother in the spring of 1890. 'I do wish they could have had one more happy summer with Uncle Hensleigh at Idlerocks but for many reasons it is better the last illness should have been in London.'[28]

Hensleigh himself had spoken to Effie of Idlerocks during this illness: 'I should have liked to have gone down once again.'

'It's a great disappointment to poor Hope,' Effie told him.

Then, after a long pause, he said: 'Perhaps it is better as it is.'[29]

It was not his last illness. He surprised everyone, including himself, by defying his doctor's gloomy prediction and recovering from his third bout of bronchial pneumonia. With the doctor's permission and accompanied by a manservant whom Snow had found with the help of Etty Litchfield, he did make another trip to Idlerocks in July of 1890. Godfrey and Hope had just returned from what Hope described as a 'honeymoon in York'. Godfrey was in a happier and more optimistic frame of mind than usual.

In August Snow and the Farrers also came to Idlerocks. Effie later told Ida Farrer Darwin that the three sisters were closer to their father then than at any time since their childhood. The only thing that would have added to her father's happiness, she noted, would have been the presence of Aunt Emma.

Now that Emma and Hensleigh were the only Wedgwoods or Darwins remaining in their generation they were even closer than they had been earlier. In the autumn the Litchfields took Hensleigh with them to Cambridge. And, in the spring of 1891, Emma made a brief trip to

London. Hensleigh again had suffered from the cold winter and had grown more frail, though apparently he suffered nothing more specific than the aches and pain of old age. Along with Effie and Hope, he became a vegetarian, and he was finicky about his diet. He continued his investigation of psychic phenomena with the enthusiasm of a much younger man. Four days before his death a case-study of automatic messages prepared by him was read at a meeting of the Society for Psychical Research.

On 1 June 1891, Hensleigh died peacefully in his sleep at the age of eighty-seven. He was buried with his wife and father-in-law in the Mackintosh tomb under the yew tree at St John's in Hampstead. Later, in his memory, Snow donated to the church a charcoal portrait of him by Edward Clifford, done when he was aged seventy-five. She also donated a portrait of her grandfather, Sir James Mackintosh. These and portraits of other eminent Victorians associated with the Hampstead church hung in the vestry for half a century until they were forgotten by parishoners and descendants alike.

An obituary of Hensleigh published in the *Journal of the Society for Psychical Research* noted that his outstanding intellectual achievements and his fame had been overshadowed by the eminence and celebrity of his cousin and brother-in-law, Charles Darwin, 'but in moral nature he was not easily to be surpassed; — in the candid uprightness, the unobtrusive beneficence, the immutable spirit of honour, which made one feel if all men were like him, how simple and noble a matter the life of man might be.'[30]

There were many tributes from the famous and from those whose names were known only to a few. W. R. Grove, an old friend who was also in his eighties, wrote to Snow: 'You have done all that love and duty could enjoin and as all must die, no death could be less painful than your Father's to himself and others.... Nearly all my old friends are now gone; of none have I a more grateful recollection than of your parents.'[31]

Hensleigh's death was probably sadder for Emma than for anyone else in the family. She had observed earlier that it was 'a great loss to be the youngest in a family'. Now there was no link with her past life.

Godfrey was an executor of Hensleigh's will. Like his brother Frank, Hensleigh had made a number of shrewd investments and was worth considerably more than any of his children had supposed. The estate was divided equally among the five children, the three exceptional daughters and the two disappointing sons. Alfred returned to London, but died a few months later at the age of fifty, having conceived a third child who was born five months after his death. Mary Ernest also became pregnant and in July of 1893 gave birth to a son, another Allen Wedgwood.

While involved in settling his father-in-law's estate and while also becoming more deeply involved with the Manchester School for the Deaf and Dumb, Godfrey finally severed all connections with the pottery. A new agreement was drawn up in the autumn of 1891 with Laurence, Cecil, then aged twenty-seven, and Clement's son, Francis Hamilton (Franky), then aged twenty-four, as equal partners. The business was improving, though still making a loss. The strong-minded Lucie had informed both Cecil and his father that she was unwilling to have children until the business was making a profit and until Cecil was able to purchase an appropriate house. Meanwhile they kept as pets a pair of Staffordshire bull terriers named Tady and Parks. They were particularly vicious dogs who frightened and angered neighbours in the street of small row houses in Chapel Chorlton. After two pet cats in the neighbourhood, injudiciously crossing the Wedgwood back garden, were killed by the dogs, the neighbours registered a protest. This was particularly embarrassing to Hope who, following in the footsteps of her mother and grandmother, took an active part in the Society for the Prevention of Cruelty to Animals. She was at the time mounting a campaign against blood sports and was greatly opposed to dogs that were trained to hunt and kill.

Godfrey attempted to persuade Cecil and Lucie to give away the two dogs and to make peace with their neighbours, some of whom worked at the pottery. Lucie would agree only to parting with one dog. Godfrey was, however, more successful in persuading them that with the inheritance that would be Cecil's through the estates of both his Hawkshaw and Wedgwood grandfathers, they could now afford to move into a house more appropriate to a partner in the Wedgwood factory. Thus, Lucie and Cecil moved to Leadendale. A new generation had begun to assert itself, making demands for a future structured to its own wishes.

32

The End of an Era
(1892 – 1897)

The 1890s was a decade of social and political upheavals, of gaiety and tragedy, of contrast and ambiguity. Out of step with the foreign policy of the other major European powers, England proudly viewed her position in the world as one of 'splendid isolation'. Ignoring serious, stuffy politics, the popular press christened the era 'the Gay Nineties'. London was suddenly fashionable and cosmopolitan. There was the beginning of café society, and stylish authors like Oscar Wilde and Frank Harris frequented the Café Royale in Regent Street. Even socialists like Shaw and Wells had a thoroughly metropolitan outlook. A new era was being born.

When Tennyson died in 1892, having reigned as Poet Laureate for forty-two years, William Morris was offered the post and declined. Morris was not only a literary cult-figure; he had brought a new look to furniture, fabrics and interior design which revolutionized Victorian taste and paved the way for external as well as internal changes.

Leonard Darwin, who after twenty years had resigned his commission in the Royal Engineers, stood as Liberal Unionist candidate for Lichfield, winning a Parliamentary seat in the general election of July 1892. Cecil and Frank took the day off from the factory and, according to Hope, drove drunken voters to the polling place to vote for their cousin. Ernest Wedgwood who differed from the rest of the family in being a Tory—he had even hoped to run for Parliament himself, but received no encouragement from the family—wrote to congratulate Leonard. The letter, as Emma wrote to her daughter Etty, was 'neat in feeling and expression as well as in handwriting'.[1]

Politics interested the Wedgwoods and the Farrers as well as the Darwins. In the autumn of 1893 the second Home Rule Bill got through the Commons but was thrown out by the Lords. Gladstone finally retired permanently on 3 March 1894, and Lord Rosebery became Prime Minister. He soon bestowed a peerage on Theta, who became Lord Farrer of Abinger.

The Litchfields were visiting Idlerocks at the time, as was Margaret Vaughan Williams and her twenty-two-year-old daughter Meggie. Litchfield had retired from his post on the Ecclesiastical Commission in the

87 Down House, home of Charles Darwin

88 Leith Hill Place, home of Josiah Wedgwood III

89   Thomas Carlyle

90   Jane Carlyle

91   John Ruskin

92   George Eliot

93   Elizabeth Gaskell

94   F.D. Maurice

95   Harriet Martineau

96   Henry Wadsworth Longfellow

97   Clement Wedgwood

FOURTH AND FIFTH
GENERATION DIRECTORS
OF THE ETRURIA WORKS

98   Godfrey Wedgwood

99   Laurence Wedgwood

100　　Cecil Wedgwood

101　　Francis Hamilton Wedgwood

102　　Kennard Laurence Wedgwood

103
Cecil Wedgwood, aged three
Oil by Emile Lessore, 1866

104
Mary Euphrasia Wedgwood,
aged six

105   The Upper House, Barlaston, built by Frank Wedgwood in 1845

106   Idlerocks, built by Godfrey Wedgwood in 1888

107
Cecil Wedgwood's coming-of-age party, Caverswall Castle, 1884

108
Cecil and Lucie Wedgwood in the garden at Idlerocks, 1890

109   Lord Farrer

110   Erasmus Alvey Darwin in old age,
c. 1879

111 Josiah C. Wedgwood and Meggie
Vaughan Williams, *c.* 1876

112 Godfrey Wedgwood *(right),* with Meggie Vaughan
Williams in Egypt, 1895; photographed by Effie
Farrer

113   Hope Wedgwood, Fanny Hensleigh Wedgwood
and Eva Mackintosh, with T.H. Farrer and his first
wife Fanny (*née* Erskine), at Abinger, *c.* 1871

114   Godfrey and Hope Wedgwood *(left and top right),*
Effie and Lord Farrer, *c.* 1890

115   Charles Darwin, 1868
Photograph by Julia Margaret Cameron

116   Emma Darwin, 1881

117   Frank Wedgwood

118   Hensleigh Wedgwood
Pencil drawings by Edward Clifford, 1882

119   Snow Wedgwood at her writing desk, *c.* 1896

120-121   Etruria in 1895: the ovens, and *(below)* the village

122   The Etruria works, 1895

spring of 1892 and now spent his time sorting through family letters and papers. He and Etty had raised the Victorian cult of illness to an art which often complicated other people's lives but simplified their own existence. One or the other of them was always ill—though never dangerously so. These mysterious illnesses protected them from unwelcome intruders and provided a convenient excuse for avoiding unpleasant duties. When she was thirteen and had a fever, a doctor had told Etty to have her breakfast in bed; she never had breakfast anywhere but in bed for the next seventy-one years.

During the Litchfields' visit to Idlerocks the unfortunate Margaret and Meggie came down with influenza, and Godfrey and Hope, the other pair of eternal invalids, were also ill. With guests and host and hostess all suffering from a variety of complaints and all confined to their rooms, the house must have seemed like a hospital. Twelve-year-old Mary wrote to her Aunt Snow that her mother was recovering from a fever and had '...draw'd a big bath the heat of the water being 30,000,000° of heat so that no one could come near her. That was on Tuesday. On the same day Father celebrated his fifty-ninth birthday by a swig too much claret, a dose of quinine and an extra meal, at least that was what I have been made to understand...'.[2]

The variety of illnesses and the range of cures were not always easy to understand. A Darwin niece described her Aunt Etty as

> always going away to rest, in case she might be tired later on in the day, or even the next day.... And when there were colds about she often wore a kind of gas-mask of her own invention. It was an ordinary wire kitchen-strainer, stuffed with antiseptic cotton-wool, and tied on like a snout, with elastic over her ears. In this she would receive her visitors and discuss politics in a hollow voice out of her eucalyptus-scented seclusion, oblivious of the fact that they might be struggling with fits of laughter.[3]

Richard Litchfield was a mild-mannered man whom, rightly or wrongly, Etty had decreed to be extremely delicate. Not one to argue, he obliged her. 'If the window had to be opened to air the room in cold weather,' the same niece recalled, 'Aunt Etty covered him up entirely with a dust sheet for fear of draughts; and he sat there as patient as a statue till he could be unveiled.'[4] Both indoors and outdoors, in winter and summer alike, both Litchfields draped themselves in scarves, chuddah shawls and rugs. A hot-water bottle was as necessary as an arm or a leg.

The hypochondria among the Wedgwoods and the Darwins bounced from one extreme to the other. Sometimes fresh air was let into the house at scheduled intervals and whatever the weather or the temperature; at other times, windows were sealed so that no contaminating foreign airs could enter during the entire winter. Sometimes daily exercise was required; at other times all forms of exercise were forbidden. Sometimes cold baths were taken twice daily; at other times baths were taken only once a week and then the temperature of the water had to be at least 75°F.

A month after their stay at Idlerocks the Litchfields' London house burned. They and their servants escaped without injury, but the house was gutted and they lost all their possessions. For two days after the fire they moved in with Snow in Gower Street. Then they left for The Grove in Cambridge.

Unlike the Litchfields, Emma at the age of eighty-four was in astonishingly good health. Though she had had infinite patience with Charles's invalidism and had virtually encouraged hypochondria and dependence in her own children, Emma was apparently annoyed by Litchfield's weakness and by Etty's precautions about his health. He also struck her as dull, and, however tolerant she might be in other matters, Emma did not suffer fools lightly. Furthermore, that he had so little interest in political matters was almost more than she could endure. She could not imagine how anyone could *not* open the post the moment it arrived each morning. His sitting quietly in the drawing room for an hour without bothering to look at *The Times* was beyond her understanding. Among the next generation she enjoyed the companionship of Snow far more than that of her daughter and son-in-law.

In 1894 Snow completed *The Message of Israel*, which was received politely by the critics and indifferently by the reading public. In the six years that had lapsed between publication of *The Moral Ideal* and *The Message of Israel*, the tastes and interests of the intelligentsia had changed. Snow was no longer in step with the times; her preoccupations were those of a generation now grown old. 'You asked me about *The Message of Israel*, 'Emma wrote to Etty; 'it did draw my attention to some sublime bits in the Prophets and Psalms, and I enjoyed her abuse of Esther.'[5]

Emma enjoyed it more than anyone else in the family. Effie and Hope thought the book tiresome and old-fashioned, but for once they refrained from giving Snow their criticisms. Snow went to Cambridge with the Litchfields for Christmas of 1894, to be with her Aunt Emma and all the Darwin brothers and their families. She wrote to Hope that Aunt Emma was the most active and remarkable eighty-six-year-old woman she had ever known. Her face was lined and her fingers gnarled with arthritis, but her eyes were the same clear, piercing blue, and her hair, with no touch of grey, was still the colour of tobacco leaves.

The Farrers spent the Christmas of 1894 at Idlerocks with, as Hope expressed it, 'all sorts & editions of children — real own — step — law — grand — and nieces and nephews with the addition of Mabel who comes under the category of children she is so cheerful and unparticular'. Mabel, Godfrey's youngest sister, adapted Hans Christian Andersen's story 'The Swineherd' as a play for the young people. The drama was so successful at Idlerocks (where the cast was larger than the audience) that the 'Wedgwood Players' performed it again at the local school for the villagers. Laurence's son Kennard was the swineherd. Clement's eighteen-year-old daughter Cecily was the Queen. Berry and Jem were courtiers, and fourteen-year-old Mary, said her mother, was 'a diminutive but outspoken Princess who enquired if we [the audience] heard the smacks of her twenty kisses to the swineherd Kennard'.

Laurence, Godfrey, Lily von Hafen and eleven of the young actors were being taken in a bus to the school, but 'when they got alongside the millpool the wheel slid on a sheet of ice dragging the horses back until they were all hanging over the water and the elders had a most unpleasant few minutes while the horses with great struggling managed to right the bus. Lily on the box had the full benefit. Those inside planning agonisedly how to poke children through the small windows.' But it all ended happily. The bus did not sink into the pond. No one was drowned. And, the show went on and was a great success. So much so that Hope joked to her Aunt Emma that they were thinking of 'apprenticing the children to the stage now that poor dear Pots are no longer profitable'.[6]

In 1894 the Wedgwood Pottery suffered another severe financial loss. There were now first cousins from three branches of the family involved in the business. With future generations the company would be divided even further. Though neither Frank nor Laurence's elder son Kennard was married, Cecil and Lucie already had two baby daughters, Phoebe, born in 1893, and Doris Audrey, born in 1894. Whether anyone in the next generation would have either aptitude for or interest in the pottery was a matter for speculation, unlikely to be answered for another quarter of a century. The family no longer seemed the cohesive unit it had appeared twenty-five years earlier. Nor did it seem likely that the business could continue much longer without making a profit. The arrangement of one son succeeding his father, and a perpetual three-way partnership of first cousins, then second cousins, then third cousins and so on through succeeding generations, no longer seemed as sensible as it had four years earlier.

In early 1895 the family agreed to the pottery being incorporated as Josiah Wedgwood & Sons, Ltd, a private company under the Limited Liability Act. The number of shareholders was limited to fifty, and shares could not be sold outside the family without first being offered to other members of the family. All of the shares were immediately and loyally taken up by the family. The company created £20,000 of 4 per cent mortgage debentures and authorized a capitalization of £100,000 — £33,000 in preferred shares and the balance in ordinary shares. Thus the pottery was still owned by the family, though actual ownership and management could be divided without changing the structure of the company. For the first time and, arguably, for the last time, the Wedgwood family acted in agreement and with responsible concern for the preservation of the heritage of the pottery and for its profitable continuation.

The timing of this major change in the structure of the Wedgwood company was symbolic and done in full awareness of its significance. The year 1895 was the centenary of the death of Josiah Wedgwood I. If the centenary of his birth had gone virtually ignored by his country and by his family, both had become more appreciative over the ensuing sixty-five years. The family and the factory received congratulations from all over the world — including a large floral tribute from a German customer accompanied by a letter expressing admiration for that 'truly excellent man Sir Josiah Wedgwood'. Such tangible good will and sincere appreciation prompted Hope to observe: 'One must acknowledge that some foreign ways are nicer than ours....'[7]

The *Staffordshire Advertiser*, which was celebrating its own centenary, published a special edition on Josiah Wedgwood and his achievements. The Wedgwood Company took a large advertisement in this special edition. 'We have made an exception in our rule of not advertising on this occasion and intend to do so every centenary 'till further notice,' Hope told her Aunt Emma, who was now the only surviving grandchild of Josiah I. 'All firms [Staffordshire potteries] that had been established over a century are advertising in it, and I am surprised to find how many there are.'[8]

Frederick Rathbone, a London antique dealer and private collector of Wedgwood, held an exhibition of Wedgwood in his Kensington shop. Pieces were displayed from his own collection and also borrowed from the collection of Sir Joseph and Lady Hooker. Many of the pieces were from the period of the first Josiah. The exhibition, however, ranged over a period of 150 years and included contemporary pieces for sale. Those who could not afford the old Wedgwood generally found a modern piece within their means and went away satisfied. The Rathbone exhibition attracted large crowds. Lady Hooker, who always gave modern vases and plaques as marriage presents, informed Godfrey that the Wedgwood displays at the Army & Navy Stores 'were so untastefully crowded that they did not look to advantage'.

Also timed to coincide with the centenary was a biography of Josiah Wedgwood by Samuel Smiles, who was then eighty-two years old and more satirized than respected in literary circles, though his books still commanded a substantial popular following. Smiles's biography highly offended the Wedgwood family. Hope was incensed that anyone should pay 'six shillings for that wretched twaddle'. The rest of the family agreed.

Godfrey and Hope and Effie began to pressure Snow to write an accurate account of their great-grandfather, but Snow said she no longer felt capable of the mental and physical exertion required for a major work. Her sisters felt that this was merely a temporary withdrawal after the disappointing reception given to *The Message of Israel*. Godfrey kindly and truthfully pointed out to her that after a quarter of a century her life of John Wesley was still the most admired of the numerous Wesley biographies.

In September of 1895 Snow went to spend a week at Down with her Aunt Emma. Leonard Darwin had been defeated in the general election of 1895. Joseph Hooker and Leonard Huxley had both been at Down acquiring material for works about their respective fathers. Emma, who was 'wonderfully well and cheerful', also encouraged Snow to write Josiah's biography. In her opinion a member of the family could be truthful without giving offence, whereas an outsider might be overly extravagant in praise or else unsuitably critical. Emma had never really forgiven Eliza Meteyard for implying that her Uncle Tom was insane. The Mayer – Meteyard papers which Godfrey had purchased at auction and given first to Hensleigh, who had then forwarded them to Emma, were also at Down. George Darwin had read them, and Hooker wrote to Godfrey that 'he [George] thinks there is a good deal of interest in them, especially connected with Josiah's early work'.[9]

Hooker and Godfrey had become close friends over the years, keeping up a steady correspondence. Hooker's interest in Wedgwood ware and Hope's interest in gardening cemented further a family friendship begun with Hooker's father and Charles Darwin. Hooker encouraged Hope to send to him at Kew samples of plants from Idlerocks for identification and naming. Like her Darwin relatives and her great-uncle John Wedgwood, Hope had a genuine talent for horticulture. She was forever importing exotic plants from various parts of the world.

Hooker had commissioned a new medallion of his father. Upon his return from Down in September of 1895, he found a letter from Godfrey accompanied by a box of medallions as a gift. Hooker replied: '... I wonder if it would be possible to restore the art — I feel sure that if people knew they could have a wax medallion likeness to be reprinted in Wedgwood ware, many would take advantage of it.'[10] Hooker also described to Godfrey a visit to Ipswich where he met the Egyptologist Flinders Petrie, who was soon going to Egypt again for further excavations. Godfrey was planning a cruise on the Nile, and Hooker thought he might like to meet Petrie in Egypt.

Egypt had been a source of fascination for educated Englishmen ever since the British invasion and occupation of the country in 1881. During the 1880s the firm of Thomas Cook & Sons provided a postal service as well as military transport between England and Egypt, and archaeologists such as Flinders Petrie and Howard Carter had taken advantage of this. French and German as well as British archaeologists had astounded the western world with the opening of the temples at Karnak and the tombs of Rameses and Queen Nefertiti, the wife of Amenhotep IV.

In the 1890s the most fashionable trip abroad that a wealthy European or American could take was the Nile cruise from Cairo through Luxor and Aswan to Wadi Halfa and back. This was a Cook's tour on a dahabeah, an Egyptian houseboat which could accommodate as many as eight passengers; the crew of twenty included a Reis or captain, a courier, a dragoman, two chefs, two waiters and a laundress.

In the winter of 1895-6, Godfrey, the Farrers, Margaret Vaughan Williams and twenty-six-year-old Meggie Vaughan Williams took a four-month Nile cruise and Egyptian tour, leaving England on 21 November 1895, and returning home again on 18 March 1896. As usual, the unadventurous Hope elected to remain behind in Staffordshire, but she requested that Godfrey, instead of writing letters, keep a journal which he could mail home at regular intervals with watercolour sketches he made of various scenes. She intended to have the journal bound as a book for the Idlerocks library and to frame some of the sketches. At the time of the Egyptian tour Godfrey was sixty-three and Theta Farrer seventy-eight years of age. Farrer, on the whole, stood up well to the physical demands of climbing through the ruins of Der el Bahari, Edfou and Silsilis, and of riding a camel through the hot desert for up to six hours at a time. Godfrey, fifteen years younger than Theta, suffered considerably with his leg and became quite lame.

The last pages of Godfrey's journal recorded their return through Italy to Lucerne and Basle.

At Basle we three elderly folk preferred a night's rest to a continuous

journey on. So the young and ever fresh Margarets went on in the thro'
train, getting to Leith Hill Place on Wednesday evening. We slept at
Hotel Euler.... Leaving at 10:30 a.m., we travelled very comfortably,
stopping every hour or so for twenty minutes to get dejeuner, dinner or
what not, and got to Calais about 1 a.m.... A fresh breeze awaited us &
the wretched little steamer jumped & tossed about the whole 2½ hours to
Dover. Fortunately we had not lost our sea legs & found on reaching
Dover that we had got thro' the night without seasickness. At Charing
Cross at 7:00 a.m. Thursday the 19th I bid farewell to the Farrers & feel-
ing very much of a wreck of our 4 months happy party, made my way to
Euston and home.[11]

During the summer of 1896 practically all of the Darwins and Wedgwoods
spent at least a few days at Down. The Litchfields, who were now living at
31, Kensington Square, surrounded by William Morris wallpaper and art
nouveau clutter, took Snow with them to Down for a week in August. Snow,
too, had moved from the large house in Gower Street to a much smaller
house in Lansdowne Road, Notting Hill.

The Farrers came over to Down from Abinger for two days. Hope and
Godfrey stopped overnight on their way back from Leith Hill Place, where
they had visited their other Wedgwood cousins, Margaret Vaughan
Williams and her sister Sophy Wedgwood. Sophy was now aged fifty-four,
unmarried and a recluse, with many of the bizarre symptoms that had
affected her mother before her spontaneous recovery. She dressed badly,
was very narrow in her sympathies and refused to eat properly. Having
developed a strange, squirrel-like habit of hiding biscuits, pieces of fruit
and other bits of food in cupboards and drawers throughout the house, she
would wait until everyone was seated at the dinner table, then tell the cook
to cancel the dinner and serve each person only a single orange. Even the
vegetarian Hope found this an irritation. Sophy had become so miserly that
she regularly went through the dustbins to see what her sister or the servants
had thrown out. Upon finding an old bottle of pills which Margaret, not
knowing what they were, had discarded, Sophy accused her of wastefulness.
When Margaret protested, Sophy popped all of the pills in her mouth
rather than have them go unused. Unfortunately they were a strong emetic.

Margaret's son, Ralph Vaughan Williams, had been at Trinity College,
Cambridge, with Clement's son Ralph Wedgwood. The two cousins became
close friends and with Ralph's brother, Felix Wedgwood, were frequent
visitors at the Darwin households in Cambrige as well as at Down in the
summer. After coming down from Cambridge, Ralph V.W. (whom the
Darwins thought had not the slightest talent for any instrument and ought
to be discouraged from his musical obsession) attended the Royal College of
Music, where his closest friend was another aspiring young composer,
Gustav Holst. Debussy, Delius and Elgar, all then in their thirties, were
their idols. In the summer of 1896 Ralph Vaughan Williams told his family
of his engagement to Adeline Fisher and of his plans for a lengthy honeymoon in Germany, where he would continue his musical studies. He was the
first Wedgwood, apart from his cousin Effie and his great-aunt Emma, to

show the slightest gift for music — and the only one to be greatly impressed that Emma had taken piano lessons with Chopin in Paris.

Emma, now well into her eighty-eighth year, still played the piano for her grandchildren, teaching them nursery tunes and her 'galloping songs'. Like her brothers Frank and Hensleigh, she was capable of enjoying her old age, and gave generously to those less fortunate than she. For some fifty years she had practised her own system of giving away penny bread-tickets to beggars and poor people who rang the doorbell at Down. These tickets were redeemable in bread at the village bakery. During the last few years, however, the number of requests for free bread-tickets had increased greatly, and in the spring of 1896 she was finally persuaded to discontinue the practice, which her sons believed encouraged tramps and vagrants to take advantage of her generosity and to make nuisances of themselves.

During the summer of 1896, when the whole family was in and out of the house at Down, the press was full of accounts of preparations for the Queen's Diamond Jubilee, which would take place the following summer. In direct contrast to the stodgy and ponderous *Times* was a new newspaper called the *Daily Mail*, selling for a half penny a copy. The 'gutter press' which concerned itself with crime and scandal and rousing patriotism captured the public's interest with as much fervour as the Evangelical literature had done half a century earlier. The trial, subsequent conviction and imprisonment of Oscar Wilde the year before had absorbed the attention of the whole country. Meanwhile church attendance, especially in the cities, was declining sharply. Sin — or the discussion of it — was far more popular than goodness and was openly acknowledged to be so.

Naturally Emma Darwin continued to read *The Times*, not the *Daily Mail*. In a critical mood, she was reading Henry James, Hardy and Shaw at alternating intervals in the morning, afternoon and evening of Sunday, 27 September 1896, when she was suddenly taken ill. On Monday she seemed to recover, made an entry in her diary and wrote a letter to an old friend. For over a decade now she had kept to the habit of writing a letter daily to one or other of her children, to various nephews and nieces, to old friends and to former servants. On Tuesday evening she had a relapse, and died without regaining consciousness on 2 October 1896.

The death of her Aunt Emma was a painful break with the past for Snow. No one was left in the generation that had preceded her. Now in her early sixties, she herself was among the oldest members of the family. Childless, she had neither past nor future to sustain her. The death after a long illness of her most intimate friend, Emily Gurney, grieved her deeply; they had drifted apart in their later years, and the mere sight of her letters to Emily, returned after her death, brought memories of a past heavily laden with pain. Snow was as bereft as she had been eight years earlier when Browning's letters were returned to her. Not one of the relationships in her life which had meant the most to her had turned out happily. The next event of personal importance to her seemed likely to be her own death. In an article on her life and literary career for an American women's magazine, she wrote that 'my life ought to have been so much more than it has been'.

Twenty-five years earlier, Emily had asked that Snow's letters be typed so that they might eventually be published, a scheme which Snow recalled 'with a tender smile' and no longer approved. There were six bound volumes of these, and a small case of letters which had been left unedited. Snow's first impulse was to burn them all without rereading them. But, as she glanced through them, her eye fell on several passages which still rang true and which stirred her writer's vanity: 'We love best when we need least.'[12] That was worth preserving. Or, on the comparison of pain and joy, 'I felt that pain should be something different — something hidden — something in which I was alone with God, not something that lowered the temperature all around me and chilled other lives. This has been a true description of my life — God grant it may not be so at the end.'[13]

Upon reading that sentiment, which seemed the more relevant with the end of her life so much nearer, she decided to edit the letters herself, not with any intention of publication but to be kept privately for Effie and Hope and for women of future generations whose sufferings might be lessened by the awareness of similar suffering on the part of one who had gone before. In the early part of 1897 Snow set herself to this task, beginning with a new introduction to the correspondence: 'To My Sisters of the Flesh and Spirit ... In reading what I have written after the interval of a generation I am penetrated afresh by the wonderful love which was not alienated by confidences as monstrous and depressing as many which I have committed to the flames, as some which I have set apart for possible perusal for a sympathetic reader warned of their contents, as one or two which I leave here....'[14]

While working on the letters, she began to feel unwell. She, who had none of the family hypochondria and had always had a seemingly endless reserve of energy, suffered a tiredness which did not abate however much she slept or rested. She curtailed her activities, seldom going out except with the Farrers. She continued to receive weekly a few members of her literary circle. Among them was C. H. Herford, Professor of English at Aberystwyth, and later her editor, as well as her close friend and confidant at this time.

In May she went to see a doctor whose diagnosis was 'a probable malignancy'. Her response was to reorganize her life with a view towards completing some of the tasks over which she had procrastinated. She determined to confront death 'as an actual need with reference to our work in this world' and thus not to come to it 'utterly unprepared with none of the habits of mind that are demanded for that gradual dying & yet cannot be wasted if we are spared that heavy trial!'[15]

Thus she declined to attend the Queen's Diamond Jubilee festivities to which the Farrers had invited her. Instead, on the very day that the celebrations began, she took a train north to Staffordshire. In an old valise which had belonged to her father were her letters to and from Robert Browning, Emily Gurney and Thomas Erskine. There were several bundles of letters to and from her Mackintosh grandfather, which her mother had saved. She also took the cardboard portfolios of Josiah Wedgwood's correspondence which Eliza Meteyard had organized and which George Darwin had given her, to encourage her to tackle a new Wedgwood biography. Well, she would tackle it. She would also try to put together for her niece Mary a comprehensive history of their family and its place in the history of the country that today was celebrating the greatest empire the world had known and the longest reign of any monarch in English history. For her own sake, Snow was returning to the country of her forebears to seek out her roots, and to make some historical sense of a life 'that ought to have been so much more than it has been'. That was the real purpose of the journey back to Staffordshire.

33

An Appreciable Trace
(1897)

Three days after Snow at Idlerocks had begun burning and sorting papers, Godfrey received a letter from Hope who, after the Jubilee festivities in London, had gone back to Abinger for several days with the Farrers. Young Mary also received in the same post a letter from her Aunt Effie. Both letters were read aloud over tea.

Effie said how delighted they were that Hope and Lily had come to London after all, when she and Theta really weren't expecting them. 'Our hearts did ache for want of you to enjoy the magnificence of the scene all together,' she told Mary.

> The beauty of the horses alone was a sight to be seen with joy — the fine men — the splendour of all the trappings and uniforms — cheers of the spectators especially at the fine Colonial troops — gradually increasing as the one hundred gorgeously clad 'equerries' including foreigners of all sorts — Indians were specially welcomed — rode in front of the sixteen Royal State carriages containing all the grandees — Colonial and Home ... and then the gravely moved, expressive face of the Queen. We saw deep feeling in her face and in the contrast of her black and white little old figure as an apex to all the splendour of the troops — it was most striking — she attempted no smile, no bow and her presence was all the more impressive for that ... the whole thing was far more splendid and moving than I ever imagined it could be and no one could doubt that there exists a very strong personal devotion to the Queen — not much misnamed by Lord Salisbury as 'Devotion.'[1]

Godfrey received in the same post the 22 June edition of *The Times*. From it he read aloud to Snow and Mary the letter delivered by Special Ambassador Whitelaw Reid to the Queen from the President of the United States. After expressing sincere felicitations from the American people to the Queen upon the sixtieth anniversary of her accession to the crown, the President concluded with: 'May liberty flourish throughout your Empire under just and equal laws, and your Government continue strong in the affections of all who live under it! and I pray that God may have your Majesty in his holy keeping. Your good friend William McKinley.' Godfrey thought the letter struck the right note of respect, appreciation and friendship. He was glad that he had been to America, seen Washington and visited the White House. This week he was particularly disappointed that he, the inveterate traveller and sightseer in the family, was unable to get to London for the Jubilee festivities—or, even more important, to see the naval review at Spithead on Saturday. Now it was impossible. He didn't want to be a burden to Hope or to the Farrers. He could only walk a few steps at a time with two sticks. Soon, he feared, he would have to have his right leg amputated—like his great-grandfather before him. Fortunately in this modern age there was chloroform.

Hope returned home on Friday, 27 June, while Effie and Farrer and Farrer's son Noel took one of twenty-eight special trains running from Waterloo to Portsmouth. They had bought tickets for the naval review at eighteen guineas each from Thomas Cook & Sons. Included in the price of the ticket was the train journey down and back, all meals and two nights aboard the 5,000 ton Union Castle passenger ship *Guelph*, which was a part of the fleet to be reviewed by the Prince of Wales. Effie complained that they had been given a second-class cabin with cockroaches when Cook's had assured them that all accommodations were first-class. Farrer was critical of the food and wine—certainly not up to the standard Cook's had provided on their dahabeah on the Nile. Noel told them both that 'you can never believe anything about a ship any more than about a horse'.[2]

In Staffordshire Snow, Hope and Godfrey compared Effie's description of the naval review with the report in *The Times*. Thousands of ordinary people who could not afford tickets watched from the shore in a line that extended for five miles. At some points the people stood from fifty to a hundred deep. The conditions under which they waited were far worse than Effie's second-class cabin on the *Guelph*. At an early hour in the morning of 26 June a storm raged. Thunder and lightning and torrents of rain delayed the opening proceedings. Many people on the shore took no shelter for fear of losing choice places they had established for themselves. At half-past nine the storm abated. The Prince of Wales and his party went out of the harbour in the Royal Yacht preceded by half a dozen small 'privileged boats' to make up the procession.

British war vessels gathered for the review numbered 173. They were arranged in four lines, each about five miles in length, along the anchorage between Portsmouth Harbour and the Isle of Wight. Outside were the other lines, one composed of warships sent by foreign powers and the other of special merchant vessels and passenger ships, such as the *Guelph*, which were crowded with guests and visitors. At the end of this row were half a dozen private yachts, the most impressive of which was owned by the flamboyant American entrepreneur Cornelius Vanderbilt. Effie wrote that 'The Prince of Wales must have got dreadfully tired of *God Save the Queen* taken up at each ship as he passed along the lines up and down but the ILLUMINATION—that was an eighteen guinea sight and no use trying to say a word about it!'[3] This was the most sophisticated display of fireworks ever held in England. Taking place over the dark water under a black sky where mist masked most of the stars, it was a spectacular ending to a spectacular occasion, the like of which would not be seen again.

The Victorian age was over. The Queen, now suffering from arthritis, sciatica and dim vision, again appeared on the balcony of Buckingham Palace in her wheelchair to receive the cheers from the crowd. She would 'soldier on' for four more years quite aloof from the forthcoming century with its experimental and expansive and sometimes vulgar ideas. For some it was still possible to pretend that this was the most perfect of imperfect worlds. Yet, in spite of the pomp and circumstance out front, behind the scenes the Government of England was (in the words of a later historian) 'headed by a couple of ageing recluses: an old Queen in her late seventies who could hardly see and hardly walk and a prematurely aged Prime Minister in his late sixties who was liable to fall asleep in the middle of framing a dispatch or a memorandum'.[4]

Snow saw herself as much of a recluse and an anachronism as were the Queen and Lord Salisbury. With a historical perspective which extended beyond the range of vision of other members of the Wedgwood family, she saw that the country and the world at large were changing. The days of power and of the glories of exotic empire were fading.

The Farrers and Godfrey and Hope still envisioned far-flung imperial adventures for the future. They were proud to have Cecil, Franky, Kennard and Berry serve as officers in the Boer War—though Godfrey wrote to Chamberlain that it would be convenient to have each returned after a year of active duty and to make certain that all were not abroad at one time. Someone, understandably according to the family's needs, had to stay at home and manage the pottery.

Almost symbolically, it seemed, the Wedgwood Company was not only sliding backward in terms of profits but the factory itself was literally sliding into the ground. At exactly the time of the Jubilee, the Etruria works, which were situated over a coal mine, began to subside. Part of the factory sank below the level of the canal which passed in front of it. Wedgwood was the most famous and prestigious pottery in the world, yet just below the surface were dangerous faults which might cause either a dramatic collapse or a gradual decline.

In the late summer afternoons Snow rested in the lovely garden at Idlerocks with Hope and Godfrey and Mary. Godfrey read Kipling's 'Recessional' to them. Next month Lily was taking Mary up to London to see a revival of the D'Oyly Carte production of Gilbert and Sullivan's *H.M.S. Pinafore*. Mary's life was all before her. What new, world-shattering events—like Uncle Charles's theory of evolution—would occur in her life time and influence the next century Snow could barely imagine. The Wedgwood family was no longer the closely knit entity it had seemed in Snow's childhood; there was no longer a loyal and important and influential circle of friends as there had been in the time of her parents and grandparents. Her beloved friend Browning long ago had written: 'Time's wheel runs back and stops; Potter and clay endure.' Perhaps this was so.

She would not burn Browning's letters or hers to him no matter what sinister interpretation a future generation might place upon them. Only letters which might cause pain or embarrassment she could and would destroy. To please Effie and Hope, she had started to write the biography of their great-grandfather. To please herself, she had begun to sort and put aside notable letters, drawings and photographs to be preserved in the scrapbook for Mary.

Two months later Snow had selected all of the letters and portraits and illustrations for the first volume of a two-volume scrapbook, which she annotated with her own recollections. The Preface, which she wrote in purple ink, began:

> My dearest Child, the collection which I here offer you is one of heterogeneous interest. It contains all letters in my possession which throw light upon the experience or character of those persons among our friends or kindred who have left an appreciable trace on our lives or the life of the world. The gathering thus made covers a space of more than a century, starting with a letter from your Great-Great-Grandfather, and closing with some which may revive your own earliest recollections.... I have had much pleasure, mixed with some sadness, in arranging the volume for you & I like to think that you may one day read it with some share in the former feeling and only that faint tinge of the latter which I can hardly desire to be absent from the perusal of records touching on the hopes, disappointments and regrets of those who have passed away. Even at the distant date when you will fully understand these words, I shall remain, my dearest child, your loving Aunt,
>
> FRANCES JULIA WEDGWOOD[5]

It was the best legacy she could give to a new generation in a changing world.

Epilogue

Snow did not complete the second volume of the Scrapbook. But her encounter with death was not as near at hand as she had supposed during the glamorous, fading summer of the Diamond Jubilee. She lived on for sixteen more years, dying in London on 26 November 1913, at the age of eighty. Though she underwent successfully an operation for the cancer she so feared, the last years of her life were clouded by slowly encroaching blindness. This, coupled with her deafness, meant she was isolated even more from those she loved and from the world of books in which she had found so much solace throughout her life.

Her surviving brother, Ernest Hensleigh, died in August of 1898 at the age of sixty-one, after a long illness of the sort that Snow had feared for herself. His three sisters helped to educate his young son Allen at Marlborough, though they had little to do with his widow, Mary.

Godfrey's right leg was amputated below the knee in 1898. Like his great-grandfather Josiah, he was fitted with a wooden leg. The workmen of the Etruria factory presented him with a handsome address, illuminated in gold, on their sincere joy at his recovery. He wrote to them that he was touched by their kindness to him during his life-long ill health and that he was particularly gratified by this last expression of their concern since he had ceased to have any active connection with the Etruria factory ten years before.

That you should still feel so kindly towards me and shew me the signal mark of your sympathy and esteem is a circumstance that both touches me and makes me feel proud. I had hoped to invite you here this summer, and to thank you by word of mouth, but I have not been and am not yet, well enough to entertain so large a party, for though I am in better health than before my illness, I am much disabled by the loss of my leg — a loss which entitles me to the same nickname my great-grandfather was known by on the works, viz, 'Owd Woodenleg'. In the meantime it has occurred to my wife that a photograph, taken of me on the first occasion on which I rose from my bed after the amputation, might

352

be acceptable to you and serve as a small token of the connection begun forty-eight years ago, and the friendly feelings it has bred between us....[1]

Godfrey drew amusing caricatures of himself as 'Owd Woodenleg' for his young granddaughters Phoebe and Audrey. His brother-in-law and old rival, Lord Farrer, died peacefully in 1899 at the age of eighty-one. Shortly afterwards Effie came to Idlerocks to live with Hope and Godfrey and Mary, the three people who, next to her Uncle Ras, had loved her the most.

In 1901, after both Cecil and Frank had served for more than two years in South Africa, the Etruria factory suffered a net loss of over £6,000. From Cape Town Cecil wrote to his father:

I need not say how bitter has been my disappointment in Etruria not paying. Not only this loss of income & my feeling that whatever you have done for me I have still been an expense to you, but more the feeling that the old firm of which we are all proud and fond should have suffered during my time there. You know I have not shirked my work, any more than the others have, but one blow after another has struck us, the sinking, the bad times, the lead question [poisoning among the workmen from handling lead glaze], until I begin to despair of ever making things go well.... Of course I speak positively without figures before me, but I am inclined to feel that we should stop before we lose more money and before we are too old to take up something else.... I hate giving in and confessing that we cannot make the Works go, but these are the facts & I see very little prospect of altering things.[2]

Godfrey, Effie, and Clement's sons Ralph and Josiah Clement, all of whom had taken shares in the company, persuaded Cecil and Frank and Kennard to carry on for a few more years even if the pottery made a loss. Each of the three directors then agreed to forgo his annual salary of £500 until the factory became profitable. In 1904 the company showed a small profit—but continued on a marginal or fluctuating profit—loss basis for the next decade, until the expanding economy in America began to provide a steady market.

Godfrey never saw the turn-about in the company's fortunes. He died in 1905 at the age of seventy-three and was buried near Idlerocks in the churchyard at Moddershall. On his tombstone are the words, '... with thankfulness for the example of a character shining with the light of unselfish love ... "Neither shall there be any more pain." Rev.XXI.'

His brother Laurence died in 1913, a fortnight after he and his nephew Frank had welcomed King George V and Queen Mary to the works. Six years earlier Kennard had gone to America to establish a branch office of Wedgwood in New York.

In the Great War, both young Allen Wedgwood, aged twenty-two, and Cecil, then aged fifty-two and a major in the Army, were killed in France. Cecil's death was a severe blow to the pottery. His widow Lucie joined the board of directors; his daughter Audrey took on the job of company secretary, and his cousin Frank succeeded him as managing director.

At Leith Hill Place Sophy Wedgwood's behaviour grew more eccentric. She suffered several seizures and spent the last few years of her life in a helpless, mindless state. In fine weather a nurse would wheel her into the garden in her Bathchair, then lift her head so that she might see the daffodils. Sadly, her niece Meggie Vaughan Williams, who had shown so much zest for life on the Egyptian cruise and who had helped her brother Ralph to establish the Leith Hill Music Festival, suffered a similar fate. She died in 1931, having retreated both physically and mentally from the active world a decade earlier.

Her brother Ralph Vaughan Williams became the most outstanding English composer of the first half of the twentieth century. He broke with the German tradition which had dominated British music for the past two centuries, establishing a purely English style inspired by native folk-songs. In 1944, after the death of his brother Hervey, he inherited Leith Hill Place, which he gave to the National Trust. His cousin and close friend Ralph Wedgwood, who was chairman of the Railway Executive, applied for the tenancy and was accepted. Ralph's brother Josiah Clement Wedgwood represented Newcastle-under-Lyme in Parliament for thirty-five years, first as a Liberal, then as a Labour and finally as an Independent Member. Two years before he died, he was elevated to the House of Lords as Lord Wedgwood of Barlaston.

On the Darwin side of the family, three of Emma and Charles's five sons—George, Francis and Horace—became eminent scientists, were elected Fellows of the Royal Society and given knighthoods. William was a successful banker and Leonard, after abandoning his political career, became president of the Royal Geographical Society and of the Eugenic Society.

Snow Wedgwood did not finish the biography of her great-grandfather, though she worked on it intermittently up until the time of her death. It was completed by her editor and friend, C. H. Herford, and published two years later with a memoir of her as a Preface. Honoured and respected in her time, she outlived her fame. Although *The Moral Ideal* went into a second edition in 1908, her reputation as a novelist, literary critic and historian diminished in the twentieth century where, in truth, she was something of an anachronism. And she knew it. In spite of her mysticism, her endless intellectual searching and her romantic idolization of a series of father-figures and beautiful young women, her real passions were for righteousness and truth. Her great-grandfather, grandfather and father would have approved of those sentiments, if not always their expression. The first Josiah would certainly have been dismayed at her leaving a large share of her considerable fortune to the Anti-Vivisection League—a dismay shared by some later relatives as well.

In her final years, as illness and old age began to draw around her, she seldom went anywhere or saw anyone apart from her family and a few close friends. She spent more time at Idlerocks with her widowed sisters Effie and Hope, over whom she effused with expressions of love which seem quite astonishing to later generations. At her death, and according to her wishes, she was cremated and her ashes interred at Moddershall parish church beside Godfrey. On the headstone of her grave are the words: 'Her words spoken or written enlightened and consoled many hearts.' The Biblical verse on the headstone is 'Thou hast chastened me sore but has not given me over unto death.'

The first volume of the Scrapbook which she had so lovingly put together for the young Mary Euphrasia found its way into the library at Idlerocks where little Wedgwood cousines of the fifth, sixth and seventh generations were occasionally allowed to take it from the shelf and to turn its pages carefully. Effie and Hope both lived to the venerable age of ninety-one. They did not lose their interest in the occult, continuing to hold seances at Idlerocks and providing an intriguing topic of gossip for their more earthbound neighbours.

Like Snow and many of their Allen ancestors, Effie and Hope became quite deaf in their old age. Both used ear trumpets with long black, snakelike tubes. When the mouthpiece of the tube was thrust into an unsuspecting hand with the command, 'Say something!', younger members of the family were often frightened clean out of their wits.

In the Great War Mary went to Italy, where she worked for the Red Cross, running a canteen and meeting hospital trains coming from the front. She was awarded a Croce al Merito di Guerra and an M.B.E. This was the happiest period of her life. When she returned, it was to a suffocating routine of leisure, duty and good works—to which she was ill suited. She did not marry until after her mother's death, when she herself was in her sixties. Then, like many of her predecessors, she married a cousin, Will Mosley, a relative of her paternal grandmother, Fanny Mosley. It was not a happy marriage.

For most of her life Mary remained the lonely, lost child, out of step with the times. As her Aunt Snow, that most Victorian of Victorian women, had foreseen, changes for better or worse would occur. What Snow wrote about the drawbacks of the intellectual life in the late nineteenth century is equally applicable to the business world in the late twentieth century. 'It is surely a good thing to remember that when you are going towards the North, you must not expect the productions of the South ... indeed, it is a part of the condition of things, in this tangled and imperfect world, that whatever shuts out much evil must shut out some good.'[3]

During the late 1920s and early 1930s, four cousins, all great-great-great grandsons of Josiah I, joined the staff at Etruria and eventually became directors of the company. After Frank's sudden death of a throat infection, in London in 1930, Kennard became chairman of the company as well as continuing as president of the American subsidiary. Times were changing. The eighteenth-century workshops were no longer adequate for the needs of the twentieth century, and there was no room for expansion. The factory suffered from atmospheric pollution and mining subsidence from near-by collieries. The buildings had sunk eight feet below the level of the canal.

The example of the first Josiah was followed by his fifth-generation descendants. A new factory was built six miles away on 500 acres of parkland near the village of Barlaston. Opened in 1940, this factory was as innovative for its time as Etruria had been 171 years earlier. If Watt's steam engine had seemed revolutionary then, so indeed was the introduction into the British pottery industry of firing the wares electrically in tunnel ovens.

The Second World War brought a turn-about in the company's fortunes. Increased export sales once again made the pottery profitable. After the war, however, the world changed permanently. Neither industry nor the country itself could successfully return to the way it had been. Old institutions, old methods, old attitudes were superseded by new technology, marketing and management. The first Josiah Wedgwood would have anticipated the changes and approved.

In 1967 Wedgwood changed from a private to a public company listed on the London Stock Exchange. The following year, the managing director, Sir Arthur Bryan, became the first chairman of Wedgwood who was not a direct descendant of Josiah Wedgwood I. When the Ivy House works began in 1759, Josiah I employed 15 workmen; a decade later, when the Etruria works opened, 300 workmen were employed. Now, more than two centuries later, Wedgwood — once a family business employing 1,500 people — has become the largest ceramic tableware group in the world, employing more than 10,500 people. Barlaston is one of the largest, most modern factories of its type in the world today.

Nothing but the 'Round House' remains of the old Etruria factory, which was sold to industrial developers. Etruria Hall, now an office building, stands alone as a solitary reminder of an age past. The Etruria gardens, of which Josiah I and his son John were so proud, are slag heaps from a near-by colliery. The Etruria Grange is a sludge pool used by an iron works.

Wedgwood, a legendary name, endures. Old patterns, old shapes, the old back-stamps continue, even though there are no longer any of the family in the active management of the company. What remains of the Wedgwoods, who left an appreciable trace on the history of their country, are pictures, books, letters and pots — all 'records touching on the hopes, disappointments and regrets of those who have passed away'.

Notes on Sources

Unless otherwise stated, all documents cited are in the Wedgwood Archives at the University of Keele. The following abbreviations have been used for sources cited frequently:

<blockquote>

CFL H. E. Litchfield, *Emma Darwin: A Century of Family Letters*, 2 vols. (Cambridge, 1904).

Group Eliza Meteyard, *A Group of Englishmen* (1871)

Life Eliza Meteyard, *The Life of Josiah Wedgwood from his private correspondence and family papers*, 2 vols. (1865)

LS Robert E. Schofield, *The Lunar Society of Birmingham* (Oxford, 1963)

RB/JW *Robert Browning and Julia Wedgwood*, ed. Richard Curle (New York, 1937)

SL *Selected Letters of Josiah Wedgwood*, ed. Ann Finer and George Savage (1965)

UC Julia Wedgwood and Emily Gurney, Unpublished Correspondence, 5 vols.

</blockquote>

Place of publication is London unless otherwise indicated. The family Scrapbook, cited frequently, is unpaginated.

  W = Wedgwood   JW = Josiah Wedgwood

PROLOGUE

1 UC,III, 81.
2 Quoted Julia W, *Nineteenth Century Teachers and Other Essays* (1909), 328.

1. IN THE BEGINNING

1 Quoted *Life*, I, 265.
2 ibid., 22.
3 Josiah C. W, *The Wedgwood Family History, 1299-1908* (1908), 123.
4 Preface to First Experiment Book.

2. EXPANDING HORIZONS

1 JW to T. Bentley, 15 May 1762.
2 ibid., 26 Oct. 1762.
3 ibid., 16 June 1763.

4   JW to John W, 11 Nov. 1763.
5   JW to T. Bentley, 9 Jan. 1764.
6   ibid.
7   ibid., 23 Jan. 1764.
8   ibid., 17 Oct. 1767.
9   JW to John W, 17 June 1765.
10 ibid.
11 JW to T. Bentley, 2 Aug. 1765.

3. CANALS AND CLAYS

1   Joseph Banks's Journal: quoted *Journal of Royal Society of Arts*, May 1975, 375.
2   JW to John W, 11 Mar. 1765.
3   Quoted *LS*, 41.
4   JW to R. Griffiths, 11 Mar. 1765; quoted *Life*, I, 363.
5   JW to T. Bentley, 7 Oct. 1765.
6   ibid., 15 Oct. 1765.
7   ibid., 26 Sept. 1765.
8   ibid., 11 Nov. 1765.
9   JW to John W, 4 June 1766.
10 JW to T. Bentley, 25 Sept. 1766.
11 ibid., 19 Sept. 1766.
12 ibid., 12 Sept. 1772.
13 ibid., 22 Feb. 1768.
14 ibid., 2 Mar. 1767.
15 ibid.
16 ibid., undated, prob. May 1767.
17 ibid.
18 ibid., 17 July 1767.
19 Quoted *LS*, 61.
20 JW to T. Bentley, 20 May 1767.
21 ibid.
22 ibid., 31 May 1767.
23 ibid.

4. A TIME OF CRISES

1   JW to T. Bentley, 13 June 1767.
2   ibid., 14 June 1767.
3   JW to R. Griffiths, 4 July 1767.
4   JW to T. Bentley, 26 July 1767.
5   ibid.
6   ibid., 5 Aug. 1767.
7   Quoted *Life*, II, 56.
8   Quoted A. Moilliet, *Sketch of the Life of James Keir* (1868), 46.
9   J. Leslie, unpub. MS biography of JW.
10 JW to T. Bentley, 10 Nov. 1767.
11 ibid., 24 Dec. 1767.
12 ibid., 15 Mar. 1768.
13 ibid., 24 Mar. 1768.
14 ibid.
15 Quoted *Life*, II, 56.
16 P. Swift to W. Cox, 31 May 1768.

17   Quoted *Life*, II, 41.
18   ibid., 42.
19   JW to T. Bentley, 20 June 1768.
20   ibid., ? June 1768.
21   ibid., 20 Nov. 1768.
22   ibid., 11 Feb. 1769.

5. THE ETRUSCAN ARTS ARE REBORN.

1   JW to T. Bentley, 9 Apr. 1769.
2   ibid., 27 Sept. 1769.
3   ibid., 1 Oct. 1769.
4   ibid., 2 Jan. 1770.
5   ibid.
6   ibid., 29 Dec. 1769.
7   ibid., 1 Jan. 1770
8   ibid., 15 Jan. 1770.
9   ibid., 3 Sept. 1770.
10   ibid.
11   ibid., 11 May 1771.
12   ibid., 26 Sept. 1769.
13   Quoted H. W. Dickinson, *Matthew Boulton* (Cambridge, 1937), 81.
14   Quoted S. Smiles, *Josiah Wedgwood* (1895), 82.
15   JW to T. Bentley, 26 Dec. 1770.

6. THE LUNAR CIRCLE

1   R. L. Edgeworth, *Memoirs* (1820).
2   JW to T. Bentley, 2 Mar. 1769.
3   ibid., 18 Sept. 1772.
4   ibid., 26 Dec. 1772.
5   ibid., 16 Mar. 1773.
6   *Wedgwood's Letters to Bentley*, ed. K. E. Farrer (1903), II, 134.
7   ibid., 156.
8   Quoted G. C. Williamson, *The Imperial Russian Dinner Service* (1909), 33.
9   JW to T. Bentley, 3 Sept. 1774.
10   ibid., 10 Nov. 1774.
11   J. Priestley, *Autobiography* (Bath, 1970), 78.
12   JW to T. Bentley, 14 June 1773.
13   ibid., 18 June 1773.
14   ibid., 21 June 1773.
15   Quoted *LS*, 116.
16   ibid., 117.
17   ibid., 36.

7. A SEED OF CONSEQUENCE

1   Quoted *LS*, 137.
2   JW to T. Bentley, 5 Nov. 1775.
3   Quoted 'Josiah Wedgwood's Journey into Cornwall', ed. Geoffrey Wills, *Proceedings of the Wedgwood Society*, II (1957), 95.
4   ibid., I (1956), 37.
5   ibid., II, 85.
6   ibid., II, 95.

7   ibid., I, 57.
8   JW to T. Bentley, 26 Aug. 1769.
9   ibid., ? Apr. 1778.
10 ibid., 7 Sept. 1776.
11 ibid., 19 Mar. 1778.
12 ibid., 7 Sept. 1776.
13 Susannah W to Mrs JW, 23 June 1777 (Down Archives).
14 Susannah W to JW, 27 Dec. 1777 (Down Archives).
15 Quoted E. Krause, *Erasmus Darwin* (1879), 102.
16 ibid., 115
17 JW to T. Bentley, 12 May 1778.
18 ibid., 22 June 1778.
19 ibid., 28 July 1778.
20 ibid., 24 Aug. 1778.
21 ibid., 19 Aug. 1778.
22 ibid.
23 ibid., 24 Aug. 1778.
24 ibid., 5 May 1778.
25 ibid.,10 Sept. 1778.
26 ibid., 6 Oct. 1778.
27 ibid.
28 ibid., 25 Feb. 1779.
29 ibid., 3 July 1779.
30 ibid., 19 Dec. 1779.
31 R. L. Edgeworth to JW, 10 May 1779.
32 JW to T. Bentley, 21 Oct. 1780.
33 R. Griffiths to JW, 25 Nov. 1780.

8. WEDGWOOD AFTER BENTLEY

1   Quoted R. Bentley, *Thomas Bentley, 1730-1780* (1827), 83.
2   JW II, unpub. notes for a biography of Thomas W.
3   JW to J. Watt, 15 May 1782.
4   Quoted J. Thomas, *Josiah Wedgwood as a Pioneer of Steam Power in the Pottery Industry* (*Transactions of the Newcomen Society*, 1936), 15.
5   Quoted *LS*, 250.
6   ibid., 251.
7   Quoted I. B. Hart, *James Watt and the History of Steam Power* (1958), 200.
8   JW to J. Watt, 17 Sept. 1785.

9. THE POWER AND THE GLORY

1   R. L. Edgeworth to JW, 20 Mar. 1786.
2   Quoted R. L. Edgeworth, *Memoirs*,
3   Quoted *Group*, 204.
4   JW to R. L. Edgeworth, 24 Dec. 1786.
5   Quoted *LS*, 215.
6   ibid.
7   Quoted *Correspondence of Josiah Wedgwood*, ed. K. E. Farrer (1906), 14.
8   Quoted *Life*, II, 577.
9   Quoted Julia W, *The Personal Life of Josiah Wedgwood* (1915), 175.
10 John W to JW, 23 Nov. 1786.
11 ibid., 3 Dec. 1786.
12 Quoted Julia W, *Personal Life*, 244n.

13   JW to M. Boulton, 23 Feb. 1787.
14   Quoted S. Smiles, *Josiah Wedgwood*, 309.
15   JW II to JW, 3 Mar. 1788.
16   Quoted H. Pearson, *Dr Darwin* (1930), 206.
17   ibid., 204.
18   ibid., 215.

10. WEDGWOOD, SONS & BYERLEY

1   John W to JW, 26 Apr. 1788.
2   JW II to JW, 7 June 1790.
3   ibid., 12 Apr. 1791.
4   Quoted *SL*, 325.
5   Quoted R. B. Litchfield, *Tom Wedgwood* (1903), 11-12.
6   Quoted I. B. Hart, *James Watt*, 222.
7   JW to E. Darwin, ? July 1789.
8   Quoted *LS*, 361.
9   JW II to JW, 20 July 1791.
10   Quoted S. Smiles, *Josiah Wedgwood*, 269-70.
11   JW to R. L. Edgeworth, ? Oct. 1791.
12   JW II to JW, 20 Aug. 1792; quoted *Correspondence of Josiah Wedgwood*,
      ed. K. E. Farrer, 202.
13   JW to John W, 17 June 1793.
14   JW to T. Byerley, 14 Dec. 1792.
15   Quoted D. King-Hele, *Erasmus Darwin* (New York, 1963), 26.
16   E. Darwin to JW; quoted *Life*, II, 610.

11. THE THREE BROTHERS

1   E. Darwin to R. L. Edgeworth, ? Feb. 1795.
2   Tom W, Journal.
3   Tom W to JW II, 12 Aug. 1799; quoted R.B. Litchfield, *Tom Wedgwood*, 5.
4   R. Southey to Tom W, 12 July 1799; quoted *Group*, 85.
5   Tom W, Report; quoted R. B. Litchfield, op. cit., 38-9.
6   Quoted M. O. Tremayne, *The Value of a Maimed Life* (1912), 41.
7   Tom W to JW II, April 1799; quoted *Group*, 109.
8   T. Beddoes to Tom W, 12 Nov. 1799; quoted R. B. Litchfield, op. cit., 36.

12. A PROMISE UNFULFILLED

1   JW II to Tom W, 28 Feb. 1800; quoted *Group*, 86.
2   Catherine W to Tom W, 14 Mar. 1800.
3   John W to Tom W, 14 Mar 1800.
4   JW II to John W, May 1800.
5   John W to JW II, July 1800.
6   ibid.
7   Quoted *Group*, 28.
8   J. Leslie to Tom W, 10 Feb. 1800; quoted R. B. Litchfield, *Tom Wedgwood*,
      81-4.
9   T. Poole to JW II, 10 Sept. 1800.
10   M. Baillie to JW II, 3 Apr. 1802.
11   R. Darwin to Tom W, 9 Apr. 1802.
12   S. T. Coleridge to Tom W, 3 Nov. 1802.
13   Quoted Mrs H. Sandford, *Thomas Poole and His Friends* (1888), II, 116.

14   Catherine W to Tom W, undated (1803).
15   Tom W to JW II, ?20 Dec. 1802.
16   S. T. Coleridge to Tom W, undated, prob. February 1803.
17   ibid., 17 Feb. 1803; quoted Joseph Cottle, *Reminiscences of Samuel Taylor Coleridge and Robert Southey* (1847), 464.
18   Tom W to T. Poole, 29 Aug. 1803.
19   S. T. Coleridge to Tom W, 27 Jan. 1804.
20   Quoted M. O. Tremayne, *Value of a Maimed Life*, 57.
21   ibid., Introduction.
22   Tom W to JW II, 15 May 1804.
23   ibid.
24   Tom W to JW II, undated, prob. January 1805.

13. HIS BROTHER'S KEEPER

1   Sir J. Mackintosh to JW II, 28 Feb. 1806.
2   JW II to Sir J. Mackintosh, 7 Feb. 1807.
3   JW II to Tom W, 13 May 1805.
4   T. Byerley to JW II, February 1802.
5   JW II To Sir J. Mackintosh, 16 Sept. 1805.
6   Sir J. Mackintosh to JW II, 28 Feb. 1806.
7   T. Byerley to JW II, 4 Jan. 1808.
8   Quoted E. Krause, *Erasmus Darwin*, 79.
9   Quoted Mrs H. Sandford, *Thomas Poole and His Friends*, II, 219.
10   JW II to R. L. Edgeworth, ? May 1807.
11   Bessy W to JW II, 27 July 1810.
12   ibid., ?25 July 1810.
13   ibid., 31 July 1810.

14. THIS EVIL DESTINY

1   John W to JW II, 13 Aug. 1810.
2   ibid., 25 Aug. 1810.
3   ibid., 15 Sept. 1810.
4   Jane W to JW II, 28 Sept. 1810.
5   John W to JW II, 2 Oct. 1810.
6   ibid.
7   J. Byerley to JW II, 1 Dec. 1810.
8   John W to JW II, 19 May 1811.
9   J. Byerley to JW II, 29 Feb. 1812.
10   John W to JW II, 19 Sept. 1811.
11   Draft of letter, JW II to John W, ? Nov. 1811.
12   John W to JW II, 16 Nov. 1811.
13   JW II, to John W, 26 Nov. 1811.
14   John W to JW II, 24 Nov. 1811.
15   JW II to John W, 7 Dec. 1811.
16   John W to JW II, 11 Dec. 1811.

15. THE GAME OF LIFE

1   John W to JW II, 1 Sept. 1813.
2   Bessy W to JW II, 25 July 1812.
3   JW II to JW III, 5 Nov. 1811.
4   JW III to JW II, undated, prob. January 1812.

5   JW II to JW III, 28 Nov. 1811.
6   D. Wordsworth to JW II, 30 Mar. 1813.
7   Quoted R. Mackintosh, *Life of Sir James Mackintosh* (1836), II, 262.
8   Jessie Allen to Elizabeth W, 31 July 1813; quoted *CFL*, I, 52.
9   ibid.
10   Quoted R. Mackintosh, op. cit., 264.
11   ibid., 267.
12   Quoted E. Hubbard, *Little Journeys to the Homes of Famous Women* (New York, 1897), 214.
13   Quoted *CFL*, I, 50.
14   ibid., 51.
15   Quoted R. Mackintosh, op. cit., 269.
16   Quoted *CFL*, I, 59-60.
17   ibid., 55.
18   ibid., 62.

16. RETURN TO ETRURIA

1   R. Darwin to JW II, 28 Aug. 1813.
2   JW II to R. Darwin, 23 Aug. 1813.
3   R. Darwin to JW II, 28 Aug. 1813.
4   JW II to R. Darwin, 23 Aug. 1813.
5   ibid., 1 Sept. 1813.
6   Sarah W to JW II, undated, prob. autumn 1813 or 1814.
7   Quoted *CFL*, I, 6.
8   ibid., 86.
9   Quoted R. Mackintosh, *Sir James Mackintosh*, II, 313.
10   JW III to JW II, 13 Dec. 1814.
11   ibid.

17. NEW WAYS FOR OLD

1   M.B. Synge, *A Short History of Social Life in England* (1908), 324.
2   Scrapbook: C. Rich to Mary Rich, undated, prob. 11 Mar. 1815.
3   John W to JW II, 5 May 1815.
4   JW II to John W, 29 July 1815.
5   Susan Darwin to JW II, 21 Nov. 1815.
6   ibid.
7   John W to G. Templer, 16 Sept. 1815.
8   Bessy W to Fanny Allen, 3 Jan. 1816.
9   Bessy W to Emma Allen, 24 Feb. 1816; quoted *CFL*, I, 122.
10   JW III to JW II, 20 Aug. 1816.
11   JW II to John W, 2 Mar. 1816.
12   John W to JW II, 29 May 1816.
13   JW II to John W, 29 May 1816.
14   Sarah W to JW II, undated, prob. July 1816.
15   Jane W to JW II, 14 Aug. 1816; quoted *CFL*, I, 128.
16   Bessy W to her sisters, 22 Aug. 1816; quoted ibid., 130-1.

18. A WISE AND MASTERLY INACTIVITY

1   JW II to R. Darwin, 1 Mar. 1817.
2   Scrapbook: Sir J. Mackintosh to R. L. and Maria Edgeworth, undated, prob. second week of June 1817.

3   Catherine W to JW II, 13 July 1817.
4   Sarah W to JW II, dated 'Thursday', prob. 16 July 1817.
5   Draft of letter, JW II to R. Darwin, 17 July 1817.
6   JW II to R. Darwin, 3 July 1817.
7   Quoted R. Mackintosh, *Sir James Mackintosh*, II, 352.
8   ibid., 358.
9   Elizabeth W to Fanny Allen, undated, prob. latter part of 1817.
10   Jessie Allen to Bessy W, 1 Dec. 1818; quoted *CFL*, I, 161.
11   Bessy W to Jessie Allen, 6 Dec. 1818; quoted ibid., 163-4.
12   Quoted E. Inglis-Jones, 'A Pembrokeshire County Family in the Eighteenth
     Century', *Journal of the National Library of Wales*, XVII (1971/2), no. 2,
     236-7.
13   Bessy W to Jessie Sismondi, 16 May 1820.
14   Quoted C. M. Alexander, *Baghdad in Bygone Days* (1928), 297.
15   Sarah W to JW II, undated, prob. autumn 1820.
16   ibid., undated, prob. November or December 1820.
17   ibid., 7 June 1821.
18   John W to JW II, 7 Oct. 1820.
19   JW II to John W, 17 Feb. 1821.
20   Bessy W to JW II, 17 Apr. 1821.
21   Bessy W to Jessie Sismondi, 8 Apr. 1822.
22   Sarah W to JW II, dated only 'Shrewsbury, Tuesday', prob. the first week in
     August 1823.

19. ADVANCED CHRISTIANS

1   Bessy W to Elizabeth W, 7 Mar. 1824; quoted *CFL*, I, 202.
2   Scrapbook: Footnote to a letter from Lady Mackintosh to Emma Allen,
     October 1802.
3   Jessie Sismondi to Bessy W, 28 Jan. 1824; quoted *CFL*, I, 199.
4   Quoted ibid., 254-5.
5   ibid., 210-11.
6   Bessy W to Fanny Allen, 6 Oct. 1824.
7   Quoted *CFL*, I, 294.
8   ibid., 231.
9   ibid., 224.
10   ibid., 242.
11   ibid., 269.
12   ibid., 287.
13   Scrapbook: Sir J. Mackintosh to John Allen, 3 Dec. 1827.
14   Quoted *CFL*, I, 293.
15   ibid., 295.
16   R. Darwin to JW II, 26 July 1829.
17   Quoted *CFL*, I, 298.

20. COUSINS AND LOVERS

1   Hensleigh W to Fanny Mackintosh, 10 Sept. 1831.
2   ibid., 24 Aug. 1830.
3   JW II to John W, 15 Oct. 1829.
4   Bessy W to Jessie Sismondi, 6 Oct. 1828.
5   JW II to JW III, 21 May 1829.
6   JW III to JW II, undated, prob. last week in May 1829.
7   JW II to Hensleigh W, 7 Oct. 1829.

8   Hensleigh W to Fanny Mackintosh, 21 Jan. 1830.
9   Quoted *SL*, 313.
10   Hensleigh W to Fanny Mackintosh, 7 Mar. 1830.
11   ibid., 2 Mar. 1830.
12   Hensleigh W to Sir J. Mackintosh, 4 Mar. 1830.
13   Hensleigh W to Fanny Mackintosh, 29 Sept. 1831.
14   ibid.
15   ibid., 24 Aug. 1830.
16   ibid., 26 Sept. 1830.
17   ibid., 9 Oct. 1830.
18   ibid., undated except 1830.
19   ibid., undated, prob. June 1830.
20   Hensleigh W to JW II, 15 Jan. 1831.
21   R. Darwin to JW II, 13 June 1831.
22   Hensleigh W to Fanny Mackintosh, 6 May 1831.
23   Quoted *Life and Letters of Charles Darwin*, ed. F. Darwin (1887), I, 195.
24   C. Darwin to R. Darwin, 31 Aug. 1831.
25   Hensleigh W to Fanny Mackintosh, 18 Sept. 1831.
26   ibid., 29 Sept. 1831.

21. BEGINNINGS AND ENDINGS

1   Fanny W to Frank W, 11 Jan. 1832.
2   Hensleigh W to JW II, April 1832.
3   Emma W to Jessie Sismondi, 16 Dec. 1832.

22. THE QUIET PATH

1   JW II to the Sismondis, 21 Dec. 1833.
2   Hensleigh W to Fanny Mackintosh, 29 Sept. 1831.
3   Quoted *CFL*, I, 340.
4   Fanny Hensleigh W to Elizabeth W, 4 Nov. 1835.
5   Quoted *CFL*, I, 376.
6   Fanny Hensleigh W to Elizabeth W, 3 May 1835.
7   Scrapbook: Maria Edgeworth to Fanny Hensleigh W, 26 Oct. 1835.
8   John W to JW II, 22 Nov. 1833.
9   Fanny Hensleigh W to Elizabeth W, 21 Oct. 1835.
10   Elizabeth W to Mrs W. Roscoe, 28 Apr. 1836.
11   ibid.
12   ibid.
13   ibid., 13 May 1836.
14   Frank W to Hensleigh W, 24 Apr. 1836.
15   Fanny Allen to Fanny Hensleigh W, 6 July 1836.
16   Quoted *CFL*, I, 383.
17   ibid., 382-3.
18   ibid., 384.

23. THE NEW VICTORIANS

1   C. Darwin to W. D. Fox, 7 June 1837.
2   ibid., 11 Dec. 1837.
3   JW II to the Sismondis, 21 Dec. 1833.
4   JW II to Hensleigh W, 23 Nov. 1837.
5   Scrapbook: Hensleigh W to JW II, undated, prob. early December 1837.

6 ibid., JW II to Hensleigh W, undated, prob. early December 1837.
7 Fanny Allen to Fanny Hensleigh W, 15 Dec. 1837.
8 Memo, marked 'To Hensleigh, May 1837', from JW II.
9 Quoted M. Allan, *Darwin and His Flowers* (1977), 121.
10 R. Darwin to JW II, 13 Nov. 1838.
11 Emma W to Fanny Hensleigh W, 3 Nov. 1837.
12 Jessie Sismondi to Emma W, 23 Nov. 1838.
13 ibid.
14 C. Darwin to Emma W, 2 Jan. 1839.
15 R. Darwin to JW II, 17 Jan. 1838.
16 Elizabeth W to Jessie Sismondi, 5 June 1839.
17 ibid.
18 Emma Darwin to Jessie Sismondi, 7 Feb. 1840.
19 Quoted *CFL*, I, 465.
20 Julia W to Fanny Hensleigh W, 6 Dec. 1841.
21 Harriet Martineau to Julia W, 17 Feb. 1841.
22 Emma Darwin to Jessie Sismondi, 7 Feb. 1840.
23 Quoted *Life and Letters of Charles Darwin*, I, 301.
24 Emma Darwin to Jessie Sismondi, 7 Feb. 1840.
25 Quoted *CFL*, II, 14.
26 ibid., 36.
27 ibid., 40.
28 ibid., 20.

24. UNCONSCIOUS PERSONS

1 Sarah W to Elizabeth Moore, 29 Jan. 1841.
2 Sarah W to Jessie Allen; quoted *CFL*, I, 140.
3 Jessie Sismondi to Elizabeth W, June 1844; quoted ibid., II, 66.
4 Quoted H. Atkins, *Down, the Home of the Darwins* (1976), 21.
5 Quoted M. Allan, *Darwin and His Flowers*, 142.
6 Quoted *Mrs Longfellow: Selected Letters and Journals of Fanny Appleton Longfellow*, ed. E. Wagenknecht (New York, 1956), 143.
7 Quoted 'Illustrated Catalogue of the Industry of All Nations', *Art Journal* (1851), 14.

25. A GLORIOUS PRETENCE

1 Julia W to Fanny Hensleigh W, 3 Oct. 1851.
2 Julia W to Mackintosh W, 16 May 1852.
3 Julia W to Mary Rich, 7 Aug. 1852.
4 Godfrey W to Julia W, 26 Nov. 1852.
5 Quoted W. Irvine and P. Honan, *The Book, the Ring and the Poet* (1975), 326.
6 ibid., 402.
7 Julia W to Effie W, 24 Oct. 1856.
8 ibid., undated, prob. autumn 1856.
9 Quoted *CFL*, II, 178.
10 Hensleigh W to Julia W, undated, prob. summer 1856.
11 E.A. Darwin to Fanny Hensleigh W, 25 Sept. 1857.
12 ibid., undated, prob. 1852.
13 ibid., ? July 1858.
14 Scrapbook.
15 Julia W to Effie W, 19 Sept. 1855.

26. TRUE DILETTANTES

1   É. Lessore, *Five Years in the Potteries* (1863).
2   C. Darwin, *On the Origin of Species by Means of Natural Selection* (1859), 5.
3   Hensleigh W, *On the Origin of Language*: Introduction to *A Dictionary of English Etymology* (1872), 7-8.
4   *Life and Letters of Charles Darwin*, I, 313.
5   Emma Darwin to Hensleigh W, 12 May (?)1859.
6   ibid.
7   Fragment of a poem in Longfellow's handwriting in the Wedgwood archive at the University of Keele; attached is a note in another hand, 'Composed by Longfellow for Mrs Frances Wedgwood of Barlaston during her visit to him'.
8   Louisa W to Effie W, ? June 1859.
9   Julia W to Effie W, 28 Apr. 1858.
10   Julia W to Mary Rich, 27 July 1862.
11   ibid.
12   Godfrey W to Eliza Meteyard, 18 Oct. 1862.
13   Julia W to Effie W, August 1858.
14   Speech of the Rt Hon. W. E. Gladstone at Burslem, 26 Oct. 1863.

27. A ROMANTIC INTERLUDE

1   Julia W to Effie W, 13 July 1863.
2   Quoted in *RB/JW*, 4.
3   ibid., 2.
4   ibid., 6
5   ibid., 8-9.
6   ibid., 10.
7   ibid., 22.
8   ibid., 30.
9   ibid., 10-11.
10   ibid., 13.
11   ibid., 30.
12   ibid., 18.
13   ibid., 19-20.
14   ibid., 79.
15   ibid., 32.
16   ibid., 35.
17   Scrapbook.
18   *RB/JW*, 25.
19   ibid., 26.
20   ibid., 38-9.
21   ibid., 51.
22   ibid., 19.
23   ibid., 32.
24   ibid., 117-18.
25   ibid., 120-1.
26   ibid., Preface, xviii-xix.

28. SOME REFRACTED WORDS

1   *Letters of Thomas Erskine*, ed. W. Hanna (Edinburgh, 1877), II, 153.
2   Julia W to Emily Gurney, 29 July 1870; UC, III, 80.
3   ibid., IV, 34.

4   ibid.
5   ibid., II, 63
6   Julia W to Mary Rich, 17 June 1866.
7   ibid., 23 June 1866.
8   *RB/JW*, 127.
9   Emile Lessore to Godfrey W, July 1866.
10   Frank W to Godfrey W, 23 Feb. 1866.
11   ibid.
12   ibid., 22 June 1866.
13   Quoted *RB/JW*, 131.
14   ibid.
15   ibid., 134
16   ibid., 182.
17   Julia W to Mary Rich, undated, prob. May 1867.
18   Frank W to Godfrey W, 1 June 1868.
19   ibid.
20   Quoted *RB/JW*, 185.
21   ibid., 181.
22   Quoted M. Ward, *Robert Browning and His World* (1968-9), II, 24.
23   Quoted *RB/JW*, 188.
24   ibid., 195.

29. LEAD KINDLY LIGHT

1   Frank W to Godfrey W, undated, late spring 1870.
2   ibid.
3   Julia W to Emily Gurney, 7 Mar. 1870.
4   Julia W to Mary Rich, undated, summer 1870.
5   Julia W to F. D. Maurice, 30 May 1870.
6   Julia W to Emily Gurney, UC, III, 13.
7   Harriet Martineau to Julia W, 2 July 1871.
8   Julia W to Mary Rich, 14 Sept. 1871.
9   E.A. Darwin to Henrietta Darwin: quoted *CFL*, II, 242.
10   Julia W to Mary Rich, 31 Aug. 1871.
11   ibid.
12   Emma Darwin to Eliza Meteyard, 29 Apr. 1871.
13   Eliza Meteyard to Emma Darwin, 3 May 1871.
14   Fanny Hensleigh W to Emma Darwin, 28 Apr. 1869.
15   Ernest Hensleigh W to Julia W, undated, summer 1872.
16   ibid.
17   Julia W to Emily Gurney, 4 Dec. 1872.
18   Quoted in Effie W's private journal, written at Plymouth Grove, Manchester, November 1871.
19   ibid.
20   ibid.
21   Julia W to Emily Gurney, November 1872.
22   Godfrey W to Mr Keary, 14 Sept. 1871 (draft).
23   Vernon Derbyshire to Godfrey W, 5 Feb. 1874.
24   Julia W to Emily Gurney, 9 July 1874.
25   Fanny Allen to Emma Darwin, 30 June 1874.
26   H. G. Allen to Emma Darwin, 7 May 1875.
27   Quoted *CFL*, II, 274.

30. GENTLEMEN AMATEURS

1   Quoted *CFL*, II, 260.
2   Quoted in Julia W to Mary Rich, undated, prob. spring 1875.
3   Quoted in Julia W to Jane Gourlay, April 1878.
4   Julia W to Emily Gurney, 5 Dec. 1875.
5   Emily Gurney to Julia W, 11 Sept. 1876; UC, V, 131.
6   ibid,; note added by Julia W, prob. 1897.
7   Julia W to Mary Rich, 25 July 1876.
8   Frank W to Godfrey W, 17 Oct. 1876.
9   ibid.
10   ibid., 14 Sept. 1878.
11   ibid., 8 Apr. 1878.
12   ibid., 18 May 1879.
13   Cecil W to Hope W, 19 Dec. 1881.
14   Frank W to Godfrey W, 14 Nov. 1877.
15   ibid., 17 Sept. 1879.
16   Quoted *CFL*, II, 294.
17   ibid.
18   ibid., 288.
19   Quoted G. Raverat, *Period Piece* (1952), 202.
20   Quoted in Frank W to Godfrey W, 9 Nov. 1880.
21   ibid.
22   E. A. Darwin to Hope W, 4 Oct. 1880.
23   Harry W to Emma Darwin, 6 May 1879.
24   E. A. Darwin to Godfrey W, 11 Jan. 1880.
25   Quoted M. Allan, *Darwin and His Flowers*, 292.
26   E. A. Darwin to Hope W, 9 May 1881.
27   Margaret Vaughan Williams to Hope W, 24 Aug. 1881.
28   Caroline W to Fanny Hensleigh W, 27 Aug. 1881.
29   Appended to letter from G. Darwin to Hope W, 27 Aug. 1881.
30   Frances Julia W, letter to the Editor of *The Spectator*, 3 Sept. 1881.

31. DEPRESSIONS AND RECESSIONS

1   Godfrey W's Greek Journal, 10 Mar. 1883.
2   Godfrey W to Hope W, 6 Mar. 1883.
3   Quoted *CFL*, II, 347.
4   ibid., 348.
5   Frank W to Godfrey W, 14 Oct. 1883.
6   ibid., 3 Feb. 1884.
7   Joseph Chamberlain to Lady Farrer, 18 Nov. 1884.
8   Frank W to Godfrey W, 3 Feb. 1884.
9   Emily Gurney to Lady Welby, 30 May 1884.
10   Quoted *CFL*, II, 380.
11   Hope W to Julia W, 10 June 1887.
12   Quoted CFL, II, 380.
13   Caroline W to Emma Darwin, 19 Nov. 1887.
14   Lucie Gibson's diary, Thursday, 9 Sept. 1887.
15   ibid.
16   ibid., 10 Sept. 1887.
17   Frank W to Godfrey W, 19 Jan 1888.
18   ibid., 3 Feb. 1884.
19   ibid.

20 Godfrey W to Lucie Gibson, 19 Mar. 1888.
21 Hope W to Lucie Gibson, 22 June 1888.
22 Quoted *CFL*, II, 349.
23 ibid., 386.
24 ibid., 387-8.
25 Emma Darwin to Henrietta Litchfield, 2 July 1888.
26 Hensleigh W to Emma Darwin, 6 Jan. 1890.
27 Hope W to Julia W, 22 Sept. 1887.
28 Henrietta Litchfield to Emma Darwin, 6 Apr. 1890.
29 ibid., 5 Apr. 1890.
30 *Journal of the Society for Psychical Research*, June 1891.
31 W.R. Grove to Julia W, 18 June 1891.

32. THE END OF AN ERA

1 Quoted *CFL*, II, 421.
2 Mary Euphrasia W to Julia W, 25 Jan. 1892.
3 G. Raverat, *Period Piece*, 123.
4 ibid., 125.
5 Quoted *CFL*, II, 434.
6 Hope W to Emma Darwin, wrongly dated 5 Jan. 1894 — actually 1895.
7 ibid.
8 ibid.
9 Sir Joseph Hooker to Godfrey W, 17 Sept. 1895.
10 ibid.
11 Godfrey W's Egyptian Journal.
12 Julia W to Emily Gurney, 5 Dec. 1872; UC, IV, 80.
13 ibid., Good Friday, 1873; UC, IV, 151.
14 Undated Introduction to UC, prob. written spring 1897.
15 Julia W to Jane Gourlay, 7 Oct. 1876.

33. AN APPRECIABLE TRACE

1 Lady Farrer to Mary Euphrasia W, undated, prob. 24 or 25 June 1897.
2 Lady Farrer to Hope W, 1 July 1897.
3 ibid.
4 L.C.B. Seaman, *Victorian England* (1973), 451.
5 Scrapbook: Preface.

EPILOGUE

1 Godfrey W to the Etruria Workmen, care of Mr Whittaker, 17 Oct. 1898.
2 Cecil W to Godfrey W, 31 Mar. 1901.
3 Julia W, *Nineteenth Century Teachers*, 413.

Select Bibliography

Place of publication is London unless otherwise indicated.

Alexander, Constance M., *Baghdad in Bygone Days* (1928)

Allan, Mea, *Darwin and His Flowers* (1977).

Atkins, Sir Hedley, *Down, the Home of the Darwins* (1976).

Bate, Walter Jackson, *Coleridge* (1969).

Bentley, Richard, *Thomas Bentley, 1730-1780, of Liverpool, Etruria and London* (1827).

Blackman, John, *A Memoir of the Life and Writings of Thomas Day* (1862).

Blair, Alexander, *Sketch of the Life of James Keir, Esq., F.R.S.* (1870).

Bolton, H.C., *Scientific Correspondence of Joseph Priestley* (New York, 1892).

Briggs, Asa, *The Age of Improvement* (1959).

Briggs, Milton, and Jordan, Percy, *Economic History of England* (1962).

Bunting, James, *Charles Darwin* (Folkestone, 1974).

Burton, Anthony, *Josiah Wedgwood* (1976).

Burton, Elizabeth, *The Early Victorians at Home, 1837-1861* (1972).

Burton, William, *Josiah Wedgwood and His Pottery* (1922).

Buten, Harry M., *Wedgwood and Artists* (Buten Museum of Wedgwood, Merion, Pa., 1960)

—— *Wedgwood Counterpoint* (Buten Museum of Wedgwood, Merion Pa., 1962)

Butler, Marilyn, *Maria Edgeworth, a Literary Biography* (Oxford, 1972)

Byatt, A. S., *Wordsworth and Coleridge in Their Time* (1970)

Campbell, Ian, *Thomas Carlyle* (1974)

Campbell, James Dykes, *Samuel Taylor Coleridge, a Narrative of the Events of His Life* (1894)

Chancellor, John, *Charles Darwin* (1973)

Chapple, J.A.V., and Pollard, Arthur, *The Letters of Mrs Gaskell* (Manchester, 1966)

Church, A. H., *Josiah Wedgwood* (1903)

Clarke, Desmond, *The Ingenious Mr Edgeworth* (1963)

Colp, Ralph, Jr., *To Be an Invalid* (Chicago, 1977)

Cottle, Joseph, *Reminiscences of Samuel Taylor Coleridge and Robert Southey* (1847)

Crowther, J. G., *Josiah Wedgwood* (1972)

Curle, Richard, ed., *Robert Browning and Julia Wedgwood* (New York, 1937)

Daiches, David, *Sir Walter Scott and His World* (1971)

Darwin, Charles, *On the Origin of Species by Means of Natural Selection* (1859)

Darwin, Francis, ed., *Life and Letters of Charles Darwin*, 3 vols. (1887)

de Selincourt, Ernest, *The Letters of William and Dorothy Wordsworth*, 4 vols. (1967-78)

Dickinson, H. W., *Matthew Boulton* (Cambridge, 1937)

Dunbabin, John P. D., *Rural Discontent in Nineteenth-Century Britain* (1974)

Edgeworth, R. L., *Memoirs of Richard Lovell Edgeworth, Esq.*, concluded by Maria Edgeworth (1820)

Emden, Cecil S., *Poets and Their Letters* (1959)

Farrer, Katherine Eufemia, Baroness Farrer, ed., *Correspondence of Josiah Wedgwood, 1781-1794* (1906)

—— *Wedgwood's Letters to Bentley*, 2 vols. (1903)

Finer, Ann, and Savage, George, eds., *The Selected Letters of Josiah Wedgwood* (1965)

Fletcher, Harold R., *The Story of the Royal Horticultural Society, 1804-1968* (1969)

Forster, E. M., *Marianne Thornton* (1956)

Gibbs, Frederick W., *Joseph Priestley* (1965)

Gorley, Jean, *Wedgwood* (New York, 1950)

Graham, John Meredith, and Wedgwood, Hensleigh Cecil, *Wedgwood, a Living Tradition* (New York, 1948)

Grant, M. H., *The Makers of Black Basalt* (1967)

Gregory, Frances W., *Nathan Appleton, Merchant and Entrepreneur* (Charlottesville, Va., 1975)

Gridley, Roy E., *Browning* (1972)

Grisewood, Harman, ed., *Ideas and Beliefs of the Victorians* (New York, 1966)

Hackwood, F. W., *Staffordshire Customs, Superstitions and Folklore* (Wakefield, Yorks, 1974)

Hadfield, Charles, *The Canals of the West Midlands* (Newton Abbot, Devon, 1966)

Halliday, F.E., *Robert Browning, His Life and Work* (1975)

Hankin, Christiana C., *Life of Mary Anne Schimmelpenninck* (1859)

Hanna, W., ed., *Letters of Thomas Erskine from 1800 to 1840*, 2 vols. (Edinburgh, 1877)

Hart, Ivor B., *James Watt and the History of Steam Power* (1958)

Hartley, Sir Harold, *Humphry Davy* (1966)

Henderson, Philip, *Tennyson, Poet and Prophet* (1978)

Hill, Christopher, *Reformation to Industrial Revolution* (Harmondsworth, 1969)

Hower, Ralph M., 'The Wedgwoods—Ten Generations of Potters', *Journal of Economic and Business History*, vol. IV, nos. 2 and 4 (February and August 1932)

Hubbard, Elbert, *Little Journeys to the Homes of Famous Women* (New York, 1897)

Huxley, Julian, and Kettlewell, H. B. D., *Charles Darwin* (1965)

Irvine, William, and Honan, Park, *The Book, the Ring and the Poet* (1975)

Jewitt, Llewellyn, *Life of Josiah Wedgwood* (1865)

Jones, Elizabeth Inglis, 'A Pembrokeshire Family in the Eighteenth Century', *National Library of Wales Journal*, vol. XVII (1971/2), nos. 2, 3, 4

Keith, Sir Arthur, *Darwin Revalued* (1955)

Kelly, Alison, *The Story of Wedgwood* (New York, 1963)

Kennedy, J., *The Manor and Parish Church of Hampstead and Its Vicars* (1906)

Keynes, Geoffrey, *Blake Studies* (1949)

King-Hele, Desmond, *Doctor of Revolution* (1977)

—— *Erasmus Darwin* (New York, 1963)

Klingender, Francis D., *Art and the Industrial Revolution* (1947)

Knoepflmacher, U.C., *Religious Humanism and the Victorian Novel: George Eliot, Walter Pater and Samuel Butler* (Princeton, N.J., 1970)

Krause, Ernest, *Erasmus Darwin* (1879)

Kriegel, Abraham D., *The Holland House Diaries* (1977)

Lansbury, Coral, *Elizabeth Gaskell, The Novel of Social Crisis* (1975)

Lawrence, Berta, *Coleridge and Wordsworth in Somerset* (Newton Abbot, Devon, 1970)

Lessore, Émile, *Five Years in the Potteries* (1963)

Litchfield, H. E., *Emma Darwin: A Century of Family Letters*, 2 vols. (Cambridge, 1904)

Litchfield, R. B., *Tom Wedgwood* (1903)

Mackintosh, R, J., *Memoirs of the Life of Sir James Mackintosh*, 2 vols. (1836)

McKendrick, Neil, 'Josiah Wedgwood: An Eighteenth-Century Entrepreneur in Salesmanship and Marketing Techniques', *Economic History Review*, vol. XII, no. 3 (April 1960)

—— 'Josiah Wedgwood and Factory Discipline', *Historical Journal*, vol. IV, no. 1 (1961)

Meteyard, Eliza, *Choice Examples of Wedgwood* (1874)

—— *A Group of Englishmen* (1871)

—— *The Life of Josiah Wedgwood from his private correspondence and family papers*, 2 vols. (1865)

—— *Memorials of Wedgwood* (1874)

—— *Wedgwood and His Work* (1873)

—— *Wedgwood Trio* (1873)

Miller, Betty, *Robert Browning* (New York, 1973)

Moilliet, Amelia, *Sketch of the Life of James Keir...with a selection from his correspondence* (1868)

Moore, N. Hudson, *Wedgwood and His Imitators* (New York, 1909)

Moore, Ruth, *Charles Darwin* (1957)

Nevill, John Cranston, *Harriet Martineau* (1943)

Pearson, Hesketh, *Dr Darwin* (1930)

Plumb, J. H., *Men and Places* (1963)

Pollard, Arthur, *Mrs Gaskell, Novelist and Biographer* (Manchester, 1965)

Priestley, Joseph, *Autobiography* (Bath, 1970)

Rathbone, Frederick, *Old Wedgwood* (1898)

Raverat, Gwen, *Period Piece* (1952)

Reader, W. J., *Life in Victorian England* (1964)

Reilly, Robin, *Wedgwood Jasper* (1972)

—— and Savage, George, *Wedgwood, The Portrait Medallions* (1973)

Richardson, Joanna, *The Pre-eminent Victorian, A Study of Tennyson* (1962)

Robinson, Eric, 'The Lunar Society: Its Membership and Organization', *Transactions of the Newcomen Society*, vol. XXXV (1962-3), pp. 153-77

Sandford, Mrs Henry (Margaret E. Poole), *Thomas Poole and His Friends*, 2 vols. (1888)

Schofield, Robert E., *The Lunar Society* (Oxford, 1963)

—— 'The Lunar Society of Birmingham: A Bicentenary Appraisal', *Notes and Records of the Royal Society*, vol. XXI, no. 2 (December 1966)

Seaman, L. C. B., *Victorian England* (1973)

Sellers, Ian, *Nineteenth-Century Nonconformity* (1977)

Selley, W. T., *England in the Eighteenth Century, 1689-1815* (1962)

Smiles, Samuel, *Josiah Wedgwood* (New York, 1895)

Synge, M. B., *A Short History of Social Life in England* (1908)

Thomas, John, *Josiah Wedgwood as a Pioneer of Steam Power in the Pottery Industry* (from *Transactions of the Newcomen Society*, 1936)

Tingsten, Herbert, *Victoria and the Victorians* (1972)

Tremayne, Margaret Olivia, *The Value of a Maimed LIfe* (1912)

Trevelyan, G. M., *English Social History* (1942)

Wagenknecht, Edward, *Henry Wadsworth Longfellow, Portrait of an American Humanist* (Oxford, 1966)

—— , ed., *Mrs Longfellow: Selected Letters and Journals of Fanny Appleton Longfellow* (New York, 1956)

Ward, Maisie, *Robert Browning and His World*, 2 vols. (1968-9)

Warrilow, E. J. D., *History of Etruria* (Stoke-on-Trent, 1952)

Weatherill, Lorna, *The Pottery Trade and North Staffordshire, 1660-1760* (Manchester, 1971)

Wedgwood, Hensleigh, *On the Origin of Language* (Introduction to *A Dictionary of English Etymology,* 1872)

Wedgwood, Josiah C., *Staffordshire Pottery and Its History* (1913)

—— *The Wedgwood Family History, 1299-1908* (1908)

—— and Wedgwood, Joshua G. E., *Wedgwood Pedigrees* (Kendal, 1925)

Wedgwood, Julia, *Nineteenth Century Teachers and Other Essays* (1909)

—— *The Personal Life of Josiah Wedgwood* (1915)

West, Anthony, *Mortal Wounds* (1975)

Williamson, George Charles, *The Imperial Russian Dinner Service* (1909)

Index of Names

JW = Josiah Wedgwood

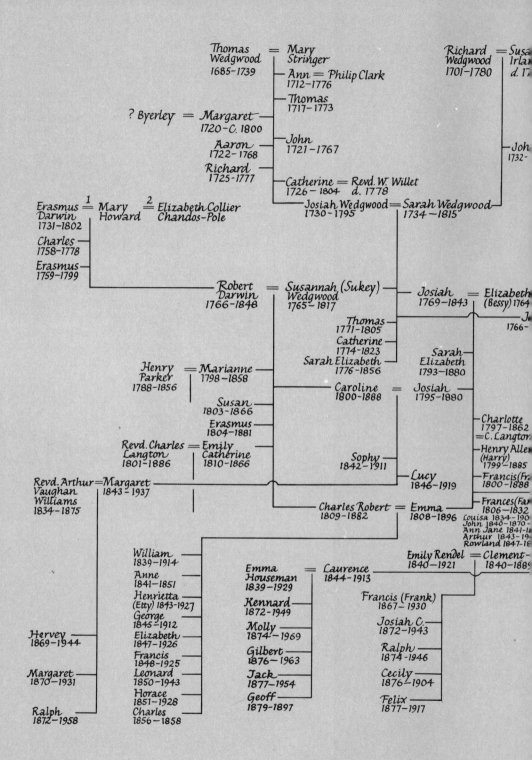